EUROPEAN FOREIGN POLICY DURING THE COLD WAR

Daniel Möckli is a Senior Researcher at the Center for Security Studies at ETH Zurich (Swiss Federal Institute of Technology).

European Foreign Policy
during the Cold War

Heath, Brandt, Pompidou and
the Dream of Political Unity

Daniel Möckli

I.B. TAURIS
LONDON · NEW YORK

Published in 2009 by I.B.Tauris & Co Ltd
6 Salem Road, London W2 4BU
175 Fifth Avenue, New York NY 10010
www.ibtauris.com
Published with the support of the Swiss National Science Foundation
and the Center for Security Studies, ETH Zurich

In the United States and Canada distributed by Palgrave Macmillan
a division of St Martin's Press
175 Fifth Avenue, New York NY 10010

ISBN: 978 1 84511 806 8

A full CIP record for this book is available from the British Library
A full CIP record for this book is available from the Library of Congress

Library of Congress Catalog Card: available

Typeset by Jayvee, Trivandrum, India
Printed and bound in Great Britain
by TJ International, Padstow, Cornwall

Contents

Acknowledgements

Doing research in the field of International History can be a challenging endeavour. Different languages and archival idiosyncrasies often make work time-consuming; the multiplicity of actors may render the storyline all too complex; and extensive stays abroad can well be ruinous to the young researcher. I have been privileged to receive much support in writing this book. My first expression of gratitude belongs to Kurt R. Spillmann, who raised my interest in contemporary history and the challenges of multilateral cooperation, and who has accompanied my research with great competence and patience. I am also much indebted to Andreas Wenger, who has drawn my attention to issues of West–West relations during the Cold War and has given me many helpful comments on earlier drafts of this manuscript. During my research in Britain, France, and Germany, I have been fortunate enough to receive advice from Christopher Hill (University of Cambridge), N. Piers Ludlow (London School of Economics and Political Science), Anne Deighton (University of Oxford), Georges-Henri Soutou (Paris-Sorbonne), and Helga Haftendorn (Free University of Berlin).

Interviews with Henry Kissinger, Michael Palliser, Crispin Tickell, Egon Bahr, Etienne Davignon, and other former ministers and diplomats have greatly helped me refine my arguments. For comments on individual chapters of the book, I thank Stephan Bojinski, Christiane Callsen, John A. Fanzun, Thomas Fischer, Cornelius Friesendorf, Anna Locher, Christian Nünlist, Jeronim Perovic, and Daniel Trachsler. With their skilful proofreading, Lisa Watanabe and Christopher Findlay have greatly improved the quality of the text, while Marco Zanoli has resolved many mysteries in my computing world. Special thanks belong to Victor Mauer, who has supported my research in many ways. A generous grant by the Ecoscientia Foundation and the Academic Trainee Fund of the University of Zurich enabled me to focus on this project for an entire year. The Jakob-und-Emma-Windler Stiftung was kind enough to cover many of my extra expenses abroad.

My grandparents, Marianne and Hans Möckli, and my mother and sister, Ebeth and Soraya Shademan, have given me every kind of support I could have wished for. Finally, I owe my deepest gratitude to Katharine Weder, whose unfailing support, understanding, and counsel provided me with the kind of environment that enabled this book to be written in the first place.

Daniel Möckli
Center for Security Studies, ETH Zurich, Switzerland

Acronyms and Abbreviations

AA	Auswärtiges Amt
AAPD	Akten zur auswärtigen Politik der Bundesrepublik Deutschland
ABM	Anti-Ballistic Missile
ACDP	Archiv für Christlich-Demokratische Politik
ADMAE	Archives Diplomatiques du MAE
AdsD	Archiv der sozialen Demokratie
AN	Archives Nationales
ANL	Direction d'Afrique du Nord et Levant
BA	Bundesarchiv
BK	Bundeskanzler
BKA	Bundeskanzleramt
BMF	Bundesministerium der Finanzen
BMWi	Bundesministerium für Wirtschaft
CAB	Cabinet Office Records
CAP	Common Agricultural Policy
C.A.P	Centre d'Analyse et de Prévision
CBM	Confidence Building Measure
CDU/CSU	Christlich Demokratische Union/Christlich-Soziale Union
Cent.	Europe Centrale
CFSP	Common Foreign and Security Policy
CO	Cabinet Office
COREPER	Comité des représentants permanents
COREU	Correspondance européenne
CSCE	Conference on Security and Cooperation in Europe
CSSR	Czechoslovak Socialist Republic
DBPO	Documents on British Policy Overseas
DELFRA Bruxelles	Représentation Permanente de la France auprès des Communautés Européennes

EB	Egon Bahr papers
EC	European Community
EDC	European Defence Community
EEC	European Economic Community
EID	European Integration Department
Elysée	Secrétariat-Général de l'Elysée
EM	Entretiens et messages
EMU	Economic and Monetary Union
EPC	European Political Cooperation
ESDP	European Security and Defence Policy
Etats-Unis	Direction d'Amérique: Etats-Unis
EU	European Union
EUROGERMA	Ständige Vertretung der Bundesrepublik Deutschland bei der EG
FCO	Foreign and Commonwealth Office
FDP	Freie Demokratische Partei
FPA	Foreign Policy Analysis
FRG	Federal Republic of Germany
G6 / G7	Group of Six/Group of Seven
GATT	General Agreement on Tariffs and Trade
GB	Europe: Grande-Bretagne
GDR	German Democratic Republic
Gén.	Direction Europe: Généralités
HSA	Helmut Schmidt Archiv
IEA	International Energy Agency
IMF	International Monetary Fund
KF	Katharine Focke papers
Levant	Sous-Direction du Levant
MAE	Ministère des Affaires Etrangères
MBFR	Mutual and Balanced Force Reductions
MOD	Ministry of Defence
MPT	Multilateral Preparatory Talks
NATO	North Atlantic Treaty Organisation
NATOGERMA	Ständige Vertretung der Bundesrepublik Deutschland bei der NATO
NENAD	Near East and North Africa Department
NNA	Neutral and non-aligned countries
NSC	National Security Council
OAPEC	Organization of Arab Petroleum Exporting Countries

Occ.	Sous-Direction d'Europe Occidentale
OECD	Organization for Economic Cooperation and Development
OPEC	Organization of Petroleum Exporting Countries
Ori.	Sous-Direction d'Europe Orientale
PA	Politisches Archiv
Pactes	Services des Pactes et du Désarmement
PLO	Palestine Liberation Organization
PMO	Prime Minister's Office
PREM	The Papers of the Prime Minister's Private Office
RDF	Regional Development Fund
REPAN-Bruxelles	Représentation Permanent de la France au Conseil de l'Atlantique Nord
RFA	République Fédéral d'Allemagne
SALT	Strategic Arms Limitations Talks
SPD	Sozialdemokratische Partei Deutschlands
SvB	Sigismund von Braun papers
UK	United Kingdom
UKDEL	UK Delegation
UKMIS NY	United Kingdom Mission New York
UKREP Brussels	United Kingdom Permanent Representation to the EC
UN	United Nations
UNEF	UN Emergency Force
WBA	Willy Brandt Archiv
WED	Western European Department
WEU	Western European Union
WOD	Western Organisations Department
ZA	Zwischenarchiv

Introduction

This book is about the dream and the enormous challenges of Europe speaking with one voice in world politics. It covers the very beginnings of the efforts at conducting a European foreign policy in the early 1970s, which were marked by remarkable initial achievements and a subsequent dramatic collapse of joint vision, ambition, and action. In 1969/70, the member states of the European Community (EC) set up European Political Cooperation (EPC), with a view to forging collective involvement in international diplomacy. By 1973, the Europeans were already the single most effective actor group at the Conference on Security and Cooperation in Europe (CSCE). They also became involved in the search for peace in the Middle East, negotiated with the US on a reorganisation of the West and a new European–American bilateralism, issued a declaration on their common identity, and even discussed European defence cooperation.

However, much of this proved unsustainable. Europe's quest for a distinct foreign policy provoked a sharp American reaction, with the severe transatlantic crisis of 1973/74 bearing some striking similarities with the feud over Iraq in 2003. As EPC lost its dynamic and declined into crisis in 1974, the limits of a European foreign policy were painfully revealed, and it became clear that the high-flying plans for a European Union (EU) and a European foreign ministry by 1980 would remain unrealisable. Bereft of any common defence identity, Europe remained unable to engage in power politics in any traditional sense, and evolved one-sidedly into what François Duchêne at the time coined a 'civilian power'.[1] Moreover, the concept of separate 'pillars' for economic integration and foreign policy cooperation, originally conceived as a provisional structure, became quasi-permanent due to lack of consensus about the purpose and structure of the European project.

Examining the formative period of European diplomacy between 1969 and 1974, the book analyses why the Europeans were successful at joint diplomacy during a brief period in the early 1970s, but still failed in the long run to establish Europe as an effective and acknowledged political power during the Cold War. Adopting a historical perspective, the study will primarily provide insight into the origins and dramatic early developments of EPC within the context, particularities, and complexities of the time. But by examining the extraordinary constellation of factors that made possible the remarkable performance of EPC in the early 1970s, it will also seek to advance understanding about the general conditions of effective European foreign policy-making. If Stanley Hoffmann has a point in comparing Europe's struggle towards a common foreign policy with the work of the unfortunate Sisyphus, how did this 'European Sisyphus' manage to move the stone of cooperation so far up the slope at the very beginning of political cooperation?[2]

Framework of analysis

The analysis focuses on three key actors in EPC: France and the Federal Republic of Germany (FRG), as the traditional driving forces of European unification, and Britain, whose accession in 1973 gave the EC more political weight and rendered the issue of Europe's role in the world more virulent. If the three big European powers alone could not guarantee progress in an intergovernmental framework such as EPC, consensus among them was a precondition for any meaningful collective European diplomacy. The roles and policies of other EPC members will, however, be discussed where possible and appropriate.

The evolution of European foreign policy cooperation will be examined in three chronological parts, covering the years 1969–72, 1973, and 1974, respectively. Part I spans the period from December 1969, when the six EC member states (France, West Germany, Italy, Belgium, the Netherlands, and Luxembourg) at their historic summit at The Hague agreed on an ambitious programme of widening and deepening the Community, to the end of 1972, when Britain, Ireland, and Denmark became official members of the EC.[3] Political Cooperation was launched within the context of a general *relance européenne*, with the Six finally succeeding in overcoming their deep divisions that had paralysed the Community in the late 1960s. EPC became operational in November 1970, with the EC candidate countries joining in spring 1972, after they had signed their EC accession treaties. Although EPC's balance sheet by the end of 1972 was as yet mixed, the decision of the Nine at their first common summit in Paris in October 1972 to transform their relations into a

European Union with an Economic and Monetary Union (EMU) and a foreign policy component became a strong symbol for their eagerness to render the 'New Europe', as the enlarging Community was often labelled, a powerful political entity.

Part II deals with the subsequent rise of EPC, which this study, for the sake of convenience, equates with the year 1973, but which has foundations that can be traced back to the period of 1969–72, and which reverberated well into 1974. The first issue to address here is the CSCE, and in particular the question why and how the Nine during these multilateral negotiations on détente in Europe succeeded in wresting numerous concessions from the Soviet Union and making Moscow subscribe to a broadened notion of security that incorporated human rights. Attention will then shift to the matter of how the Europeans, over the summer of 1973, used the US-sponsored 'Year of Europe' initiative that called for strengthened transatlantic relations as a catalyst for advancing their own political unity. Rather than complying with the US quest for a new Atlantic Charter, the Nine asked the US to acknowledge them as a second decision-making centre in the West, embarked on a policy of speaking to Washington with one voice, and started a process of defining their collective identity as a basis for their interactions with other political entities in the world. In response to the October War and the oil crisis in the autumn of 1973, the Europeans moved even closer together when they published their first ever declaration on the Arab–Israeli conflict and decided to expand their presence in the Middle East through a Euro-Arab dialogue. Also indicative of Europe's rise in 1973 were the talks between London, Bonn, and Paris on expanding cooperation to the defence realm and the secret Anglo-French discussions on nuclear cooperation. When at the close of the year, the Nine assembled for their summit in Copenhagen, they focused for the first time mainly on foreign policy affairs, rather than Community matters.

Finally, part III of the book covers the abrupt decline of EPC in the first half of 1974. Europe's fragmentation began when the Nine failed to establish a common energy policy in early 1974 and, at the Washington Energy Conference in February 1974, ended up openly divided on whether to tackle the oil crisis in an Atlantic or European framework. The Nine subsequently also gave up their attempt at formulating a common policy vis-à-vis the US. In the so-called 'Gymnich Agreement', they subordinated the effectiveness of EPC to transatlantic cohesion and US leadership. In June 1974, the 'Year of Europe' ended with the 'Ottawa Declaration' of the North Atlantic Treaty Organisation (NATO) and a general reinvigoration of political consultations within the Alliance. As for their Middle East policy, the Europeans withdrew again from trying to influence the Arab–Israeli peace process and decided to eschew all political issues in the Euro-Arab dialogue. They also stalled their deliberations on defence, with the CSCE emerging as the sole policy field where EPC continued to work smoothly. In a development that was symbolic for Europe's diminished political ambition, the Nine had de facto ceased their efforts at defining and preparing for European Union by the summer of 1974, shifting the work in this field from the EC and EPC institutions to a single person, Prime Minister Leo Tindemans of Belgium.

In order to be able to identify the distinct forces that influenced EPC's performance over time, the analysis will be guided by three categories of factors, relating to either the 'extra-European', the 'intra-European', or the 'individual' level of European foreign policy-making. While these categories do not structure the narrative of the book, they will be taken up at the end of each chapter to determine the major enabling and restraining factors shaping European diplomacy between 1969 and 1974.

The extra-European factors refer to developments in the international environment of EPC, that is, those that were situated outside the specific context of relations among the Six and later Nine, but had an effect on intra-European relations. One such development in the early 1970s was détente. Although the East–West antagonism continued to be the most dominant political structure of the international system, the confrontational relations of the early Cold War were gradually superseded by an era of East–West dialogue, cooperation, and negotiation. Détente was both a bilateral and a multilateral phenomenon. It took place between the superpowers, as well as within Europe. Indeed, it had many faces and meant different things to different actors. Yet, while its essential purpose from a Western point of view was to prevent further conflict with the East and modify Soviet behaviour, détente also evoked suspicion among the allies and, ironically, often affected intra-Western relations as much as it changed inter-bloc affairs. From a Western European point of view, the essential external factor concerning détente was the US rapprochement with the Soviet Union. Superpower détente, desired by Washington in view of both the growing strategic parity between East and West and the objective of withdrawing US troops from Vietnam, could potentially bring more stability to Europe. Yet, intimate American–Soviet relations could also negatively affect vital European interests and diminish the credibility of the US security guarantee in NATO.

Related to the issue of how the US would reconcile its policy of superpower détente (and triangular diplomacy with China) with its role of leadership in the West was the question of Washington's attitude to the process of European unification. While the US had traditionally been supportive of the principle of European integration, it had become more critical of European realities, such as the protectionism of the Common Agricultural Policy (CAP). The prospect of enlargement implied that the Community would become an economic giant and that transatlantic competition and friction were bound to increase. Accordingly, the American response to this development, as well as to Europe's new foreign policy aspirations, constituted an essential extra-European factor for the viability of EPC.

The *economic* international system was also marked by profound changes during this period. The early 1970s witnessed repeated international monetary turbulences and the collapse of the Bretton Woods system. The shift from a system of fixed parities to floating currencies could either boost European monetary unity or strain relations within the European Community, but it was bound to have an effect on European cooperation and, thus, on EPC. Also, after decades of boom and unprecedented prosperity, all industrialised countries were affected by new tides of inflation and economic disruption in the 1970s. Such symptoms of crisis were reinforced when the oil crisis of 1973/74 threatened to paralyse the Western economies, in a development that starkly exposed the dependence of consumer societies on Arab oil and raised awareness of a new North–South dimension in world politics. Economic and monetary issues increasingly came to dominate the international political agenda and became part of 'high politics',[4] which again was likely to influence European unity and European political cooperation in one way or another.

The intra-European level of EPC comprises factors relating to relations between the Six/Nine, that is, factors that emanated from one of the EPC (or candidate) countries and affected the policies of European partner countries or of EPC at large. Two particularly important factors of this kind were West Germany's own version of détente, referred to as *Ostpolitik*, and the evolution of Anglo-French relations. Chancellor Willy Brandt was determined to complement Konrad Adenauer's legacy of anchoring the FRG in the West by normalising relations with the East. This policy both represented the basis for multilateral détente in Europe and provided the West German government with more freedom of manoeuvre in international politics. However, the emerging German–Soviet détente also caused fears in Europe that Bonn might be tempted to resolve the 'German question' in a separate agreement with Moscow and choose neutrality. If the specific consequences of *Ostpolitik* for the FRG's *Westpolitik* and the evolution of European unification were uncertain, its repercussions on EPC were bound to be profound.

As for Anglo-French relations, the British refusal to join the project of European unification in the 1950s and French opposition to British accession in the 1960s were important reasons why all efforts at getting *l'Europe politique* under way ended in failure prior to 1969. The fact that Paris in 1969 finally lifted its veto on EC enlargement did not necessarily mean that the sources of suspicion and rivalry between France and Britain had been removed. How these two European great powers arranged themselves within the 'New Europe' was therefore certain to influence the viability of EPC to a significant extent. Also relevant was the question of whether the Europeans – and France, Britain, and the FRG in particular – pursued at least partly congruent conceptions and visions of the widened Europe's future role in the world.

The individual level of European foreign policy-making concerns the role of specific national decision-makers or bureaucratic entities. Although, strictly speaking, it constitutes a sub-category of the intra-European level, it is treated here as a separate set of factors, so as to draw attention to the impact of individuals on EPC. It is worth noting that a new generation of actors came into power in Europe in 1969/70. The changes of government in France, the FRG, and Britain all symbolised breaks with the past and, to varying degrees, marked a change in national foreign-policy preferences. While the presidency of Georges Pompidou in France (1969–74) still stood in the tradition of Gaullism, French foreign policy – as conducted by two successive foreign ministers, Maurice Schumann (1969–72) and Michel Jobert (1973/74) – became less doctrinaire and ideological and generally more supportive of European integration than had been the case under President Charles de Gaulle (1958–69). The chancellorship of Willy Brandt ushered in a new era in West Germany, both because of *Ostpolitik* and because the Social Democratic Party (SPD, Sozialdemokratische Partei Deutschlands) managed for the first time in the FRG's post-war history to replace the Christian Democrats (CDU/CSU: Christlich Demokratische Union, Christlich-Soziale Union) as the ruling party. The SPD's coalition partner during Brandt's term in office (1969–74) was the liberal party (FDP, Freie Demokratische Partei), headed by Walter Scheel, who became vice-chancellor and foreign minister. Finally, in Britain, the new Conservative government under Prime Minister Edward Heath and Secretary of State Sir Alec Douglas-Home (1970–74) pursued a pro-European course unmatched by any other British government before or since. Although it was a coincidence that Heath, Brandt, and Pompidou were all out of power again by mid-1974, their departure from office marked a caesura that further supports the timeframe of this study.

Two additional individuals worth drawing attention to are Richard Nixon, US president between 1969 and 1974, and Henry Kissinger, assistant to the president for national security affairs (1969–75) and US secretary of state (1973–77). Although the US is treated as an external factor rather than a primary actor in the analysis, Kissinger, in particular, came to have a strong impact on the early history of EPC, which is why he will occupy a prominent place in this book. Conversely, the roles of transnational groups, such as Jean Monnet's Action Committee for the United States of Europe, or of EC institutions, such as the European Commission or the European Parliament, are not taken into account systematically in this study. Andrew Moravcsik's contention that political elites within the process of European unification enjoy much more leeway in shaping national preferences in foreign and security policy than in the realm of economics certainly holds true in the case of EPC, which emerged as a strictly inter-governmental and highly secretive forum during the early 1970s.[5]

Understanding the 'psychology of cooperation'

Thematically, this study lies at the crossroads of European Integration History and Cold War Studies. With its focus on a multilateral issue and its multinational perspective, it belongs to the field of International History.[6] Epistemologically, the analysis stands in the tradition of hermeneutics. Ontologically, it is based on an individualistic interpretation of social phenomena. It recognises that forces external to agency limit and affect an individual's actions and that agency and structure are irreducible to each other. However, it primarily looks at political, economic, and ideational structures through the prism of the perception of the agents, assuming that what is essential for understanding an individual's behaviour is how he or she interprets these forces and constraints.[7] This perceptionist paradigm is not to say that the developments on the extra-European and the intra-European levels of EPC outlined above eventually all qualify as belonging to the individual level. But it does suggest that the way they are perceived by the relevant decision-makers and bureaucratic elites matters greatly for how and to what extent they influence EPC.

To gain insight into the challenges of intergovernmental cooperation, historians can benefit from work done in the discipline of Political Science. Although historians and political scientists differ in their approaches and goals – the former, to put it crudely, aiming at understanding in complexity, the latter at explaining in parsimony – they still have much common ground in the study of international relations, which is why there is a strong case for cross-fertilisation.[8] It is striking that relatively few political scientists so far have developed specific theories relating to Europe's foreign policy.[9] Nevertheless, political science studies of both the way in which national foreign policies are forged and the conditions under which states may cooperate offer valuable insights for a historical analysis of European diplomacy.

With its focus on reasoned rather than rational choices, the field of Foreign Policy Analysis (FPA) is of particular importance to this book.[10] Building on the notion of agency perception and on cognitive and psychological aspects of foreign policy decision-making, FPA (in its variant of Political Psychology) builds on two basic features, namely, beliefs (or belief systems) and role conceptions. Beliefs relate decision-makers to their environment, define it for them, and help them to establish goals and preferences. Such beliefs relate to the essence of the political world, the nature and characteristics of the international system, and to images of adversaries and allies.[11] The notion of role conception refers to the question of how political elites and individual decision-makers view the role of their political entity in the international environment, that is, in our case, the role of their country within Europe, and of Europe in the world.[12] Another important aspect is the Bureaucratic Politics variant of FPA, which emphasises the impact of governmental bureaucracy on the formation of foreign policy preferences, drawing particular attention to the importance of the perceptions and roles of non-elected officials, and to the group dynamics and special interests and cultures of bureaucratic entities.[13]

If FPA makes the important point that foreign policy-making is to a considerable degree influenced by psychological phenomena, this finding can be extended to multilateral cooperation. Studying the changing effectiveness of an intergovernmental forum such as EPC is also about studying its changing 'psychology of cooperation'. Effective multilateralism has to do with how involved actors perceive their own and other participating actors' interests in cooperation, whether there is a certain congruity of beliefs and role conceptions, and, above all, whether these actors trust one another. The relevance of the notion of trust for effective multilateral cooperation has been underlined by research within the field of International Relations. Neorealists are generally sceptical about the feasibility of cooperation because, in their eyes, the anarchy of the international system creates a lack of trust and certainty that compels states to maximise their security and satisfy their interests through self-help, that is, by striving for power and independence. Neoliberal Institutionalists, who – like the Neorealists – treat the state as a unitary, rational actor, are more optimistic about the prospects of cooperation, as distrust in their eyes can be overcome by means of institutions, which enable information and communication, reduce transaction costs, and allow for endurable multilateralism. Constructivists are also more optimistic than Neorealists concerning multilateral cooperation. Focusing on ideational and normative rather than material structures, they argue that identity can shape interests. Transnationally shared ideas in the sense of 'communities of values' raise the likelihood of regime formation, with socialisation by means of interaction providing a basis for trust and, thus, for effective and sustainable cooperation.[14]

In this book, I will argue that while numerous factors shaped the course of EPC, the changing psychology of cooperation was particularly important. The growth of mutual trust in the early 1970s among key decision-makers and officials was an essential condition for EPC's remarkable rise. As I will show, this trust had much to do with the beliefs, role conceptions, and European policies of Heath, who succeeded in forging close relations with Pompidou and Jobert. This Anglo-French axis, a rare exception in European post-war history, laid the basis for the extraordinary constellation of trilateral Anglo–French–German leadership in Europe that lent much dynamic to European foreign policy cooperation and allowed the EC countries to pursue common political aspirations.

State of research

This is the first monograph to deal with the phenomenon of European foreign policy cooperation based on primary sources, with most of the relevant archival documents released only recently. Accordingly, there is no well-established historiographical framework into which a historical examination of EPC could be embedded. However, there is a valuable body of political science literature and contemporary studies of the 1970s that provides some insight into the issues of interests here. Also, some historical studies on individual actors or topics covered in this book are available now for the first time, carrying historical research on the process of European unification during the Cold War into the 1970s.

There are a number of political science studies dealing with such issues as EPC's institutional development, the decision-making process, EPC–EC relations, national perspectives and inputs, and case studies on specific policies.[15] There are also three useful accounts on EPC by officials involved at the time.[16] With regard to the general development of European integration between 1969 and 1974, the first edited volumes are available now,[17] but it is still indispensable to consult the main textbooks on European unification to gain a more comprehensive picture.[18]

Of the three countries under investigation in this book, historical research on the respective foreign policies is most advanced in France. The 'Pompidou Years'[19] are covered reasonably well with regard to French policies towards Europe, West Germany and détente, the US, and the economic transformations that marked the international system.[20] Most of these publications rely heavily on the personal papers of Pompidou. There also exists a well-documented political biography on the French president, as well as an analysis of Jobert's foreign policy based on privileged access to some of his personal papers.[21] In contrast, little is known on the role and ideas of Schumann, and much research is still required on Franco-British relations during the early 1970s. As for the foreign policy of the FRG, although document-based research has so far been dominated by publications on *Ostpolitik*, more and more publications are now also available on Bonn's *Westpolitik*.[22] Like in France, many of these writings strongly focus on the role of the chancellor, whose papers, like those of Pompidou, have been declassified earlier than usual. While biographies on the charismatic Brandt are likely to remain popular,[23] there is a need for a more detailed examination of the roles of other cabinet members, such as Scheel and Helmut Schmidt (minister of defence from 1969 to mid-1972, minister with combined economic and finance portfolios in the second half of 1972, and minister of finance in 1973/74). German–British and German–US relations also require investigation, as do West German views on strategic issues and the role of NATO. Until more archive-based assessments of the FRG's foreign policy in the early 1970s are available, it is useful to consult some of the earlier publications on this period.[24]

It is surprising how little research interest the late 1960s and early 1970s have stimulated in Britain to date. There are a few analyses on Prime Minister Harold Wilson's policy towards European integration between 1964 and 1970, and especially on the British decision for a second EC application in 1967.[25] With regard to the Heath era, however, few historians so far have tackled Britain's European policies, the entry negotiations with the EC, the rapprochement with France, or the British plans for European defence cooperation.[26] There is also a lack of publications on the special relationship between the US and Britain during this time. Again, there are some informative non-historical works on the Heath government and its foreign policy,[27] as well as a biography on the prime minister that gives prominence to his European zeal.[28]

The performance of EPC at the CSCE was assessed immediately after the Helsinki Final Act in a dissertation that based its interesting findings on numerous interviews.[29] Personal accounts of European diplomats engaged in the CSCE process are available too.[30] On Europe and the Middle East, we still know little about the Nine and their response to the Arab–Israeli conflict.[31] Some contemporary evaluations discussed the reverberations of the oil crisis in 1973/74 on Europe's economic and political solidarity.[32] Regarding the 'Year of Europe', historical research has only recently gotten under way.[33] While there is an extensive body of literature on Kissinger and US foreign policy in the early 1970s,[34] Europe does not figure prominently in these studies. Three broad examinations of European–US relations were published in the early 1970s, however, offering valuable insights into the economic, political, and strategic debates.[35] Finally, although little material is available so far about the debates on European defence and Anglo-French nuclear cooperation in the early 1970s, some of those publications that do cover the issue are of noteworthy quality.[36]

Much of the substance of this book is based on archival research pursued in Britain, France, and Germany. US sources were used very selectively only where the relevant documents in European archives were missing. The memoirs and personal writings of decision-makers and diplomats were also taken into account.[37] Finally, interviews were conducted with Henry Kissinger and several Europeans involved in EPC, which shed additional light on the story of the turbulent beginnings of European diplomacy.[38]

Part I

Towards a European Foreign Policy, 1969–72

MUNICH, West Germany, Nov. 19 [1970] – The six member countries of the European Economic Community agreed here today to establish a system of consultation aimed at coordinating their foreign policies as much as possible. Foreign Minister Walter Scheel of West Germany, who presided over today's session, […] said the hope was Western Europe 'will speak one day with one voice.' The initial discussions, he said, provided ground for the belief that 'rapprochement of viewpoints is possible.'

'Common Market to Seek to Align Foreign Policy',
New York Times, 20 November 1970

European unification has always been a political project. Geopolitical and security considerations have been essential driving forces behind European unity. The economic motives of expanding markets and modernising domestic industries have obviously been relevant too. Yet, it was the sharp decrease of European power and influence in world politics, as much as the inability of the traditional balance of power system to provide peace in Europe, that most starkly revealed the functional deficits of the European nation states after 1945 and the imperative of a new, collective approach. European unity was, above all, a response to Europe's self-destruction in two devastating world wars, the loss of its colonial empires, and the rise of extra-European superpowers that marked the end of the century-old Eurocentric international system. It was also a strategy to prevent future wars in Europe, resolve the 'German question', and contain Soviet Communism.

All this pointed to the need for some form of political organisation of Europe and for coordination and harmonisation of national foreign and security policies. Yet, by the late 1960s, after two decades of European integration, the Europeans were further away from political unity than at any time before. All plans and negotiations to that end had failed, and the hopes and ambitions of the early years had been superseded by deep divisions and distrust. Throughout the 1960s, Europe had been paralysed by clashing visions of its unity and purpose. While it was one of the world's most dynamic growth areas economically, politically it remained impotent and fragmented. Europeans became so polarised that the economic integration process itself was negatively affected, with the European Community repeatedly plunging into crisis in the second half of the 1960s. It was only at the very end of the decade that the Europeans finally succeeded in overcoming their paralysis. At their summit at The Hague in December 1969, the Six charted an ambitious course for the EC's first round of widening and deepening. After years of resistance, France at last lifted its veto on accession negotiations with Britain and other candidate countries. The Six also subscribed to the goal of setting up an Economic and Monetary Union, and they tasked their foreign ministers with writing a report on how to get political cooperation started. It was the beginning of a comprehensive *relance européenne*, in the context of which the old dream of European political unification could finally be translated into reality.

European Political Cooperation was established and became operational between 1970 and 1972. It was a start without fanfares. The divisions of the 1960s had not been forgotten, nor had they all been resolved, which is why policy-makers approached the issue with caution. Moreover, other issues dominated the political agenda and the headlines at the time, with the public taking little notice of EPC initially. Concerning the EC, all eyes were set on the enlargement talks. For all the atmospheric improvement accomplished at the Hague Summit, any sustainable relaunch of the European project was critically dependent on whether these talks would succeed. It was only in early 1972, when the accession treaties were signed and enlargement was officially scheduled for 1 January 1973, that any doubts about the EC's widening were dispelled. *Ostpolitik*, Brandt's policy of reconciliation with the East, also drew a lot of attention, being implemented between 1970 and 1972/73 with breathtaking speed and vigour. The FRG's bilateral treaties with the Soviet Union and Poland of August and December 1970, the Quadripartite Agreement on Berlin of September 1971, and the Basic Treaty with the German Democratic Republic (GDR) of December 1972 ushered in a new era in European post-war history. As Bonn de-facto recognised the territorial and political status quo in Europe, accepted the post-war borders in Eastern Europe (including the Oder–Neisse line), abandoned the FRG's claim of exclusively representing the German nation, and signed agreements on the mutual renunciation of force, the ground was prepared for détente to unfold across the continent – and for the two German states to join the United Nations (UN).[1] Washington's own attempt to reduce East–West tensions and improve relations with the two Communist giants, the Soviet Union and China, was watched equally attentively in Europe. The Sino–American rapprochement, especially Nixon's trip to Beijing in February 1972, was as spectacular as the US–Soviet summit that took place in Moscow in May 1972. As superpower détente kept up with détente in Europe, speculations increased as to whether Nixon's declared policy of moving from an 'era of confrontation' to an 'era of negotiation' might yet result in overcoming the antagonistic system of the Cold War.[2]

If EPC was set up in the shadow of such epoch-making international developments, this was only to its own advantage. Had there been higher expectations or more pressure to deliver, it may well be that the sensitive endeavour of harmonising Europe's national foreign policies would not have gotten very far. As it turned out, EPC had an unspectacular, but successful start. Some Europeans may have been disappointed when the Six in 1970 decided to begin with a very modest scheme involving only non-binding political consultations. After all, the 'Davignon Report', named after Belgian Political Director Etienne Davignon who presided over the elaboration of the study mandated at The Hague, diverged sharply from the grand designs of political unification that had been characteristic of the 1950s and the early 1960s. Most of those involved in conceptualising EPC, however, were well aware that developing any more ambitious tool would simply have been unrealistic. When the EC foreign ministers met for their first round of consultations in November 1970, the predominant feeling was thus one of relief, coupled with more than a little excitement that the great adventure of forging a European foreign policy could finally begin.

Over the following two years, EPC evolved from an untested idea to a tool that demonstrated its large potential. Consultations proved more effective overall than many had anticipated, although the degree of success varied according to the respective subjects. Perhaps more important even, the initial lingering distrust of EPC in the aftermath of the clashes of the late 1960s was gradually giving way to new relations of trust and a shared belief that a common European voice in world politics was actually feasible. If diffidence had still marked the elaboration of the Davignon Report in 1970, the Nine already revealed a noteworthy degree of self-confidence and political ambition at their first common summit in Paris in October 1972.

In this first part of the book, I will examine the emergence and consolidation of EPC in the period from Europe's relaunch at the end of 1969 to the EC's enlargement on 1 January 1973. Chapter 1 will analyse those factors that enabled the creation of EPC in the first place, and it will investigate the reasons for the marked improvement in the Nine's team spirit and confidence between 1970 and 1972. Chapter 2 is about EPC's first two years of practical policy har-monisation and the normative debates on Europe's role and structure in 1971/72, which culminated in the Paris Summit of October 1972 that set an ambitious programme for the 'New Europe' of the Nine.

Chapter 1
New leaders and the relaunch of Europe

In 1969, Europe was in a deadlock. As France refused any negotiations on EC enlargement, some of its Community partners, together with Britain, blocked all progress à Six. Ideas began to circulate about cooperation outside of the established framework of European integration. French President Charles de Gaulle brought up the possibility of political great power cooperation between France, Britain, the FRG, and Italy, which implied a weakening of the EC structures. Britain, eager to force its way into the EC, was busy convincing the Five (i.e., the Six without France) to isolate de Gaulle by pushing political consultations without French participation. The West Germans, intensely wooed by both Paris and London, uneasily wavered between the two poles and, being divided themselves, found it impossible to show a way forward. It was a time of deep distrust and frustration, and of widespread fear that the integration project might yet collapse.

Three years later, Europe was in a very different shape. The EC was the acknowledged nucleus of European integration again, and was on the eve of its first round of enlargement. With its goal of creating an EMU, it had embarked on a very ambitious course that, it was hoped, would take the integration process to a much higher level. The parallel project of European Political Cooperation promised to give a long-awaited political dimension to European unification. Anglo-French relations had dramatically improved, paving the way for trilateral leadership in Europe by Paris, London, and Bonn. As the decision at the Paris Summit to build a European Union by 1980 demonstrated, Europe now was much more self-confident and full of élan, willing to finally realise its full potential.

This chapter is about the dramatic change that occurred in the course of European unification between 1969 and 1972. Its main argument is that new leaders in France, the FRG, and Britain played a seminal role in the relaunch of the European project. The growing economic and political strength of West

Germany was the single most important factor that compelled Europeans to search for ways of overcoming their deadlock. Yet, while de Gaulle in 1969 sought to move closer to Britain outside the EC structures, Pompidou as his successor preferred to enlarge the Community to contain Germany's power. Also relevant was the change of leadership in the FRG, where Brandt's European role conception and policies were much more compatible with those of Pompidou than had been the case under Kurt-Georg Kiesinger, West German chancellor between 1966 and October 1969.

Although the general *relance européenne* that was initiated at the summit in The Hague was mainly facilitated by Pompidou and Brandt, this chapter will argue that Edward Heath's election victory in spring 1970 was critically important for the positive evolution of EPC during its first years. Harold Wilson might be credited for building up pressure on Paris in the late 1960s, which contributed to the French decision to lift the veto on enlargement negotiations. Nevertheless, his anti-French policies and doubtful European credentials ruled out any genuine Anglo-French rapprochement. Only Heath's achievement of winning Pompidou's confidence cleared the way for Europe's dynamic development in the early 1970s, and for EPC to move from diffidence and caution to rapid progress and ambition.

In the following, I will first look at the crisis situation of the late 1960s and analyse the breakthrough compromise at the Hague Summit in December 1969. I will then show how EPC was conceptualised in 1970 in a climate of continuing distrust. The third section of this chapter deals with the impact of Heath on EPC's evolution between 1970 and 1972, with some concluding remarks assessing the significance of the emerging trilateral leadership in Europe.

Pompidou, Brandt, and the EC's first widening and deepening

On 2 December 1969, the six leaders of the EC member states issued a communiqué after a two-day summit at The Hague that was to mark a milestone in the process of European integration. They sketched a comprehensive programme to relaunch the Community and leave the recent past of European confrontation and stagnation behind. Having decided to lay down a definite financial agreement for their Common Agricultural Policy and to move on from the transitional period to the final stage of the Common Market, the Six now sought to build a 'united Europe capable of assuming its responsibilities in the world of tomorrow and of making a contribution commensurate with its traditions and its mission'. This meant, above all, a widening of the EC, with the member states welcoming negotiations on enlargement, provided that the applicant states – Britain, Ireland, Denmark, and Norway – 'accept the treaties and their political finality' and 'the decisions taken since the entry into force of the treaties'. It also meant a deepening of the Community, most notably by working out a plan to create an EMU. Finally, with the political objectives of the Community reaffirmed, attention was drawn to Europe's role in 'promoting the relaxation of international tension and the rapprochement among all peoples, and first and foremost among those of the entire European continent'. The foreign ministers were, thus, instructed to 'study the best way of achieving progress in the matter of political unification, within the context of enlargement', and to report their findings before the end of July 1970.[1]

The reference to political unification in the communiqué was remarkable in two different ways. On the one hand, it was much more timid and vague than the decisions to consolidate the Common Market, launch enlargement negotiations, and work towards monetary union. The mandate for the foreign ministers was laid out in the penultimate paragraph only and was formulated in such a low key way that, as Christopher Hill and Karen E. Smith have pointed out, '[e]ven the interested observer might have been forgiven for failing to notice'.[2] As the foreign ministers were merely asked to 'study' the issue, without any obligation to actually achieve progress in their report, institutionalised foreign policy cooperation of the Six was no more than a possibility even after the memorable Hague Summit.

On the other hand, it was surprising that the reference made it into the communiqué at all. Given the severe crisis the Community had fallen into, the Hague Summit was first and foremost about securing the EC. This required resolving the enlargement issue, which accordingly was the focus of the pre-summit negotiations as well as of the meeting itself. Political cooperation was hardly discussed during these talks, as the disputes of the 1960s had made it abundantly clear that progress in this field would only be feasible once the problem of Britain's accession to the EC could be resolved. The fact that the six leaders nevertheless eventually commissioned a report on political unification reflected both a sense of urgency to begin with foreign policy cooperation as soon as possible and widespread hopes that the upcoming enlargement negotiations would eventually succeed. The decision appeared the more surprising since the British, who had been mere bystanders at The Hague, had explicitly asked the Six to delay deliberations on the political dimension of unification until after enlargement – or to include the candidate countries from the start. Though the British side may have been satisfied at the prospect of accession talks, in the field of political cooperation it was set to miss yet another bus, just as it had done with its belated reorientation towards the Common Market in the early 1960s.

In order to assess the significance of the Hague Summit – the general relaunch of the European project as well as the specific mandate to study political unification – we need first to take a brief look back at the previous EC crisis and the reasons why European political union never materialised in the 1950s and 1960s. This will provide the basis for the subsequent analysis of how Pompidou and Brandt managed to break the EC deadlock in the second half of 1969.

The vision of unity, the reality of fragmentation: De Gaulle's legacy

It was not for lack of effort or political will that by 1969, the Europeans had still not managed to establish a political roof over their unification process. A multitude of designs for political unity were proposed in post-war Europe, and several rounds of respective intergovernmental negotiations did take place. While in the late 1940s the notion of a European Third Force was particularly popular,[3] the first extensive negotiations on a European defence and foreign policy occurred between 1951 and 1954. Having just launched the integration process with the founding of the European Coal and Steel Community, France, the FRG, Italy, and the Benelux countries began to negotiate on a European Defence Community (EDC) with common European forces, common institutions, and a European solidarity clause. There was also an ad hoc assembly working out a draft treaty on a European Political Community as an overarching framework for all European organs, but these talks were suspended once the French parliament rejected the EDC.[4]

In the mid-1950s, plans were considered to change the Western European Union (WEU) into a forum for European politico-military or even nuclear cooperation. Such ideas evaporated in the aftermath of the Suez Crisis however, as Britain opted for a special defence relationship with the US while France began to reverse its diplomatic alignment with London and against Bonn.[5] Although the European Economic Community (EEC) of the Six in 1957 was not explicitly geared towards foreign policy and defence cooperation, its proclaimed goal of an 'ever closer union among the peoples of Europe' still nourished expectations that political integration was about to follow.[6] The EEC foreign ministers did indeed hold meetings on foreign affairs during a brief period in 1959/60. However, these meetings were discontinued when the Six started talks on the so-called 'Fouchet Plans', and they were never resumed again.[7]

The Fouchet Plans, named after the French diplomat Christian Fouchet who chaired the respective commission, gave rise to the most intensive

European negotiations on political unity throughout the Cold War and became paradigmatic for all subsequent debates. The original Fouchet Plan, put forward by France in 1961, suggested an 'indissoluble' union run by an intergovernmental Council composed of either heads of governments (every four months) or foreign ministers (every two months). A European Political Commission, located in Paris and formed by senior officials of the foreign ministries, was to assist the Council and could set up working bodies as it considered necessary. Major aims included a common foreign policy 'in matters that are of common interest to member states' and a common defence policy to 'strengthen, in cooperation with other free nations, the security of member states against any aggression'. The treaty was to be reviewed after three years, with a view to 'centralising' the EEC to the Political Union. As negotiations on 'Fouchet I' and several other French drafts failed to produce consensus, a new text was tabled by the Five in 1962 that sketched a European Union with its own constitution, an independent executive, and majority decision-making. However, no consensus could be found on this draft either, which is why the Fouchet talks left the Europeans bitterly divided.[8]

The failure of all these initiatives was all the more frustrating since the case for Europe's political unification was compelling. The end of the Eurocentric world and the bipolarity of the Cold War, marked by the dominance of two extra-European superpowers, meant that the Europeans could only hope to be heard again in international politics if they cooperated and succeeded in speaking with one voice. Moreover, while the formation of a Western bloc based on NATO and US leadership was vital for protecting Western Europe from the Soviet Union and for containing West Germany, uncertainty about the American security guarantee repeatedly pointed to the need for Europe to reduce its near-total dependence on US nuclear weapons and ground forces. Against the background of an emerging nuclear equivalence between Washington and Moscow, could the US not one day be tempted to decouple its strategic arsenal from the defence of Europe and forfeit European interests for the sake of stable superpower relations? Once the EEC was launched, the growing discrepancy between Europe's economic might and its political impotence became a third major motive for political unification. As an economic power with a customs union, common trade interests, and a growing number of preferential agreements with third countries, Europe required an institution to place its technical deliberations into a bigger political setting. Progress in this field was the more important since the US made it clear that it would tolerate economic discrimination only as long as there was a prospect for European political unity.[9]

Although many factors contributed to the Europeans' lack of success in forging a political unity, three points were crucial: they disagreed about the role of a united Europe within the West, about the role of Britain within Europe, and about Europe's organisation and decision-making structure. Interestingly, in all these issues, a major dividing line could be traced between the Five and France. It would be wrong, however, to one-sidedly attribute blame to the French. After all, France as the main sponsor of the EDC and of the Fouchet Plans had shown more interest in political unification throughout the post-war period than many of its partners. Rather, the failure of the European countries to construct a common political identity should be understood as being caused by diverging conceptions of their respective national role conceptions. There were simply too many discrepancies between the various policy-makers' key perceptions, belief systems, and policy preferences in decisive moments for a common European stance to emerge.

Divisions between France and the Five were, of course, accentuated once de Gaulle was president. In the Gaullist grand design, Western relations were to be restructured and responsibilities redistributed. France was to be the pivotal point between two systems of cooperation: global tripartism with the US and Britain; and European political unity of the Six, as laid out in the Fouchet Plans. Because he disapproved of American hegemony in NATO, de Gaulle instead advocated an autonomous Europe – *l'Europe européenne* – without British membership. He also called for a return of both European and transatlantic cooperation to an intergovernmental basis. Convinced that France, after its humiliating wartime experience, decades of domestic instability and frustrating colonial wars, required above all new moral purpose and a sense of *grandeur*, de Gaulle confronted Jean Monnet's 'logic of integration' with his own 'logic of diversity'.[10]

Of the three major contentious issues, the most divisive was clearly Europe's role vis-à-vis NATO and the US. France's partners considered any French-led European security architecture too weak to contain the Soviet Union and to protect them from any resurgent German nationalism. Rather than postulate a degree of emancipation from the US, they sought to improve their security mainly by requesting a bigger say in the Atlantic Alliance. In their view, European political unity should reinforce the West and strengthen NATO. The FRG was particularly dependent on the US, not just for its security but also for its longer-term goal of German reunification. Furthermore, for smaller powers such as the Dutch, a remote American hegemon might well be easier to bear than domination by neighbouring European powers. Also important in this context was the fact that Washington actively discouraged any European defence autonomy, promising a more equal Atlantic partnership and nuclear sharing instead.[11]

The second question of Britain's role in Europe by the 1960s had become closely linked to the issue of relations with the US. In the 1950s, Britain's self-exclusion from the European project had a strongly negative impact on the efforts towards political unification, as France felt too weak to deal with the FRG alone. Yet, once Britain applied for talks on entry conditions to the EEC in July 1961, France was no longer willing to let London share its leadership in Europe. Britain's special relationship with the US had left the French convinced that London would act as a Trojan horse for US interests in Europe and seek to dilute and adapt the Community in a way that would be detrimental to French geopolitical interests and agricultural needs. Since the other EC countries, with varying degrees of enthusiasm, supported the British application, a rift was opening both between France and the Five and between France and Britain.[12] As for the third point of disagreement concerning the structure and organisation of Europe, the French insistence on a confederal model of unification contrasted with the preference of most other European governments for a more supranational scheme. In this context, however, the differences were less profound than in the other two cases. As the Fouchet negotiations revealed, the Five were willing to consider intergovernmental forms of cooperation, if only Britain was on board to counter any French hegemonic ambitions.[13]

The consequences of all these divisions were far-reaching. After 1962, disillusionment prevailed as to the possibility of political union. There were no more negotiations on the issue, and the differences in role conceptions for Europe became even starker. De Gaulle's *double non* on 14 January 1963 to Britain's EEC candidacy and to a US offer to assist the French nuclear programme in return for Paris assigning its *force de frappe* to a NATO Multilateral Force pointed the way to a further radicalisation of French European and defence policies. France's long-planned withdrawal from NATO's integrated military structure in 1966, which split the West into 14 NATO defence members and 15 members of the broader political Alliance, rendered a full-fledged European political union ever more improbable.[14] The empty-chair policy that France pursued in the EEC in 1965/66 also alienated the Five, who had to concede that the Commission would remain a technical body rather than a political nucleus, and that Community decision-making would essentially be unanimous.[15] The gap between the flamboyant visions of Europe and its frustrating everyday realities grew further when de Gaulle on 27 November 1967 vetoed negotiations on a second British application for membership in what by now was called the Economic Community.[16] His reasoning that Britain was still too 'Atlanticist' in its political outlook and economically not stable enough to join the EC caused so much irritation in Europe that the EC now definitely plunged into acute crisis.

And yet, the need for the EC countries to cooperate politically did not go away. Events such as the Six-Day War in the Middle East in 1967 and the Soviet intervention in Prague in 1968 painfully revealed just how helpless the Europeans were even in crises that affected their own interests and security. Fear of superpower collusion at the expense of European interests mounted with improving prospects for détente and the US government's wooing for Soviet assistance in Vietnam. While the nuclear issue was becoming less acute with the creation of a consultative Nuclear Planning Group in NATO, uncertainties about America's engagement in Europe did not die down, but shifted to the issues of US troop withdrawals and insufficient US backing of the Bretton Woods monetary system. Furthermore, even though NATO did overcome its crises of the mid-1960s and gained new legitimacy with the 'Harmel Report' of 1967 (named after Belgian Foreign Minister Pierre Harmel) by complementing its defence function with the new political purpose of defusing East–West tensions, it could not make up for the lack of a European forum to forge a specifically European point of view.[17]

In order to raise the likelihood of any progress in the political field, the Europeans after 1963 shifted the debate from grand ideas of political union to the more modest concept of foreign policy cooperation.[18] Yet, even such limited cooperation, officially proposed by France and the FRG at the EC summit in 1967, failed to materialise. The prime obstacle here was the 'British question'. London succeeded in persuading at least some of the Five to reject any European political cooperation without British participation. It therefore tied the notion of a European foreign policy firmly to its own accession to the EC. Europe now fell into a deadlock – a deadlock that went so deep that its first generation of post-war leaders proved unable to resolve it.[19]

The 'German question' and enlargement: Wilson's anti-French approach

De Gaulle and Harold Wilson's Labour government shared one common challenge that urged them to overcome Europe's state of paralysis: the constant rise of West German power. In the shadow of all European quarrels, the FRG's economy witnessed phenomenal growth rates throughout the 1960s, with the D-Mark becoming the leading currency in Europe. This raised concerns that leadership in the Europe à Six would increasingly switch from France to the

FRG.[20] Also, the French withdrawal from NATO left Bonn with a bigger say in the Alliance, which became dominated by a German–American axis. Most importantly, although West German foreign policy was still restrained by domestic divides between 'Atlanticists' and 'Gaullists', and between those advocating non-recognition of the GDR and those supporting a partial rapprochement, it seemed only a question of time before Bonn would embrace its own policy of détente. As the FRG with a new *Ostpolitik* was bound to liberate itself from legacies of the past and enter into dialogue with the Soviet Union, its diplomatic space of manoeuvre and international weight was certain to further increase.[21] In early 1969, de Gaulle reacted to this resurging 'German question' with an attempt to resolve the 'British question'. However, the approach he chose for achieving a limited Franco-British rapprochement was as ill-conceived as the Wilson government's reaction to it. The resulting so-called 'Soames-Affair' became what Hugo Young has called 'the most incandescent bilateral row' in Anglo-French relations since 1945, with the two sides more divided than ever.[22]

When de Gaulle decided to reach out to Britain, French foreign policy was in a mess. The May 1968 upheavals had shaken the domestic basis of the general's ambitious geopolitical aspirations. The Soviet intervention in the Czechoslovak Socialist Republic (CSSR) a few months later threw into jeopardy his policy of détente and his vision of a new European security system from the Atlantic to the Urals. Worst, perhaps, France was beset with monetary instability, and it could only note with consternation that the FRG was resisting all pressure from Washington, London, and Paris to revaluate the D-Mark.[23] It was against this background of French weakness that on 4 February 1969, in a conversation with Christopher Soames, Winston Churchill's son-in-law and British ambassador to Paris, de Gaulle proposed Franco-British talks on new structures for an enlarged Europe. Repeating his traditional claim that the Common Market could not take in more members, he sketched his idea of a large European free trade zone with special arrangements for agricultural products and a small inner council of a European political association, consisting of France, Britain, the FRG, and Italy. He insisted that it was now time to find out whether London and Paris were able to achieve real cooperation that would not be based on a war alliance, but on a shared desire to build Europe. In response to Soames' question of whether he thought it necessary for Britain to leave NATO, de Gaulle replied in the negative. But he added that once there was a truly independent Europe there would be 'no need for NATO as such, with its American dominance and command structure'. Regarding procedure, he asked for a gesture from Wilson indicating such talks to be desirable, which he would then approve. The French president finished by urging the British to keep this conversation secret until decisions on talks had been taken.[24]

De Gaulle's proposal was impracticable, little thought out, and too defiant of the EC institutions to resolve Europe's crisis. At the same time, half-hearted though it may have been, it was a step towards Wilson and an indication that Paris was willing to search for a modus vivendi with London. Soames, a Conservative politician and well-known European, was intrigued and encouraged his Labour government to respond favourably to the offer.[25] This was not how Wilson and his secretary of state, Michael Stewart, chose to go about it, however.

It had taken Wilson several years in office to realise that there was no viable alternative to joining the European unification process if Britain was to finally reverse the marked decline in its power. Yet, once he had taken his twin decisions in 1967 of applying for EC membership and withdrawing British troops from east of Suez, he had vigorously pursued the goal of compensating for Britain's loss of empire by a leading role in Europe.[26] Wilson himself was unenthusiastic about the Common Market, and his EC application had partly been motivated by opportunistic party considerations. But by refusing to take de Gaulle's repeated 'no' for an answer, the British prime minister succeeded in keeping the issue on the agenda and placing pressure on France to lift its veto against enlargement. Given the context of France's previous uncompromising position, it is understandable that Wilson deeply distrusted de Gaulle's proposal and suspected that the French general intended to abuse Anglo-French discussions to upset London's relations with the Five.[27] Yet, rather than decline the French offer through diplomatic channels, the Labour government decided to further escalate the bilateral conflict, to disclose de Gaulle's initiative, and to embarrass him publicly.

This confrontational strategy towards France had been designed in autumn 1968, when Wilson and Stewart had decided to 'continue to invest the EEC citadel', but also to 'consider all other possible means of manoeuvre outside and around the citadel' to increase de Gaulle's isolation. The prime minister's idea at that time had been to relaunch the Fouchet Plans to demonstrate Britain's European posture to the Five, reveal how 'ridiculous de Gaulle's policies and opposition were', and influence the French domestic scene in a way that made sure that the general would not be succeeded by another Gaullist like Pompidou or Michel Debré. Stewart, however, had argued for an even more aggressive anti-French policy of actively sowing discord between Bonn and Paris and luring the FRG over to the British camp.[28] Despite Wilson's scepticism, the Foreign and Commonwealth Office (FCO) had its way. Henceforth,

Britain's priority was to work towards a 'showdown' with France and 'increasingly strained relations and perhaps an open breach between Germany and France',[29] with a view to what Stewart came to call turning 'the four–two combination in Europe into a five–one combination'.[30]

De Gaulle's secret proposition provided just the kind of opportunity the FCO had been waiting for. The British not only informed the Five and the US of the French plan, but on 21 February 1969 also leaked it to the press, with the 'Soames Affair' causing a sensation all over Europe.[31] Moreover, Stewart in particular gave such a distorted account of the Soames–de Gaulle conversation that the French, outraged and in the defensive, launched a fervent diplomatic counter-offensive.[32] But Stewart would not leave it there. Parallel to the 'Soames Affair', he also went to great length to isolate France within the WEU, making sure that Anglo-French relations would deteriorate further.

Ever since de Gaulle's *double non* of 1963, the WEU had served as a point of liaison between the EC-Six and Britain, providing for quarterly ministerial meetings to exchange information on political and economic issues.[33] After de Gaulle's second veto in 1967, there had been several initiatives to make these exchanges less sterile and to strengthen the WEU as a platform for European political consultations as long as the EC was paralysed.[34] Such ideas had made little headway initially, as France had suspected that Britain would use the WEU to rally the Five behind it, and since Britain had shown no particular interest in pursuing them. Yet once Britain had embarked on its decidedly anti-French course, the WEU was moving into the centre of its attention. Stewart untiringly promoted it as a forum for far-reaching political consultations. Encouraged by the Five's growing frustration with de Gaulle's obstructionist policies, he hoped to persuade them, and the FRG above all, to go ahead with Britain in the WEU even if France declined, as was to be expected.[35]

At the WEU ministerial meeting on 7 February 1969, Stewart indeed managed to persuade the Five to start serious consultations on the Middle East and to use the WEU permanent representatives in London to that end.[36] When French Foreign Minister Debré, who had been absent at the WEU meeting, shortly thereafter underlined that France rejected consultations below the level of ministers and would consider them illegal, Stewart convinced the Five to go ahead with the disputed sessions anyway and even attended the meeting in person.[37] Debré, furious and humiliated, reacted with an empty-chair policy in the WEU, insisting that France would only return if Britain and the Five stopped their consultations and refrained from using the organisation as a 'war machine' (*machine de guerre*) against France.[38] Labour's WEU manoeuvre, together with the 'Soames Affair', had definitely led Anglo-French relations to a new low point. As Debré told Stewart on 11 April 1969: 'The thread is broken' (Le fil est cassé).[39]

Labour's objective of outflanking France in Europe appeared to be accomplished. Yet to what avail? The emerging British historiography on Wilson's European policies during the later 1960s tends to be surprisingly favourable. N. Piers Ludlow has stressed that by putting Britain's EC membership firmly on the international agenda, Wilson paved the way for his successor to take the country into Europe.[40] Similarly, Melissa Pine has argued that Wilson succeeded in ensuring meaningful cooperation with the Five, preventing harmful developments in the Community, and creating an environment conducive to the eventual lifting of the French veto against EC enlargement. The 'Soames Affair', according to Pine, was a 'storm in a teacup' and had mainly positive ramifications for Britain, raising the profile of its application.[41] There is no doubt that Wilson's insistence on keeping the application on the table was a prerequisite for France lifting its veto on enlargement. However, it could well be argued that with their excessively anti-French course, Wilson and Stewart not only failed to increase Britain's chances for EC accession but actually complicated things further.

Four critical observations are in place. First, Labour failed to lure Bonn away from Paris. Wilson and Stewart no doubt misunderstood and underestimated the significance of the Franco-German rapprochement for Bonn. Neither Chancellor Kiesinger nor Foreign Minister Brandt would risk sacrificing West Germany's most significant post-war achievement for whatever short-term benefits. While the West German bureaucracy at times leaned strongly towards the British, the political establishment refused to side with any anti-French coalition. There was surprise in Bonn at how Wilson was dealing with the Soames issue.[42] Kiesinger reassured de Gaulle that he was getting tired of warding off attempts to bypass France in Europe and complained that far too much time had already been invested in the 'British question'.[43] As for the WEU, once the West Germans realised that France would resist the British initiative, they became less than lukewarm about these consultations and, in fact, decisively blocked the organisation from developing into a new European-lead forum.[44] Bonn also refused to subscribe to a substantial bilateral Anglo-German declaration on Europe as proposed by the FCO,[45] and the German government generally made clear to London that French leadership could not simply be substituted by Britain in Europe.[46]

Second, Labour's escalatory approach also failed to influence the French domestic scene in a way conducive to British interests. When de Gaulle stepped down at the end of April 1969, after having lost a referendum on a domestic issue, Britain's preferred successor, Valéry Giscard d'Estaing of the French Independent Republicans, declined even to stand for election.[47] As for Alain Poher, the president of the European Parliament and most important alternative candidate to Georges Pompidou, he had no chance of winning. Promising a break with Gaullist foreign policy, Poher stood for an enlarged and politically united Europe, an end to the 'empty-chair' policy in the WEU, a revived leading role for France in the Atlantic Alliance, and an integration of French and British nuclear forces in a European defence organisation.[48] Yet, Pompidou's sweeping victory left no doubt that as much as the French electorate appeared tired of de Gaulle's eccentric leadership, it was still in favour of the general's basic policies.[49]

Third, the fact that the enlargement question was imbued with new dynamics after spring 1969 had little to do with British policy. De Gaulle's resignation can hardly be related to British pressure politics. More importantly, if all major French presidential candidates in 1969 declared themselves in favour of Britain's entry into Europe, there is no evidence that this was because of Labour's 'European approach'. Stewart's claim in his memoirs that developments subsequent to de Gaulle's resignation provided ample evidence that he had 'backed the right horse' with his offensive policies therefore appears unfounded.[50] Rather, as argued above, the structural changes of the international environment, and the rise of the FRG especially, were the main factors that led France to modify its foreign policy. The Wilson government, however, failed to understand this. While its policy of sitting de Gaulle out and adhering to its application was appropriate, its distinctly anti-French course was both unnecessary and counterproductive.

Fourth, Britain did have to pay a price for cornering France. Labour's reputation remained tarnished in Paris even after de Gaulle's resignation. Stewart's expectation that London would finally get a 'straight yes' from Paris, complete enlargement negotiations before the next general elections in Britain (due in 1970), and convince the French to 'put the past behind us',[51] turned out to be over optimistic. By further nurturing a climate of distrust in Anglo-French relations, the 'Soames Affair' and Britain's WEU manoeuvre prompted the new French government and the French bureaucratic elite to approach the issues of enlargement and political cooperation with extreme caution.[52] As will be shown, Wilson's discrediting of France provoked a more thorough exclusion of Britain from the subsequent bargaining on the European relaunch, and on the definition of the principles underlying the negotiations on enlargement, than would likely have been the case with a more conciliatory policy. More significantly for our purposes, Britain also became marginalised in the debates on political cooperation. In the second half of 1969, France not only succeeded in ascertaining the prevalence of the Six over the WEU, but also insisted that EPC would start without the EC candidate countries, as it wanted to make sure that Britain no longer could misuse a platform of political cooperation for the purpose of forcing its way into the Community. This was a serious blow to London, and it is doubtful that the FCO at the end of 1969 would still have confirmed its earlier credo that 'good relations with France are of less importance to us than good relations with the US and Germany'.[53]

Breaking the deadlock: A fragile consensus at the Hague Summit

Leadership changes were essential in overcoming Europe's crisis. De Gaulle's resignation obviously was key, but new German Chancellor Willy Brandt also played a vital role in finding a compromise solution. However, with Wilson still in power, Franco-British relations continued to be marked by distrust. Pompidou only lifted the French veto against enlargement negotiations at the EC summit at the end of 1969 because it was the lesser of two evils. For all the excitement and relief that the breakthrough in The Hague prompted, the consensus was still very fragile, and it was not until Heath's election victory in 1970 that the French came to see a widened Europe as a scheme with much potential.

Even though the 'British question' was at the centre of attention in the second half of 1969, Britain was conspicuously absent from the bargaining process that led to the breaking of the deadlock. Pompidou chose to negotiate the relaunch of Europe with his back turned on London, not without hinting at French disappointments in dealing directly with Wilson. Britain did try to engage again with France once de Gaulle was gone. In autumn 1969, Soames proposed a bilateral dialogue on enlargement and offered Stewart's word that Whitehall would keep the talks secret this time. But Pompidou laconically replied that Britain should stop trying to tear the EC walls down and argued that the only way into the Community would be through the gate.[54] He also turned down Brandt's idea of a summit of the Seven, which many perceived as the most obvious way forward.[55] Instead, Pompidou insisted that it was up to the Six to decide about the parameters of Europe's future. The compromise package of The Hague was, accordingly, mainly agreed between him and Brandt.

Pompidou had run for the French presidency based on the campaign slogan of 'change within continuity' (le changement dans la continuité).[56] Once in power, he did preserve some of his predecessor's basic policies, most notably the primacy of national independence in defence matters and the notion of privileged relations with the Soviet Union.[57] Yet, he also considered modifications in French foreign policy to be both inevitable and desirable. On the one hand, Pompidou lacked the stature of de Gaulle that would have allowed him to pursue a similarly eccentric course. He was not a 'historic' Gaullist with roots in the French *Résistance*, and he had never joined the institutional Gaullist movement. A former teacher and man of letters (who had edited an anthology of French poetry), he had repeatedly worked for de Gaulle during the 1950s. But he also had pursued a career in banking, and it came as a surprise when de Gaulle appointed him as French prime minister in 1962. During his years at the Matignon until 1968, Pompidou had been able to build his own political profile, assisted by the so-called 'Pompidou Boys', notably François-Xavier Ortoli, Jacques Chirac, and Edouard Balladur.[58] Still, as president he was impelled to build a broader power base and reach out to French centrists and moderates.

On the other hand, Pompidou also had different role conceptions than de Gaulle with regard to both France and Europe. He was less concerned with prestige politics and geopolitical pretensions than with a thorough modernisation of the French economy, as he believed that French power depended primarily on rapid industrial growth. This implied a general move towards greater modesty and pragmatism in international affairs, and an end to excessive ideological rows with Washington. While sceptical of American predominance in Europe, Pompidou aimed at a rapprochement with the US, not least because of his fear of a resurgent Germany.[59] Yet the biggest difference between him and de Gaulle concerned the EC. De Gaulle had tolerated the Common Market mainly because of its benefits for French agriculture. Pompidou, however, not only considered it an indispensable tool for French economic modernisation, but also valued it in its own right. The new French president too supported an *Europe européenne*, and he rejected a political role for the Commission. Yet, contrary to de Gaulle, he thought it perfectly possible that the EC would still be viable after enlargement, and he was anxious to advance European unity. Pompidou's main interest and expertise related to the economic dimension of unification, and he regarded monetary union as a key project both for strengthening Europe and for binding the FRG to the West. While he was sceptical about the feasibility of political unification under the political circumstances of 1969, he considered a modest form of foreign policy cooperation desirable – as long as the British could not abuse it again for their own purposes.[60]

Pompidou's positive attitude towards Europe was reflected in the composition of the new French government. Maurice Schumann replaced Debré as foreign minister, to the surprise of many. Well-known as France's spokesman in London during World War II, Schumann was a genuine Anglophile and avowed European. Debré himself, a Gaullist hardliner, was only offered the defence ministry, which he grudgingly accepted. Jacques Chaban-Delmas, the new prime minister, had already fought for the European cause at the Congress of Europe in 1948 and was a stout defender of EC enlargement. Finally, it was particularly significant that Pompidou offered the key Ministry of Economy and Finance to Giscard d'Estaing, a non-Gaullist, who was even a member of Jean Monnet's Action Committee for the United States of Europe.[61]

As for the way out of Europe's crisis, Pompidou (who was quick to take the reins of French foreign policy into his own hands) formulated his policy in a hand-written annotation of 8 July 1969: first, to complete the CAP with a definite financial agreement; second, to talk about reinforcing the Community; third, to think through with the Five the consequences of enlargement and establish a joint negotiating position.[62] The French president left no doubt that his priorities, presented to the public in the form of the catchy triptych of 'completion, deepening, enlargement' (achèvement, approfondissement, élargissment), were in that order. He did accept the need for enlargement, not just to counterbalance West German power, but also to get the EC going again and to win British support against calls for supranationalism. But he insisted that the Community be consolidated beforehand, so as to rule out that Britain could subsequently modify its very foundations.[63]

The West German response to the French proposal was initially cacophonous. Foreign Minister Brandt and the SPD emphasised the primacy of enlarging the Community and advocated a conception of Europe that was not too far away from Pompidou's triptych. Conversely, Chancellor Kiesinger and the CDU/CSU were mainly interested in complementing the Common Market with a political and security framework. Only after Brandt's election victory of 28 September 1969 did a coherent West German position emerge. As his conception was much more in touch with the realities of the time, the leadership change in Bonn raised the chance for a viable compromise in The Hague.

Although supportive of British membership in the EC in the long run, Kiesinger was very concerned about the effects of enlargement on the cohesion of the Six. He shared de Gaulle's view that the Community with Britain would turn into something different, and he had doubts as to London's motives for joining the European project. While never explicitly speaking out against enlargement, he publicly made it clear that Europe could not be built 'with states that failed to keep their affairs in order and were not sound and stable',[64] an obvious warning that Britain would first have to resolve its economic weakness before accession to the EC would be conceivable. Kiesinger's top priority in the months prior to the summit was progress in the realm of political cooperation. Fearful of the rise of China as a third nuclear power, and unwilling to rely solely on the US for the defence of Europe, Kiesinger pleaded vigorously for urgent efforts at moving towards a collective European will in matters of foreign and defence policy. Although he admitted that he did not have a blueprint for political unification, he was critical of Pompidou's economic priorities and urged that regular meetings of the heads of government and their foreign ministers begin as soon as possible.[65]

The SPD regarded such far-reaching ideas as wishful thinking and came up with quite a different policy for The Hague.[66] Brandt portrayed himself as being in favour of European political unity and collective solidarity in world politics, not least because, as he once admitted, it could serve as a substitute for the lost German fatherland (*Ersatz-Vaterland*).[67] But he called for pragmatism and patience in this respect, coining the phrase that 'the desirable must not prevent us from doing the possible'.[68] Brandt thus argued for a modest beginning in political consultation, emphasising the primacy of enlargement instead.[69] If the SPD, like large segments of the bureaucracy in the Auswärtige Amt (the West German foreign ministry), for a number of reasons had long been supportive of Britain's membership in the EC,[70] in 1969 one major new motive moved to the foreground: *Ostpolitik*. A wider and prosperous Community was important for Brandt to anchor his new Eastern policy firmly in the West and defuse fears that a new 'Rapallo' in the sense of a separate Soviet–German reunification deal was in the offing. As the SPD had originally been sceptical of European integration, Brandt now sought to demonstrate that his policy of reconciliation with the East would complement rather than undermine Adenauer's policy of integrating the FRG into the Atlantic Alliance and the EC. A relaunch of European unification based on a widening of the EC was an ideal opportunity to underline his credo that *Ostpolitik* would begin in the West. Moreover, a more dynamic European integration project was bound to become a magnet for Eastern European countries.[71]

Brandt's 'Small Coalition' of social and liberal democrats epitomised a change in the FRG's history in more than one way. The coalition marked the first time that the SPD was the major governing party, thereby paving the way for the new *Ostpolitik*. It also represented a shift from the authoritarian leadership of the Adenauer era to the much more participatory and cooperative style of Brandt. The rise to the chancellery of this charismatic, inclusive, and highly popular public figure – who had been a leftist revolutionary in his youth, was the illegitimate child of a proletarian mother, and had emigrated to Scandinavia during the Third Reich – was a manifestation of the profound change of societal values that had taken place during the 1960s. Brandt himself cultivated the myth of a second 'zero hour' in 1969, arguing that his election victory was final proof that Adolf Hitler had definitely lost the war.[72]

As for the FRG's *Westpolitik*, the priority shifts concerning EC enlargement and political unification under Chancellor Brandt were less far-reaching than in the case of *Ostpolitik*, and little taken note of. Continuity prevailed in the sense that Brandt and Scheel were committed to the European integration process, just as their predecessors had been. Scheel, one of the few Liberals who had voted for the Treaty of Rome despite Britain's self-exclusion, was indeed an ardent European who indicated from the start that he planned to invest most of his time in the European project.[73] Still, the differences between the new government and Kiesinger were significant. Brandt never pressed Pompidou to move towards European political unity, and he readily accepted the bargain proposed by France, trading his major summit objective, that is, enlargement, for the French president's top priority, that is, the consolidation of the – much disputed – CAP.

Already in July 1969, Brandt had hinted during a visit in Paris at the possibility of agreement with the French compromise package, a position he reconfirmed once he became chancellor.[74] He also accepted Pompidou's refusal to specify a date for opening enlargement negotiations – a position the French president insisted upon so as to make sure that completion would be achieved without falling prey to delaying tactics. Brandt did so because he knew that the FRG could counter any French non-compliance with enlargement by not ratifying the CAP measures.[75] The difficulty, however, was how to multilateralise the deal among the Six. In three preparatory meetings for the summit, and after numerous bilateral conversations, the EC foreign ministers managed to agree on the triptych agenda, a limited participation by the Commission, and the obligation for potential new EC members to take over the entire *acquis communautaire*. At the same time, there were ongoing clashes over the need to fix a date for opening talks with the accession candidates.[76]

There was, therefore, a pervasive atmosphere of anxiety when the six leaders gathered in The Hague on 1 and 2 December 1969. Many believed that failure to reach consensus risked provoking the disintegration of the Six and the recurrence of balance-of-power politics in Europe. As if to raise tensions further, the summit had a bad start. Pompidou gave a very reserved opening speech that outlined the problems, but failed to offer solutions. Although his reticence was a deliberate tactic,[77] it put him immediately into the defensive, the more so since Brandt sketched an impressive European action programme and self-confidently reminded his interlocutors that the best way to counterbalance the FRG's waxing strength was by widening the EC.[78] With discussions in the afternoon being strained by disagreement whether to tackle enlargement or the CAP first, the decisive breakthrough did not come until Brandt and Pompidou held a bilateral conversation over dinner. Once the French president, as witnessed by Gaston Eyskens and Pierre Werner (the prime ministers of Belgium and Luxembourg), gave his word of honour that enlargement negotiations would start in 1970, his partners no longer insisted on being given a more precise date.[79] When Pompidou surprised his interlocutors the next morning with a comprehensive programme for the deepening of the Community, the tense atmosphere finally gave way to a mood of reluctant optimism and relief. Continuing resistance against the compromise package by both French officials and Joseph Luns, the Dutch foreign minister (who wanted a concrete date), indicated that the deep-rooted distrust among the Europeans could not be swept away with a single summit.[80] Still, the top-level agreement gave reason to hope that the deadlock had at last been broken.

As for the issue of political cooperation, it had not been a key theme either during the pre-summit bargaining or during the summit itself. It was clear that significant progress in this field was contingent on agreement to enlargement negotiations, and the ongoing WEU crisis had made further progress difficult. The British had been well aware that the WEU would be no long-term solution, and after de Gaulle's resignation, they had been quick to subordinate the WEU issue to their main priority of accession to the Common Market. Still, the FCO had remained interested in maintaining the dynamics of this London-based organisation, which it now wanted to use as a tactical instrument for keeping the Five on the British side and continuing to deny the Six consultations without Britain.[81] However, although some low-key consultations had taken place during the French 'empty-chair' policy, the WEU had remained largely ineffective. The Belgians had joined the FRG in blocking progress in the absence of French participation. Also, the WEU had run into financial trouble, as France refused to pay its share of dues. And even the British had to admit that the French absence was unhealthy for the organisation, particularly with regard to its task of monitoring West German armament restrictions.[82]

If Britain had failed to sustainably strengthen the WEU à Six in the autumn of 1969, efforts by Harmel as chairman-in-office to bring France back in had been equally unsuccessful.[83] Against this background of a continuing stalemate in the WEU, debates on political cooperation had gradually shifted back to the EC-Six. In France, the WEU crisis came to be seen as an opportunity for reviving the idea of foreign policy cooperation à Six. Even though the French had no blueprint at hand, Schumann suggested to Brandt in September 1969 that France was interested in the matter and that a start could be made with institutionalised meetings of the six foreign ministers. He added, however, that he would prefer the FRG to take the initiative, with France promising support.[84] Well aware of the difficulty of starting without Britain, the French were obviously anxious not to be rebuffed again as in 1962. Another problem for the Quai d'Orsay was the cautious stance of Pompidou. In the autumn of 1969, the French president discarded his earlier proposal that the six heads of state and government should hold frequent meetings, not least because of accusations that he was out to weaken the EC institutions.[85] Accordingly, he also asked for restraint when Schumann and Chaban-Delmas made the case for a French Fouchet-type proposition during the internal summit preparations.[86]

Accordingly, it was the West Germans who took the operative lead concerning political cooperation prior to the summit. Before Schumann's visit, there had been no agreement in Bonn how to approach the issue. Brandt had spoken in favour of political consultations by as many European countries as possible, Kiesinger had favoured a small core group, and officials in the Auswärtige Amt had sketched a Fouchet design for the Seven.[87] But when France forced the FRG to choose between continuing inaction and another attempt at cooperation between the Six, Bonn opted for the latter and, accordingly, placed EPC on the summit agenda during the first preparatory meeting of the six foreign ministers.[88]

When conceptualising a concrete summit proposal regarding political cooperation, the officials in the Auswärtige Amt decided to proceed very cautiously. Their experience of regular bilateral consultations within the framework of the Elysée Treaty and in the German–French Study Group on questions of European security had given them ample evidence how difficult it was to find common ground in many issues even with France alone.[89] Moreover, Brandt's tour of European capitals in the summer of 1969 had reconfirmed his view that the only chance for the Four to accept political cooperation à Six was an agreement offering the prospect of later participation by Britain.[90] Consequently, the FRG's idea was to propose that a study be pursued under the hypothesis of enlargement and to be completed within six months. Such a modest proposal should induce the Four to give up their principled resistance against starting à Six, while allowing the French to cease their opposition against allowing candidates to join later.[91]

During the summit, the FRG did table its plan, which indeed was included in the summit communiqué. Brandt during his speech made the case for turning the Community into an 'exemplary scheme' (*eine exemplarische Ordnung*) that would become an element of a pan-European structure of peace. Urging Europe to unify its resources and to be empowered to stand up against the superpowers and preserve its own identity, he called for 'qualified political cooperation' (*qualifizierte aussenpolitische Zusammenarbeit*) beyond the normal WEU-type exchange of views. To the surprise of many, Pompidou responded with his own initiative. Conceding that Europe indeed had a political vocation, albeit a pacific and non-provocative one, he suggested that there should be regular – but not too frequent – meetings of the EC foreign ministers. The French president argued that the EC members should discuss foreign policy problems, most notably Europe's relations with the US and Eastern Europe, and they should perhaps try to harmonise some policies.[92]

Pompidou put forward his suggestion mainly as a defensive measure, hoping to keep the initiative with the Six and rule out any prospect of immediate consultations with the candidate countries.[93] France, therefore, was not unhappy when its partners favoured Brandt's more cautious idea of starting with a non-committal study only. Various statements during the summit revealed just how diverse individual viewpoints still were on the issue. Eyskens, Werner, and Italian Prime Minister Mariano Rumor called for Europe's political unification in terms that went much beyond either Brandt's or Pompidou's suggestions, whereas the Dutch seemed unenthusiastic about the whole idea and, with their call for full participation of the Community institutions in a European foreign policy, made sure that no consensus would be in immediate reach.[94]

Hence, the essential result of The Hague with respect to political cooperation was simply that a reference to it had made it into the communiqué. After two decades of inconclusive debates and negotiations, the topic finally was back on the EC agenda. In the aftermath of the compromise package on the EC's widening and deepening, the idea of a European political identity began to look more feasible again. It remained unclear whether the study would ever lead to a concrete agreement, just as nobody could tell whether the enlargement negotiations would actually succeed. But there was at least a possibility again that progress could finally be made.

For the British delegation, the outcome of the Hague Summit was ambivalent. On the one hand, the door for accession talks had finally been opened. But on the other hand, the CAP had been cemented, which greatly embarrassed the Wilson government. For all their rhetoric of accepting this key policy of the Common Market, Wilson and Stewart were actually hoping to reform it. Whitehall could only express regret that this major issue had been negotiated without a British seat at the table.[95] The British were also irritated to realise that the Six were to launch talks on political unification. For the Labour government, the mandate to work out a study on political unification was an 'unwelcome decision'.[96] Despite numerous protestations from the British government stating that it felt, as Stewart once put it, 'entitled to object to any proposal that the Five should engage in any way in political consultation [...] with France in a forum from which we were excluded',[97] Britain had to realise that all of its efforts to persuade at least one of the Five to veto such a proceeding at the summit had been in vain. It was, as the FCO put it, 'a reverse for Her Majesty's Government, and for the Secretary of State personally'.[98] Having done much to isolate Paris in the first half of 1969, London ended up marginalised itself when it came to sketching a political framework for Europe. There is no doubt that at the Hague Summit, Europe had taken a big step towards overcoming its paralysis. Still, a large measure of uncertainty persisted, concerning both the durability of the *relance européenne* as such and the ability of the Europeans to establish consensus on a new political dimension of unification. The difficult relations between London and Paris had much to do with either.

The Davignon Report: Starting EPC à Six

After the summit of The Hague, there was finally movement again in the process of European unification. Talks on how to set up a monetary union started in early 1970, and an expert group headed by Pierre Werner was tasked with proposing a way forward. Described by Brandt as the new 'Magna Charta' of Europe, EMU was widely perceived as the ideal vehicle for further integration.[99] The EC-Six were also busy defining their position for the accession negotiations with Britain, Ireland, Denmark, and Norway, which were scheduled to begin at the end of June 1970. As for the commissioned study on political unification, it was on the negotiation table right from the beginning, the summit communiqué having asked for its completion by July 1970.

Whereas the EC-related work of the Six in Brussels became characterised by a growing spirit of optimism and cooperation, the parallel deliberations on *l'Europe politique* took place in an atmosphere of ongoing distrust and tension. Disagreement about the role of Britain in producing the study continued to be a major problem. The fact that the study was to be worked out just when *Ostpolitik* entered into its operative phase proved to be a second major obstacle. If Brandt's policy towards the East and the 'German question' were essential motives behind EC enlargement, they became a hindrance for Europe's political unification. Nevertheless, the Six eventually managed to agree on a common text regarding political cooperation. Although the provisions in the so-called Davignon (or Luxembourg) Report were conspicuously modest, the decision to get EPC started at all was a success in itself.

A climate of distrust: Britain's exclusion

Given the vagueness of the Hague mandate to study progress in this field 'within the context of enlargement', it comes as no surprise that heated debates took place in the early months of 1970 as to how to actually interpret this phrase. The British argued that the contentious clause could only mean that the Six should take no decisions in the political field without London's involvement. They came up with a well-concerted, month-long campaign in favour of an early involvement in the respective deliberations. In a note to the Six of March 1970, George Thomson, chancellor of the Duchy of Lancaster, insisted that Britain regarded the objective of political unification as of 'historic importance' and demanded that London should be involved in the talks on 'full and equal' terms at least as soon as enlargement negotiations had opened, that is, one month before the study was due.[100]

The French were having none of this. Ruling out any British involvement in EPC prior to enlargement, they said that the clause 'within the context of enlargement' simply meant defining a model of cooperation that would be compatible with an enlarged Community and would not hinder the process of enlargement. The Quai d'Orsay indefatigably defended the principle of 'compulsory correlation' (corrélation obligatoire) between belonging to the EC and participating in EPC, which, according to them, had already been accepted during the Fouchet negotiations and was vital to protect the Community.[101] The French fear that Britain would use EPC as a 'court of appeal'[102] to influence the (economic) enlargement negotiations certainly was not unfounded.[103] There was also concern in Paris that the British might drop the goal of EC membership as soon as they were allowed into EPC, being satisfied with participation in the political Europe. Furthermore, Stewart's increasingly federalist rhetoric in early 1970 left the French wondering whether Britain might in fact support a scheme of foreign policy incompatible with French interests. Finally, France also thought it essential to sustain the political momentum within the circle of the Community countries in order to justify the inadmissibility of neutral and non-democratic countries to the EC, and to exclude interested countries such as Turkey from any new forum of political consultation.[104]

When Thomson lamented in Paris in April 1970 that Britain did not want to miss yet another bus in Europe's unification, Schumann laconically replied that Whitehall 'would be kept fully informed of where the bus was going and the bus route would be straight'.[105] Yet it was not so much French stubbornness, but rather the FRG's support for the French position that eventually led the Six to proceed in their study despite British reservations. The West Germans had initially assured the British that the applicants would be free to join the study carried out by the Six as soon as negotiations on enlargement had begun.[106] But once they had realised that French resistance was insurmountable, they preferred going ahead à Six to not going ahead at all – just as in autumn 1969, when they had placed EPC on the summit agenda despite British objections (see above). Consequently, when Thomson asked for support for the British point of view, he met with a rebuff in Bonn and was even advised to subsequently refrain from offensive tactics and exercise more caution in dealing with the Six.[107]

By the end of April 1970, the FCO effectively gave up its effort to either join the Six in their study or delay political cooperation of the Community countries. As Soames advised Thomson, this was 'no time for trouble-making'.[108] The principal objective of British policy being to 'create a favourable atmosphere for the opening of negotiations',[109] the FCO decided to step back in matters of political cooperation for the sake of European (and particularly French) goodwill. London was hoping that the Six might suspend the beginning of EPC until after enlargement, a possibility that Pompidou and Schumann had hinted at several times.[110] And, should the Six decide to proceed anyway, the thinking was that the government could always 'rely on the Dutch to block things for us'.[111]

It was this kind of reasoning that led the British to also resolve the WEU crisis, largely on French terms. In the first months of 1970, the FCO had still been eager to strengthen the WEU as an instrument for delaying EPC à Six.[112] By June, however, it accepted that the WEU Permanent Council would hold no political consultations unless unanimously mandated and that issues relating to EC enlargement would not be tackled. If France in return ended its 'empty chair' policy,[113] this did not mean that the WEU would gain more relevance again. On the contrary, after an 18-month period of reactivation and drama, the organisation was finally relegated to its previous status of 'hibernation'. Since Britain no longer used it for tactical purposes, all efforts concerning European political consultations were now refocused on the Community framework.

As will be shown below, Britain was mistaken in its assumption that the Six would not begin harmonising their foreign policies before enlargement. At the same time, London's exclusion from the talks on political unification did contribute to the timid nature that came to characterise the study à Six. The old equation that had haunted Europe in the 1960s was still valid during the working out of the Davignon Report: while France might have been able to keep the British out, Britain's absence fostered caution and disunity among the Six.

New uncertainties: Ostpolitik and Westpolitik

A second factor with a negative impact on the working out of the study was the FRG's *Ostpolitik*. There were several reasons for this. Starting with Bonn, one problem was simply the limited capacity of the Brandt/Scheel government to deal with EC matters in early 1970. After the Hague Summit, Brandt and Egon Bahr, the architect of his *Ostpolitik* and foreign policy adviser, were immediately preoccupied with launching their new Eastern policy. Although Brandt appointed a new parliamentary state secretary for European affairs, Katharina Focke, to the chancellery to signal his determination to guide the course of *Westpolitik*, this measure had limited effect, as Focke proved unable to give major impulses.[114] As for Scheel, he suffered from a lack of experience in foreign policy issues in his first few months in office, and it would take him some time to get the kind of domestic and international recognition that would be commensurate with Bonn's diplomatic weight.[115] As a result, bureaucrats in the foreign ministry came to dominate the elaboration of the study, just as the chancellery ran the key aspects of *Ostpolitik*.[116] While this did not prevent the FRG from playing an active role in discussing the Hague mandate, the lack of involvement of the political decision-makers limited the scope of what Bonn would want to negotiate.

Ostpolitik also posed certain conceptual constraints on the FRG's *Westpolitik*. Recent research has pointed out that *Ostpolitik* as conceived by the SPD implied the long-term goal of ideologically undermining the East by exposing it to Western ideas. Labelled 'Change through Rapprochement' (*Wandel durch Annäherung*), this policy aimed at diminishing Soviet hegemony in Eastern Europe, with a peaceful change of the Eastern power structures, perhaps leading to German reunification.[117] But if the FRG's recognition of the status quo in Europe was only intended as a means towards overcoming it, this circumstance implied consequences for European unification. Bahr, flirting with the idea of reunification within a pan-European security system that was to replace NATO and the Warsaw Pact (and would be guaranteed by the two superpowers), strongly opposed European political unification in principle.[118] Brandt, who mockingly described Bahr as a 'Prussian patriot' who was 'colour-blind towards Europe' and 'ignorant of where France lay in Europe',[119] tended to view Western European integration as a focal point for a subsequent pan-European security system, which is why he saw less contradiction between his *Westpolitik* and his *Ostpolitik*. Still, he did give orders to the Auswärtige Amt to keep the political construction of Europe within certain limits and avoid anything that could give the impression of political bloc formation.[120] His argument that Europe should focus on 'strong political co-operation' and leave real political unification 'for generations ahead of us' was no doubt largely inspired by a sober analysis of intra-European relations in the spring of 1970.[121] But it also very likely had to do with his determination not to provoke criticism from Moscow at a time when the FRG sought a rapprochement with the East.

France, too, was unwilling to sacrifice détente for the sake of the political unification of Europe. As Pompidou told Aldo Moro, the Italian foreign minister, now that *Ostpolitik* was clearing the way for an all-European détente, would it not be foolish to build another block in the West?[122] Yet, much more even than the promises of pan-European détente, it was the uncertainties related to *Ostpolitik* that convinced the French president to approach the issue of European political unification with caution. Although he trusted Brandt and was in favour of the short-term operational phase of *Ostpolitik*, Pompidou was deeply concerned about the prospect of future German–Soviet collusion.[123] But rather than *l'Europe politique*, he emphasised enlargement and EMU as means of containing any renascent German nationalism. As for political cooperation, he gave instructions to the Quai d'Orsay to keep any scheme to a minimum and not to stick any 'flashy posters to an empty boutique' (*panneaux provocants sur une boutique vide*).[124] As he explained, he 'played a subtle game' in Europe (*je joue un jeu subtil*) and wanted to await further developments in *Ostpolitik*, European détente, and Britain before taking any bigger steps. A genuinely political Europe might be a target for the 1980s or later, but it would certainly not materialise as long as the 'German problem' remained unresolved.[125]

Defining machinery rather than purpose

Ostpolitik did also have a *positive* impact on the study. As the Auswärtige Amt noted, the more the FRG moved towards the French policy of '*détente, entente, cooperation*', the more agreement Bonn and Paris found with regard to the political unification of Europe.[126] The fact that both the FRG and France emphasised caution in how they approached the study was an important key to success, particularly since it contrasted with the much more ambitious proposals put forward by Belgium and Italy.[127] Also, domestic and international concern about *Ostpolitik* prompted the Auswärtige Amt to take a lead role in producing the study, as the FRG was eager to demonstrate its attachment to the West.[128] While Davignon was officially in charge of the report (Belgium acting as the presidency of the EC in the first half of 1970), the West German bureaucracy did much to support him in devising a scheme for cooperation.

The making of the Davignon Report can be divided into three phases: an initial phase of informal bilateral deliberations that started with a kick-off meeting of the foreign ministers on 20 January 1970 and lasted until their first substantive exchange of views on 6 March 1970; a main phase of multilateral bargaining and of conceptualising EPC that resulted in the Six provisionally accepting a draft report on 20 July 1970; and a final phase where the Six cleared the text domestically and invited the four EC candidates to offer their own views, ending with the EC foreign ministers officially approving and publishing the report in Luxembourg at the end of October 1970.

The process was launched with visits by Paul Frank, the political director of the Auswärtige Amt, to his European counterparts in early 1970 to learn about respective national views and expectations.[129] These efforts resulted in a West German *Aide Mémoire* that focused on setting up a light mechanism for harmonising national foreign policies. The paper was characterised by a high degree of pragmatism. It recommended that cooperation be non-binding, with two annual meetings of foreign ministers and the heads of state and government, alternately. Three levels of cooperation were envisaged: a level of national experts who would jointly work out analyses and options, independent of national directives; a committee of the national political directors to evaluate the work of the experts and prepare the ministerial consultations; and the ministerial and summit meetings. All levels would be supported by a coordination service. The European Parliament and the Commission would be associated with the consultations. As the proposed mechanism was only intended as a first step towards a more comprehensive political union, it was suggested that the report should be approved as a solemn declaration only, with a proper treaty following at a later stage.[130]

It was this *Aide Mémoire* that became the – unofficial – basis of negotiations. At the ministerial meeting on 6 March 1970, important first decisions were taken: consultations would not become compulsory and have no judicial basis; no secretariat would be established; and summit meetings would take place only under extraordinary circumstances.[131] Furthermore, the political directors of the Six were officially mandated to work out the study. It was in the course of several day-long negotiations of this group, soon to be called the 'Davignon Committee', that the study took shape.[132] Only where no consensus could be achieved would the foreign ministers themselves take up bargaining and try to hammer out compromise solutions.[133]

One immediate controversy related to the scope of the study. While the Belgians and the Italians complained that the West German paper one-sidedly focused on machinery rather than defining the end state of political unification, the French argued that Bonn overemphasised a possible evolution of cooperation. A compromise was found by starting with foreign policy only, but including two dynamic parts in the report: a preamble indicating the goal of political union (which became part I of the report), and an additional provision to continue to study the question and provide a second report within two years after EPC became operational (part III). Again, lengthy debates took place on how precise the preamble should be. France refused any reference to a supranational evolution of Europe, and, together with the FRG, it made sure that no explicit statement on the need for a European defence identity was included. Conversely, Paris failed to insert a reference on the goal of a *Europe européenne*, with the net result being that part I of the report contained little more than cloudy rhetoric on Europe's 'duty' and the 'necessity' that it 'exercise its responsibilities'.[134]

Regarding the precise scheme of cooperation, which became the second and most important part of the report, the basic West German three-level approach was accepted. However, France presented its own paper and succeeded in turning the already cautious West German proposal into an even more government-controlled design. Experts were to receive directives from the Political Committee; extraordinary meetings could be summoned only by consensus; the Commission was only to be invited 'to make known its views' where its activities were affected; and the European Parliament was merely to be associated by a biannual colloquy with its Political Commission and by an annual oral report of the chairman of the Six to the plenum on progress in the study on political unification.[135]

Finally, much time was invested in establishing a consensus on part IV of the report concerning the procedure and timing of associating the applicant countries to EPC. Whereas France had originally proposed that the British and the other applicants be informed via other institutions, such as the WEU or the Council of Europe, the West Germans presented the so-called 'Scheel Formula', according to which consultations by the Six would be immediately followed by a day of information and exchange of views with the applicants. French wariness of excessive British involvement was eventually assuaged by a compromise solution suggested by the Belgians, which involved holding the two kinds of meetings several days apart.[136] The point at which the candidate countries could fully participate in EPC remained open, however, as the report only stated that the exchange of views would be intensified once the EC accession agreements had been signed.

The most striking feature of the Davignon Report was clearly its minimalist conception. The stated objectives of EPC were merely to ensure better mutual understanding of international problems through regular exchanges of information and consultation; to strengthen solidarity by promoting the harmonisation of national views and by coordinating positions; and, 'where possible and desirable', to come up with common actions. There was no talk of a common European foreign policy, and no permanent institutions of cooperation were envisioned. Also, EPC was largely decoupled from the EC. If the distinction between foreign policy cooperation and economic integration was an important lesson learnt from earlier attempts at political unification and a precondition of success in 1970, it came to be criticised by federalists, in particular, as a key weakness of the Davignon Report.[137]

Conversely, the modesty of the design had the distinct advantage that the EC candidates had no difficulties with accepting the report. The British were not unhappy with the 'meagre content' of the study.[138] In their official comment, they did express their discontent with the arrangements for association. But, like all candidate countries, they generally approved of the report, paving the way for the Six to launch EPC operationally.[139] Furthermore, there was one procedural novelty in the Davignon Report that appeared promising. By involving the national bureaucracies, EPC aimed at sorting out differences and harmonising policies on a long-term basis. Its inter-diplomatic approach based on the Political Committee of the national political directors differed from the sort of multilateral diplomacy exercised in NATO and the UN, where permanent representatives played a central role in consultations. Regular meetings of the heads of the national bureaucracies promised to be an effective forum for consultation, even more so since these meetings were complemented by national working groups of those responsible for individual foreign policy issues.

This brief outline of the genesis of the Davignon Report demonstrates that the conventional wisdom, according to which France played a leading part in setting up EPC, is at odds with the picture that emerges from the archives. It may well be that France was hoping to use EPC as an instrument with which to safeguard a leadership role in Europe; it is possible that it sought to reduce US influence on the FRG with EPC; and it cannot be ruled out that one of its motives with EPC was to balance enlargement with a distinctly Gaullist foreign policy mechanism.[140] However, as outlined above, France pursued an essentially defensive strategy during the working out of the study, its negotiating position being dominated by aloofness, uncertainty, and a conspicuous sense of disorientation. As for the FRG, its vital role in getting EPC started has been more adequately reflected in the historiography. Nevertheless, in this context, some of the motives identified as driving the FRG's interest in political cooperation must be questioned. The arguments that Bonn accepted EPC as a concession for French approval of enlargement or saw it as an instrument to bring the French around with respect to enlargement are untenable in light of the archival sources.[141] On the other hand, the view that the West Germans sought to embed their foreign policy in a multilateral framework to enhance the FRG's international influence and better deflect external criticism seems plausible, even though it is difficult to substantiate it with concrete evidence.[142] The archives do, however, disclose a whole variety of other motives. Other than counterbalancing *Ostpolitik*, these include the danger of an impending US disengagement, the desire to assuage US complaints about economic discrimination, the prospect of a possible pan-European security conference, as well as the wish to recapture the imagination of the youth in Europe.[143]

The documents also reveal one of the reasons why the West Germans played a much more active part in setting up EPC. At this stage, they were simply more optimistic about the feasibility of cooperation than France. Pompidou accepted the Davignon Report, but suspected that efforts at coordination would remain 'futile' and 'cat food'.[144] The FRG, in contrast, urged the Five to begin practical cooperation as soon as possible, and convinced them to hold a first ministerial meeting as early as November 1970.[145] As the non-binding and procedure-oriented character of EPC obviously rendered its viability dependent on the political will of the participating governments, the question of whether France would eventually come round to abandon its pessimism and reluctance was thus of seminal importance for the emergence of a common European identity.

Heath and the unblocking of *l'Europe politique*, 1970–72

EPC could well have remained an anaemic and unsuccessful tool if it had not been for the unexpected election victory of the Conservatives in Britain in the spring of 1970. Edward Heath deserves much credit for giving added dynamic to the project of political cooperation by accomplishing a genuine Anglo-French rapprochement and taking Britain into Europe. More than anything, it was the credibility of his commitment to the EC that convinced France of

Europe's large, untapped potential and ushered in what Pompidou came to call a 'new era of mutual trust' between Paris and London.[146]

A revolution in British foreign policy

It is not easy to understand why the Heath government has only aroused little academic interest so far. One reason might be that many of its domestic policies came to be regarded as a failure. It may also have to do with Heath's uncharismatic personality. The lifelong bachelor has been described as a hardworking 'one-dimensional robot',[147] who lacked essential qualities of leadership and was 'one of the least inspiring speakers in modern times',[148] and his famous passions for organ music, yacht racing, and French literature did little to bring him closer to the British people. Heath's foreign policy, however, can hardly be the cause of this negligence, for it has been justly labelled as 'a revolution'.[149] Three aspects were particularly remarkable: the deemphasising of the special relationship, Heath's genuine belief in the European cause, and his prioritisation of close Anglo-French relations.

In the traditional British dilemma of how to secure the country's global influence after decolonisation, Heath was the only leader to ever unambiguously opt for the European option rather than for close Anglo-American relations. When he took up office in June 1970, he informed an astonished US President Nixon that he no longer wished to talk of a 'special relationship'.[150] Convinced that the relevance of Britain for the US was bound to diminish anyway,[151] his declared priority was British commitment to Europe. Although special links to the US in the nuclear and intelligence field were to be retained, overall relations had to lose their traditional intimacy.[152] Heath stressed that Britain would not want to appear as a Trojan horse for the US in Europe, and that European consultations would in the future have to precede Anglo-American deliberations, prompting Kissinger to conclude that the US 'faced in Heath the curiosity of a more benign British version of de Gaulle'.[153]

Heath's zeal for the European idea set him apart from many other British politicians. His strong belief in the ideal of unification originated in his interwar travels to Nazi Germany and his experience of World War II, which led him to conclude that European unity was the only path to European reconciliation. European unification in his view would also restore the 'old world's' weight in global politics, which he regarded as indispensable, not to preserve past glories, but to build a just and peaceful future. A second notable aspect of Heath's role conception was that he had supported British participation in Europe from the very beginning, arguing already in his maiden speech in the House of

Commons in 1950 that London should be involved in the negotiations of the Six.[154] His idealism aside, he considered it in Britain's very best interest to join Europe in order to regain its strength and leading role, and to tie West Germany firmly to the West.[155] As an ardent advocate of a comprehensive political Community with a common foreign and defence policy, Heath considered EPC to be a laudable start, but hoped that its artificial distinction from the EC would one day be overcome. If he wanted the EC to become the focal point of all issues of European concern, he was not in favour of a federalist structure, but regarded the intensification of intergovernmental cooperation as the political core of Europe.

France played a key role in Heath's role conception of Europe. Having always deplored that nothing had come of Churchill's proposed union between France and Britain in 1940,[156] the new prime minister, a genuine Francophile, was very eager to build the 'New Europe' on a strong Anglo-French basis. Far from wanting to exclude Brandt from a leading role in Europe, he was well aware that close and trustful relations between London and Paris were the key to progress in Europe – which is why he regarded his relationship with Pompidou as a top priority of his foreign policy. Just how far Heath was prepared to go in his rapprochement with Paris was revealed in his famous proposal in the late 1960s to pool British and French nuclear weapons to form a joint deterrent to be 'held in trusteeship for Europe as a whole'.[157]

Importantly, large segments of the FCO both shared Heath's enthusiasm for Europe and were ready to abandon the anti-French stance of the late 1960s. Of course, there were always those, such as Permanent Under-Secretary Denis Greenhill, who were more Atlanticist than European in their outlook and viewed Britain's accession to the EC with some concern.[158] Yet the predominant mood in the FCO was clearly pro-European in the early 1970s, as reflected in its numerous studies on a common European foreign policy that may well stun the reader with the high expectations they reveal.[159] The anti-French tendencies in the FCO were rapidly declining, both because the first generation of pro-European top officials, marked by the struggle with de Gaulle, were gradually leaving office, and because Heath himself gave instructions to change policies vis-à-vis Paris.[160]

For all the FCO's support, however, Britain's European policy became largely dominated by Heath himself, with Douglas-Home being in charge of all other matters of foreign policy, notably the Commonwealth and transatlantic relations. This was not just because Douglas-Home, a former prime minister, was less single-minded in his pursuit of European policy than Heath. It also had to do with the fact that Heath was very experienced in EC affairs, having been Britain's chief negotiator during the first accession talks in the early 1960s.[161]

Anglo-French rapprochement

It was one thing for Heath to be eager to improve relations with France. But it was quite another question whether Pompidou would be receptive to such a move and would trust that Britain was serious in its approach. It was during the first bilateral summit between the two leaders in Paris on 19–21 May 1971 that the ice was finally broken in Anglo-French relations. Watched attentively all across Europe and beyond, this was the single most important meeting between any two Western European statesmen in the early 1970s. Secretly prepared for months by Downing Street and the Elysée,[162] its positive outcome meant that the fragile *relance européenne* accomplished at The Hague finally became consolidated, and that the era of distrust was overcome.

The summit had become necessary because by spring 1971, the enlargement negotiations were stuck. It is worth noting that these accession talks were a rather technical affair. The great issues of European unification were not discussed. In the case of Britain, the central problems to sort out were Commonwealth sugar, New Zealand butter, fisheries, and Community finance. London was in a very vulnerable position in these negotiations, the only major negotiable aspect being transitional measures and periods. As Con O'Neill, the British head of delegation below ministerial level, put it in his masterly retrospective report on the negotiations, the precept was to '[s]wallow it, and swallow it now'.[163] Having argued for years that it was too late for Britain to change the basic structure of the Community, Heath underlined that he was ready to accept the Community as it was. Still, the negotiations turned out to be highly difficult and often frustrating. While the talks were officially to be held between the candidates and the Community, they were in effect mainly an affair between France and Britain, the latter soon being confronted with, as O'Neill vividly described it, French 'frost and fog and drizzle'.[164]

Although economic interests were one reason for the French tactics of stonewalling, the basic problem was the deep-rooted distrust in Paris concerning British intentions. Although he did not really see any alternative to enlargement, Pompidou was very worried about what would become of a Community that included Britain, a country he was unfamiliar with and whose language he did not speak. Was London seeking to join Europe in order to strengthen or to block it? Was it prepared to defend European economic and political interests even against the US? It was obvious that a political understanding between

France and Britain on the purpose and shape of the future Europe was the key to unblocking the accession talks, which themselves became, 'peripheral, accidental, and secondary',[165] in the words of O'Neill.

The summit discussions were characterised by remarkable intimacy and unusual intensity. Aside from the interpreters, no staff were present during the four rounds of conversations, which were to last more than 11 hours.[166] Both Pompidou and Heath, who each had undergone extensive briefing sessions, signalled with exceptional gestures their determination to make this a groundbreaking meeting. The French president invited his guest to two meals instead of one at the Elysée, and, even more extraordinarily, went to dine at the British embassy. Heath, for his part, had given his first public speech upon arrival in French and, by staying longer with Pompidou than planned, he forfeited participating in a famous yachting race. He was not to regret it. As Soames put it, referring to Heath's boat, 'what may have proved *Morning Cloud*'s loss was at least, and emphatically, Europe's gain!'[167]

The first key point of debate was the future role of Europe in the world, an item suggested by the British. In a spirited opening speech, Heath expressed his disagreement with those in Britain who had emphasised the 'special relationship' after the war. He argued that any hope of satisfactory relations with the US were illusionary, if only because of the latter's sheer size. Only a strong Community could provide the European states with the means to defend their interests against the superpowers and a rising China, which is why Britain sought a durable marriage with the EC. After Heath had further outlined his conception of Europe, Pompidou replied that he shared the prime minister's European drive and that if Britain were, indeed, willing to use its political weight and vocation for the sake of Europe, this could well open up new possibilities. Heath then assured Pompidou that Britain no longer wanted to play a balancing role in Europe. The debate on this point ended with Heath accepting the French president's wish to discuss the difficult subject of defence at a later stage, not without indicating, however, that France and Britain should not postpone a common evaluation of nuclear cooperation for too long.

The second item on the agenda, on EC decision-making, was a key French concern. Here, consensus was quickly established. When Pompidou began to explain the French position that Community decisions on issues where vital national interests were at stake should, in practice, be reached by unanimous agreement, Heath immediately indicated his complete approval and backed the French model of a confederal Europe. The talks then moved to monetary policies and the future role of the Pound Sterling. These matters were more complex and the debates particularly extensive, but Heath did promise that Britain would join in fully in EMU. Further points discussed included the Community preference schemes, development aid, and the crucial remaining issues of the enlargement negotiations. One particularly interesting subject of debate was the future of the French language in the Community institutions. Internal French documents reveal just how concerned Paris was about the prospect of a 'linguistic balkanisation' of the enlarged Community.[168] Pompidou was all the more relieved when Heath indicated early on in the talks that French should remain the major working language in Brussels, and promised that British officials appointed to the Community would be able to carry out business in French.

Heath also agreed to list the main points of agreement in a secret joint document so as to give France some guarantee that he really meant business.[169] Once this was done, French satisfaction was complete. The summit ended with a joint press conference in the Elysée Palace's Salle des Fêtes. Where de Gaulle had announced his infamous veto in 1963, Pompidou and Heath now performed long handshakes for the cameras and proudly informed the European publics of their successful consultations, with Pompidou concluding:

> Many people believed that Great Britain was not and did not wish to become European, and that Britain wanted to enter the Community only so as to destroy it or to divert it from its objectives. Many people also thought that France was ready to use every pretext to place in the end a fresh veto on Britain's entry. Well, ladies and gentlemen, you see before you tonight two men who are convinced of the contrary.[170]

As a British diplomat later recalled, it was a most moving occasion, with very loud applause, and few eyes dry in the Salle.[171]

A boost to EPC

The meeting of minds between Pompidou and Heath at their Paris summit marked the beginning of what the press came to celebrate as a new *entente cordiale* in Franco-British relations.[172] To be sure, not all parts of the summit agreement would actually materialise: the understanding on the use of the French language was to prove futile in view of Irish and Danish resistance to speaking French in the Community;[173] also, as will be outlined below, Britain was incapable of joining Europe's monetary agreements for longer than a few weeks. However, what counted most was that Pompidou was now convinced, as he immediately wrote to Brandt after the summit, that Heath was sincere in his policy of joining Europe to strengthen it and keep it really European.[174] The legacies of de Gaulle and Wilson were about to be overcome, and great efforts were subsequently taken to create a pattern of cooperation between Paris and London.[175]

The decisive breakthrough in the enlargement negotiations was achieved only four weeks after the summit.[176] Then, after winning domestic approval in the marathon six-day 'Great Debate' in the House of Commons in October 1971, Heath finally signed the accession treaty in Brussels on 22 January 1972, surrounded by people such as Jean Monnet, Paul-Henri Spaak, Harold Macmillan, and George Brown. It was, as he stated in his memoirs, the proudest moment of his life.[177] It could be argued, of course, that Pompidou would have been compelled to let Britain into Europe even under a Labour government. This may well be so, although Wilson's sharp reprobation of the conditions of entry and his confrontational opposition course against Heath's European policy suggest otherwise.[178] What is certain, however, is that Wilson would never have been able to convince the French political elites that he was genuinely committed to Europe and, accordingly, that there were new opportunities for a widened Europe. Heath's commitment to Europe, in contrast, came to be judged as trustworthy and reliable in Paris.

This credibility would also give a boost to EPC. For one thing, with enlargement agreed and Franco-British relations repaired, the French came to accept British participation in EPC prior to the EC's official widening already. London joined EPC in February 1972, with the other candidate countries following two months later.[179] More importantly, Heath succeeded in convincing Pompidou of the feasibility and great benefits of European foreign policy cooperation. The French president began to realise just how much Europe could achieve now that two of its great powers – with veto powers in the UN Security Council, nuclear capabilities, special rights and responsibilities in Germany, and generally worldwide interests – were finally closing ranks. In the aftermath to the Paris summit, he explained to Brandt that the most important consequence of the Anglo-French rapprochement might well relate to the new perspective it opened for Europe's political determination.[180] Even in public, he now showed much more interest in EPC, for example when he in a television appearance pointed out on a world map the enormous potential that a united Europe might have as a new factor in world politics.[181]

The change of leadership in Britain was not the only reason for the French president's change of mind in 1971/72. Another important factor drawing his attention to EPC was the early crisis of EMU, Pompidou's pet project in Europe. Although monetary cooperation had been launched in the spring of 1971, it had been quickly disrupted by repeated international monetary crises.

The weakness of the Dollar and recurring US balance of payment deficits prompted increasing amounts of unwanted dollars to flow into the reserves of European countries, with speculative flights becoming so drastic that the FRG in particular felt compelled to float the D-Mark. As France rejected the FRG's idea of a collective European float against the Dollar, the leading industrialised countries worked out a worldwide realignment of fixed parities in December 1971. Based on this 'Smithsonian Agreement', the first stage of EMU was relaunched in March 1972, with the Europeans halving the margin within which currencies were allowed to move against one another from the 4.5 per cent of the Smithsonian Agreement to 2.25 per cent for their own currencies. Yet, this system, referred to as the European 'currency snake' in the 'Smithsonian tunnel', by June 1972 became disrupted too when the Pound Sterling was forced to leave the 'snake' and was floated. As the US, having suspended the convertibility of the Dollar into gold and refusing to defend a fixed dollar rate, no longer seemed to back the Bretton Woods system, it became increasingly clear that the forging of a European monetary personality would become much more difficult even than had been anticipated.[182]

For Pompidou, foreign policy cooperation became an alternative path to progress in Europe, therefore. By 1972, he famously referred to EPC as 'Europe's great hope' and compared it to a small vacillating flame that had to be kindled with patience and insistence.[183] As will be outlined in the next chapter, he now even came up with his own EPC initiative, proposing a political secretariat for Europe. It was a clear sign that his perception of political cooperation had dramatically improved – a development of utmost importance for the future course of EPC.

Towards trilateral leadership

Against the background of Europe's crisis and polarisation in the late 1960s, the emergence and consolidation of EPC between 1969 and 1972 was an accomplishment that could by no means be taken for granted. In this chapter, I have argued that leadership changes in France, the FRG, and Britain constituted the single most important factor enabling this accomplishment.

It might be tempting to point first to developments on the extra-European level of the international environment to explain why EPC came into being. After all, nuclear parity between the superpowers implied a growing importance of economic power and a multipolarisation of the international system, which gave regional units greater manoeuvrability and provided Europe with the option of forging its own political identity. Equally, superpower détente raised the likelihood that the US might forfeit European interests for the sake of East–West stability, a concern that seemed the more justified since the Nixon government was morally weakened by Vietnam and confronted with an increasingly isolationist domestic climate. Yet, the problem with this argument is that both the opportunity and the need for Europe to develop a capacity for pursuing its own foreign policy had been acknowledged long before. Superpower détente had been in the making for several years already, and uncertainties about the US security guarantee had troubled the Europeans throughout the post-war period, without ever prompting a *Europe politique*.

The main reason why the Europeans succeeded in starting EPC in the early 1970s was that they were able to overcome their internal deadlock that had prevented them from progressing to political unification earlier. The Anglo-French conflict over Britain's accession to the EC had been the major obstacle to European political cooperation in the 1960s; this 'British question' was resolved primarily because of the recurring 'German question'. The FRG's economic power and its *Ostpolitik* called for a new Anglo-French counter-weight in Europe and prompted the French search for a new modus vivendi with Britain. However, although the pressure to act stemmed from developments on the intra-European level, Europe's relaunch would have been impossible without parallel changes on the level of individual decision-makers.

De Gaulle's departure from office was decisive for finding a new consensus on Europe. Although the general had come to accept the need of a rapprochement with London by early 1969, he was incapable of devising a solution acceptable to either Britain or the Five. It was Pompidou's EC-based conception of cooperation that paved the way for enlarging the Community. The election victory of Brandt, while comparatively less important for Western Europe's fate, was significant too, as the SPD's EC priorities were more compatible with Pompidou's European triptych than those of Kiesinger and the CDU/CSU had been. Finally, the fragile Franco-German compromise on a *relance européenne* at the Hague Summit was only really substantiated once Heath replaced Wilson in Downing Street. Labour's counterproductive anti-French course in early 1969 had further nourished distrust in Paris and made any bilateral rapprochement impossible as long as Wilson was in power. Conversely, Heath's credible European commitment and his pro-French bias provided the conditions under which a new Franco-British axis of cooperation and trust could be forged, convincing Pompidou that enlargement was more than a necessary evil and might, in fact, raise interesting new perspectives. Also important, Brandt supported the new entente between Paris and London for the sake of European unity, despite the reduced influence it might imply for Bonn in the EC.

The creation of EPC in 1970 having been a function of the general *relance européene*, the timid nature of the Davignon Report was primarily the result of intra-European factors, notably the ongoing Anglo-French strains and the imponderabilities of *Ostpolitik*. In this case, an external factor, the global monetary turbulences, contributed to improving the prospects for EPC in 1971/72, encouraging a French shift in attention from monetary to political cooperation. But the key to that shift and to the atmospheric improvement in EPC was again the coming to power of Heath, who convinced Pompidou of the potential for an enlarged Community to become a powerful actor in international affairs. As I will show in Chapter 2, political cooperation in practice proved challenging throughout 1971/72, producing mixed results. Yet, given that EPC's minimalist conception meant that political will was an essential factor of success, the apparent common ambition of the leaders in France, Britain, and the FRG for the 'New Europe' to speak with one voice in diplomacy gave cause for optimism.

The constellation of a British prime minister zealous about Europe, a French president trusting British intentions, and a West German chancellor encouraging close Anglo-French cooperation was indeed a rare and promising phenomenon in Europe's post-war history. It provided the basis for trilateral leadership in Europe, not in the sense of a hegemonic great-power directorate, but in terms of relations of trust and at least partly compatible role conceptions of Europe. On the eve of enlargement, this emerging trilateral leadership was Europe's greatest asset. If the post-Hague period in the process of European unification has been aptly coined the Europe of the 'second generation',[184] this term might as much refer to the new fields of cooperation that emerged as to the new leaders that injected so much dynamism into the common project, and into EPC in particular.

Chapter 2
Political cooperation: Operative beginnings and normative debates

EPC became operational on 27 October 1970, when the EC foreign minis-ters officially instated the Political Committee consisting of the six national political directors.[1] The first ministerial consultations took place in Munich on 19/20 November 1970. It was a successful inauguration meeting in terms of both substance and the cordial atmosphere that prevailed. The Six identified the CSCE and the Middle East as EPC's first two topics of consulta-tion. They mandated the Political Committee to deal with these issues further and report to the next ministerial meeting that was to take place under the French presidency in the first half of 1971. They also agreed that their embassies in third countries and international organisations should be involved in consultations, and they constituted a working group to evaluate further progress in the field of political unification, as mandated by the Davignon Report.[2] As the first exchange of views with the four EC candidate countries a few days later went well too,[3] the process of policy harmonisation among the Six could finally start in early 1971. The Political Committee appointed working groups on the CSCE and the Middle East and instructed them to draft first joint studies. Although it was unclear at the time where all this would lead to, the great adventure of defining a European foreign policy had at last begun.

Having previously examined EPC's emergence from the top-down per-spective of the level of leaders, I will now analyse its practical beginnings and everyday realities in 1971/72 from the bottom up. Indispensable though the improvement in the psychology of cooperation under Brandt, Heath, and Pompidou was, this factor alone was clearly not strong enough to enable Europe to speak with one voice in international diplomacy. It was the foreign ministries that were responsible for EPC, and it was between their bureaucra-cies that the bulk of consultations were being held. Enquiring into the European efforts at forging common positions, therefore, also requires tracing consultation processes that predominately took place on the level of officials.

A second point to be discussed in this chapter concerns the normative debates on the 'New Europe' which took place during the same time period and which culminated in the Paris Summit of the Nine in October 1972. With the enlargement issue settled and the EC crisis overcome, the other two major points of contention of the 1960s, that is, Europe's purpose and structure, resurfaced. The Paris summit communiqué, with its decision to build a comprehensive European Union, became an impressive manifestation of the ambition of the Nine to become a powerful international actor. But it also papered over ongoing disagreements over the specifics of Europe's identity, which is why this chapter will end with a mixed verdict on the state of EPC on the eve of enlargement.

A first success: Preparing the CSCE

The decision to choose the CSCE as a topic for EPC was both obvious and surprising. It was obvious because the pan-European conference was bound to directly affect Western European interests, and the uncertainties as to its timing and substance gave further cause for the EC countries to stand together and formulate joint policies. But it also caused surprise, since Western preparations for the conference had already been going on within NATO, an organisation that in 1967 had complemented its traditional objective of Western defence with an additional focus on détente and which was now engaged in a remarkable diplomatic dialogue with the Warsaw Pact on the conditions and specifics of the CSCE. It was all the more noteworthy that in 1971/72, the EC countries gradually took the lead from NATO in hammering out a Western position. When the delegations of the EC countries left for Helsinki in November 1972 to participate at the Multilateral Preparatory Talks on the agenda and procedures of the CSCE, they did so with a common brief on all major issues at stake. Preparations for the CSCE, therefore, can justly be labelled EPC's first major success. In the following, I will examine why and how the EPC countries 'became the motor' and 'sat at the steering wheel' of intra-Western preparations for the CSCE.[4] The role of the Community members at the Multilateral Preparatory Talks (MPT, lasting from November 1972 to June 1973) and the CSCE itself (lasting from July 1973 to July 1975) will be covered in chapter 3.

Disunity as a starting point

The idea of a pan-European security conference had originally been put forward by the East. Beginning with the famous Soviet call for a European collective security system in 1954, the Warsaw Pact had repeatedly advocated such a gathering to deal with the major military and political issues of post-war Europe. The West, however, had remained sceptical about Soviet pan-Europeanism, mainly because these proposals failed to include the US and Canada, seemed to aim at destabilising Western Europe, and implied Western recognition of the GDR. Prospects for a conference improved only at the end of the 1960s, when the Warsaw Pact revealed greater flexibility concerning the agenda of discussions in its Budapest Appeal of March 1969. As the East shifted its objective from dissolving the military alliances to securing Western recognition of the political and territorial status quo in Europe and no longer appeared to view East–West negotiations as simply a propaganda stunt, the Western camp began to show reluctant interest.[5]

With its 'Signal of Reykjavik' of June 1968, NATO had placed Mutual and Balanced Force Reductions (MBFR) on the East–West agenda, indicating its emphasis on the military dimension of détente. Still, it responded positively to the Budapest Appeal and promised to study the feasibility of such a conference as well. It was the start of an inter-bloc dialogue with the Warsaw Pact by means of ministerial communiqués. In the course of this dialogue, the Warsaw Pact came to accept US and Canadian participation in the conference, as well as an agenda item on cooperation that would include 'cultural relations'.[6] With this last term, the East responded to NATO's demand of discussing the 'freer movement of people, ideas, and information', as first mentioned in the ministerial communiqué of December 1969.[7] The Western Alliance, in return, agreed to discuss the principles governing relations between states, an Eastern desideratum designed to get confirmation of the status quo.[8]

In December 1971, NATO proposed to the Warsaw Pact four major areas of discussion: questions of security, including both the principles and certain military issues; freer movement issues; cooperation in the fields of economics, science, and technology; and cooperation to improve the human environment.[9] At the same time, however, its agreement to holding the conference remained qualified. Already at the Rome meeting in May 1970, NATO had made the CSCE contingent upon a successful outcome of the FRG's *Ostpolitik*, a satisfactory Quadripartite Agreement over Berlin, and progress in the Strategic Arms Limitation Talks (SALT).[10] As this policy of linkages revealed, for NATO the CSCE represented as much a useful bargaining tool for other purposes as a policy goal in itself, and it was only in May 1972 that the Western Alliance officially agreed to launch the MPT by the end of the year.

The instrumental value of the CSCE was particularly stressed in the chancellery in Bonn. Brandt and Bahr had their doubts about the value of the CSCE as such, which, according to the chancellor, could be expected to produce little more than long speeches.[11] Considering MBFR to be more relevant to security in Europe than the CSCE, Brandt and Bahr were particularly anxious not to allow the CSCE to turn into a belated peace conference on Germany, which is why they insisted that it could only succeed Bonn's *Ostpolitik*.[12] If they accepted the idea of a CSCE as early as 1970/71 nevertheless, it was mainly to improve the atmosphere for their bilateral negotiations and get a lever to advance their own agenda with Moscow.[13] Scheel and the Auswärtige Amt, in contrast, were much more optimistic about the potential of the CSCE. They believed that constructive results might be obtainable, especially in the wide field of cooperation. As the FRG was likely to be directly affected by many issues in a conference on East–West relations, the Auswärtige Amt launched a major bureaucratic effort to establish a position on the CSCE as early as the end of 1970. Emphasis was placed on the notion of human contacts, where West Germany, as part of a divided nation, possessed a great deal of first-hand expertise and hoped to achieve concrete improvements in inter-German relations.[14] With an expert team at its disposal that was far larger than in any other foreign ministry of the Nine, Scheel's ministry had worked out guidelines for the conference by early 1972,[15] at a time when many other governments had hardly begun to deal with the specifics of the CSCE yet.

A case in point was the British government, which distrusted Russian calls for détente as much as it was worried about *Ostpolitik*, and which would have much preferred to advance European integration before opening any significant East–West negotiations.[16] According to London, the CSCE was likely to become a propaganda battle, which promised little substantive results and had much to do with pleasing public opinion in Europe. The FCO regarded the conference as 'inevitable rather than desirable', depicted it as 'largely irrelevant to British national interests', and warned against hopes that it would 'usher in a brave new world'.[17] Heath, in particular, feared that the CSCE would only weaken the coherence of the West, with détente diminishing public acceptance of the Alliance's defence expenditure, rather than being able to achieve anything for the people in the East.[18] As Britain needed West German backing for entry into the EC, the Heath government did not speak out against détente in Europe and left it to Bonn to set the pace for *Ostpolitik* and a CSCE.[19] But it is remarkable that in 1971, at a time when many European statesmen planned visits to Moscow to improve relations with the East, London boldly expelled more than 100 officers of the local Soviet Trade Delegation, accusing them of intelligence activities, which heavily strained Anglo-Soviet relations.[20]

The French were much more positive about the CSCE. After initial reluctance, Pompidou and Schumann had become strong proponents of a conference by mid-1970 at the latest.[21] De Gaulle had already repeatedly discussed with the Soviets the desirability and feasibility of a conference on European security in the late 1960s, without really helping Moscow to press the case, however.[22] If Pompidou believed much less in a Europe from the Atlantic to the Urals than his predecessor, he still came to back the CSCE for two reasons. First, he sought to document France's close relations with the Soviets and reconfirm its pioneering position in the process of détente.[23] Second, the French government came to strongly believe that the conference could actually be transformed to the advantage of the West. With the major Soviet quest for Western recognition of the post-war realities in Europe being already to a large extent met through Brandt's *Ostpolitik*, Pompidou viewed the CSCE as an instrument to weaken the Soviet grip on Eastern Europe. A pan-European conference, he hoped, would allow the West a 'peaceful penetration of ideas' in the East in order to 'spread the virus of liberty'.[24] The CSCE, hence, provided an opportunity to export the French ideal of independent national personalities to the whole of Europe. The Quai d'Orsay talked of hollowing out the Communist monolith in Eastern Europe, while Schumann himself behind closed doors described the French goal as nothing less than 'peaceful rollback'.[25]

Taking the lead from NATO

It comes as no surprise that France from the outset played a leading part in the efforts at jointly preparing the CSCE within the framework of EPC. When the Belgians proposed the CSCE as an EPC topic in November 1970, they received strong backing from Paris.[26] Although the French at that time were still doubtful concerning the feasibility of European political cooperation, they much preferred EPC to consultations in NATO. Being sceptical of a political role of NATO as a matter of principle, they argued that a bloc-to-bloc approach to the CSCE would only strengthen the Soviet grip on Eastern Europe. While they agreed that the Alliance should collect materials and ideas in preparing the CSCE, they did not want to give it a role at the actual conference.[27]

The FRG initially was more ambivalent about attributing a role to EPC in the Western deliberations on CSCE. Even though the upcoming conference had been one of the reasons why Bonn in 1969/70 had been eager to launch political consultations of the Six, there was some concern in the Auswärtige

Amt now not to alienate NATO and the US with intra-European consultations. There were also worries about French intentions in EPC, as well as fear that the Five might want to get a say in Bonn's *Ostpolitik*. On the other hand, the Auswärtige Amt wanted to avoid an early EPC crisis at all cost, which is why the FRG too accepted the Belgian proposal.[28] As for Britain, it was important that the Heath government chose not to obstruct the Six in their consultations on the CSCE. This was partly because in the case of the CSCE the British had only, as Philip Williams put it, 'limited interests at stake, limited expectations, and limited aims'.[29] But it was also because they hoped that EPC would reduce competition in the race for Moscow in which London was bound to lose. Moreover, the FCO saw it as an opportunity to both advance political cooperation and get more control over West Germany's Eastern policy.[30]

Why did EPC evolve from a supplementary body of consultation to the dominant Western institution of policy formulation in the case of the CSCE preparations? Certainly, the general political will to make this forum a success and French disinclination to working within NATO were important factors. Yet more relevant was the fact that NATO had difficulties of its own in preparing for the CSCE, which prompted even those initially reserved in EPC to refocus on the European framework. Even though NATO's main concern in the early 1970s was MBFR, it did analyse many individual aspects of a CSCE and functioned as an important bazaar for member states to popularise ideas and proposals. The result of these intensive consultations was a voluminous report, which provided the basis upon which the foreign ministers of the Fifteen proposed the four topics for negotiation outlined above in December 1971.[31] The crux of the matter was that while NATO succeeded in identifying a vast number of options, it often failed to agree on concrete preferences. Divergences related not only to specifics and tactical questions of the conference, but also to its fundamental objective: should the West approach the East with maximal demands for propaganda purposes, or should it work towards serious negotiations and aspire to genuine results?[32]

Part of the problem was lack of US leadership. Kissinger and Nixon seemed little interested in the CSCE, which in their eyes involved too many actors to yield any substantive results and which they even regarded as a potential loser for the West.[33] Fearful of bilateral moves of European governments towards Moscow, and sceptical of a specific European détente in the form of the multilateral CSCE, the White House repeatedly warned its European allies that it was, first and foremost, up to the US to play the game of détente.[34] Although the State Department was less hostile about the conference and US officials in NATO still tried hard to provide leadership, the lack of support from the top echelons in Washington was an important factor behind the lack of direction in NATO preparations.[35] Kissinger's disregard for the CSCE was particularly disappointing to all those Europeans who had so long fought for US involvement in the conference. Worse, his preference for bilateral détente between the superpowers, which was apparent by 1972, became a serious source of concern among the Europeans. When in May 1972 the US, without consulting its allies, agreed with the Soviets to separate the CSCE and MBFR and defined a schedule for the further proceedings of the respective negotiations, this step left not only the French speechless.[36] Fears that the US might subordinate the CSCE to superpower détente and, for tactical purposes, could even accept Soviet conference proposals detrimental to European interests, confirmed the Europeans' decision to prepare for the CSCE in an additional forum of their own.

A second factor negatively affecting NATO's ability to effectively prepare the CSCE was the changing emphasis of the conference from military to political aspects of security and, generally, from issues of security to issues of cooperation. With MBFR taken away, the notion of confidence building measures (CBMs) was the only agenda item left that belonged to NATO's core competence. If the key question of the conference from a European point of view soon became how much liberalisation the Soviets would be willing to accept in Eastern Europe in return of Western recognition of the political and military status quo,[37] NATO was constrained in dealing with this issue. For one thing, concepts such as human rights and freer movement were not part of the US conception of détente à la Kissinger, who was concerned with managing superpower relations and getting Soviet support in Vietnam and remained sceptical as to the Soviet system's susceptibility to change.[38]

Also problematic, there were member states in NATO such as Greece, Turkey, and Portugal that found it difficult themselves to accept detailed proposals for freer movement.[39] Greece, in particular, with its military junta and martial law, was an embarrassment to the Alliance, which since its founding had striven to be a community of political values but was forced to compromise this objective for the sake of effective Western defence. Although the Scandinavians, in particular, at ministerial meetings often spoke out against the Greek government in the early 1970s,[40] there was a basic consensus that NATO would be vulnerable without its flank countries and that human rights and NATO membership, therefore, had to be treated as two separate issues.[41] The result was that NATO preparations on freer movement were less precise than some European governments would have liked.

As a non-military actor, the EC obviously found it easier to act as a community of values. From the outset of the integration process, the Europeans had emphasised human rights and fundamental freedoms as core constituents of their unity.[42] In the case of Greece, they had been quick to freeze the EC association agreement in 1967.[43] The European desire to place human rights on the CSCE agenda and render it a legitimate issue in relations among states was therefore an important reason for increasingly shifting consultations from NATO to EPC.[44] At the same time, it is important not to overstate this point. For one thing, some EPC members too were inclined to use the issue of freer movement mainly for propaganda purposes to embarrass the Soviet Union in 1971/72. Moreover, although it was indeed the Europeans who came to define the essential specifics of the freer movement dossier, they would not have been able to do so without the large-scale compilation effort of NATO in this field. The main issues, such as travel impediments, family reunifications, radio jamming, circulation of Western newspapers and books, working conditions for foreign journalists, access to libraries, etc. had all been on the table in NATO.[45] What had been lacking was agreement on Western objectives and tactics.

One other advantage of EPC compared to NATO was that it was a smaller and more homogeneous group and did not have to see-saw between the extreme views often put forward by the US and the Scandinavians, on the one hand, and NATO's southern flank countries, on the other hand. At least in the British perception, consultations in EPC were of a different quality and often more 'business-like' than those that took place in NATO. This was also because the EPC model of gathering those responsible from the various capitals, rather than representatives posted to Brussels, proved particularly fruitful in a field as complex and diverse as the CSCE, allowing problems to be discussed freely and in a spirit of give and take, rather than along the lines of often rigid instructions.[46]

NATO's deficiencies in dealing with the CSCE preparations had a marked effect on the FRG in particular. In 1971/72, the West Germans evolved from being brakesman to a major driving force behind EPC consultations on the CSCE. So active did the FRG become that the British began to feel overwhelmed by its 'mass production of memoranda'.[47] To be sure, there were additional reasons for the change in Bonn's attitude. Progress in *Ostpolitik* brought about the desire to multilateralise its results. Also, there was hope in the Auswärtige Amt that the CSCE would become a tool to advance European integration. Moreover, the West Germans could note with satisfaction that harmonising CSCE policies in EPC meant more than just following French directions and could result in meaningful compromise solutions.[48] But NATO's inability to agree on concrete measures to improve the lives of people in Eastern Europe was a central factor.[49] Needless to say, with the FRG firmly on board, the prospect for effective European policy harmonisation improved markedly.

United to Helsinki

European consultations on the CSCE between 1970 and 1972 were not free from conflict either. As in NATO, there were initially profound differences on basic issues. The Italians and the Dutch came into EPC with the defensive and propagandistic approach predominant in NATO, and they were difficult to persuade, at least in the beginning, to work out constructive conference briefs.[50] Views also diverged as to the preconditions of a conference, with the French pressing for an early MPT and the FRG trying to establish more linkages between issues than its partners would accept.[51] Perhaps the biggest point of contention concerned the question of a link between MBFR and the CSCE.[52] Yet, all these disagreements could be overcome in the course of EPC consultations or were otherwise defused, as when the two superpowers decided in May 1972 to run MBFR and the CSCE separately, but in parallel.

EPC started with a small selection of CSCE topics only. This was mainly because the FRG insisted on a restrictive mandate. Bonn wanted to focus exclusively on EC-relevant aspects of the CSCE and suggested starting with the twin questions of whether the conference could negatively affect the Community and whether it could be of instrumental value in obtaining Soviet recognition of the EC. Belgium, by contrast, wanted to pre-coordinate all CSCE issues in EPC before going into NATO. A compromise solution tabled by the French presidency was finally agreed according to which EPC would tackle EC-related questions plus issues where discussions of the Six promised to have added value.[53]

At its first meeting on 1 March 1971, the EPC working group mandated to deal with the CSCE agreed on a division of labour among the national foreign ministries, each of which (except Luxembourg) was to produce an issue-specific study for discussion.[54] The French were clearly the driving force behind these early deliberations and, with their paper on the preparations and procedures of the CSCE, broached one of the most sensitive and disputed topics of intra-Western coordination right from the beginning. Although no immediate agreement was reached on the French conference model, it was addressed as an option in EPC's first joint report on the CSCE of May 1971. This report, which was based on revised versions of the studies, already reflected a remarkable degree of consensus and was greeted with satisfaction by the foreign ministers.[55]

A second report of November 1971 identified EPC objectives and principles concerning the CSCE, further scrutinised the procedural aspects of the MPT and the conference, drafted a conference agenda, examined the potential of economic East–West cooperation, and studied the pros and cons of a permanent pan-European body as a follow-up to the conference.[56] In the process of working out this report, EPC had refined its structures: a so-called 'ad hoc group' had been set up to involve the European Commission in the examination of economic questions, with the original working group, renamed the 'sous-comité', subsequently concentrating on political and security aspects of the conference.[57]

EPC's third report on the CSCE of May 1972 mainly dealt with draft guidelines for the MPT,[58] which were honed in the months thereafter. The intensity of consultations now reached a climax, with the Nine moving towards working out a common position on all major aspects of the CSCE.[59] Final preparatory efforts focused on defining tactics with regard to freer movement; specifying the wording of the conference agenda; formulating draft mandates on the objectives and tasks of commissions and sub-commissions to be appointed to deal with the individual topics during the actual conference; and, on the basis of a British comparative description of the preparatory work done in NATO and EPC, sorting out all kinds of remaining differences among the Nine.[60]

Impressively, EPC had agreed on a policy for the MPT and had already drafted texts for vital elements of the CSCE itself by November 1972.[61] Incorporating the EC candidate countries in this process went rather smoothly. Other than problems with the French language, the main challenge in the spring of 1972 was to bring the new participants up to speed on the issues to be discussed.[62] Impressed with the convergence of ideas among the Six and the fact that EPC consultations were based on assumptions not yet accepted in NATO, Britain adopted EPC positions without any major objections.[63] Although it did not play a significant role in shaping the Nine's policies prior to the MPT, the fact that it backed these policies gave the Nine the necessary weight required when they presented them to the Atlantic Alliance.

That was to occur on 16 November 1972, a date that marked a caesura in post-war transatlantic relations. For the first time, the EPC countries appeared collectively in the NATO Council, with the Dutch EPC presidency submitting a joint report of the Eight (without Ireland) on the MPT and inviting the seven non-EC countries to comment on it.[64] While individual EPC countries had introduced national papers into NATO since European consultations had begun, here was a comprehensive policy brief tabled by a group of important allies, in which positions had been formulated on issues that were still being inconclusively debated in NATO. The show of unity between EPC countries in NATO did not fail to make an impression. As the French permanent representative proudly reported to Paris, some non-EPC delegations were truly stunned at the cohesion of the Eight in the defence of their report.[65] Indeed, the EPC study was accepted as a basis for discussion in NATO,[66] and, as will be outlined in Chapter 3, it was successful in positively influencing Western deliberations.

The most important point of the presented EPC position concerned the conference model. By the end of 1972, the EC partners collectively supported the French scheme of a limited preparatory phase followed by a main conference on two levels and in three stages. Following the MPT, the CSCE was to be formally launched at the level of foreign ministers. The bulk of work should then be done by commissions and sub-commissions composed of diplomats and experts, who were to discuss every agenda item in depth over an extensive period of time. The conference would end again on the political level, where the decisions would be reviewed and approved.[67] The significance of the model was that it implied thorough pan-European discussions and aimed at concrete results. It contrasted with the US model, which foresaw that most substantive discussions and the working out of texts would be done in two 'exploratory' and 'preparatory' phases, with the actual CSCE conference amounting to little more than a quick rubber stamp conference.[68]

Another important point was the European concept concerning the scope and procedural arrangements in the MPT. Approval to hold a CSCE was dependent on whether Western objectives in the MPT were met in terms of substance, agenda, and methods of work. The key was to get approval for the idea of commissions, and to negotiate for each commission and sub-commission terms of references that would provide clear mandates for the main phase of the conference.[69] The Nine also advocated countering the Eastern proposal of an agenda item of economic cooperation and culture with the Western position of separating the economic and human components. The underlying idea was to reduce state control in freer movement issues and to signal the importance of a non-state level of security.[70]

With respect to individual agenda items, EPC contributed little to the Western position in the field of security. NATO's synopsis illustrating the various principles that could be negotiated was discussed in EPC, but the bulk of the work remained with the Alliance. Similarly, the task of overcoming the divergences on specific CBMs was left to NATO.[71] Conversely, in the economic field, the lead was clearly taken by the ad hoc group of the Nine. Here, expectations had been decreasing in the course of consultations. Examination of a West German proposal to offer Eastern Europe industrial cooperation had led to growing awareness of the many technical difficulties of East–West cooperation and the political problem of discrimination vis-à-vis other partners, such as the US. Another FRG initiative that involved making an attractive offer of economic concessions in return for political concessions of the Warsaw Pact had been rejected within EPC.[72] Still, the Nine were in possession of a comprehensive inventory for the economic field, which included both possible agenda items and initiatives of the West and an analysis of likely Eastern proposals.

Finally, as already indicated, a major contribution was made by EPC in the field of freer movement and culture. Even though the degree of muddling among the Europeans had long been just as great as that in NATO, the Nine emerged with a joint position with regard to objectives and tactics on this topic by the end of 1972. Rather than supporting the proposed US objective of focusing public attention on the closed nature of the Soviet system, the Nine supported confidential matter-of-fact discussions. Rather than making any East–West cooperation dependent on progress in the freer movement field, they preferred parallel talks on all issues and a step-by-step approach to the freer movement question that did not start with the most sensitive demands.[73] Significantly, the Nine agreed to propose at the MPT a commission with the neutrally worded heading of the 'development of contacts between people, increase in cultural and educational exchanges, and broadening of the dissemination of information', instead of using the provocative US title of 'free movement of people, ideas and information'.[74]

On the eve of the MPT, European cooperation in preparing the CSCE had demonstrated both the feasibility and the benefits of harmonising policies and acting together. This also had positive reverberations for EPC at large. The success story of the CSCE preparations contributed to the increasingly positive assessment of EPC in France. Schumann declared more decidedly than ever at the NATO ministerial meeting in December 1972 that the Alliance was a military grouping, and called on the non-EPC members to respect the Nine's emerging prerogative in the political field.[75] EPC's positive performance convinced the FRG of its usefulness in protecting Bonn's interests in East–West negotiations. It caused the British to perceive, in the words of the FCO, a 'growing political consensus among the members of the enlarged Community, born of a natural feeling of shared interest'.[76] And it generally became an important source for the newfound European self-confidence and ambition, which provided the basis for EPC's further rise in 1973.

Just how effectively the Nine would act at the MPT and the CSCE remained to be seen. For one thing, EPC's relationship with NATO remained as yet undefined. Misgivings in the Alliance about being presented with a fait accompli by the EPC countries had been uttered ever since European consultations had begun, and they had become accentuated now that the EC countries came up with concrete proposals.[77] While ad-hoc cooperation between the two bodies had gone smoothly enough in the case of the CSCE preparations, future frictions and demarcation disputes seemed likely in the absence of general provisions.[78] This was the more so since substantive disagreements regarding the CSCE persisted, with the US rejecting both the European three-stage model and the reformulation of the 'freer movement' formula.[79] A second point of concern was that the unity of the Nine with regard to the CSCE was still rather fragile too. Their common brief was the outcome of a series of hard-fought compromises and many hours of heated discussions, and its status remained disputed. The French insisted that the Nine should stick to their texts and should not accept any amendments, except if agreed by all. Their threat to 'go it alone' in Helsinki if any of the EPC partners broke ranks in NATO was countered by a West German refusal of any take-it-or-leave-it approach. There were also the Dutch, who had long been unwilling to depart from US positions, declared the EPC brief non-binding, and so far had played a rather erratic role within the European consultations on the CSCE.[80] As it turned out, most of these concerns proved unfounded. As Chapter 3 will show, the CSCE became EPC's best field of performance in the early 1970s – as well as beyond.

An early row over the Middle East

The decision by the Six to put the Arab–Israeli conflict onto EPC's agenda demonstrated their seriousness about forging a relevant European foreign policy. As today, the crisis in the Middle East constituted one of the most pressing problems in international affairs in the early 1970s. Then as now, it was a highly complex, emotional, and polarising issue. Starting with this topic was not without risk, therefore, as nothing could do more damage to EPC than early disharmony and paralysis. As will be argued in this section, Europe's initial efforts at defining a common position on the Middle East were marked by both a noteworthy amount of substantive agreement and dissention as to what to do with a collective policy. Lack of consensus about the desirability of any European role in the Arab–Israeli conflict prevented the EPC countries from taking common action in 1971/72, without bringing consultations to a halt, however.

In the early 1970s, the situation in the Middle East was marked by an impasse following the Six-Day War of June 1967.[81] In a pre-emptive strike against its Arab neighbours, Israel had occupied the Golan Heights and the Sinai from Syria and Egypt, and had driven Jordan out of the West Bank and the Old City of Jerusalem. Hopes for peace after the war had centred on the UN Security Council's Resolution 242 of 22 November 1967. Advocating a land-for-peace solution, the resolution essentially called on the Arab states to acknowledge Israel's right 'to live in peace within secure and recognized borders', in return for withdrawal of Israeli forces 'from territories occupied in the recent conflict'.[82] The problem was that the resolution in 1967 had only been passed because of its ambiguous wording, the consequence being that it effectively could do little to bring the parties closer together.

The single most disputed aspect was the extent of Israel's required withdrawal. Did the phrase 'from territories' mean complete withdrawal to the pre-1967 borders, as the Arabs claimed? Or, did it allow for withdrawal plus minor border adjustments, as others such as the US claimed? Or, would 'secure and recognized borders' imply a right to enforce significant border changes, as the Israelis saw it, arguing that their pre-1967 borders had never been secure? Also contended were the conditions of negotiations. The Arabs wanted Israel to accept their territorial demands prior to any diplomacy. Conversely, Israel insisted that the Arabs first had to recognise its right of existence before negotiations could take place. It insisted on face-to-face talks with the Arabs, who for their part refused any direct contact and were hoping for outside involvement in any settlement. Matters were even more convoluted since some of the more radical Arab states, such as Syria, refused to consider recognising Israel at all. Another major point of disagreement related to the question of whether a comprehensive solution on all major controversies should be aspired, including the occupied territories, control over Jerusalem, and the fate of the refugees; or whether a piecemeal approach promised to yield more results, as Israel maintained.

After 1967, the international community was involved in various ways in trying to break the stalemate. There was the 'Jarring Mission', named after Swedish diplomat Gunnar Jarring, a UN special representative, who was tasked with assisting the parties to implement Resolution 242. Jarring, however, could do little to reconcile positions that were becoming more and more irreconcilable. By 1969, Israel and Egypt were engaged in an ugly war of attrition again, and by 1971, the 'Jarring Mission' was completely deadlocked.[83] There was also a Four-Power forum comprising the US, Britain, France, and the Soviet Union, which had sought to work out common solutions and to back Jarring at the level of deputy UN permanent representatives since February 1969. Again, this forum could not live up to its purpose, and by the end of 1970, it was no longer in the forefront of deliberations, not least because Washington – in view of Israel's rejection of involvement of outside powers other than the US – never put its whole weight behind it.[84]

The US State Department under William Rogers also pursued Two-Power talks with Moscow, and it did come up with unilateral initiatives, which were also, however, bound to fail. The 'Rogers Plan' of December 1969, calling for a return to the pre-1967 borders with only insubstantial adjustments, was rejected by Israel. Later US attempts to establish an interim disengagement along the Suez Canal came to nothing either. In part, this had to do with the aloofness of the White House. Although Nixon and Kissinger permitted Rogers a more active role in the Arab–Israeli conflict than in most other foreign policy issues, they did not really back his efforts. They neither believed that his initiatives would amount to anything substantial, nor were they willing to add the Middle East to their already demanding agenda of withdrawing from Vietnam and advancing détente with China and the Soviets.[85] By the early 1970s, then, no viable road to peace was in sight.

Europe's first report on the Arab–Israeli conflict

By the time the Six decided in 1970 to deal jointly with the Middle East crisis, European political and economic predominance in the region was a thing of the past. The process of decolonisation had swept away British control over Egypt, Iraq, Jordan, and the Persian Gulf Region, as it had ousted the French from Syria, Lebanon, and the Maghreb. Although Europe had ceased to be a dominant power in the Middle East after the Suez Crisis in 1956, France and Britain, in particular, continued to have numerous economic, political, and cultural interests in the region.[86] Moreover, all European countries were deeply worried about the security implications of the Arab–Israeli conflict. Mounting Arab radicalism had fostered an increasing Soviet presence in the Mediterranean, which was to culminate in Moscow's Friendship Treaty with Egypt in May 1971. Soviet military supplies to countries such as Egypt, Syria, and Iraq were indicative of how a matrix of Cold War rivalry was gradually laid over the regional Arab–Israeli dispute.[87] In view of these developments, Europe felt increasingly vulnerable on its southern flank – a perception that was further accentuated in 1972/73 in view of growing concerns about energy supplies, as will be discussed in Chapter 5.

It was the Quai d'Orsay that instigated Middle East consultations in EPC. The more that the Four-Power talks faded into irrelevance, the more the French leaned towards the European option. Having themselves initiated the

Four-Power forum to secure a hand in any settlement on the Middle East, the French risked being cut off from any potential negotiations again by late 1970.[88] NATO political consultations on the issue were not really in the French interest, and, besides, they so far had produced little agreement. As Manlio Brosio, NATO secretary-general from 1964 to 1971, put it, dealing with the Middle East within the Alliance often amounted to nothing more than 'an embarrassing and perfunctory discussion, strewn with banalities and silences'.[89]

Pompidou, in line with his generally sceptical attitude towards EPC in 1970, did not give the Six much credit when they decided to deal with the Arab–Israeli conflict. He put his faith in US mediation efforts instead, which Nixon had promised to intensify during their bilateral summit in February 1970.[90] But he accepted that France would also attempt to resolve the issue within EPC. Initially, there was some reluctance in the Quai d'Orsay too as to whether the topic should really be introduced into EPC, as the Five were seen to have only sporadic and superficial knowledge of the Middle East crisis.[91] Yet, with its own idea of a peace initiative having been superseded by unilateral, unannounced new proposals from Rogers in the summer of 1970,[92] there really seemed to be no viable alternative left. The French foreign ministry was not thinking of any major European action or initiative at this point. Rather, it regarded dealing with the Middle East in EPC as an 'educative process', that is, as a chance to assemble the weight of the Five behind French positions and thereby strengthen the French stance in the Four-Power talks and elsewhere.[93]

French policy concerning the Middle East had undergone a significant reorientation after the Six-Day War. Prior to that, France had cultivated privileged relations with Israel, including cooperation in the military field. However, with Tel Aviv ignoring French warnings that any pre-emptive measures would only result in mounting Soviet influence, a weakening of moderate Arabs, and an escalating Palestinian problem, de Gaulle decided to change course after 1967. France imposed a military embargo on all conflicting parties and through a network of bilateral contacts re-established close relations with the Arab world, of which it became a privileged Western partner.[94] Pompidou continued de Gaulle's policy of realignment. Despite domestic and international criticism, he even approved selling French military planes and tanks to the radical Colonel Muammar al-Qadhafi in 1970, arguing that Libya did not belong to the conflicting parties and had pledged not to deliver the *Mirages* further to Egypt.[95] As for a solution to the Arab–Israeli conflict, France advocated a comprehensive settlement, with a complete withdrawal from all the occupied territories being identified as a key condition for peace.[96]

When Schumann suggested the Middle East as a topic for EPC in November 1970, the FRG was immediately supportive.[97] In fact, Bonn had been signalling to the French since early 1969 that it wanted the Arab–Israeli conflict to be included as a subject of discussion in European consultations.[98] There were two major reasons for this. First, the West Germans were worried that instability in the Middle East could negatively affect the process of détente in Europe. Therefore, they advocated treating the two areas as one strategic area.[99] Second, their own Middle East policy had run aground in the mid-1960s, which had put them in a very delicate situation. In response to Bonn taking up diplomatic relations with Tel Aviv, and in protest against secret West German weapons deliveries to Israel that had been disclosed, ten Arab countries had broken off their diplomatic ties with the FRG in 1965.[100] The FRG subsequently considered itself a primary target for terrorist activities of Palestinian extremists.[101] To make matters worse, relations with Israel, which had been historically strained anyway, also worsened in the second half of the 1960s, as Bonn discontinued the weapons deliveries to Tel Aviv out of fear that Arab countries might recognise the GDR diplomatically.[102] The goal of the Brandt/Scheel government to repair relations with the Arabs without further diminishing ties with Israel implied the need for a clarified position on the Arab–Israeli conflict. This, again, was much easier for the FRG to accomplish within a multilateral framework, which would leave it less exposed to criticism and offered a way of contributing to peace in the region.

The British were initially unhappy about the prospect of the Six dealing with the Middle East. They considered the 'Jarring Mission' and the Four-Power talks the most viable path to success and were worried that the 'ganging up' of the Six, as an FCO note called it, might do more damage than good to the prospects for peace.[103] Furthermore, in the case of the Middle East, Britain felt particularly entitled to be involved in European deliberations. Ever since the Balfour Declaration of 1917 advocating a Jewish homeland in Palestine, the British had been more deeply involved in the Arab–Israeli conflict than any other European country. They not only had vital trade and oil interests at stake in the conflict, but also possessed large expertise on the area and a wide network of relations, especially with Egypt.[104] Nevertheless, the Heath government resisted all calls from the FCO to urge the Dutch to block EPC consultations on the Middle East. The Conservatives did not want to put extra strain on Anglo-French relations. Moreover, they actually welcomed the idea of a common European position on the Arab–Israeli conflict.[105]

One major reason for this was a change in British policy in the autumn of 1970. In contrast to Labour's effective pro-Israel stance, the Heath government soon decided to 'move into a more uncommitted position, with all due caution and less blatantly and cynically than the French had done'.[106] As the FCO had already argued in its first briefing note to Douglas-Home in June 1970, British dependency on oil supplies from Arab countries meant that Britain's association with the US and Israel was proving increasingly costly.[107] With Douglas-Home effectively advocating an Israeli troop withdrawal to the pre-1967 borders (without, however, explicitly calling for a retreat from '*the territories*') in his Harrogate Speech in October 1970, Britain was moving to a position close to the French one, the remaining differences being matters of emphasis rather than substance.[108] Since this shift was bound to provoke criticism, embedding it in a – French-inspired – European context seemed desirable. And, with France promising to continue bilateral exchanges on the Middle East and inviting Britain to present its views to the Six, London refrained from any obstructionist measures against EPC consultations.[109]

In spite of the shared desire of the three great powers to formulate a common European position, the EPC working group in question that had been tasked with finding common ground was struggling to produce anything substantial, at first. The Dutch, in particular, proved extremely reluctant to define common positions. Faced with a domestic public that was sensitive to the question of Israel, the Dutch government did not see much benefit in the Six getting involved in the Arab–Israeli conflict.[110] However, thanks to West German and Belgian backing, the French finally convinced their partners to try to identify the terms of a viable Arab–Israeli peace by interpreting key aspects of Resolution 242. Similarly to the CSCE preparations, each government except Luxembourg was assigned a specific topic to study: the FRG and the Dutch were to deal with freedom of navigation through international waterways, the least sensitive matter; Belgium chose the refugee problem; Italy the status of Jerusalem (a problem not mentioned in 242); which left France with demilitarised zones and the border questions, the most controversial issue discussed at the time.[111] Based on the discussions of the respective national papers, a joint report was produced, which was presented to the foreign ministers at their second EPC meeting on 13 May 1971, after having been cleared by the Political Committee.

The contents of this report were remarkable. Within a few months, the Six had been able to work out common positions on some basic issues of the Arab–Israeli conflict. Most importantly, the report made the case for a retreat from *the* occupied territories, with minor border rectification possible if agreed by the conflicting parties. This formula came close to the French position, but qualified it with the notion of adjustments, as advocated by the US.[112] Since many other points were also close to the French point of view, the report was particularly well received in Paris, where officials exulted that the Five were now assembled behind the French Middle East policy and wondered what potential EPC may still hold for French foreign policy. But, interestingly enough, the West Germans too were pleased with the result.[113]

What remained controversial, however, was the question of what to do with the report. During the ministerial meeting, Schumann called upon his five colleagues to officially approve the document, hand it to their respective ambassadors and interested governments, and inform the UN secretary-general. Moro initially declined to take any political responsibility for the report and complained that recent consultations had evolved too fast to evaluate the results thoroughly. Luns too expressed scepticism. Pointing to Europe's political and military impotence, he rejected any distribution of the study beyond the UN permanent representatives of EPC governments. Scheel and Harmel, in contrast, backed Schumann and urged diplomatic action and further evaluation of a possible European initiative. A compromise was finally reached when the Six approved the report, but decided to hand it only to their ambassadors and the UN representatives as a basis for their conversations on the Middle East. It was less than the French had hoped for, but it was definitely more than most of those involved had initially dared to expect. With EPC's first report on the Arab–Israeli conflict, the Six had formulated a position that was idiosyncratic in substance and gave reason to hope that Europe might soon play a role in advancing peace in the Middle East.[114]

West German back-pedalling, French fury

Such hopes proved to be premature. Disharmony among the Six re-emerged as soon as the EPC ministerial meeting had ended. For one thing, several member states became irritated when they learnt the degree of detail with which the French permanent representative at the UN had briefed the UN secretary-general on the contents of the report.[115] Much worse and more serious, however, was a Franco-German row over the report that evolved in the context of a visit of Scheel to Israel in early July 1971. In the wake of this row, EPC came to the brink of a crisis, and European efforts at a common policy vis-à-vis the Middle East crisis received a first serious blow.

Ever since EPC consultations on the Middle East had started, the FRG (and, to a lesser extent, the Benelux and Italy) had been confronted with vehement protests from Tel Aviv. Israel's Ambassador Eliashiv Ben-Horin, always well-informed about the secret deliberations of the Six, in several visits to the

Auswärtige Amt had forcefully denied that Europe had the right to deal with the Middle East and meddle in Israeli affairs. Warning the Germans against falling into line with the anti-Israeli French policy, he had emphatically demanded that Tel Aviv be informed about the consultations, or even be invited to join in the talks.[116] Similarly, Foreign Minister Abba Eban had argued in a letter to Scheel that Europe would only complicate negotiations in the Middle East and that the consultations of the Six would not be able 'to aid Israel in the dire dangers to its security' anyway. He, therefore, felt 'bound to request that this process should not be continued' and alluded to the 'special context of German–Israel relations'.[117]

Some countries, such as Italy and Belgium, appear to have given way to such pressures, to the extent that they qualified the significance of the document.[118] Not so the West Germans. Although Scheel was aware that he would come under intense pressure over EPC during his upcoming visit to Tel Aviv – the first visit of a West German foreign minister to Israel – he promised Schumann that he would defend the right of the Europeans to deal with the issue.[119] His assurances turned out to be over-optimistic. No sooner had the West German delegation landed in Israel than they were taken, in deviation from protocol, to a Holocaust memorial. There, Gideon Hausner, chief prosecutor at the Eichmann trial, warned them that West Germany's only way to repent was to assure Israel's survival, which implied abstaining from interfering with the def-inition of what its secure boundaries should be.[120] Psychological warfare con-tinued during subsequent talks with Eban and Prime Minister Golda Meir, where Scheel faced accusations of deserting Israel for oil interests and open waterways.[121]

Although it is difficult to establish what Scheel actually said in Israel and what Israeli media added to it, there is no doubt that the West German foreign minister was gradually forced into minimising the status of the report. While he vigorously defended EPC and maintained that the report had been approved unanimously, he came to describe it as a mere working paper, emphasised its difference to the French position on the question of borders, and eventually conceded that the borders of 1967 ought to be subject to negotiations by the conflicting parties.[122] Matters became even worse when the West German gov-ernment spokesman argued that the FRG continued to support the 242 for-mula 'from occupied territories' and implicitly dismissed the relevance of the EPC report.[123]

The French were outraged. It was not just that they felt betrayed by Scheel. Rather, it was their boastful public comments prior to Scheel's trip, to the effect that EPC had accepted the French position on the Arab–Israeli conflict and that the West German foreign minister would speak for the Six in Israel, that embarrassed them. Schumann now threatened to publish the EPC report in order to reveal the provisions on withdrawal, lest the FRG failed to publicly correct its position. He even went so far as to insinuate the possibility of terminating EPC.[124] The affair reached a climax when the West German Axel Springer media group, which was hostile to the report, disclosed large parts of it.[125]

Back to a low profile

Cynics could point to some undeniable merits of the leak. The French could demonstrate to the world that the Five had, indeed, moved fairly close to their own position. For their part, the West Germans profited since the clause on '*the occupied territories*' in the 'Schumann Paper', as the EPC report soon came to be called, helped them strengthen ties with the Arabs. When Scheel, in the aftermath of the affair, confirmed West German adherence to Resolution 242 and to the specifications in the EPC report, the way was cleared for most Arabs to take up diplomatic relations with Bonn again.[126] However, with regard to Europe's Middle East deliberations, the éclat of the summer of 1971 posed a severe setback. For several months, consultations lost much of their dynamism and were marked instead by reticence, irritation, and distrust. Faced with domestic criticism after the disclosure of the report, the Dutch refused to produce further common documents for the rest of the year and would only accept oral reports from the president of the working group or the Political Committee to the next higher level.[127] The FRG, too, became more reluctant to deal with the specifics of a peace arrangement after the diplomatic crossfire it had encountered. Its zeal for European initiatives had decidedly vanished. When the working group, in compliance with the mandate it had already received prior to the Franco-German row, eventually came up with two new studies on the relatively uncontroversial issues of guarantees for a peace accord and the formalities of a peace treaty by the spring of 1972, Bonn insisted that these documents were not to be referred to in any talks with third parties.[128]

Europe's disorientation of how to proceed did not change significantly when the EC candidates joined the EPC consultations in the spring of 1972. While Britain and the other candidates were generally supportive of the principles agreed by the Six, they were not willing to subscribe to papers they had not contributed to.[129] EPC's Middle East consultations only gained some new verve when Egypt's President Anwar el-Sadat expelled more than 15,000 Soviet military advisers in July 1972, obviously disillusioned with Moscow's half-hearted support. Since the Europeans had received signals from the Arabs that greater European involvement in the Middle East would be desirable,[130] the idea of a European initiative re-emerged. But such plans again failed to materialise in 1972. In the economic field, the idea of advancing peace in the Middle East by tying Israel and the Arabs close to the European Community proved to be time-consuming when it came to practical implementation. Although the EC launched a Global Mediterranean Policy to promote free trade and technical cooperation in 1972, visible results were still years away.[131] Preparations for a potential political initiative soon petered out, too. Convinced that France and Europe did not have enough to offer, Pompidou asked a disappointed Schumann to discontinue all secret preparations for a Middle East peace conference that the Quai d'Orsay had initiated along with Egypt in the summer of 1972.[132] And even if there had been a window of opportunity for Europe in the summer of 1972, it quickly closed again after the 'Munich massacre' of 5 September 1972, when Palestinian terrorists killed 11 Israeli athletes during the Olympic Games in West Germany. The lack of Arab expressions of regret and the anti-terrorist measures in Western Europe caused a marked deterioration of Arab–European relations.[133] Bonn, in partic-ular, came under heavy fire from the Arab media, facing accusations of apply-ing Nazi methods in tightening terms for Arab immigration and residence in the FRG.[134] To make matters worse, the Brandt government, after freeing the captured terrorists seven weeks later in response to the hijacking of a Lufthansa passenger aircraft, also faced strained relations with Israel again.[135] In such a tense atmosphere, the Europeans once more proved incapable of agreeing on a common action when France proposed an EPC declaration to deplore the harsh retaliatory measures taken by Israel in Lebanon and Syria.[136]

After two years of consultations on the Arab–Israeli conflict, the Europeans found themselves in a delicate position on the eve of enlargement. They had been able to put down on paper common positions on key aspects of a settle-ment, which was an achievement per se. But the relevance of these documents remained disputed, and national policies on the Middle East still differed in practice. Worse, no agreement was yet in sight as to an active European engagement in the search for peace. When the Italians urged their partners dur-ing the fifth EPC ministerial meeting in November 1972 to speed up their involvement, they received a cacophonous answer. Douglas-Home and Schumann argued that Europe should await further events, while the Dutch insisted that the conflicting parties alone would be able to find a solution.[137] There was one silver lining in that EPC cooperation at the UN General Assembly in 1972 had begun to yield positive results, with the Europeans collectively influencing the formulation of the resolution on the Middle East.[138] But generally speaking, the Europeans remained on the sideline of events. This was all the more deplorable because the situation in the Middle East was deteriorating further. While Europe continued to struggle with formulating a common policy, the Arabs began to threaten Israel with war again, and concerns about an oil crisis were mounting.

Defining the 'New Europe': Ambition and division

If EPC's operative beginnings in 1971/72 revealed both the potential and the challenges of foreign policy cooperation, a similar verdict can be applied to the normative debates regarding the 'New Europe' that went on during these same years. The prospect of EC enlargement nourished new discussions on both the end state of European integration and Europe's political identity. Key issues were the conceptual design of the future Europe, the institutionalisation of *l'Europe politique* by means of a political secretariat, European–American relations, and the notion of a European defence identity. With the exception of defence, all these debates found a first endpoint in the Paris Summit of the Nine in autumn 1972, which resulted in an impressive declaration that stunned the public and reflected Europe's new ambition. However, when analysed against the background of the preceding discussions, the Paris communiqué also reveals significant ambiguities and omissions that served to paper over ongoing differences among the Nine as to Europe's larger purpose. In the following, I will briefly look at the summit itself, before putting its outcome into the perspective of the debates of 1971/72.

The Paris Summit of October 1972: Towards European Union

When the national leaders of the Nine gathered in the *Centre de Conférences Internationales* in Paris for their first joint summit on 19/20 October 1972, public interest was enormous. This was partly because it was a special moment in the history of European integration, as the British, Irish, and Danish were sitting as equal partners at the European table at last. But it was also because people were curious what the Europeans would accomplish at their enlargement summit. With the Community due to widen in ten weeks, the Nine faced the exciting task of forging a common vision of Europe's future. Summit preparations had been extensive but inconclusive. While France had launched the summit idea in August 1971 with a view to fixing Europe's monetary problems only, it had come to accept its partners' preference for a broad agenda.[139] However, with national ideas and initiatives proliferating, the Nine had found it difficult to find agreement on the details.[140] Pompidou had repeatedly warned that he would not host a summit that was merely about posturing and drinking champagne, and it was only after much French pressure to substantiate the preparatory work that he had sent out his invitation in mid-September 1972.[141] Still, the many last-minute meetings, letters, and exchanges of draft communiqués had betrayed a sense of continuing trepidation, and it was clear that real negotiation were still required during the summit if the Nine were to fulfil the high expectations placed in them.

Although Pompidou opened the summit by assuring that he did not intend to prolong the meeting deep into the night, as had too often been done in Brussels, the wives of delegates and French dignitaries eventually found themselves alone at the closing buffet.[142] Final editing work turned out to be a protracted affair, with the nine leaders hammering out compromises on the remaining brackets in the draft text by themselves.[143] Yet once it was all done with, the result presented to the more than 1,000 journalists assembled was remarkable. The Nine came up with a long communiqué on the future priorities and the international role of the Community that comprised many specific decisions and deadlines as well as broader visionary aims.[144]

To be sure, not all parts of the communiqué were equally substantial. Provisions strengthening the EC's institutions were thin, with two reports mandated on improved decision-making procedures for the Nine and on institutional consequences of EMU. More solid, if less spectacular, was the coverage of the EC's external relations with individual groups of countries, where the Community commissioned studies on better development aid, announced a common commercial policy towards Eastern Europe, and expressed its will to 'maintain a constructive dialogue with the US, Japan, Canada and its other industrialised trade partners'. A first positive surprise was the decisions on EMU. Despite the international monetary crisis, the Europeans confirmed their intention of reaching the second stage of EMU on 1 January 1974. They also agreed that this required common measures in the industrial, scientific, and technological realms, with respective action programmes to be worked out in 1973. In this regard, top priority was attributed to having a Regional Development Fund (RDF) operative by the end of 1973, its purpose being to correct structural imbalances within the EC.

Yet by far the biggest summit breakthrough related to the provisions on Europe's political future. The announcement of the Nine that they intended 'to transform before the end of the present decade the whole complex of their relations into a European Union' caused both astonishment and excitement. Rather than make the traditional reference to the 'political finalities' of the EC, here was an expression of Europe's collective will to strive for a political union. The summit communiqué even outlined a process of how to reach the target, with the Community institutions being asked to submit a report before the end of 1975.

The statement appeared to be all the more sensational since it was accompanied by other provisions on *l'Europe politique*. The Nine acknowledged the 'growing world responsibilities' incumbent on them and argued that Europe ought now to 'affirm its personality [...] and establish its position in world affairs as a distinct entity', with a view towards making 'an original contribution commensurate with its human, intellectual and material resources'. They specifically decided to intensify EPC consultations at all levels, with the foreign ministers subsequently meeting four times a year. Additional improvements were promised for inclusion in a second report on EPC scheduled for 30 June 1973. Furthermore, it was stressed that EPC should henceforth not only deal with current problems, but also increasingly 'formulate common medium and long-term positions, keeping in mind, inter alia, the international political implications for and effects of Community policies under construction'.

The goal of building a European Union and becoming a powerful actor in international affairs contributed decisively to the positive verdict of the summit. It caught the public imagination, underlined the Nine's new self-confidence, and gave the Paris meeting a distinct air of optimism and progress.[145] Two leaders who were particularly relieved upon this success were Pompidou and Heath. The French president had suffered a grave disappointment a few months earlier when the French electorate responded to a national referendum on EC enlargement with large-scale indifference and a less massive 'yes' than he had anticipated. Having called the referendum to get a mandate for a more active French European policy, Pompidou could now base his claim for a leadership role among the Nine on the positive outcome of a summit he had hosted.[146] As for Heath, a serious economic crisis at home and widespread domestic scepticism towards the Community had put him under pressure to provide evidence that EC membership was in Britain's interest. While pleased with the political provisions, he was especially relieved about the RDF, as the British hoped that the concept of transferring money into industrially backward areas would be as beneficial to them as the CAP was to the French.[147]

Nevertheless, the governments assembled in Paris were well aware that the glowing summit communiqué also concealed ongoing differences and projected a bigger sense of unity than had already been achieved. This was less obvious to the public, as the previous debates on Europe's future had only rarely been conducted in the open. But to the historian, even a brief look back at these debates in 1971/72 is sufficient to recognise a gap between the impressive vocabulary of the summit and the practical difficulties in defining the specifics of a common European identity.

The controversies behind: Dropping the political secretariat

One such gap concerned the actual high point of the summit. As the archives reveal, the provision on EU was as much an expression of ambition as a last-minute measure to plaster over disagreement on the final conception of Europe. The federal–confederal debate had re-emerged in January 1971, when Pompidou surprised his press audience by sketching his own design of Europe. This *Plan française* foresaw a confederation of states, with the Council of Ministers evolving into a European government controlled by a European Parliament. Although it was a defensive measure to make sure that the member states would retain political responsibility even in the case that EMU became a success, Pompidou could not prevent the issue from being taken up in the context of the general debate on the 'New Europe'.[148] Initially, France's partners had responded with polite silence to Pompidou's initiative in order to avoid controversy. But as soon as the question of Europe's future structure was put on the summit agenda, heated discussions resurfaced. Several delegations were ready to accept confederal interim solutions, but insisted on a federal long-term scheme that would unite both economic and political integration.[149] With no rapid consensus in sight, the discussions soon switched to procedural suggestions such as launching a second 'Operation Spaak', that is, a report on the political unification of Europe by an eminent personality, comparable to the procedure that had given birth to the EEC in the mid-1950s.[150]

While the British remained passive throughout this debate, the FRG, confronted with domestic opposition to *Ostpolitik*, was eager to make progress. Brandt proposed to confirm the goal of a European government at the summit and underline Europe's intention of moving beyond economic unification by giving it a new name with more 'political sex appeal'. But he insisted on replacing the goal of 'confederation' with the more ambiguous term of 'union', and specifically suggested to incorporate the WEU into the EC and label the entire new European body 'Western European Union'.[151] Even though Pompidou agreed to compensate for the lack of substantive agreement by using the power of the word, he stubbornly stuck to the term 'confederation' throughout the summer of 1972. It was only immediately prior to the Paris gathering that

Balladur, now the deputy secretary-general of the Elysée, came up with the formula of 'European Union', a compromise solution that made it into the French
draft communiqué.[152]

When the Danes as freshmen expressed concern during the summit that
'European Union' could mean anything, it was pointed out to them by
Pompidou, Heath, and Scheel that the Delphic phrasing was precisely the
beauty of it. Still, it is worth noting that the concept of EU was more than a simple rhetoric trick. The date of 1980, as proposed by France, was left unques-
tioned during the summit negotiations, and all but the Danes supported the
Belgian insistence on defining a procedure for the steps ahead. Remarkably,
Pompidou was one of the stoutest defenders of a robust phrasing of the EU
paragraph, and he even went so far as to accept that the report mandated for
1975 would be worked out by Community institutions and in the fullest respect
of the treaties – a concession unthinkable under de Gaulle. Thus, the political
will to define the political finality of Europe and to take the unification process
a big step further was clearly present, the ongoing disagreement over the
specifics of the EU notwithstanding.

A debate relating to the federal–confederal issue concerned the idea of institutionalising and strengthening EPC through a political secretariat. This discussion turned out to be even more explosive, which is why it was not reflected
in the Paris communiqué at all. The interesting aspect here is that the principal
case for a secretariat, laid out in a West German memorandum in November
1971, was broadly supported.[153] Setting up a political secretariat was even a top
priority on the French summit agenda once Pompidou had become more optimistic about EPC (see Chapter 1).[154] When the Italian and Belgian delegations
suggested establishing a complementary European analysis unit to study international issues from a European perspective, no noticeable objections were
made either.[155]

But the devil was in the details. The question of the secretariat's location
proved unsolvable in 1972, which was unsurprising inasmuch as it raised the
fundamental issue of Europe's future conception. France insisted that the secretariat had to be located in Paris rather than Brussels, and Pompidou invested
so much public prestige into this matter that it became inconceivable for him
to climb down. The French came up with a whole variety of reasons in favour
of their capital. They did not want EPC structures to be located too close to
NATO, as this would hamper European détente and prevent the evolution of
a European identity distinct from that of the US. They also felt entitled to host
the EPC bodies in return for their support of enlargement, and they pointed
out that Paris had been accepted as the seat of political cooperation during the

Fouchet negotiations. But the key French consideration, and the major point of contention among the Europeans, concerned the twin issues of EPC–EC relations and EPC's ultimate purpose. Pompidou was dead set on keeping EPC separate from the Community institutions and reducing the Commission's role in foreign policy cooperation to the minimum possible. He agreed with the warnings of orthodox Gaullists that a secretariat in Brussels would open the floodgates to demands for political integration in the sense of supranational unification.[156] As much as he came to support the goal of European Union, the French president was determined not to mix up the economic and the foreign policy aspects of the European project.[157]

Britain and the FRG, by contrast, wanted to place EPC under a single Community roof in the long term. Both Heath and Brandt were willing to concede that for an interim period, EPC and EC could remain what the West Germans began to call the two 'pillars' (*Säulen*) of the European construction.[158] Nevertheless, they were convinced that establishing Paris as seat of the secretariat would set a definite precedent against later combining these two pillars into a single comprehensive community. And was it not probable that a separated EPC, once matured, would draw away all political substance from the Community institutions – as de Gaulle had intended with his Fouchet Plan? Needless to say that London and Bonn were also worried about excessive French influence over European affairs once Paris was accepted as Europe's political centre. Moreover, divorcing EPC from Brussels could only accelerate the fragmentation of Europe, with other great powers coming under public pressure to demand their own European institutions.[159]

By June 1972, Europe was deeply split in this matter. Whereas Ireland, Norway, and Denmark leaned towards Paris, Belgium and the Netherlands backed the Anglo-German campaign for Brussels.[160] Although Pompidou and Brandt for lack of consensus decided to remove the political secretariat from the summit agenda again,[161] France had not really given up yet. After the French president unexpectedly won Italian support for Paris to host the secretariat, he sent Schumann to Brandt and Heath for one last round of negotiations on 23/24 August 1972. This French diplomatic offensive ended in failure too, however, not least because the West German chancellor and the British prime minister coordinated their positions via telephone.[162]

With the secretariat no longer being an issue, summit preparations focused on alternative ways to strengthen EPC. While the idea of more frequent consultations proved uncontroversial, more sensitive topics were left for the second report on EPC, which had been mandated by the Davignon Report and was due in 1973.[163] During the summit itself, it was Heath who had the greatest impact on the discussions on EPC. Not only did he urge the foreign ministers to come up with a formula that would allow for a truly common foreign policy, but he also raised the taboo of improved EC–EPC relations when he argued that the foreign ministers needed to better attune their two 'hats' as members of the Council of Ministers and EPC. Pompidou initially deprecated the idea of mixing 'fruits and vegetables', but ended up accepting a formula on taking Community matters into consideration in EPC. This formula was very vague, however, and did not provide for any institutional linkage, which is why Soames correctly predicted in his after-summit report that the French were 'likely to still give the Community a lot of trouble over this'.[164]

Although the summit provisions on *l'Europe politique* were noteworthy, EPC-specific institutional progress remained limited without the secretariat. Also remarkable, although hardly noticed at the time, was that the two processes of foreign policy cooperation and political unification were implicitly separated in the summit communiqué. As the summit communiqué commissioned the second report on EPC to focus on improving political cooperation only, the lead in working out political union was now clearly with the Community institutions. This did not necessarily prejudice the effectiveness of EPC. But it meant that rather than bringing EPC closer to the Fouchet design, as the French might have hoped for, the Paris meeting effectively meant a step away from it.

Finally, a third debate worth looking at in the context of the summit concerned European–American relations – the only topic culminating in an open confrontation during the Paris meeting. Although this issue had preoccupied both sides of the Atlantic since the very beginning of European unification, it gained new virulence with the prospect of the Community's widening and deepening in the early 1970s. The FRG, more than any other EC member, became a strong proponent of an institutionalised European–American dialogue to make sure that the Community's success did not come at the expense of transatlantic relations. Bonn was convinced that the present situation – with a US ambassador in Brussels, a Community mission in Washington, and Commission contacts with the US lower-level bureaucracy – did not meet the political needs of the time.[165]

However, internal disagreement between the chancellery and the Auswärtige Amt on the scope of the consultative machinery as well as concerns about French repudiation meant that the FRG came up with very vague conceptual suggestions only, such as building an 'organic link'.[166] Yet even these ideas went too far for Pompidou, who feared that any form of institutionalised dialogue would lead to a US *droit de regard* in EC affairs that would result in Europe's subordination and tutelage. The French president stressed that he was by no means anti-American and did not intend to build Europe against the US. But as much as he sought to improve bilateral Franco-American relations (see below), he considered it premature to define a collective European position vis-à-vis the US, which he regarded as the biggest challenge in forging any common European identity.[167]

Interestingly, most of the FRG's other partners seemed to welcome the idea of consultations in the abstract but, with the exception of Belgium, did little to back Bonn during the summit preparations. Britain again kept a rather low profile during these discussions and indicated a preference for a pragmatic solution, proposing simply to express in the communiqué the will to 'maintain close and continuing contact with the US'.[168] Matters became even worse for the FRG during the actual summit, when Heath openly sided with Pompidou in rejecting institutionalised ties with the US. This meant that the vague phrasing of a 'constructive dialogue' relating to trade only became the lowest common denominator. But Brandt flatly refused to accept any wording that collectively referred to industrialised countries without singling out the special importance of the US to Europe, and a French compromise solution was only adopted after much haggling that would list the US with other key trading partners of Europe.[169]

The summit struggle over formulations emphasising either a distinct European identity or an outward-looking Community mirrored the general lack of agreement among the Nine over the specifics of the 'New Europe'. As much as the new possibilities for Europe were recognised after the settlement of the 'British question', no clear vision of Europe's purpose and structure had yet emerged. Debates had become much less confrontational and were generally conducted in a climate of growing optimism and trust. Nevertheless, all that glittered was not gold at the Paris Summit, and the Nine approached the year 1973 with as much ambition as uncertainty.

European defence: Soldiers for the Common Market?

One final normative debate that resurfaced in 1971/72 and deserves attention here concerns the notion of European defence. So sensitive was this issue that it did not make it onto the summit agenda and was initially only discussed on the bilateral level, largely between the Big Three. Yet these – secretive – deliberations on a European defence identity and Anglo-French nuclear cooperation were highly relevant for EPC, as the credibility and effectiveness of any common foreign policy was also related to the availability of European hard power. Unsurprisingly, differences in this field were even more basic than in the other normative debates. Whereas Britain and the FRG were eager to advance defence cooperation, Gaullist France continued to question the desirability of a European defence component as a matter of principle. But there were also some first signs of movement in Paris, giving cause for hope that progress was within reach.

It was not just the new opportunities resulting from the *relance européenne* that brought the issue back on the table. Equally important were perceived needs deriving from changes in the strategic environment. The eroding credibility of the US nuclear deterrent and the expected increase in the relative conventional strength of the Warsaw Pact posed growing challenges to Western Europe's security. The prospect of unilateral US troop withdrawals and declining European defence budgets threatened to undermine NATO's strategy of flexible response. Furthermore, it is notable that nuclear parity seemed to contrast more and more with what François Duchêne called an 'imparity in political will between the two superpowers', by which he referred to the growing isolationism within the US and the parallel perceived Soviet expansionism, especially in the Mediterranean.[170] While it was out of the question in the early 1970s to revive plans for a European defence union that would be fully autonomous of the US, there was a heightened sense of urgency that Europe should play a bigger role in securing its own defence.

It was Britain that took the lead in pushing the issue in 1971/72. As Heath was more worried about the Western defence posture, more sceptical about Soviet intentions, and more enthusiastic about a Community defence policy than any other leader of the Nine, Britain's goal was to 'persuade members of the EEC to tackle defence cooperation as systematically and whole-heartedly as they have economic co-operation'.[171] In November 1970, the prime minister mandated two interdepartmental working parties to study the prospects of both multilateral defence cooperation and Anglo-French nuclear collaboration. To his great disappointment, however, his bureaucrats proved unable to come up with a clear way forward in either case.

The report on multilateral cooperation, despite an extensive revision process, contained only meagre policy recommendations and, in the words of Heath, 'failed to produce a solution commensurate with the problem'.[172] This was mainly because the FCO and the Ministry of Defence (MOD), while agreeing on the need for European defence, differed strongly on how to go about it. The MOD recommended a gradualist conception of strengthening the existing schemes of cooperation, that is, the Eurogroup in NATO (see below) and bilateral defence talks. Conversely, the FCO favoured a new 'Organization for the Co-ordination of European Defence', based on a treaty and built on the same membership as the EC. Even though Heath clearly sided with this more radical approach, the FCO found it impossible to muster MOD support for jointly working out a respective British initiative, which left the Conservative government bereft of any conceptual foundations for its defence ambitions.[173]

As for the second report, it was rather discouraging too, as it pointed to numerous barriers that stood in the way of Anglo-French nuclear cooperation. The study agreed that there was a case for such cooperation, not just with a view to building Europe and strengthening European security, but also because the SALT negotiations between the superpowers entailed the risk that US support for British nuclear weapons might erode. At the same time, the differences in the French and British nuclear systems, equipment, and strategies rendered a joint approach very difficult. The scope for cooperation seemed all the more limited since Britain was extremely dependent on the US in the nuclear field and was legally prohibited from passing on the information and supplies it received for its sea-borne Polaris system. Issues such as targeting and deployment, which were considered of the biggest interest to France, were also the most sensitive areas of Anglo-American cooperation, with the effectiveness of the British nuclear deterrent being heavily dependent on US intelligence. Politically, cooperation was thus only conceivable with US backing, while the only possible field for a technical joint venture was the development of a successor system for the time after the mid-1980s.[174]

Heath had obviously underestimated the complex challenges involved in nuclear cooperation. Still, he was far from giving up. He had always been critical of how Britain had chosen to one-sidedly lean towards the US in its nuclear policy in 1961/62. During his years as opposition leader, he had even publicly proposed an Anglo-French nuclear deterrent to be held in trusteeship for Europe, complemented with a NATO-like European nuclear planning group.[175] Anglo-French nuclear cooperation was Heath's pet notion, and he was determined to investigate with Pompidou at least the possibility of a long-term project on a successor system. Similarly, the prime minister decided to pursue further the idea of European defence cooperation, irrespective of the bureaucratic deadlock between the FCO and the MOD.[176]

The FRG was surprisingly receptive to the idea of Community-based defence. While reluctant to talk about it openly as long as *Ostpolitik* was in its operative phase, behind closed doors Brandt and Scheel fully acknowledged the need for a European defence identity. In July 1971, the chancellor tried to convince Pompidou that it was only logical for defence cooperation to follow now that EMU and EPC had been launched, and he suggested an EC solution to defence by 1980. During their next bilateral summit, he added that the FRG could not take an initiative in this field, but would be supportive of any French ideas.[177] The British were assured by Bonn that although 'Bahrisch' tendencies made things difficult for Brandt, the chancellor was in fact considering the notion of Community soldiers for the 1980s.[178] As for the Auswärtige Amt, it pondered over the possibility of bringing the European defence ministers and chiefs of staff into EPC and shifting the Eurogroup's functions into the Community once enlargement was accomplished. It did not work out any blueprints for European defence yet, but Scheel already informed the US that the foreseeable problem of duplication between EPC and NATO ought to be addressed sooner rather than later.[179]

As for Anglo-French nuclear cooperation, reactions from Bonn were more ambiguous. Scheel and Rainer Barzel, the opposition leader, promised a surprising degree of support. Brandt seemed at least open about it, but indicated that the FRG could not subscribe to any defence concept that involved West Germany providing infantry whilst other Europeans were in charge of nuclear deterrence.[180] Defence Minister Helmut Schmidt, however, openly opposed what he called an Anglo-French 'nuclear condominium' and predicted that without an US nuclear umbrella, the FRG would go neutral. In his eyes, the 'trust for Europe' notion was not credible, since neither Paris nor London would expend their nuclear forces in retaliation against a Soviet attack on the FRG, as this would leave them with no nuclear capacities left to deter a subsequent nuclear onslaught on their own territories.[181]

The French response to the British ideas was the opposite of the German position. Paris showed no interest yet in multilateral European defence but, hesitantly, accepted a dialogue on nuclear cooperation. As Pompidou was not particularly interested in defence issues during his first years in office, Debré exerted a big influence on French policy in this field, which accordingly remained more marked by orthodox Gaullism than other aspects of France's European course. Debré's case against European defence was simple. He was convinced that the US, out of pure self-interest, would refrain from withdrawing its troops from Europe. He also did not consider a multilateral solution feasible, as France and Britain from his point of view were the only European powers willing and capable of defending themselves. He believed that a divided Germany was bound to be an unreliable partner, and the small powers were notoriously keen on freeloading when it came to providing security. Furthermore, he was unwilling to sacrifice France's policy of independence for a project that was devised to strengthen NATO only.[182] Pompidou himself was perhaps less resolute than Debré in ruling out defence cooperation. But he remained evasive on the issue and merely maintained that a common defence identity could only be the last step in European unification.[183]

Concerning nuclear cooperation, the French had some doubts too. Their independent *force de frappe* represented much more than a nuclear deterrent and provided the basis of national self-respect. They were also sceptical about Britain's excessive dependence on the US, and they were anxious not to strain their good relations with Moscow. Perhaps their biggest concern was the role of the FRG in any European deterrent, as the exclusion of West Germany from nuclear weapons was a basic principle of French security policy.[184] Still, France did have an interest in a dialogue with Britain. Despite its enormous costs, the French nuclear programme was far less developed, with major deficiencies – according to British sources – including second-strike capabilities and intelligence.[185] Moreover, the French shared the British concern that SALT might result in the superpowers pressuring third countries to abandon their nuclear weapons.

Thus, when Heath raised the idea of probing cooperation concerning second-generation nuclear systems during a bilateral summit in March 1972, Pompidou, after a lengthy debate, came out in favour of such an Anglo-French dialogue, provided that it be conducted in complete secrecy.[186] Remarkable though this agreement was, its practical significance remained as yet limited. Although an initial exchange did take place at the military level in July 1972,[187] the dialogue appears to have been put on hold again thereafter. Two factors are likely to have played an important role. One was the fact that the US too offered France a military and nuclear dialogue just when Britain was trying hard to arouse French interest. The extent to which this was a deliberate US move to counter European advances in the nuclear field cannot be assessed from European archives. On the one hand, Nixon twice assured Heath that he had no objections to Britain broaching the subject with France. 'You should feel that you have a great deal of running room on this,' he argued in December 1970, adding one year later that Heath should 'just do it and don't tell anybody'.[188] On the other hand, the US offered little concrete help when the British enquired just how much they could tell the French, and Washington made it clear that the Congressional Joint Atomic Energy Committee would have to be involved at an early stage in any Anglo-French transfer of know-how.[189] At the same time, the US entered into direct talks with France on missiles and safety procedures, and by mid-1972 even delivered very sensitive and important data on Soviet anti-ballistic missile (ABM) defences to Paris.[190] Even though Britain never received much information on this Franco-American dialogue, it was painfully aware that it could hardly become an attractive partner for France as long as Pompidou received key information first-hand from Washington.[191]

The second factor was related to internal re-evaluations in Britain itself. In 1972, it had become clear that as a result of the improved Soviet ABM defence, the Polaris system required short-term improvement to secure the credibility of British deterrence. The choice between the available improvement options was relevant to the Anglo-French dialogue in so far as it affected the time scale of the introduction of the successor system and, consequently, the possibilities of cooperation. Obviously, the Heath government had to take many factors into account in its deliberations, the possibility of cooperation with France being perhaps only a subordinate one. But until February 1973, when their decision was due, there was little point in talking to the French about any specific successor systems.[192] Having said that, the British were well aware that Anglo-French nuclear cooperation was the 'strongest and perhaps only bait' to attract French interest in European defence, and Heath remained determined to knock at the French door again in this matter in 1973.[193]

By the end of 1972, then, discussions on European defence remained inconclusive. They had been substantive enough to provoke a Soviet campaign against the idea of 'soldiers of the Common Market'.[194] But agreement seemed still a long way off even among the FRG, France, and Britain. Apart from the fragile Anglo-French nuclear dialogue, the only discernible examples of progress in 1971/72 were a strengthening of the Franco-German politico–military study group and the launching of a new Franco-British equivalent.[195] While these developments underlined the growing political will to tackle the issue once more, they hardly indicated any multilateral solution to European defence yet.

Therefore, Eurogroup remained the only European forum dealing with defence in 1971/72; however, it had little to do with forging a common European defence identity. An informal caucus within NATO consisting of biannual informal dinners of European defence ministers and a series of working groups, Eurogroup had been launched by the Wilson government in late 1968 in response to US calls for greater burden-sharing in the Alliance. In the early 1970s, it did serve the important purpose of averting immediate US troop withdrawals by maximising the visibility of European defence efforts by means of a European Defence Improvement Programme that made a positive impression on the US Congress. Yet it was widely acknowledged that Eurogroup could not serve as a nucleus for adding a defence capability to the European project. This was partly because it comprised non-EC members, such as Turkey and Greece. But its major handicap was that France categorically refused to participate, on the grounds that it was too close to NATO.[196] Whether French attitudes about European defence would evolve was indeed of critical importance for the prospect of building European hard power. For the time being, the idea of a defence component to European unification was bound to remain just that: an idea.

A mixed balance sheet on the eve of enlargement

Overall, EPC had a satisfactory start in 1971/72. By the eve of enlargement, it had become a consolidated tool for diplomatic concertation and an acknowledged part of European unification. Its operative beginnings demonstrated that working out joint European positions was a feasible endeavour and could lead to substantive results. Practical consultations thus at least partly confirmed the optimism derived from the generally improved conditions of European foreign policy-making as elaborated in Chapter 1. At the same time, EPC consultations and the parallel normative debates on the 'New Europe' brought to light some significant shortcomings and ongoing divisions. Such negative aspects were reasons for caution regarding the prospects of a European foreign policy, suggesting a mixed verdict on EPC after its first two years of existence.

On the positive side of the balance sheet, the everyday realities of European cooperation in 1971/72 indicated a growing political will and an improved psychology of cooperation not only among the leaders of Britain, France, and the FRG, but also in the Europe of the Six and later Nine. The large majority of European governments definitely shared the desire of Heath, Pompidou, and Brandt to render Europe a powerful actor in international affairs. The first topics chosen for political consultation were highly relevant and demanding, and the Europeans did not shy away from again addressing normative issues that had bitterly divided them in the 1950s and 1960s. It is also important to note that the bureaucracies of the foreign ministries turned out predominantly in favour of EPC.[197] Strikingly, there were many more meetings of the Political Committee and of most working groups in 1971/72 than had been anticipated. Consultations by the EPC embassies in non-EC countries and international organisations had also been established successfully. Furthermore, a practice of *information communautaire* had emerged, according to which the host foreign ministry kept the embassies of EPC partners informed about any meetings with other governments. While consultations led to occasional rows and irritation over problems such as leaked documents,[198] a good degree of socialisation and a 'coordination reflex'[199] among national officials became discernible already during these early years. It was also encouraging to note that the EPC members had shown their ability to translate their political will into common substance. The preparations for the CSCE were a big first success in this regard. Consultations on the Middle East had proven more difficult and had been less harmonious. But even here, the Europeans had been able to find a surprising amount of common ground concerning key aspects of a potential peace agreement in the Arab–Israeli conflict. The Nine also were in agreement on building a political union, and they acknowledged the need to further strengthen EPC.

As for the negative side, numerous factors emerged during 1971/72 that had the potential for spoiling the effectiveness of EPC. The bulk of these challenges related to intra-European disagreements both about specific EPC policies and about the broader issues of Europe's political identity. True, some obstacles concerned the individual level of European foreign policy-making, as in France, where orthodox Gaullists such as Debré continued to be uneasy about EPC and where officials in the Quai d'Orsay tended to regard non-adoption of French positions in EPC as failed consultations. Also, extra-European factors occasionally contributed to problems of cooperation. Although the US, being preoccupied with Vietnam and superpower détente, had been little involved in European affairs in 1971/72, it could make things more difficult for the Europeans in those cases where it did intervene, as in the Franco-British nuclear dialogue. This already pointed to potential transatlantic frictions over Europe's role within the West, an issue that came to the forefront in 1973/74.

Yet the predominant problem clearly was the lack of intra-European consensus on Europe's foreign policy. Apart from substantive differences on specific questions regarding the CSCE and the Middle East, no strategic consensus had yet been established about the desirability of an active European role in resolving the Arab–Israeli conflict. Similarly, although national role conceptions of European states had become more congruent in the sense of a shared broad vision of Europe speaking with one voice in global diplomacy, basic divergences remained. Disputes about the relations between the EC and EPC and the location of the political secretariat mirrored a larger disagreement on the conceptual end state of Europe. Consensus was also lacking on European relations with the US and NATO, as well as on European defence cooperation. Such differences not only raised doubts about the feasibility of a common foreign policy, but also had negative practical consequences for EPC. Without access to the EC's economic instruments, and lacking any military capabilities, EPC was as yet bereft of any proper power base. And without a secretariat to relieve the rotating presidency from the increasing burden of work, some inconsistency of effort seemed inevitable. Another problem was that the Danes and, above all, the Dutch were less enthusiastic about EPC than their partners and repeatedly had to be dragged along. Whether the Nine could preserve cohesion in EPC once they moved from internal deliberations to public policy remained to be seen, therefore.

Still, for all these weaknesses, the Europeans had good reason to look towards the first year of the enlarged Europe with confidence. This was also because by the end of 1972, trilateral Anglo–French–German leadership was beginning to show in the practical experience of European cooperation. The new distribution of power within the Community was openly reflected at the Paris Summit, where the delegations sat around one long table, the centre of which was occupied by Pompidou and Brandt on one side and Heath on the other side. As Soames observed at the time, this 'triangle was the heart of the action, in stature the rest were nowhere'.[200] If the Paris Summit could justly be identified as the symbolic starting point for the rise of EPC in 1973, it was not just because of the European ambitions and self-confidence indicated in its communiqué, but also because the constellation of triangular leadership became visible for the first time.

Part II

External Challenges and the Rise of Europe, 1973

> As we enter 1973, we see the exciting prospect of a European Community equal in size and influence to the other great powers, a Community which will enable us to improve the prosperity and quality of life of all our peoples, a Community which will be a force for reconciliation in the wider world, a Community committed to assisting those less fortunate than ourselves in the developing countries.
>
> Telegram Heath to Brandt, 1 January 1973 (WBA BK 52)

With enlargement accomplished, the European Community had become an economic giant by 1973. It now represented 10 per cent of the world's population, about 20 per cent of global production, more than 25 per cent of world trade, and nearly 40 per cent of monetary reserves.[1] These figures rendered the EC an economic entity comparable to the two superpowers. With Britain on board, it was not only expanding its position as a key competitor within the industrialised world, but was also evolving as a magnet for many other countries, particularly in the Third World. Despite recurrent monetary instabilities and some worrisome inflation, most of the European economies were still booming. Thus, the prospects for the EC appeared promising, and many in Europe were as excited as Heath about the Nine's growing power and opportunities.

One of the major questions at the beginning of 1973 was whether the Nine would be able to translate their economic power into political influence in world affairs. Would they succeed in progressing towards a common foreign policy and a European Union as they had declared at the Paris Summit? So far, EPC had not yielded any visible results to the public, and even those directly involved in political consultations could not be certain at this stage where their joint efforts at speaking with one voice would yet lead to. However, as shown in part I, the changes of government in Britain, France, and the FRG had brought about a constellation of decision-makers in Europe that gave ground for optimism. Importantly, the reorientation towards *l'Europe politique* continued in both Bonn and Paris in early 1973, which further raised the chances for the 'New Europe' to acquire a political profile commensurate with its economic weight.

After his triumphant re-election in the autumn of 1972, Brandt was indefatigable in pointing out that European unification was now the FRG's unequivocal priority. Accordingly, in his official policy statement for his second term in office, he placed the EU and EPC at the very top.[2] Even more significant for the prospects of EPC was the fact that control over West Germany's European policy was further shifting from the chancellery to the Auswärtige Amt. This was by no means a deliberate move by Brandt. Rather, it was a reflection of a generally diminishing cohesion of the West German government and Brandt's own loss of authority, caused mainly by more frequent and extensive periods of depression and exhaustion. His absence from the negotiations on the post-election cabinet reshuffle resulted in important gains for the FDP coalition partner and the foreign ministry. The post of parliamentary state secretary for European affairs was transferred from the chancellery to the Auswärtige Amt, and the ineffective Focke was replaced with Hans Apel. The chancellery was further weakened when Bahr, after the accomplishment of the bilateral phase of *Ostpolitik*, suffered a circulatory collapse (*Kreislaufkollaps*) and was absent from the scene for several months.[3] Conversely, there was the remarkable rise of Scheel, who had become increasingly popular and competent as foreign minister. The fact that this Euro-enthusiast had established himself as a senior figure in the government and presided over an ever-stronger ministry could only be to the advantage of EPC.

The French reorientation towards the political unification of Europe was also accelerated by a cabinet reshuffle, and much more directly and decisively than in West Germany. Pierre Messmer, who had replaced Chaban-Delmas as prime minister already in July 1972, after the parliamentary elections of 11 March 1973 formed a new government that no longer comprised either Debré or Schumann. As a primary obstacle to progress in political and defence cooperation prior to 1973, Debré was basically ousted by Pompidou, who accused him of having remained too 'Gaullist' and, subsequently, replaced him with Robert Galley, a little-known minister, formerly responsible for issues such as telecommunications and transport.[4] Schumann, for his part, unexpectedly lost his seat in the elections and was replaced by Michel Jobert, Pompidou's closest adviser.

Jobert's nomination as head of the Quai d'Orsay was of seminal importance for EPC. As secretary-general of the Elysée since 1969, this confidant of Pompidou had been a key figure in the Franco-British rapprochement in the early 1970s. His more than 30 secret meetings with Soames up to the end of 1972 (when Soames became EC commissioner in Brussels) had laid the foundation for the close relations that had emerged between Pompidou and Heath.[5] Jobert himself had been an old acquaintance of the British prime minister since they had met during their holidays on the Spanish Riviera in the early 1960s, which is why his nomination implied a further strengthening of Anglo-French relations and accordingly was welcomed in Whitehall.[6] As for the West Germans, they too were pleased with this surprise move of Pompidou, preferring Jobert's polite and unobtrusive style to Schumann' occasional extravagancies and vanity.[7]

The major significance in the change from Schumann to Jobert lay in their different role conceptions for Europe. The former had seemed more interested in enlargement of the Community than in EPC and had often been preoccupied with French relations to the Soviet Union and Eastern Europe. Jobert, in contrast, had already fought hard for the European Defence Community when he was official in the cabinet of Pierre Mendès-France in 1954. Being ardently in favour of a European foreign policy, he sought to promote and intensify EPC. His advent to executive power was thus an important asset in the Nine's endeavour to extend the process of unification to the political realm. Essential in this respect was that the new French foreign minister, contrary to his predecessor and contrary to expectations, managed to preserve a noteworthy room for manoeuvre and soon developed what came to be called a 'diplomatie jobertienne'.[8] This had much to do with the deteriorating health of Pompidou, who suffered from Waldenström cancer and, like Brandt, became less directly involved in the everyday making of foreign policy. The more authoritative position of Jobert did not mean that he would have been in a position to pursue an entirely different course from the Elysée. But the important thing was that there was now congruence between Paris, Bonn, and London in the sense that the foreign ministries, as the main operative carriers of EPC, were all in strong positions to promote and accentuate political cooperation, with Pompidou, Brandt, and especially Heath backing and protecting their efforts.

If 1973 turned out to be an extraordinary year for European foreign policy, witnessing the remarkable rise of EPC and astonishingly successful débuts of the Nine in world affairs, the political will of France, the FRG, and Britain to work out common positions and act collectively was a necessary precondition. Yet, the real trigger catapulting Europe onto the diplomatic stage and accelerating its political development was a series of external challenges in 1973 that provided both opportunities and necessities for the Community countries to act as a unity. It is these challenges and their impact on EPC that are at the heart of the following three chapters, which will trace and analyse the dynamic evolution of EPC in the course of 1973 from the rather unspecific ambitions at the beginning of the year to the substantive outputs culminating in a Declaration on European Identity in December 1973.

Chapter 3 deals with the role of the Nine at the CSCE. It differs from the other two chapters in that its time frame is not limited to a few months in 1973, but covers a wide period from the end of 1972 to mid-1974 and, albeit in a summary fashion, even briefly stretches beyond to the end of the conference in 1975. Unlike the other issues examined in this part of the study, the multilateral East–West negotiations in Helsinki and Geneva were a long and static affair, which is why it seems sensible to deal with them in one chapter. It is noteworthy, however, that the CSCE for EPC had different implications at different times. The success of the Nine at the CSCE preparatory talks in Helsinki during the spring of 1973 *did* provide the initial boost leading to the dynamics and confidence that came to characterise EPC in 1973, which is why the CSCE chapter is located at the beginning of this part. However, the continuing successful cooperation at the CSCE also provided an important background when other issues preoccupied the Nine after the summer of 1973. Moreover, the endurance of EPC cohesion in this field stood in sharp contrast to the general decline of EPC's effectiveness after mid-1974, which renders the insights from this chapter an important reference point at the end of this study, when the specific conditions of success in foreign policy cooperation in the early 1970s will be discussed.

As for the subsequent chapters, covering those challenges which successively accelerated and advanced EPC in 1973, Chapter 4 will deal with Europe's remarkable response to Kissinger's 'Year of Europe' initiative of April 1973. Chapter 5 will subsequently focus on how the October War of 1973 and the ensuing oil crisis prompted the Nine to further harmonise their position on the Arab–Israeli conflict and take measures to generally strengthen Europe's capacity to act in world affairs.

Chapter 3
Facing the Soviet Union: The Nine at the CSCE

In the history of European foreign policy, 15 January 1973 was a memorable day. Submitting joint proposals for a CSCE agenda and for mandates on each issue at the Multilateral Preparatory Talks in Helsinki, the Community countries for the first time acted as a united body on the international stage. It was an impressive demonstration of their ambition to move towards a common foreign policy, and of the unity they had already achieved in matters relating to the MPT and the envisaged conference. The collective move of the EC delegations surprised both the Warsaw Pact and the Neutral and Non-aligned countries (NNA). It has justly been described by a delegate as EPC's true hour of birth.[1] Importantly, it was the first manifestation only of what was to become a highly successful scheme of cooperation between the Nine throughout the CSCE process.

In this chapter, I will examine the role of the Nine at the MPT in Helsinki (November 1972 to June 1973) and at the CSCE in Geneva (September 1973 to July 1975). I will argue that the Nine were a key driving force in making the Soviet Union subscribe to an expanding notion of security, with Moscow eventually acknowledging human rights as a principle of international relations and the security of individuals as a complement to the security of states. Conversely, the CSCE also had positive repercussions for EPC, becoming a major catalyst for the rise of the Nine as an international actor with a distinct foreign and security policy.

Since one of the findings of this chapter is that the two projects of the CSCE and European foreign policy cooperation strongly interacted with each other, the chapter will start with an analysis of the general link between détente and European unification in the early 1970s. Reviewing the relationship between superpower détente, *Ostpolitik*, MBFR, and the CSCE, on the one hand, and the process of European integration, on the other hand, will allow placing the examination of the role of the Nine at the CSCE into a bigger context. I will subsequently investigate why the Nine could become the collective actor with the single biggest impact on the substance of the CSCE. As the Soviet Union during the conference left the Warsaw Pact countries (with the partial exception of Romania) much less space of manoeuvre than the Europeans had initially hoped, Moscow became the Nine's major negotiating counterpart. Consequently, the main issue to address here is how the EPC countries succeeded in wresting from the Soviets the kind of concessions that allowed them to incorporate most of their concerns into the Helsinki Final Act, which was signed by 35 heads of state and government on 1 August 1975. As the CSCE differed from the other EPC issues in that the Nine continued to perform effectively even when EPC otherwise fell into a crisis in 1974, particular attention will be paid to the central factors of success, which in this case will be discussed in an entire sub-chapter rather than in the concluding remarks. In the last part of the chapter, I will finally take a reverse perspective and cover the impact of the CSCE on the Nine.

Détente and European unification

Three structural elements to a large extent determined Europe's security system in the Cold War era: the Soviet military presence in Eastern Europe, the US military presence in Western Europe, and the FRG's integration into the West.[2] This constellation for a long time appeared relatively stable. The fact that the Western Europeans in the 1950s and 1960s had not been able to agree on building their own defence capabilities implied that only the two superpowers and West Germany effectively disposed of political options to change the European security system. However, in the late 1960s and early 1970s, two major developments occurred that threw Europe's security system into a state of flux and seemed likely to modify it in one way or another.

The first development was a growing sense of US weakness. The Vietnam War, the dollar crisis and lack of monetary leadership and domestic pressure for an isolationist US foreign policy left many in Europe concerned that Washington might withdraw its troops and decouple its own security from the security of Western Europe. If there had always been uncertainty in Europe as to the reliability of the US security guarantee, such worries now appeared to reach new heights. The second development referred to the process of détente, which involved all three key actors of European security. With both the FRG and the US seeking to put relations with the Soviet Union on a new basis, *Ostpolitik* and superpower détente, in particular, entailed the possibility of radically transforming the parameters of European security. This too, at times, caused great concern in the capitals of Western Europe.

I have discussed in the previous two chapters how these developments affected European unification between 1969 and 1972, particularly with regard to the Community's enlargement, the evolution of the EMU project, the formation of EPC and the re-emergence of concepts of European defence cooperation. What is important here is that the nexus between perceived US weakness and the process of détente, on the one hand, and the evolution of European unity, on the other, became stronger even in 1973. This partly had to do with the Watergate scandal, which made Nixon a lame duck six months after his sweeping re-election in November 1972, and threw the US back into domestic turmoil four months after Washington had finally signed a peace accord with North Vietnam.[3] But, above all, it had to do with the advancements of détente, and, in particular, with intensified superpower relations and the beginning multilateral East–West negotiations in the form of MBFR and the CSCE.

In the following, I will focus on the link between individual facets of détente and European unification in 1973, leaving an examination of the effects of Watergate on Europe until Chapter 4. Both the bigger European leeway stemming from superpower détente and the growing European fears of a superpower condominium and of negative consequences of MBFR and the CSCE prompted the Western European governments – and especially the French – to intensify European political unification. The particular aspect about the CSCE was that it represented the only manifestation of East–West rapprochement that allowed the EC countries to get involved collectively. The CSCE was Europe's one opportunity of participating in the negotiations on restructuring the international system, which is why it was only here that détente and European integration interacted in both ways.

The spectre of a superpower condominium

European concerns that the US might increasingly subordinate the interests of its allies to stable and intimate relations with the Soviet Union came to a new peak in 1973. Above all, it was the American–Soviet 'Agreement on the Prevention of Nuclear War', signed by Nixon and Leonid Brezhnev, secretary-general of the Soviet Communist Party, during their summit at Washington on 22 June 1973, that sent shock waves through many European capitals.[4] Despite US reassurances that it was no more than a banal statement according to which the objective of superpower détente was peace, this agreement inadvertently accelerated Europe's quest for a distinct political identity, provoking a policy change in France, in particular.

Kissinger gave a vivid account in his memoirs of how the agreement had been secretly negotiated since the summer of 1972. The Soviet Union had initially proposed a bilateral nuclear non-aggression treaty, with Moscow and Washington renouncing the use of nuclear weapons against each other. Although nuclear weapons according to Soviet interpretations were still feasible in the European theatre, they could no longer be employed against the territory of the superpowers. Kissinger was well aware that this cynical call for a bilateral alliance to the detriment of NATO was designed to both promote neutralism in Europe and lend the Soviets a free hand in an attack against China. Nevertheless, he was unwilling to give Moscow a flat rebuff in this matter, mainly because the US needed Brezhnev's support in achieving peace in Vietnam and, consequently, wanted to be seen ready for détente. The White House, therefore, gradually transformed the Soviet proposal in the course of the negotiations into a declaration of principles of political restraint that proscribed the threat of any force. The avoidance of nuclear war in this way no longer implied any obligations, but became a mere objective of diplomacy. The resulting agreement, in Kissinger's view, represented a diplomatic victory for the US. While there was still little in the document that could be beneficial to the West, the most important thing, according to him, was that Washington had succeeded in taking the teeth out of what had been a dangerous Soviet manoeuvre.[5]

This was not, however, how most Europeans saw it. Although interpretations of the agreement among the Nine varied, the predominant perception was that European interests and security had been severely compromised. Of the three big European powers, Britain was the one least worried. This was because it had been in close and regular touch with Kissinger about the negotiations and had, in fact, at the request of the US, secretly produced the bulk of what Washington handed to the Soviets as an American draft. The Heath government had been perplexed as to why the White House would ask the British rather than its own Department of State to deal with such a sensitive matter. But even though it felt awkward about Kissinger's insistence on absolute secrecy, it responded favourably to the US request for assistance and, under the codename 'Hullabaloo', studied ways and means of diffusing the Soviet proposal.[6]

The FRG and France had never been actively consulted about the drafts. They had been kept informed about the negotiations sporadically and at the top level only, and on the condition of not involving their bureaucracies.[7]

Accordingly, Bonn and Paris were both negatively surprised by the contents of the final agreement. Concerns related to both security and political implications of this new form of US–Soviet rapprochement. On the one hand, it seemed likely that the agreement might further weaken the US commitment to the nuclear defence of Europe. On the other hand, there were also fears that the bilateral consultative machinery of the superpowers envisaged for times of crisis could challenge the primacy of allied consultations and the relevance of the UN Security Council, ushering in a new international system based no longer primarily on regional alliances and collective security but on what a West German scholar at the time labelled an American–Soviet 'duopoly'.[8]

The US argument that Western deterrence was unaffected by the agreement since NATO's right to employ nuclear weapons in case of Soviet conventional attack remained unimpaired, became at least partially accepted in the FRG, following intensive US–German consultations. In the case of France, however, similar American efforts to placate Pompidou proved futile.[9] The French president and Jobert remained deeply suspicious about the agreement not only because it dealt a serious blow to their relations with Moscow, but also because it appeared to provide for a worldwide 'condominium' and a 'new Yalta' by the superpowers. The US–Soviet declaration of 22 June 1973, from the French point of view, posed a direct threat to France's nuclear role, to the relevance of its status as permanent member of the UN Security Council, and to the autonomy of Western Europe, which is why it shook the political establishment in Paris so violently.[10] An enraged Pompidou left Brezhnev, during the latter's stop-over in France following his summit with Nixon, in no doubt that the agreement would force France to adapt its foreign policy.[11] Jobert, for his part, publicly warned of secret American–Soviet aspirations for global hegemony and denounced the 'fake security' of superpower détente in a sensational speech at the CSCE opening session in July 1973.[12]

The key French response to the menace of US–Soviet collaboration was a marked shift towards unifying the Nine politically in the summer of 1973. While such a shift had already been in the offing in 1972, and had become even more pronounced with Jobert's move to the Quai d'Orsay in April 1973, it would not have become manifest so quickly and forcefully as it did. It resulted in France seeking to advance EPC on the occasion of both Kissinger's 'Year of Europe' initiative and the October War in the Middle East in the autumn of 1973, as I will outline in Chapters 4 and 5. It also gave new impetus to the notion of European defence cooperation, as again will be covered in Chapter 5.

MBFR and German neutralism

In the case of the multilateral project of MBFR, the link between détente and European unification was more complex. There was again a shared sense of uncertainty about what East–West negotiations on reducing the level of troops in Europe might imply for Western Europe's security, and this did provide an incentive for advancing European unity. However, of greater importance were the Europeans' fundamentally different assessments of the risks and opportunities of MBFR. While the FRG primarily perceived MBFR as a chance to promote military détente in Central Europe, Britain and France were much more sceptical about the whole process and, moreover, were concerned about West German intentions at the conference. Similarly to *Ostpolitik* in 1969–72, fear of MBFR leading to a neutral Germany prompted London and Paris to emphasise European unity as a counter weight, with Bonn, in turn, supporting such efforts to promote greater Western European cohesion as a means of demonstrating its loyalty to the West.

The MBFR negotiations that took place in Vienna between 1973 and 1989 are a largely forgotten affair today. Unlike the CSCE, they never led to any tangible result. Nor does it seem likely that there ever was a chance of East and West finding consensus as to what 'balanced' reductions meant. Whereas Western allies sought to redress the existing imbalance in ground forces in Europe through unequal reductions to a common ceiling, the Warsaw Pact countries were naturally unwilling to forfeit their advantage and insisted on reductions of equal proportions.[13] Against the background of this incompatibility of goals, it seems that the only reason the parties to the conference did not discontinue these talks earlier was because the negotiations allowed governments to underline their support for détente and, at the same time, ward off domestic calls for unilateral troop cuts. Seen in this light, MBFR did fulfil an important purpose.

It is important to point out, however, that such an interpretation is marked by hindsight and does not correspond with how decision-makers perceived MBFR at the outset. In 1973, during the MBFR exploratory talks between February and June, as well as once the conference started in the autumn, there seemed to be a real chance that MBFR would, in some way or other, affect Europe's security system. True, the exploratory talks had already turned out to be much more troublesome and frustrating than the parallel talks on the CSCE.[14] Yet, at the same time, it was clear that in negotiations on military security the stakes were much higher than in negotiations on political security and cooperation. Moreover, with the Nixon administration showing an eagerness to begin MBFR as soon as possible in order to embed domestic pressure for troop withdrawals in a multilateral framework, it seemed probable that the conference would result in some kind of reductions.[15] Hence, when the US, Canada, Britain, the FRG, and the Benelux countries, together with the Soviet Union, Poland, the CSSR and the GDR, launched the negotiations on 30 October 1973, MBFR in its early phase received at least as much governmental attention as did the CSCE.

There was no European agreement concerning the objectives of MBFR and the preferred course of negotiations. The FRG did support Washington's goal of using the conference to prevent unilateral troop cuts. However, it also saw in MBFR a guarantee against the European security system being determined by the superpowers alone.[16] Most importantly, the Brandt/Scheel government insisted that reductions comprised not only the stationary troops of the US and the Soviet Union, but also national, that is, European, contingents. There was disagreement within the government as to when to include German troops in the reductions. Social democrats, such as Bahr, Schmidt, and Georges Leber (who in July 1972 had replaced Schmidt as minister of defence, with Schmidt becoming minister of finance) urged involvement from the beginning, while Scheel and the Auswärtige Amt argued that national contingents should only follow after initial US–Soviet reductions. Nevertheless, all West German decision-makers underlined that even if non-stationary forces were to be cut in a second phase only, such a second reduction should at least be negotiated together with the first phase.[17]

Britain and France were seriously troubled about the implication of Bonn's MBFR policy. Even though other European powers, such as the Dutch, partly for budgetary reasons, were also in favour of including European troops in MBFR,[18] the case of the FRG was different, since it was in a position to significantly change the parameters of European security. There were many reasons why London and Paris were generally sceptical about MBFR. The British were convinced that the notion of any model of reduction being compatible with undiminished Western security was nothing but a 'pipe dream'.[19] If they still participated in the conference, it was mainly for defensive reasons, as well as to help the US cope with their domestic problems.[20] The French, for their part, stayed away from MBFR entirely. They refused to be drawn into anything that could result in French forces being put under external control or, worse still, in French troops having to leave German territory. They were also deeply concerned about negative implications of a special zone of reduced force levels in Central Europe for European security and European unity. From the French perspective, European security would be diminished, since the US would have to withdraw behind the Atlantic while the Soviets would only move further East. Also, the Western Europeans would have to reduce qualitatively good troops for worse Eastern contingents. Furthermore, the Europeans would become discriminated compared to the superpowers, with the former disarming, while the latter would only have to withdraw. As to the risks for European unity, the French were concerned about any zone of reduction dividing the Nine between 'ins' and 'outs', as well as about a Soviet say in the further evolution of Western European unification.[21]

Yet, the biggest concern in Paris and London related to MBFR's impact on the FRG. As Pompidou had already frankly confessed to Brezhnev in October 1971, fear of German neutralism was the basis of French disinclination towards MBFR.[22] If *Ostpolitik* in 1971/72 had defused some essential points of contention between East and West and in that sense had brought more stability to the Cold War international system, it also had nourished some disquiet within the West. Freeing the FRG of historic burdens, unresolved border issues, and Soviet defamations, *Ostpolitik* meant that Bonn no longer was a key object in East–West relations only but increasingly found itself in a position where it could assert its own course. The fact that the FRG had become one of Moscow's most privileged partners during this process had raised fears in France and Britain of German neutralist tendencies – fears that mounted further when Bonn in 1973 still insisted on including its own troops in the MBFR process. It was not that all FRG arguments in favour of cutting German troops would have been unreasonable. There was, indeed, a point to the argument that downsizing stationary troops alone would leave the Bundeswehr too powerful in Europe.[23] Moreover, Brandt's credo that fewer troops in Central Europe would mean more stability and peace, although not shared in Paris and London, did not per se overly worry the French and the British, since they trusted the chancellor's commitment to the West.

Yet, there was also Bahr, who openly identified a Soviet withdrawal from the GDR as Bonn's negotiating goal, proposed a reduction of US nuclear weapons in Europe from 6000 to 200, and continuously refused to acknowledge the need for or feasibility of Western European political unity as a precondition for pan-European cooperation.[24] Bahr's position appeared even more worrisome after one of his planning papers of the late 1960s was leaked to the West German press in the summer of 1973, which made public proposals for major troop withdrawals, the dissolution of the alliances, and the creation of a new security system.[25] It was this type of foreign policy thinking – coupled with press images showing Brezhnev charmingly kissing Frau Brandt's hand during his stay in the FRG in May 1973, or West German celebrations of GDR victories during the Olympics in 1972 – that sent shivers down the spines of French and British decision-makers.[26]

Could it not be possible that those strands within the SPD who, as an FCO analysis put it, 'see Germany as having a special role between East and West, who pay lip service to NATO but whose thoughts turn to Rapallo' may work towards neutralising Germany in order to make its reunification possible and use MBFR to that end?[27] Both the British and the French did not rule this out, wondering whether Brandt with *Ostpolitik* might not have mounted a horse he may not be able to control in the long run.[28] They did welcome the fact that the Soviet Union had discontinued its anti-Bonn propaganda and had stopped issuing disinformation about the FRG. However, what worried them was that parts of the political elite in the FRG, in return, increasingly seemed to stop telling the truth about the Soviet Union.[29]

Such uncertainties about the implications of MBFR for Europe and about Bonn's role in the context of East–West negotiations again led both France and Britain to intensify efforts at building the Europe of the Nine. Although convinced that no legal construction would ever be able to contain a strong popular current in favour of German–Soviet rapprochement,[30] Pompidou, nevertheless, regarded an attempt to tie the FRG more closely to the West as the best option available.[31] The West German government, for its part, confirmed the need for strengthening European unity. In the Auswärtige Amt, it was, above all, recognition of the risks entailed in MBFR and German–Soviet relations that led to efforts of deepening the Community.[32] In the chancellery, emphasis lay more on the desire to diffuse distrust as to Bonn's reliability as a partner in Western Europe and, as in 1970, to complement the FRG's active role in East–West negotiations with an equally active part in *Westpolitik*. The specific ways in which the FRG and France, in particular, sought to advance *l'Europe politique* in the second half of 1973 will be discussed in Chapter 5.

The CSCE and EPC: Opportunities and interactions

Of all manifestations of détente, the CSCE posed the most direct challenges to European unification. At the same time, it also constituted Europe's chance at collectively shaping détente, which is why it also became associated with great opportunities. The immediacy of such challenges and opportunities had much to do with the fact that the CSCE and European unification were two processes with remarkable similarities: both were multilateral security projects seeking to diffuse tension and prevent further conflict in Europe through cooperative, non-military means, with the 'German question' being a key underlying issue. With its all-European dimension, the CSCE potentially represented an alternative design for the Western European framework and, to some extent, stood in a competitive relation with it. This called for a joint position by the Nine to defend their collective interests. Concomitantly, as the CSCE was in its formative period only, the Community countries also saw a chance of exporting some of their established parameters of cooperation to the pan-European level.

There was agreement among the Europeans during their preparations for CSCE that in pressing for a pan-European conference the Soviet Union had been partly motivated by the goal of demolishing Community solidarity and slowing down the process of European unification. Moscow was expected to challenge European unity in both economic and political terms at the CSCE. Economically, it was likely to promote a system of all-European trade and to attack the Community as a discriminatory bloc. Politically, its campaign in favour of creating a permanent political organ and formulating a binding set of principles of state behaviour revealed an aspiration of modifying the existing European security system. Institutions beyond bloc structures were bound to diminish the relevance of NATO and the Community, and to give the Soviet Union a say in the development of Western Europe.[33]

In view of such dangers to the European Community, there were prominent figures speaking out against Western Europe consenting prematurely to a CSCE in the early 1970s. Especially active in this respect was Richard Coudenhove-Kalergi. Warning that the CSCE was a Communist strategy to place European unification under Soviet hegemony, the founder of the Paneuropean Union was indefatigable in urging the Western Europeans to accomplish their political union prior to any negotiations with the East.[34] Coudenhove's suggestion of delaying the CSCE was seen as overcautious by most policy-makers. Yet, there are indications that the decision at the Paris Summit to build a European Union by 1980 was in part motivated by the upcoming CSCE.[35] At any rate, there was consensus among the Nine that the best way of coping with the Soviet challenges was by facing Moscow collectively at the CSCE.

Beyond such negative incentives for the EC countries to act together, the CSCE for the Nine provided interesting opportunities too. As indicated in Chapter 2, the CSCE offered the Nine a chance of involving the Soviet Union in a dialogue about the division and security of Europe and bringing the two parts of the divided continent closer together. Above all, it was an opportunity for the EC countries to confront Moscow with their dynamic conception of détente that was based on respect for human rights and aimed at improving the plight of everyday life under Communist regimes. A proactive role for the Nine at the CSCE seemed all the more desirable since the exclusive US–Soviet dialogue inherent in superpower détente threatened to deal with issues of European security without any European involvement. Furthermore, since the Nine appeared an obvious actor group in this multilateral process, given the EC-specific risks emanating from the CSCE, was this not an opportunity to make their presence as a unit felt and show the reality and potential of their foreign policy cooperation?[36]

The impact of the Nine on the CSCE

The CSCE in several ways was an ambiguous affair. It was politically important in that it was the first post-war gathering of all states in Europe (plus Canada and the US), except Albania. It was relevant to the security of Europe in that it dealt with both the factual geopolitical status quo and the normative dimension of what security and détente should mean. It was symbolically significant as the first conference with open participation by both Germanies. And, it was unprecedented in its multitude of topics. At the same time, the CSCE avoided the key issue of troop levels in Europe. It only took place once other important aspects of European security, such as West Germany's Eastern borders and the status of Berlin, had already been handled elsewhere. It turned out to last over two years and gradually lost the attention of the public and even of many governments. And, with its results being legally non-binding, its impact and meaning was in doubt for a long time.

This is not the place to examine the historiography of the role of the CSCE in the evolution of East–West relations. Suffice it to point out that its relevance has only been fully recognised with the fall of the Berlin Wall. While the extent of its contribution to the demise of the Soviet Union remains disputed, it is today widely acknowledged that the CSCE did play a role in bringing the Cold War to an end. It encouraged dissent in Eastern Europe by legitimising it. As it rendered human rights a principle of international relations and specified operative standards for states to facilitate human contacts, access to information, and cultural exchanges, the CSCE fostered domestic social mobilisation in Eastern Europe and initiated a dynamic that gradually hollowed out the Communist regimes on a normative level.[37]

The Nine had a large share in lending the CSCE this dynamic dimension. Having become the primary forum for intra-Western coordination in 1971/72 (see Chapter 2), they now functioned as the major Western body to confront the Soviet Union during the CSCE, wresting important concessions from Moscow. Before examining their role and performance in Helsinki and Geneva, however, it is necessary to sketch the general course of the CSCE, so as to provide a framework for the subsequent analysis.

Anatomy of a conference: Towards the Final Act

When the 34 delegations gathered in Helsinki on 22 November 1972 to jointly prepare the CSCE, they had little idea of what awaited them. As it turned out, the MPT did not evolve as the kind of informal consultations among local ambassadors that many had expected. Rather, it gradually transformed into a major international conference of its own, with 200 participants, and with formal and informal working groups proliferating. Numerous controversial debates took place, with the negotiations dragging on for more than half a year. Officials and expert advisers from capitals were soon to replace most ambassadors, who were overwhelmed by both the variety and the details of issues addressed.[38]

The MPT came to be structured into four rounds of talks. The first phase was taken up by long procedural controversies and initial statements by the heads of delegations.[39] In the second phase, after Christmas, participants came forward with specific national propositions, which were grouped into four main subject areas, or 'baskets'. Concrete negotiations followed in the third and fourth phases,[40] which resulted in the 'Final Recommendations of the Helsinki Consultations' of 8 June 1973. This text, also referred to as the 'Blue Book', specified the organisation, agenda and procedures of the CSCE. It was of tremendous importance, since nothing that was not included in it could be negotiated thereafter.[41]

The Blue Book foresaw a conference in three stages: an initial meeting of the foreign ministers to launch the CSCE was to be followed by the actual negotiations on the level of officials, with the final texts to be approved on a political level to be decided. With regard to the agenda, four fields of discussion were recommended: security (basket I), economic and technical cooperation (basket II), 'cooperation in humanitarian and other fields' (basket III) and a possible follow-up to the conference (basket IV). Three committees were to be set up for baskets I to III, with the actual negotiations on specific issues taking place in 11 sub-committees. There were two sub-committees for basket I, tasked with working out a decalogue of already identified 'principles which each participating state is to respect and apply in its relations with all others participating states', and to submit proposals on CBMs, respectively. Basket II

comprised five sub-committees on commercial exchanges, industrial cooperation, science and technology, the environment, and other areas, such as transport and migrant labour. Finally, there were four sub-committees in basket III,
looking at human contacts, information, culture, and education. For all the
committees and sub-committees, the Blue Book listed detailed terms of
references.[42]

The actual CSCE opened in Helsinki on 3 July 1973, when the foreign ministers approved the Blue Book by acclamation and one after the other offered
their own views of what the conference should achieve.[43] Already at this first
stage of the CSCE, it became obvious that the negotiations were to be more
complex and last longer than particularly the Soviet Union had wished. The
sheer number of committees and sub-committees, the agreed procedure of
consensus decision-making, as well as the battles over substantive issues
fought between East and West even during the MPT pointed to extensive discussions to come. Still, when the by now 35 delegations (with Monaco joining
in) on 18 September 1973 came together in Geneva to begin the actual substantive work, hardly any participant would have expected the conference to
last nearly two years rather than a few months.[44]

Even more than had been the case with the MPT, the Geneva negotiations
turned into a trench war. By Christmas 1973, any popular euphoria had disappeared; in mid-spring 1974, the CSCE was for the first time facing a near-complete stalemate; and when the conference had to adjourn in July 1974 for a
six-week summer recess, there was no doubt left that these negotiations would
become, as the British put it, a 'long haul'.[45] An atmosphere of confrontation
and a sense of frustration became characteristic of much of the negotiation
period. Tough battles took place on almost every adjective and comma in the
various texts that were to be worked out in accordance with the Blue Book.[46]

Some figures might convey an idea of how complex these negotiations
turned out to be. There were up to 400 delegates in Geneva, most of them
highly specialised and responsible for a single topic only in the wide panoply of
CSCE issues. Five negotiating sessions were needed to reach agreement, with
2341 official meetings, 761 of which dealt with basket III issues alone. In addition, there were many more meetings of informal groups. It was largely in these
informal groups with perhaps a dozen delegations, as well as in corridor discussions and bilateral contacts, that the actual bargaining took place, and especially so with regard to basket III.[47]

The CSCE had gradually become, to quote a participating diplomat, a
'detached, […] rather obscure debating society'.[48] It was only after mid-
February 1975 that the conference began high-pressure negotiations again,

with the delegations managing to hammer out the essential compromises in the end. The resulting 'Final Act', signed in Helsinki at the summit level on 1 August 1975, was a voluminous document.[49] It contained all substantive provisions agreed during the negotiations and, thus, put flesh on the thematic skeleton as defined during the MPT. The Final Act marked both the end point of an extraordinary conference and the beginning of the 'CSCE process' that culminated in the 'Charter for a new Europe' in 1990 and the creation of the Organisation for Security and Cooperation in Europe (OSCE) in 1994.

The CSCE not only brought new issues to the security agenda and expanded the concept of security itself. Despite being an essentially East–West affair, the conference also brought new actors onto the stage of international security. While there were several issue-specific, loose formations at the CSCE, such as the Berlin Group, the Mediterranean Group, and the Nordic Caucus,[50] two groups played more persistent roles and had a remarkable impact on the course of the conference. One of these groups comprised the NNA countries, which came up with joint contributions during the conference and were individually much more active than had been expected. These NNA countries did not arrive at the CSCE with harmonised policies and came to coordinate their positions only in the course of negotiations. They also were less cohesive than the Eastern and Western camps, as they were a politically and ideologically heterogeneous group and pursued different objectives. Yet, there were fields such as security where their interests were compatible. And, most importantly, they played an invaluable role in dragging the negotiations forward, be it through substantive compromise packages to build bridges between Eastern and Western positions, or through the provision of good offices, such as presiding over the informal working groups.[51] The Nine obviously were the other new group to make an impact at the CSCE, and it is to their role that we now turn.

Shaping the agenda in Helsinki

At the onset of the MPT already, the major objectives of East and West were clear. The Soviet Union as the long-time driving force behind the CSCE was in a position of *demandeur* and pursued a largely conservative agenda. Moscow initially might have had more dynamic goals in mind, seeking to oust the US from Western Europe and set up a new pan-European security system. However, while its hope to gain more influence in Western Europe did persist, its paramount objective by the end of 1972 had become defensive. The predominant Soviet request by that time was Western acknowledgement of the political and territorial status quo in Europe, which would allow Moscow to stabilise its hegemonic system in Eastern Europe. Accordingly, a declaration of principles emphasising the inviolability of frontiers and a pan-European political organ were two key results that the Soviets aspired to. Moscow, thus, strove for a short, declaratory CSCE ending at summit level, and it wished to bring the MPT to an early conclusion.[52]

The West did not categorically rule out formally acknowledging what had been a reality for decades anyway. Yet, it was willing to do so under certain conditions only. It wanted to make sure that peaceful changes of frontiers remained feasible and that overcoming the division of Europe remained a possibility. The EC countries, in particular, asked of the Soviet Union to accept a conception of détente that referred to peoples as well as states and comprised practical improvements for the citizens of states under Communist rule. They were supported by the NNA countries in these demands, which in addition were keen to discuss certain aspects of military security in Europe. The story of the MPT is essentially about how the non-Communist participants succeeded in wrenching concessions from the Soviet Union in terms of the CSCE's agenda and procedures, or, to put it the other way round, how Moscow came to pay a remarkable price for getting the actual conference started. Given that Eastern and Western objectives were obviously irreconcilable, with the Soviets asking the West to acquiesce in their sphere of influence in Eastern Europe and the West seeking to penetrate precisely this sphere, the West at the end of the MPT came out, as a British delegate put it, 'in a position of clear advantage'.[53]

The EPC countries in the course of the MPT made the single biggest impact on the procedures and agenda of the CSCE. They had to give very little away on the substance of their joint position, and where they did they achieved major Soviet concessions in return. Their de facto leadership did not take place in opposition to NATO and the NNA countries, with which they closely cooperated. But it was the Nine who mainly shaped the outcome of the MPT. The first thing they managed to get through was their *conference model*. The three-stage organisation with committee work in-between was accepted in the first round of talks already. The East insisted at first that the third stage must take place at summit level, but came to accept that this was to be decided in the course of the conference only. The US was more tenacious and initially failed to support the model, on the same grounds as during NATO preparations in 1971/72. However, in view of the overwhelming majority in favour, Washington too gave way.[54]

With their concerted surprise move on 15 January 1973, the Nine had a tremendous impact on both the subsequent work of the MPT and the content of the CSCE. In three consecutive presentations, Belgium as acting EPC presidency, Italy, and finally Denmark tabled comprehensive proposals by the Nine for a *conference agenda*, as well as *terms of references* for all issues to be discussed.[55] It was the fruit of the intensive preparatory work that the Nine had done in 1971/72, allowing them to put their mark on the substantive discussions from the very beginning. Their approach of separating the economic and human realms as two distinct agenda items came to be accepted by the Soviet Union at the end of the second round of talks.[56] They also managed to get through the idea of mandates for each CSCE topic, which represented a midway solution between the Soviet intention of identifying a broad agenda only and the US approach of negotiating the entire substance before the actual conference.[57] The Soviets lamented that the EPC mandates were too long and too detailed, but they focused on watering down the language of these texts rather than fighting the principle. By April 1973, Moscow even conceded that all issues would be addressed in-depth during the CSCE in sub-committees and accepted every sub-committee proposed by the Nine. The joint working out of terms of references for these sub-committees, thus, became one of the major tasks of the MPT. It compelled the Eastern delegations to take a stand on sensitive issues already prior to the conference. More importantly, it meant that the Communist delegations would be unable to circumvent these issues during the CSCE itself.[58]

In order to make sure that the Eastern delegations would have to comment upon all Western proposals, the Nine suggested that the MPT should apply an inductive, *bottom-up method* of discussing all propositions in a single, open-ended working group before jointly drafting the terms of references and labelling the respective agenda items.[59] The Soviet Union at first insisted on speeding up the work by running individual groups for each basket and leaving out proposals where consensus was unlikely anyway. But, again it came round to accept the bottom-up approach. However, channelling all work into one group soon turned out to be too inflexible an organisational structure for the MPT. When the Swiss came up with the idea of setting up informal drafting groups or so-called 'Mini–Groups', the EPC countries initially reacted dismissively. Yet, they finally gave way in March 1973, well aware that the bottom-up approach in principle had become established.[60]

With respect to the substance of the individual agenda items, the biggest battles were fought over issues linked to baskets I and III. Remarkably, the Nine prevailed again in the large majority of cases, and it is here that they wrested the biggest concessions from Moscow. Concerning the *basic principles*, it is worth noting that most of the principles on the table were uncontested, as they already figured in the UN Charter or other international declarations. The

Soviet Union, however, was keen to establish the 'inviolability of frontiers' as an additional principle of international relations. All the more irritated were the Eastern delegations when the Nine coupled the notion of inviolable borders with the principle of 'non-use of force' in their draft proposal of 15 January 1973, which implied that border changes were still possible by peaceful means. Worse still, the catalogue of principles proposed by the EC also contained references to 'human rights' and 'national self-determination'. These too were new principles, only this time contrary to Soviet interests, not least because they challenged the Brezhnev Doctrine. Accordingly, Moscow criticised both principles sharply, arguing that human rights were a domestic rather than international affair and that self-determination was a topic relevant for colonies, but not Europe.[61]

The Nine were well aware that they would not be able to deny the East its key objective of making the inviolability of frontiers an independent principle. If they eventually accepted decoupling the inviolability principle from the 'non-use of force', they traded this concession for two significant Soviet counter-concessions. First, there was no reference implying that inviolability of frontiers could mean freezing the territorial status quo by making borders immutable. This was relevant both to the West Germans, who were determined not to accept any provisions at the CSCE that went beyond the Moscow Treaty, and to the EC at large, which strove towards a common market without internal borders.[62] Second, their own two principles were incorporated into what became a decalogue. Human rights as a CSCE issue continued to be a source of irritation to the Soviets, to the extent that it occasionally became a non-expression during the negotiations and was replaced by 'penguin' as a synonym and code.[63] Nevertheless, not least because of the support by the neutrals, it became the longest and best defined title of the principles in the Blue Book, being referred to as 'respect for human rights and fundamental freedoms, including the freedom of thought, conscience, religion or belief'.[64] Moreover, with the Soviets accepting the notion that all principles were equally relevant and applicable, the Nine were also successful in preventing them from rendering the inviolability of frontiers the status of a super-principle at the CSCE.[65]

The single biggest achievement of the Nine at the MPT was the explicit and extensive terms of references in *basket III*. This basket was by far the most innovative aspect of the CSCE agenda, laying out what the principle of human rights should mean in practice.[66] Its meaningless title '[c]operation in humanitarian and other fields' reflected the enormous struggle involved in getting this issue on the agenda at all. It plastered over the basic divergences between East and West as to how to approach this field. While the East preferred to talk about – state-controlled – improvements in cultural exchanges, the West insisted on including freer movement issues as well, which is why all-important Western demands were hidden behind the 'other fields' notion.[67] The more noteworthy were the mandates that figured beyond the basket's heading.

The first sub-committee in this basket was to deal with 'human contacts' and had to prepare proposals to 'facilitate freer movement and contact, individually or collectively, privately or officially, among persons, institutions and organisations', with specific fields of study such as reunification of families, marriages, and travel. The second sub-committee was asked to bring forward suggestions as to the 'freer and wider dissemination of information of all kinds'. The fact that this provision made it into the Blue Book is particularly remarkable, since Soviet resistance in this matter originally was stronger than anywhere else.[68] There were two more sub-committees on 'cooperation and exchanges in the field of culture' and 'cooperation and exchanges in the field of education'. Debates here had been comparatively less acrimonious, but had largely evolved to the advantage of the non-Communist delegations, which had made sure that the mandates comprised references to exchanges not only between government agencies, but also between 'non-governmental bodies'.

To be sure, not all topics listed for basket III in the Blue Book originated with the Nine. But while the NNA countries and other NATO members too succeeded in raising issues in this realm, it fell largely to the EC countries to function as the fortress of Western interests and stave off Eastern attempts to water down these provisions. The Soviet Union initially was ready to accept sub-committees for human contacts and information only on the condition that their respective mandates were circumscribed by a preamble referring to the principles of non-interference and national sovereignty, and to national laws and customs generally. The Nine, however, refused to go along with this and insisted that the preamble referred to all principles. They were successful in turning the preamble to their own advantage by inserting a reference to the applicability of the proposals 'irrespective' of the political, social, and economic systems, and by calling for 'new ways and means' appropriate to the aims listed in basket III.[69]

Finally, the EPC countries also ensured that those topics that could potentially allow Moscow to increase its long-term influence in Western Europe were kept vague. Concerning *basket IV*, the Soviets themselves, perhaps in anticipation of Western resistance, had submitted a proposal that was much less threatening than had been feared, calling for a permanent consultative committee to exchange information and prepare other conferences only.[70] The

Nine diffused the sensitivity of the issue further by insisting that any follow-up would be considered only on the basis of progress during the CSCE negotiations and that the matter would, therefore, not be dealt with in a sub-committee but in the general co-ordinating committee that was to orchestrate the whole conference. As for *basket II*, the Nine rejected the Eastern demands for economic non-discrimination and most-favoured nation status. They generally kept the issue low-key and acted rather defensively, postponing any potential Community offer to stage II of the CSCE. Emphasising principles such as reciprocity, information, and business contacts, they were content with terms of references that allowed for a thorough examination of specific issues.[71]

By the end of the MPT, the CSCE had definitely become a project of the non-Communist delegations, and of the Nine especially. The NNA countries too put their mark on the MPT, be it by procedural proposals, such as the basket idea and the 'mini group' approach or by adding substantive issues to the agenda such as the Swiss suggestion to 'undertake the elaboration of a method for the peaceful settlement of disputes'.[72] Yet, these countries as a group obviously were not strong and cohesive enough to get their entire – heterogeneous – agenda accepted. They were forced to give way especially in fields where they received no collective backing from the West, as was the case with proposals for more far-reaching measures in the realm of military security or with the Austrian idea of putting the Middle East conflict on the agenda. With respect to NATO, the only area where the Fifteen as a group played a significant independent role within intra-Western coordination was in the field of CBM, the inclusion of which in the CSCE agenda was also a success for the non-Eastern participants, its vague language notwithstanding.[73] Overall, however, it was the Nine who had been in the lead of defining and defending Western positions throughout the MPT and who by summer 1973 had well established themselves as a key actor of European détente, underlining their aspiration of shaping the CSCE according to their own interests.

Expanding the notion of security in Geneva

An analysis of the role of the Nine at the CSCE – with its multilateral dimension, its multi-issue approach, and its countless formal and informal negotiating sessions – could easily fill the space of a book itself. For our purposes, it is sufficient to summarise the impact of the EPC countries on the course and the outcome of the conference, without scrutinising every position of the Nine in every debate in every sub-committee. Attention will be focused on those issues that were most contentious during the conference and, ultimately, gave the CSCE its particular character and relevance.

There were some striking similarities between the CSCE negotiations and the MPT. Not only were the same battles fought again, but they were also fought in the same constellation of actor groups that had emerged in Helsinki, leaving it to a considerable extent to the Nine to negotiate with the Soviet Union and seek to wrench whatever concessions possible from the Eastern hegemon. Another similarity was the fact that it was the Eastern delegations who, again, made the essential concessions in the end, after the Soviet leadership, with its self-imposed deadlines, had put them under renewed time pressure in early 1975. The resulting disorderly Eastern retreat from some of their basic and long-defended positions in baskets I and III meant that the non-Communist delegations were successful in inserting many of their demands into the Final Act, with the balance sheet of the Nine being especially positive.[74]

However, there were also two major differences between the CSCE and the MPT. For one thing, the Communist delegations in Geneva for a long time refused to be in a position of *demandeur* and no longer urged the West to make haste. As a delegate from Eastern Europe put it bluntly in the autumn of 1973: 'If you have the money, we have the time.'[75] This determination of the East to bear the challenge of a long struggle thwarted the Nine's strategic calculation to bargain Soviet concessions for an early completion of the conference at summit level, rendering the CSCE an ordeal that only came to an end once Moscow lost patience again in early 1975. The second difference refers to the role of the US. Although for the most part inactive as during the MPT, the Nixon administration came to actively support positions of the Nine towards the end of the Geneva negotiations and managed to obtain key concessions from the Soviet Union in bilateral superpower talks. While the Nine, supported by NNA and individual NATO countries, again bore the brunt of negotiations at the CSCE, the US this time had a bigger share in securing the success of the non-Communist delegations than in the case of the MPT.

Unsurprisingly, the most controversial debates during the negotiations related to the respective key priorities of East and West. They concerned the specifications of the two principles of the 'inviolability of frontiers' and 'human rights', as well as the applicability and authoritativeness of basket III. With regard to the *basic principles*, the Soviet Union for a long time rejected any reference to the right for peaceful border changes and was particularly hostile to including such a clause in the inviolability principle, as proposed by the Nine in their draft decalogue of October 1973.[76] The ensuing deadlock, which paralysed work in basket I for months, could partly be overcome in April 1974, when the Spanish delegation came up with an interim compromise to register the 'peaceful change' formula simultaneously with the inviolability principle, but on a separate piece of paper. Accepting the separation of the two notions amounted to a major Western concession and did not go without internal strain among the Nine.[77] Yet, the West also got something in return, as the Soviets had to concede that the 'peaceful change' clause would figure somewhere in the decalogue. Much of the remaining debate was, therefore, about where to put this floating sentence, with the Nine and the US eventually jointly managing to insert it into the first principle of 'sovereign equality'.[78]

The provision that 'frontiers can be changed, in accordance with international law, by peaceful means and by agreement', was essential in complementing the static, Soviet-inspired principles in the Final Act with a dynamic notion of change. If it did not stand where the EPC countries had originally wanted it to, its mere inclusion and its prominent place in the Decalogue still left them satisfied. More resounding even was their success in the case of the 'human rights' principle. Contrary to the principle of 'self-determination of the peoples', which as a result of resistance even from NATO delegations, such as Turkey and Canada, remained short and vague,[79] this second principle advocated by the Nine emerged as containing the longest explanatory text of the entire decalogue. Debates in this matter even surpassed the inviolability issue in intensity and length, with the Soviet Union attempting to water down the drafts wherever possible and limit the coverage of the principle to the freedom of religious belief.[80] Yet, the Nine eventually managed to get accepted a whole series of detailed provisions on the duty to respect and promote human rights, as well as references to the non-Marxist conception of human rights deriving from the 'inherent dignity of the human person', and to the respect for the universal significance of human rights as an 'essential factor for [...] peace'.[81] The principle was of tremendous importance. By rendering human rights an issue of inter-state relations, it undermined the notions of sovereignty and non-interference, that is, the very basis of the Westphalian state system.[82]

Basket III witnessed both the most tedious and the most sterile debates during the CSCE and some of the biggest scoring points for the Nine. The goal of the EPC countries in this basket was clear: rather than try to strengthen the rights of individuals, as the UN had attempted to in several declarations, the focus was on defining guidelines for behaviour of the state vis-à-vis its citizens, with a view to lowering barriers to cooperation and mobility in fields where problems had been especially virulent.[83] To this end, the Nine, together with other non-Communist delegations, during the first few months of the CSCE swamped the conference with proposals for practical improvements. None of these proposals in themselves were very provocative or ideological, but it was hoped that together they would have a tangible impact.[84]

In order to obtain concrete results, the Nine again sought to apply the bottom-up approach of avoiding any drafting in basket III and in the decalogue of basket I before all proposals relating to basket III had been thoroughly discussed with the East. Yet, such delaying tactics this time proved unproductive. The so-called 'General Debate' in the autumn of 1973 degenerated into what a participating US diplomat described as 'shadowboxing', with the Nine insisting on substantive discussions of freer movement issues, while the East sought to keep specific comments to a minimum.[85]

Already after the speech by the Soviet Foreign Minister Andrei Gromyko at the CSCE opening ceremony in July 1973, there had been concerns among the Nine that the East might try to turn the clock back in Geneva to pre-MPT and try to reintroduce caveats eliminated during the talks in Helsinki.[86] The ever harsher Soviet campaign against dissidents, such as Andrei Sakharov and Aleksander Solzhenitsyn, in the summer of 1973 had given further indication that Moscow would not make too much out of basket III and would continue to consider a policy of repression at home perfectly compatible with a policy of détente abroad. In fact, things turned out worse than any of the Western delegates could have expected. With a whole variety of methods, including threats, attempted extortion, and lamentations that they would lose their jobs, Communist delegates sought to introduce limitative formulations into basket III to rob the specific proposals of their practical significance. Most serious for the Nine was the Eastern insistence on a preamble in basket III, designed to emasculate its entire content.[87]

It was this controversy about a preamble that by early 1974 brought the negotiations to a quasi-standstill, with stonewall tactics on either side. Moscow refused to draft any texts in baskets III before a preamble had been formulated and insisted on including references to the principles of 'sovereignty' and 'nonintervention in internal affairs', as well as to national laws and customs to limit its obligations. The Nine, analogous to the MPT, did not rule out a preamble, but demanded to address the operational parts first. Moreover, they wanted the preamble to contain general introductory phrases and a collective reference to all principles only, well aware that language which negatively affected the authoritativeness of the provisions in basket III would seriously endanger the general balance of gives and takes in baskets I and III.[88]

It was largely owing to Western European stamina and tenacity that the Soviets, despite indefatigable efforts and intensive pressure, failed to significantly water down basket III. The NNA countries did play an important part in this basket in that their procedural and substantive compromises prevented the negotiations from completely collapsing.[89] And, again, if it had not been for the eventual effort of the US government to bilaterally negotiate the so-called 'global initiative' with Moscow, where the Nine offered some concessions in the fields of human contacts and information in order to obtain their essential points, it is unlikely that so many provisions by the EPC countries would have made it into the Final Act.[90] Yet, it was the Community countries that were not only at the origin of the majority of proposals, but also functioned as the major fortress defending them during the CSCE. That basket III in the end contained the longest explanatory texts of all, including such diverse provisions as lowering fees to enable the reunification of families, improving the working conditions for journalists in foreign countries, and increasing the places to sell foreign newspapers, was one of their biggest and most important achievements.[91]

Throughout the CSCE, *basket II* was much less controversial than the other fields of discussion. Here, negotiations yielded steady progress, but they remained in the shadow of the other baskets and led a life of their own.[92] This was because the Nine and the Warsaw Pact countries, as the two main protagonists in this basket, decided early on against giving too much weight to the economic dimension of European détente. The Soviet Union showed less interest in technological cooperation than the West had expected and generally refrained from being *demandeur* in this basket. As for the Nine, they came out against any Community offer. Some of the EC countries had remained generally sceptical towards the idea of trade negotiations with the East. The CSCE also turned out to be an unsuitable forum for negotiations affecting only specific groups of the participants. Most importantly, the Soviet Union came to acknowledge the existence of the EC in 1973/74, irrespective of the CSCE negotiations.[93] And, since the Nine continued to oppose the Eastern objective of non-discrimination and the Soviets equally stubbornly resisted all detailed references to increased business contacts and information, there really remained little of any significance for the CSCE to do.[94]

The one field where the EPC countries as a group continued to play a subordinate role both within intra-Western coordination and in the actual negotiations was the CBM-section of basket I. In the course of the CSCE, the Nine came to deal more frequently with the issue, but they left the lead to NATO.[95] Since several NATO members and the Soviet Union remained opposed to specific and ambitious CBMs, this field, in fact, became very much an issue of the NNA group, which surprised all other delegations in February 1974 with its first joint substantive proposal at the CSCE. NNA countries eventually succeeded, with the active help of some EPC and NATO members, in inserting into the Final Act the notion that political and military aspects of security were complementary. Yet, as far as practical propositions were concerned, references to such measures as the notification of military manoeuvres and military movements remained vaguer than many non-Communist delegations had hoped.[96]

Two final fields where the Nine did play a major role were related to the structure of the conference texts and the question of a follow-up. Whereas the Soviet Union was making the case for each basket leading to separate documents and for the texts of baskets II and III to be signed by lower-level officials only, the Nine continuously refused to give the decalogue a special status and advocated collecting all agreements in a *single compendium* and signing collectively what they proposed could be called the 'Final Act'.[97] It was the Dutch who, in February 1974, submitted on behalf of the Nine (and after consultation with NATO) a draft structure of such a 'Final Act' to the other conference participants, who at last came to embrace the concept of a single document.[98] As for *basket IV*, the Nine countered the Eastern concept of a consultative committee with a proposal, tabled by Denmark in April 1974, which foresaw an interim period of several years, followed by a meeting of senior officials in 1977.[99] The intention behind this proposal was to make any follow-up dependent on whether the East implemented the provisions they signed up to in the Final Act. The resulting controversies were peculiar in that some neutrals too opted for a permanent organ, which in their eyes was essential to control the implementation of the Final Act and which, for them, provided a unique platform to remain involved in the European security dialogue.[100] Yet, the Nine eventually had their way again.

The large impact of the Nine on the CSCE becomes particularly evident when assessed against an analysis of the overall conference outcome. The Final Act did acknowledge the post-war political status quo in Europe and the inviolability of frontiers, as the Soviet Union had wanted. However, Moscow had to pay a heavy price for its desperate quest for legitimacy. With its 'peaceful change' clause, the CSCE left the possibility of overcoming the division of Germany and Europe open. In addition, it broadened the notion of what European security was about, rendering the respect and promotion of human rights a condition for peace, acknowledging the security of individuals as a legitimate subject of international affairs, and introducing CBM as a new element of stability. With its basket III, it also provided a specific barometer for the state of détente. Furthermore, while no permanent organ was set up that could enable the Soviet Union to increase its influence in Western Europe, the role of the US and Canada in European security was explicitly acknowledged. The major provisions of the Final Act, therefore, despite lack of public recognition at the time,[101] turned out to be distinctively in the West's favour, with the NNA countries also tending to be on the winning side, not least because the Helsinki Charter recognised the right to neutrality in Europe.[102]

Significantly, with the exception of the neutrality and CBM issues, the Nine had a decisive share in shaping all these key results of the CSCE. This is all the more surprising since the economic dimension of the CSCE, which originally had been a primary reason for the Nine to prepare the conference collectively, turned out to be of little importance. What this underlines is that the Nine were successful both in developing a joint overall policy with respect to the political dimension of détente in Europe and in defending large parts of their common conception during the conference negotiations. If one of the original Soviet motives in advocating a European security conference had been to weaken the West, the rise of EPC as a new cohesive caucus of Western interests in the context of CSCE was an unexpected and remarkable development.

Factors of success

Examining the reasons why the CSCE turned into a major success story for EPC is essential for understanding the potential, as well as the limitations, of European foreign policy-making in the early 1970s. In accordance with the framework of analysis applied throughout this study, this section will identify those factors relating to either the extra-European context, the intra-European dimension, or the individual level of European foreign policy-making that had a marked effect on the Nine's performance at the CSCE. I will argue that US benevolence and the nature of the CSCE were two particularly important reasons why the Community countries in the case of this conference managed to pursue a common foreign policy, assert their common interests, and establish themselves as a respected actor in international affairs.

A favourable international environment

An obvious factor enabling EPC's effective performance concerns Soviet tactical mistakes and disadvantages during the conference negotiations: recurring self-imposed time limits compelled the East time and time again to make important concessions; because of the less than half-hearted US engagement in the CSCE, such concessions were perhaps considered less serious in Moscow than they turned out to be; and even if their significance had been recognised by Soviet decision-makers, it would have been very difficult for the Kremlin to abandon the conference without doing enormous damage to both détente in Europe and Soviet prestige. Important that this aspect of Soviet negotiating deficiencies is, it will not be addressed here further, as it reveals little about the general conditions of effective European foreign policy cooperation in the early 1970s. Rather, when it comes to the extra-European level of EPC, it is the attitude of the US and NATO towards the role of the Nine at the CSCE that must be in the centre of attention. In addition, relations with the NNA countries need to be taken into consideration, as their views towards the Nine too could have an effect on EPC's ability to act effectively in a multilateral setting such as the CSCE. The fact that Washington accepted Europe's lead role within the West and that the NNA group approached the Nine constructively provided for a distinctly favourable international environment for the EC countries to play an influential role at the CSCE.

The US recognised the validity of a distinct EPC position at the CSCE despite the considerable differences in the European and American conceptions of détente that the intra-Western preparations for the CSCE had brought to light (see Chapter 2). Nixon and Kissinger, pursuing a realist perspective of international relations, were much more concerned about 'hard power' and the military realities on the ground than the rather lofty, more abstract issues addressed at the CSCE. They viewed détente as a device to manage superpower relations, rather than a pathway to change in Europe as many Western Europeans saw it. Consequently, they continued to be little interested in the CSCE during much of the negotiations in Helsinki and Geneva. Indeed, the more superpower détente advanced in 1973/74, the less inclined was the American administration to expose itself at this pan-European conference and risk any unnecessary collision with Moscow.[103] It was only when the bilateral détente between Washington and Moscow was waning that Kissinger paid more attention to the CSCE, without, however, ever making it a policy priority.

Importantly, the lack of US interest and commitment allowed the Nine to play a leading role within the West even when they were at odds with the White House over the purpose and substance of the CSCE.[104] Kissinger more than once got very frustrated with the Nine and their conference policy. He continued to call the CSCE a 'mistake' and argued vis-à-vis the Nine that the Soviet system, having survived for 50 years, could not be changed simply by putting Western newspapers on sale on a few kiosks in Moscow.[105] More troubling for the Europeans was his criticism that they were being 'thoroughly unhelpful' to Washington, since their ambitious conference policy threatened to obstruct superpower détente.[106] In the summer of 1973, Kissinger asked the Community countries to let the Russians, as sponsors of the CSCE, 'have what they wanted', make the conference 'short' and 'snappy', and accept that little progress was possible.[107] The CSCE should by no means give the impression that it would be able to resolve issues of 'cosmic importance',[108] which is why he asked the Europeans not to transform the conference into a 'Wagnerian drama'[109] and to prevent it from becoming a spectacular success. The CSCE's outcome, according to Kissinger, ought to be 'virtually meaningless',[110] with its third stage taking place by October 1973 in order to give positive impulses to the then commencing MBFR negotiations.[111] In the summer of 1974, Kissinger, increasingly weary of the stubbornly slow negotiating tactics of the Nine, shocked the Europeans by asking them to reduce their demands to a minimum of essential points, so as to enter into rapid global negotiations with the Soviet Union based on a Western minimum requirement list.[112] This proposal caused much concern in Europe, particularly against the background of a bilateral US–Soviet summit communiqué of June 1974. In this communiqué, Washington agreed that substantial progress had been made in the CSCE and already subscribed to the assumption that the conference would be concluded at the highest level, much to the consternation of the Nine, who considered this superpower statement to be full of Soviet phraseology and to read like a Soviet draft.[113]

Yet, for all his impatience, Kissinger always kept his pressure moderate. He neither combined pressure with threats, such as withdrawal of US troops from Europe, nor did he menace to go it alone in case of European non-compliance. His one attempt, with the help of Egon Bahr, to actively undermine the CSCE policy of the Nine and render it more compatible with Soviet demands in early 1973 faced a dead end in the West German chancellery and petered out without any visible impact.[114] Therefore, the great deal of anxiety in Europe during the peak of superpower détente in 1973/74 that Washington might break ranks with Western positions and make premature concessions,[115] much that it contributed to cohesion among the Nine, proved largely ungrounded. The US seems to have considered the CSCE not worth a row with the European allies, which is why the Nine in this case could go their way without seriously risking damaging transatlantic relations.

With Kissinger being happy, as the French once put it, to 'leave to the Europeans the role of the infantry' in the CSCE,[116] the US delegation kept a low profile and remained largely passive both in Helsinki and Geneva. As it often seemed to lack detailed instructions from Washington, it usually supported the positions of the Community countries and remained a loyal partner to its European allies throughout the conference.[117] Even when Kissinger by late 1974 came to play a more active role and bilaterally negotiated with the Soviet Union on some key issues of the CSCE, he frequently defended provisions as developed by the Nine and did not himself reformulate basic Western positions.[118]

Significantly, the US in the case of the CSCE accepted not only a European lead in the formulation and implementation of Western policy, but also the precedence of EPC over NATO as the major forum of Western coordination. The procedure that had marked the final weeks of intra-Western preparations in 1972, with the Nine developing the specific draft texts and tactical guidelines in EPC before tabling them in NATO, became the dominant pattern during both the MPT and the negotiations in Geneva. Some confusion had initially reigned in NATO when it had become clear that the US was anxious to let the Europeans do the running in CSCE matters, which left the Canadians sensitive and the Greeks, Turks, and Portuguese confused.[119] By early 1973, however, the non-EPC members of NATO appeared to rally willingly to a lead from the Nine, who, as a West German official noted enthusiastically, increasingly found themselves able to effectively 'pre-programme' the position of their Alliance partners.[120]

A largely non-competitive and constructive relationship between EPC and NATO undoubtedly facilitated the Nine's claim to a lead position within the West. NATO as an organisation did not become operational in Helsinki and Geneva, and the NATO council in Brussels and the 15 NATO delegations on the ground were engaged in much fewer coordination meetings than the equivalent bodies of the Nine.[121] Nevertheless, there was a system of close cooperation between the Nine and the Fifteen, with the Community countries regularly presenting the positions they had worked out in EPC.[122] Depending on the subject, the respective discussions in the Alliance could still amount to substantial consultations, as was frequently the case with politico-military issues. In other cases, as regarding basket II, they were of a more formal kind, designed to keep the US and other non-EPC members happy.[123] There was also a scheme of bilateral partnerships in place, with individual EPC countries being responsible for informing individual NATO members about the state of EPC deliberations and the outcome of specific EPC meetings.[124]

A similar, if less intensive scheme, was also built up by the Nine to manage relations with individual NNA countries.[125] The fact that these delegations recognised the Nine as a distinct and relevant actor group worth cooperating with was important in enabling the EPC members to obtain as much as they did at the CSCE. EPC and the NNA group, for all their differences, had enough in common to render them obvious partners during the conference: they did not represent military blocs, they were eager to limit the Soviet hegemonic position in Eastern Europe, and they often represented positions in the respective baskets that the other side found easy to support.[126] In particular, the views on human rights and basket III issues of the four neutrals – Austria, Finland, Sweden, and Switzerland – were similar to the Nine, which is why cooperation with them was more substantial than with the non-aligned. These neutrals took care never to be seen too close to the Nine. They were eager to preserve their own identity at the conference, which is why no joint initiatives were ever taken in the negotiations. Nevertheless, behind closed doors, a great amount of orchestration went on, with delegates being on the telephone for days on end to discuss common positions.[127] The Nine also occasionally handed their draft texts to the neutrals in advance and on a confidential basis, and they generally took care to incorporate into their papers those requests of the neutrals that corresponded with their own views.[128]

We can conclude that on the extra-European level conditions for a common European policy were distinctly favourable, as there was no basic opposition from either the US, NATO, or the NNA countries to the Nine acting as a distinct group at the conference. Such a positive external constellation, however, was only a necessary, but by no means a sufficient, condition for the Nine's success. The effectiveness of their performance at the CSCE also depended on their ability to maintain cohesion and push through their propositions during the negotiations.

Internal cohesion

The cohesion of the Nine at the CSCE was remarkable in terms of both its comprehensiveness and durability. It contributed much to EPC's effectiveness at this pan-European conference. There were, of course, advantages in acting jointly in a multilateral exercise such as the CSCE. Although the Nine tabled their proposals as national contributions, because of the principle of sovereign equality of each delegation at the CSCE, their collective support for each proposition enabled them to exert a degree of influence unattainable for any individual delegation.[129] Common positions were particularly valuable in the informal meetings, where only two to three delegations represented the Eastern, Western, and NNA groups.[130] Moreover, a joint standing also rendered each of the Nine less vulnerable against domestic or external challenges to their CSCE policies, since they could always refer back to their collective commitments.

Still, unity of the Nine in this first effort at a common foreign policy was anything but a given and remained potentially vulnerable throughout the conference. It was a major achievement for the Community countries to be able to formulate and implement common policies over such an extensive period of time. Equally, it was a great success for them to effectively stand up to the Soviet Union as their major negotiating counterpart. Two main features provided the basis for the EPC countries' remarkable cohesion at the CSCE: a shared perception of interests, and stable political will to act jointly. The broad convergence of views among the Nine concerning the challenges and opportunities of the CSCE and their shared understanding of the specific objectives to be pursued provided for a community of interest rare in the history of European foreign policy. Equally noteworthy is the continuation of political will to see through the often tedious and seemingly never-ending negotiations. Both features were reflected in the ways in which EPC worked in the case of the CSCE. In the following, I will first examine these ways in more detail, before analysing the underlying intra-European and individual factors that enabled them.

A first noteworthy feature of the Nine at the CSCE was the extraordinary intensity of their consultations. The sous-comité and the ad hoc group consulted in quasi-permanence in Helsinki and Geneva. They were in charge of defining the interests and positions of the Nine and orchestrating the actions of the delegations.[131] Being EPC's main organs on the ground, they regularly reported, through their acting presidencies, to the Political Committee of the Nine, which in turn issued further instructions where necessary. In rare cases, disputed issues went up to the ministerial level in order that compromise solutions could be hammered out.[132] In Geneva, additional EPC working bodies were set up for each of the 11 sub-committees in the baskets. Add the meetings of the head of delegations and the extra working groups convoked to deal with specific problems and you come up with as many as 15 committees regularly engaged in coordinating the policies of the Nine at peak times.[133] The frequency of meetings in each body obviously varied, but the overall amount of official EPC gatherings for each six-month EPC presidency lay in the hundreds.

Unsurprisingly, this complex structure of consultation posed occasional problems. It took several months for the Nine to adapt to the mushrooming of committees and sub-committees at the beginning of the Geneva negotiations.[134] The proliferation of CSCE bodies also threatened to diminish EPC's efficiency if a weak and disorganised presidency was in charge.[135] And, there was always the human factor, with, for example, the eccentricities or ineptness of individual officials prolonging decision-making seemingly indefinitely at times.[136] Yet, overall, EPC's sophisticated consultative system worked very efficiently and enabled the Nine to develop and maintain a shared perspective on both substance and tactics.[137]

In the course of these consultations, the Nine worked out numerous internal collective reports. Some of these reports laid out the position of the Nine with respect to immediate tactical questions or specific CSCE topics.[138] Others were progress reports providing an inventory of outstanding issues and defining the respective positions of the Nine.[139] There was also the basic report on 'the objectives and strategy of the Nine' of November 1973, which gave a comprehensive overview over the Community countries' general aims at the CSCE and provided the delegations with guidelines for each basket.[140] What is striking about all these reports is the sense of 'we-feeling' and common identity they reflect. The Nine were commonly referred to as 'we', with phrases such as 'we must take into consideration that' or 'our objective is' being characteristic of how common policies and approaches were defined.

With so many issues on the agenda, occasional substantive disagreements in the process of policy formulation were inevitable. The desirability of a Community offer in basket II was the most contentious issue among the Nine. Another point concerned the right of non-participating Mediterranean states to contribute to the CSCE.[141] Opinions also diverged with regard to the follow-up, where the FRG, especially the chancellery, was more open about continuing machinery than the other Eight.[142] Moreover, CBM continued to pose problems, with the FRG and Benelux being more supportive of such measures than France.[143] However, in the large majority of cases, such conflicts could be resolved internally, either by compromise packages or by those countries in the minority coming to respect the views of the majority.[144] It is noteworthy how, in the case of the CSCE, all of the Nine gave clear priority to a collective EPC position, and were willing to subordinate and adapt national preferences where necessary.[145]

Such an EPC prerogative became characteristic for the Nine throughout the CSCE. It corresponded with a high degree of flexibility and tolerance with regard to policy implementation. Some delegations supported positions of others even when they considered them less important or unfeasible. The notion of peaceful change, for example, was much more important to Bonn than to anyone else, but was defended by all. Similarly, the human rights principle was pushed primarily by the FRG, Denmark, and Ireland, but was loyally supported by less engaged delegations also.[146] Flexibility also meant room of manoeuvre for individual delegations to act outside the framework of the Nine, be it by tabling additional, purely national propositions, linking up with other like-minded countries, or bargaining bilaterally with non-EPC delegations, especially with the Soviet Union.[147] The essential if unwritten rule in this regard was that any extra position and bilateral bargaining should respect rather than undermine or even contradict the common body of substance that the Nine had elaborated.[148]

It was this kind of flexibility which allowed the Nine to preserve their cohesion despite their national idiosyncrasies. The West Germans, interested in preserving good relations with the Soviet Union, might have leaned more towards making concessions to the East than others and, at times, irritated their partners by trying to be the privileged partner of both East and West.[149] However, they were never disloyal to the Nine and, on the contrary, contributed greatly to EPC's prominent profile during the CSCE. In fact, Scheel and the Auswärtige Amt repeatedly used the cohesion of EPC as an argument to fend off inclinations by Bahr to manage the CSCE through back channels between the great power chancelleries and be over-accommodating to Soviet demands.[150] France too initially oscillated between unilateralist leanings and a leadership role among the Nine. Occasional criticism by French delegates that coordination among the Nine was excessive did, indeed, nourish an undercurrent of suspicion that they might take up a maverick role in the negotiations.[151] Yet, although it was certainly true that the French, as the British put it, 'fancy themselves as East/West bridge builders',[152] they too, like the West Germans, never deserted European policies for the sake of bilateral dealings with the Soviet Union. In fact, France became one of the most active defenders of EPC positions, to an extent that heavily strained its relations with Moscow.

There were also the Dutch and the Italians, who belonged to EPC's hardliners and frequently supported a strategy of conflict with the Soviet Union. Serving generally as a useful anchorman with their uncompromising stance, the Dutch more than once, in the eyes of several delegations, overdid it and failed to recognise when the time had come to lift the anchor.[153] While during the MPT they could eventually be talked into supporting EPC's compromises necessary to establish agreement for holding the CSCE, they did not always comply with the position of the majority in Geneva.[154] The Italians also occasionally worried their partners, mainly when they combined their hard-line approach with what others regarded as inconsistent arguments.[155] Yet, even if these two delegations might have been among the most difficult partners to drag along, they never seriously threatened to undermine the unity of EPC and generally played along as loyal and constructive members of the Nine.[156] As the British delegation put it in a metaphorical account of the CSCE as a football match between the 'Brussels Casuals' and 'Warsaw Park', Italian dribbling did at times prove 'more confusing to friend than foe', and Dutch bicycle-kicks remained fruitless. Even so, neither did much harm to the team, and, as the same report concluded, one could not but admire the courage of the Dutch striker's willingness to 'take on the whole Park defence in head-on confrontation'.[157]

The intermediary role that Britain came to play within the Nine was important in allowing the EPC countries to preserve their unity despite individual national peculiarities. Being less interested in the substance of the CSCE than in the ability of EPC to perform effectively, the British frequently went to great lengths to make sure that all of the Nine were on board and ready to defend a Community position.[158] They remained more sceptical than other Europeans about the possibilities of the CSCE, viewing the conference rather defensively as an occasion to 'squeeze the Russian lemon very hard to demonstrate to public opinion how little juice there is in *détente à la russe*'.[159] Yet, it was precisely because the British professed less emotional affinity to specific CSCE issues than many of their partners that they were in a suitable balancing position in the middle of the pack. Whenever the Nine seemed in danger of losing the initiative at the CSCE as a result of internal disagreements, London was willing to take the lead in finding common ground. Such was the case in the later days of the MPT, for example, when the British delegation, concerned about 'the detached position of the French, the special preoccupations of the West Germans, the eccentricity of the Italians and the public silences of Benelux' for the first time decided to give up its initially cautious role and put the Nine on track again.[160]

Apart from a high degree of flexibility, a division of labour also contributed to the effectiveness of joint action by the Nine in the CSCE. The Nine established a *chef-de-file* system during the conference, where individual delegations, according to their interests, took the lead in specific issues, being in charge of internal reporting and coordination, as well as external contacts in this matter.[161] The FRG, for example, took prime responsibility for human contacts and industrial cooperation, the British were in charge of CMB, information, and tactics, while the French dealt with the basic principles and cultural exchanges.[162] Such a system of national specialisation allowed the Nine to keep up with the multitude of parallel negotiations and give sufficient attention to all issues at stake, an achievement that many other non-Communist delegations found difficult to accomplish, due to the enormous resources required.

Strikingly, the Nine tenaciously clung to their position, and in their reports repeatedly called for 'patience and firmness',[163] even at times when they themselves felt a sense of fatigue and were gloomy about the prospect of ever achieving anything substantial at the CSCE.[164] Related to their stamina, they also demonstrated a remarkable resilience to external pressure designed to modify their course. The Soviet Union more than once attempted to break the cohesion of EPC by offering France and the FRG secret dealings to hammer out the basic CSCE compromises outside the multilateral framework. In early 1973, Brezhnev tried to convince Pompidou and Brandt (as well as Nixon) to keep the MPT phase short, refrain from working out terms of references, and to jointly discuss the draft of what the Soviets thought should become the final CSCE declaration.[165] In the summer of 1973, the Soviet leader again took great pains to obtain their approval of closing the CSCE by the year's end.[166] An even bigger diplomatic campaign took place in early 1974, when the Soviets in a series of letters and visits sought to both intimidate and cajole key Western leaders into dropping the practical provisions of basket III and CBM, as well as closing the conference within months and at the top level.[167] Yet, for all the Soviet assertions that it would be ridiculous and futile to try to undermine the social systems in Eastern Europe, and for all their complaints that it was incomprehensible why the West would answer an Eastern offer for consolidating peace by seeking to compel Soviet citizens to read the *New York Times*,[168] EPC's three lead powers would not be divided by the Soviet Union. If there was at times socialising in the evenings (*Kameradschaftsabende*) between the French, West Germans, Soviets, and Americans,[169] there is no indication that anything substantial resulted from it.

Similarly, pressure exerted by the US, as discussed above, failed to persuade the Nine to change their course. Kissinger's CSCE policy did at times have a dispiriting effect on the Nine. However, instead of accepting the logic of Kissinger's arguments, the Europeans questioned his ability to understand what the CSCE really was about.[170] Although the Nine internally did produce an inventory of key issues in response to Kissinger's urgent call to proceed to the final bargaining in 1974, they rejected his wish to use it as a basis for negotiations and prolonged the issue-by-issue approach until well into 1975.[171] Only then did they come around to final bargaining, with the US government by that time, in view of generally deteriorating superpower relations, unambiguously representing the interests of the Western camp again. As much as Kissinger's self-restraint at the extra-European level represented an important condition for EPC's effective performance at the CSCE, the common determination of the Nine to continue their policy despite US dissatisfaction was a notable characteristic at the intra-European level.

The Nine's resilience against external pressure, together with the high intensity of their consultations, the large body of common reports, the EPC prerogative, their high degree of flexibility, their division of labour, and their stamina are all *reflections* of the remarkable community of interests and the common political will that characterised their performance at the CSCE. But what were the underlying factors that facilitated the emergence of these features in the first place? One important element of success clearly was that the CSCE constituted a relatively new foreign policy issue. Vested interests of individual Community members had not yet crystallised when it became an EPC topic, which implies that the CSCE was much more about jointly developing policies than seeking to harmonise previously established ones.[172] Furthermore, with the exception of the FRG, none of the Nine considered core national interests to be at stake during the CSCE, which made it easier for them to speak with one voice. Domestic social expectations relating to détente in Europe also played a role, compelling the Nine to continuously press for dynamic elements such as greater freedom of movement or CBM, even at times when they themselves doubted the feasibility of their policy.[173]

Even more important, however, was the peculiar nature of the CSCE. Three idiosyncrasies of this conference enabled the Nine to play an effective role and allowed for the fact that EPC's deficiencies did not become a major handicap in this case. First, the CSCE provided the Nine with a permanent framework of consultation. Its character as a long-term multilateral negotiating forum constituted an invaluable advantage to the EPC countries, as they otherwise disposed of no permanent structures for political cooperation and still lacked a secretariat.[174] Second, the 'philosophy' behind the CSCE corresponded well with the means the Nine had at their disposal to engage in international diplomacy. Debating about norms and other aspects of 'soft security' and working out declarations was very much concordant with the European approach to foreign policy-making. This was partly because it reflected basic assumptions of the Europeans' own conception of unity. Yet, it was also because they had not yet moved to the defence field of cooperation and lacked the kind of 'hard power' indispensable to be recognised as a credible actor in many fields of international politics.

Third, the CSCE essentially was a bureaucratic project. The formation of interests and policies in this case was less closely tied to specific governments and politicians than in other EPC fields, which allowed for a continuity of cohesion and political will unattainable elsewhere. This finding indicates that conditions conducive to a successful European engagement in the case of the CSCE also existed on the individual level of European foreign policy-making

– an observation that is of particular relevance for the purpose of this study and will be explicated further in the following.

The CSCE as a bureaucratic project

Previous chapters have paid particular attention to the roles of individual decision-makers in enabling or hindering European foreign policy cooperation. Indeed, it has been a key proposition of the first part of this book that EPC's emergence in the early 1970s was closely related to the trilateral leadership in Europe provided by Brandt, Heath, and Pompidou. The chapters in this second part will demonstrate that trilateral leadership also had a large share in EPC's rise in 1973. Within this broad assumption, however, a differentiation can be made between the CSCE, on the one hand, and the 'Year of Europe' discussions and the Middle East issue, on the other. The influence of national leaders on the CSCE policy of the Nine was comparatively smaller than in the other two cases (see Chapters 4 and 5). While their general intention of rendering Europe as a powerful actor in international diplomacy was an important foundation for the Nine to approach the CSCE collectively, their personal beliefs and role conceptions mattered less here, and they were less directly involved in the actual process of policy formation than in the other EPC fields. This relative insignificance of specific individuals at the CSCE was a major reason why this particular policy field of Europe's foreign policy endeavour did not get negatively affected even when Brandt, Heath, and Pompidou left the scene and EPC fell into crisis in 1974.

In other words: an important individual-level factor of success in the case of the CSCE was that it was a bottom-up, bureaucracy-driven project. There were several reasons why political leaders gradually lost their grip on the conference proceedings: the multitude of topics, actors, and interests involved made the CSCE an extraordinarily diffuse matter for them; the complexity and interrelatedness of the specific bargaining in the baskets further contributed to their difficulty in making out what was going on in the conference; and the duration of the CSCE and the kind of abstract problems it treated sooner or later prompted them to focus their attention on other, more pressing issues.[175] Kissinger's characterisation of the CSCE as 'a case of multilateral diplomacy run amok'[176] mirrors well how this conference had evolved in a way that made it comprehensible to a select group of experts and diplomats only.

Kissinger's frustration was EPC's gain. The triple shift of the lead role in the CSCE from the political to the bureaucratic level, from the national bureaucracies to the officials on the ground, and from the formal negotiating fora to small private sessions meant that it was a small nucleus of permanently involved EPC representatives that effectively took the lead in defining the Nine's CSCE policy and kept them on track.[177] Political decision-makers did come into the picture occasionally, of course. They had to take strategic decisions and give directives concerning basic matters, such as the follow-up issue or the response of the Nine to the US demand of working out a minimum requirement list.[178] In some instances, they also had a role to play at the tactical level, such as when the foreign ministers publicly expressed their disappointment about Soviet intransigence at the CSCE in a press conference after an EPC ministerial meeting in June 1974.[179]

Yet, as most leaders found it very difficult to personally encroach upon the specific course of the negotiations or the position of the Nine, the large majority of decisions were taken by the officials on the ground. Significantly, even the directives issued by the nine foreign ministers had usually been previously worked out by the sous-comité in Helsinki and Geneva. And, it was often the officials in charge of the delegations on the ground who during their return visits to the capitals also formulated the guidelines for the next steps to be taken.[180] As a result of this far-reaching autonomy of officials involved in the CSCE, the Nine remained largely immune to changes of individual decision-makers and governments throughout the conference.

Undeniably, political decision-makers would have been in a position to interrupt or even terminate EPC's engagement at the conference if they had really wanted to. This is why it was relevant that they shared, at least to some extent, a basic consensus regarding the Community's collective interests, kept the cooperation going, and protected it from outside challenges. But it fell to an anonymous group of diplomats and experts to carry the burden of seeing the cumbersome negotiations of the CSCE through, and it is them who deserve the main credit for rendering this conference a success story for EPC. The bureaucratic character of the CSCE not only contributed to the fact that détente in Europe outlived the much more personalised, back channel-based superpower détente between Nixon and Brezhnev. It also meant that EPC's effective performance in the case of the CSCE was much more sustainable than elsewhere.

The impact of the CSCE on EPC: 'The Mighty Nine'

Having analysed the role and performance of the EC countries at the CSCE, I will finally reverse the perspective and look at the CSCE's impact on the Nine, and on EPC in particular. The interactions between the pan-European confer-ence and European unification had two major consequences for the develop-ment and psychology of European political cooperation in its infant years. On the one hand, the CSCE contributed to the strengthening of EPC by linking it more closely to the EC pillar. On the other hand, and more importantly, it provided the Nine with a tremendous moral boost, corroborating their faith in the feasibility, potential, and desirability of collective European foreign policy-making.

By practical necessity, the CSCE partly accomplished what the EPC mem-bers in their normative debates in 1971/72 had been unable to agree upon: it brought the intergovernmental pillar of EPC closer to the European Commission as the central Community institution and, hence, qualified the previously rigid separation between the political and economic dimensions of European unity. It is worth noting that this rapprochement related to the CSCE-dimension of EPC only and that even there important barriers remained. Still, by setting a precedent, it was of great importance to the devel-opment of EPC as a whole, marking the beginning of a piecemeal process that is still going on today. Of the three great powers examined here, the FRG and Britain from early on were hoping to use the CSCE as a means of improving EPC and overcoming its dissociation from the Commission.[181] Unsurprisingly, France was a much more retarding element in this regard, seek-ing to keep the Community organs out of EPC as much as possible. The two basic questions of the participation of the Commission and the competence of the Community in the CSCE kept EPC busy on all levels throughout the con-ference and were resolved only after lengthy theological disputes.[182]

As previously noted, an ad hoc group was set up in EPC during the intra-Western preparation phase as an extra working group besides the sous-comité to deal specifically with the economic aspects of the CSCE and integrate Commission representatives. The Commission played an active role here and came up with its own reports and proposals, which the EPC representatives did take into account.[183] This ad hoc group remained operational throughout the CSCE, which is to say that with respect to policy formulation, the Commission was always involved in and associated with EPC deliberations. The EC organ was kept at bay, however, from the sous-comité and, hence, from basket I and III matters. Concerning the Commission's role in the nego-tiations, a very restrictive solution was chosen for the MPT period, with the presidency of the Nine also speaking in the name of the Community in cases where issues affecting Community competence were at stake.[184] Further agree-ment at that time proved impossible, not least because the Commission itself came up with demands that in the opinion of most EPC members were exaggerated. In particular, its proposal that it should speak on behalf of the Nine in the CSCE sub-commission responsible for trade caused acrimonious debates and angered even its loyal supporters, such as the British, who considered it 'unfortunate that the commission still chooses to act as a sort of adversary of the nine within the machinery of political co-operation'.[185]

It was only in the course of the actual CSCE negotiations that remarkable progress was achieved in bringing the Community in. During stage I, the Danish foreign minister as acting EC president issued a statement announcing that as basket II included subjects which among the Nine were under the competence of the EC, the 'Community may become involved [...] in the future work of the Conference and that the implementation of any possible outcome of negotiations on these subjects will depend on agreement with the Community'.[186] Most importantly, the Nine in September 1973 agreed to allow the Commission to participate in the CSCE by placing its officials in the delegation of the acting presidency.[187] Odd that it was for the Commission representatives to change their 'nationality' every six months, this approach allowed the Nine to comply with the procedural rules of the CSCE, according to which states alone could participate in the conference. Eastern delegations at first denied the Commission the right to take the floor at the CSCE, decrying as hair-splitting the Nine's argument that the Commission was speaking in the name of a national delegation rather than the Community.[188] But by publicly shaking hands with the Commission representative, the Soviet delegate in October 1973 indicated consent to a Community role at the conference,[189] which no longer was questioned by the East thereafter.

The culmination of Community involvement in the CSCE undoubtedly occurred when Aldo Moro signed the Final Act at the Helsinki Summit on 1 August 1975 not only as prime minister of Italy, but also 'in his capacity as President in office of the Council of the European Communities'.[190] The expediency of such a clause had also initially been disputed among the Nine.[191] Moreover, once the EPC members had agreed that an interpretative declaration similar to stage I was insufficient for stage III and should be complemented by an official presence of the Community in the Final Act, it still took intensive negotiations to get the approval of the other delegations.[192] Yet, it is hard to exaggerate the significance of the finally attained double signature, which reflected the Nine's collective contribution to the CSCE as much as the role of the Community as an acknowledged entity, both within the Nine and at the conference generally.

Equally important for the development of EPC, if less palpable, was the general boost it received from the successful performance of the Nine at the

CSCE. EPC members could note with satisfaction that they were recognised as an important actor group in the conference. It might not have been without an undercurrent of irony that the Soviets in Geneva used to refer to the EPC countries as 'the Mighty Nine'.[193] However, the fact is that Moscow tended to treat the Community countries as a group during the negotiations, approached them as a clearing unit for the positions of the West, and addressed only the respective lead country when seeking to bargain with EPC delegations on a specific issue.[194] Urgent Soviet invocations that it was in the hands of the Nine to determine whether anything would ever come out of the CSCE indicated an acknowledged role of the Community countries at the CSCE, as did Soviet accusations that the Nine would constitute a new bloc within NATO, and that their common position would make the negotiations much more complex.[195]

The CSCE gave ample evidence to the Nine how valuable and effective common foreign policy-making could be. With much contentment, and no little vanity, they publicly declared at the end of the conference that the CSCE had been marked by their concerted contribution and had become a 'shining example' of their cooperation.[196] This kind of positive self-assessment was preponderant throughout the negotiations and was especially relevant during the first half of 1973 and after mid-1974. In the former case, the recognition that the Nine had done well in the MPT as the enlarged Community's first foreign policy test provided an important psychological boost for EPC's remarkable rise in 1973. As regards the latter period, the reassurance gained from the CSCE that foreign policy cooperation remained feasible was invaluable at a time when other fields of cooperation in EPC stagnated or even collapsed.

We can conclude, then, that the CSCE not only was to a significant extent shaped by the EPC countries' contributions, but also served as a catalyst for establishing the Nine as a foreign policy actor. The interaction between the two processes of the CSCE and European unification, hence, brought about important changes in the European security system in terms of both an expanded notion of security and in the rise of the Nine as a new entity in international diplomacy. As it is this rise that concerns us most here, and as this rise after mid-1974 proved less enduring in subject areas other than European détente, it is time to turn our attention to these other areas and to the dramatic developments that ran parallel to the CSCE and strongly affected the evolution of EPC in 1973/74.

It is with a view to reintegrating this chapter into the overall chronology of the study that it shall end with reference to the ubiquitously positive assessments of the Nine with regards to their own performance at the MPT in the first half of 1973. There was a widespread feeling in European capitals that

EPC had passed its first test, as the British put it, 'with flying colours'.[197] The Nine were convinced that it was they who could claim much of the credit for the concessions wrested from the Soviets, and they were generally satisfied with how smooth cooperation in Helsinki had been.[198] Scheel proudly asserted in a public article that EPC had done so well in Helsinki that it was now definitely on its way to political union.[199] Jobert called EPC's performance at the MPT 'the best example to show the reality of progress in Europe'.[200] Perhaps most pleased of all were the British, who noted with excitement that the challenge of the MPT and the low profile the US had chosen to adopt had cast the Nine into a 'more heroic role' than they could have expected, a role they performed 'extremely' well.[201]

The recognition stemming from the Helsinki talks that EPC worked in practice clearly accentuated the kind of self-confidence that had already gained shape among the Nine in the months prior to enlargement and that had found early reflection in the Paris summit communiqué of October 1972. This self-confidence laid the basis for the remarkable leap forward that the Nine came to make in response to the multiple challenges that confronted them in the course of 1973. One such challenge was Kissinger's proposal to reorganise transatlantic relations, which is what the following chapter is about.

Chapter 4
Facing the US: Kissinger's 'Year of Europe' and the reorganisation of the West

On 25 September 1973, Knud Andersen, Danish foreign minister and acting president of EPC, went to see Kissinger in New York, where he discussed on behalf of the Nine a draft declaration on European–American relations produced by the Community countries. It was another memorable date in the formative period of EPC. For the first time, the Nine acted united and spoke with one voice outside the CSCE framework. Remarkably, they did so vis-à-vis the United States, the Western hegemonic power and key protector of European security. As relations with the US traditionally had been the most sensitive issue in defining a European foreign policy, Andersen's meeting with Kissinger represented a great move forward in the development of EPC. Most noteworthy, however, was the substance of the draft that the Danish envoy brought along: the EC member states, expressing their will to act collectively in international diplomacy, asked the US to acknowledge the Nine as a distinct entity in world politics and suggested a new bilateralism between a uniting Western Europe and Washington.

The European draft was a first, unexpected answer by the Nine to Kissinger's 'Year of Europe' initiative. Addressing the editors of the Associated Press at the Waldorf-Astoria hotel in New York, Kissinger on 23 April 1973 had proposed to redefine Atlantic relations so as to adapt the Alliance to the conditions of détente and growing European economic power. The intention of the US national security adviser clearly was to strengthen Atlantic unity. Yet, from a European perspective, the question he implicitly raised of how to reorganise the West brought the issue of the Nine's emerging political identity to the forefront.

The 'Year of Europe' initiated a debate on European–American relations both among the Nine and across the Atlantic. It was to last for more than a year and placed the issue of the role of the Nine within the West firmly on the European agenda. Indeed, the fate of EPC in 1973/74 became closely tied to the meandering course and final outcome of this US-sponsored initiative. Inadvertently, the 'Year of Europe' became a catalyst for advancing the foreign policy efforts of the Nine and giving a boost to EPC in 1973. However, it also brought about some of the most acrimonious controversies in post-war Atlantic relations, and it contributed greatly to EPC's stagnation and decline in 1974. All remaining chapters in this study are, thus, in one way or another related to the 'Year of Europe'. This present chapter covers the first phase of this initiative, which lasted from Kissinger's speech in April to late September 1973, when the Nine presented their joint draft to the Nixon administration and embarked on collective negotiations with Washington. Why did the Nine, contrary to US wishes, decide to respond collectively to the initiative and come up with a draft declaration on relations between the EC countries and the US rather than a 'new Atlantic Charter', as Kissinger had suggested?

The American challenge: Expanding Atlantic relations

The US 'Year of Europe' initiative did not come unexpected to the Europeans. The Nixon administration from late 1972 onwards had given public and private signals that Europe would be its primary area of attention as soon as peace was established in Vietnam. Still, Kissinger's speech in April took the Europeans largely by surprise. They had neither expected such far-reaching proposals nor their public articulation. Moreover, they were concerned that the American proposal for expanding Atlantic unity might be at the expense of Community interests, which is why their initial response was much less enthusiastic than the US had hoped.

Kissinger's initiative

'1973 is the year of Europe,' started Kissinger in his seminal speech on 23 April, 'because the era that was shaped by decisions of a generation ago is ending.'[1] New realities, such as the revival of Western Europe and Japan as major power centres, the strategic nuclear parity between Washington and Moscow, and the relaxation of tensions between East and West, had produced a 'dramatic transformation of the psychological climate in the West' and required a 'fresh act of creation'. Economically, Europe's transformation from a recipient of US aid to a strong competitor caused friction and turbulence in EC–US relations. Although Washington still supported European unity and benefited from economic integration, the Community's protectionist policies and emphasis on its 'regional personality' provoked increasing criticism in the US, especially at a time of chronic and growing US balance of payment deficits. Concerning defence, NATO's strategy of flexible response was little more than a 'slogan wrapped around a defense structure' that emerged 'from lowest common denominator compromises driven by domestic considerations'. NATO forces and doctrine had not been adequately adapted to the requirements of strategic equality between East and West. In addition, the Europeans feared that Washington might abandon them militarily, while the widespread view in the US was that the Europeans did not do enough to carry the burden of defence. With regard to diplomacy, Kissinger argued, the success of détente had created its own problems, most notably in the form of European fears that the US might sacrifice the interests of its allies for the sake of superpower détente. Warning against 'drift, escapism, or complacency', he urged the Europeans to seek with the US 'an understanding of what should be done jointly and of the limits we should impose on the scope of our autonomy'.

The challenge, Kissinger continued, was 'whether a unity forged by a common perception of danger can draw new purposes from shared positive aspirations'. He declared that common interests and positive values beyond security should now be identified, and shared ideas and common purposes be reinvigorated. A 'unifying framework' should be set up to manage Atlantic diversity and strike 'a new balance between self-interest and a common interest'. Kissinger suggested specifically that 'a new Atlantic Charter setting the goals for the future' ought to be worked out and be signed during Nixon's trip to Europe towards the end of 1973. He asked for a broad political approach to upcoming economic negotiations, a 'rational posture of defence' and a 'new consensus on security addressed to the new conditions', as well as a 'clear set of common objectives' in bilateral and multilateral relations and negotiations with the East.

Hidden in various parts of his speech, Kissinger did sketch elements of the kind of transatlantic bargain he had in mind. In his view, the Europeans would have to recognise several parameters: economic, military, and political issues at stake were all 'linked by reality' and had to be approached comprehensively; these issues should not be left to 'technicians', but should be addressed at the highest level; Japan ought to be a principal partner in the proposed enterprise; Europe had 'regional interests' only, whereas the US had global interests and responsibilities, which would not automatically be identical; and, finally, European unity was 'not an end in itself but a means to the strengthening of the West' and a 'component of a larger Atlantic partnership'. The Nixon administration for its part was ready to make further concessions for the sake of

European unity if there was a 'spirit of reciprocity'. Moreover, it would not withdraw US forces from Europe unilaterally, provided the Europeans agreed to a fairer distribution of the defence burden.[2]

It was a very ambitious initiative. Echoing the 'Atlantic Charter' of 1941, when Franklin D. Roosevelt and Winston Churchill had defined key principles for a new post-war international order, Kissinger called for a comprehensive overhaul of Atlantic relations. His appeal comprised policy-specific proposals, as well as an ideational aspect of reinvigorating the Alliance and lending it new purpose by expanding it politically and economically. The implications were far-reaching and dramatic. As Kissinger indicated in his memoirs, the approach deliberately resembled the Marshall Plan speech of 1947, which had inspired the Europeans and had been a caesura in marking the beginning of close transatlantic cooperation.[3]

With the 'Year of Europe' speech, the US government revealed a series of concerns about the state of Atlantic relations. While it acknowledged that US pre-eminence had come to an end not only in relation to the Soviet Union but also within the West, it seemed worried about how European–American relations would evolve. Bickering over trade and monetary issues had already strained Atlantic relations in 1971/72. Now that the Community was enlarged, economic rivalry was certain to increase. Politically, the Nixon administration expressed uneasiness about European versions of détente. Kissinger's reassurance in his speech that the US would 'welcome the participation' of its allies in an East–West dialogue could hardly disguise the lingering, if nostalgic, US aspiration of keeping control of and taking the lead in dealing with Communist powers.[4]

Also manifest in the speech were concerns about the domestic mood of isolationism in the US. Congressional pressure to reduce American overseas commitments, as reflected in the annual resolutions of Senate Majority Leader Mike Mansfield, had put the White House on the defensive. The call for greater allied support in the 'Year of Europe' could, thus, be interpreted as a warning to the Europeans that it was in their own interest to help the US government cope with its domestic difficulties. Indeed, when reading the speech together with Nixon's fourth annual foreign policy report to Congress that came out only ten days later, this kind of warning emerged as the overarching message the US seemed eager to convey. In this report, Nixon insinuated that the principle of Atlantic unity in defence and security could hardly be reconciled any longer with Europe's economic regionalism.[5] In other words: the Nixon administration seemed to expect the Europeans to be mature enough to make economic concessions in order to allow the US to maintain domestic support for a strong commitment to NATO.

American dissatisfaction with NATO too was mirrored in the 'Year of Europe' speech. If strategic nuclear parity rendered conventional defence more relevant, the Europeans, from an American point of view, were not resolutely enough drawing the right conclusions. They were reluctant to raise their troop levels and defence expenditures, because of domestic resistance and because augmenting their own forces risked accelerating an American withdrawal. Moreover, in order to avoid a war on European territory, they were still keen on rapid escalation and an early response with nuclear weapons, which led to transatlantic disagreement, especially concerning the use of tactical nuclear weapons. US frustrations also touched upon the political state of the Alliance, which, despite the Harmel Report of 1967, had never been able to establish consensus as to its purpose and priorities. As Nixon put it in his report to Congress: 'For almost a decade the Alliance has debated questions of defense and détente – some urging one course, others a different priority. Now the debates should end. We must close ranks and chart our course together for the decade ahead.'[6]

Finally, it appears that Kissinger launched the 'Year of Europe' also under the assumption that Europe was waiting for a gesture of commitment by the US. The Nixon administration during its first term had devoted its attention almost exclusively to putting relations with the Soviet Union and China on a new basis and disengaging from Vietnam. In early 1973, Kissinger had repeatedly apologised for this neglect of Europe, which had contributed to an economic estrangement and a frequent lack of political consultation. The US press too warned the US government that it was high time that it reinvigorated European–American relations. As the *Washington Post* put it: 'President Nixon and Henry Kissinger had better get cracking. Events are running very fast and in a very negative fashion for the Atlantic Alliance.'[7]

Interestingly, the speech comprised no procedural suggestions as to how to approach this complex exercise. Kissinger, perhaps in deliberate imitation of the former US Secretary of State George Marshall, seemed to leave it to the Europeans to take up the initiative and organise the proceeding. It is doubtful that he was aware of the enormous procedural challenge with which he confronted the Europeans. Economic and defence issues in Europe were treated in separate institutions, with eight of the thirteen European NATO allies belonging to the EC and one EC member, Ireland, being neutral and staying outside NATO. There was also the European Commission, which represented the Community competence in trade matters, which is why it had a role to play in the 'Year of Europe'.

With regard to substance, it is significant that no mention was made in the speech as to the political aspirations of the Nine. Kissinger's only respective reference was that the US erroneously had expected European political unity to follow economic integration. There was no mention of the Paris Summit goal of a European Union, or of EPC and the European attempt to harmonise national foreign policies. The political dimension of Atlantic problems as identified by Kissinger was limited to autonomous détente policies, and even here he was likely to have had in mind *Ostpolitik* and French–Soviet bilateralism, rather than the Nine's collective CSCE policy. Such American ignorance of, or disregard for, the enlarged Europe's pursuit of a political identity became a major reason why the 'Year of Europe' was to evolve so differently from what Kissinger had expected.

The Nine baffled

The official public European reactions to Kissinger's speech were noncommittal but friendly.[8] Still, the immediate response to the 'Year of Europe' did not accord with Kissinger's expectations. As he put it, no ally seemed to rush 'to get on the bandwagon', in sharp contrast to the Marshall Plan, when British Secretary of State Ernest Bevin had organised a constructive, substantial European reply.[9] Part of the problem was that the Europeans were irritated about what they considered a gross lack of advance consultation on such a monumental initiative. Jobert, Heath, and Brandt all came to complain that the exercise had been launched as a surprise move, the absence of preliminary deliberations in their eyes being responsible for much of the subsequent transatlantic strain.[10] In his memoirs, Kissinger dismissed such criticism and insisted that the initiative had been well prepared. The speech, according to him, had been established over a month in advance. An outline of it had already been given to the French on 13 April 1973, while the British had even received a copy of it four days in advance. In Kissinger's view, the allies had generally been broadly consulted on the US endeavour several months prior to the speech.[11] Archival evidence, however, reveals a different picture. More than once, Kissinger apologised to the Europeans that he had only been able to finish the speech on the day before it was given. While he did, indeed, outline elements of his address to the French,[12] he never gave a text to London. Most importantly, what Kissinger referred to as consultation in early 1973 amounted to little more than him laying out his analysis of Atlantic problems and indicating that the US would soon want to deal with these problems.

As early as September 1972, the US had announced that it hoped, as Kissinger put it during a press conference, 'to resume most intense consultations with our European friends on how to put relationships between Europe and the United States on a new, even more dynamic and constructive basis' in 1973.[13] From that day on, Washington had not ceased in stressing that it aimed at a new Atlantic partnership and that 1973 from its perspective would be the year of Europe. In mid-February 1973, Nixon sent a special envoy, Peter Peterson, to Europe for talks on European–American relations.[14] At the same time, Kissinger informed the Europeans that the US was planning to take an initiative on Atlantic relations and that it then would hope for a 'generous response'.[15]

Kissinger had even initiated secret bilateral dialogues on Atlantic relations with Britain, France, and West Germany prior to his speech. Each of these dialogues had been based on personal contacts with confidants of the respective leaders: in the case of Heath, it was Cabinet Secretary Burk Trend, with whom he had held regular meetings on sensitive security issues since 1972; as for Pompidou, Kissinger chose Jacques Kosciusko-Morizet, French ambassador in Washington; concerning Brandt, the obvious choice was Bahr, with whom he had already employed a back channel for several years. To each of these interlocutors, Kissinger had given assurance that he was America's preferred partner in Europe, with whom the US would want to pre-discuss Atlantic relations before multilateralising the debate. Of these three dialogues, talks with London had become the most advanced at the time of the 'Year of Europe' speech. When Heath had visited Nixon in February 1973, he was the first European statesman to learn that the US planned to launch a concrete initiative to revitalise Atlantic relations. Although Heath had maintained that Europe should first develop further its own institutions before entering into a new partnership with Washington, he had given way when Kissinger one month later had proposed to jointly work out a 'conceptual framework' to 'institutionalise the Atlantic relationship' on the political, military, as well as economic level.[16] Yet, when Trend had gone to Washington to discuss a British draft paper on 19 April 1973, Kissinger had not even studied it and, while browsing through it, had dismissed it as 'mild fatalism'.[17] Arguing that a symbolic impetus beyond 'traditional liturgies' was required, Kissinger had urged instead that a series of bilateral working parties be set up to jointly study the future of the Atlantic relationship.[18]

The dialogues with Paris and Bonn had been comparatively less intense. During a visit to Paris on 8 December 1972, Kissinger had briefly suggested to Pompidou the idea of an Atlantic summit meeting in 1973.[19] When Kissinger had launched his dialogue with Kosciusko-Morizet in March 1973, the initial French reaction had not been hostile. Tactically clever, Kissinger had emphasised the need to construct a better Atlantic framework to finally end 'German ambiguity' (*l'ambiguité allemande*). Once 'a Mitterand' or 'a Palme' came to dominate Europe, according to Kissinger, it would already be too late.[20] By April 1973, Paris had accepted his proposal of bilateral talks and agreed to a summit between Nixon and Pompidou in Reykjavik. The West Germans by that time had already agreed on a bilateral summit to discuss Atlantic relations too, despite Brandt's concern that the US might want to divide the Europeans.[21] However, Kissinger's dialogue with Bahr had been difficult, with the latter explicitly criticising the US argument for a new 'concept' to 'formulate the political, defense and economic components of the European–American partnership'. Bahr had been sceptical of rendering NATO more political, not only because this might hinder his Eastern policies but also because he believed that the military alliances as a consequence of superpower détente would lose relevance anyway.[22]

The major problem with these secret dialogues, and the primary reason why the three European powers were so surprised at the 'Year of Europe' speech, was that Kissinger confused a general discussion on Atlantic problems with actual consultations on his planned initiative. By the time he came out with his speech, he had only informed the Europeans that Atlantic relations should be redefined and had asked them to secretly cooperate with him, but had left them largely in the dark as to what exactly he had in mind.

European concerns

There is no little irony in the fact that Kissinger called for a new Atlantic Charter and European–American partnership without serious advance consultations. However, if lack of consultation contributed to the reserved initial European response, substantive misgivings about the Kissinger proposals played an even bigger role. It was not that the Europeans would not have been aware themselves that transatlantic relations needed rethinking. After all, they had been deliberating on new consultative machinery between the EC and the US since 1970 (see Chapter 2). If the Paris Summit had only brought consensus on the vague formula of a 'constructive dialogue' with Washington, the issue had remained on the table thereafter. This was especially so since Nixon in late 1972 had announced his intention to travel to Europe in the spring of 1973. Both Britain and the FRG wanted to use this opportunity to express Europe's emerging personality, which is why they had suggested that the individual bilateral summits with the US should be complemented with a collective meeting of the Nine with Nixon. France, at that time, had considered it premature for the Nine to jointly face the US, and the matter had lost some of its urgency again when in February 1973 Nixon had postponed his visit indefinitely, in response to European criticism of the US 'Christmas bombing' of North Vietnam in 1972.[23] Nevertheless, the Nine in March 1973 had agreed on a substantive exchange of views on European–American relations, with Davignon circulating a paper among European capitals that offered both an analysis of the transatlantic situation and raised a series of questions that should guide the intra-European debate.[24]

Yet, if the Europeans were well aware that not all was well with transatlantic relations, they disagreed with essential parts of Kissinger's proposal. Four major points of criticism figured prominently in all European analyses and internal reactions. The Nine considered the call for a new Atlantic partnership premature; they rejected the concept of issue linkage; they suspected the Nixon administration of seeking to subordinate European unity to Atlantic prerogatives and US leadership; and they regarded Kissinger's move as, at least in part, domestically motivated, with the Watergate scandal being about to unfold.

'In an ideal world, we would have chosen a different timescale. We would have preferred that the new Community of Nine had time to shake down and find its way forward towards common positions with greater deliberation'.[25] Douglas-Home's remark in his public response to the 'Year of Europe' epitomised a common European perception that Kissinger's initiative came at an inconvenient time for the Nine. With the enlargement of the Community only just accomplished, the year of 1973, from a European point of view, should have been a period of consolidation. In view of the many goals and self-imposed deadlines set at the Paris Summit in 1972, the Nine were fairly self-absorbed at the time of Kissinger's appeal. The Atlantic challenge also appeared premature as it failed to take account of the state of European unity. As Brandt wondered, how could all the issues raised by the US be solved in one text within the few months available before Nixon came to Europe?[26] Even Kosciusko-Morizet, who according to Kissinger had been fully consulted prior to the speech, warned the US national security adviser that it would be very difficult for Europe to respond to such vast an agenda.[27]

Kissinger's concept of linking trade, monetary, and defence issues in Atlantic negotiations was a second point of shared European concern. In 1971/72, the Europeans had noted with relief that Kissinger had rejected calls by representatives of US economic interests, such as US Secretary of the Treasury John Connally, for global negotiations of economic and defence issues, warning that such a linkage would negatively affect the cohesion of the Alliance.[28] All the more worried were they now that Kissinger too had come round to this 'one ball of wax' approach. Well aware of the strong leverage the Nixon administration possessed in view of Europe's security dependence, the Community countries were unwilling to buy US grain for allied defence, as Pompidou put it.[29] Brandt and Heath essentially embraced the Gaullist argument that it was in Washington's own interest to defend Europe against the advance of Communism.[30]

A third European concern was that the 'Year of Europe' might well be a hidden US challenge to European unity. Was Kissinger really out to promote an Atlantic partnership, with two equal American and European poles? Or did he not have in mind a multipolar Atlantic community under strong US leadership instead, where Atlantic cooperation would necessarily have to grow at the expense of European cooperation? Even some respected US observers leaned to the latter interpretation. Stanley Hoffmann saw the 'archaeo-Atlanticism' expressed in Kissinger's speech as an attack on European unification, while Robert J. Schaetzel, generally hostile to Nixon's European policy, recognised in the initiative a quest for a new 'pax Americana'.[31] Indeed, the speech contained several indications that the US might seek to reaffirm American preponderance in the West. The fact that Kissinger identified European unity only as a function of Atlantic strength and suggested including Japan in the exercise gave the impression that he was out to integrate the emerging regional powers into his overall design and subordinate European–US and Japanese–US relations to his triangular diplomacy with the Soviet Union and China. His implicit claim of a US prerogative in managing Western détente also conveyed the idea that the Nixon administration was seeking to move Western Europe into place with its global policies. Kissinger's biggest provocation to the Europeans, however, turned out to be his contrasting of US global interests and responsibilities with Europe's regional interests and, seemingly, non-existent responsibilities. This encountered sharp objections from the Nine. Even the West Germans, who previously had signalled to Kissinger that Europe had regional interests only, now rejected the distinction, pointing to Europe's new sense of responsibility with regard to both East–West relations and the Third World.[32] Although Kissinger was quick to apologise for his blunder by arguing that his statement had been descriptive rather than prescriptive and that the US would welcome a global role for Europe,[33] the Europeans remained sceptical as to his support for their unification project.

Finally, it is important to note that the Kissinger initiative was also interpreted in Europe against the background of the evolving Watergate crisis in the

US. By the autumn of 1972, it had become clear that the burglary into the offices of the Democratic Party's National Committee at the Watergate apartment in June 1972 had been linked to a campaign of political spying in the context of Nixon's re-election effort. In March 1973, there had already been allegations of a cover-up by the White House, and the crisis peaked for the first time at the end of April 1973, when Nixon, denying prior knowledge of the break-in, announced the dismissal of John Dean and the resignations of John D. Ehrlichman and Harry R. Haldeman, all top White House officials.[34] The extent to which Watergate had already – more than 15 months before Nixon's resignation – become a national obsession in the US was reflected in how the American press covered the 'Year of Europe' speech. As Kissinger deplored in his memoirs, the media focused more on his few comments on Watergate than on the substance of the initiative, which failed to get the domestic attention he had hoped for.[35]

With a Senate committee beginning to investigate the case, Watergate was bound to affect US foreign policy. Accordingly, many European governments regarded Watergate as a major reason why Kissinger brought transatlantic discussions abruptly into the public domain. They considered it likely that Kissinger's unexpected, spectacular move was in part inspired by a desire to deflect from the domestic upheavals.[36] As Trend argued vis-à-vis Heath one day after Kissinger's speech, Nixon was now 'a man in a hurry', as Watergate threatened to affect his moral authority. Yet, if Nixon's need to shift to a more presentational style of foreign policy had possibly inspired the 'Year of Europe', how seriously should the US challenge then be taken?[37] Moreover, Watergate heightened concerns in Europe as to the reliability of the American commitment to the defence of Europe. As Heath put it to Pompidou in May 1973, would Nixon, given his declining influence on Congress, remain strong enough to carry through his foreign policy commitments?[38]

For all their objections to Kissinger's initiative, and despite their preference for the status quo in Atlantic relations, the Europeans were well aware that they could not simply ignore Kissinger's appeal. No matter how awkward they might have considered it to get engaged with a tarnished American president in a process aimed at reaffirming the moral unity of the West, some constructive response to the 'Year of Europe' seemed necessary, if only to help Nixon cope with his domestic difficulties. Yet, coming up with a collective answer to the American challenge turned out to be a protracted and tangled affair for the Nine. As much as the Europeans agreed in their basic analysis of the US initiative, they were initially divided over how to respond.

Struggling for a joint position

In the first two months after Kissinger's speech, the essential debates on how to go about the 'Year of Europe' took place in multiple bilateral consultations between the three leading European powers and the US. Although there were multilateral deliberations in EPC too, they were not leading anywhere, largely because France was sceptical about any collective European response and because Kissinger sought to work out the basics of a new Atlantic Charter via the bilateral dialogues he had built up. Gradually, however, these bilateral dialogues turned into dead ends. With France reassessing its European policy in the summer of 1973, the path became cleared for a concerted European answer to Kissinger's initiative. The 'Year of Europe' became an EPC project, with the Nine in July 1973 deciding to address the US with one voice and work out a document on Europe's identity as a basis for their evolving foreign policy.

Bilateral diplomacy

It fell to the FRG to be the first European power to discuss the 'Year of Europe' with the US, since Brandt's visit to Washington, engineered by Kissinger prior to his speech, was due only days after the initiative had been launched. There was widespread scepticism in the government about US intentions in the proposed exercise. The West German ambassador in Washington warned that Kissinger's speech reflected an American nostalgia of the unchallenged hegemony of the 1950s and 1960s and that the US was out to subordinate Europe and reinvigorate its own leadership. Herbert Wehner, influential leader of the SPD parliamentary party, publicly called the initiative the outline of a 'monster' and internally warned Brandt that the initiative reflected the 'wishful thinking of a great power' (*Grossmachtwunschdenken*), with the US viewing world politics only from its own perspective.[39]

The chancellor had many doubts too. Yet, he was well aware that in view of West Germany's overwhelming dependence on the US he could not afford to treat an initiative of the FRG's major ally in purely negative terms. Besides, Brandt, as well as the Auswärtige Amt, also identified opportunities with the exercise. On the one had, the West Germans could hope that the initiative would result in the kind of 'constructive dialogue' between the Nine and Washington that Bonn had long been advocating.[40] On the other hand, 'the Year of Europe' also promised a chance of advancing the political dimension of European unification. According to the West German leaders, the Nine should use the challenges inherent in Kissinger's initiative to further develop and strengthen EPC. They should respond to Kissinger collectively and demonstrate their emerging profile as an actor in world affairs.[41]

In order to make the US familiar with the European realities, the chancellor prepared his talks with Nixon by memorising phrases of the Paris Summit communiqué of October 1972. Amazed that Nixon appeared badly informed about Kissinger's initiative and conceived of Europe as a net of bilateral relations only, Brandt emphasised that he had come to Washington not as a spokesman *of* Europe but at least *for* Europe, and he almost exclusively referred to the Nine rather than German–US relations.[42] Insisting on a degree of 'regional European autonomy' (*regionale Eigenverantwortung*) and 'global co-responsibility' (*weltpolitische Mitverantwortung*), he asked Nixon to treat the Nine as if they were already one big partner and their political unity largely accomplished.[43] Concerning the 'Year of Europe', Brandt remained vague in his proposals. He convinced Nixon to drop the label 'Atlantic Charter' – which had been directed against Germany in 1941. Furthermore, he suggested that Nixon ought to visit not only NATO and some bilateral partners when travelling to Europe to sign the declaration, but also the Nine. He flatly rejected a global approach in any upcoming transatlantic negotiations, and he succeeded in inserting into the joint communiqué references to Europe's 'enlarged responsibility in international politics' and the need for a 'balanced partnership' between the uniting Western Europe and the US.[44]

The West Germans were more than a little satisfied with their performance in Washington.[45] Indeed, their domestic press was so enthusiastic about what became commonly described as Brandt's victory in the US that Kissinger indignantly wrote to Bahr that the US had not understood the talks with the chancellor 'to be an encounter of which one side had the objective of dissuading the other from an erroneous line of policy'.[46] Still, Brandt and Scheel remained thrilled at how they had transformed the 'Year of Europe' from a vague transatlantic framework to a project that stressed a collective role for the Nine. When the chancellor wrote to Heath and Pompidou about the outcome of his summit, he underlined that he had spoken to Nixon as a European and urged that the Community members should now collectively receive the US president, possibly within the EPC framework. Brandt also informed his colleagues that Kissinger's proposals were improvised and should not be accepted uncritically. Two weeks after his return from the US, he maintained even vis-à-vis Brezhnev that a European personality distinct from the US was now emerging.[47]

Both the British and the French governments must have been astonished at the briskness with which Brandt had confronted the American administration.

However, London and Paris initially differed sharply about the West German proposal of making the issue of Europe's emerging role in world politics a central topic of the 'Year of Europe'. Whereas Whitehall favoured a common European position in the upcoming talks with the US, the French expressed serious doubts. When Brandt on 17 May 1973 discussed with Douglas-Home his impressions of his trip to Washington, the British secretary of state immediately agreed that Nixon ought to deal with 'the new Europe'.[48] In fact, ever since they joined the Community, the British had held the view that the EC-Nine should deal with the US as a Community, since bilateral discussions with Washington on matters such as economics and monetary policies could only leave Europe as the loser.[49] Already in January 1973, George Rowland Cromer, British ambassador to Washington, had warned the FCO of Kissinger's preoccupation with 'horse-trading across different categories of issues' in European–American relations and had argued that 'the need for political, as well as technical, economic and military, coordination of European positions could scarcely be more obvious'. With remarkable foresight, Cromer added that the US inclination for linkages and 'divide and rule' tactics might perhaps represent 'a sufficient challenge to Europe to enable the move towards political consultation and integration to proceed a few steps further'.[50]

In many ways, the British were even more critical of Kissinger's proposals than the West Germans. After a preliminary examination, the FCO contended that Kissinger's analysis was 'unnecessarily disparaging' of the work already in hand in institutions such as NATO, the General Agreement on Tariffs and Trade (GATT), and the International Monetary Fund (IMF). The US may be inviting the Europeans to sacrifice their economic interests for 'the political exigencies of Washington' and seemed to ask for burden-sharing on a scale unaffordable to Britain. Moreover, the FCO warned, Britain had to 'be wary of any US attempt to drive a political wedge between ourselves and our European allies or to use us as a stalking horse for Washington's purposes in Europe'. In a complementary analysis, the MOD also maintained that Kissinger had 'exaggerated' the military deficiencies in the Alliance and seemed ignorant of the essential work being done in NATO institutions.[51]

Heath himself was more upset about Kissinger's approach than any other European statesman. He considered the timing of the speech unfortunate and its terminology bad. Just when Britain was anxious to prove its European credentials, Kissinger called for a new Atlantic design. Even more irritating, in his opinion, was that an American took the liberty of announcing a 'Year of Europe'. For Britain, every year in the early 1970s was a year of Europe. As Heath noted in his memoirs: 'For Henry Kissinger to announce a Year of

Europe without consulting any of us was rather like my standing between the lions in Trafalgar Square and announcing that we were embarking on a year to save America!'[52] Europe, Heath complained to Walt Rostow, Kissinger's predecessor as national security adviser, could do with less preaching about burden-sharing and more recognition of what it was already doing. The American trade deficit had little to do with the Community, but stemmed largely from Japan and Canada, according to the prime minister. As the United States, like Britain in previous decades, was going through a process of decline, it was time it no longer ignored Europe's existence.[53]

Yet, even though Heath remained unconvinced of the need to redefine Atlantic relations, he was not out to obstruct the 'Year of Europe'. Although occasionally he had to be asked by Douglas-Home to tone-down his public criticism of Kissinger,[54] he was willing to help Nixon. Moreover, Heath agreed with Brandt and his own officials that Kissinger's appeal represented an opportunity for the Nine. As the FCO put it, with the speech being 'strongly PR oriented' and Nixon being in need of a success, Europe was now in a strong bargaining position: 'We should adopt a sympathetic and constructive stance but play things cool and long, decline to be hustled, and progressively force the Americans to redefine their objectives in face of the difficulties'.[55] The 'Davignon Committee', as the British still referred to EPC, seemed the appropriate forum to coordinate a European position, because NATO, with members such as Greece and Portugal, as in the case of CSCE, was not suitable for an exercise of stressing common values.[56]

However, the Heath government was disinclined to take the lead in organising a response to the US initiative. As the American challenge was likely to be divisive and the French reaction to both the 'Year of Europe' and the idea of a collective European response bound to be critical, the British preferred to stay 'benevolently neutral' and keep their heads down.[57] So, when Kissinger visited London on 10 May 1973, Whitehall remained vague about how to approach the exercise. Heath suggested a four-power steering group. Trend too talked about a 'smaller political directorate', while Greenhill proposed a European/Atlantic committee and ad hoc groups to address specific topics. Douglas-Home, for his part, made no procedural suggestions whatsoever and seemed preoccupied with the eyeglass case that Kissinger had put on the table during the course of meeting – which he took for a tape recorder.[58] Kissinger's final hint at joint Anglo-American leadership in the 'Year of Europe' was politely countered with the argument that it should be down to the US, not Britain, to push France in the right direction.[59]

The key to progress in the 'Year of Europe' now clearly lay in Paris. As for Heath and Brandt, they looked to France to get support for organising a European response. Conversely, from Kissinger's perspective, the Franco-American dialogue and the upcoming Nixon–Pompidou summit in Reykjavik represented his last bilateral channel left to finally kick off serious work on redefining Atlantic relations. As it turned out, France left both sides dissatisfied in this early phase of the 'Year of Europe'. French analyses of Kissinger's speech reveal that they were unhappy about many aspects. Jean-Bernard Raimond, Pompidou's diplomatic adviser, called it an 'imperious text' (*un texte impérieux*) designed to install 'an Atlantic world under American leadership' (*un monde atlantique à direction américaine*).[60] Challenging the more positive verdict of the initiative by Kosciusko-Morizet, he argued that from a US perspective, Washington's audacious foreign policy left room for one centre of decision-making only.[61] Jobert too identified an 'imperious will' (*volonté impériale*) in the speech, with Kissinger treating the Europeans 'like a subset of client states' (*comme un sous-ensemble d'Etats clients et vassaux*).[62] The Quai d'Orsay added that Kissinger wanted to share burdens rather than responsibilities and with his inclusion of Japan was to constitute a block of the rich incompatible with French interests. Worse still, from a French point of view, was that the 'Year of Europe' appeared to threaten both France's preeminence in Europe and independence in the Alliance. If Paris leaned towards a European response to Kissinger, the US was bound to get involved with the Nine and dilute French leadership. If the US had its way with a multilateral Atlantic solution, there was the double risk of the Alliance becoming more political than Paris would want and France being pressured to fully participate in NATO.[63]

When Heath came to Paris in late May 1973 and suggested that Pompidou should draft the declaration called for by Kissinger, the French president 'indicated dissent with a deprecating smile' and assured his counterpart that France would not move an inch. Heath warned that if the Europeans did not define their own concept, the US would be able to simply impose its ideas. He argued that he would accept four-power talks with Washington, but insisted that the Nine should also meet, particularly to discuss Europe's role within transatlantic defence. As it was difficult for the Community countries to produce a text from scratch, he encouraged the French to take the lead. Yet, Pompidou remained unconvinced. He still considered it premature for EPC to deal with defence. Moreover, he flatly rejected a meeting of the EC countries with Nixon, arguing that such a gathering would amount to the US president holding court with the Nine.[64]

Having long argued that defining a distinct European personality vis-à-vis the US would be the most difficult part of working out a European identity, Pompidou feared that the unity of the Nine would still be too fragile for a common European position towards Washington. Rather than lead to US recognition of Europe's political role, as London and Bonn hoped, the French were concerned that a meeting with Nixon would only expose European fragmentation or, worse, dissociate the Eight from France.[65] The French consequently refuted the British argument that '[e]ven if it were the case that the American wolf wanted to eat the European lambs, surely he could do it more easily one by one than if they all stood together'.[66] They were also sceptical about a common European approach since the goal of coordinating on such a wide range of issues threatened to suck the still fragile political consultation mechanism into the much stronger EC machinery, thereby prejudicing the still undecided structure of the future Europe.[67] Therefore, Pompidou rejected both Heath's call for French leadership and Brandt's proposal of a meeting between the Nine and Nixon.[68]

The Nixon administration did not get anywhere with the French either. Kissinger's preparatory talks in Paris in mid-May 1973 for the Franco-American summit in Reykjavik gave no indication yet of how much resistance the US would encounter in Iceland. Well familiar with Jobert from the time of his Vietnam negotiations in Paris, Kissinger's first two talks with the new French foreign minister, who spoke fluent English, were cordial, if rather confused and vague. Kissinger assured Jobert that the US considered France its key partner in Europe, was in favour of secret nuclear cooperation, supported French autonomy, and regarded French absence from the integrated command of NATO as a technical question only. Jobert, for his part, asked for an informal paper by Kissinger on what the US expected from the bilateral summit and indicated that France might well be supportive.[69] With Pompidou himself, Kissinger conducted what the French historian Georges-Henri Soutou has called the most substantive talks between the French president and a US representative ever.[70] Being more forthcoming about the substance of the 'Year of Europe' than either Heath or Brandt, Pompidou argued that he had been less irritated about Kissinger's references to Europe's regional role and the idea of globalisation than some of his colleagues. The Nine's major zone of influence would, indeed, be Europe, the Mediterranean, and Africa, Pompidou maintained, and keeping account of the big picture while negotiating in individual institutions was necessary. The French president admitted, however, that he was very concerned about the implications of superpower détente for Europe and China, which prompted Kissinger in turn to give a detailed and very open account of his strategic considerations behind triangular diplomacy.[71]

However, the atmosphere between France and the US became more negative once the specifics of the US initiative were discussed in Reykjavik at the end of May 1973. Kissinger's promised advance memorandum on what the summit should achieve could have done little to placate the French decision-makers. The US asked for nothing less than a bilateral agreement on an Atlantic summit during Nixon's trip to Europe, an understanding of what kind of principles the Atlantic declaration should contain, and a joint position on how to approach the 'Year of Europe' procedurally. Regarding this last point, the note proposed a triple approach of continuing bilateral talks, secret discussions among the four major Atlantic powers at the level of presidential assistants, and more formal coordination on the level of the deputy foreign ministers of all countries involved.[72]

Already during their preliminary meeting in Iceland, Jobert confronted Kissinger with a long list of French misgivings about the US proposals and turned the 'Year of Europe', from Kissinger's perspective, into a 'wrestling match'.[73] Pompidou, who could hardly conceal his illness to the press any longer when stepping off the airplane, in his talks with Nixon was equally restrictive, if less emotional. Seemingly unimpressed by Nixon's adulations and the insinuation that the US might be willing to give the Poseidon missile system to France, he sharply criticised the US monetary policies and called Kissinger's whole Atlantic initiative into question. Why redefine the goals of the Alliance? Pompidou warned against launching a process of reform, as some allies, such as the Dutch and the Danish, already neglected defence and pursued a one-sided policy of détente. Furthermore, why a declaration that linked the issue of defending the free world with US–EC economic problems? And, with EMU still in trouble, political unification only just started, and Heath being the only European he knew in Britain, why should 1973 become an extraordinary year for Europe?[74]

Concerning procedures, Pompidou rejected four-power talks, signalling that smaller EC partners already assailed him for discussing the 'Year of Europe' with the US bilaterally. Would anyone believe that four presidential advisers would only meet for common recreation in hot spring resorts? Thus, all Pompidou was ready to accept was continuing bilateral consultations of Kissinger with his three European counterparts, under whatever pretext. Nixon's final, shy return to the idea of a meeting of the deputy foreign ministers within the framework of the Alliance encountered no response.[75] The near-complete failure of the summit became apparent when the French and the US delegations publicly differed in the concluding press briefing even on the tiny common denominator they thought to have achieved. While the French spokesman generally emphasised bilateral consultations and indicated that upcoming technical discussions in individual institutions would be complemented by meetings of deputy foreign ministers on a bilateral basis, Kissinger insisted that these latter meetings would take place on a multilateral level. As the British justly observed, the American version of how to proceed seemed to be based on 'wishful thinking', rather than on what France had actually conceded.[76]

After a month of multiple bilateral discussions, no consensus was in sight on how to approach the 'Year of Europe'. Given the stark divergences both among the Europeans and across the Atlantic, it was only logical that the multilateral deliberations that ran in parallel to the bilateral dialogues made no headway either. In the Alliance, the first exchanges of views were marked by puzzlement, with Donald Rumsfeld, US ambassador to NATO since January 1973, admitting that he was ignorant of what a new Charter should accomplish.[77] Discussions on the 'Year of Europe' during NATO's ministerial meeting in June 1973 according to the British had 'some air of unreality', with Rogers declining to defend Kissinger's initiative and Jobert coming up with the lapidary advice not to fumble with what he considered was still a good Alliance.[78]

As for EPC, the collective discussions on Kissinger's initiative in the Political Committee in late April and May 1973 revealed a deep split between the Eight and France, with Paris responding to its partners' eagerness to emphasise the political aspirations of the Nine in the 'Year of Europe' with a fivefold 'no'. The French delegate, insinuating apologetically that he had the most restrictive brief imaginable, rejected Davignon's proposal of an ad hoc group of EPC and EC officials to discuss the US initiative; a common European response to Kissinger; a meeting of the Nine with Nixon; the working out of a paper on European–US relations to prepare the next EPC ministerial meeting; as well as the Dutch idea of a common communiqué at that meeting stating that the Nine would now prepare a 'constructive dialogue' with Washington. An Italian appeal to de Gaulle's credo that Europe could only have a foreign policy when it had a joint position on the US achieved as little in bringing the French round as bilateral exchanges by the Belgian presidency with Paris.[79]

Thus, when the nine foreign ministers themselves discussed Kissinger's speech for the first time in early June 1973, the meeting became a rather unpleasant affair. Above all, it was bedevilled by French suspicions that the

Eight were out to blur the distinction between EPC and the Community organs by means of the 'Year of Europe'. Jobert insisted that all further deliberations should be limited to EPC and suggested several extra ministerial meetings over summer, not without complaining that things would be much easier if a political secretariat had been set up. Others argued that work should be done by the Political Committee, in cooperation with either the EC permanent representatives or the Commission. Eventually, one extra ministerial meeting in July was agreed, with Jobert, under strong pressure, conceding that the Political Committee identify specific questions for the foreign ministers 'in accordance with common procedures', which might or might not mean in cooperation with the EC. There was some support for the French compromise solution of Nixon meeting the two respective presidents of the EC Council of Ministers and the Commission. However, the basic difficulty remained. As the British put it, 'Jobert showed no desire to get down to work on preparing a common European position'.[80] For all their common analysis of Kissinger's initiative, the Nine remained divided as to a European response.

A French policy change

By early summer 1973, Kissinger began to show irritation at how slowly and unenthusiastically the Europeans approached his initiative. If it had taken him two weeks to transform relations with China, he complained to the Italians, and three weeks to do the same with the Soviets, why should a redefinition of Atlantic relations take so much longer?[81] Kissinger deplored that allied relations appeared to be in a permanent state of 'guerrilla warfare', whereas relations with adversaries were constantly improving and marked by dramatic diplomatic achievements. Why could the Europeans discuss a CSCE summit, but be so recalcitrant about a preceding Atlantic gathering?[82] As he wrote to Jobert in mid-July 1973:

> [A]ll of us will suffer, and Europe perhaps more than we, if it turns out that we can engage in multilateral conferences and bilateral meetings, and sign agreements and reach understandings, with the East, such as CSCE, MBFR, SALT, etc., but are unable to do so among ourselves. I say this as a historian more than as one concerned with current affairs, because in the latter capacity one can always find ways to muddle through.[83]

Kissinger admitted that he had based his speech on the misconception that the Europeans felt neglected. At the same time, he threatened that the Europeans would be making a grave miscalculation if they believed that the US engagement in Europe would remain unchanged without any action on their side. Indeed, Nixon might well abandon the 'Year of Europe' and cancel his trip to Europe in the autumn. While this would not really affect US national interests, Kissinger boldly claimed, Congress was likely to legislate 75,000–90,000 troops out of Western Europe by the end of 1973.[84]

Although many Europeans were in doubt as to whether Kissinger's warnings of grave consequences should be taken seriously – and whether, for that matter, a favourable European response would make any difference to Congress at all – there was some tangible unease at how a European rebuff might affect Atlantic relations.[85] France, accordingly, came under ever-growing pressure to give up its policy of negation. A remarkable French policy change did, indeed, come about in June/July 1973, which eventually allowed the Europeans to respond collectively to Kissinger's speech. This change, however, did not occur in reaction to European or US pressure but went far deeper than that, amounting to a fundamental overhaul of France's foreign policy.

In the previous chapter, I have outlined how improving German–Soviet relations and superpower détente caused much concern in France and contributed to a French shift towards *l'Europe politique*. In particular, I have argued that the Soviet–American 'Agreement on the Prevention of Nuclear War' of 22 June 1973, which the French interpreted as a 'new Yalta' that fundamentally challenged both French and European autonomy, provoked a policy change in Paris. Importantly, this perceived threat of a superpower condominium peaked precisely at the time when the Europeans discussed their response to Kissinger's 'Year of Europe'. Jobert became convinced that this US initiative was only a function of the nuclear agreement between Washington and Moscow, with the US seeking to subordinate allied relations to the new prerogative of superpower détente.[86] The question of how to respond to Kissinger's speech, therefore, became part of the wider issue of how to defend French and European interests in the context of the Soviet–American collusion. Although some French officials were inclined to drown the whole project of a European foreign policy as a result of the deep split in EPC,[87] Jobert, determined to strengthen Europe's role in the world, did not consider this an option. Rather, he decided to take the bull by the horns and try and use Kissinger's initiative as an instrument to advance European political unity.

For all the procedural wrangling in EPC, the French were struck by how angered their partners seemed to be about Kissinger's proposals and how keen they were on expressing Europe's global responsibilities and aspirations. Already previous to the American–Soviet nuclear agreement, Paris had wondered whether this was not an opportunity to be exploited, in the sense of transforming the 'Year of Europe' into a test for the readiness of the Nine to become a truly independent political actor.[88] It was largely for this reason that France in the bilateral dialogue with the US had put off a concrete response to the initiative throughout June 1973, with Jobert in fact gradually taking the initiative away from Kissinger. When the latter in Paris on 8 June 1973 offered France a free hand at defining Europe's role in the Atlantic declaration and indicated that the US would accept a solid confirmation of Europe's distinct identity, Jobert began to sense his chance. Calling Kissinger a great strategist, but ignorant of tactics, he suggested that the public impression of a difficult, biting dialogue was only to the advantage of the 'Year of Europe', lending it significance and emotion. Promising to do some drafting for their next meeting at the end of the month, Jobert insisted that the US by then should have its own draft ready, and insinuated that the dialogue could later be multilateralised. Kissinger expressed confusion as to whether his counterpart was genuine in his offer or laying a trap to endlessly put off the declaration. Denouncing the NATO bureaucracy as a 'liturgical nightmare' (*cauchemar liturgique*), he at first tried to talk Jobert into a trilateral dialogue with London, but he eventually expressed agreement with the French insistence on continuing bilateralism.[89]

However, when Jobert was received by Nixon and Kissinger in the Western White House in San Clemente at the end of June 1973, he brought along no substantive or procedural ideas, was generally evasive about the 'Year of Europe', picked up two draft proposals for an Atlantic declaration prepared by National Security Council (NSC) staff and the State Department, and simply asked for patience.[90] With such delaying tactics, the French foreign minister had won both the initiative and another month for internal and intra-European reflections. While it was a risky strategy that did nothing to soothe Kissinger's irritation, it gave Paris the time required to find out whether a common position of the Nine that would not contradict basic French perceptions was feasible in the 'Year of Europe'.

The key meeting that brought France round to a joint European approach took place in London, where Jobert on 2 July 1973 made a stopover upon his return from San Clemente to attend Douglas-Home's seventieth birthday party. In an internal meeting on 20 June 1973, the British had made two basic choices about the 'Year of Europe'. First, Heath had accepted the FCO argument that there should be two declarations: one on the Atlantic Alliance, signed by the Fifteen; the other on relations between the Nine and the US. Second, refuting the first respective drafts of the FCO, he had asked his officials to pursue what could be called a 'Europe-first' approach and to regard

European unity as a precondition for a transatlantic understanding: the drafts according to Heath had to be acceptable to all European partners and should represent a statement of European requirements, rather than being tailored to US wishes. While they should contain constructive language, they should offer no concessions of substance. Most importantly, in order to be able to defend European interests in both processes, the Nine should work out a third, internal, document on their own collective identity.[91] Heath's instructions reflected three things: his wish to provide Nixon with an answer, his genuine European zeal, and his preoccupation with close Anglo-French relations. In particular, the idea of combining the Atlantic exercise with the project of defining the European identity was an expression of the new British policy of, as the FCO put it, 'giving as much thought to likely French reactions to our decision as we have in recent years to likely American reactions'.[92]

Although Jobert began his talks in London by rejecting both the need for a European paper and a summit with Nixon, he came to realise how much Heath's views 'could facilitate the nascence of Europe and preserve its identity from the American fatality'.[93] With a two-declaration approach, France would be able to circumvent global negotiations and the thematic expansion of Atlantic cooperation. And, was British backing of a European personality distinct from Washington not a Gaullist dream come true? While Jobert left London reassured about the potential of Franco-British cooperation, he still had doubts about the FRG's attitudes towards the 'Year of Europe'.[94] By mid-July 1973, however, these doubts were dispelled too. With one of his manoeuvres, Jobert himself contributed to the emerging Franco-German understanding. Unlike the British, who in early July had decided to put their bilateral dialogue with the US on hold,[95] the FRG was complying with a White House request for further confidential talks in Washington. Yet, by hinting to Scheel that Kissinger had asked Bahr to go to Washington, Jobert created a West German row over prerogatives that resulted in Scheel replacing Bahr in the German–American dialogue.[96] This was significant in so far as Scheel was distinctly European-minded and ever since Kissinger's speech had been urging the Nine to make the US initiative a test for EPC and define a common policy vis-à-vis the US as a step towards the EU.[97]

Scheel's talks in Washington on 12 July 1973 were the only occasion where any of the three European powers in their bilateral dialogues with the US lay the outline of a possible declaration on the table. Kissinger was thrilled. He gave Scheel his own two drafts and asked him to turn the German draft into an official document. However, the German–American understanding was less thorough than Kissinger might have hoped. Procedurally, Scheel already advocated the two-declaration approach and invited Nixon to meet the Nine in a gathering with the two presidencies of the Commission and the EC Council and the nine foreign ministers. What was more, Scheel undoubtedly took Kissinger's encouragement for the Nine to act as a unit and emphasise their special role in the declaration much more literally than Nixon's adviser could have intended.[98]

Scheel's draft, at any rate, was never delivered to Washington in its final form. Moreover, the West Germans after their trip to the US reported to Paris and London that Nixon was desperate for a success and willing to underwrite, as the FCO recorded, 'virtually any definition of the European personality which the Europeans wanted to put in a declaration'.[99] Bonn's keenness on taking advantage of the US desire to have a declaration and expressing the distinct personality of the Nine obviously reinforced the change of thinking in Paris, with the path towards serious work in EPC on the 'Year of Europe' being finally cleared.[100]

The Nine unite

The French policy change was the main reason why deliberations in Europe on how to respond to the US challenge in the summer of 1973 shifted from the bilateral to the multilateral level of EPC. Two additional factors contributed to this process: dissatisfaction with Kissinger's working methods, and with the substance of the US draft declarations. Of the three big European powers, at least the British and the West Germans by July 1973 had definitely become fed up with Kissinger's penchant for bilateralism and secret diplomacy, which had produced misapprehension and distrust between the Three and seriously strained political cooperation among the Nine. London and Bonn became increasingly irritated at what they regarded as Kissinger's attempt to play the Europeans off against each other. By insisting on secrecy, only Nixon's security adviser ever knew the full score, while placing his European counterparts in the awkward position of hiding their discussions with Washington from their partners.[101]

There was, for instance, great confusion among the Federal Republic, Britain, and France about the US draft declarations, which Kissinger had confidentially given to Jobert on 29 June, to Cromer in early July, and to Scheel on 12 July 1973. The West Germans, long dismissive of rumours that France had received these drafts,[102] must have felt duped when they realised that Kissinger had been less forthcoming with them than with Paris and London. The British, for their part, became annoyed when Jobert revealed in London on 2 July 1973 that he had received US drafts and that Kissinger had decided not to give them to anyone else. Even the French foreign minister, generally well-disposed to diplomatic manoeuvres himself, prematurely suspected the British of being in possession of the drafts and accused them of having feigned ignorance when they had expressed surprise that France should have received draft proposals by the US.[103]

Kissinger's secretive style, Britain and the FRG agreed, might have been adequate to deal with Communist autocracies, but it was totally at variance with both the domestic and the EPC dimensions of decision-making in Europe. Given the European parliamentary systems, neither Heath nor Brandt enjoyed the degree of centralised and personal authority of a Brezhnev. They could not act without involving large parts of the political elites and the bureaucracy.[104] Furthermore, by being asked to keep their dialogues with the White House confidential, Kissinger compelled the Europeans to break with the EPC information practices following bilateral talks with third powers. Those European powers not privileged to have bilateral talks with Kissinger showed increasing impatience and concern at great power consultations. The Belgians warned the FRG in July 1973 that if it were true that Scheel had given the US a West German draft declaration, this would amount to a gross violation of the spirit of EPC, while the Italians even headed to Washington themselves to demand a first-hand account by Kissinger on what had been discussed so far.[105] The British became particularly embarrassed when they realised that 'whenever we have been asked to maintain secrecy about a given talk, we have done so only to find subsequently on a few occasions that the fact of our having these bilateral talks has been disclosed [by Kissinger] to some of our partners'.[106] If Kissinger's working methods had posed an occasional source of irritation to the Europeans well before the 'Year of Europe', they now seriously threatened to undermine the unity of the Nine. There was no doubt in London and Bonn that it was high time that the Europeans finally got out of the 'procedural morass' and put an end to clandestine bilateral consultations.[107]

The fact that the FRG, Britain, and France all came out with highly negative internal assessments of the US draft declarations further induced the Europeans to get together and do their own drafting. From a West German point of view, the two US papers were 'fundamentally unacceptable', while the FCO considered them 'badly drafted, unfortunate in tone in places, and markedly obscure in others' and bemoaned that they embodied substantial European concessions to US views without offering equally substantive concessions in return.[108] The French were particularly unimpressed by the White House draft, which in their eyes overemphasised the linkage principle and

Atlantic solidarity, asked for total French reintegration into NATO, and condemned efforts at developing special relations with adversaries. In an acerb letter to Kissinger on 14 July 1973, Jobert pointed out that such US drafts would not receive any backing in Europe. Asking for more realistic documents, he impertinently argued that he could not keep his promise of presenting his own draft, since its contents would only embarrass Washington.[109]

Although the winds now unmistakably turned in favour of a European draft, EPC deliberations in the weeks before the extraordinary ministerial meeting of 23 July 1973 were still not as smooth and effective as in other fields of cooperation, such as the CSCE. France still participated only reluctantly, with public Danish criticism of French nuclear tests provoking irritation in Paris.[110] The French also stubbornly continued to insist on a rigid separation of EC and EPC operations. This resulted not only in the Commission being excluded from the upcoming EPC ministerial meeting. It also led to the foreign ministers gathering in Copenhagen (the capital of the acting Danish EPC presidency) on the morning of 23 July to discuss the 'Year of Europe', before rushing to Brussels for an afternoon meeting in their capacity as members of the EC Council of Ministers – a procedure that naturally represented a scoop for the press and became widely quoted in analyses of EPC to illustrate Europe's political immaturity.[111] Conversely, however, the French representatives were now more constructive in the debates on substance. They were also cooperative in the working out of a list of key questions on the European–American dialogue to prepare the ministerial meeting, which generally brought about a more relaxed atmosphere in EPC.[112]

Even though the ministerial discussions in Copenhagen were rather confused, with the Danish chairman never putting the list of questions to the ministers, the Nine were eventually able to make a series of important decisions. Unsurprisingly, Jobert started off by stressing the significance of the proposed paper on European identity. He argued that Europe should first affirm its identity 'in all directions, on all issues, and for herself'[113] and put off work on a European–American declaration and preparations for Nixon's visit until the end of 1974, when the unity of the Nine would be more solid (and, he omitted, France would preside over the EC). If the US now seemed worried about the changing balance between its policy of superpower détente and its Alliance policies, it behaved, according to Jobert, like a 'pyromaniac fireman' (*pompier pyromane*) and ought not be allowed to dictate the speed of Europe's answer.[114] Some ministers, such as Aldo Moro (Italy), Gaston Thorn (Luxembourg), and Max van der Stoel (Netherlands), expressed some sympathy with Jobert's line of reasoning. By contrast, Douglas-Home and Scheel insisted that a preliminary answer would have to be given to Nixon by the autumn of 1973.

The resulting compromise solution was very much commensurate with what the British had anticipated in late June 1973. The Nine agreed on a collective European response to the 'Year of Europe' and asked the Political Committee to prepare a report on potential subjects of a European–American dialogue until the next ministerial meeting on 10 September. They favoured a two-declaration approach to the 'Year of Europe', one relating to European–American affairs and one to Atlantic relations of the Fifteen. They also agreed to work out a document on their collective identity, which in time should provide the basis for their dialogue with Washington. This document should comprise both a political evaluation of European relations with the US and define the responsibility and place of the Nine in world politics. On top of these decisions, which were made public, the Nine on a confidential basis also agreed to subsequently exchange all information obtained in bilateral dealings with the US, to coordinate their position (excluding Ireland) in the context of a NATO declaration of the Fifteen, and, ad referendum, to jointly meet Nixon during his visit, in a form to be determined.[115]

Fragile that its compromise outcome was, the Copenhagen meeting of 23 July 1973 marked a first milestone in the EPC discussions on relations between the Nine and the US. Three months after Kissinger had launched his initiative, the Nine, after several heated rounds of debates, finally embarked on the venturesome course of defining both their collective relations with their key ally and the peculiarity and normative basis of their foreign policy. For the Community countries to agree on tackling two of the most sensitive issues of European foreign policy-making was remarkable. The initiative in the 'Year of Europe' now lay definitely with the Nine, who had transformed the US challenge into an opportunity to put forward their own vision of Europe's role within the West, and in the world. As Jobert observed, perhaps 1973 would still become the year of Europe – albeit not in the sense that Kissinger had envisaged.[116]

Speaking with one voice to the US

In August and September 1973, the Nine were confronted with two major challenges regarding the 'Year of Europe:' to put flesh on the principle of a common European position; and to get US approval for negotiating with the Europeans collectively, and on the basis of their own view of how to redefine

Atlantic relations. As it turned out, getting Washington's approval for the Nine to speak with one voice vis-à-vis the US was even more difficult than establishing a European consensus on what to say in a European–American dialogue. In the following, I will first examine the US objections to a collective European role in the 'Year of Europe', before dealing with how the Nine succeeded in working out a common draft declaration. The negotiations of the Nine on defining their common identity will be covered in Chapter 5, since the 'Declaration on European Identity' was not completed before December 1973.

Mid-summer theatre: A first transatlantic row

Before the Europeans could begin studying how to proceed from their Copenhagen meeting, they had to face some scathing criticism from the White House. This criticism first occurred in reaction to letters from the British and the FRG informing the US about the decisions taken by the nine foreign ministers. Heath not only provided Nixon with a detailed account of the outcome of the Copenhagen meeting, but also made it clear that the Nine would henceforth exchange all information they received from the US. Arguing in favour of ending Anglo-American bilateralism on the 'Year of Europe', he implied that US violations of its own request for secrecy about meetings with Britain had resulted in French accusations of London failing to keep its partners informed. The prime minister added that he would advise against the US idea of an extra Atlantic summit of all 16 NATO and Community members (on top of the meetings with the Nine and the Fifteen), of which he had only learnt indirectly from the West Germans and the Italians and which was unlikely to find sufficient support among the Nine.[117]

As for Brandt, he combined his report to Nixon with a renewed appeal for an equal partnership between Europe and the US, advising the US president to await the results of the work of the Nine, which, he assured, would be beneficial to all.[118] In his parallel account to Kissinger, Scheel went even further when he emphasised the importance of the emerging European drafting process, asked the US not to interrupt these European deliberations, and suggested that Washington should publicly welcome the decisions of Copenhagen and express appreciation of the growing global significance of European unity. The West German foreign minister also noted that the US draft had been badly received in Europe and, adding insult to injury, that he had decided against giving the US the completed West German draft since renewed bilateral exchanges could easily bring about 'debilitating misunderstandings'.[119]

It did not take long for the White House to answer these letters, which had all mixed their factual accounts with implicit criticism of the US policy in the 'Year of Europe' or with pleas that Washington should back the line adopted by the Nine. Heath was to receive the harshest reply. 'I must tell you frankly that I am quite concerned about the situation in which we seem to find ourselves', Nixon began his letter. He criticised the Europeans for appearing able enough to contemplate collective and bilateral East–West summits, but at the same time enmeshing intra-Western relation 'in a complex procedural web'. It was 'hard to understand', Nixon continued, why the Europeans refused to discuss their mutual relationships with the US, adding that the procedure chosen by the Nine appeared 'almost like adversary bargaining'. He also rejected the European proposal to meet the Community foreign ministers and insisted instead, the lacking institutional role of the heads of state and government in the EC notwithstanding, on being received by the Nine at summit level. Blaming Heath's decision to end the bilateral dialogue for Britain's ignorance about a possible summit of the Sixteen, Nixon stressed that it would have never occurred to him that Europe after months of preoccupation with procedure argued that it 'cannot devise the extraordinary forum that would be appropriate for this important endeavor'. He concluded by warning that without commitment at the highest level 'the injury to the interests of all our countries could be severe and lasting'.[120]

Nixon's answer to Brandt was less extensive, though still crisp enough for the chancellor to give orders not to disclose its existence, let alone its substance. After expressing, 'in all candor', his surprise that the Nine were shutting down all channels of communication until mid-September and seemed to turn an initiative designed to create a new spirit of Atlantic solidarity 'almost into a European–American confrontation', the US president declared that he would now take no further initiatives, but would await the product of the Nine. Should the European document not be substantive and the proposed procedure for the European–American dialogue not be consistent with cooperative Atlantic relations, he would cancel his trip to Europe, Nixon added, underscoring again that he could not 'consider meetings in multilateral forums in which my European colleagues do not find it possible to participate'.[121] Scheel, who only a week earlier had been assured by Kissinger that the US welcomed the collective debates of the Nine on the 'Year of Europe' and was flexible on procedures,[122] now too received a rebuff, albeit less strongly worded. Obviously frustrated that his initiative had been turned into a bureaucratic exercise, Kissinger drew a grim picture of Atlantic relations. He refused to accept that time pressure had been artificially created by the US, purported that he had chosen bilateral dialogues 'in deference to European wishes', and pessimistically claimed that a declaration might now do more damage than good.[123]

In his memoirs, Kissinger confirmed that the US viewed the Copenhagen meeting as a turning point in Atlantic relations, as the Nine had moved to put these relations into a 'straitjacket of legalistic formalisms' and had taken the unprecedented decision of putting an US initiative on ice and cold-shouldering a presidential visit to Europe.[124] Yet, neither his retrospective analysis nor the US letters to London and Bonn reveal as lucidly the essence of US objections to the course on which the Nine had embarked as Kissinger's poignant remarks in his long conversation with Trend in Washington on 30 July 1973. It fell to the deplorable British cabinet secretary, Atlanticist of long standing, but loyal to Heath's European prerogatives, to be the first European representative to meet Kissinger after Copenhagen and encounter first-hand the wrath of the still agitated security adviser.[125]

Kissinger started off his outburst by announcing that the 'Year of Europe' was 'over'. Should an 'adversary relationship' develop, the Europeans had to accept the consequences, and they would be 'very painful'. If old friends treated the US government like that, the US would deal with them 'as they did with Luxembourg'. Not a single European politician had given whole-hearted endorsement to his initiative, and it remained a mystery to him what the French were really up to. The content of any declaration was now 'almost unimportant', and while it was up to the Europeans to do something about it, the US would reject any 'statement of banalities'. Kissinger added that he would no longer put up with public European criticisms of US motives behind the 'Year of Europe'. Should these continue, the US would retaliate in kind.

The gist of Kissinger's subsequent, specific points of criticism was twofold. First, the US government 'had never intended to use this initiative to build Europe'. It had sought to 'build Atlantic unity', and it was 'not possible to do both'. The US had been hoping for a coordinated Atlantic response, not a European response. An Atlantic declaration should have preceded the work on European political unity, but the Nine had reversed the order. Second, the procedure chosen was 'incorrect'. The US resented the fact that it was now excluded from European deliberations. It had hoped to handle the 'Year of Europe' with Britain, France, and the FRG, but was now told that it would not receive any drafts or ideas until they had been 'discussed with Norway [!], Luxembourg and even Ireland' and that Washington was then expected to deal with the Danish foreign minister, whose name he did not know and who would be no more than a 'messenger boy'. Scheel had committed an 'act of bad faith' when he had withdrawn his draft, Jobert had 'totally misled' him, and British behaviour had been incompatible with the special relationship and 'even insulting'.[126]

The meeting was to stand out as a low point in post-war Anglo-American relations. Despite Kissinger's pressure, the British delegation throughout this painful session refused to let the White House have the FCO drafts prepared for discussion among the Nine. What the talks primarily revealed was that, as Douglas-Home noted upon reading the record, Kissinger had not persuaded himself that the Nine were an entity with whom Washington would have to deal.[127] When the British briefed their European partners, the surprise at Kissinger's devastating criticism was ubiquitous. Was it not contradictory for the US to constantly demand that Europe speak with one voice, but complain about a fait accompli as soon as the Nine embarked on such an endeavour?[128]

As if to test whether Nixon shared Kissinger's rejection of a collective European role in the 'Year of Europe', Brandt and Heath wrote again to the US president in early August 1973. Pointing out that the Europeans were in a difficult learning process, the chancellor argued that the US should not harbour a 'wrong feeling of exclusion' when the Nine attempted to hammer out a common position among themselves.[129] Heath more pointedly maintained that it would 'surely be judged one of the greater ironies of history if, just at the moment when [...] nine of the countries of Western Europe are at last emerging as an entity, the United States should be tempted to reject the concept of an equal partnership which all their efforts for nearly 30 years have been designed to create'.[130] Yet, the answer from the White House was not encouraging. 'I have no objection to the Europeans arriving at common positions', Nixon replied to Brandt. But, raising an issue that was to dominate transatlantic debates in the first half of 1974 especially, he underlined that the US would want to be consulted before European thinking solidified into an agreed policy. 'Considering the close relations between the United States and Europe for 25 years', Nixon added, 'it seems inconceivable that our allies will no longer be engaged in a joint Atlantic process but in a negotiation between the United States, on the one hand, and the EC Nine on the other'.[131]

Franco-British lead: Towards a European draft declaration

The US message was clear. But how should the Nine react? In early August 1973, Heath wrote to Pompidou and Brandt that perhaps the moment for a major European initiative had come. He suggested an informal trilateral summit at the end of the month to make sure that the next EPC ministerial meeting in Copenhagen on 10 September 1973 would be a success.[132] With both the Elysée and the chancellery considering such a gathering too dramatic, a West German proposal to send to Paris two top officials of the FCO and the Auswärtige Amt for parallel talks with Jobert was finally accepted.[133] Heath and Brandt were well aware that the key to an effective EPC performance continued to lie in Paris.[134] While Britain and the FRG widely concurred in their own analyses of the situation, the French reading of the cold shower by the Nixon administration was likely to be different – which made it ever more uncertain whether the Nine would be able to agree on both a substantive position and a procedure of how to negotiate with the US in the limited time available.

London and Bonn were both alienated by Kissinger's explosion. The FCO found it increasingly frustrating to work with the 'mercurial and unpredictable' decision-makers in the White House.[135] The West Germans resented being scolded in the 'tone of a world power' (*Ton einer Weltmacht*),[136] especially since two years earlier they had been told by Kissinger that he 'wanted to be able to lift up the telephone, get through to Europe and ask what their view was on a certain subject'.[137] Even Brandt came to suspect now that there was a mutual agreement between the superpowers not to have a strong, unified Western Europe.[138] Britain and the FRG agreed that US attitudes and behaviour were largely responsible for the transatlantic rift. As Heath put it in his letter to Pompidou and Brandt: 'Unless and until the United States Administration recognises the nature of the Community and the extent to which we all feel bound to reach a Community position before getting into detailed discussions with the US […] we shall not achieve better understanding'.[139] London and Bonn also believed that if Kissinger now placed the blame on Europe, this was only a pretext with which to deflect from the fact that his methods had failed to frighten the Europeans into a position more in line with US interests.[140]

At the same time, even though they considered part of Kissinger's irritation to be a bluff, Britain and the Federal Republic were concerned about the impact of the transatlantic crisis on European security. Whitehall had been shocked at Kissinger's question about how the US nuclear deterrent could be credible if there was a feeling in the US of the Europeans being adversaries.[141] Bonn was especially worried about an accelerated withdrawal of US troops.[142] The tangible anxiety in both countries primarily related to a perceived likeliness that Watergate could have an ever more baleful influence on US foreign policy. After the uncovering of a secret tape-recording system in the Oval Office in July 1973 that was expected to contain evidence of his involvement in the White House cover-up, Nixon had refused to release the tapes and, instead, embarked on a major legal battle with Congress. With an impeachment process looming, Heath and Brandt wondered what all this would yet imply for Europe.[143]

The French, by contrast, felt little urgency to help Nixon. Having received no scornful letter from Washington, they were generally less concerned about the US reproach after the Copenhagen meeting. France interpreted Kissinger's eruption as largely tactical and refuted the Anglo-German argument that there was now an increased time pressure for Europe to act. The US would stay in Europe no matter how grave the domestic crisis, Jobert remained convinced, sarcastically arguing that American nuclear deterrence had lost all credibility anyway in view of the emerging superpower condominium.[144] How could France be persuaded to make haste and constructively participate in working out a European proposal? It is here that Brandt and Heath came up with different answers. The West Germans, who got cold feet, were now eager to accommodate US requests and attempted to threaten France into line. They sought to complement principles about the political significance of the Nine, which had already figured prominently in their Atlantic draft declaration of July 1973,[145] with more Atlantic statements that would express a 'special relationship' between Western Europe and the US. Also, given that it was improbable that declarations of historical significance could be worked out before Nixon's visit, they suggested that the trip of the US president should only mark the beginning of a continuous dialogue.[146] Irritated about Jobert's slow pace,[147] Bonn warned Paris of the incalculable risks a failure of the upcoming EPC ministerial meeting would contain for West German foreign policy. The West German public, so the argument went, was likely to respond to any security vacuum emanating from reduced US protection of Europe by pressing for an arrangement with Moscow, rather than for a deepening of European integration.[148]

The British pursued a more seductive approach. On 11 August 1973, they delivered their own drafts for a European–American declaration and for a document on the European identity to the Quai d'Orsay. Both papers, which had been mandated by Heath on 20 June and had met the approval of the British Cabinet on 25 July 1973, caused much surprise in Paris. From a French perspective, the draft on European identity was 'very well done' (*fort bien rédigé*), particularly since it insisted on every page that the Nine should define their own goals and interests, rather than seek to placate the United States. Its 'European' spirit, the French were amazed, stood in stark contrast to the Atlantic inclinations that Paris had always associated the British with. The declaration on European–American relations, according to the French assessment, would not pose any problems either, as its language was constructive at the same time as being vague.[149] The British draft declaration on relations between the Nine and the US had obviously been designed to reflect the highest common European denominator on the issue. It laid emphasis on what had already been agreed rather than breaking new ground and used numerous phrases of the Paris Summit communiqué of 1972 and an earlier EC–US trade declaration of February 1972. Importantly, one of its longest and most explicit principles asked the US to recognise Europe's political role in the world:

> The European Community, in establishing its position in world affairs as a distinct entity, will make a contribution commensurate to its human, intellectual and material resources. The United States, recognising that the creation of the Community has enhanced the stability of Europe, will be glad to see the Community speaking with a single voice in international contexts.

Other principles on general cooperation, trade, money, energy, and the environment were drafted in such a broad, abstract fashion that they implied no European concessions and at the same time were difficult to rebut.[150]

London's approach was successful in getting the French on board. In a secret meeting with Heath during his vacations in Southern England, Jobert urged his counterpart to now build Europe jointly with France and indicated his readiness to work towards a declaration with the US.[151] His ministry had already some days earlier strongly argued in favour of subscribing to the British approach, not least to prevent London from leaning towards Bonn.[152] France, in fact, now definitely took the reigns in the 'Year of Europe'. When the two representatives of the FCO and the Auswärtige Amt came to Paris on 29 August 1973 for their agreed parallel talks with Jobert, the French foreign minister indicated to the British envoy, Deputy Under-Secretary of State Thomas Brimelow, that France would support the FCO draft in EPC, provided that Douglas-Home did not allow it to be 'massacred' – a condition the British accepted.[153] Once the US would receive the draft of the Nine, Jobert added, it would become clear where the Western superpower stood: 'Either they were for Europe or against it'.[154]

At the same time, Jobert and his top officials succeeded in wresting agreement from Paul Frank, the West German state secretary, to work out the declaration on the basis of the British draft, which Bonn, because of its lack of Atlantic zeal, could hardly believe had been written by the FCO.[155] Frank was reminded that a European identity could only be defined in distinction to the Americans, who according to the French now appeared to be out to destroy European integration. Brandt's envoy was then bombarded with wild accusations: by behaving like a satellite, West Germany would block the unification of

Europe; in its panic about the declining US security protection, it ignored the fact that French and British nuclear submarines would be able to destroy two-thirds of Soviet territory; and it betrayed its French partner, which, contrary to the US, had loyally supported *Ostpolitik*, only to witness a relapse of Bonn's *Westpolitik* into the Atlantic years of Ludwig Erhard (chancellor between 1963 and 1966). Puzzled about the new French eagerness to draft a declaration, and worried that it might eventually be the West Germans who would annoy the US by delaying intra-European deliberations, Frank upon his return in Bonn proposed to let the French and British have their way. The FRG should no longer expose itself in the controversies over European–American relations, avoid the recurrence of the Franco-German disputes of the 1960s, work towards improving the British draft, and, if necessary, reject responsibility for a failure of the Nine and make clear that it would have preferred a more substantial declaration.[156]

Although it was the West Germans who deviated most from their course after these triangular exchanges, all three powers in late August and early September 1973 became satisfied with the manner in which the Nine prepared the upcoming seminal ministerial meeting in EPC. With respect to the draft declaration, the FRG was pleased that the British document became markedly extended and enriched in the course of the multilateral deliberations. The West Germans themselves inserted a clause about the 'lessons of history' demonstrating the need for close links between Europe and the US. They also put through, together with the Belgians, a reference to European security, and they managed to fend off attempts to efface references to a 'constructive dialogue' and work in 'harmony'.[157] To their own surprise, the French too managed to further shape the British draft to their liking.[158] They removed the notion of 'interdependence' and accentuated the principle which asked the US to acknowledge the Nine's global significance, which now read:

> The United States, recognizing that the creation of the Community is an event of great international importance and has enhanced the stability of Europe, welcome the intention of the nine to insure that the Community establishes its position in world affairs as a distinct entity.[159]

Generally, the French were extremely pleased at how the preparations evolved: 'Never, to my knowledge,' the French delegate reported to Jobert, 'had there been such an authentically European spirit in an endeavour dealing primarily with the US.'[160] The British, for their part, relieved that the French were now cooperative and that the West Germans 'kept their Atlantic preoccupations under control',[161] focused their attention to mediating and keeping the Nine together. In the words of an FCO official, who used the image of a convoy to describe the Nine in their relations with the US: 'The Federal Republic was leading the convoy and the French were lagging behind and the British destroyer was moving up and down the column keeping it reasonably together and in order.'[162] All nine governments also agreed to start the declaration by contrasting 'the United States of America on the one hand' with 'the European Community and its member states on the other hand'; to include in the preamble references to the EU project and to human rights; and to emphasise the essential and distinct role of the Nine with respect to détente, referring especially to their 'constructive contribution' at the CSCE.

If the Nine in their EPC preparations could only deal with the non-EC relevant aspects of the declaration, they also managed to agree on a procedure for the drafting in those fields which touched upon the competence of the Community, with the *Comité des représentants permanents* (COREPER) being tasked to work out respective principles. The EPC members further established consensus on how to negotiate their draft with the US, as France lifted its reservations about the nine political directors gathering with their US counterpart and accepted at least one such meeting at the end of September 1973. Importantly, all of the Nine, at French request, vowed not to support US proposals for changes in their draft other than by consensus. Finally, they also completed, based on a West German proposal, a list of ten subjects as an agenda for their talks with Nixon.[163]

When the nine foreign ministers, attentively observed by the media, reassembled in Copenhagen on 10 September 1973, they were in a position to reap the fruits of what had been the most intensive preparation of an EPC meeting up to that point.[164] There were still prolonged discussions among the ministers, not least because Andersen as chairman was, as Douglas-Home reported to London, 'his usual inept, if genial, self'.[165] In the end, the list of subjects, at French insistence, could only be communicated orally to Washington. Also, there was still no agreement about the form of the meeting with Nixon. Those two issues apart, however, the degree of consensus of the Nine was impressive. It reflected an enormous step forward for EPC. The Nine had developed both a common substantive position and a procedure to engage as a collective actor in negotiations with the US on a redefinition of European–American relations. By practical necessity, they had also come to agree on a closer link between EPC and EC, which was reflected in the fact that Commission President Ortoli participated in this meeting.[166] Moreover, as will be outlined in Chapter 5, they had already been able to take note of an interim report about their project of defining the European identity.

The photo shoot with the foreign ministers after the EPC meeting was reportedly characterised by unusual blithesomeness[167] – and, one would assume, great sighs of relief. Scheel talked of a turning point in European politics, while Douglas-Home spoke of a 'new kind of diplomacy'.[168] Perhaps the most joyful of all ministers was Jobert. He had been only too aware that some partners, such as the Italians, had kept Kissinger confidentially informed about all discussions going on in EPC in preceding weeks. But, as he lavishly recalled in his memoirs, he was all the more enthusiastic now that the Nine had still managed to define a common policy in the 'Year of Europe' primarily inspired by European, rather than US considerations.[169] There is, indeed, no doubt that the decisions taken at the September meeting in Copenhagen were a great accomplishment and marked an essential moment in the 'rise' of EPC in 1973. However, one key issue was yet to be answered: how would the Nixon administration take it?

A little French manoeuvre: Bringing NATO in

Having added to their draft declaration the economic principles worked out in the EC machinery, the Nine sent their document to Washington on 19 September 1973. Five months after Kissinger had launched his initiative, Europe was finally presenting a collective answer. Ahead of the Nine lay what the West Germans, perhaps ironically, coined a 'week of Europe' (*Europawoche*),[170] with several Community countries being scheduled to meet Kissinger in New York at the fringes of the UN General Assembly between 24 and 29 September 1973. Andersen, as EPC's acting president, was to officially discuss the draft on behalf of the Nine, while others such as Scheel, Douglas-Home, and Jobert were set to have a general exchange on the 'Year of Europe'. A meeting of the Political Committee with US representatives to discuss the European draft was also planned.

It was to be a week of seminal importance for EPC. The Europeans had little idea of what the US would make of their proposal. They headed to New York in the hope that the Nixon administration would eventually come round to support their effort to act as a collective political entity. As Brandt, who parallel to the nine foreign ministers stayed in the US because of the FRG's accession to the UN, argued in a speech in Chicago: the Community countries sought to convince their American partner that the 'new European confidence' would be mutually beneficial and that their goal was 'constructive competition', rather than 'destructive rivalry'.[171] Yet, the Nine could not rule out that the debates would become acrimonious again. Kissinger's forceful warning, only days before the New York meetings, that the Europeans would be grossly mistaken if they assumed that Nixon would sign any declaration just because of Watergate seemed to forebode new division.[172] The fact that the draft had been leaked to the US press before it had even reached the US government could have done little to calm tempers in the White House.[173]

As it turned out, the 'week of Europe' became a great success for the Nine. To be sure, Kissinger, who had become US secretary of state earlier in the month, did not spare the Europeans from criticism. In his talk with Andersen, he considered the draft feeble and showed disappointment that it neglected most US requests, while asking the US to endorse the European decisions of the Paris Summit in 1972. He also indicated that the US would make its final verdict of the draft dependent on the substance of the complementary draft to be worked out in the Alliance. And, he left no doubt that in the long run it would be unacceptable for the US to deal with the Nine via an envoy who was not authorised to negotiate.[174] There was also an element of US threat again, with Brandt being reminded by Nixon of the terrible price to be paid if Congress gained the impression that the Europeans were ganging up on Washington.[175]

And yet, Kissinger accepted the two-document approach, and he agreed to negotiate a European–American declaration with the Nine on the basis of their own draft. Remarkably, Kissinger even publicly lauded the European contribution in a press conference on 26 September 1973:

> With respect to the declaration that the European Nine have developed and that was presented to me yesterday on behalf of the Nine by Foreign Minister Andersen of Denmark, let me say that the United States recognizes that this first attempt by Europe to speak with one voice on a political matter of transatlantic relationships is an event of the greatest significance [...] It may be that in historical retrospect this meeting of the European Nine in Copenhagen will be seen as one of the decisive events of the postwar period.[176]

Although it is difficult to account fully for Kissinger's noteworthy change of attitude, several factors plausibly played a role. The assurance by both London and Bonn that close and confidential relationships could now be restored and run parallel to the emerging multilateral dialogue was received with cheers in the White House.[177] Also, now that the Nine had at last managed to speak with one voice, it was politically difficult for the US to repudiate their endeavour altogether; the more so since Kissinger, challenged by Douglas-Home to suggest a better procedure for the Nine to make a reality of a European common policy, had to admit that this was a 'tough' problem, which he had not really thought through.[178] Yet, the decisive impulse most probably came from a bilateral conversation Kissinger had with Jobert just before the press conference.

It was the usual bizarre kind of discussion between these by now major two protagonists of the 'Year of Europe'. Both Kissinger and Jobert seemed attracted by their counterpart's intellect, but at the same time distrusted each other's intentions. Both stressed their personal friendship, but regarded themselves as rivals. Both liked to exchange compliments for their diplomatic skill, while simultaneously trying to trick each other. This time, it was Jobert's turn. Good-humoured, Kissinger started the conversation by admitting that Jobert had really 'out-manoeuvred' him. Jobert confessed being a 'mischievous spirit' and repaid the compliment by calling the US secretary of state an 'agitator'. When Kissinger warned that Europe was currently playing 'Russian roulette', the French foreign minister urged him not to 'destroy' what the Nine were just about to build up. He then put on the table what Kissinger in his memoirs called 'the most constructive gesture of any European minister'[179] in the Atlantic dialogue: a French draft declaration on Atlantic relations of the Fifteen.[180]

It was the product of what Jobert internally had called his 'idea of a manoeuvre'.[181] In early September 1973, he had tasked the French permanent representative to NATO, François de Rose, to secretly draft a substantive declaration on allied relations. The document should be worked out without involving the Quai d'Orsay, which he regarded as too critical of the Alliance and which in August had come up with a draft he disliked. Jobert's idea was, as he informed de Rose, to please the US with an impressive declaration of the Fifteen in order to get Washington's approval for the European draft on relations between the Nine and the US. Nixon and Kissinger should subscribe to Europe's political emancipation in return for a strong text on allied defence.[182]

Kissinger could hardly believe his eyes when he read the French draft, which de Rose, in all secrecy, had translated into English once Jobert had cleared the text with Pompidou. The document, eye-catching even by its eloquent language, naturally contained references to issues that were important to Paris: it interpreted the superpower agreement on the prevention of nuclear war in a way that reconfirmed the US deterrence guarantee for Europe; it stated why it was in American self-interest to keep their troops in Europe; and it stressed both the European contributions to allied defence and the dissuasive effect of French and British nuclear weapons. However, the draft also comprised surprising French concessions to US requirements: it emphasised the indivisibility of allied security; identified common defence as an indispensable requisite of détente; pointed to the need to adapt NATO's strategy; and committed the Europeans to maintain sufficient force levels.[183]

Kissinger could only congratulate Jobert on his 'admirable effort'.[184] Even though the French foreign minister resolutely rejected the US proposal to strengthen the clause on allied consultations and further add references to MBFR, burden-sharing, and the need to improve forces, Kissinger agreed to start negotiations on an allied declaration on the basis of the French draft.[185] With France tabling its draft in the Alliance on 3 October 1973,[186] discussions among the Fifteen, therefore, also eventually gained momentum. Debates in NATO on the 'Year in Europe', despite draft proposals by several delegations,[187] had been marginalised by great power bilateralism and had become effectively blocked in the summer of 1973 by the disinclination of the US and France to get down to serious work prior to the EPC September meeting.[188] Only when the French eventually presented their draft were all allies willing to start negotiating – and did Kissinger seem to believe again that his initiative could still yield worthwhile results.

The French manoeuvre, there is little doubt, had its share in persuading the US to let the Nine have their own declaration. Accordingly, the first-ever collective political negotiations between the Community countries and the US started in a friendly and constructive atmosphere. It was on 29 September 1973 that the EPC Political Committee gathered in the Danish mission at the UN for a preliminary exchange of views with the US, represented by Walter Stoessel, assistant secretary of state for European affairs, and Helmut Sonnenfeldt, an NSC member and confidant of Kissinger (also referred to as 'Kissinger's Kissinger'[189]). The US delegates still criticised the European draft as 'thin' and came up with a long list of amendments. In particular, they proposed inserting the notions of 'partnership' and 'interdependence;' calling for 'new means' of consultation rather than improving existing ones; including Japan in the economic aspects; and referring not only to the CSCE, but also to MBFR. Nonetheless, they officially agreed to negotiate on the basis of the draft of the Nine, with a first round of negotiation being scheduled for mid-October 1973. The Nine, for their part, kept to the procedure agreed, with their Danish chairman conducting the proceedings and all others adding their comments. Throughout the meeting, the Nine managed to stand together as if there had never been any division between them. It spoke volumes for EPC's success and gave reason to optimistically look ahead. As the British after the 'week of Europe' contentedly noted: 'The show is on the road.'[190]

The rise of European diplomacy

By early October 1973, the Nine had reason to be content with their perform-ance in the 'Year of Europe'. They had managed to transform an Atlantic ini-tiative, which they had regarded as largely incompatible with their interests, into a European–American project that promised to accentuate their own role both within the West and in world politics. They had begun to develop a com-mon policy and speak with one voice vis-à-vis Washington. They had been able to seize the initiative from the US and with their two-declaration concept had become the linchpin of inter-allied deliberations. And, significantly, they had eventually succeeded in getting Kissinger's approval for their approach, which in itself gave cause to rejoice.

As in the case of the CSCE, several factors contributed to this remarkable advance of European Political Cooperation. At the extra-European level of the international environment, the US initiative to vastly expand Atlantic cooper-ation posed a direct challenge to European unity. It conflicted with the goal set by the Nine to further strengthen the economic and political unification of the enlarged Community and generally called into question the viability of a dis-tinct European actor in international affairs. The 'Year of Europe' compelled the Nine to move together in defending common interests. This implied the need to finally address the two crucial issues of defining the Nine's relations with the US and identifying the idiosyncrasies of their own collective identity. It also provided an opportunity for Europe to assert its political ambition. Kissinger's initiative, thus, became a catalyst for European unity.

Détente too played an important role. The absence of an immediate Soviet threat to European security meant that the Nine were no longer in a position where they were essentially obliged to comply with American designs and poli-cies at all costs. The EC countries continued to be dependent on Washington for their security and still had an overarching interest in good relations with their major ally. However, in 1973, they had more leeway to negotiate the specifics of transatlantic relations with the Western hegemonic power than at anytime before in the Cold War. At the same time, superpower détente prompted the Europeans, and especially the French, to intensify their political cooperation, both to stand their ground in international diplomacy and to effectively articulate their needs to the US.

Watergate was a third external factor fostering the advance of EPC. With the White House being increasingly discredited on Capitol Hill, uncertainty as to the reliability of US foreign policy was rapidly mounting. This induced many Europeans to help Nixon in his domestic struggle, not least by responding to

Kissinger's appeal. Conversely, the fact that Nixon was in dire need of a foreign policy success also gave the Nine some leverage as to the substance of the declarations. Nixon and Kissinger had to realise that assembling the Europeans to deliver aid to them, as in 1947, was a much easier task than assembling them to ask for aid. As Watergate made it difficult for the US to abandon its initiative, the Nine found it easier to transform the 'Year of Europe' to their own advantage than would have been the case under normal circumstances.

As for the intra-European level, the collective will of the Nine to use the unexpected US initiative as a means with which to forge European unity was an important factor in Europe's political progress in the summer and autumn of 1973. In his memoirs, Kissinger contemptuously labelled the Nine a 'coalition of negation' welded together by Jobert, whom he accused of having exploited 'the smaller countries' uneasiness about dictation from the Big Four, West Germany's reluctance to inhibit *Ostpolitik* within a larger grouping, and Heath's determination to demonstrate his 'European vocation'.[191] There is no doubt that the French foreign minister shaped the timetable of Europe's response and had more than a little share in assuring that the European draft was not more forthcoming to US requirements. Yet, it is important to note that all Europeans shared a predominantly negative assessment of White House intentions with the 'Year of Europe', that the Eight had made the case for a common European response much earlier than France had, and that all Nine, rather than just France, were eager to use the initiative to Europe's purposes and contrast Kissinger's Atlantic design with their own desire to expand European unity.

A shared perception by the Nine that European and American interests diverged significantly not only in the economic realm, but also in key foreign policy fields, such as the Middle East and the CSCE, gave further reason for them to amplify their own political efforts. Another important factor at the intra-European level was the collective recognition the Nine had gained from the CSCE that political cooperation could be an effective and worthwhile endeavour. This kind of reassurance provided a solid foundation from which to venture on the much more sensitive territory of defining a European policy with respect to the US. As Douglas-Home told Ortoli after the Copenhagen meeting on 10 September 1973, the astonishing success of the Nine in defining European–American relations would have been impossible had it not been for the mutual confidence they had obtained during their cooperation in Helsinki.[192]

The individual level of European foreign policy-making was also relevant for the rise of EPC in this first phase of the 'Year of Europe'. Without Jobert, it seems unlikely that France's reassessment of its European policy under conditions of superpower détente would have resulted in such a stark move towards the political unification of Europe. It is also improbable that the French would have come to view the US initiative as an opportunity to advance their own European priorities. As for Britain, Heath's 'Europe-first' policy in the 'Year of Europe' was immensely important to bring France on board. The fact that even the FRG, the most vulnerable partner of the Nine, despite US pressure stuck to the concept of a European draft and, after a brief period of unease, actively contributed to its formulation, also had to do with personalities, as well as individual beliefs and aspirations. Without Scheel's enthusiasm for and Brandt's resolute support of a new bilateralism between the uniting EC-Nine and Washington, no common European position on how to redefine Atlantic relations is likely to ever have emerged.

The one big issue that remained unresolved was whether the US would accept and support Europe's quest for a distinct political profile in the long run. Such US benevolence obviously was a *sine qua non* condition for the Nine to succeed. To be sure, Kissinger had become reconciliatory and had agreed on European–American negotiations. Yet, as Cromer in a letter to London in early October 1973 warned, the winds could easily change direction again and 'bring some pretty sharp squalls with it'.[193] The unpredictable consequences of Watergate constituted one reason why the Europeans could not rule out once again becoming the focus of Nixon's scorn. Several other uncertainties that troubled the Nine related to the short-term problem of finding agreement with the US on the specific products of the 'Year of Europe': What would happen if they proved unable to agree on concessions demanded by the US, which was bound to insist on a less cursory treatment of transatlantic problems? What would happen if they failed to achieve consensus with Washington on amendments to the Alliance draft that was so important to the White House? Moreover, would they be able to eventually meet US expectations with regard to the level and form of Nixon's meetings in Europe?

Yet, the biggest European concern related to the more general issue of the future of European–American relations. There was agreement among the Nine that most of the transatlantic strain that had occurred in recent months could be attributed to Kissinger's own doings. If Kissinger now had come to accept collective negotiations between the Nine and the US on the European draft, there was no indication yet that he would go along with a degree of European emancipation in the field of foreign policy. Nor were there any signs that he would be supportive of the European decision to identify the US, out of all states, as the first Western government to be addressed collectively by the Nine.

The urgency of these issues for the EPC countries increased further when the US in the course of the autumn of 1973 became gradually less preoccupied with the economic–defence link in the 'Year of Europe' and, instead, shifted its attention to Europe's foreign policy ambitions and the question of how to link EPC deliberations into the larger framework of Atlantic consultations. For several reasons, economic tensions over the Atlantic receded in the second half of 1973. At the onset of a new round of GATT negotiations in Tokyo, the EC and the US had managed to establish basic agreement on the course of further trade liberalisation. Another accord had been hammered out at the IMF annual meeting in Nairobi in September 1973, where it had been decided to accelerate the creation of a new international monetary system. A sharply increased demand for grain on the world market had meant that the US lobby against the CAP had begun to wane. Most important of all, a further 10 per cent devaluation of the US Dollar in February 1973 had caused a dramatic turnaround in the US balance of payments, which now was on its way back into surplus and positively influenced other US economic indicators.[194]

With domestic economic pressure in the US diminishing, the issue of the Nine's role within the West was gradually coming to the foreground during the autumn of 1973 in the 'Year of Europe'. Of course this had much to do with the Nine's own bold performance and their request that Washington acknowledge their distinct role in international diplomacy. Yet, Kissinger's insistence on including the US in the formative period of EPC decision-making left the Nine wondering how they could ever formulate their own policies.[195] From their perspective, the issue boiled down to the question of whether Nixon and Kissinger would lend their support to the further advancement of the European project or whether they would perceive the growing unity of the Nine as an unwelcome bloc within NATO and a potential obstacle to US foreign policy and their aspired structure of peace. At least the British and the West Germans were optimistic that the Nine would gain US backing if only Nixon and Kissinger developed a better understanding of how EPC worked and what the Europeans tried to achieve. The deliberations of Heath and Brandt during their bilateral summit of 6 October 1973 on how to best educate the US government in this respect were abruptly interrupted, however.[196] As war broke out again in the Middle East, international events unfolded that came to pose another formidable challenge to the Nine – and brought frictions back into Atlantic relations and the 'Year of Europe' negotiations.

Chapter 5
Into the Middle East: The October War, the oil crisis, and Europe's political identity

The last three months of 1973 constituted a period of tension and drama in international politics. The October War and the related oil crisis brought further instability to the Middle East, heavy strain on superpower détente, and new ruptures in transatlantic relations. They also caused a severe economic crisis, with inflation rapidly mounting and recession looming. The world with bated breath was witnessing how a series of events in quick succession invalidated several topoi of both diplomacy and the world economic system. First, there were the coordinated surprise attacks of Egyptian and Syrian forces on Israeli forces in the Sinai and the Golan Heights of 6 October 1973. Launching the fourth Arab–Israeli war, they belied the belief that Israel's ever-growing military superiority would deter the Arabs from reclaiming the occupied territories by military means. Then, there were the grave US–Soviet tensions over violations of the cease-fire of 22 October 1973, which culminated in the Nixon administration staging a nuclear alert. Escalating to the most dangerous East–West crisis since the early 1960s, this superpower confrontation appeared to put the whole rapprochement between Washington and Moscow in jeopardy. Finally, there was the oil crisis, which put enormous financial strain on oil-consuming countries and provoked a new sense of vulnerability among industrialised nations, bringing back a feeling of want to societies shaped by consumerism and accustomed to cheap energy and constant economic growth.

These turbulent developments also inevitably threatened to affect the security of Europe. Any military clash between the superpowers over the Middle East was bound to involve European territory. Politically, a collapse of superpower détente was likely to have adverse effects on détente in Europe too. Most tangible and menacing, however, was the crippling effect the Middle East crisis had on European economies. Being much more dependent on oil imports than the US, the Nine came under enormous pressure by the Arab challenge. For the first time in post-war history, Europe felt primarily threat-ened not by the military might of the Soviet Union, but by economic policies of a peculiar group of developing countries, which introduced a new North–South dimension into European security. The challenge for the Nine was the more complex since the Arab oil producers did not treat them as a group, but differentiated their export cuts according to the degree of support given by individual EC members to the Arab cause.

In the face of such external pressures, EPC took another remarkable leap forward. Against the background of the dire straits in which they suddenly found themselves, the Nine considered it imperative to now get involved in finding a solution to the Arab–Israeli conflict. On 6 November 1973, they issued a Declaration on the Middle East that contained a common policy on the Arab–Israeli conflict. Parallel to this breakthrough in policy harmonisa-tion, further efforts were made to generally strengthen Europe's political weight in the world, by bringing the heads of state and government into EPC, and by intensifying the discussions on European defence. By the end of the year, EPC reached a peak in its dynamic development, reflected in the publica-tion of a Declaration on European Identity by the Nine in mid-December 1973. This positive development occurred not least because France, in reac-tion to Europe's marginalisation during the October War, paid prime attention to EPC, which it now regarded as the royal path to European unification.

However, the growing political unity of the Nine also became exposed to new pressures and sources of friction towards the end of the year. There were renewed sharp European–American rows over the Middle East, with threat perceptions, interests, and policies of the Nine and the US being glaringly divergent. Negotiations on the two declarations of the 'Year of Europe' in this poisoned climate quickly stagnated. By the end of the year, Kissinger came up with new proposals to rebuild and reinforce the Atlantic partnership, which reopened the debate on Europe's role within the West with a vengeance. Moreover, there was a mounting economic crisis within the EC. Key projects of the Community, such as EMU and the RDF, failed to make progress for lack of agreement, which made the ambitious programme of the Paris Summit look increasingly unattainable. Inability to agree on effective economic policies to deal with the oil crisis acerbated the strained climate in Brussels, with accusa-tions of lack of solidarity threatening to undermine the very basis of European integration.

The summit of the Nine in Copenhagen in mid-December 1973, originally called by Pompidou to discuss the future of European foreign policy, under these circumstances turned into a crisis meeting, concerned mainly with damage limitation. From an EPC perspective, its results were not bad. Yet, the meeting largely ignored the transatlantic issues and failed to deal resolutely with the economic challenge. It remained unclear, therefore, as to whether Europe would proceed with new dynamism in 1974 or would fall into a prolonged crisis.

Tarzan speaks!

There is no doubt that EPC dynamics during the autumn of 1973 profited from both the October War and the oil crisis. The external pressure deriving from these crises gave a triple boost to European foreign policy cooperation: it led the Nine to further elaborate and harmonise their policy vis-à-vis the Arab–Israeli conflict; it induced the French to fully back further progress in EPC and defence cooperation; and it prompted the beginning of the Euro-Arab dialogue, a French idea launched in December 1973, which came to fruition in early 1974. Also important, after their debut in multilateral diplomacy in the context of the CSCE and their confidential deliberations in working out a common policy concerning the 'Year of Europe', the Nine with their Middle East declaration published for the first time a joint substantive diplomatic statement in November 1973. Three years after EPC had been launched, European publics bore witness to how the EC–Nine, whom Davignon had repeatedly compared to Tarzan, that is, muscular commercially, but with fairly scanty speech,[1] eventually began to express themselves with one voice in world politics.

Energy and European security

The October War, also referred to as Yom Kippur War (the Arab attack occurring on the Day of Atonement, the most important Jewish holiday), caught both Israel and the US by surprise. Although there had been intelligence about Egyptian and Syrian war preparations and a great deal of Arab war rhetoric throughout 1973, Tel Aviv and Washington took these signs as a bluff.[2] In view of the gross military inferiority of Israel's neighbours, they ruled out any military operation as self-defeating. However, the rationale of the Egyptian leader Anwar al-Sadat was different. Unlike Hafez al-Assad, his radical Syrian ally, who was out to recapture the Golan Heights and would never accept Israel's right of existence, Sadat sought a limited war only. He was well aware that it would be impossible for Egypt to regain militarily the territory that had been lost in 1967. Yet, he considered an attack on Israel's occupation zones indispensable to building up a stronger posture for a subsequent diplomatic solution. By going to war Sadat hoped to overcome Arab humiliation and restore self-respect. Moreover, he aimed at eventually bringing the White House in to mediate between the conflicting parties, since Nixon and Kissinger, despite promises to the contrary, had continued their hands-off policy towards the Middle East following the 1972 US elections.[3]

Sadat achieved both goals. It is true that he lost the October War militarily. By mid-October 1973, Israel had launched a decisive counter-offensive, forcing the Syrian army back and subsequently pushing the Egyptians over the Suez Canal again. Led by General Ariel Sharon, among others, the Israeli army by 20 October had not only regained the temporarily lost territories, but was even on its way to Damascus and Cairo. Yet, Sadat won the war psychologically, with the Arab troops fighting much better than expected. Both the Israeli government of Prime Minister Golda Meir and the Nixon administration were convinced that Israel would win an overwhelming and rapid victory within two or three days. Yet, Israeli losses during the first days were staggeringly high, which shocked Tel Aviv and destroyed the myth of Israeli invincibility. Even more important for Sadat, he also won the war diplomatically. The October War put the Arab–Israeli conflict immediately on top of the US foreign policy agenda, with Kissinger emerging as the key player of the peace process that got underway once the cease-fire of 22 October 1973 took hold.[4]

During the war, Kissinger's foremost concern was the support and protection of Israel. At various times he stalled or pushed for cease-fire resolutions at the UN, very much in accordance with Israeli policy preferences. Moreover, once it became clear that Israel would militarily remain on the defensive much longer than predicted, Washington launched a massive airlift to re-supply Israeli capabilities.[5] Kissinger's second major preoccupation was escalation control with the Soviet Union. From his perspective, the October War, beyond its regional implications, was a test for superpower détente. There was, indeed, much consultation going on between Washington and Moscow during the fighting. Significantly, UN Security Council Resolution 338 on a cease-fire, which became finally accepted on 22 October 1973, had been jointly worked out between Kissinger and Brezhnev in the Kremlin. It called for the implementation of Resolution 242 and for immediate negotiations 'between the parties concerned' under 'appropriate auspices'.[6] However, superpower relations were also marked by intense competition and strain during the war. At the UN, both the US and the Soviet Union gave priority to representing the interests of their respective clients over jointly seeking to stop the fighting. Furthermore, both sent thousands of tons of war materials daily to support their allies in the battlefield.

In addition, they almost clashed over violations of the cease-fire on 24/25 October 1973, causing shock among publics unprepared for such an escalatory development. The war, in fact, turned into a major East–West crisis after the Israeli had taken Kissinger's hint that they might fight just a little longer after the cease-fire as green light to continue their offensive against Egypt. While it remains unclear which side violated the cease-fire first, the result was that Egypt's Third Army became surrounded and cut off, with the US experiencing great difficulty in refraining Israel from working towards the complete defeat and humiliation of Sadat. The new Resolution 339 urged the parties to return to the lines of 22 October and mandated UN observers to supervise the cease-fire.[7] Yet, it failed to stop the fighting, which provoked Sadat to call for the intervention of US and Soviet troops. Brezhnev, who was furious about Israeli non-compliance with the cease-fire, pressed Nixon in several letters to exert his influence on Israel. On 24 October 1973, he even threatened to act unilaterally to enforce the cease-fire if the US failed to play its part. Although considered by many observers as a Soviet bluff, the Nixon administration reacted harshly, putting its troops on the highest peacetime alert, before rejecting both unilateral Soviet and bilateral Soviet–American intervention in the Middle East. The next day, a new UN resolution, Resolution 340, was passed as if nothing had happened, calling for an immediate cease-fire and creating a UN Emergency Force (UNEF) to secure its implementation.[8] Moscow had accepted that UNEF would be composed of forces other than those of the five UN veto powers, which quickly defused superpower tensions again. As the fighting on the ground too came to a halt, peace talks could finally begin.

It was in this post-war diplomacy that Sadat received what he wanted, as Kissinger began to tour the Middle East in search of peace. Unlike Nixon and Brezhnev, who both supported a joint American–Soviet role in putting pressure on the parties to agree to a comprehensive settlement, Kissinger's strategic post-war objective was to exclude Moscow from the peace process and render the US the major peace-broker in the Middle East. Sadat supported Kissinger's quest for US unilateral diplomacy and also accepted his preference for a step-by-step approach. Following an initial Egyptian–Israeli agreement on non-military supplies for the Third Army and a release of war prisoners resulting from direct military talks at km 101 on the Cairo–Suez road, the US secretary of state embarked on his famous 'shuttle diplomacy' in the Middle East. This led to an Egyptian–Israeli disengagement agreement in January 1974, and an agreement to disengage Syrian and Israeli forces on the Golan

Heights in May 1974.[9] Parallel to this, a multilateral peace conference was convened in Geneva in mid-December 1973, with delegations from the US, the Soviet Union, Israel, Egypt, and Jordan taking part (there was also an empty Syrian seat). Yet, this turned out to be a largely symbolic act, as Kissinger's parallel bilateral diplomacy and piecemeal approach prevailed. While the Geneva talks on a comprehensive settlement in early January 1974 were adjourned indefinitely, Egypt and the US were beginning to form a strategic relationship, which changed the parameters of the search for peace in the Arab–Israeli conflict and foreshadowed the Camp David accords and Israel's withdrawal from the Sinai in 1978/79.[10]

Europe was absent from all these efforts at peacemaking. During the October War, two European powers, France and Great Britain, as members of the Security Council were involved in the UN attempts at establishing a ceasefire. However, their role was a largely formal one, as the real negotiations took place between the superpowers. After the war, the Europeans were also excluded from the Geneva Conference, and they had no direct impact on Kissinger's unilateral diplomacy in the Arab–Israeli conflict. Europe's absence from diplomacy in the Middle East weighed all the heavier since vested European interests were at stake in the region. It was not just that countries such as France or Britain were anxious about a further erosion of their traditional ties and spheres of influence in the Arab world; more relevant and worrisome to the Nine as a unit were the threats to European security that emanated from the escalating conflict in the Middle East. Situated in Europe's proximity, the Arab–Israeli conflict had always caused concern in Europe as to its repercussions on regional and global stability. In the early 1970s, Western Europe had become increasingly afflicted by terrorist attacks of radical Palestinians extending their fight against Israel to the industrialised world. Furthermore, the prominent role of the superpowers in the October War added an East–West dimension to the conflict that both further reduced Europe's influence in the region and threatened to bring about new superpower confrontation and jeopardise European détente. The biggest danger for European security, however, stemmed from the oil crisis, which emerged in parallel to the October War and was partly related to it. The Middle East was of strategic relevance to Europe in terms of energy supplies, which is why the Nine became heavily affected by the developments of October and November 1973, and began to try to actively shape the politics of the Middle East.

The oil crisis of 1973/74 had two major components. On the one hand, the Organization of Petroleum Exporting Countries (OPEC) wrested control from the multinational oil companies over crude oil prices and production levels in the autumn of 1973, with the Persian Gulf producers on 16 October 1973 deciding to increase the price of oil by 70 per cent, and a further OPEC price increase occurring in December 1973. This change of sovereignty over oil supplies was not specifically tied to the Arab–Israeli conflict, but was the culmination of a process that had been going on for several years. While a consortium of seven large oil companies, the so-called 'Seven Sisters', had previously exerted a de facto monopoly over the oil market, the producing countries by the late 1960s had begun to assert their own rights to the oil wealth. The rise to power of Qadhafi in Libya had triggered a development in the course of which the producing countries had gradually taken over the ownership of and operational control over oil from the Western enterprises. Since the demand for oil in the industrialised world had been rapidly rising at the same time, the OPEC decision ushered in a new phase of post-war history: at a time when the industrialised countries were becoming ever more dependent on oil, they lost access to guaranteed cheap energy supplies.[11]

The second component of the oil crisis was the 'oil weapon' applied by Arab oil producers, with a view to forcing the consumer nations, and the US in particular, into supporting the Arab point of view with respect to the resolution of the Arab–Israeli conflict. This component was directly linked to the October War and a measure taken in support of the Egyptian–Syrian cause. On 17 October 1973, one day after the OPEC decision, the Organization of Arab Petroleum Exporting Countries (OAPEC) in Kuwait agreed on immediate production cutbacks of 5 per cent, followed by further monthly cutbacks until Israel withdrew to its 1967 borders. On 4 November 1973, the decision was modified insofar as production cuts of 25 per cent of the September levels were made. These production cuts applied to countries judged neutral in the Arab–Israeli conflict. Those countries considered 'hostile' to the Arab position faced a complete embargo, while 'friendly' countries were destined to receive supplies as normal.[12]

The cumulative effect of both developments was extremely serious. Oil prices soared, with a fourfold increase between October 1973 and January 1974. The world economy, already suffering from inflation, slid into the worst recession for decades, with unemployment rapidly rising. The new wealth of petrodollars of producer governments brought further instability to the international economic system and negatively affected the balance of payments of consumer countries. If today it is clear that there never was a serious shortage of oil supplies in 1973/74, as the oil companies quietly distributed oil and spread the damage fairly evenly among consumer countries, there was a feeling of want at the time and a perception that the decade-long rise in prosperity was about to be reversed.[13]

Thus, oil became a matter of national security in 1973/74, especially in Western Europe. In contrast to the US, Western Europe was highly dependent on oil supplies from the Middle East. In 1973, it imported 62.9 per cent of its energy supplies, compared to 17.4 per cent in the case of the US. Some 45 per cent of its energy needs were covered by Arab oil, compared to only 5 to 6 per cent in the case of the US.[14] In the FRG, for instance, oil made up more than half of West German energy consumption, with about 71 per cent of oil imports stemming from Arab producers.[15] As governments in industrialised countries in the early months of the crisis focused much more on the production cutbacks than on the price rises, the lack of large national stocks of oil was considered to be particularly problematic. In most Western European countries, measures such as speed limits, bans on Sunday driving, or bans on late-night television were introduced to save energy. Voluntary restraint measures, such as restricted heating or car-pooling, were also encouraged. In Britain, street lighting was curtailed, and petrol-rationing books were even issued as a contingency measure.[16]

At the risk of comparing apples with pears, it could be argued that Western Europe's economic security was as dependent on Arab oil as its military security was dependent on the US nuclear umbrella. This dependency on imports from the Middle East was the more remarkable as it was starkly one-sided. Moreover, the oil crisis not only threatened Western Europe's economies, but also posed a direct political challenge to the unity of the Nine, with OAPEC treating individual members of the Community differently with its 'oil weapon': France and Great Britain were regarded as 'friendly' nations and received normal oil supplies; the Dutch, like the US, were confronted with an oil embargo; and the remaining Six were grouped as 'neutral' and faced phased production cuts.[17] To make matters worse, OAPEC ministers threatened further sanctions against any country assisting embargoed countries by reallocating oil.[18] The differentiated economic treatment of the Community countries by the Arab oil producers was a glaring expression of the failure of the Nine to develop a common political approach towards the Arab–Israeli conflict prior to the outbreak of the October War. At the same time, once the fighting had begun, the Nine were repeatedly called upon by Arab leaders to get diplomatically involved in peacemaking and urge Israel to withdraw from the occupied territories.[19] Some of them also received sharp letters from Qadhafi, the most radical of all Arab leaders, who threatened Europe with severe consequences if it stayed passive, and even went so far as to secretly ask Pompidou for nuclear weapons to get the upper hand in the fight against Israel.[20]

Given the manifold challenges to the security and unity of the Nine that originated from the oil crisis and the October War, pressure was mounting for the Community members to get together and act on two fronts. On the diplomatic front, there was a need to finally come up with a joint policy on the Arab–Israeli conflict, not so much to appease the Arabs, but because all of the above-mentioned challenges, except OPEC's new strength as a producer cartel, were directly related to this perennial antagonism. On the economic front, an adequate response to the energy crisis and the Dutch embargo was required, which was linked to the issue of a Community energy policy. In the following, I will deal with Europe's diplomatic response to the double crisis, covering the issue of an EC energy policy further below.

Crises foreseen: Europe's triple frustration

For the Nine, the months prior to the outbreak of the October War were marked by anxiety with regard to the Middle East. Compared to the Nixon administration, the West Europeans were much more pessimistic about the effectiveness of Israeli–American deterrence against further Arab military attacks. Related to this negative assessment, they were more worried than the US about a coming energy crisis and the use of the 'oil weapon' by the Arabs. They were, thus, greatly alarmed about developments in the Middle East. However, their sense of urgency contrasted sharply with their inability to act. The Nine found it impossible to do anything to prevent either the resumption of hostilities or the oil crisis that was to hit them so badly. Consequently, their frame of mind on the eve of the double crisis was marked by a sense of frustration. They were dissatisfied with US Middle Eastern policies, with Israeli stubbornness, as well as with their own weakness.

There was great disappointment in Europe that the Nixon administration, despite earlier promises, continued to be unwilling to try to break the diplomatic impasse in the Middle East.[21] Being convinced that only US pressure would bring Israel to a more compromising stance that could lead to a mutually satisfactory settlement, the Europeans were worried about the consequences of the apparent White House policy of providing the Israelis with ever-more military goods, while putting the Egyptians off with words and shunning any mediating role.[22] They became ever more gloomy when the US as the only Security Council member vetoed a resolution in July 1973 that called the Israeli occupation of the occupied territories 'illegal', seemingly being indifferent to Sadat's warning that this was Egypt's last attempt at searching for a diplomatic solution.[23]

European frustration with the US had to do with their divergent assessments of the likelihood of another military confrontation in the Middle East. The Nine took the Arab sabre-rattling in the early months of 1973 very seriously. It is not that they would have understood Sadat's rationale for going to war any more than Kissinger; rather, they considered it possible, and increasingly likely, that Egypt could resort to the last desperate measure of all-out confrontation in response to its economic destitution and political humiliation, and under the pressure of its agitated masses. As the FCO put it: 'In logical terms it is hard to believe that the Egyptians would launch an attack. But logic was not always a true guide to the Middle East.'[24] Of course, there were nuances in the perceptions of the EPC members: France, Britain, Denmark, and the Dutch were particularly pessimistic about another war, whereas the FRG, for example, held a more optimistic view.[25] Nevertheless, all Nine agreed in a joint EPC report of 22 May 1973 that another Arab–Israeli confrontation was a 'plausible hypothesis' and could not be ruled out even for the second half of the year.[26]

Countries such as Britain were, thus, indefatigable in their efforts to convince the US of the growing dangers of war. On 10 May 1973, Douglas-Home rejected Kissinger's argument that 'the strongest leverage on Arabs was the danger of another crushing defeat' and, instead, warned that 'the whole Middle East might flare up' again.[27] Yet, the British had to realise that Washington did not even deem a settlement necessarily desirable. It was common European thinking that the absence of an Arab–Israeli settlement was detrimental to Western interests, as it threatened to further radicalise the Arabs, who in their frustration might increasingly look to the West for scapegoats and lean to the Soviet Union for support. The US, however, seemed to consider the Soviet Union the only strategic gainer from a settlement, as Moscow would get free access through the Suez Canal to its fleet in the Indian Ocean. Moreover, the Americans argued, Arab elites might prove more difficult to control following a settlement. They would no longer have to vie for Western support for their cause, and they could no longer distract their domestic audiences from their own incompetence and corruption by referring to the struggle with Israel, which was bound to provoke more radical revolutions.[28]

European and American perceptions of the issue of oil supplies also diverged. In 1972/73, recognition was growing on both sides of the Atlantic that an energy crisis was looming, with OPEC growing ever stronger. There was disagreement, however, as to the probability of the Arabs applying the 'oil weapon'. The Nixon administration argued that in circumstances short of hostilities, the Arabs were unlikely to tap off oil supplies, which is why Israel's deterrence capabilities should be further strengthened. The West Europeans, in contrast, feared that Arab frustration could lead to the interruption of energy supplies from the Middle East, even if Egypt chose not to go to war.[29] Again, assessments among the Nine were not identical. The West German foreign ministry agreed that Europe needed to prepare, but its Middle East experts in September 1973 still estimated that the 'oil weapon' was not likely to be used in the immediate future. France, by contrast, sensed a more acute threat, with Pompidou already warning Nixon at their Reykjavik summit in May 1973 that the Arabs had finally become conscious of their power and might well begin to blackmail consumer nations.[30] Yet, no one was more aware of the imminent danger than Heath. Whether in Bonn or in Paris, the British prime minister alerted his colleagues during his visits that the Arabs would 'soon use their commercial position for political means' and could put the very 'basis of industrial power in Western Europe' into jeopardy.[31] In a letter to Nixon, Heath once more urged the US to use its 'unique influence' over Tel Aviv to facilitate progress in the search for peace in the Middle East, forecasting that 'unless Israel can be persuaded to show a greater willingness to withdraw from the territories she occupied in 1967, vital Western interests will soon be at risk'.[32]

Israel was, indeed, the second focal point of European frustration, proving even more immune than the US to the European argument that the situation in the Middle East was less stable than might seem. The Israeli stubbornly stuck to the view that the status quo gave them the security they wanted and denied any need to negotiate with the Arabs, except on their own terms. Tel Aviv continued to insist on direct talks and rejected the Arab demand of committing Israel to withdrawal prior to any negotiations. Golda Meir's explanation to Brandt that it might appear presumptuous if a small country such as Israel believed itself to be always in the right, but that this was indeed the case, reflected an improvidence and self-assuredness characteristic of Israel's policy in the summer of 1973.[33] Meir's uncompromising position was all the more troubling for the Europeans since her country continued building more settlements in the occupied territories, which was set to render an already complex conflict even more intractable.

Europe's biggest frustration, however, related to its own incapacity to avert the impending crises. In the months prior to the October War, the Nine pursued four different paths to meet the looming Arab challenge. None of these paths led anywhere, however, as internal disunity constrained the Europeans in taking effective action. First, there was the idea for the Nine to jointly approach the US and urge Europe's major ally to get involved in Middle East diplomacy. This never materialised, as some EPC members considered it inappropriate to demand of Washington to put pressure on Israel, while others did not believe that external signals would do anything to clear away the domestic obstacles in the US to pushing Tel Aviv towards peace negotiations.[34] Second, there was an Italian proposal in the spring of 1973 for a European initiative towards Egypt, with the Community injecting $5 billion over ten years for the reconstruction and rehabilitation of the Egyptian economy. Here too disagreement prevailed. Some, like the British, considered it naïve to think that economic progress would defer the Egyptians from going to war. There was also resistance from national treasuries. Other arguments against the economic approach were the exclusive assistance to one Arab country; the fact that results would only become visible in the long run; and the expected difficulties in assembling private sector money for the public–private partnerships as foreseen in the Italian *Aide Mémoire*.[35]

More disturbing from a European perspective than the failure to take specific action was the double inability of the Nine to further refine a common European position on the Arab–Israeli conflict and to formulate a common energy policy, the third and fourth of the European approaches referred to above. Starting with EPC's Middle East consultations, the meetings in 1973 prior to the outbreak of the October War did not yield any concrete results. EPC's stagnation in this field, which contrasted with the marked successes of the Nine concerning the CSCE and the 'Year of Europe', was the consequence of a somehow over-ambitious start in 1971 (see Chapter 2). In the first nine months of 1973, there *were* some encouraging signs concerning the feasibility of a common Middle East position. Most notably, the Dutch, traditionally the most pro-Israeli country in EPC, began to move away from their one-sided support of Tel Aviv to a more balanced position in view of an ever-hardening Israeli policy.[36] However, at the level of EPC experts, this did not yet translate into any progress towards a common policy. Several experts judged the risk of provoking another internal or external row to be far greater than the prospect that a more detailed and explicit European position could contribute anything constructive to the mitigation of tension in the Middle East. As for the ministerial level of EPC consultations, the Arab–Israeli conflict quickly lost priority after April 1973, since the foreign ministers became preoccupied with formulating an answer to Kissinger's 'Year of Europe'.[37]

One particular problem was the continuing volatility of the FRG's policy. In 1973, Bonn went to great lengths to improve its understanding of Middle Eastern politics, launching bilateral dialogues on the issue with both the Foreign Office and the Quai d'Orsay.[38] Officials of the Auswärtige Amt also repeatedly travelled to Arab capitals in the first half of 1973, trying not only to restore relations after the Munich massacre of 1972, but also to get a better idea of the Arab position vis-à-vis Israel.[39] With regard to the Middle East conflict, the FRG government, in view of what Scheel called the 'weight of history',[40] continued to be at pains to maintain a balanced position between the two conflicting parties, which was reflected in parallel visits by Brandt and his foreign minister in the late spring of 1973 to Israel and the Arab world, respectively.[41] Yet, violating their own guiding principle of avoiding any unilateral political engagement in the Middle East, Brandt and Scheel during their visits in the region incautiously encouraged their interlocutors to apply the lessons of *Ostpolitik* to resolve the Arab–Israeli conflict. While they presumably meant well, their implicit recommendations of sacrificing territory for the sake of peace and embarking on direct negotiations between adversaries were obviously anathema to Arab leaders as they, in effect, implied that Bonn was subscribing to the Israeli position. When Brandt even publicly called for direct peace talks in his speech to the UN in September 1973, Arab relations with the FRG, or at least with the SPD, deteriorated sharply once more. While underlining the inappropriateness of action outside the EPC framework to the FRG government, it also negatively affected cooperation efforts by the Nine, as one of their major members had lost credit in the Arab world again.[42]

Britain and France could only lament Europe's continuing disunity and powerlessness. Their own positions had become almost identical by 1973, with Britain under Heath having gradually moved closer to the French view that peace in the Middle East required a withdrawal of Israel from most occupied territories. Yet, although their bilateral consultations were very productive, both London and Paris were well aware that any bilateral initiative was out of the question, not least because of the omnipresent memories of the Suez crisis of 1956.[43] Concerning EPC, the French had effectively given up their efforts of uniting the Nine in their attitudes towards the Arab–Israeli conflict. The British, for their part, were dissatisfied with the 'aimless and inconclusive' expert meetings of the Nine.[44] The Seven, as far as the FCO was concerned, were 'babes in the Middle East wood' still 'learning their ABC', whereas France and Britain were 'sixth formers'.[45]

Nevertheless, the FCO and the Quai d'Orsay continued to consider EPC consultations on the Arab–Israeli conflict imperative. If for the moment it was not possible for the Nine to undertake a major initiative on the Middle East, there was still merit in trying to accentuate a common European position, if only as a damage-limiting measure to fend off potential Arab pressure. The mildly pro-Arab stance that had crystallised from EPC work in 1971/72 promised a valuable basis to that end. As the FCO bluntly put it in June 1973, the objective in the short term could no longer be 'to fashion a Community instrument for solving the Arab/Israel problem but to work towards a harmonised attitude amongst all the nine which would be sufficiently sympathetic to the Arabs not to expose the Community as a whole or any individual members to an unacceptable risk of hostile Arab reaction against its interests'.[46] Britain and France took additional unilateral measures to talk the Arabs out of turning against Europe in the case of new violence in the Middle East, with London seeking to multiply and strengthen its economic and political ties with the Arabs and France even selling new military equipment to Libya. Both were, of course, aware that Israel would be displeased with such policies. However, both risked alienation from Tel Aviv. To quote the FCO once more: 'To put it crudely, our national interest is far more heavily engaged with the Arabs than with Israel.'[47]

As regards the European handling of the energy issue, fragmentation among the Nine was even more pronounced. Predominantly a topic of the EC rather than EPC, the European Commission had come up with several proposals for a common energy policy from the late 1960s onwards. While the focus had initially been on cheap oil, attention of the Commission had gradually shifted to secure supplies in the early 1970s. Proposals included external measures, such as cooperation with other consuming nations and oil producers, as well as internal measures, especially the setting up of a Community oil market. The EC Council for the first time in three years dealt exclusively with the energy problem on 22 May 1973. Yet, even after an 18-hour marathon meeting, the Nine could only state their profound differences as to how to approach the energy issue.[48]

France had refused to consider a decision on external energy policy without prior agreement on a common market for oil that included controls on imports, investments, as well as prices. Paris sought to transfer essential principles of its national energy approach – government-influenced national oil companies and bilateral deals to secure oil supplies independent from the 'Seven Sisters' – to the European level. Britain, the Netherlands, and the FRG, in contrast, were sceptical about market dirigisme. They preferred looser forms of cooperation and wanted at least parallel progress in external energy relations, with the Dutch putting emphasis on cooperation with the US, while Britain drew special attention to consumer–producer relations. London's attitude was shaped by the prospect of large indigenous oil reserves in the North Sea that would be ready to be drilled in a few years, as well as by its coal reserves and its large stakes in two of the multinational oil companies. The Dutch too had a major stake in one of the 'Seven Sisters' and, hence, an interest in the existing international oil regime, whereas the West German resistance to an over-regulated Community market had more to do with their general preference for liberal economic models. On top of such divergent interests, it is important to note that even the individual Community members were only in the process of formulating comprehensive national energy policies in 1972/3, which made the search for a Community policy all the more difficult.[49]

For all their anxiety about a coming energy crisis and escalation of tensions in the Middle East, the Europeans by early October 1973 remained in a very vulnerable position. Only when both crises hit them even faster and harder than they could have expected was a new dynamism injected into their efforts to formulate joint answers.

A common policy in the Arab–Israeli conflict

European disunity about the Arab–Israeli conflict became apparent in the way in which EPC members individually apportioned blame for the outbreak of hostilities at the onset of the October War. The Dutch publicly accused the Arabs of aggression. Jobert, at the other end of the spectrum, held Israel responsible for the war. By famously asking media representatives on 8 October 1973 whether trying to return 'home' (*chez soi*) would necessarily constitute an aggression, he became very popular in the Arab world. Subsequently known as 'Jobert of Arabia',[50] he also criticised the role of the superpowers, especially the fact that Brezhnev, 'the champion of détente', and Kissinger, 'winner of the Noble Peace Prize', were shaking hands at the same time as their countries sent thousands of tons of arms to the battlefield.[51] Other Europeans, such as Britain and the FRG, took a more neutral line in public, even though the Heath government and the Middle East experts in Bonn subscribed to the French view that the war was primarily a result of the obstinacy of the Meir government.[52]

During the war, Britain, France, and the FRG all shared an inability to exert any impact on the course of events and, at the same time, were confronted with considerable criticism for their national policies. From the very beginning, London was eager to stop the fighting and get negotiations started so as to prevent the Arabs from applying the 'oil weapon'. The idea of the FCO was to jointly table a resolution with France at the UN that would call for a cease-fire and a peace conference about the implementation of Resolution 242, with the participation of the parties to the conflict and the five veto powers of the Security Council. This British initiative failed, as did a similar French plan to reactivate the concept of a peace conference that Paris had discussed with Egypt in the summer of 1972 (see Chapter 2). In both cases, it was Sadat who declined, insisting instead on a resolution calling for full Israeli withdrawal to its 1967 borders.[53]

Britain and France also encountered sharp domestic criticism and accusations from Israel during the war, largely as a result of their policies on arms sales. The Heath government placed an embargo on the supply of armament and equipment to Syria, Egypt, Iraq, Libya, and Israel. The pro-Israeli Labour party, as well as the majority of the media, viewed this measure as one-sidedly favouring the Arabs, since Tel Aviv had been in the midst of receiving tanks from Britain and was in need of spare parts during the war. Consequently, the embargo caused heated debates in parliament, and it provoked Meir to publicly proclaim that Douglas-Home seemed not to have learnt the lesson of the Munich Conference he had attended 35 years earlier, that is, that peace could not be won by sacrificing small nations.[54] A similar dispute raged in Paris, where the government came under particularly heavily attack once Israel announced in mid-October 1973 that it had shot down two Libyan Mirages, which France had promised would not be re-exported by Qadhafi to other Arab countries. Even though the Israeli army was unable to furnish conclusive proof to support its allegations, the French government found it difficult to win public backing for its policies. As in Britain, the pro-Arab policy of the government collided with the pro-Israeli attitude of large segments of the public.[55]

During the hostilities, the FRG did not try to engage in the diplomatic search for peace. Nonetheless, it faced even more criticism for its policy than Britain and France and found itself in a deplorable squeeze between American, Arab, and Israeli expectations. The major point of contention in the case of the FRG related to the US military airlift, which also took place from American bases in West Germany. As long as the fighting continued, Bonn tolerated such supplies, in spite of Arab accusations that this violated its policy of neutrality. The real trouble began when the government learnt from the media that the US was continuing its supplies after the cease-fire had been agreed, loading military equipment at Bremerhaven onto Israeli ships. This put the FRG in an embarrassing situation, as deliveries now took place directly from West German soil (instead of US bases) and went straight onto Israeli ships (instead of US ships and planes). Angry about the lack of US consultation, and recalling how the Arabs in similar circumstances in 1965 had broken off diplomatic relations, Bonn demanded that Washington immediately bring a halt to the exercise.[56] This led to a fierce German–American row (see below). At the same time, it proved too late to prevent another clash with the Arabs, whom the FRG had promised that no supplies would occur after a cease-fire. Accusing the FRG of being the only country other than the US to materially support Israel, OAPEC members, and above all Qadhafi, threatened to punish Bonn with an oil embargo.[57]

To make matters worse, the FRG was simultaneously confronted with strong Israeli criticism. General accusations of the FRG's neutral course from Jewish lobbies had receded after Brandt had confidentially drawn their attention to the fact that he, in all secrecy and contrary to West German laws, had authorised re-supplying the Israeli army with a key electronic device, which had been lost during battle and which the *Bundeswehr* alone had been able to provide in due time.[58] Yet, this did not prevent Israeli newspapers from attacking Bonn again once it had intervened against the US shipments. The West Germans found themselves accused of nothing less than facilitating genocide with their policy and 'murdering for oil as they had once murdered for ideological reasons'.[59]

Bearing in mind its weak position, it comes as no surprise that the FRG was one of the major driving forces behind a collective European response to the October War. From the beginning of the hostilities in the Middle East, EPC was functioning well in that ambassadors of the Nine in Arab capitals, Israel, and Moscow, as well as at the UN, were in regular contact and shared their assessments of the local situation.[60] However, the FRG also wanted the Nine to stand together and attempt to formulate a joint public position vis-à-vis the war.[61] This desire was shared by all of Bonn's partners. Public expectations, new élan from EPC's 'Year of Europe' success, and, particularly, the great dangers emanating from the constellation in the Middle East to Europe's security were all reasons prompting the Nine to consult on joint measures from early on during the war.[62]

With national Middle East experts being too busy to leave their desks, it was the political directors themselves who made a first attempt to hammer out a common European statement on the war. Emerging from this was a European call for a cease-fire, which was issued on 13 October 1973. It was nothing spectacular, with the Nine appealing to the parties 'to agree to stop the hostilities' and linking a cease-fire to subsequent negotiations according to Resolution 242.[63] Its formulation had, nevertheless, proved rather difficult, with the Dutch and the Danish insisting on several amendments to the proposed French draft: both wanted to avoid the impression that the Nine were *demanding* a cease-fire (hence the inelegant inclusion 'to *agree to* stop'); and both rejected a sentence implying that France and Britain could also speak in the name of the Nine at the UN.[64] The European call did not achieve any discernible effect, with Egypt insisting on the complete withdrawal of Israel, and Tel Aviv responding dryly by condemning Britain's arms embargo and the French Mirages in Libya.[65] Nonetheless, it was a notable statement in that it was EPC's first ever public communiqué on a political issue. Although thin on substance, the important thing was that a common text had been agreed. This was only made possible by changes in the Dutch and Danish positions during the course of the negotiations. They shifted from their original, US-inspired approach of linking the cease-fire with a call for the parties to return to the lines of 6 October 1973 (which implicitly denounced the Arabs for their aggression) to a more forward-looking position of a comprehensive peace settlement.[66]

The communiqué, therefore, already pointed to the further harmonisation of views among the Nine that was to find reflection in their declaration of 6 November. Unlike the declaration, however, it only expressed the need for peace and did not lay out components of a settlement. Referring to the war rather than the underlying parameters of the Arab–Israeli conflict, it did not yet represent a substantive common policy. In fact, as long as the hostilities continued, the Nine failed to come up with any further joint measures. A Belgian proposal of 16 October 1973, according to which the Nine should discuss ways for Europe, in the capacity of a 'third force', to take an initiative and bring about a cease-fire, did not materialise, as both the FCO and the Quai d'Orsay considered such an undertaking unrealistic.[67] It was agreed, however, that the Middle East working group should finally meet and evaluate whether there was anything more the Nine could do. As the nine experts by coincidence met on 22 October 1973, just after UN Resolution 338 had finally been passed, they attempted to issue a statement on the cease-fire. Out of this came a text, based on a British draft, which welcomed the resolution, called for a comprehensive peace, and indicated the readiness of the Nine to contribute to it. The French, however, argued that a European statement should do more than simply paraphrase the UN resolution and offer 'applause for the superpowers'. They insisted on a further paragraph stating that the Nine 'trust that the massive supplies of arms to the combatants will cease as soon as possible', which turned out unacceptable to Denmark.[68] With the Netherlands also being reluctant to insert any elements not covered by the resolution itself, the draft had to be dropped altogether.

It was, therefore, only after the cease-fire of 22 October 1973 that the Nine managed to make any real progress in their effort to formulate a common position concerning the Arab–Israeli conflict. Their ability and willingness to do so was influenced by three major factors: dissatisfaction with Kissinger's crisis management; the growing threat to European security emanating from the oil weapon; and Arab calls for Europe to play a bigger role in the region. The realisation by the Nine that Washington perceived the October War very differently from them was undoubtedly crucial. Whereas the Community countries saw in the war a primarily regional conflict between the Arabs and Israel that could potentially have further great power implications, the US appeared to view it mainly through Cold War lenses. Whereas Europe was mainly concerned about its economic security, the US was focusing its attention on global security and the balance of power between East and West.[69] These differences in perception and priorities made the Nine aware, more than ever, that their interests were not adequately represented by the US Middle Eastern policy. When Kissinger advised the Europeans immediately after the cease-fire to leave it to him to implement what he had set up in Moscow,[70] this was anything but reassuring for the Nine, who profoundly disagreed with several components of US post-war diplomacy. They did not like the fact that the 'auspices' mentioned in Resolution 338 obviously comprised Washington and Moscow only and, consequently, implied the exclusion of both the UN and Europe from the upcoming peace negotiations.[71] In addition, the Nine also felt disavowed by the fact that Kissinger made sure that no European ally could participate at the UNEF mission to secure the cease-fire. British and French contingents were barred from joining when the US secretary of state, eager to prevent Soviet troops from entering the Middle East, pushed through the exclusion of forces from permanent members of the Security Council from the UN force in Resolution 340. A Belgian proposal that the remaining Seven should offer contingents to the UN in the name of the Nine had to also be abandoned, as Kissinger feared that a Community contribution would only open the door for Warsaw Pact countries to insist on participating in UNEF. As only neutral Ireland eventually was considered suitable to participate in the UN force, Europe's presence on the ground was reduced to a much smaller scale than had been initially envisaged.[72]

From a European perspective, the most dissatisfying element of Kissinger's post-war diplomacy was his apparent disinclination to work towards a comprehensive peace settlement. Kissinger's approach to proceed on a country-by-country and issue-by-issue basis was far from promising as far as the Nine were concerned. Concerns among the Nine grew further once they realised how obsessed the US secretary of state was with diminishing Soviet influence in the region, which made many in Europe wonder whether the US had a proper concept for peace at all and whether its bilateral diplomacy would not end up forfeiting an opportunity to resolve the conflict.[73]

European disagreements with Kissinger's approach to peacemaking weighed all the heavier since the Nine knew that the cuts in oil supplies, which the Arabs had decided towards the end of the war, would hit them much more drastically than the US. The French were certainly more cynical than their partners when they argued that the US might have even encouraged the Saudis to apply the oil weapon so as to domestically get through a crash programme for the development of alternative energy sources and simultaneously weaken a recalcitrant Europe.[74] Yet, all the Nine agreed that the energy crisis rendered it more important for Europe than for the US to establish progress towards peace in the Middle East. They were further encouraged to get involved more actively in international diplomacy by talks with Arab representatives, who led them to believe that Arab governments had only conceded under pressure to a dominant role for the superpowers in the quest for peace and would welcome a bigger role for the Nine. Europe, Sadat's foreign minister argued during a visit to London, had much more experience in the Middle East than Kissinger, who had bewildered his host during his first trip to Egypt by asking to visit the Pyramids in Cairo.[75]

At French insistence, the Nine met again at the end of October to begin work on a declaration. There was some initial procedural wrangling, as Davignon at first objected to the French proposal that consultations should be conducted by the resident ambassadors in Copenhagen so as to avoid publicity.[76] All the Nine, however, agreed that another joint statement was now desirable. As Douglas-Home put it: 'Europe is too large and its vital interests too closely involved for it to sit silent while great events take place over their heads'.[77] The result of the Copenhagen meeting, marked by French leadership and countless telephone calls between ambassadors and their respective capitals, was a short text agreed ad referendum. It expressed the firm hope that peace negotiations would at last begin, based on Resolutions 242 and 338 and in the framework of the UN, and it recalled that principal responsibility for international peace and security lay with the Security Council, thereby criticising implicitly both Kissinger's step-by-step approach and his circumvention of the international community. It also referred to international guarantees to back any settlement, reinforced by the dispatch of peace-keeping forces to demilitarised zones. Moreover, it pointed out that this was only the first contribution on the European part to the search for a comprehensive solution, thereby signalling the Nine's intention of getting steadily more involved in the matter.[78]

Although governments approved the Copenhagen draft on 2 November 1973 and agreed that it should be published at a special EPC ministerial meeting four days later, that was not the end of it. On the basis of a British initiative, the text was significantly elaborated by the Political Committee on

5 November 1973 to include a common European position both on the violations of the cease-fire and, most importantly, on the specifics of a peace settlement. Denmark and Ireland were initially reluctant to go any further, whereas the Netherlands, previously the main stumbling block in EPC, now actively sought to spur additional progress.[79] Just before the Political Committee met, there was a demarche by the US government to all EPC members except Britain and France, which expressed interest in hearing Europe's view on the peace process, suggested close and permanent consultation about the issue, and indicated that the Nine could play an important role in the Middle East through consultations with Washington. Yet, as far as the Nine were concerned, this looked too much like a US last-minute manoeuvre to dissuade the Europeans from further elaborating their Copenhagen draft.[80]

The final text of the 'Declaration on Middle East', issued by the nine foreign ministers in Brussels on 6 November 1973, in addition to the contents of the Copenhagen draft, strongly urged the forces of both sides to 'return immediately to the positions they occupied on 22 October', in accordance with UN Resolutions 339 and 340. It also listed four points on which a peace agreement should be based: the inadmissibility of the acquisition of territory by force; the need for Israel 'to end the territorial occupation which it has maintained since the conflict of 1967', respect for the sovereignty of every state in the area and their right to live in peace within secure and recognised boundaries; and recognition that in the establishment of a just and lasting peace account must be taken of 'the legitimate rights of the Palestinians'. The declaration ended by recalling the ties of all kinds which had long linked Europe to the littoral states of the south and east of the Mediterranean and by reaffirming that the Community had embarked on a Global Mediterranean Policy in 1972 in order to redefine economic bilateral relations with these states.[81]

This declaration was a breakthrough in the evolution of EPC. It marked the beginning of a distinct European policy vis-à-vis the Arab–Israeli conflict, and it represented Europe's first substantive public statement. Also noteworthy, having been issued at the fringes of a Council meeting, the declaration signified that EPC was moving closer to the EC, continuing the trend of qualifying the rigid separation between the two bodies by practical necessity. Of course, the declaration still left several details of a peace deal aside and was not yet comparable to comprehensive schemes for a settlement as elaborated by Britain or France, for example.[82] Nevertheless, it did contain key elements of an agreement and was specific enough to attract Israeli criticism for leaving little left to negotiate. The most important clauses included the call for Israel to end its occupation and the reference to the Palestinians. As a result of Danish resistance, the text did not explicitly ask for an Israeli withdrawal. However, it did make clear that the Nine regarded international guarantees as more promising for Israel's security than a policy of occupation. Using a new and genuinely European (i.e., neither French nor British) formula, the declaration actually made a strong case for complete withdrawal, given that it did not even refer to the possibility of border adjustments. By also linking peace to the fate of the Palestinians, the Nine took up an issue long advocated in UN General Assembly resolutions, though they did not go as far as mentioning what specific rights the Palestinians should have.

The European declaration met with harsh criticism, notably from Israel. The text contained several elements that were anathema to Tel Aviv. The call to a return to the lines of 22 October supported the Egyptian view that it should evacuate those territories captured in violation of the cease-fire. Moreover, a UN role in the peace talks did not conform to Israeli views, and neither did the references to guarantees, the end of occupation, and the rights of the Palestinians. In an official statement, the Israeli Foreign Minister Eban argued that the Nine had disqualified themselves from any further contributions to the peace process with their declaration and alleged that the theme of the text was 'Oil for Europe rather than Peace for the Middle East'.[83]

Not only Israel, but also large parts of the media in Europe accused the Nine of giving in to blackmail and appeasing the Arabs to safeguard their oil supplies.[84] Yet, it would be simplistic to attribute the declaration merely to the 'oil weapon'. The October War and the oil crisis undoubtedly had accelerated the process of policy harmonisation. What is more, it was certainly a result of these crises that countries such as the FRG were prompted to finally go public with matters previously considered too sensitive for the public domain. However, it should be recalled that even the Dutch had begun to show signs of frustration with Israel's uncompromising course already prior to the outbreak of the hostilities. Most importantly, it must be underlined that the EPC members in 1971/72 had already confidentially agreed on a number of substantive points that featured in the text of 6 November 1973 (see Chapter 2). Hence, the declaration mainly accentuated and enhanced a policy that had been worked out in the years prior to its formulation.[85] In this, it contrasted with a similar declaration that Japan issued later in the month. Whereas Japan, even more dependent on Arab oil than Europe, came up with a sharp policy change from a low-profile, business-first approach to a strong pro-Arab political statement, the declaration of the Nine to a greater extent reflected a reassertion than a reappraisal of policy.[86]

The main reason why the European declaration received a predominantly negative reception by the European publics was the lack of public knowledge about EPC's earlier work on the Middle East. The secrecy that West Germany and the Netherlands had previously imposed on EPC consultations concerning the Arab-Israeli conflict became a handicap once the Nine went public with their positions in response to the crisis. Under such circumstances, the pro-Arab dimension of the declaration could all too easily be regarded as a knee-jerk reaction and a submission to pressure. Significantly, however, the Community governments themselves appeared mostly content with the declaration.[87] In the FRG, for example, where the government came under particularly heavy domestic pressure, Brandt strongly defended the text in a speech to the Bundestag and the Bundesrat, arguing that each of the Nine had been forced to make compromises and that it was in the interest of both Europe and the Middle East for the Community to gain political weight and influence.[88]

There was agreement among the Nine that their Brussels statement should be the starting point for further common action. To this end, Britain took the initiative on 10 November 1973 and proposed a joint letter by the nine foreign ministers to Arab capitals. The idea of the FCO was to make use of the positive response that the declaration had received in the Arab world and declare the readiness of the Nine to contribute to peace diplomacy in the Middle East. While the letter intended to arouse Arab interest in closer relations with Europe, it aimed, above all, at indicating that Euro-Arab cooperation would not be supported by European publics as long as the oil weapon was applied against the Nine.[89] The Political Committee and the Middle East experts, who jointly considered the idea on 13 November, eventually transformed it into a collective demarche to be communicated by one European ambassador in each Arab capital. They did so in order to avoid the impression of Europe applying pressure and to make sure that the measure gained no publicity. As the British reported from Copenhagen, the drafting of the demarche took place in a tense atmosphere, with some bitter exchanges, cigar butts growing stale in the ashtrays, and officials haggling over wording well into the small hours.[90]

Consensus on the substance was finally established, but two obstacles had to be removed before the demarche could take place. The French failed for an entire week to give the operation a green light. This was because renewed public criticism of French nuclear tests by Denmark, Ireland, and the Dutch had caused indignation in Paris. Furthermore, there was resistance within the economic department of the Quai d'Orsay to France risking its stake as a 'friendly' country to the Arabs for the sake of Community partners affected by the oil production cuts.[91] Furthermore, once Jobert came around to authorising the demarche, it was Denmark that stalled. The reason for this was that Israel had approached the Nine with an *Aide Mémoire* of its own that had caused a great deal of surprise and confusion in European capitals. As if it had not just decried the declaration of the Nine, Tel Aviv now claimed that it was 'prepared to enter into confidential diplomatic contact' about the peace process and Europe's role in it.[92] Jobert immediately suspected a trap and proposed to his colleagues to ask the Meir government a few questions about its views on the legitimacy of a European contribution to peace in the Middle East before accepting a dialogue. Although this procedure was approved, there was no agreement about the tone of the European reply, which, in turn, led Denmark to block the Arab demarche. It was not before 22 November 1973 that Copenhagen too, despite the unresolved issue of Israel, lifted its reserve and, as EPC presidency, commissioned the collective European demarches in the Arab capitals to be put into effect.[93] Although unnoticed by the European publics, and severely delayed because of intra-European differences, this was another noteworthy step in the Nine's nascent Middle East policy, representing the first joint diplomatic European action related to the Arab–Israeli conflict.[94]

The October War and the oil crisis not only fostered Europe's ability to speak with one voice in the Middle East, but also caused the Nine to progress from joint statements to joint initiatives. From a European perspective, this was certainly a welcome development. Progress became visible, for example, in the European voting behaviour at the twenty-eighth session of the UN General Assembly, where the Nine supported resolutions criticising Israel in line with the spirit of their declaration, voted against resolutions condemning Israel beyond the limits of this declaration, and abstained on issues where they had not yet formulated a common policy.[95] It was also reflected in the fact that the FCO was now much more impressed than in the summer of 1973 by the performance of the EPC Middle East experts, and not just because of the French representative's skill, lavishly reported, of being able to make his cigarette-end bob up and down on his lips as he talked.[96]

At the same time, EPC's achievement should not be exaggerated, as Europe's common position had not yet translated into much impact on the international course of events. Their statement had not rendered the Nine an acknowledged player in the search for peace yet. Worse still, their attempt at bringing the Arabs round to lifting the 'oil weapon' had not yet paid off. The Arab oil ministers did announce in Vienna on 18 November 1973 that the 5 per cent production cutback for December would not apply to the EC countries, in appreciation of their Middle East declaration. But the Arabs refused to end the embargo on the Dutch, thus continuing to discriminate between the Nine.[97] Moreover, they soon showed themselves unimpressed again by Europe's diplomatic efforts.

Despite the confidential Europe demarche, the Arab summit at Algiers on 26 November 1973 approved four resolutions relating to the EC countries: the Nine should be called upon to go beyond their first declaration; to cease economic and military aid to Israel; to supply the Arabs with weapons; and to exert more pressure on the US.[98] That the Arabs were serious about these demands became painfully clear when Arab emissaries came to European capitals for bilateral talks after the summit in Algiers and asked for such outlandish measures as Europeans joining Arab soldiers in their fight against Israel.[99] On 8 December 1973, OAPEC in Kuwait went a step further and decided that the cuts deferred from December would be re-imposed in January 1974 if the Community countries failed to provide more concrete evidence of their friendliness than a declaration.[100] These were frustrating developments for the Nine. They underlined that Europe needed more political weight and more means at its disposal, if it really wanted to make a difference in international diplomacy and achieve a tangible impact with its emerging common policies. It was, therefore, no coincidence that the autumn of 1973 also witnessed important initiatives to strengthen EPC as a whole.

Invigorating Europe's foreign policy

Of all EC member states, France was the country most shaken by Europe's inability to influence events during the October War and the oil crisis. In a speech to the French National Assembly on 12 November 1973, Jobert relentlessly delineated Europe's powerlessness in the Middle East and urged the Nine to draw the right consequences from it. Arguing that the crisis had confirmed the existence of a superpower condominium, the French foreign minister decried the monopolisation of the peace process by Washington and Moscow, and insisted that Europe's exclusion from the search for peace was a mistake. He then, in a famous passage, both deplored Europe's undeniable weakness and appealed to Europe to finally rise:

> Treated like a 'non-person', humiliated in its inexistence, Europe, through its dependency on energy, is also affected by the second battle of this Middle-East war. A forgotten victim of the conflict, but a victim nevertheless, even though it had perpetually denounced the perils, its distress and its bitterness are obvious. But it also noted that it was more of a pawn than an instrument or an asset in the arbitration of the great powers. It can, it should learn a basic lesson from this. Many people expect, not its jolt, but its nascence.[101]

Jobert concluded his speech by pointing to the notable achievements EPC had already accomplished. Calling for enthusiasm, he left no doubt what the priority of French foreign policy would subsequently be: to advance and accelerate the political construction of Europe.[102] In this endeavour, Jobert was backed by Pompidou, to whom the October War had become a *révélateur*, that is, an eye-opener and trigger, for the need to make haste with European unification. Previously, the French president had blocked ideas promoted by Jobert to invigorate the political profile of Europe, such as the concept of giving Europe a voice and a face by nominating annually one of the nine leaders as Europe's unique spokesman and representative.[103] Now, by contrast, he was more receptive to his confidant's suggestions and actually went public with a French initiative to strengthen EPC himself.

'Treated like a non-person': A French initiative for EPC summitry

On 31 October 1973, after a French Ministerial Council, Pompidou issued a statement that comprised a double initiative to buttress EPC. Referring to the Nine's political absenteeism from the Middle East peace process, Pompidou argued that it was now absolutely necessary for the Nine to prove their solidarity behind the construction of Europe and their capacity to help in settling world problems. Accordingly, he proposed, first, regular European summits on foreign policy issues, so that the nine leaders could harmonise their own outlooks and give EPC more authority and strategic focus; and, second, the adoption of a mechanism that would enable the Nine to hold emergency meetings during times of crises and respond more swiftly and decidedly to imminent challenges.[104]

Pompidou and Jobert were thinking of a new kind of working meeting on foreign policy by the nine European leaders. These summits should be family gatherings (*au coin de feu*), without officials and other ministers, which from a French point of view constituted the best way of working out policies resolute enough to lend Europe's ambitions and declarations credence and weight. If things developed well, a small secretariat might later be set up. Gradually, EPC summits could point the way to European Union, as these meetings might evolve into a sort of European Cabinet Council and mark the shape of a European confederation.[105] As for the crisis mechanism, Pompidou and Jobert envisaged a flexible mechanism, run perhaps by special state secretaries. They advocated a system of consultation not unlike the UN Security Council, except that instead of resolutions the EPC representatives would work out proposals at the disposal of the nine leaders.[106]

Other European leaders strongly agreed with the French analysis of the situation and the call for giving Europe the means it needed to defend its interest. This was particularly true for the FRG. In an address to the European Parliament in Strasbourg in mid-November 1973, Brandt depicted the further unification of Europe as essential to survival between the giants and argued that 'in a world whose destiny cannot and should not be determined by two superpowers alone, the influence of a united Europe has become indispensable'.[107] In a conversation with the Italian Prime Minister Rumor, Brandt went even further when he argued that there would be times when superpower relations were better than European–American relations, which demanded that the Nine should develop their own political capacity.[108] At the time of Pompidou's initiative, the West Germans had, in fact, been working on a European initiative for several months themselves. The idea had originated in July 1973 with the chancellery, which had made the case for comprehensive West German proposals in Community as well as EPC matters. The initiative had failed to materialise, however, mainly because of resistance by Minister of Finance Schmidt to endlessly pump more money into the EC.[109]

All the more keen was the FRG to support the French proposals, therefore. Indicative of Brandt's positive attitude, and EPC's high prestige in the autumn of 1973, was the chancellor's order in mid-November that the Auswärtige Amt should subsequently inform him about all proceedings in the Davignon machinery so that he could give appropriate guidance.[110] Pompidou's initiative evidently received backing from the Conservative government in London too, which had long pressed for the rapid development of a common foreign policy. In November 1973, Douglas-Home also agreed with Scheel that Kissinger's unspoken goal of establishing a worldwide power structure, whose two centres – Moscow and Washington – would be linked in friendship posed an intrinsic threat to the Nine and called for European action.[111] However, the one thing that troubled decision-makers in both Britain and the FRG about the French summit idea was that Pompidou saw these meetings as an extension of the EPC machinery only. From their perspective, this could have far-reaching consequences in that it prejudiced the future shape of the EU. Regular EPC summits without equivalent meetings in Community affairs were bound to shift the balance in the process of unification to intergovernmental forms of cooperation. This would cut across the thesis, held in London and Bonn, as well as in most other EC countries, that the EU should eventually be built upon the EC. Was it Pompidou's intention, the Dutch and others wondered, to bring the Fouchet Plan of the early 1960s back on the table?[112]

One reason why France's partners were concerned was because of Pompidou's obstinate resistance to close links between the EPC machinery and the EC in the context of the working out of the second report on EPC. This report had been approved by the EPC ministerial meeting in Copenhagen in July 1973, which is why it came to be known as the Copenhagen Report.[113] It had brought some improvements to EPC's working methods, setting up a Group of Correspondents of national EPC officials to assist the Political Committee and implement EPC decisions, and establishing a telex network (COREU – *Correspondance européenne*) to link the foreign ministries in a common communication system. It had also doubled the colloquies with the European Parliament to four per year. And, it had stated that 'each state undertakes as a general rule not to take up final positions without prior consultation on EPC issues', coming one step closer to compulsory consultations, as long advocated by Italy and others.

Yet, the Copenhagen Report had otherwise been a rather modest achievement, and it had been particularly thin on EC–EPC relations. Britain, supported by the FRG, Italy, and the Benelux countries, had been fighting hard to bring the two machineries closer together. Although Douglas-Home had never liked the idea of the foreign ministers 'wearing two hats' (as members of the Council and of EPC), arguing that he had only one head,[114] Britain had always accepted a certain separation between EPC and EC. But, it had aimed at establishing much closer cooperation between the two, with the Council machinery becoming responsible for the political matters of the Community policies; with both bodies being able to request reports and assistance from the other side; and with ad hoc groups between EPC political directors and EC permanent representatives working out joint reports.[115] France, by contrast, generally petrified at the spectre of Community rules spilling over to EPC, for a long time had not even accepted a text which put the two pieces side by side. Backed by Denmark and Ireland, it had rejected any convergence between EPC and the EC and had emphasised the different natures of the two machineries instead.[116]

Eventually, the Copenhagen Report merely provided for the Commission to be invited by EPC to make known its views (in accordance with the existing practice); for the Council to be informed by the EPC presidency of agreed EPC conclusions to the extent that these conclusions related to EC issues; and for ministers (rather than the Community) to be able to instruct EPC to prepare studies on 'certain political aspects of problems under examination' in the EC. What might have looked at first glance as a compromise solution was, in effect, a victory for Pompidou. Therefore, while Britain, the FRG, and the Danish presidency accepted Pompidou's summitry initiative, they suggested that these meetings should give strategic direction not only to Europe's foreign policy, but also to the Community's internal development. They did so to make sure that European summits would diminish, rather than acerbate the chasm between EPC and the EC. Another strong motive was that the economic crisis of the autumn of 1973 from their point of view called for urgent decisions by the European leaders as well (see below).[117]

There was no visible resistance from Pompidou against expanding the summit with pressing Community issues.[118] Hence, the revised summit concept came close to an idea that Jean Monnet had already secretly discussed with decision-makers in Paris, London, and Bonn in September 1973. At that time, Monnet, having pondered the idea of regular summits since 1969, had come forward with a confidential memorandum on the 'Constitution and Action of a Provisional European Government', suggesting that the nine leaders should subsequently meet every three months to execute the Paris Summit decisions, discuss EPC, and give guidance to the development of the EU.[119] If Pompidou had proposed the EPC side of the idea only, Brandt and Heath from the perspective of Monnet's memorandum simply put the second half of the memorandum back on the table again.

The Nine finally agreed to hold their summit in mid-December in Copenhagen, and to regard this summit as an extraordinary meeting from which to decide how to proceed. They were compelled to label it extraordinary since, even after their consensus to deal with both EPC and EC matters, differences as to the purpose, scope, and frequency of these meetings remained. Whereas Pompidou sought informal talks in all confidentiality, Heath called for more business-like debates resulting in specific actions. Whereas the British prime minister suggested holding one summit in every presidency, Brandt was reluctant to institutionalise meetings, since he feared that this might deter the ministers from working hard enough to establish agreement in the Council and EPC.[120] Moreover, all countries except France, Britain, and the FRG insisted that the foreign ministers should accompany the nine leaders, be it because their constitution attributed the responsibility for conducting external relations to the foreign minister (Netherlands); because several parties of a coalition government wanted to be represented at the summit (Italy); or because the prime minister in their political system was much more involved in managing internal policies than foreign policy (Belgium). Similarly, most countries wished to have a specific agenda of the summit talks, not least because they were aware that Pompidou as a consequence of the French presidential system was more familiar with the specifics of many issues than their own leaders.

Eventually, it was agreed that foreign ministers would hold parallel sessions at the Copenhagen meeting, and that talks would be inspired by a list of issues.[121]

The French naturally were not very happy with this solution, and Jobert would later complain that the cats that Pompidou had thrown out by the door with his initiative simply sneaked back through the window again.[122] Nevertheless, there was reason to hope that a compromise could be found at the upcoming Copenhagen meeting as to the future of the summit approach. And, most importantly, for all the restrictions France's partners had imposed on Pompidou's initiative, there remained the encouraging prospect of the nine heads of state and government finally getting involved in European foreign policy-making, which was bound to give EPC additional authority and impetus. The fact that the summit was to deal with European foreign policy in itself gave ample demonstration of the progress EPC had made in the course of 1973 – and of the perceived need and desirability that it ought to be developed still further.

Jobert calls for European defence, too

Parallel to the discussions of how to strengthen EPC, the autumn of 1973 also witnessed renewed efforts at getting European defence cooperation under way. Here too France played a seminal role, as it was the French policy change towards *l'Europe politique* that gave the debates on a defence component to European unification new impetus. Interestingly, Paris had signalled to its partners as early as the summer of 1973 that it was ready to modify its policy of strict national defence autonomy, which is why talks on European defence already had re-emerged prior to Pompidou's EPC initiative. Yet, these talks received a decisive boost by the experience of the October War and the oil crisis, and they acquired a remarkable quality and frequency in the weeks before the Copenhagen Summit.

If concepts in the FCO and the Auswärtige Amt for a Community defence pillar in the first half of 1973 looked like wishful thinking in view of continuing lack of French interest (see Chapter 2),[123] this changed with Jobert's first speech at the French National Assembly on 19 June 1973. In this address, Jobert deplored that the Europe of the Nine was disarmed, warned that it would suffer more and more from its lack of defence autonomy, and suggested that the 'Year of Europe' should, above all, be used to think about European defence. It was a sensational speech, nourishing expectations in European capitals that France might at last draw the consequences of the mounting threats to European security that emanated from such diverse factors as MBFR,

Watergate, and superpower bilateralism.[124] There were additional signs of encouragement in that respect when the French included passages on European defence in their draft declarations on European Identity (see below) and Atlantic relations (see Chapter 4). Moreover, French Minister of Defence Galley admitted quite frankly that French defence policy was shot through with internal contradictions and would need to be adjusted to present circumstances.[125]

Again, this French overture was strongly welcomed in Europe. Interestingly, however, in both Britain and the FRG there was disagreement between the defence ministries and the foreign ministries as to the conclusions to draw from it. On the one hand, the defence ministries still saw no alternative with regard to European defence but for France to join the Eurogroup. They considered any European defence identity without a link to NATO's integrated defence planning unreasonable, and any potential French goal of a defence organisation not dominated by the US, but compatible with a US military presence in Europe, unrealistic. They, thus, leaned to a strategy of pressing ahead with the Eurogroup and making France feel uncomfortable about its exclusion, with a view to convincing Paris of the Eurogroup's benefits.[126] The foreign ministries, by contrast, not only regarded French participation in the Eurogroup unlikely, but also saw in the French appeal a long awaited opportunity to take up the issue of Community defence.[127] The Auswärtige Amt was particularly enthusiastic about the French policy shift and began to resolutely make the case for harmonising security and defence in the framework of the Nine, that is, as an extension to EPC.[128] With Brandt and Heath sharing the view of their foreign ministries, both the FRG and Britain, therefore, secretly engaged in dialogues with the French on the new possibilities of European defence.

Only two days after Jobert's speech, on the occasion of his six-monthly meetings with Pompidou, Brandt came forward with the most insisting and specific attempt to discuss defence with France of any West German chancellor since Adenauer.[129] Brandt, in fact, raised three fundamental issues simultaneously: French relations with NATO; the implications of the present French nuclear strategy for the defence of the FRG; and the prospect of European defence in the context of European Union. He enquired into such sensitive fields as French nuclear targeting, asking whether any French nuclear weapons would point to German, and especially West German, territory. He also indicated that the time might have come to talk about defence of the Nine. In his parallel talks with Jobert, Scheel too addressed the topic of a European security and defence policy by 1980, which could have left no doubt in Paris that the West German government was serious about it.[130]

Other than an assurance that there were no French targets on West German soil, Brandt and Scheel did not yet get any concrete answers. Pompidou talked of French solidarity with NATO in case of war and hinted at Europe's dependence on the US for its defence. He accepted that the bilateral study group should henceforth deal with the issues raised by Brandt. Yet, he remained vague as to European defence and insinuated that French thinking was still in a state of flux. As for Jobert, he agreed that there would be no common European foreign policy without a common defence policy and that the issue must be tackled now rather than in 1979. Instead of offering ideas as to how to proceed, however, he merely warned that the Nine were about to lose their room for manoeuvre as a result of superpower détente and emphasised that Paris would neither join the Eurogroup nor support a reform of the Alliance.[131]

It was only during a second round of talks between Scheel and Jobert that the fog over French thinking began to disappear. The West German foreign minister via his ambassador in Paris on 19 September 1973 proposed to his French counterpart to secretly continue their dialogue on how to 'unearth the treasure' *(den ungehobenen Schatz)* of European defence cooperation.[132] Jobert immediately accepted, but because of the October War it was only on 9 November 1973 that the two could finally take up the issue in Paris, over a private dinner and, as Jobert recalled, a good bottle of Bordeaux.[133] It was a remarkable conversation. Referring to Europe's marginalisation in the Middle East, Scheel insisted that a process leading to European autonomy in defence should now get started. He added that this would not have to be contradictory to loyalty to the Alliance, and that Europe would remain tied to some extent to the US, even after 1980. In the longer term, however, the Nine should liberate themselves from this dependence, which is why the EU, in his view, needed a common defence, including a European nuclear element. The process towards a later European defence ministry should now be launched, Scheel concluded, suggesting that initial cooperation in this field could work analogous to cooperation in EPC. Previous French foreign ministers of the Fifth Republic would likely have either panted for air or burst out with laughter in the face of such suggestions. Not so Jobert. He did not go as far as Scheel. But he accepted to proceed in stages towards common defence, underlined that Pompidou's summit initiative would pave the way for a European executive that could also deal with defence, indicated that, in his view, the EU could well have a federal structure after 1980, and agreed at last that defence cooperation could possibly start with EPC. In a second meeting after dinner, Jobert added that Pompidou too accepted the West German analysis, with Scheel promising a paper with a more detailed outline of his views, in return.[134]

A dialogue on European defence also began to take shape between France and Britain. In this case, the driving force was Jobert. In August 1973, he authorised the staff of his *Centre d'Analyse et de Prévision* (C.A.P.), a new personal planning unit he had set up at the Quai d'Orsay one month earlier,[135] to get into touch with the British planners about defence. At Jobert's insistence, these talks were conducted according to the 'Kissinger rules', that is, they had to be kept completely secret (even from the French foreign ministry) and on an informal, non-committal basis. They began with a first exchange of views in Paris in mid-September, with a follow-up meeting in London five weeks later. The British participants were not wholly satisfied with how these discussions proceeded, as their French counterparts refused both to take in politico-military experts and to extend the talks to a tripartite level with the FRG. Yet, they received a fascinating insight into the kind of ideas Jobert seemed to be working on. The French planners were talking of a Council of European Defence Ministers parallel to, or as part of, EPC. There could also be a permanent secretariat for defence cooperation. WEU could be reactivated too, and some steps should be taken towards a specialisation in arms procurement in Europe. Eurogroup, by contrast, was out of the question, for reasons of 'theology' and French domestic factors.[136]

By early November 1973, substantive talks on European defence cooperation had, thus, finally got off the ground. As in 1971/72, they were still limited to the bilateral level, and they were restricted to the Big Three. However, the major difference in 1973 was that now France too accepted the necessity of progress. It is worth pointing out in this regard that at the same time as the prospect for European defence improved, the option of Anglo-French nuclear cooperation effectively faded away. This had been by no means obvious in the first half of 1973. During his summit with Pompidou in Paris in May 1973, Heath had finally been successful in getting the French president's approval of approaching the matter. He had told Pompidou that Britain needed to make urgent decisions about how to modernise its nuclear deterrent in order to ensure its continuing credibility, and that his decision would be influenced by the French view of the possibility of Anglo-French cooperation on a successor system.[137] Pompidou had initially remained vague and negative about Heath's renewed appeal for cooperation, pointing, as in previous talks, to Britain's dependence on the US, Soviet sensitivities, and the problem of the FRG. However, when Heath had stubbornly stuck with the issue, the French president had suddenly become more forthcoming. Committing his counterpart to complete secrecy, he had laid out France's 15-year plan for the development of its nuclear force, underscoring that the political defence interests of the two countries were, indeed, identical and their destinies inseparable. Pompidou then had declared: 'This is why, if the British government wishes it, I consider that the issue has now been raised and needs to be addressed, contrary to what the French attitude has often been.'[138] He had added that a joint study on a new generation in 1985 could be undertaken, and that expert talks on a joint research effort should get under way.

To the great disappointment of Heath, however, no French deeds ever followed these words. The Elysée's answer to an enquiry by Heath in mid-June 1973 about how to proceed had simply been that cooperation was a distant prospect only.[139] If Pompidou had at least suggested that both capitals produce national calendars of their production programmes, no such calendar was ever delivered to Whitehall. The British accordingly gained the impression that France did not really seem to care about its choice of how to modernise their deterrent.[140] They no longer attempted at talking France into a joint nuclear approach and, indeed, faced criticism in parliament for having ever tried to do so.[141] The reason why France backed out again is difficult to establish. Clearly, however, the US played a role, mimicking the developments in 1971/72 (see Chapter 2). Just ten days after Pompidou had signalled readiness to embark on a nuclear dialogue with Heath, Nixon had offered him in Reykjavik to finally get a Franco-American dialogue started and had proposed that France sent experts to Washington to that end. At that time, Pompidou had indicated that he would not sell his soul to Britain for a 'pot of lentils' (*une plate de lentilles*), but that he would be interested in cooperation with the US.[142] Accordingly, he had been quick to send Galley and some defence officials for first talks to the US Defence Department. Thus began a process of covert US assistance to French nuclear weapons, inspired by the principle of negative guidance, that is, French specialists making known their ideas and their US counterparts indicating whether they were on the right course. To be sure, the dialogue in the autumn of 1973 was quickly interrupted again as a result of worsening Franco-American relations, to be resumed at the end of 1974 only. Yet, from a French perspective, it was still a more promising path than Anglo-French cooperation, which by necessity would have required some involvement of the US, but because of this trilateral dimension would have been more difficult for Paris to control.[143]

Although, or perhaps rather because, the nuclear option was withdrawn from the table by November 1973, France, Britain, and the FRG were now sedulously trying to hammer out agreement on where discussions on European defence should start. In a speech to the WEU Assembly on 21 November 1973, Jobert somehow disappointed his partners by publicly proposing to use the WEU as a platform for initial discussions.[144] He did so because Denmark and neutral Ireland were sceptical about the Nine talking about defence. As the other Seven constituted the exact membership of the WEU, this forum appeared as a viable alternative. Also, Pompidou cautioned Jobert not to put the cart before the horse and suggested to go for the WEU until it became clearer whether the political unity of the Nine would lead anywhere. In his summit with Heath on 16 November 1973, the French president did have a first substantive exchange on what European defence in the future could consist of. However, he was obviously more sceptical about the readiness of the Nine to take on this issue than his foreign minister was.[145]

Aware that Bonn did not like the WEU, which had been set up to control West German rearmament, Pompidou suggested in his next meeting with Brandt on 26 November 1973 that the WEU treaty ought to be revised and offered to drop all restraints concerning West German defence other than those relating to weapons of mass destruction. The chancellor replied that he would not rule out the WEU and be flexible about the forum as long as a sovereign European defence would result from it.[146] Scheel, however, continued to make the case for a common security and defence policy of the Nine. Being convinced that resistance from Ireland and Denmark could be overcome, he now more enthusiastically than ever talked of a single representation by the Nine within the Alliance by 1980.[147] Bonn's cacophony became complete when Defence Minister Leber, just after Jobert's speech in the WEU Assembly, came up with exuberant praise for Eurogroup, which he continued to see as the best way towards European defence.[148] Britain was comparatively more united than the FRG in its negative response to the French WEU proposal. It remained pragmatic, however, as to whether future European efforts should focus on the Nine or Eurogroup. In its public reaction to Jobert's speech, it referred to the advantages of the Eurogroup. Internally, by contrast, Heath and Secretary of Defence Peter Carrington argued that while Eurogroup was suitable to deal with procurement, talks on European defence should take place within the Community framework.[149]

By the end of November 1973, the different institutional preferences as to how to deal with European defence threatened to slow down the dynamic that had emerged with the French policy change. This, however, was contrary to the interests of France, Britain, and the FRG, which now all shared a political will and sense of urgency about making progress in this field. Although Pompidou, Heath, and Brandt agreed that European defence should not become an issue of the Copenhagen summit, because of sensitivities of the Danish presidency,[150] it was hoped that this meeting would, nevertheless, give further impulse to-this matter and reveal ways of how to proceed. Such expectations were grounded especially on hints by French decision-makers that France would really mean business in European defence if this summit proved that a *volonté politique* among the Nine really did exist.[151]

Thus, the notion of European defence clearly was in the air in the weeks before the Copenhagen summit. What was promising with respect to a potential security and defence dimension to the process of European unification was that the EPC members had already begun to deal with a series of specific topics in this realm in the course of 1973, albeit in a rather patchy way. Starting in February 1973, the Political Committee had discussed in several meetings, often based on Italian papers, the implication of MBFR on European unity. What initially amounted to little more than an embarrassed 'general murmuring [...] over the brandy glasses', by the end of the year became rather substantive debates already.[152] Another significant development was the decision, proposed by France in early July 1973, to set up an ad hoc working group to analyse the diverse security implications of the American–Soviet agreement on the prevention of nuclear war for Western Europe. Even though the respective experts found it difficult to produce a report with a common assessment, their meetings were still important in bringing security issues closer to EPC's range of topics.[153] It is also worth noting that some consultation and coordination among the permanent representatives of EPC members in NATO had been launched, especially in the context of the 'Year of Europe' declarations.[154] Finally, a precedent of discussing European defence in EPC had been set when the French unexpectedly brought up the matter in the process of formulating the Nine's paper on European Identity.

The Declaration on European Identity

The Copenhagen summit in mid-December 1973 represented a kind of test case for whether the Nine's intention of building up the means and capabilities with which to give more weight to their foreign policy ambitions could actually be translated into practical measures. For concepts such as EPC summitry, and perhaps even European defence, it was potentially the first step towards what many hoped would be a rapid development of the further political unification of Europe. In the case of the identity paper, however, the situation was different. Here the summit marked the culmination and end point of a process that had started in the summer of 1973. Issued by the nine foreign ministers on the occasion of their Copenhagen meeting, the 'Declaration on European Identity' of 14 December 1973 constituted an attempt to define the foundations of a

European foreign policy and formulate specific objectives concerning Europe's role in the world. It came about as a response to the mounting external challenges that the Nine had encountered in recent months and became the most manifest expression of EPC's progress in the second half of 1973 outside the realm of the policy-specific achievements in the context of the CSCE, the 'Year of Europe', and the October War. It was more than just a situational reaction to specific challenges. Being the EC countries' first monothematic statement on the European identity, it was a pioneering document in what has become a very prominent topic that has occupied European institutions, national governments, and academics alike since the end of the Cold War. What is striking is the similarity between those discussions and the debates today, despite the progress that the unification of Europe has made since.

As shown in Chapter 4, the origins of the declaration lay in Britain, where the FCO came up with the idea in June 1973 that the Nine should define for themselves the European identity as a basis for working out a common European position in a joint declaration with the US in the 'Year of Europe'. From a British perspective, the identity paper was, above all, to be a device to convince the French to participate in the Kissinger exercise. Yet, the debates on European identity took on a life of their own. It turned out to be impossible to define the Nine's identity quickly enough to use it as the basis from which to elaborate a European–American declaration. Whilst the transatlantic row in August 1973 made it imperative for the Nine to act fast, an initial exchange of views among the Nine revealed that there was disagreement on both the purpose and the substance of an identity paper.[155] Work on this issue, therefore, only began to take off once the Nine had approved a draft declaration on their relations with the US in early September. This had the advantage of reducing the time pressure placed upon the Nine. The Group of Correspondents, which was tasked with producing the paper, could put together their heads to discuss how Europe's identity was to be defined over a period of nearly three months.

Initial national differences about how to approach the exercise became apparent in three very disparate drafts that Britain, Ireland, and France submitted to the Correspondents. The FCO came forward with a 20-page paper that focused almost exclusively on European–American relations. The narrow focus was justified with the argument that a EU with a common foreign policy would make little sense without a common European attitude towards the US. Defining Europe's identity, so the paper argued, should allow the Nine to be generally prepared for the external pressures they were bound to face in the coming decade; to get ready for the specific talks with the US on trade, monetary, and defence matters; and to be able to respond adequately to the 'Year of

Europe'. The draft did briefly refer to the possibility of defining Europe's identity vis-à-vis the US by trying to differentiate distinct values and choices of methods of either entity. Yet, its major purpose was to provide a guide to how to tackle European–American affairs in the context of the Kissinger challenge. It was mainly concerned, therefore, with identifying a set of general principles for relations between the Nine and Washington. Thus, the British paper stated that agreement among the Community countries should always precede agreement with the US; that it was more important for the Nine's identity to be defined by early agreement among themselves than for this identity to be acceptable to the US; and that the Nine should resist any suggestion that the evolution of their relations and their common policies would be subject to any kind of prior agreement with the American administration. It concluded that the Nine should not make any material concessions in their upcoming negotiations with the US, but should remain conciliatory in their attitudes, in accordance with the motto: *suaviter in modo, fortiter in re.*[156]

The Irish draft was much more conceptual in its approach. It defined the European identity via the existing EC institutions and the achievements of EPC and put it into the dynamic perspective of the EU of 1980. Its emphasis was on the internal development of the Community, rather than on Europe's role in the world. It also explicitly ruled out that the Nine would aspire to become a superpower.[157] The draft put forward by France was different yet again. It built on the two earlier papers by Britain and Ireland, but rejected the view that the Nine's identity should appear as a function of their relations with the US and made the case for a general approach instead. The French draft, hence, proposed two different sections on the 'constitutive elements' of the European identity, as well as on the European identity vis-à-vis the 'rest of the world'. In the former section, the singularity of the identity of the Nine was depicted by the fact that they all had different national cultures, while concomitantly being heir to a common civilisation with shared legal, political, and moral values and ever more similar ways of living. It was also claimed that Europe had common interests, deriving from factors such as its history, geography, population size, and exchanges with the world. As the individual nation states had lost their dominant international positions only European unity could enable the voice of Europe to be heard again, the French draft argued, adding that the Nine also required an adequate defence if they wanted to preserve their independence. As for the 'rest of the world' section, the will of the Nine was emphasised in playing a dynamic role in international politics and progressively defining common foreign policy positions. The Nine's relations with individual states or groups of states were then briefly characterised, dealing respectively with Africa and the Mediterranean; other developing countries; the US; Japan and Canada; the Communist East; and China. What was striking about the French draft was that it failed to ever mention the Community, in stark contrast to the nearly 50 such references in the British paper.[158]

Although elements of the British and Irish drafts made it into the eventual EPC text, the Correspondents agreed to work on the basis of the French document. The majority of delegates came out against focusing on the US alone, be it because they considered the substance of the FCO paper too sensitive and the risk of leakage too large, because they disagreed with its rather critical attitude towards the US, or because they simply agreed with France that Europe's identity needed a more comprehensive basis.[159] The British paper also looked increasingly inappropriate since discussions on European–American relations proceeded separately from the work on the Nine's identity. Moreover, it soon turned out that most EPC members favoured publishing the identity paper as a declaration, which naturally gave it a very different character from what the Heath government had originally envisaged.[160] Britain tried in vain to convince its partners to at least approve the principles of relations with the US as a confidential country annex to the declaration, to be subsequently complemented with similar guidelines for the Soviet Union and other political entities. While it did gain the support of the French, most other EPC countries considered it too risky to do anything that might provoke renewed wrath from Washington.[161]

Once the basic decision on the purpose and scope of the paper was taken, negotiations on the wording of the text went smoothly. Obviously, there were still national differences of emphasis. The West Germans and the Dutch, for example, would have preferred to work on the basis of phrases already agreed in previous European statements, but eventually gave way to the appeal of the French and the Italians to project the European identity into the future.[162] Some, such as the British, would have liked to have the goal of a 'common' European foreign policy explicitly stated, but had to accept that others wanted to proceed more slowly and stick to expressions such as 'with one voice'. The FRG was also wary about describing the Nine as a new 'power' in global diplomacy, which others, such as France, had to take into account for the sake of an overall compromise.[163] Yet, the only item that provoked protracted and heated discussions and had to be decided at the level of foreign ministers was the issue of defence. Whereas some, such as the Irish and the Dutch, were generally nervous about the idea of raising the topic of defence in an EPC document, others, such as the Italians and the British, supported the French paragraph, but sought to complement it with references to the Alliance and the US. Ireland, however, did not want to mention the Alliance, while Denmark objected to an explicit formula of 'European defence'. Many compromises were, thus, necessary before everyone could subscribe to a common text, which ironically resulted in the defence paragraph becoming much longer than the French had originally intended.[164]

The 'Declaration on European Identity' was finally published as a fairly coherent, slim statement on the internal factors which provide the common foundations of the Nine, the reasons why it was imperative for them to act as one in international politics, and the broad principles of their external relations and foreign policies.[165] It was structured in three parts on the 'Unity of the Nine Member Countries of the Community', 'The European Identity in Relation to the World', and 'The Dynamic Nature of the Construction of a United Europe'. Part I closely followed the French draft and contained six major features. It started off with the common European civilisation and the diversity of cultures, but went on to describe the unity of the Nine as a 'basic necessity' to ensure the survival of this common heritage. Concerning the common values of the Nine, it identified representative democracy, the rule of law, social justice, and respect of human rights as 'fundamental elements' of European identity. A third aspect of this identity was the determination to take part in the construction of the united Europe, with the EC, EPC, and the emerging EU being open to others who share the same 'ideals and objectives'. The Nine, then, pleaded for 'joint solutions to international problems' and argued:

> International developments and the growing concentration of power and responsibility in the hands of a very small number of great powers mean that Europe must unite and speak increasingly with one voice if it wants to make herself heard and play its proper rôle in the world.

After an assurance that the Community was not inward looking, the first part ended by referring to defence:

> The Nine, one of whose essential aims is to maintain peace, will never succeed in doing so if they neglect their own security. Those of them who are members of the Atlantic Alliance consider that in present circumstances there is no alternative to the security provided by the nuclear weapons of the United States and by the presence of North American forces in Europe; and they agree that in the light of the relative vulnerability of Europe, the Europeans should, if they wish to preserve their independence, hold to their commitments and make constant efforts to ensure that they have adequate means of defence at their disposal.

Part II began by underlining that European unification was not inspired by a 'desire for power', but would constitute an international 'element of equilibrium'. It added that the Nine would play their active role in world affairs in accordance with the UN Charter principles. Alluding to the ongoing 'Year of Europe' discussions, it requested that in the case of collective negotiations of the Nine with other countries, the institutions and procedures chosen should 'enable the distinct character of the European entity to be respected'. The declaration, then, discussed the relations of the Nine with other countries or regions, following a more differentiated categorisation than had featured in the French draft. Remarks on the US were more detailed than those on other actors, but were unspecific and came only in fourth place. The Nine referred to the 'common heritage' and 'shared values and aspirations' with the US and indicated their willingness to preserve close ties and maintain a constructive dialogue, but also reaffirmed their determination 'to establish themselves as a distinct and original entity'. They added that cooperation should be developed on the basis of equality and in the spirit of friendship.

Finally, in part III, the Nine pointed out that their identity would evolve further as a function of the dynamic construction of the EU. They implied that they had only just embarked on a process that they expected would take them much further. This concluding remark was characteristic of the general tenor of the declaration, which was marked by self-confidence and political ambition. To be sure, the text did remain vague in many ways, and it was much stronger on values and intentions than on more material factors, such as defence and the real distribution of capabilities at the time. What is more, for all its emphasis on self-reliance, it did have to admit that Europe's security was dependent on the protection from the US as an outside ally, which is why it has justly been called 'an impressive cheque made out for the future but uncovered in terms of power'.[166] Nevertheless, it is striking how the declaration identified the political will of the Nine to act as a distinct entity in international politics as a core component of the European identity. It was this assertion that linked this document to the European–American declaration and the 'Year of Europe' again and gave it its contemporary significance at the end of 1973. Assured by EPC's success stories in the CSCE, the Kissinger exercise, and the Middle East declaration, and compelled by the changing international environment, the Nine were more convinced than ever at the close of the year of the need and benefits of speaking with one voice in global diplomacy and of Europe acquiring some degree of political autonomy.

A twofold challenge to Europe's political unity

Seen from the US, it must have seemed ironic, and even provocative, that 1973 closed with a declaration by the Nine on their identity. Ironic, because the only visible product resulting from the 'Year of Europe' was a document asserting Europe's political aspirations rather than a redefinition of Atlantic relations. Provocative, because European–American relations had dramatically worsened again in the course of the October War and the oil crisis. In the autumn of 1973, the Nixon administration, in fact, showed increasing signs of disenchantment with Europe's foreign policy efforts, which as a result of EPC's growing success obviously began to affect US interests as well. At a time when EPC was heading towards a new peak in its development, American frustration about it, thus, began to pose a serious challenge to the viability of any distinct European foreign policy. In parallel, a mounting economic crisis of the Community also threatened to gradually undermine the unity and solidarity of the Nine from within. Neither the external nor the internal challenge in 1973 decisively inhibited the evolution of EPC at this point. Yet, the clouds that would build up to a storm and sweep away much of Europe's political ambition in 1974 were already gathering on the horizon.

The transatlantic crisis: Clashing over the Middle East

In the history of the Atlantic Alliance, the Middle East traditionally represented the single biggest focal point of dissent. From the Suez Crisis in 1956 to the Iraq War in 2003, allies time and again were at loggerheads over the right kind of policies vis-à-vis challenges relating to this region. In 1973, a bitter clash occurred over how to respond to the October War and the oil crisis. This rift was repeatedly referred to as 'Suez in reverse', as some observers, including Kissinger, read into the European lack of support for Washington's policy an act of retribution for America's opposition to the Franco-British intervention in 1956.[167]

As indicated above, differences between Europe and the US related to the war, the question of how to resolve the conflict and structure a peace process, as well as the nature of threat that emanated from the Arab–Israeli struggle. Whereas the Europeans pursued a policy of neutrality during the war, the US became actively involved in it by supplying arms to Israel. Whereas the Europeans argued that in view of its illegal occupation of territory it was primarily up to Israel to make the necessary concessions to allow diplomacy to progress, the US refrained from putting any such demands on Tel Aviv.

Whereas the Europeans supported a UN peace conference and a comprehensive settlement of the conflict, the US emphasised its unilateral undertaking and a step-by-step approach. And, most significantly, whereas the Europeans were mainly concerned with threats to their economic security resulting from the Arab 'oil weapon', the US perceived the Arab–Israeli confrontation mainly through an East–West lens, being preoccupied with the conduct of the Soviet Union and the global balance of power.

Such divergent positions and priorities resulted in numerous confrontations over specific issues, which together amounted to one of the most profound transatlantic crises during the Cold War. The Europeans generally refused to be associated with Kissinger's Middle East policies, since they considered that they had warned Washington for long enough of the consequences of US non-involvement in the search for peace and now had to bear the brunt of the energy crisis. Moreover, they considered the extent to which the US interpreted the Arab–Israeli conflict as an extension of the East–West antagonism excessive. Kissinger, for his part, accused Europe of giving in to Arab blackmail and being blind to the Soviet threat. In his view, European behaviour during the double crisis confirmed that Europe had regional interests only and lacked any sense of global responsibility.[168]

Differences between the US and the Europeans already emerged during the first two days of the war. While Kissinger intended to introduce a resolution at the Security Council calling for a cease-fire and a return to the pre-war borders, the British and French wanted the cease-fire to be linked to negotiations according to Resolution 242 – which the US secretary of state denounced as supporting Arab aggression and land grabbing.[169] On 12 October 1973, London and Washington clashed again over a potential UN resolution. This time, Kissinger asked Britain to table a resolution calling for a cease-fire in situ, indicating that the Soviets had assured him that Egypt would acquiesce to such a proposal. Whitehall, however, knew from Sadat that Egypt would accept no such resolution unless Israel agreed to withdraw to its 1967 borders. Accordingly, Douglas-Home, after double-checking with Cairo, declined to take any initiative that was bound to compromise British interests in the Arab world. This, again, provoked the wrath of Kissinger, who stressed that the US could not recall any crisis in the last three years where Britain had been with the Americans 'when the chips were down',[170] and that his only consolation was that they would all go down together and that at least they would now do it 'with the worst possible grace'.[171]

A next point of contention concerned the US airlift to Israel. In order to preserve their neutrality in the war, all EPC members, except the Netherlands and the FRG, dissociated themselves from the US transports by banning over-flights over their territories and refusing permission for the US to use their air bases and other facilities in Europe.[172] If this attitude caused general indignation in Washington, it provoked a sharp reaction when the Brandt government publicly asked the US after the cease-fire to stop loading Israeli ships on West German territory too. Bonn received not only a strong US note hinting at 'disastrous consequences' if the West displayed disunity, but also a public warning by US Secretary of Defence James Schlesinger that the US might have to review its policy of maintaining troops in the FRG in view of West Germany's uncooperative attitude.[173] Brandt, conversely, internally complained that Washington treated the FRG like a colony, and in a letter to Nixon he implied that he was less than convinced of the US case for a continuing airlift to Israel.[174]

The issue of whether NATO had a collective role to play in the crisis also caused temperatures to rise on both sides of the Atlantic. On 16 October 1973, Rumsfeld asked the Europeans in a strongly worded statement in the NATO Council to join the US in an 'organic policy that would make clear to the Russians the damage that would be done to their interests if they damaged ours'.[175] He proposed that the allies slow down or suspend participation in the CSCE, take economic measures against the Communist East, and review their bilateral agreements with the Soviet Union in protest to Soviet support of the Arab aggression. This met with a rebuff from the Europeans, however, who were not willing to sacrifice détente in Europe for the sake of US policies in the Middle East.[176] Kissinger, on the other hand, considered the European argument that Alliance responsibilities did not extend to the Middle East legalistic and could not understand that the Europeans would refuse to participate in the containment of Soviet expansionism in the Middle East, given that they would suffer much more from a radicalised Arab world than the US.[177] Chance remarks by Schlesinger that the Alliance should be readier to use force to make sure that the industrialised nations would not continuously be submitted to the whims of the 'under-developed countries' did nothing to narrow such differences and calm the situation.[178]

After the cease-fire of 22 October 1973, another row broke out over the US nuclear alert. There were two major reasons for this. First, the Europeans were taken by complete surprise by the apparent escalation of tensions between the superpowers and felt inadequately consulted on the US measure. While the British were at least officially informed via their ambassador one hour after the US decision was taken, most other Europeans learnt of the alert from the media, with Rumsfeld only belatedly issuing a statement in NATO.[179] As

Washington's allies soberly realised, gone were the days when John F. Kennedy had sent out emissaries with photographic evidence to European capitals to muster allied support during the Cuban missile crisis.[180] Second, many in Europe remained unconvinced after the event as to whether the US alert had been justified. The perception was widespread that Moscow had no intention of intervening militarily in the Middle East and had supplied arms to the battlefield in order to prevent complete Arab defeat only.[181] Even the French and the British, to whom Kissinger showed Brezhnev's letter that had prompted the US reaction, internally continued to express doubts about the commensurability of the measure, noting that the one threatening Soviet sentence in the letter had been accompanied by a series of reassurances of cooperation.[182] Europe continued to suspect the US of having been, at least partially, motivated to use an alert to prove that its foreign policy continued to be operational in the face of the increasing domestic turmoil that beset the Nixon administration. Was it simply a coincidence, the press speculated, that such a drastic US action should occur only days after the resignation of Vice President Spiro Agnew over a financial scandal and, in particular, after the 'Saturday Night Massacre', that is, Nixon's firing of the special prosecutor in the Watergate scandal, as well as of the US attorney general and his deputy?[183] Kissinger was naturally outraged at the lack of European support for a measure which the US, according to him, had taken to defend the global equilibrium. He did not care what Belgium thought about it, he told Cromer in Washington, but at least one or two of the major allies should have supported it. Kissinger acknowledged a deficit of consultation, not without adding, however, that the US could not have accepted a different judgement under the circumstances anyway.[184]

Finally, there was the declaration of the Nine on the Middle East of 6 November 1973, which caused major irritation in the US both because of its timing and because of its substance. As for the timing, the declaration was not only issued right at the beginning of Kissinger's first trip to the Middle East, but also despite the fact that the US had loudly and resolutely vituperated the Europeans for their policies in the crisis. During a press conference on 26 October 1973, a bad-tempered Nixon had pointed out that 'Europe, which gets eighty per cent of its oil from the Middle East, would have frozen to death this winter' if it had not been for American mediation to stop the fighting.[185] Four days later, he had warned Brandt in a letter that by 'disassociating themselves from the US in the Middle East, our Allies may think they protect their immediate economic interests, but only at great long term cost. A differentiated détente in which the Allies hope to insulate their relations with the USSR can only divide the Alliance and ultimately produce disastrous consequences for Europe.'[186]

In acrimonious conversations with the French, British, and West German ambassadors to Washington on 25/26 October 1973, Kissinger had left no doubt that the Nixon administration was 'fed up' with Europe.[187] Since the Europeans had behaved as 'hostile powers', had revealed a 'total absence of a sense of responsibility',[188] and had insisted on unity in matters of defence while acting non-cooperatively on other issues, there would now be a complete re-evaluation of transatlantic relations.[189] Time and again, according to Kissinger, the US had offered to consult and work out common positions, only to receive in return the conspicuous dissociation of allies, which had happened 'with too much consistency, too many times'.[190] After this 'blatant show of disunity', the West might now well go down the path of ancient Greece, which he, as a historian, could only observe with melancholy.[191]

As for the substance of the declaration, Kissinger left no doubt in his memoirs as to how much he resented it. According to his devastating criticism, the declaration was a wholesale endorsement of the Arab interpretation of Resolution 242. With its insistence on a return to the lines of the cease-fire of 22 October 1973, it reduced Sadat's room for manoeuvre. Being a flirtation with the radical Arab position, it encouraged intransigence that threatened to prolong the war, as well as the 'oil weapon'. Its comprehensive approach to a peace solution was out of touch with reality and undermined the position of moderate Arabs, who had accepted the US piecemeal approach. The whole declaration was, thus, a direct challenge to US policy, which would 'either undercut US diplomacy or demonstrate Europe's irrelevance'.[192]

It was again the British who became involved in the sharpest exchanges with Washington. In a heated meeting with Carrington on 7 November 1973, Schlesinger accused Britain of pursuing a policy of 'decayed Gaullism' and insisted that London could no longer count on the special relationship being maintained.[193] During a dinner with US correspondents, Heath retaliated that Kissinger could not expect the Europeans to fall into step behind him if they disagreed with US policy. Washington should learn to understand, so the prime minister argued, that there were two Europes. Although the US constituted a major ally in NATO, it was not a member of the Nine, which could legitimately hold a position different from that of Washington and which might express themselves through a Danish spokesman, whether Kissinger liked it or not. The Americans had long urged the EC to speak with one voice, Heath added, but they now did not seem ready for it.[194]

To be sure, not everyone in Europe took the US threats at face value. Jobert, for example, dismissed the American expressions of dissatisfaction by laconically comparing Kissinger to 'a saucepan of milk which boiled over from time to time'.[195] However, there was growing anxiety among the Nine as to the future of the 'West', even more so since the oil crisis was anything but over and diverging interests of Europe and the US were bound to cause further transatlantic strain.[196]

The 'Year of Europe' blocked – and new American proposals

It comes as no surprise that the European–American rift also had negative repercussions on the 'Year of Europe'. Although the negotiations on the two declarations took place in a constructive atmosphere at the level of officials, basic differences on the substance of the texts remained. These differences gained all the more weight in the course of the autumn of 1973 as they found expression in practical politics, most notably in the transatlantic disputes over the Middle East. Indeed, the discussions on how to redefine and strengthen the West against the background of the transatlantic turmoil began to look surreal. At the same time, European–American clashes gave additional meaning to the view that something was deeply wrong with the Alliance, which caused Kissinger to come up with new proposals at the end of the year to reinforce the Atlantic Community.

Negotiations on the European–American declaration in October 1973 began quite well for the Nine. After two intensive internal rounds of deliberations,[197] the Political Committee was able to agree on a joint reaction to the amendments proposed by Stoessel and Sonnenfeldt in late September 1973 (see Chapter 4). In their revised draft, prepared for the first round of negotiations with the US in Copenhagen on 18/19 October 1973,[198] the Nine did take up some of the American requests. But they remained firm on the basic issues. They inserted a reference to the Alliance, and they also gave more weight to the close ties between Europe and the US. Yet, there were still no references to 'interdependence' and 'partnership', which France, in particular, considered to be Atlanticist jargon reflecting a notion of the West that left no room for an autonomous European foreign policy.[199] Furthermore, the Nine developed two common briefs for an exposé by the Danish political director at the beginning of the negotiations, in which they explained why they were not able to accept the US amendments on the issues of defence and consultations. References to defence, they argued, would reintroduce a global approach and link all issues, which they opposed. As for consultation, they were ready to intensify the existing habits. But their unity was not yet developed enough for them to accept any new machinery for more institutionalised consultations.[200]

When the negotiations with the US representatives took place, all nine EPC members came to note with satisfaction how united they were and how impressed the US appeared by their resolute performance.[201] The French delegation was surprised at how firmly the West Germans rejected the concept of 'partnership'; how insistently the Danish warned Stoessel and Sonnefeldt not to press the Nine into a club of Ten; how much the Italians and the Belgians emphasised the priority of the European identity over US–European relations, which could be a function of this identity only; and how decidedly the British defended the autonomy of European détente. They reported enthusiastically to the Quai d'Orsay that they themselves had hardly had to intervene in the negotiations, and that solidarity among the Nine had reached such a level that France was even informed by its partners of advance manoeuvres by the State Department designed to convince some of the Nine to engage in a concerted effort to press Paris into accepting the notion of 'partnership'.[202]

Whereas the Nine were content with the meeting, Kissinger was displeased with the result. What good was it to wrangle over commas in the declaration, he argued, if in practice there was conflict only between the two sides?[203] Europe, Kissinger asserted, was fighting 'the wrong battles on the wrong battlefields', and the West in this condition would hardly survive another five years.[204] By the end of October 1973, the US secretary of state indicated that he was 'sick and tired' of the declaration, which, he insinuated, should possibly be dropped.[205]

The Europeans, for their part, suspended work in NATO on the Atlantic declaration on 26 October 1973 as a measure of protest against non-consultation on the US nuclear alert.[206] Discussions between the Fifteen on this declaration had been substantial throughout October, but had failed to really lead anywhere. This was because key US amendments to the original French draft were unacceptable to Paris. France was eager to stress Europe's particular vulnerability and the increasingly specific character of the defence of Europe as a result of the nuclear parity of the superpowers. Washington, in contrast, insisted that all allies remained equally vulnerable and that the defence of Europe was becoming more complex, rather than more specific. The US further rejected the notion that it was only 'at present' that there was no alternative to US troops and nuclear weapons to defend Europe, which France, in turn, read as an objection to the goal of any future European defence cooperation. Another point of dissention was the French interpretation of the American–Soviet agreement on the prevention of nuclear war, which the US wanted to omit from the text. Finally, France was also unhappy with the Nixon administration's seeming attempt to place the reference to the

European Union into an Atlantic, rather than an autonomous European framework.[207]

Once discussions on this declaration resumed, the Franco-American gap seemed to widen, rather than narrow. On 14 November 1973, France tabled a revised draft in the NATO Council that contained additional references to human rights, economic cooperation, and, in a vague allusion, to MBFR, as requested by the Dutch, the British, and the West Germans, respectively.[208] Yet, with the partial exception of MBFR, the new draft took little account of most US proposals, with the respective alterations being more cosmetic than substantial. A third French draft, issued later in the month, did take into account some further US suggestions, most notably in the field of burden sharing. But it was obviously still way below the expectations of the US, which in turn confidentially submitted further amendments to Paris that could only make negotiations even more difficult.[209]

With work on the Atlantic declaration stagnating, progress in the parallel discussions on the European–American declaration in November 1973 became inconceivable. Despite a personal letter from Jobert to Kissinger that asked the US to accept the European draft as it stood,[210] the US delegates came forward with the same kind of requests again in a second round of negotiations in Copenhagen on 14 November 1973. While Stoessel and Sonnenfeldt professed to understand the difficulties of the Nine to refer to 'partnership', 'interdependence' and new consultative machinery, they indefatigably tried to get the concepts behind these terms into the draft by new vocabulary. Moreover, there were now additional differences on the economic part of the text coming to the fore.[211]

Kissinger expressed ever-greater frustration towards the end of the year at how European–American relations and the 'Year of Europe' were evolving. This was also because the Nine had officially invited Japan to work out a bilateral declaration with Europe in mid-November, despite the fact that both Washington and Tokyo had strongly argued in the autumn of 1973 in favour of a chapeau declaration including Japan once the first two declarations had been settled.[212] While the Nine disliked the idea of a declaration of all industrialised democracies that might reduce the relevance of the original two declarations, Kissinger seemed to resent the fact that the EC countries were becoming more and more the linchpin of the 'Year of Europe'. Additional annoyance was caused by the leakage to the press of both the revised draft on European–American relations (with the US amendments) and the first and second French draft on Atlantic relations.[213] Furthermore, the US found it hard to understand why it was refused a say in the working out of the identity document, remaining unhappy about the British argument that it could no more expect to be consulted about the drafting of a unilateral European policy statement than the Nine could hope to influence Nixon's annual reports to Congress on American foreign policy.[214]

In a conversation with Cromer on 24 November 1973, Kissinger made it clear that the Europeans would not get away with their behaviour. Deploring that there was no more Anglo–American–German lead in NATO, he accused Britain of leaning too much towards France and decried the West Germans as unreliable, with the US having 'hair-raising intelligence' about what the FRG was telling the Russians. He then argued that the Nine's relations with the US were now dominated by the French, who sought to construct Europe on an anti-American basis and on the 'cold-blooded assessment' that they could drive Britain to share in this. Yet, the French assumption that the Americans would not retaliate against such an undertaking was 'the worst decision since the Greek city states confronted Alexander', Kissinger warned.[215] What the US secretary of state had in mind became apparent two weeks later, when he, on four different occasions during the NATO ministerial meeting in Brussels and a subsequent speech in London, uttered strong criticism of how EPC was developing and came up with several new proposals of how to reinforce Atlantic ties. All these meetings took place in a cool and petulant atmosphere. The fact alone that NATO ministers for the first time in years discussed European–American relations rather than East–West affairs gives ample illustration of the sense of transatlantic crisis that prevailed at the time. As the FCO summed up the encounters, after all that had happened since Kissinger's 'Year of Europe' speech, fireworks could be expected in Brussels, and they 'duly took place'.[216]

On the traditional quadripartite dinner on the eve of the NATO meeting, Kissinger started by admitting that the Franco-British position on the Arab–Israeli conflict prior to the outbreak of the October War had been correct and that he would even personally support the European position on Israeli withdrawal. Describing his mediating efforts in the Middle East as a 'heart-breaking, miserable, dirty business', he assured his interlocutors that he had no intention of marginalising Europe in the area, but failed to give a convincing answer as to why he had not pressed for a European seat at the table of the peace conference in Geneva. Kissinger then lamented that Europe only seemed to unite to take positions against the US and accused the Heath government of being more Gaullist than de Gaulle himself. Pointing out the 'total difference of perception' between the Nine and the US, he sharply attacked the text of the European–American declaration, in which he would no longer be interested. As a remedy to the transatlantic malaise, Kissinger proposed to link or combine the consultative machineries of EPC and NATO, which obviously found little support among his three interlocutors. His request to be regularly informed about the weekly results of the West German *Bundesliga* was, however, met with approval, this being a task which Scheel immediately accepted.[217]

During the actual NATO ministerial meeting on 10/11 December 1973, Kissinger bemoaned that some Europeans had 'analysed to death' his April initiative and had turned it into an 'adversary process'. He, then, bashed the Nine for turning the refusal to consult with the US into a principle, which he contrasted with the occasional 'oversights and mistakes' of the Nixon administration with regard to consulting Europe. This time speaking out in favour of completing both declarations, the US secretary of state suggested that NATO consultations should be improved in terms of both procedure and substance. Procedurally, the political directors from capitals should at regular intervals join the NATO Council in permanent sessions; in terms of substance, NATO consultations should begin to cover more issues outside the Alliance territory. When Jobert launched another assault on the superpower condominium in his own speech and called for European defence cooperation, Kissinger, as he recalled in his memoirs, used the 'rarely exercised right of reply for a sharp rebuttal'.[218] So much tension was now in the air that NATO Secretary-General Luns called for a private meeting after the plenary session to ease off the situation. While the meeting failed to achieve this purpose, it did witness another proposal by the Danish Foreign Minister Andersen that NATO should adopt the consultation method of the Nine, with ministers discussing freely issue by issue, rather than reading out set speeches.[219]

On the afternoon of 11 December 1973, there was an additional exchange of views between Kissinger and the foreign ministers of the Nine. Taking place in Andersen's hotel suite in Brussels, it was a historical meeting in the evolution of EPC, as it marked the first official encounter between the Nine and the US at the foreign minister level. In terms of substance, however, Kissinger was right when he later wrote that 'the meeting will not be recorded in diplomatic history as having added to anybody's store of knowledge except that of the puckish Irish foreign minister, Garret FitzGerald, who had never before witnessed transatlantic tribal rites'.[220] Initially planned to discuss the European–American declaration, the meeting in the two weeks before the Brussels gathering had not even been guaranteed to take place, as neither side had wanted to be seen as *demandeur* by proposing to hold the session. When it did proceed, with FitzGerald, allegedly by coincidence, being in town too, the atmosphere was friendlier than in NATO. However, the conversation was more about mutually pouring out grievances, rather than consulting on the draft. The one novelty was Kissinger's request to make the declaration shorter, less formal, and more eloquent. Interestingly enough, Kissinger confidentially asked Jobert again to do the job, the two secretaries of state having sorted out their differences over a private bilateral breakfast.[221]

Finally, Kissinger also used the opportunity of a public speech he was scheduled to make at the Society of Pilgrims in London on 12 December 1973 to air his assessment of the crisis and demonstrate his willingness to give new impetus to Atlantic relations. Invited by a host who was critical of the deterioration of Anglo-American relations under Heath,[222] Kissinger offered Europe a special relationship with the US akin to that which existed between Washington and London. Europe and the US, he argued, should not be two distinct entities, but members of the same community. Recalling the reasons for the 'Year of Europe', and assuring his support for an independent European identity and a global political role of the Nine, Kissinger then listed his grievances about EPC, which culminated in the warning that 'Europe's unity must not be at the expense of Atlantic community'. The Nine, he continued, now had to choose between 'creativity together or irrelevance apart'. After suggesting that the declarations should be finished and consultations improved, he eventually came up with yet another proposal, with a view to illustrating the kind of partnership he had in mind. Europe and the US, he proposed, together with Canada and Japan, should set up an Energy Action Group, composed of senior national representatives, in order to tackle the energy crisis as a common Atlantic enterprise.[223]

Kissinger's mixture of verbal sticks for EPC and substantive carrots concerning Atlantic cooperation could not but be interpreted as an assault on the way European foreign policy-making had evolved. His ideas of bringing EPC closer to NATO, transforming the Alliance into a comprehensive forum for European–American cooperation, and including the Political Directors – a term so far only used by EPC – in NATO consultations, caused alarm bells to ring, and not only in Paris. At the same time, it was undeniable that the US was reaching out its hand to Europe once more. The energy proposal was particularly important in this respect, as Kissinger's offer of American cooperation came at a time when the Nine were at loggerheads with each other as to how to tackle the energy crisis. His Atlantic initiatives were, thus, bound to be divisive, and it was hardly a coincidence that he made them just days before the European summit at Copenhagen that was to cover EPC and energy issues. At the end of this chapter, I will describe how the Nine dealt with Kissinger's proposals at Copenhagen. Before I come to that, however, it is necessary to shed light on the second challenge that threatened to put EPC's further rise into jeopardy.

The EC crisis: Europe's economic base weakened

For all the excitement that prevailed about the prospects of the EC at the beginning of 1973, the first year of the enlarged Community on the economic level became a rather difficult one. Major aspects of the ambitious Paris Summit programme, such as EMU and the RDF, could not be implemented, with the negotiations in Brussels being increasingly marked by polarisation and stagnation. Worse, divergent conceptions of how to deal with the oil crisis in the autumn of 1973 led to serious fissures in the EC and threatened to undermine the solidarity of the Nine from within. Many of the problems that beset the EC over the year could be interpreted as normal consequences of enlargement, with national interests clashing over issues such as the geographic distribution of development aid, the price of grain, or sugar subsidies. However, as even the FCO self-critically acknowledged, key conflicts among the Nine were caused or at least accentuated by the minimalist approach Britain pursued vis-à-vis the development of Community policies. From the FCO point of view, the fact that the Treasury, rather than the FCO, had its way in shaping British policies towards EMU, RDF, and, to a lesser extent, the energy crisis proved disastrous for the search for common ground in these fields.[224]

It was clear to all in the Heath government that since Britain as *demandeur* in the enlargement negotiations had been compelled to more or less accept the terms of entry as they stood, it would have to follow Monnet's famous advice of 'joining first and negotiating afterwards'.[225] Yet once in, stark differences emerged between the Treasury and the FCO as to how to assure that Britain too could benefit economically from EC membership. The Treasury's approach, to put it crudely, was to ensure immediate short-term advantages in order to convince the critical public of the benefits of the Community, and to give priority to the maintenance of British national freedom to control the economy. The FCO, by contrast, argued that Britain should associate more intimately with the development of EC policies. It was convinced that Britain would benefit from a further deepening of the Community in the medium term, as London would most likely be able to partly direct the EC's evolution and then exploit it just as France was exploiting the CAP. Denying the EC its dynamic perspective, according to the FCO, would be detrimental to British interests and could well mean that London would be forced to renegotiate the terms of accession within three years. Although time and again overruled by the Treasury in its argumentation, the FCO would not cease during 1973 in pointing to the success of its approach in EPC, which contrary to EC policies had become a 'growth industry'.[226]

Most irritating to Britain's partners was the Treasury's persistent failure to return to the European currency 'snake', which made any progress towards EMU impossible. In March 1973, Brandt came forward with a very generous offer to help Britain get on board the EMU project. While a new acute monetary crisis in February 1973 had been temporarily resolved by a devaluation of the Dollar, it had become ever more clear to the Europeans that in view of Nixon's unwillingness to stop the Dollar from sliding, a restored system of fixed exchange rates was becoming infeasible. Brandt, therefore, proposed reintegrating the British currency into the 'snake' again and going for a joint European float. The chancellor was willing to pay a high price for what would have constituted a quantum leap towards EMU, offering large financial support and guarantees to Britain, and accepting measures that the FRG had previously rejected.[227] Yet, Britain declined the offer. Although Heath leaned towards it, his chancellor of the exchequer, Anthony Barber, made acceptance dependent on such unrealisable conditions such as unlimited financial support and non-obligation to repay that Britain could only be seen as being unprepared to adopt a fixed parity again for the Pound Sterling within the 'snake'.[228] In consequence, the six members of the 'snake' decided in mid-March 1973 to jointly float without Britain, Ireland, and Italy. This meant that they maintained fixed exchange rates among each other, but ceased defending the fixed parity of the Dollar, thereby constituting a 'snake' without the previous tunnel of the Smithsonian Agreement (see Chapter 1). This time, France accepted such a model, since the D-Mark had been devalued. As the US in parallel abolished the Dollar's fixed relation to gold, the Bretton Woods system had definitively come to an end, with any future monetary system being as yet indiscernible.[229] The effect of all this was that the goal of establishing EMU by 1980 looked ever more unrealistic. The lack of progress on the harmonisation of both monetary and economic policies made the plan of entering a second phase of the EMU project in 1974 obsolete. This, in turn, became a great problem for Britain, as the RDF was part of this second phase. Heath's strategy of rendering Community support in the modernisation of Britain's industries the equivalent to French benefits from CAP came under threat, therefore. Ironically, it was precisely those three countries which failed to enter the 'snake' that now strongly argued in favour of setting up the RDF anyway, be it by moving to some kind of interim phase of EMU or by taking RDF out of the bigger EMU design.[230]

Unsurprisingly, this evoked little enthusiasm in Paris and Bonn. In France, Pompidou was frustrated that his cherished monetary union was blocked. Moreover, French officials were irritated by the manner in which Britain had brought a sense of pragmatism to Brussels that France perceived as detrimental to its interests. Several reports arrived at the Quai d'Orsay, according to which British officials seemed little concerned about a strict interpretation of the treaties and a separation of competencies, with Douglas-Home in his very first appearance at the Council of Ministers bemoaning that the EC should discuss important political issues much more than trifles such as Norwegian fish.[231] As regards the FRG, there was a growing unwillingness, particularly manifest with Schmidt and large parts of the West German media, to continue to be the Community paymaster as long as no further progress in European integration could be achieved.[232]

Still, both Pompidou and Brandt were willing to help Heath with his domestic troubles. Yet, in the midst of discussions of what to do with the RDF, new tensions came into the Community over how to tackle the energy crisis. At the end of October 1973, the Dutch requested from its Community partners an agreement to pool Europe's oil supplies and share them if necessary. The Hague declared its appeal for European solidarity a test for the general viability of the Community and the nascent common identity of the Nine.[233] It received strong backing from the FRG and smaller EC members, who all regarded such a measure as a first step towards a common energy policy. Bonn now was even ready to accept a less liberal model of a common energy market than it had long advocated, as long as the Nine could finally reach consensus on this key policy field.[234]

However, Britain and France were extremely reluctant to display any Community solidarity in the oil realm. Being the only two European powers declared 'friendly' by the oil producers, they argued that a European oil allocation system could only provoke the Arabs to enlarge the embargo and make other Europeans 'join the Dutch in the dog-house',[235] which would do no good to anyone. Pompidou in particular was irritated at the demand by the Netherlands, which had always rejected his advice of building up oil stocks for times of crisis and had blocked a common European position in the Arab–Israeli conflict, but now insisted that its problems be shared by all.[236] Both he and Heath were well aware that some action was required to prevent the Community from falling into a deep crisis. Yet, they preferred to focus on diplomatic efforts by EPC to bring the Arabs round and, in addition, to confidentially ask the international oil companies to redistribute oil supplies silently, rather than public economic measures.[237]

At the EC Council meeting on 6 November 1973, Douglas-Home and Jobert did accept a short Community energy statement to be issued parallel to the declaration on the Middle East. It was, however, a bland text about the interdependence of EC economies only, remaining well below the expectations of both the Netherlands and the FRG. Moreover, both Britain and France also refused to publish the Commission's proposals on oil solidarity and to allow them to be formally taken up by the Council.[238] Conversely, they appear to have been able to convince their partners of the merits of a policy of quiet solidarity. According to Heath's memoirs at least, silent sharing of oil did take place.[239] Indeed, it is notable that warnings from the Dutch to France that they might have to curb their exports of natural gas (on which the Parisian region, in particular, was highly dependent) vanished in the second half of November 1973, with The Hague indicating publicly its satisfaction with a 'common position' found.[240] Then again, press reports were soon emerging that Britain and France would put pressure on the oil companies not to divert oil to The Hague, which nourished accusations that they egoistically put national interests first and pursued a policy of *sauve-qui-peut*.[241]

With the energy question far from being settled, and basic EC issues such as EMU and RDF unresolved, the Copenhagen summit was obliged to place a considerable accent on Community topics. The Heath government was now in a particularly desperate need of an economic success at the summit. At the end of 1973, Britain was, as Barber said in Cabinet, facing 'the gravest economic crisis since the end of the war'.[242] Apart from the oil crisis, it had already been suffering from a profound economic decline, with high unemployment, a wave of industrial action, and sharply rising prices. To make matters worse, there was an additional coal crisis, with the National Union of Miners striking for higher wages. The government responded to these challenges by declaring a state of emergency and a three-day working week to conserve energy.[243] Heath, however, came under mounting public pressure for his pro-European policies, which many in Britain blamed for the country's economic problems. With Labour under Wilson campaigning aggressively for a renegotiation of Britain's entry terms to the EC, he was compelled to bring home something positive from Copenhagen. This meant, above all, a substantial RDF. If prior to the summit he had won French and West German general support for the establishment of such a fund by 1 January 1974,[244] the contentious point remained how substantial it should be.

At the EC Council on 4 December 1973, Schmidt made it clear that the FRG, which had been less severely hit by the economic turmoil and which was expected to pay the lion's share of the RDF, would only reconsider its minimalist position regarding the fund if the Community balanced its national supplies of oil and moved towards a common energy policy.[245] This explicit linkage was part of a wider West German offensive in favour of *Öl-Solidarität*. As Bahr publicly argued during a visit to Paris, there was no point in trying to persuade Washington and Moscow that Europe existed if the Nine were not willing to say the same thing in Arab capitals. Brandt internally went even further when he claimed that the concept of an EU would be useless if burdens could not be shared equally in the context of the oil crisis.[246]

The Copenhagen Summit: The Nine at the crossroads

The European summit of 14/15 December 1973 was a crisis summit. The stagnation of the EC, the continuing oil crisis, and the transatlantic low left no time for the Nine to develop joint visions and reflect on the future of Europe and the course of EPC on a strategic level as originally foreseen. Rather, Europe's leaders were under pressure to deliver concrete answers to urgent problems, with the publics expecting a strong display of the Community's capability and will to act. Originally conceived as a fireside chat, the meeting at the Bella Center in Copenhagen turned into a full-fledged summit. While on the first day exclusive sessions of the heads of state and government did take place, more and more chairs were carried into the conference room, with advisers, experts, and the foreign ministers gradually participating. As more than a thousand journalists were waiting outside for results to report, the Nine could not but issue a summit communiqué, the key passages of which were argued over by the chiefs themselves in endless drafting sessions.[247] It all resembled, as a West German diplomat recalled, a diplomatic fair (*diplomatischer Jahrmarkt*),[248] which looked all the more improvised since it had not been prepared as a major conference and since it was run by a weakened Danish presidency that had just encountered a severe election defeat.[249]

One of the curiosities of the summit was the appearance of four uninvited Arab ministers, who, mandated by the Arab summit of late November 1973, asked to be received by the Nine. Although France had previously informed its partners of the Arab plan,[250] the question of how to deal with this request took up a disproportionate amount of time on the first day. After a long procedural wrangle, with Brandt insisting on receiving the Israeli ambassador as a balancing measure, it was decided that the foreign ministers would take the delivery of the Arab message and report back to the nine leaders. The sheer fact that the Europeans agreed to receive the Arabs at all signified the new power of the oil-producing countries. Despite their long sermons in their meeting with the foreign ministers on the evening of 14 December, the four emissaries actually had little to say, other than that the Nine should now take concrete measures to advance peace in the Middle East and should work closely with the Arabs. Nonetheless, they were influential enough to effect an official answer by the Danish prime minister the next day, who on behalf of the Nine signalled interest in European–Arab cooperation, while at the same time pointing out how harmful the 'oil weapon' was to any such endeavour.[251]

Given these adverse circumstances, the Copenhagen summit did achieve noteworthy results, both in the field of EPC and with respect to Community issues. The major issues of discussion were the Middle East and the energy crisis, whereas transatlantic questions were only marginally covered. With regard to EPC, Pompidou's initiatives both met approval. The foreign ministers were tasked to deal with crisis management and the joint assessment of crisis situations in their next meeting. Concerning foreign policy summitry, the Nine decided to 'meet more frequently' and under the responsibility of the presidency, although they refrained yet from institutionalising their summits and deciding whether to permanently integrate EC issues too.[252] The bulk of the discussions on EPC, however, focused on the present, rather than the future, and on the Middle East in particular.

After a fairly long debate on the Arab–Israeli conflict, the Nine agreed on a text that endorsed the Declaration of 6 November 1973, welcomed the peace conference in Geneva, asked for the full implementation of Resolution 242, and expressed Europe's readiness to assist in the search for peace and the guaranteeing of a settlement. They, thus, confirmed by and large the policy as developed by EPC. Conversely, British and French attempts to go beyond the status quo failed to get unanimous approval. A proposal by Heath to ask Israel to 'give a commitment on withdrawal comparable to commitments given by certain Arab States on peace' was strongly backed by Pompidou, but was opposed by Brandt, as well as the prime ministers of the Netherlands, Denmark, and Luxembourg. Despite a tiring search for a compromise and a dire warning by Pompidou that the Nine would come to regret the omission of this phrase, no further elaboration of Europe's policy towards the Arab–Israeli conflict could be achieved.[253]

Instead, an additional decision was taken to enter into negotiations with the Arab oil-producing countries on comprehensive arrangements concerning the economic and industrial development of these countries and stable energy supplies at reasonable prices to the Community members. The idea for such a Euro-Arab dialogue had already been discussed between Jobert and the governments of Tunisia, Egypt, and Saudi Arabia in November 1973.[254] Jobert's rationale was to compensate for Europe's exclusion from the peace process and secure European interests in the Middle East through a long-term cooperation scheme with the Arab world. Deliberate future Arab interruptions of oil supplies should be averted by increasing the interdependence of Arab and European economic interests, and by European support for the modernisation and industrialisation of the Middle East.[255] Although the summit communiqué did not yet embrace Jobert's suggestion of a conference between the EC and the Arab League, France's partners did subscribe to the general idea of intensifying European–Arab ties.[256]

This was all the more remarkable since Kissinger had, prior to the summit, warned not to launch any European dialogue with the Arabs without US participation.[257] It is generally noteworthy how little the Nine dealt with the transatlantic crisis and the American challenge to EPC in Copenhagen. There were no references in the communiqué to Kissinger's December proposals. The energy initiative of the Pilgrim speech was not mentioned at all. Rather, the Nine pointed to the Organization for Economic Cooperation and Development (OECD) as the traditional forum of cooperation among oil-consuming countries. A British suggestion to refer to the European–American declaration was rejected by Paris.[258] All that the communiqué said, therefore, was that the growing unity of the Nine would strengthen the West as a whole and would be beneficial to European–American relations. There is no doubt that awareness of Kissinger's sensitivities about EPC prevented some of the Nine from going further on the issue of the Arab–Israeli conflict. After all, the US secretary of state was touring the Middle East at the time of the summit, and the peace conference in Geneva was to open within days. Yet, it would be too much to argue that American disgruntlement, as expressed in Brussels and London just before the Copenhagen summit, had left a heavy mark on the decisions of the Nine. The issue was simply put off.

A similar verdict can be made with regard to the economic challenge the Community was facing. Although here too some progress was achieved at the summit, one essential decision was again avoided. The breakthrough in this part of the summit talks was the decision to make energy a common European issue.[259] In an annex to the communiqué dedicated to energy, the heads of state and government asked the Commission to present proposals for a common energy market, on which the Council would decide by the end of February 1974. Individual elements of such an energy policy were discussed intensively, but were not as yet included in the summit statement.[260] It was also decided to produce comprehensive energy balance sheets on the energy situation in

Europe. Importantly, the Council was requested to adopt provisions to ensure that all states introduce 'on a concerted and equitable basis' measures to limit energy consumption. This was not quite the explicit expression of Community solidarity that the FRG and the Netherlands had been pressing for, but it went a long way towards indicating that the Dutch would not be left in the lurch and satisfied both Bonn and The Hague.[261] At the same time, the delicate issue of RDF was eschewed. Although it was agreed to launch the RDF on 1 January 1974, it was left to the Council to decide at its next meeting on 17/18 December 1973 on the size and distribution of the fund. To the great disappointment of Britain, Brandt was obviously unwilling to overcome the opposition of his economic and finance ministries to settling the issue during the conference.[262]

Overall, the Copenhagen summit did not really give reliable indication on where the Nine were going. If it was plain to all that Europe was at a crossroads, the meeting with respect to EPC had neither produced a big boost nor a major drawback. On the one hand, the Nine still professed self-confidence and ambition. They confirmed their distinct policy vis-à-vis the Arab–Israeli conflict and the Middle East, and they also backed the goal of strengthening EPC institutionally. The political will to make progress was also reflected in the summit decision to speed up the work on the EU and task the presidency with making proposals to that end. The fact that the Declaration on European Identity was published on the occasion of the summit further underlined the Nine's desire to act as an autonomous entity in world politics. Nevertheless, the basic challenges EPC was confronted with in the autumn of 1973 were not really comprehensively addressed at the summit. Similarly, it was left to the Council to hammer out the specifics of both the common energy policy and the RDF. From a legal point of view, this was the regular procedure, as the summits were still not an official component of European integration. Politically, however, it was a risky thing to do, as it was far from certain that the organs in Brussels would be able to work out the necessary compromise solutions, without firm leadership from the top.

The immediate assessments of the summit in Bonn, Paris, and London were predominantly positive. The West Germans rejoiced on the decisions on energy, Pompidou praised the manifest political will of the Nine to march towards political union, and the FCO too was more or less pleased with the overall outcome.[263] Yet, such positive verdicts turned out to be premature, and it comes as no surprise that the contentious issue was the RDF. In Copenhagen, Brandt had proposed the sum of 50 million units of account as the FRG's offer for the RDF. It was a ridiculously low sum, which he had put forward, as he recalled in his memoirs, mainly as a protest measure against his own government.[264] Britain obviously became greatly alarmed at this behaviour and, prior to the decisive Council meeting on 17/18 December 1973, went to great lengths to win Bonn's support for its demand of a fund of 3,000 million units for the period 1974–76. Heath personally telephoned Brandt to remind him that Britain had complied with Schmidt's requests in the field of energy and now hoped to get the promised West German concessions concerning RDF in return. 'If this does not materialize,' Heath warned the chancellor, 'then I am afraid it will turn really very bad indeed.'[265]

And, so it did. Although the FRG did augment its offer to 600 million units at the Council meeting, it was still well below what Heath could accept in order to avoid domestic criticism. With no agreement in sight, the clocks were symbolically stopped until the subsequent Council meeting on 7 January 1974, so that there was still a possibility for the RDF to be set up in time. Britain, however, now reversed Schmidt's linkage and blocked any European energy measures until a substantive RDF had been agreed.[266] The result was not only an open British–German confrontation, but also an evident incapability of the Nine to implement basic decisions of the Copenhagen summit. The bogeyman in both London and Paris was Helmut Schmidt, who was seen as portraying himself egoistically as the guardian of West German prosperity and being more interested in establishing himself as the leading contender to succeed Brandt as chancellor than in contributing to European unity.[267]

Thus, the year 1973, having witnessed a remarkable rise and performance of EPC, ended in conspicuous uncertainty. There were still numerous factors favouring a continuing rise and evolution of EPC. Yet, there were also increasing signs of stagnation, polarisation, and disruption. Ambiguities encompassed all levels of analysis. At the extra-European level of the international environment, the October War and the oil crisis represented a new challenge to Europe of a magnitude that provoked another significant boost to EPC. The Nine took a decisive leap forward in their common policy towards the Arab–Israeli conflict. By enhancing the substance of this policy and making it public, they now disposed of a distinct position with regard to establishing peace in the Middle East and were ready to play a role in the diplomatic search for a settlement and the guaranteeing of any agreement. Their notion of a Euro-Arab dialogue constituted an additional idiosyncratic element of their approach to the Middle East, promising to become both an instrument to improve the reliability of energy supplies to Europe and the first interregional dialogue the Community countries were embarking on.

Also on the positive side of the balance, the double crisis of the autumn of 1973 triggered debates and endeavours of the Nine to strengthen EPC's capacity to act and defend European interests, be it by foreign policy summitry, a mechanism for crisis management, or, on a less concrete level yet, European defence cooperation. Such progress had been instigated by the painful realisation how vulnerable Europe continued to be and how marginalised it was bound to remain as a result of American–Soviet détente. Conversely, the October War had also illustrated that for all the talk about détente, clashes between the superpowers were still a possibility, which again could only strengthen the case for the Nine to secure their own seat at the table of world politics.

At the same time, the Europeans had to take note that the degree of American benevolence towards EPC was undoubtedly declining, which called into question a basic condition of any viable European foreign policy cooperation. Kissinger not only expressed frustration with the Nine's Middle East policy, but also with the project of a common European foreign policy at large. The more successful EPC became, the more it had the potential of adversely affecting US interests and policies, which the US secretary of state obviously disliked. The ever more resolute American calls for advance consultation on European foreign policy decisions indicated that from the American point of view there would be limits to the measure of autonomy the Nine could expect in the realm of diplomacy. Equally disturbing for the Nine, the growing energy crisis and the deteriorating world economy confronted them with a very different kind of challenge than those emanating from the CSCE or the 'Year of Europe', for instance. These external developments affected their most basic material interests, with the goal of formulating a common response being the more difficult to accomplish since the Arabs differentiated among the EC countries in their application of the 'oil weapon'.

At the intra-European level, the odds concerning EPC's further development were similarly ambivalent. On the one hand, there was still much political will among the Nine to advance EPC and accentuate Europe's profile as a foreign policy actor. This was illustrated by the eagerness of the national leaders to get involved in EPC and lend additional credence to the tool with their own authority. Also, for the first time since the mid-1950s, there was a constellation where Britain, France, and the FRG were ready to discuss European defence cooperation. And, there was the Declaration on European Identity, as well as the still fairly united position of the Nine in the negotiations with the US on the two 'Year of Europe' declarations. On the other hand, there were also considerable differences of perception, regarding, for instance, the purpose of

European summitry and the appropriate forum for defence cooperation. What is more, while all the Nine continued to be in favour of a dynamic development of the Community, different priorities and domestic needs as to the implementation of the Paris Summit programme threatened to paralyse the EC and, in doing so, to erode a basic foundation of any European foreign policy. Such differences became compounded by the fact that the individual EC countries in the autumn of 1973 contemplated divergent strategies as to how to deal with the 'oil weapon'.

Finally, at the individual level of decision-makers, things were in motion too. On the one hand, the constellation of Heath, Jobert/Pompidou, and Brandt/Scheel was still promising in that a common desire among these key figures existed to push the political unification of Europe still further. In a sense, the prospects for Europe appeared better than ever since 1969, as Pompidou was now actively engaged with his own initiatives to advance EPC, and as Jobert and Scheel, in particular, shared Heath's zeal for cooperation in the field of defence. On the other hand, each of these exponents in the autumn of 1973 developed in directions that also began to make them look increasingly vulnerable. Heath's position became gradually weakened both at the European and the domestic level. His inability to prevent the Treasury from pursuing a minimalist course in the EC in 1973 cost him a degree of goodwill in both Paris and Bonn. Much more severely even, his failure to secure a substantial RDF against the background of the acute economic crisis in Britain gravely weakened him at home. Brandt, for his part, was widely said to suffer from a general sense of fatigue. His lack of domestic leadership in the autumn of 1973 had become so stark that even members of the SPD began to openly criticise him.[268] As for Scheel, he too felt more and more worn out and after a stay at the hospital in December 1973 decided to run for the Federal Presidency in mid-1974.[269] Pompidou's health was also deteriorating further, while Jobert seemed eager to push the Nine ever more away from the US, which France's partners watched with growing unease. At the same time, new faces began to move to the centre of European politics, who, while supportive of Europe, did not consider the political advancement of the Community as their first priority. This was especially true for the FRG. Not only was Leber keen on preserving the Eurogroup and transatlantic defence cooperation, rather than venturing into unknown, risky European territories, much more importantly there was also Schmidt, who appeared first and foremost concerned with securing national economic stability and restoring Atlantic harmony, and who was unwilling to invest an increasing quantity of West German money into a European construction whose foundation looked anything but stable at the time.

While the year 1973 turned out to be impressive for EPC, it was difficult for the EC, and agonising for Atlantic relations. Yes, it was the year of Europe, in that the Nine proved and enhanced their ability to speak with one voice in world affairs. However, EPC's fate at the end of the year was anything but settled. In hindsight, it is clear that the seeds of its rapid decline in 1974 had already been sown, even though it looked as though it still was on the rise.

Part III

US Discontent, Economic Weakness, and Europe's Decline into Crisis, 1974

> The history of the twenty years after 1973 is that of a world which has lost its bearings and slid into instability and crisis.
>
> Eric Hobsbawm (2003: 403)

If the year 1973 was, in some respects, the 'Year of Europe', 1974 has been aptly coined the 'Year of Economics'.[1] Issues such as rapidly raising inflation and growing structural unemployment, formerly regarded as low politics, moved to the top of the international political agenda. There was a profound sense of crisis in the industrial democracies, and a realisation that the post-war era of economic growth and prosperity had come to an end. With the energy crisis unresolved and the oil price quadrupled, an acute shift of capital set in from the oil-consuming nations to the producer countries, which brought about severe balance of payment deficits in most Western countries. Recessions and instability came to characterise the world economy. The economic downturn also threatened to challenge the internal cohesion of democracies, as Communist parties in Italy, Portugal, France, and elsewhere successfully exploited the combination of détente and weakened Western economies by advocating their own forms of Eurocommunism. 'We have entered the era of uncertainty', Pompidou declared at the beginning of 1974, expressing a widespread sense of malaise that became further accentuated over the course of the year.[2]

The economisation of international politics could well have been to the advantage of the European Community, allowing the Nine to augment their influence through their collective economic weight. Yet, the opposite happened. Barely one year after enlargement had nourished great confidence and expectations as to Europe's future, the Community plunged into one of its deepest crises, marked by tendencies of re-nationalisation, fragmentation, and desolidarisation. In fact, 1974 turned out to be an *annus horribilis* for the EC, ushering in a period of disillusionment and 'eurosclerosis' from which it would not recover for more than a decade. All the difficulties that had begun to strain the Community in late 1973 became further exacerbated. A first blow to the EC occurred on 19 January 1974, when France announced that it would withdraw from the European 'snake' and join Britain, Ireland, and Italy in floating its currency. It was an unexpected measure that shocked particularly the West Germans, who had offered France massive financial support to fend off further potential speculations against the Franc. Pompidou, however, decided that France needed free hands to deal with its economic and monetary difficulties. The 'snake', accordingly, became severely weakened. What had once represented a powerful symbol of European integration and had been designed to constitute the core of a later EMU now turned into a mirror of an increasingly disunited Community.[3]

Less than two weeks after the 'snake' had been skinned of any substance, emotions rose high again in Brussels when negotiations on the Regional Development Fund ran aground. After much British lobbying, the West German cabinet finally agreed to double Bonn's contribution to an RDF, despite resistance by Schmidt. Yet, while the new FRG proposal diffused Anglo-German tensions, it brought both Bonn and London into conflict with Paris, as France would have benefited much less from the modified scheme. On the decisive Council meeting on 30 January 1974, the Nine could only note their continuing disagreement on the size and distribution of the fund. The issue was adjourned, which meant a grave defeat for the Heath government, whose European policy came under ever-heavier domestic attack.[4] Lack of progress also became characteristic for the European attempts to build a common energy market. Although the British lifted their reserve on common European energy measures, despite the failure of the RDF, the Nine proved unable to transform the decisions of the Copenhagen Summit into concrete action. Neither Britain nor France were willing to reduce their national room of manoeuvre in securing oil supplies, and they were not the only EC countries to tour the Arab world in search for bilateral oil and wider economic deals. The threats emanating from the energy crisis to national security proved too severe for a common European energy policy to emerge fast enough to respond to the acute difficulties.[5]

On top of all this, it was the growing economic divergence between individual EC members which posed a formidable challenge to the Nine in 1974. As national rates of inflation varied more than 100 per cent at times, the gap between rich and poor within the Community was rapidly widening.[6] On the

one side, there was the FRG, which was relatively little affected by the economic crisis. With its continuing strong trade surplus and its huge currency
reserves, West Germany consolidated its position as the EC's economic giant
and, in fact, augmented the gap with its European partners.[7] In contrast, Italy
and Britain were hit particularly hard by the crisis. In Italy, national bankruptcy
was looming, which threatened the proper functioning of the Common
Market.[8] In Britain, the economic trends were so daunting that even the FCO
Planning Staff, which in 1972/73 had produced numerous studies on a common European foreign policy, was now preoccupied with analyses of how
Britain could best 'survive the Seventies'.[9]

In unusually explicit terms, the European Commission warned on 31
January 1974 of the consequences of mutually inconsistent economic and fis-
cal policies, competitive devaluations, and measures of protectionism. In a
solemn 'Declaration on the State of the Community', it argued that the Nine
could not reach their objectives if their unity was but a 'fair-weather phenomenon' and stressed that Europe was now 'in a state of crisis – a crisis of confidence, of will and of clarity of purpose'.[10] Yet, prospects became even gloomier
for the EC. In the spring of 1974, a new Labour government came to power in
Britain, which was much less pro-European than Heath and threatened to
withdraw from the Community unless the Tory terms of entry were renegotiated. Consequently, 1974 for the EC not only became a year of economic crisis, but also a 'year of renegotiation',[11] which provoked further disputes among
the Nine and increased the incertitude as to Europe's future. Indicative of the
sense of paralysis that prevailed in the first half of 1974 were the concepts of a
'core Europe' or 'Europe à la carte', which were contemplated for the first time
in European capitals, and particularly in Bonn.[12]

European diplomacy unsurprisingly became affected by this profound crisis of the Community. At the beginning of 1974, there was still hope that EPC's
continuing rise might compensate for the economic stagnation of Europe and
keep the process of unification going. Yet, the context was very different from
the year before. The spirit of excitement and optimism soon vanished, and the
degree of internal cohesion and mutual trust of the Nine was deteriorating. The
fact that such a divisive issue as energy came to dominate the global diplomatic
agenda in 1974 was certainly not to the advantage of EPC. Rather than declarations on Europe's identity and political standpoints, practical and urgent
solutions were now required to a problem that affected the everyday lives of
everyone in the Community.

EPC's situation was becoming the more worrisome in view of American
dissatisfaction with Europe's foreign policy aspirations. Kissinger's call to

restore the prerogative of Atlantic cooperation in December 1973 gained further weight in 1974, as the US was now in much better shape than any European country. Economically, the US balance of payments troubles, at least for the moment, were a thing of the past. Being much less dependent on the import of energy than Europe, the US was less severely affected by the rocketing oil price than the Nine, and the strength of the Dollar in 1974 stood in stark contrast to the weakness of most European currencies.[13] Politically, Kissinger was now firmly in the driver's seat of international diplomacy. Whereas Nixon was preoccupied with the impeachment proceedings of Watergate and eventually resigned on 8 August 1974, Kissinger's world reputation reached new heights. After the successful negotiations on military disengagements in the Middle East, he became what one of his biographers has called the 'first diplomatic superstar of the modern era', with US magazines celebrating him as 'Super-K' and 'Miracle Worker'.[14] The unparalleled diplomatic and military power of the US, along with its relative economic invulnerability, placed Kissinger in a strong position to, as the British put it, 'impose his will on the Nine'.[15] Indeed, much of the tensions that came to bedevil EPC in the first half of 1974 related to the issue of European–American relations. Yet, it would be wrong to one-sidedly blame US sticks and carrots for the growing European divisions. Rather, governments in Britain, West Germany, and elsewhere began themselves to wonder whether bilateral rapprochements with Washington were not a more promising way of coping with the massive challenges of the time than putting all eggs into the basket of an increasingly fragile European unity.[16]

In this last part of the book, I will analyse the decline of EPC in the first half of 1974. In Chapter 6, the period until mid-March 1974 will be covered, which can be defined as the early period of EPC's crisis. Chapter 7 will cover the remaining period from mid-March to the end of June 1974, which was characterised by the collapse of several important previous achievements and objectives of EPC. As I will argue, this decline of EPC in the spring of 1974 was brought about by a general deterioration of the conditions of European foreign policy-making, with changes of government in London, Paris, and Bonn playing an important role.

Chapter 6
The Washington Energy Conference:
The European front crumbles

On the face of it, the Washington Energy Conference was a technical affair. Held at the invitation of President Nixon on 11–13 February 1974, it assembled representatives of 13 major oil-consuming countries to discuss ways of jointly meeting the oil crisis. The gathering was the result of the energy initiative launched by Kissinger in mid-December 1973 in the context of his Pilgrim's speech (see Chapter 5). Its objective was to formulate a consumer action programme regarding issues such as the conservation of energy, demand restraint, alternative energy sources, and emergency sharing. Also on the agenda were the economic and monetary consequences of the oil crisis, such as the growing balance of payments deficits and the fight against inflation.

On closer examination, however, the conference was a highly political event. For one thing, the US quite obviously sought to build up an institutionalised consumer cartel to counter OPEC, which implied a confrontational response of the industrial democracies to the price increases and embargo measures taken by the oil producers. Moreover, and essential for this study, the meeting in Washington was as much about the notion of Atlantic cooperation as it was about energy. As the major driving force behind the conference, Kissinger repeatedly called it a test for the Atlantic partnership, and it is indicative of his political intentions that it was the foreign ministers, rather than the finance and energy ministers, who were the main addressees of the US invitation. Although Japan, Canada, and Norway were also present at the gathering, the Washington Energy Conference was, first and foremost, about the future of political relations between the Community countries and the US. It was a continuation of the 'Year of Europe' by other means, emphasising the principle of Atlantic unity and consultation in a concrete policy field, rather than in lofty declarations. The policy field being energy, that is, the most pressing security problem of the time, the question of whether the Nine were willing to support an Atlantic course or preferred again to define their own distinct approach to meet the energy challenge was of great symbolic significance, and especially so against the background of the transatlantic divisions of 1973.

The US-sponsored conference put the Nine in a difficult position. Most of them strongly favoured a cooperative, rather than a confrontational policy vis-à-vis the oil producers. When Nixon issued his invitation on 9 January 1974, the Europeans were in the midst of working out the details of a Euro-Arab dialogue, as they had agreed at the Copenhagen Summit (see Chapter 5). Although they had not yet been able to implement a common energy policy, there was still hope in early 1974 that an internal EC energy market was in the offing. At the same time, the economies of several EPC members were already severely weakened, and the view was widespread that Europe alone would not be able to cope with the challenge. Moreover, there was a growing unwillingness to risk another confrontation with the US.

As it turned out, the Washington Energy Conference became a first major setback for the political unity of the Nine. Although they had been able to work out a common mandate prior to the conference, the Community members ended up in disarray in Washington. Whereas eight governments complied with the US call for institutionalised energy cooperation, France refused to sign essential parts of the final communiqué and found itself isolated. The European split was a serious blow for EPC, whose dynamic development in 1973 had owed a great deal to a common front of the Nine against what had been perceived to be unreasonable US policies and demands. While the Nixon administration had served as an inadvertent catalyst for European unity in previous months, it now had a divisive effect on the Nine. If the Washington Energy Conference can be identified, with the benefit of hindsight, as the beginning of EPC's decline in 1974, it is important to note that this by no means seemed inevitable at the time. To the satisfaction of the French, the Nine decided on 4 March 1974 to launch the Euro-Arab dialogue, previous warnings by Kissinger that this would be detrimental to US interests and could undo the success of Washington notwithstanding. It was to be the straw that broke the camel's back. What followed was another fierce transatlantic row, which differed critically from the preceding clashes in 1973 in that the US now explicitly threatened to reduce its military protection of Western Europe in case of European non-compliance with American requirements. In one fell swoop, Kissinger called into question Europe's role in the Middle East, the autonomy of EPC, and the notion of Europe speaking with one voice to the US. The result was a sharp Franco-American polarisation, and the plunging of EPC into its biggest crisis since its beginnings.

European reservations

It would be too much to say that the Europeans were enthusiastic about Kissinger's energy initiative. Whereas editorial comments were largely positive, with comparisons being made to the Marshall Plan of 1947,[1] decision-makers in the European capitals had mixed feelings about Kissinger's idea. Their lukewarm initial reactions and subsequent evasive suggestions as to how to proceed caused dissatisfaction in Washington, with Nixon bringing matters to a head by convening a conference of important oil-consuming countries. While this compelled each European government to show its colours, the Nine went to great lengths to secure a common mandate for the meeting. This was an extremely difficult endeavour, however. Although all of the Nine subscribed to the three basic objectives of preserving European unity, taking into account the sensitivities of oil producers, and not provoking new American disenchantment, national priorities within this matrix varied. Working out a common brief for the conference in this context amounted to an attempt to reconcile the irreconcilable, which meant that the unity of purpose and policy of the Nine was already very fragile when they arrived in Washington.

The trouble with the Pilgrim's speech

Kissinger's suggestion in mid-December 1973 to make the energy problem a common Atlantic enterprise and set up an Energy Action Group of Europe, the US, Canada, and Japan to deal with the oil crisis was publicly welcomed by most European governments.[2] Internally, however, European decision-makers had severe doubts about the US idea. For one thing, they had again not been consulted about the American initiative, receiving information about the speech only hours before the US secretary of state addressed his Pilgrim audience in London. Kissinger's request in the covering letter that the US was hoping for support and active participation in the Action Group seemed all too similar to the way in which the US had launched the 'Year of Europe' in April 1973.[3] A second European reservation concerned the concept of assembling major oil-consuming countries only. The Nine considered it ill-advised to leave the oil-producers and developing (oil-consuming) countries on the sidelines, as they feared that the formation of a bloc of Western industrial democracies might provoke OPEC retaliation. Kissinger's call for the consumers to show real strength and jointly confront the challenge might have been sensible from an American point of view, as the US was not heavily dependent on oil imports and had reason to hope to reach self-sufficiency in a few years.[4] From the perspective of the Nine, however, the approach suggested by Washington contained serious risks. Europe's overwhelming dependence on Arab oil rendered constructive relations with producer countries imperative, and the economic crisis in the Community meant that additional price increases or production cuts had to be avoided at all costs. While most Europeans professed some interest in cooperating with the US on technical issues, such as developing alterative sources of energy, they had no stomach for concerted Atlantic diplomacy in the energy crisis.[5]

The British, for example, were well aware that Kissinger's offer of cooperation was 'an opportunity which we cannot afford to miss'.[6] However, they had already warned the US in October 1973 against provoking a confrontation with OPEC,[7] and they were now unhappy with the kind of ideas Kissinger appeared to have in mind. 'It rather looks as if Kissinger cannot go anywhere without taking an initiative', the FCO noted, slating the US secretary of state's seeming determination to create new Western machinery to meet the OPEC challenge.[8] Some in the FCO also saw the Pilgrim's speech as a deliberate attempt to pre-empt the planned Euro-Arab dialogue. British communications to Washington about the Kissinger proposals, therefore, stressed the need for Europe and the US to work together, but generally attributed to this Atlantic cooperation the purpose of improving relations between the consumers and producers.[9]

The fear that the US energy initiative might also be a hidden attack on European political unity constituted a third European concern about the Pilgrim's speech. Nowhere was this perception more pronounced than in France, which strongly suspected that the main motive for Kissinger's proposal was to re-establish American leadership in the West by making an example of it in the realm of energy.[10] The French were well aware that Kissinger had used the same concepts and vocabulary in his speech as in his 'Year of Europe' address. Notions such as the globalisation and interdependence of issues and new means of consultation were there again, as if no negotiations had ever taken place between the Nine and the US in 1973. French concerns that the Energy Action Group was a device to put the original US idea behind the 'Year of Europe' into practical effect and, at the same time, to disrupt the unity of the Nine loomed all the larger since Europe could only say yes or no to Kissinger's proposal, rather than hide behind ambiguous formulations as in the two declarations. During Kissinger's stay in Paris a few days after the Pilgrim's speech, the French left no doubt that they were hostile to any organised Atlantic cooperation to confront OPEC and strongly preferred their own scheme of a Euro-Arab dialogue. Conversations were polite, and Kissinger even attended the Christmas dinner of the Quai d'Orsay, arm-in-arm with Jobert.[11] But, although the French promised not to work against the US initiative, they made it clear that they would not risk the status as a 'friendly' country to OAPEC for the sake of allied unity.[12]

Finally, a fourth reservation among the Nine related to the question of Europe's representation in the proposed Action Group. Whereas Kissinger failed to come up with specifics of how to proceed after his speech, American officials responsible for energy matters indicated that the US envisaged the participation of a few key Western countries only and even thought about limiting the core of the Group to three top representatives of Europe, the US, and Japan.[13] While this latter proposition completely failed to take into account the procedural difficulty of a single European representative, the former idea of big power consultations clearly was inconsistent with the Nine's decision at the Copenhagen Summit to find yet a common answer to the energy crisis.

A way out for the Nine to avoid new Atlantic institutions that threatened to negatively affect both their own unity and their relations with the Arab world was to promote the OECD as a forum for Western discussions of the oil crisis. The OECD, in fact, already possessed institutions specifically designed to deal with energy problems. If this machinery had not so far been activated during the oil crisis, it was because countries such as France and Britain had been against the principle of consumer cooperation altogether. Now, however, consulting in the OECD seemed a lesser evil than creating a new, US-dominated institution, which was bound to provoke the oil producers. The British were particularly active proponents of the OECD. Already at the Copenhagen Summit, Heath had been a major driving force behind the communiqué paragraph referring to the OECD for energy talks (see Chapter 5). In a letter to Nixon, he subsequently praised the organisation as the 'obvious choice' to anchor the new Energy Action Group, and Britain urged the secretary-general of the OECD to come up with proposals to that end.[14] In order to meet the US requirement of limited representation, the British suggested that the Action Group should be an exalted version of the already existing OECD High Level Group, which consisted of the US, Canada, Japan, France, Britain, the FRG, the Netherlands, Italy, Norway, and the EC Commission. With a Community organ represented, so the British hoped, those EC members not included would at least have some indirect access to deliberations from which the US seemed otherwise to want to exclude them.[15] 'If it is true to say', the FCO maintained, 'that the European response to the Kissinger initiative is a valid test case, in his eyes, of transatlantic cooperation, it is no less true to say that the US reaction to our proposal that the matter should be dealt with by the High Level

Group in the OECD is a test case of whether the American Administration are [sic] serious about cooperation in these matters'.[16]

The West Germans and the French tended to agree with this view. Bonn also let the Americans know that the proposed energy talks should be related to the OECD.[17] It is worth pointing out that it had been Helmut Schmidt who, on 5 November 1973, via Bahr's back channel, had initially suggested to Kissinger that Western Europe and the US should have private talks to discuss oil and related economic matters. At that time, however, Kissinger had turned down the proposal on the ground that the 'discouraging experience of the Year of Europe' did not justify such an undertaking, which he would only contemplate once a more 'constructive and harmonious pattern of Atlantic relationships' had been established. After yet another message by Schmidt on 29 November 1973, Kissinger seems to have had second thoughts, however, as he now suggested a private bilateral meeting with the West German minister of finance in mid-December. It is difficult to discern whether the meeting ever took place. But the fact is that Kissinger's public approach was not at all what Schmidt had originally envisaged and that the confrontational policies that the US secretary of state had in mind did not correspond with the way in which Bonn wanted to tackle the issue.[18]

As for the French, they too wanted to attribute a role to the OECD in dealing with the oil crisis. However, Jobert and Pompidou viewed this Paris-based organisation as playing a less important role than was thought in Britain and the FRG. In a letter to Kissinger on 28 December 1973, the French foreign minister laid out a multi-stage scheme of how to go about dealing with the energy problem. According to this French plan, the OECD should primarily focus on energy conservation. Consumer cooperation should also take place concerning high-technology projects, such as deep-water drilling. The key French suggestion, however, was that Europe, the US, Canada, and Japan should each pursue their own autonomous energy policy and deal separately with the oil-producing countries. On top of this, a world conference should be convened to bring together all stakeholders to discuss energy matters.[19]

In the midst of these debates on how to proceed with the proposed Energy Action Group, OPEC and OAPEC came up with new decisions about the price and supply of oil that made it even more difficult for the industrial democracies to agree on a common course of action. On 23 December 1973, the Persian Gulf members of OPEC announced an unexpected, massive further price rise of crude oil. One day later, OAPEC in Kuwait reviewed its production cuts. Besides reclassifying Belgium and Japan as 'friendly' countries, the Arab oil producers cancelled the 5 per cent cutback of supplies scheduled for January 1974 in favour of a 10 per cent increase, while maintaining the embargo against the Netherlands and the US.[20]

These measures promoted different reactions on either side of the Atlantic. For Europe, the balance sheet was mixed. There was relief that the trend of reducing the supply of oil had been reverted. But the Arabs still refused to treat the Nine as a unit, and they continued the embargo against the Dutch. Perhaps even worse, the oil producers had flatly ignored a French demarche, according to which Europe would now expect stable and fair prices following the decision at Copenhagen to embrace the idea of a Euro-Arab dialogue.[21] The lesson European governments took from this demonstration of power by the producer countries was twofold. A Euro-Arab dialogue had to get started as soon as possible to deepen the relations and mutual interests between the two sides. Yet, especially for the weaker European economies, there was also an ever-growing recognition that US backing was indispensable for them to deal with their domestic economic challenges. From a European perspective, the combination of both lessons tended to reinforce the case for building on the OECD, which was hoped to foster consumer cooperation without alienating relations with producers.

From an American point of view, the interpretation of the decisions taken in Teheran and Kuwait was rather different. As Kissinger noted in his memoirs, the Nixon administration felt deceived by the Arabs. Washington had expected the embargo to be lifted or at least be eased in response to the US efforts at brokering peace in the Middle East. Instead, it was the Europeans whose oil curbs were mitigated, which implied that Europe's dissociation from the US had resulted in preferential treatment.[22] Consequently, US desire to render the Energy Action Group a political symbol of Atlantic cooperation in dealing with energy appears to have grown. The US rejected the preference of the Nine for working through the OECD. Kissinger told the FRG that the organisation was simply not political enough for the purpose. Nixon similarly wrote to Heath that the OECD was 'not best suited for giving a strong new impetus for the priority action required'.[23] Instead, the Americans now took the matter into their own hands and confronted the Europeans with the idea for a high-level political consumer conference and the choice of either embracing or declining the notion of Atlantic partnership in the sphere of energy.

Testing Atlantic solidarity: Kissinger convenes a conference

On 9 January 1974, Britain, France, West Germany, Italy, the Netherlands, Norway, Canada, and Japan all received an invitation from Nixon to send their foreign ministers to a conference in the US for discussions about the international energy crisis and the work that needed to be done. In his long invitation letter, which was released to the public, Nixon argued that the energy situation had brought consumer and producer nations to a 'historic crossroad'. According to him, the world's nations now faced a 'fundamental choice' that could 'affect the structure of international political and economic relations for the remainder of this century'. In his analysis of the scope of the challenge, the US president warned of the potentially irreparable damage to the prosperity and stability of the world. He then argued:

> Two roads lie before us. We can go our own separate ways, with the prospect of progressive division, the erosion of vital interdependence, and increasing political and economic conflict; or we can work in concert, developing enlightened unity and cooperation, for the benefit of all mankind – producer and consumer countries alike.

Nixon continued that the proposed meeting of the major industrial consumer nations, to be held in Washington on 11 February 1974, should establish a task force in order to formulate a consumer action programme. Key objectives would be to define cooperative measures designed to deal with the explosive growth of global energy demand, and a 'concerted consumer position for a new era of petroleum consumer–producer relations'. He concluded the letter by suggesting that a consumer–producer meeting could take place within 90 days after the Washington conference, and by urging his addressees to 'turn this period of crisis into one of opportunity for constructive and creative cooperation'.[24] In an extra paragraph to Brandt, whom he erroneously took for the acting president of the EC (an office performed by the foreign minister), Nixon added that he would leave it to the Community 'to decide whether and how it may wish to participate in the meeting'.[25]

In a press conference on 11 January 1974, Kissinger spelled out further what the purpose of the US initiative ought to be. The White House saw the conference as a 'test of the whole approach towards the international system' and of the 'proposition that the world has become interdependent'. Kissinger underscored that the US was not the country most dependent on a multilateral approach. Implicitly denouncing the policy of France and Britain of seeking bilateral oil deals with producer governments, he insisted that in the absence of Atlantic cooperation the US would be well placed to prevail in any competitive bilateral bidding. Yet, rather than selfishly use its economic and political strength for its own benefit only, the US considered it best to work out a common policy of all major consuming nations and was even prepared to discuss the sharing of its indigenous energy sources. Procedurally, Kissinger explained, he had in mind a three-stage design, according to which the Washington meeting was to be followed by a second conference with developing consuming nations, such as India and Brazil, before a consumer–producer gathering could eventually take place.[26]

Just how ambitious the Americans were with their initiative became obvious when they conveyed to the invitees specific proposals for the conference agenda. Besides the plenary session, four high-level working groups were suggested to deal with specific parts of the energy challenge. The foreign ministers were in charge of defining a comprehensive consumer action programme, including the institutionalisation of consumer cooperation. Finance ministers should attend too in order to consider the economic and monetary consequences of the oil crisis. A third group would be composed of energy officials, who should deal with conservation, demand restraint, emergency sharing, and the issue of alternative energy sources. Finally, science and technology officials were to meet to discuss joint research and development opportunities.[27]

From the point of view of the Community countries, there could be little doubt that all of this amounted to a thinly disguised American challenge to Europe's position vis-à-vis the energy crisis. Although the Nixon administration had accepted the British idea of inviting the constituent nations of the OECD High Level Group, the proposed new forum was to be set up outside the OECD, and the meeting to take place in Washington, rather than Paris. There were strong indications that the US had now definitely embarked on a course to break the OPEC cartel. Even though this was not made explicit in the invitation, the fact that the White House scheduled two conferences to build up consumer solidarity prior to approaching the producer countries clearly implied a policy of confrontation, or, as the British called it, of a 'ganging-up of the more important consumers against the rest'.[28] In addition, Kissinger himself remarked in conversations with European representatives that it was now high time that the consumers did something against the 'oil weapon'. It was 'basically intolerable', he told the new British secretary of cabinet, John Hunt, that 40 million 'backward people' were able to dictate to 800 million others their style of life and their standards of living.[29] Moreover, Defence Secretary Schlesinger publicly insinuated that the US might use military force if the oil embargo continued, with Vice-President Gerald R. Ford adding that Washington could also terminate its food aid to the Arab countries as a measure of retaliation against OAPEC.[30]

Equally worrying for the Nine, one evident motive for Kissinger convening the conference was to subordinate Europe's identity to his Atlantic conception. While already implicit in his Pilgrim's proposal, Kissinger's policy of ignoring the Nine as an entity was made explicit in that the US chose to invite selected EC countries only. True, the invitation letter contained the possibility of Community representation. Yet, there was little doubt that Washington had no desire for any form of Atlantic cooperation that comprised the Nine as a single unit. Again, the French were more pessimistic and outspoken than their partners when they described the Energy Conference as a political manoeuvre by Kissinger to take revenge for the 'Year of Europe' and split up the Community.[31] However, others such as the West Germans too resented that the White House had refused to approach the Nine as a whole with its proposal. The Auswärtige Amt suspected that the conference had been designed as a means for Kissinger to 'force Europe and Japan into line with US policy'.[32] Henri Simonet, the European Commissioner responsible for energy matters, thought along the same lines. As he put it to Peter Carrington, the secretary of state of the new British ministry for energy, the meeting in Washington 'had all the signs of a political exercise' designed to strengthen the Western Alliance, rather than of a plan to coordinate energy policies as such.[33]

Europe's suspicions seemed to find confirmation by remarks made by US Department of State and Treasury officials, who complained that there was much confusion in Washington as to what the US secretary of state had in mind, the more so since Kissinger refused to read any studies on the technical aspects of the oil crisis.[34] How justified the Nine were in their assessment of US intentions becomes clear in Kissinger's own later account of the conference, where he openly admitted that his predominant concern was with the European–American relationship. Being frustrated with Europe's response to his Pilgrim's speech, the wanted to ensure that the 'same interminable procedural nightmare that had thwarted the Year of Europe' would not repeat itself. In other words: 'We would now see whether we would again be faced with the insistence that the European countries would speak to us only through a single instructed representative or whether the importance of the subject would produce a more natural pattern of consultation.' Kissinger admitted that 'there was some justification for anxiety that Europe's identity might be swallowed in the institutionalisation of Atlantic unity'. However, he added that 'the energy crisis did not lend itself to regional subdivisions'.[35]

The Nine were well aware that a decision was now being forced upon them. They had little doubt that it was Kissinger rather than Nixon who had staged the challenge upon them, as the president was ever more preoccupied with Watergate and his own domestic survival. Interestingly, Nixon himself later was to distance himself from how Kissinger challenged the Europeans with the

Washington Conference.[36] Yet, this in January and early February 1974 was of little help to the Nine, who were given less than four weeks to attempt to solve the conundrum of how to secure their distinct European interests without alienating Kissinger and forfeiting American benevolence towards their unity and political aspirations.

How to reconcile the irreconcilable

Following the American invitation to the Washington Energy Conference, there was a period of hectic consultation in Europe. Although discussions took place in both EPC and the Community institutions, the key decisions were taken in the EC Council of Ministers, as the US initiative concerned not only Europe's envisaged dialogue with the Arabs and its political standing in the world, but also, and most directly, its aspiration to formulate a common energy policy. Despite some immediate positive public reactions to the Nixon letter in European capitals, the EPC Political Committee agreed that the governments of the Nine should not send any definite reply to the US before a common internal discussion had taken place. Both France and the FRG pushed for an orchestrated European answer to the White House, and they were strongly supported by those countries, such as Belgium, Ireland, and Denmark, which had not been invited to the conference.[37]

A first exchange of views in the Council of Ministers on 15 January 1974 ended with the decision that the Community should accept the US invitation, on the understanding that all of its members, together with the Commission, should be represented.[38] While Kissinger accepted to enlarge the number of participants, the unresolved issue that continued to trouble the Nine was the substance of their position. There was agreement that a joint mandate should be worked out. Yet, in addition to this, there seemed little common ground. While eight EC members shared a good degree of ambivalence about the conference, but sought, nevertheless, to play a constructive part, France was blatantly hostile about the proposed meeting and revealed little willingness to find a compromise solution with the US. Furthermore, specific national objectives, requirements, and priorities varied among the Eight too, rendering the task of hammering out a joint position ever more formidable.

Britain and the FRG sought to balance four basic, but potentially contradictory, interests. Apart from preserving Community solidarity, they wanted to avoid all possible taint of a confrontation with the producers, so as not to jeopardise their energy supplies. They were also eager not to clash with the US and risk renewed transatlantic quarrelling again. Moreover, they hoped to avoid having to choose between American and French positions.[39] London and Bonn tried to reconcile what appeared irreconcilable by seeking to limit the political scope and confrontational dimension of the conference. Both Brandt and Heath in their official acceptance letters to Nixon reinterpreted the purpose of the Washington meeting as serving the consumers to prepare their dialogue with the producers.[40] The British, who generally regarded the US proposals for the agenda and procedures of the conference 'unrealistically ambitious' and 'incautiously drafted',[41] came up with concrete suggestions for altering Kissinger's design. Whitehall proposed a follow-up meeting with producers within 30 rather than 90 days, made the case against setting up working groups during the conference, and suggested that a potential follow-up task force should be composed of ambassadors in Washington only. The British also decided to send only Carrington to the conference, with Douglas-Home being scheduled to tour Africa.[42] As for the West Germans, they suggested that Kissinger should already invite some producers to the consumer meeting in Washington.[43]

London and Bonn had their own disagreements in specific energy matters. For instance, the British were defending the concept of bilateral oil deals and argued that the conference should merely work out a code of conduct as to how to go about them. The West Germans, by contrast, and Schmidt in particular, were much more critical about oil bilateralism and preferred alternative multilateral approaches and solutions, such as oil sharing – which for Britain again was anathema in view of its future indigenous North Sea supplies.[44] Yet, the governments of Heath and Brandt held very similar views on one essential point: whatever their own differences, and whatever the specific outcome of the conference, the one 'royal' priority they could no longer afford to neglect was good relations with the US. Neither of them stated explicitly that they would prioritise their preference for American benevolence over European unity and close relations with France in case these objectives proved to be irreconcilable. Nevertheless, their internal preparations reveal that however engaged they were in working towards a common policy of the Nine, their foremost concern was to remain in Kissinger's good books.

With regard to the issue of how to approach the energy crisis on the political level, Britain was much closer to France than to the US, favouring a Euro-Arab dialogue and bilateral exchanges with the Arabs. Also, Heath continued in 1974 to attach much importance to the strategic relationship he had built up with Pompidou.[45] Nevertheless, the British came to conclude that in view of the country's dire economic situation it was the US which was most likely to be able to provide the kind of help they required. Whitehall was desperate for

American assistance in the realm of borrowing. British decision-makers, therefore, considered it unwise to get into trouble with Washington over the issues of energy and the Middle East, where Kissinger was pursuing personal initiatives and held 'most of the trump cards' in his own hand.[46] They strongly feared adverse economic consequences for Britain if they rebuffed the US at the conference. Heath also sought to accommodate the US by eventually complying with Kissinger's request that Douglas-Home attend the Washington Conference too.[47]

Moreover, the British believed that it was precisely in those fields of the energy problem where they were most interested in multilateral cooperation that they needed the support of the American ally most. Europe alone would not be able to break the oil price spiral, and it was too small an entity to master the economic and monetary repercussions of the energy crisis.[48] The US, by contrast, was publicly talking about a policy to 'roll back' the oil price, a measure which the Heath government regarded as indispensable to cope with Britain's domestic crisis.[49] To learn more about American intentions in this regard, the prime minister sent John Hunt to Kissinger at the end of January 1974 for a private conversation, the result of which was met with great satisfaction in London. In Washington, Hunt gained the impression that the US was very serious about taking measures to get the oil price down, and he could further report that the Nixon administration was prepared to help Britain with coal imports.[50]

The West Germans were less directly dependent on the US for their economic well-being. However, Schmidt, in particular, was convinced that because of the interdependence of the industrial democracies European cooperation with the world's biggest economy was a *sine qua non* for effectively dealing with the global economic turbulence. Furthermore, although there was deep resentment in Bonn that Kissinger appeared to declare each and every problem a test for the cohesion of the Alliance, there was also agreement that the FRG could not afford additional clashes with the US in view of its security dependence.[51] US support was especially required as *Ostpolitik* stagnated in early 1974, with the GDR being less cooperative in its relations with the FRG and the West than Bonn had expected.[52] Significantly, Brandt instructed Scheel to work for a European position at the Washington Energy Conference as far as possible, but to defend national interests where necessary, referring specifically to the need for very close contact with the US in matters of security and energy.[53]

The French, for their part, paid much less attention to the negative effects any failure of the proposed energy conference could have on their relations with the US. There was some recognition in Paris that France would be in a weak position if economic giants, such as the US, Japan, and the FRG, engaged in a competition to bid bilaterally for oil. Yet, French decision-makers were much more concerned about the strains on their special relations with the Arab world that their association with any institutionalised Atlantic cooperation on energy under American hegemony might cause. A major objective they pursued was to preserve Europe's autonomy in energy matters and generally make sure that the energy crisis would not reinforce American (or, for that matter, Soviet) influence on the unity of the Nine.[54]

Accordingly, France came up with a comprehensive counter scheme of how to tackle the energy crisis, in which the Washington Conference was transformed into an exploratory and technical meeting only. Essentially, France now publicly defended the same design that Jobert had proposed to Kissinger at the end of 1973. In a letter sent to UN Secretary-General Kurt Waldheim on 18 January 1974, Jobert proposed the urgent convocation of a world energy conference under UN auspices to define general principles of cooperation between producer and consumer countries.[55] In an *Aide Mémoire* to the Community countries one day later, he argued that the various problems of the energy crisis should be examined simultaneously in different international organisations. In addition to the UN conference, it was believed that Europe should focus on the Euro-Arab dialogue. Consumer cooperation should focus on common technological programmes, and consultations among consumers should generally take place in the OECD. Jobert concluded the outline of his plan by urging that the Nine should now take firm and coherent action to avoid compromising the future construction of Europe.[56]

In the weeks prior to the Washington Energy Conference, Jobert travelled twice to the Middle East, visiting countries such as Syria, Saudi Arabia, Kuwait, and Iraq. There were wild speculations in the press as to the purpose of his journey, with France being accused of bartering oil for arms deliveries. Safeguarding stable oil supplies certainly was one motive behind the trips, other objectives being to prepare the Euro-Arab dialogue and to enhance France's economic and cultural presence in countries that had become largely oriented to the Anglo-American world. Yet, there is no doubt that a major goal of Jobert's visits was to strengthen Arab support for France's Middle East and energy policies, as well as to assemble key oil producers behind him prior to the upcoming consumer conference.[57] There were two more indications that France pursued a confrontational course with the US in relation to the energy conference. First, Pompidou rejected an American request that France also send Giscard d'Estaing to the conference, since he considered his minister of finance to be too Atlanticist in his orientation. At first, Pompidou even wanted to keep Jobert from going too, with the French foreign minister himself being reluctant to attend a meeting that he believed was bound to affirm US supremacy in the West. If Pompidou finally nominated Jobert as the sole French representative in Washington, he did so not without complaining to Debré about the 'Germanic brutality' (*brutalité Germanique*) with which Kissinger sought to assemble the whole world around him.[58] Second, France officially replied to Nixon's invitation much later than its European partners, and, adding insult to injury, it did so by means of a public statement before having even informed the US administration. What was more, the substance of this reply boded ill for any agreement at the conference, as the French underlined that they would not be able to consent to the setting up of an organisation of oil consumers and argued that their decision to participate responded, in addition to considerations of courtesy, to the desire to permit Europe to take a common position on the issue.[59]

Surprisingly, the Europeans were able to agree on a joint policy for the Washington Energy Conference despite their differences. After extensive discussions in the Council of Ministers on 5 February 1974, the Nine adopted a common mandate, as well as a collective position on the specific procedural propositions put forward by the US.[60] A closer look at the substance of the European brief reveals that it leaned strongly towards the French position. General reservations shared by all of the Nine were complemented with additional restrictive points as advocated by Paris, while basic American requirements were not taken into account. Jobert's warning that the Eight would have to go alone to Washington if some basic French needs were not met in the mandate obviously had proven more credible and effective than Bonn's counter-threat that France's partners would delay the Euro-Arab dialogue in the event of French non-cooperation.[61] Another reason why the French had their way had to do with the old trick of French diplomacy to start the bargaining process with a position so restrictive that the other parties involved would greet with relief any subsequent French concessions. At the beginning of the Council session, Jobert circulated a French draft mandate as an alternative to the draft worked out by the West German presidency (which closely followed the recommendations previously presented by the EC Commission). This French paper was uncompromisingly negative in its tone, and with the very limited agenda it proposed for the conference it implied that Paris judged the meeting in Washington to be basically superfluous.[62] When Jobert subsequently accepted without too much commotion a revised draft by the presidency that included some French ideas, everyone was astonished. However, the fact was that France had made modest concessions only.[63]

In the final brief for the Nine, France conceded that the full range of topics suggested by the US would be on the agenda. It also accepted that the Nine could review their position in the course of the conference. And, there was now a provision that the Nine would not wholly exclude the setting up of short-term working groups to consider specific matters. However, the EC members explicitly stated their preference for plenary sessions only during the conference. More importantly for the French, the Nine agreed to oppose permanent follow-up machinery and the setting up of new institutions, and, in particular, rejected any international task force of senior officials to prepare for a follow-up foreign ministers' conference. Strongly welcomed by all, the mandate also expressed the objectives of avoiding confrontation with the producers at the conference, paying special attention to the needs of the developing consumer countries, and finding a procedure for a consumer dialogue with both these groups, to be launched by 1 April 1974. Moreover, the brief stressed that the conference could not resolve any particular issue in the time span available, pointing out instead that the OECD and the IMF should subsequently deal with these issues.[64]

Europe's emphasis on a prompt dialogue with producers, and its resistance to a permanent new Atlantic forum, surely did not correspond with Kissinger's conception of the Washington Energy Conference. It was a tactical success in itself for the Nine to go to Washington with a joint position. How the US would respond to it and how individual European governments would react when put under pressure at the conference remained to be seen, however. There was tangible unease in European capitals in the days prior to the meeting, as it was clear to all involved that heated discussions lay ahead, both among the Nine and between Europe and the US.

Division at the conference

Given the shaky unity of the Nine, it was little wonder that their front crumbled once the negotiations at the Washington Energy Conference began. By throwing in the full weight of the US as an economic power and security provider to Europe, Kissinger had little difficulty in dividing the Nine and getting a conference outcome largely in accordance with his wishes. Forcing the EC countries to side either with France or the US, he confronted the Europeans with a difficult choice. It was a demonstration of American prevalence, constituting one of the rare examples in post-war transatlantic history where the Western superpower deliberately seemed to encourage European division. Making a clear choice between Washington and Paris was particularly precarious for the West Germans, whose entire foreign policy was based on the two pillars of the alliance with the US and European unity based on Franco-German rapprochement. As it turned out, the FRG came to play the key role in Washington. On the one hand, it represented the weakest link in the European chain in that it was more vulnerable to US threats of withdrawal than any other member of the Community. On the other hand, as the strongest economy of the Nine, Bonn's choice was of seminal importance for Europe, which constituted another good reason why the US paid particular attention to getting the West Germans on their side. As head of the FRG delegation, Helmut Schmidt accordingly emerged as the dominant European representative in Washington, aligning closely with Kissinger and dragging his reluctant Community partners (minus France) along with him.

American sticks and carrots

There are strong indications that US perceptions of French policy became distinctly more critical in the days prior to the energy conference in Washington. At this point in time, Kissinger began to complain in conversations with European counterparts about insulting remarks Jobert allegedly had made during his trip to the Middle East. According to US evidence, Jobert had warned against Kissinger's approach of interim settlements in the Arab–Israeli conflict whilst in Baghdad. Elsewhere, he supposedly had criticised the lack of dynamism in US peacemaking efforts and predicted that the Washington Energy Conference would not become another Congress of Vienna – an ironic reference to Kissinger's academic work by which he questioned whether the proposed meeting would achieve any impact at all. Kissinger repeatedly pointed out to his European interlocutors that if Gromyko made similar statements to those Jobert had made in the Arab world, this would mark the end of superpower détente.[65]

Kissinger's patience with France seems to have come to a definite end in early February 1974. His memoirs and edited US documents reveal that the US secretary of state directly blamed Jobert for the restrictive European mandate for the energy conference and came to see the Washington gathering as an opportunity for an arm wrestling match with France. Agreeing with Sonnenfeldt's assessment that the Nine appeared only ready to break with Jobert if faced with the prospect of a break with the US, Kissinger underlined just days before the conference that he was now prepared to have a 'public confrontation' with the French, to 'end all cooperation', and to 'make every forum a contest between them and us'.[66] The US objective of isolating France at the conference began to be felt in Europe when Nixon secretly contacted Heath and Brandt in early February 1974 about the meeting in Washington, but no longer sought contact with Pompidou on the same matter. Nixon requested that both London and Bonn send a senior representative to Kissinger's immediate assistance in the final preparatory stages of the conference, as only close bilateral consultations would assure a successful outcome of the upcoming gathering. Heath and Brandt both complied with the request, with the British prime minister insisting that these deliberations remain completely confidential and would not be disclosed to the Community partners.[67]

By the time the various ministers arrived in Washington, Kissinger seems to have decided to bet primarily on the West German horse. Of all the preparatory bilateral consultations he conducted on 10 February 1974 to foster allied support for his conference objectives, the talks with Scheel and Schmidt were the most important ones. During their bilateral breakfast conversation, Scheel initially clearly failed to live up to Kissinger's expectations. Being the acting EC president, Brandt's foreign minister represented the Community rather than the FRG in Washington. This particular role, as well as his general concerns about European unity, made Scheel put much more emphasis on the need to accommodate France than Kissinger could have liked. Scheel proposed that the conference should postpone any concrete decisions until the upcoming EPC ministerial meeting on 14 February 1974, when the Nine would take a concrete European initiative, which would allow French prestige to be saved. He generally gave the impression that he would not be heartbroken if the US forgot about its entire energy project. Kissinger, however, was unwilling to let the matter be decided in EPC. In his response to Scheel, he accused the Nine of semi-neutralism and of a desire to separate from the Alliance. Although he depicted himself as conciliatory when he suggested that four of the proposed seven working groups could be inserted into existing international machinery, his basic message to the EC president was one of threat. The US administration, he argued, was not prepared to accept yet another confusing result of European–American negotiations. Rather than obscuring disagreement by clever rhetoric as in the 'Year of Europe', Washington this time would publicly announce the failure of the conference. Should a renewed confrontation between the US and the Nine occur, Kissinger warned, the Europeans would not get away with it this time. Since the White House would under such circumstances pursue a basic reassessment of the foundations of US post-war foreign policy, Atlantic cooperation was bound to change. It might not be terminated, but it would be of a different nature. An agitated secretary of state ended his exchange with Scheel by making it clear that the US could survive without Europe, but that the Nine might find it hard to thrive without their major ally.[68]

When it was Schmidt's turn to meet Kissinger at the end of the day, no further American threats were necessary to win West German support. As head of the FRG delegation, Brandt's minister of finance promised to back the American proposals and acknowledged the importance of the kind of energy programme suggested by the US. Interestingly, in the weeks before the conference, Schmidt had professed scepticism at the way Kissinger was handling the energy crisis. He had come to disagree with the way the US politicised the character of the Washington meeting.[69] These misgivings notwithstanding, Schmidt was the right man for Kissinger's purposes at the conference. He was convinced of the need for an Atlantic solution to the economic challenges, and he was much less emotionally attached to the emerging political unity of the Nine than Scheel, who was one of EPC's founding fathers. Being well aware of the impossibility of the FRG forfeiting American benevolence, Schmidt did not need the kind of admonishment Scheel had got from Kissinger to go along with the US. When his American host mentioned that the conference could become a symbol of either the decline of the West or a turning point in Atlantic relations, Schmidt underlined that he would not participate in any attempt to turn Europe against the US.[70] Additional American carrots, such as (alleged) hints by the Nixon administration that it might accept a lower figure in the ongoing bilateral negotiations over offset payments in case of Bonn's support in energy matters, might have contributed to Schmidt's loyalty towards Kissinger in Washington.[71] However, such carrots were neither decisive, nor necessary, to bring the West Germans into line with the US conference design.

As the last European minister to arrive in Washington, Jobert quickly got the impression that his Community colleagues had been subjected to 'frightful scenes' (*scènes affreuses*) by Kissinger, whom he accused of having 'reviled, mistreated, and menaced' (*morigénés, malmenés et menacés*) the Europeans.[72] When he met Scheel to review Europe's common position for the conference, he realised that the European front had already been disrupted. Jobert missed the last round of European preparatory consultations on the evening of 10 February 1974, as Kissinger paid him a visit at the French embassy.[73] With no witnesses present, there is no reliable account available of the meeting. Yet, both Jobert's and Kissinger's memoirs leave no doubt that it was a cold and unproductive exchange. According to the account of the French foreign minister, he strongly reproached Kissinger for having intimidated the Europeans and expressed his regret at ever having come to the conference. Kissinger, by contrast, recalls that Jobert sighed about Pompidou's inflexible attitude and suggested that the conference should be continued in the OECD in Paris to enable France to fully support it – a proposition rebuffed by his visitor. Whatever the specifics of the conversation, Kissinger was certainly right about one thing after the meeting: a Franco-American showdown was now inevitable.[74]

Bonn's choice between Washington and Paris

The Loy Henderson Room in the US Department of State has witnessed a great many conferences. The Washington Energy Conference that took place at this location between 11 and 13 February 1974 will not have been recorded as one of its more harmonious ones. But it was definitely a remarkable get-together, witnessing the open collaboration of West Germany with the US against France. It was a most unusual constellation in transatlantic relations during the Cold War. However, it was representative of the diverging needs and priorities among the Nine at the time, which is why it was also to become a symbol of the decline of EPC and European unity in 1974. From the very beginning, the conference met with great difficulties. The ministerial opening speeches had already led to a first Franco-German conflict, with much of the remainder of the conference being characterised by tedious intra-European consultations and confrontations. Once he had outlined the results he hoped would come from the meeting, Kissinger could basically sit back during the conference and watch the Europeans scuffling. The core point of contention among the Nine was the issue of an institutional follow-up of consumer cooperation, which had to do as much with energy as with the principle of Atlantic partnership and Europe's role in the world. Jobert was steadfastly against any new Atlantic machinery and fought for an autonomous European course, but his European partners all came to accept the US proposals and in the end openly took sides against France.

Kissinger started off the conference by provocatively situating it within the tradition of the 'Year of Europe'. Referring to the unprecedented challenges to Western prosperity and to the 'entire structure of international cooperation', he argued that the problems at stake could only be resolved by the US, Europe, and Japan together. Kissinger also warned that failure to cooperate would threaten the world with a 'vicious cycle of competition, autarky, rivalry, and depression such as led to the collapse of world order in the thirties'. He then sketched the fields of cooperation he had in mind, repeating his offer to deal with those issues already covered by international organisations through existing machinery. His main two proposals were, first, to set up a Coordinating Group of senior officials to overview the common work and, second, to have yet another consumer conference before finally convening a third conference with producers. The message was clear: consumer solidarity should precede a dialogue with oil-producing countries.[75]

As Kissinger recalled in his memoirs, '[i]t would be too much to say that the ministers assembled shared this perspective'.[76] Still, being compelled to take a stand, most Europeans showed support for the US design, in more or less explicit terms. As speaker for the Community, Scheel remained vague and attempted to do a balancing act between his mandate and Kissinger's requests. He asked not to institutionalise the conference in its present composition and to have an early dialogue with producers, but, at the same time, agreed to examine effective methods of consumer cooperation and backed short-term working groups. Scheel praised the emerging European identity and the goal of an EU, but also said that consumers should now do some common thinking on identifying key issues. It was decidedly fuzzy, but Kissinger could certainly gather from it that the EC delegate was ready to search a compromise solution, rather than rigorously defend the position defined by the Nine.[77]

As the next minister to speak, Schmidt was much more forthcoming in his support for Kissinger. He pointed out that he shared the view that confrontation with OPEC should be avoided, but reminded his fellow ministers that the consumers were already confronted with a cartel of oil producers. Schmidt then launched a ferocious attack against bilateral oil deals and added a remark which was noteworthy for the explicit threat it contained. West Germany, so Schmidt argued, was not 'worst hit' by the energy crisis and could 'at least pay its oil bill', which is why it would not fear competition 'if everybody tried to get his own way'. It was an unmistakable warning to France (and Britain) to stop pursuing beggar-thy-neighbour policies or else risk competition with the FRG, whose balance of payments and currency reserves in Europe were second to none. Schmidt continued by calling for cooperative answers to the problems of security, trade, money, and energy, which in his view were all interrelated. This observation, again, was a slap in the face for the French. But, it evidently also questioned the whole negotiating approach of the Nine in the 'Year of Europe'. Schmidt concluded his speech by acknowledging the role of the US in the Middle East, which once more implied that he had reservations about EPC and the position formulated by the Nine.[78]

After Douglas-Home had explicitly embraced the need for follow-up machinery,[79] it was Jobert's turn to address the conference. Taking exception to the speeches by Kissinger, Schmidt, as well as Scheel, the French foreign minister no longer disguised his anger behind diplomatic language. Jobert began by observing that Scheel had neglected to outline the details of the common mandate of the Nine, which he now would do himself. The Community, according to Jobert, participated at the conference as a common actor. It rejected all confrontation with the producers, as well as a new international energy regime. It also was against any follow-up machinery and new systems of consultation. Jobert emphasised that Schmidt had obviously not been present at the European discussions in Brussels and accused him of having violated the Community mandate. He also challenged Schmidt's reprobation of bilateral oil deals, encouraging the West German minister of finance to take into account diverse national situations before moralising. Turning to Kissinger, Jobert criticised the composition of the conference, which in his eyes was generally ill-conceived. Moreover, he extensively quoted a US senator, who himself had excoriated the Nixon administration's energy policy.[80]

Emotions at this stage were running high already. In internal consultations among the Nine, Scheel warned that much more was now at stake than whether or not to set up the Coordinating Group. Europe had to decide whether it was ready to cooperate with the US. If the Community remained paralysed on this matter, its entire existence would be in jeopardy, and there would be incalculable political consequences for the relations between the Nine and the US. Scheel accordingly appealed to his fellow ministers to get in touch with their governments to find a solution, which Jobert declined to do, however, on the grounds that his instructions were clear enough. Schmidt, for his part, showed little interest in jointly clarifying the EC mandate and, instead, sought to drive home to his colleagues the impossibility of an autonomous European policy. The Nine, he argued, were incapable of establishing and preserving a balance of power in Europe, let alone in the Middle East. They were simply dependent on the US.[81] According to Jobert's memoirs, Schmidt then erupted, adding: 'If I must choose between Europe and the United States, I choose the United States, let me be clear about this.'[82]

If any of the Eight were still reluctant to comply with the US requests vis-à-vis the conference outcome at the end of the first day, Nixon's address during the host nation dinner was likely to have dispelled those doubts. Calling the energy crisis the biggest challenge to the industrial democracies since World War II, the US president warned that if each nation went off on its own, this would 'drive our economies down and drive all of us apart'. He reminded his audience of the strong domestic pressure he faced to withdraw US troops from Europe and insisted that each nation present at the Washington Energy Conference would be better served by cooperation in security, trade, and energy. Nixon concluded by arguing that '[s]ecurity and economic considerations are inevitably linked, and energy cannot be separated from either'. This statement caused a great stir at the conference, coming close to saying that the US might reduce its military engagement in Europe if its allies failed to cooperate in dealing with the oil crisis.[83]

The second day of the conference was again marked by intra-European consultations, which went on for so long that the Washington gathering had to be extended to 13 February 1974. After an initial 90-minute plenary session in the morning, a working group started to draft the final communiqué, which, for lack of a joint European paper, was done on the basis of an American proposal.[84] Meanwhile, the Nine were looking for a way out of their deadlock. Although several delegations came up with compromise solutions, it proved impossible to bridge the gap between the desire of the Eight to avoid the renewed wrath of Kissinger and Jobert's insistence on adhering to the EC mandate. There were again disagreeable exchanges between Jobert and Schmidt, with the latter subsequently accusing the French foreign minister of having cared more about the French role in the world than the world economic problems, of which he had no grasp.[85]

Although Brandt via telephone rejected Schmidt's request to make a clear-cut choice between the US and France, and instructed the FRG delegation to muddle through without taking sides, the West German minister of finance now swung the Community (minus France) firmly behind the US.[86] The Eight understandably were nervous about dissociating themselves from France, which is why Douglas-Home urged Kissinger on two occasions during the day not to show them up by agreeing to some secret Franco-American deal. In a private conversation with the US secretary of state, Jobert, indeed, made an attempt to reach a last-minute compromise solution with the US. His offer that he would accept new OECD machinery to be set up at yet another conference in Paris in four weeks time and that he would even support some interim machinery prior to that was greeted with scepticism by Kissinger, however. Fearing that France would use the time to build up a new European front against the US, Kissinger asked for Pompidou's word that Paris would accept the same kind of machinery as foreseen in Washington – which the French president rejected.[87]

All that was left to do on the third day of the conference was to finalise the communiqué. With France dissociating from those parts that laid out specific tasks and follow-up procedures, the drafting negotiations occurred essentially between the Eight and the US. It was an overwhelming success for Kissinger, who obtained most of what he wanted. Besides the follow-up machinery, he also succeeded in avoiding the specification of a particular date for a conference with the producers, which according to the communiqué was to be held at the 'earliest possible opportunity' and which, if necessary, would be 'preceded by a further meeting of consumer countries'.[88] At the end of the conference, Scheel could only state that the Nine had not been capable of agreeing on a common policy, while Kissinger terminated the gathering by criticising the difficulties of negotiating with the Community.[89]

Originally, the German presidency of the EC had planned to hold a 'European press conference' after the Washington Energy Conference to demonstrate to the American public the new reality of a united Europe. Now that the Nine emerged bruised from the negotiations, Scheel's comments to the media took place on a much more modest scale. Against the background of the disaster the Community had just experienced, there was an unreal undertone to his assurances that there would be an EU by 1980 and that the Nine would soon speak with one voice in NATO.[90] Understandably, it was Jobert, rather than Scheel, who was in the limelight after the conference. The French foreign minister repeated to the press in Washington that the meeting had been about politics, rather than energy, and that he had been the only delegate to actually abide by the European mandate. Describing the conference as a clever ruse to dominate Europe, he predicted that it would barely make a dent in the pressing energy problems. Back in Paris, Jobert publicly argued that he could not possibly have subscribed to a kind of Europe that received its directives from the US. He also placed much of the blame on the FRG, deploring that Schmidt's heart had made such a clear choice between Europe and the US.[91]

'Bonjour les traîtres:' The significance of the European split

In the history of transatlantic relations, the Washington Energy Conference is a remarkable event and an interesting object of analysis, due to its emotional proceedings and its divisive outcome. Yet, what was its larger significance? What role did it play in the context of the energy crisis? And, what was its effect on the process of European unification and on European–American relations? Starting with the energy issue, the verdicts of those involved about the impact of the conference greatly vary. As the sponsor of the gathering, Kissinger, in retrospect, called it one of the most productive and effective conferences in his memory. He could point to the fact that the Washington Energy Conference set up an Energy Coordinating Group, which, in turn, became the basis of the International Energy Agency (IEA), founded in November 1974. This consumer organisation, according to Kissinger, implemented most of the measures proposed by the US and promoted the necessary cohesion among industrial democracies in the field of energy.[92] Helmut Schmidt, Kissinger's key ally at the conference, came up with a much more negative assessment. The meeting, according to him, ended without results, as France refused to participate in the follow-up and as the US rejected to involve producer countries. The OPEC cartel, therefore, remained undiminished, with the consumers being hit again by a second oil crisis in 1979.[93] Fiona Venn, a leading scholar in oil diplomacy, clearly sides with Schmidt. Consumer cooperation, Venn argues, was assured by US threats, rather than negotiations, and the Western allies continued to be divided.[94] A look at the sources confirms the view that the Washington Energy Conference did not achieve a great deal in terms of resolving the energy problems. In the months after the meeting, Kissinger seems to have lost much of his interest in institutionalising allied energy cooperation. He claimed that it had been the French who had given the conference an unnecessary political flavour, and he even declared himself ready to transfer the follow-up work into the OECD. Indeed, the US secretary of state appeared to have become so indifferent that Schmidt had to appeal to him in March 1974 not to drop the enterprise entirely. Brandt's minister of finance obviously feared losing face if it turned out that the conference had been predominantly a political exercise after all.[95]

Moreover, those Europeans who fully subscribed to the conference communiqué subsequently remained wary about overt cooperation with the US, which in the follow-up to the conference was much more eager to define a consumer emergency package for any new energy crisis than to prepare a dialogue with the producers.[96] As Kissinger himself recalls, America's allies continued to be 'torn between their desire for US financial and diplomatic support and their recurring nightmare that consumer solidarity might trigger a crisis with the oil cartel'.[97] The Washington meeting clearly expressed more unity between the US and the Eight about how to tackle the oil crisis than there actually existed. It must have been disappointing to Washington that Giscard as the new French president in the second half of 1974 decided to maintain Pompidou's position on energy. By publicly calling for a conference between consumers and producers, Giscard embarked on a head-on confrontation with Kissinger's consumer strategy. The Franco-American deal at the end of 1974 to no longer obstruct each other's approaches to the energy problems might have smoothed the ruffled feathers among the industrial democracies. Yet, it reflected the same kind of disagreements that had rendered the Washington Energy Conference such a disputed affair.[98]

With respect to European unification and relations between the Nine and the US, the conference left a heavy mark, however. Only one week after the Community had agreed on a common mandate, the Nine returned from Washington utterly divided. It was a shock to the EC, and a setback for EPC.[99] The EPC ministerial meeting scheduled for 14 February 1974 was postponed, so as to give the national governments some breathing space to contemplate the consequences of the European split.[100] Undoubtedly, the European division in Washington weakened the basis for a European political identity. Britain's break with France called the key axis of EPC's success in 1973 into question. The recognition in London that only alignment with the US might rescue the country from its severe economic difficulties was a severe blow for Heath's Europe-first approach. As the FCO came to acknowledge: 'Those who argued in Whitehall that British interests were best pursued through the Community would now find their position significantly weakened.'[101] The limits of European political unification had also been highlighted by the behaviour of the FRG, which, once it considered its security to be at stake, was quick to stress the primacy of its alliance with the US. More worrying for Bonn's European partners, West Germany in Washington had demonstrated how its economic supremacy among the Nine had begun to translate into political leadership. Schmidt's assertion that the FRG under certain circumstances could contemplate the disruption of the Community no doubt contained a good deal of bluff. Still, as an FCO official put it, 'the unsayable has been said'.[102] West Germany's dominance during the conference was bound to influence the wider political balance within Europe.

This was a particularly unwelcome development for France. Indubitably, Pompidou and Jobert were the great losers of the Washington meeting. In the course of 1973 and early 1974, France had put all its eggs in the basket of European political unity, accepting corresponding strains on the Franco-Soviet special relationship and an early end of Franco-American military cooperation. Now, however, they had to realise that a *Europe européenne* under French leadership was as difficult to accomplish as ever and that an autonomous European identity might well have been a dream with a short life. The French saw their suspicions confirmed that Kissinger was out to dominate the Nine.[103] The collision course they had followed in Washington received a good deal of domestic public backing, and Prime Minister Messmer's exclamation in Paris that France was isolated again 'just like in the good old days' reveals that not every Gaullist felt uncomfortable about what had happened.[104]

However, the fact was that French foreign policy was in shambles, with its core relations with Bonn and London tarnished. Jobert might have said in jest only that he would greet his European colleagues at their next meeting with 'welcome, traitors' (*bonjour les traîtres*).[105] The background to this comment to the French parliamentary commission for foreign affairs was very serious, however: France had been deserted at the Washington Energy Conference, since all its partners preferred a break with Paris over a renewed transatlantic crisis.

Still, it would be wrong to exaggerate the effect of the conference on Europe. It is important to note that the governments of France, Britain, and the FRG in the weeks after the Washington Energy Conference all opted to press on with cooperation in Europe and to ignore the division over Kissinger's proposals as much as possible. The French, in particular, decided not to give up and to treat 'Washington' instead as a parenthesis in the evolution of European unity. Urging his partners to still work for a Euro-Arab dialogue, Jobert even came up with new energy proposals in March 1974 and suggested that the Nine should set up a European Energy Agency.[106] The British too evaluated the consequences of the conference to be bad but not catastrophic. They recommended that the Nine should now have some 'warm sweet tea and a rest',[107] and they had some hope that the split at Washington would be a 'salutary shock' that would bring the Europeans still closer together.[108] As for the West Germans, the Brandt/Scheel government resisted calls in the domestic press to shift its attention from building an EU to constructing closer relations with the US and advancing Atlantic integration in all fields. There was no doubt among West German decision-makers that there was no alternative to close relations with France, and Brandt himself was disgruntled at how snootily Schmidt had attacked Jobert during the conference. Repairing the damage to Franco-German relations was, thus, a primary objective in Bonn after the confrontation in Washington, which constituted one of the reasons why the Nine only weeks after the European split were able to agree on complementing their Middle East policy with an important new dimension.[109]

An unexpected comeback: The Euro-Arab dialogue

In January and early February 1974, parallel to preparing the Washington Energy Conference, the Nine had intensively consulted on how to structure a Euro-Arab dialogue. These deliberations were the result of their decision, taken at the Copenhagen Summit, to examine how cooperation with the Arab countries could be intensified and institutionalised. By the time the conference took place in Washington, EPC on the level of officials had an agreed report ready on how to proceed and get a dialogue started. It was a French-inspired scheme, comprising a three-stage process that would culminate in a ministerial conference between the nine Community governments and the 20 Arab countries. The divisive outcome of the Washington gathering prevented the EPC ministers from deciding on the report as scheduled. Yet, when the postponed EPC meeting finally did take place on 4 March 1974, it became clear that Kissinger's energy initiative had only delayed rather than prevented ministerial blessing for the Euro-Arab dialogue. The endorsement by the foreign ministers of the EPC report was the more remarkable, since Kissinger after the Washington conference had gone to great lengths to make it clear that the US would not approve any ministerial meeting between Europe and the Arab world.

The surprising decision by the Nine indicated that although European unity had begun to crumble at the energy conference, the decline of EPC was by no means irretrievable. However, the US reaction to Europe's approval of a common scheme for the dialogue was strong. March 1974, accordingly, witnessed yet another serious European–American clash. Interestingly, the old 'front' of 1973 between the Nine as a unit and the US had been re-established, only three weeks after eight European governments had sided with Kissinger against France. At first, the Europeans were at a loss as to why the Nixon administration so vehemently opposed their policy, which had been modified prior to the EPC meeting to take American concerns into account. Yet, as the Nine soon realised, US misgivings ran much deeper than the specific EPC decision to embark on a dialogue with the Arabs. The main issue at stake was Europe's role within the West and the notion of an autonomous foreign policy of the Nine. Kissinger's benevolence towards the political ambitions of the Nine definitely came to an end in March 1974, which was to throw EPC into a deep crisis.

Meeting the oil challenge

The rationale behind the Euro-Arab dialogue was twofold: first, to compensate for Europe's exclusion from the Middle East peace process by augmenting Europe's presence in the region through comprehensive arrangements of cooperation; and, second, to defuse the power of the 'oil weapon' by increasing the economic interdependence between the Europeans and the Arabs so that the oil producers had a stake in the stability and growth of European economies. When in mid-December 1973 four representatives of the Arab

League unexpectedly had turned up at the Copenhagen meeting to discuss with the Europeans the situation in Middle East, the Nine had signalled their interest in an institutionalised form of European–Arab cooperation (see Chapter 5). The initial preparation of the dialogue was firmly in French hands. Even before the European leaders referred to the possibility of European–Arab cooperation in the Copenhagen communiqué, a top French diplomat discussed with Sadat in Cairo how the EC members could strengthen their ties with the Arab world.[110] On 10 January 1974, one day after Nixon had issued his invitation to the conference in Washington, the French in the EPC Political Committee tabled a paper on how to launch and structure a Euro-Arab dialogue. They proposed to start with the FRG presidency of EPC getting in touch with Arab representatives to indicate Europe's readiness to set up a dialogue and discuss the preliminaries. A second phase would consist of Euro-Arab discussions on the level of mixed working groups. These groups would cover a wide range of issues, including industry, energy, agriculture, science, and finance. Finally, the foreign ministers of EPC and the Arab League would meet at a conference towards the end of 1974 to discuss the results of the working groups and take respective decisions.[111]

Reactions in the Political Committee were predominantly positive. Indeed, the Nine attached such great importance to the idea of the dialogue that EPC's working group on the Middle East met three times between 18 January and 1 February 1974, making haste to work out a joint report on the matter. Unsurprisingly, the debates did not go without controversies. France's partners insisted that the Commission should be involved in the dialogue, which in their eyes was to become a joint EC–EPC enterprise. There were also concerns that the scheme of cooperation with the Arabs would stand in competition with the EC Mediterranean Global Policy launched in 1972, which had been devised as a framework for bilateral economic and trade agreements, and comprised a long-term perspective of cooperation as well. Then, there were the Danish, who professed little interest in building up special relations with the Arabs. The Dutch, in contrast, came up with their own initiative for the Nine to participate in the economic and social stabilisation of any peace agreement in the Middle East.[112]

There was also some disunity as to the role of oil in the talks with the Arabs. While all agreed that secure supplies of oil ought to be an objective of the dialogue, opinions diverged as to whether this should constitute an explicit issue to be addressed. Pompidou publicly argued that the proposed dialogue was mainly about oil and relations between producers and consumers. Douglas-Home too held the view that oil should be a topic in the European–Arab exchanges. The EC Commission, for its part, attached much importance to energy in its wider dimension being a key aspect of the dialogue.[113] Others, however, were reluctant about the oil issue, as they feared getting into trouble with Kissinger again. They preferred to drop the topic entirely and avoid any impression that the dialogue could be an alternative policy to Kissinger's consumer conference.[114] It was generally controversial among the Nine whether the dialogue should consist of economic content only to reach its political objectives or whether it should also deal with political aspects of European–Arab relations. The French, in particular, were strong defendants of the latter interpretation, hankering more than any of the Eight after a political role for Europe in the Middle East.[115] Finally, one last point of contention was the question of when to inform and consult with the US on the European initiative. Whereas Paris wanted to inform Kissinger only once the nine foreign ministers had agreed on the dialogue, the Eight made the case for early contact with the US and suggested that discussions with the US secretary of state could take place during the Washington Energy Conference.[116]

For all these reservations and diverging priorities, the Political Committee was able to agree at its next meeting on 6 February 1974 on a common position about the Euro-Arab dialogue and a respective *Aide Mémoire* to the Arab countries.[117] The case for attempting to engage the Arabs was compelling enough for all governments to make concessions vis-à-vis the scheme. In addition, there was a good deal of Arab lobbying for intensifying European–Arab cooperation, which is likely to have given additional impetus to opting in favour of a dialogue.[118] The EPC report adopted by the political directors stated that the dialogue required close cooperation between EPC and EC. As for the topics of the dialogue, no definite decision was made, with 'energy' remaining on the list of possible issues. Importantly, the proposal to inform the US was dropped. As Britain and the FRG continuously informed Washington informally about the European preparations for the dialogue, the FCO, in particular, estimated that the US would have 'no cause for complaint' and that the matter, therefore, 'was not worth provoking a row' with the French.[119]

It was an overoptimistic assessment. Whereas no official consultations between the Nine and the US took place during the Washington Energy Conference, Kissinger did not conceal his anger about the proposed dialogue in the bilateral preparatory talks with European ministers. It is worth noting, however, that at this stage Kissinger's criticism focused not so much on the lack of consultation as on the substance of the dialogue, and especially on the idea of a Euro-Arab ministerial conference. Kissinger rejected such a conference on the grounds that it would compromise his own peace efforts in the

Middle East. He denounced the conference as a stab in his back, as it was bound to induce the Arabs to demand more from the US than the Nixon administration was willing to give. Europe should stay out of the matter, Kissinger urged, even more so since it was certain to stay as passive as always if the Arab–Israeli conflict should flare up again. European non-compliance with his request, he told Schmidt, could provoke a 'serious crisis in the Alliance'. Jobert received a similar warning, together with an assurance from Kissinger that a Euro-Arab conference would only take place over his dead body.[120]

Such US threats did have an impact on the Europeans, and on the West Germans especially. After having been informed by Schmidt over the telephone, Brandt immediately instructed Scheel in Washington to be careful about the planned Euro-Arab conference. The Nine, according to Brandt, could not accept having the timing and substance of their political cooperation dictated to them. Still, the chancellor continued, he would strongly advise not risking any new confrontation with the US over the Middle East. Scheel replied that he fully agreed with this view and assured Brandt that he had everything under control with the Nine.[121] Indeed, it is probable that one of the major reasons why the FRG presidency postponed the EPC ministerial meeting of 14 February 1974 was the desire to avoid a decision on the EPC report on the Euro-Arab dialogue being taken immediately after Kissinger's energy conference.

The subsequent European split in Washington obviously further heightened the uncertainty as to whether the dialogue would ever see the light of day. However, to the surprise of the French,[122] the Europeans decided against dropping their initiative in the aftermath of the energy conference. In part, this had to do with French concessions concerning the substance of the dialogue. In a memorandum of 28 February 1974, Jobert expressed his readiness to remove, for the time being, the issues of oil and the Arab–Israeli conflict from the agenda of the dialogue, so as to prevent further conflict with Washington.[123] Yet, other factors played a role too. One such factor was fear of Arab wrath. As some Arab governments were already aware of the outline of the European scheme for cooperation, the Nine feared that their bottling out would be perceived as resulting from US pressure, which could provoke new Arab restrictions on their oil supplies.[124] Some, such as the West Germans, were particularly sensitive about avoiding new confrontations with the Arabs as they already had come under Arab criticism for their policy at the energy conference.[125] But there was also fear of French wrath. Having isolated France once, it is likely that many European governments would have thought twice before repelling Jobert again.[126] This, again, was particularly true for the FRG, since Brandt was out to mend fences with Pompidou.

Moreover, even those Europeans who had sided with Kissinger in Washington held the view that a constructive dialogue with the Arabs was a more promising strategy to secure an insurance policy against any further Arab use of the 'oil weapon' than building up a confrontational consumer position. Pressing on with the Euro-Arab dialogue was also a means of deflecting from the continuing Arab pressure to further specify Europe's position on Israeli withdrawal from the occupied territories (see Chapter 7). Furthermore, as the British argued, if the Nine gave in now, the US would come to believe that EPC was not serious and that American pressure was sufficient to change European policies.[127]

It is unclear whether Kissinger was aware of these European deliberations. The fact is that the US continued to put pressure on the EPC countries (though not France) to rethink their dialogue with the Arabs in the second half of February 1974.[128] During two stop-overs in London and Bonn on his way to and from Syria, Kissinger tried to persuade the British and the West Germans to at least modify the European scheme. In London, he repeated his 'grave reservations' about the conference. In his view, the Europeans would be compelled to support the line taken by the more radical Arabs at such a gathering. This, Kissinger argued, would be detrimental to the interests of the moderate Arabs, as well as the US, and all the more so since it would be impossible to avoid politics at any such meeting. Islamic summits according to Kissinger were 'liable to be even worse than European summits'. He added that all Europeans, except the British, were incapable of understanding the Arabs, whom they tended to take too literally. It is likely that the US secretary of state left London under the impression that his point had well been taken in the FCO. Douglas-Home, at any rate, concluded the meeting by indicating that the Nine would be careful about the dialogue and that he would like to postpone the conference with the Arabs 'to the Greek Kalends', that is, eternally.[129]

Kissinger's conversations in Bonn took a similar course. During his dinner with Scheel, he described the conference as a catastrophe, since it would contradict the US approach of working towards peace in the Middle East on an actor-by-actor and issue-by-issue basis. Kissinger also came up with a measure of threat again, hinting that he had begun to discuss with Nixon an American withdrawal from Europe not for domestic reasons, but as a reaction to the Nine's policy towards the Arab world. Again, Scheel's response must have been reassuring. Although Brandt's foreign minister defended the dialogue, he agreed that there should be no conference in the near future. He even pointed out that he personally did not see the point in a conference either and that the possibility of such a Euro-Arab gathering should generally be approached with great caution. Scheel also confessed that he did no longer grasp French policy, which he considered illogical and strongly marked by emotions. His state secretary added that France seemed to have a mentality resembling the one that had shaped Germany in the old days: 'many enemies, much honour' (*viel Feind, viel Ehr*).[130] After another conversation with Brandt the following morning, a good-humoured US secretary of state told the West German press how sound American–German relations were and how difficult it had been for him to find bilateral problems during his stay in Bonn.[131] He then headed for Brussels, where he was scheduled to brief the allies in the North Atlantic Council on the Middle East. By coincidence, the postponed EPC ministerial meeting took place in Brussels on the very same day. The Nine were, thus, to decide about the Euro-Arab dialogue at the same moment that Kissinger was in town.

As acting president of the Nine, Scheel opened the EPC meeting by recalling his exchange with Kissinger the night before. According to the West German record of his remarks, he argued that the US secretary of state had accepted the Euro-Arab dialogue, on the assumption that oil and the peace process remained excluded. Kissinger would continue, according to Scheel, to have some concerns about the conference, which is why he had asked that the Nine should proceed cautiously with their dialogue.[132] According to the French record, Scheel even said that Kissinger had acknowledged his misconception of the dialogue and would no longer make any difficulties, as long as the Nine stayed in touch with the US about their initiative.[133]

After Scheel's introduction, the European foreign ministers one by one expressed their support for the dialogue. There was hardly any debate after the first exchange of views. Scheel briefly raised the issue of whether the Political Committee should once more take a look at the details of the European scheme, but he accepted the argument of his colleagues that enough time had already been invested in examining the preliminaries of the dialogue.[134] His own report about Kissinger's latest views certainly helps to explain why the Nine were reassured about going ahead with their initiative. Another reason was that the Europeans had made some last-minute alterations to their *Aide Mémoire* to the Arabs in order to meet American concerns. Rather than referring to the possibility of a conference in 1974, their proposal now foresaw such a meeting only if results in the working groups justified it, with no specific timeline given.[135]

As Douglas-Home could not participate in the Brussels meeting, due to national elections in Britain, the Nine could not officially launch their dialogue with the Arabs on 4 March 1974. Eight governments adopted the EPC report formally, with any incoming British government being expected to do so by written procedure within a few days. Scheel, therefore, briefed the press after the meeting just as jovially as Kissinger had done hours earlier in Bonn. He praised the rediscovered harmony among the Nine and stressed that the meeting had finished earlier than anticipated because agreement among the Europeans had been complete. The EC countries, Scheel contended, would now contribute to stabilising the Middle East by embarking on a dialogue with the Arabs. Coming back to the division at the Washington conference, he said that expectations had simply been excessive, as even the Nine could not define a common policy in the course of a single trip to the US when it had previously taken them five years to do such a thing. He generally gave the impression that the Nine were back on track, and that both intra-European and transatlantic quarrels were a thing of the past.[136] It was a terrible misjudgement.

'They cannot have it both ways': A final Atlantic explosion

It was on the afternoon of 4 March 1974 that the happy atmosphere in Brussels, in the words of Kissinger, 'disappeared with a thunderbolt'.[137] At Scheel's request, the US secretary of state called in at the West German embassy in Brussels to be briefed by the acting EPC president on the meeting of the Nine that had taken place in the morning. Kissinger arrived in a sour mood, as he already had learnt from journalists after his briefing in the North Atlantic Council that the Nine had adopted a common scheme for the Euro-Arab dialogue. Gone was the serenity that had marked their dinner the night before.

Scheel assured his American counterpart that the Nine had taken into account US reservations and would proceed very cautiously in the dialogue. He put particular emphasis on the European determination not to disturb US foreign policy in any way. Yet, the failure of Scheel's effort to convince Kissinger could not have been more obvious. The secretary of state came up with a forceful reply. He strongly criticised the lack of advance information. The procedure chosen by the Nine to summon him only after their decision in order to merely confront him with a *fait accompli* was unacceptable, and even more so since he had been present in the same city. This, Kissinger claimed, in the long run would be incompatible with the Atlantic Alliance. Good European intentions, he continued, were irrelevant in the face of the hard facts. His peacemaking in the Middle East would be negatively affected, and whatever had been achieved at the energy conference had been more than undone by the Euro-Arab dialogue. Alluding to the new practices in the monetary field, he concluded by warning that if Europe wanted to float its foreign policy, the US would do just the same.[138]

It was the beginning of what would become, according to the French historian Pierre Mélandri, some of the most troublesome weeks in the history of transatlantic relations.[139] On 6 March 1974, Brandt received a strongly worded letter from Nixon. In this letter, the US president conveyed his 'frank reaction' to the decision of the Nine to move forward with a programme of broad cooperation with the Arab world. Nixon made three major points. First, the initiative was not welcomed by the US, as it came at an 'extremely delicate stage' in the negotiations for a peaceful settlement in the Middle East. By pursuing such a scheme on their own, the Nine would inevitably fall into a 'competitive position' with the US. Second, the White House would have expected an opportunity for 'intimate prior consultations'. As Nixon maintained: 'We have had, at best, little information, inadequate discussions and practically no opportunity for the United States to make its view known to our closest allies.' He, therefore, demanded to 'arrange a system of close consultation and coordination' between the Nine and the US so as to avoid 'the pitfalls I see in our moving ahead on separate courses'. Third, since Washington had once again been treated as an adversary, rather than Europe's partner, Nixon for the time being cancelled all US participation in the negotiations on the European–American declaration, which had been scheduled to continue in March 1974 on the basis of a revised and shortened European draft (see Chapter 7).[140]

By diplomatic standards, Nixon's criticism was unusually explicit and sharp. Yet, worse was still to come. Brandt was quick to respond to the allegations. He once more made the case for the Euro-Arab dialogue and insisted that the West German government had continuously informed the US. He promised, however, that the FRG would endeavour to develop suitable procedures among the Nine for the timely coordination of important matters of mutual interest. Concerning the European–American declaration, he urged Nixon to continue the talks and bring the work to a positive conclusion. Brandt also expressed his hope that the US president might come to Brussels in the second half of April 1974 to sign both 'Year of Europe' declarations.[141]

It is remarkable how resolutely Brandt defended the EPC decision of 4 March 1974. However, his letter achieved little good. In fact, it provoked anger from two very different sides. The French were furious that the West Germans had replied to Nixon without consulting in EPC. Brandt's letter, they argued, had signs of a collective response but contained elements that France would disagree with.[142] Nixon, by contrast, in yet another letter, complained that Bonn's assurances were insufficient. He insisted that 'the consultative process should not be made dependent on the individual occupying the Economic Community Presidency at a given moment, but should stem from a more organic relationship between the Nine and the United States'. In his view, a true consultative relationship would be the 'most natural and normal manifestation of the partnership' which had existed so long between Europe and the US in the Alliance. It seemed clear from the experience of the previous months, however, that the Nine had reservations on this score. The US president added that he was not willing to obscure these differences by compromise language in the 'Year of Europe' declarations, which is why he had decided to let the situation mature further and postpone any visit to Europe until a later time.[143]

Nixon gave further meaning to this second letter to Brandt by a public remark that again caused a great stir in Europe. On 15 March 1974, he addressed the Executives' Club in Chicago, where he stated during a nationally televised question-and-answer session:

> [A]s far as security is concerned the United States is indispensable to the security of Europe, not only our presence in Europe but also the fact of our nuclear strength. Now, the Europeans cannot have it both ways. They cannot have the US participation and cooperation on the security front and then proceed to have confrontation and even hostility on the economic and political front. And until the Europeans are willing to sit down and cooperate on the economic and political front as well as on the security front, no meeting of heads of government should be scheduled. [...] In the event that Congress gets the idea that we are going to be faced with [...] confrontation and hostility from 'The Nine', you will find it almost impossible to get Congressional support for continued American presence at present levels on the security front. [...] It does not mean that we are not going to have competition, but it does mean that we are not going to be faced with a situation where the nine countries of Europe gang up against the United States – the United States which is their guarantee for their security.[144]

These were harsh words. Hardly ever during the Cold War had an American administration threatened so openly to withdraw its military protection from Western Europe if its European allies failed to comply with US policy. The linkage between security, foreign policy, and economics, dreaded and eschewed by the Nine throughout the 'Year of Europe', had now been demonstratively invoked. Whereas Kissinger in 1973 had always argued that acknowledging the linkage was essential to avoiding economic frictions to spill over into the security field, the situation was now different. The US explicitly used Europe's military dependence to press for political concessions from the Nine.

This in itself was indicative of the success of EPC in 1973. Rather than economic issues, it was now, first and foremost, Europe's efforts to pursue a common foreign policy that troubled the White House. Yet, the linkage boded ill for EPC's future.

Nixon himself seemed to have realised that he might have gone too far. In yet another speech in Houston a few days later, he talked about his European 'friends' and argued that he had been misunderstood in Chicago. Nixon emphasised that he would not go along with Mansfield and assured that he would withdraw US troops from Europe only in parallel with reductions on the Soviet side.[145] Yet, this alone was not sufficient to calm tempers again. After all, from a European perspective, Nixon's threats were troubling not so much because of any particular strength and single-mindedness of the US president, but precisely because he was so weakened domestically.

The Europeans initially were puzzled about the violent American reaction to the Euro-Arab dialogue. They were certain that the US administration had received all the information it could have wished about the European deliberations and preparations prior to 4 March 1974. There was wide agreement among the Nine, therefore, that the American strictures were, as the British put it, 'greatly exaggerated'.[146] Davignon even went so far as to call Kissinger's accusation of lack of information the 'intellectual dishonesty of the century' (*la malhonnêteté intellectuelle du siècle*).[147]

When the West Germans confronted Kissinger on 16 March 1974 with an account of how they had briefed American officials about the dialogue prior to the confrontation between Scheel and Kissinger in Brussels, the US secretary of state came close to offering an apology. The whole affair, he now argued, had been based on a misunderstanding. Acknowledging that his department had been much fuller in the picture than he had thought, Kissinger admitted that the problem of information had been between him and his bureaucracy, rather than between the Nine and the US. Yet, the West Germans did not buy this interpretation. Rather than being a misunderstanding, they believed that Kissinger had deliberately provoked a confrontation with the Nine to address some more fundamental issues of European foreign policy-making, which were only remotely connected to the Euro-Arab dialogue.[148] Internal US documents again reveal that they were not too far from the truth: 'I want to use this as an excuse now to show that this procedure will never be accepted again', Kissinger told Sonnenfeldt in the immediate aftermath to the Brussels decision, implying that from his perspective it was now time to raise the question of EPC and its relations with the US and the Alliance at large.[149]

'Killing the Davignon committee': The struggle over Europe's role within the West

The presumption was widely shared in Europe that the dramatic US behaviour after 4 March 1974 had, in part, been motivated by Watergate.[150] As the British argued, there were obvious advantages for Nixon to talk tough to the Europeans, which is why all 'US denials that there is a domestic angle do nothing to convince us otherwise'.[151] However, it became equally clear that Kissinger was using the EPC decision about the Euro-Arab dialogue as a trigger to administer a shock to Europe. Yet, for what purpose? This was an essential question, which by mid-March 1974 preoccupied the minds of European decision-makers. If it was obvious that the US secretary of state was dissatisfied with European–American relations, it was less clear what he specifically sought with regard to the Nine. Internal European assessments of American behaviour and intentions, as well as bilateral conversations with Kissinger personally, led the Europeans to conclude that he was pursuing two major objectives: to get the Nine as a political unit out of the Middle East, and to generally diminish the relevance of EPC and restore the supremacy of allied consultations. To start with the former, Kissinger occasionally publicly ridiculed the role of the Nine vis-à-vis the Arab–Israeli conflict and the oil producers, arguing that the 'Europeans will be unable to achieve anything in the Middle East in a million years'.[152] Yet, in his exchanges with European ministers, he indefatigably attacked EPC's policy on the Middle East, which, in his view, was bound to sabotage his own strategy. During yet another stay in Bonn on 24 March 1974, Kissinger made it clear that the Nixon administration could not tolerate the Nine pursuing goals in the Middle East that were incompatible with US policy. A few weeks later, he told Thorn that the European position in this key region of international politics could only be an additional, rather than an alternative, design to his own. Even prior to the transatlantic crisis of March 1974, he had expressed concerns to Douglas-Home that the Nine might attempt to achieve a pre-eminent position in the Middle East.[153]

During his briefing in NATO on 4 March 1974, Kissinger requested that EPC issue no further declarations on the Arab–Israeli conflict and added that the Nine should prove their identity in other ways than through building up a competitive strategy vis-à-vis that of the US in the Middle East.[154] In his subsequent exchange with Scheel at the West German embassy in Brussels, he even proposed an official division of labour between the US and Europe. Washington should focus on advancing peace in the Middle East, while the Nine should take charge of initiatives in the economic field.[155] How serious Washington was about this idea became clear when Nixon too urged Brandt in

April 1974 that the Nine should stay out of politics in the Middle East, on the grounds that only the US possessed the means of helping Israel.[156] The US did recognise that a European role in the Arab–Israeli conflict might be desirable at a later stage. As Kissinger told Peter Ramsbotham, the new British ambassador to Washington, the Nine could become an invaluable factor if his personal efforts ran aground. With the Soviet Union waiting in the wings, a European initiative after any failure of the American peace effort could well be the 'saving move', which is why a contribution by the Nine should be 'held in reserve'. This, however, was certainly not what all the European consultations in EPC had been about. In the FCO, Kissinger's 'generous' concession was greeted with a short, cynical remark only: 'thank you very much!'[157]

As to EPC at large, it was less clear to the Europeans what exactly Kissinger hoped to achieve. The one thing for certain was that he was fed up with European diplomacy. Thus, Kissinger blamed the Nine for pursuing policies that were incompatible with US interests in areas he considered vital. Examples he put forward in this respect included not only the declaration on the Middle East of 6 November 1973 and the Euro-Arab dialogue, but also the offer by the Nine to both Japan and Canada to work out bilateral declarations with the Community in the context of the 'Year of Europe'.[158] Kissinger also confessed that he had come to mistrust the political intentions of the Nine, particularly since they had treated the US as merely one of many third countries in their identity paper and refused to accept terms such as 'partnership' and 'interdependence' in the negotiations on the European–American declaration.[159] Another frequent American complaint in March 1974 was that the exclusion of the US was 'built organically into the structure of Europe'. The US secretary of state revealed his anger and incomprehension at not having been invited to meet the nine foreign ministers in Brussels on 4 March 1974, and that none of his European counterparts had come to see him at NATO. This, Kissinger asserted, would have been 'unthinkable in the old days'.[160] He generally criticised the Nine for being so determined to consult without the US about world problems and even accused the EPC members of hiding the issues broached in their deliberations.[161] Related to this grievance, Kissinger condemned what he saw as a European tendency to relocate political consultations from NATO to EPC.[162] In his briefing in NATO on 4 March 1974, he made it clear even before the renewed transatlantic clashes that no ally could ask for American military protection if he refused to consult on foreign policy.[163] In a conversation with Ramsbotham two days later, he focused his attack more specifically on the Nine, accusing them of using the military institutions of the Alliance to ensure their military defence, but withdrawing into the 'closed circle' of EPC when it came to political discussions.[164]

But what would Kissinger's unmistakable displeasure with EPC mean? How far did he really want to go? Interestingly, France, the FRG, as well as Britain, all believed that Kissinger's call for a 'system of consultation' in fact hid a wider objective of, at the very least, curbing EPC's autonomy and controlling the policy-making process by the Nine. Both Paris and Bonn suspected that when Kissinger talked of consultation, he actually meant an American veto over European decisions.[165] Already in January 1974, the West Germans had recognised that the French may have been justified in maintaining that Kissinger was eager to interfere in intra-European consultations.[166] As for the British, they considered it excessive to talk of a desired American 'veto' in EPC. Nevertheless, they agreed that Kissinger sought new machinery in which the US would have a 'preponderant voice'.[167] What is more, they had to admit that by 'making such a disproportionate fuss about the Europe/Arab dialogue and by such crude assertions as 'the US must be met 100% of the way', Kissinger appeared to prove the French case that he aspired to exercise a veto over Europe.[168]

There were even fears in Bonn, London, and Paris that Kissinger was out to get rid of EPC altogether. True, the secretary of state time and again stressed that he was strongly in favour of a strong and independent Europe, and that the Nine could very well take decisions contrary to US preferences, if only Washington had had a chance to make its views known.[169] But was this any-thing more than lip service? The Europeans had their doubts. Already after Kissinger's visit to Europe in mid-December 1973 (see Chapter 5), an FCO assessment had come to question his support of European unity, concluding that Europe would not stand much chance of being acquitted 'except if it does nothing', since the US secretary of state did not wish it to play any role 'except one of subordination and unquestioning support of the US'. Since Kissinger was a 'manipulator', who regarded the world as revolving around him and hated action independent of himself, so the assessment went, he was likely to acquiesce only in the existence of a 'Europe without a real mind or will of its own' – which is why the Nine had to attempt to 'survive the years of his Secretaryship' as best as they could.[170] After the quarrel over the Euro-Arab dialogue, many in the FCO came to strongly suspect that Kissinger was determined to 'destroy the dialogue and European political consultations as well'.[171] Since the US secretary of state, nonetheless, continued to argue that Europe had to play a role in the world, the British asked him to come up with a specific example where EPC should get engaged. Significantly, Kissinger had to admit that he could not think, on the spot, of any good one.[172]

The French needed no convincing that Kissinger could not accept any independent European decision-making centre.[173] Already after the Washington Energy Conference, they had argued that Kissinger sought to reduce Europe to an 'American poodle' and to reintegrate it into his Atlantic design based on US leadership.[174] More surprising, perhaps, was that even the FRG now shared this pessimistic evaluation. By the end of February 1974, the chancellery surmised that Kissinger's concept of global political dominance (*weltpolitische Alleinbestimmung*) implied an American preference for a fragmented and weak Europe.[175] In mid-March 1974, there were serious concerns that Kissinger would blow up (*sprengen*) EPC if the Nine failed to meet his demands.[176] Bonn also realised that he no longer talked to EPC as a unit and was adamantly against the Nine speaking to the US with a single voice.[177] Anxieties about the future of EPC were further nourished when the US secretary of state proposed to have regular consultations between the Big Four (the US, Britain, the FRG, and France),[178] which could not but disrupt the political consultations of the Nine. And, what else but a rejection of EPC was Nixon's remark to Brandt on 6 April 1974 that he could accept economic rivalry between Europe and the US but no political competition?[179]

These were gloomy European analyses and concerns. How well founded they were is demonstrated by comments Kissinger made internally in the course of a few telephone conversations between 15 and 23 March 1974. Just after Nixon had made his remarks in Chicago, Kissinger exulted to Brent Scowcroft, deputy assistant to the president for national security affairs, that he was now 'winning', as the Nine would subsequently 'think three times' before tackling the US again. On 18 March 1974, he told Stephen Graubard, his biographer and friend, that he was 'going to kill the Davignon committee' and that nobody was 'going to make a decision anymore without checking' with the US. His policy, according to Kissinger, was to 'let the Europeans stew in their own juice now', and his guess was that the West Germans and the Dutch would cave in first. Two days later, he explained to Alexander Haig, White House chief of staff, that he wanted 'to isolate the French' and that he was 'going to be brutal'. Kissinger continued: 'It took me two months to get this show down started, I am not going to pull off.' Finally, assessing the impact of the tough US reaction, Kissinger came up with a positive verdict on 23 March 1974 in a conversation with McGeorge Bundy, a former special assistant for national security affairs: 'No European government is now going to vote for something that affects our interests without getting it to us.'[180]

This was a difficult situation for EPC, and European decision-makers seemed at a loss as to how to go about it. There was a good deal of resignation in European capitals as to the feasibility of an autonomous European foreign policy. As Jobert told Scheel, if Kissinger interpreted each move by the Nine towards a more united Europe as a hostile gesture against his own person, Europe could simply not be built and was bound to remain fragile and quasi-inexistent. The West German foreign minister too wondered how his European dream could ever come true in the face of such stark American opposition. How could the Nine advance their own unity without affecting Atlantic cooperation and making the US feel isolated? Moreover, if Kissinger seemed determined to deal with each European government individually as long as there was no full-fledged European Union, how should the Nine ever be able to progress towards that goal?[181]

As the FCO noted, the Europeans were now faced with a choice between two undesirable alternatives. They could make concessions to the US with respect to their political consultations, or they would have to accept worsening relations with the Nixon administration. In the words of an FCO official:

> Kissinger may well intend to use consultation as a device for dividing and ruling the Europeans, and if we pay the price he asks, European political co-operation may cease to function effectively as long as he is around. But I do not believe that our European partners, or the present British government [i.e. the new Labour government under Harold Wilson], will in any case be prepared to accept a major and continuing row with the Americans as the price of keeping political co-operation going. We are therefore faced with nothing better than the choice of a lesser evil.[182]

The matter for the Nine was the more convoluted since they were bound to disagree on which of the alternatives was worse. Whereas France under Pompidou and Jobert accepted a degree of confrontation with the US for the sake of European unity, the Eight considered it impossible to build up EPC against the opposition of their major ally and security provider. This, of course, implied a return to the constellation of the Washington Energy Conference, with the Eight finding themselves caught again between Washington and Paris.

Franco-American polarisation

At its core, the transatlantic crisis over the Euro-Arab dialogue was a Franco-American confrontation over Europe's role within the West and in the world. Differences between Paris and Washington about the desirability and auton-omy of a collective European foreign policy had become so blatant that bilateral relations in March 1974 reached what Kissinger called an 'all-time low'.[183] It was the culmination of a mutual escalation of mistrust that had set in at the end of 1973. The Nixon administration, which for nearly five years had put close relations with Pompidou at the centre of its European policy, now ran a course of open hostility towards France. Similarly, the French government after years of gradual rapprochement with the US returned to a position of orthodox Gaullism in 1974. Anti-American sentiments in France and anti-French attitudes in the US seemed to reach new heights, permeating the respective societies and public spheres as much as the realm of politics.

'[S]ince when must a host consult his parasites?' Such was the polemical concluding line of a private letter Jobert received from George Fox, president of Fox International and a major US business leader. Fox rejected Jobert's claim that the US too would have to consult more if it wanted constructive relations with Europe, on the grounds of a highly dubious and insulting interpretation of French history and politics.[184] It was illustrative of how even people outside the political arena became emotionally involved in the bitter bilateral dispute. Media reporting in both countries played a role too, containing traits of systematic anti-French and anti-American campaigns. Absurd accusations and outlandish comparisons became a regular feature and did much to further escalate the atmosphere of tension. To take just one example, the *Washington Post* not only described Jobert as 'public danger no. 1',[185] but also, and approvingly, compared the tough US policies towards France in March 1974 with the bombing of Hanoi at the end of 1972. The American broadsheet paper subsequently did agree to publish a formal protest letter by Kosciusko-Morizet, who expressed his disgust at the comparison. Yet, by printing it together with a photograph that graphically displayed Pompidou's terminal illness, it could not but provoke a new uproar in Paris.[186]

As for the relations between Jobert and Kissinger, they became marked by non-communication, a great deal of frustration, and mutual incomprehension. Ironically, both the French foreign minister and the US secretary of state continued to point out that their quarrel was not personal and that they still regarded their respective counterpart as a friend.[187] In practice, however, they seemed to do everything possible to counteract any such impression. Both left no opportunity in conversations with third parties to blame each other for the deterioration of European–American relations. Both sought to convince the other Europeans of their case to expand their respective bases of loyalty in their battle against each other. Kissinger apparently even went so far as to tell journalists that Pompidou was to die soon anyway, which would change French politics and sweep away Jobert from power without any American doing.[188]

All that seemed left between these two outstanding political protagonists of their time was a great many questions, which they conveyed to each other either through the press or their ambassadors. Did Kissinger want partners or servants in Europe, Jobert asked James Reston in an interview with the *New York Times* on 10 March 1974. Why did he become so harsh when France chose to dissent on specific issues? Why had he lectured the French at the energy conference when they had only attempted to defend a common policy by the Nine? What difference did it make whether the Europeans talked to the Arabs with or without the US? Why had he made public speeches about Europe's destiny without even talking it over with Europeans in advance? And, was the threat to no longer defend Europe militarily in order to force the Nine into compliance with US Middle Eastern policies not disproportionate? 'Thank you for visiting with a provincial politician', Jobert concluded the interview, alluding to the Roman Empire and a policy of treating other countries as vassals, rather than allies.[189] When it became public in April 1974 that the US had just concluded a giant bilateral agreement with Saudi Arabia, Jobert unsurprisingly had one more question to add: Why had Kissinger so vehemently denounced the French policy of seeking bilateral deals with Arab oil producers when he had secretly pursued the very same approach?[190]

The US secretary of state had no fewer questions to ask in response. In a long conversation with Kosciusko-Morizet on 22 March 1974, Kissinger confessed that he was at a loss to understand the rationale behind French policy. Why this systematic opposition to the US, when the Nixon administration had treated France for so long as its privileged partner in Europe? Why this hostility to his policies in the Middle East, where according to his own evidence French ambassadors even advised the Arabs against lifting the oil embargo against the US? And, what was the point of spreading fear of a superpower condominium? The French would be making a miscalculation, Kissinger claimed, if they took American self-interest in defending Western Europe as a basis for organising Europe politically against the US. He added that he was greatly concerned about the future course of European–American relations, especially since it was France's turn to take over the presidency of the Nine in the second half of 1974.[191]

For the other Europeans, the Franco-American polarisation in early 1974 was an unwelcome development. Both the West Germans and the British knew that Jobert was not innocent in the worsening of transatlantic relations. In their view, the French foreign minister had been oversensitive about Europe's autonomy from US influence and too dogmatic when pragmatism would have been required to work out a compromise solution with

Washington at the energy conference. As the British ambassador to Paris put it: Britain and France 'both agreed that there should be a distinct European personality vis-à-vis the Americans, but we want this personality to have a close and satisfactory dialogue, and they want it to behave like a young woman anxious to preserve her virginity from the GIs'.[192] Yet, both Bonn and London placed the major portion of blame for the new low between the Europeans and the US with Kissinger. In their view, the US secretary of state was simply wrong in his assumption that EPC policies were determined by France alone, rather than the Nine.[193] The FCO accordingly deplored that he appeared to have become 'hysterical' about France and to blame Jobert for everything he disliked about Europe.[194] The problems between the Nine and the US clearly ran deeper. The Europeans also disliked Kissinger's strategy of isolating France. They considered it, as the British put it, a 'dangerous game' for the US to make the other Europeans choose between Washington and Paris.[195]

The rift between France and the US represented an enormous handicap for the proper functioning and further development of EPC. It reflected a general deterioration of the conditions of European foreign policy-making in the first three months of 1974. Several factors that had been instrumental in enabling EPC's rise in 1973 were either no longer there or had transformed into elements fostering EPC's decline. On the extra-European level of the international environment, American support of a collective European role in international diplomacy, if it ever existed, had definitely disappeared. In early 1974, Kissinger approached European unity and EPC as if he perceived it as a threat to the Alliance and to US national interests. Whereas his 'Year of Europe' initiative in 1973 had become an inadvertent catalyst for progress towards the political unification of the Nine, his follow-up proposal of Atlantic energy cooperation proved highly divisive to the Europeans. This was for two main reasons. First, the issues at stake at the Washington Energy Conference were much higher than in the more normative process of defining European–American relations through declarations. Second, the US, and Kissinger in particular, this time put a great deal of effort into the matter, presumably as a consequence of the developments in 1973. The harsh American reaction to the Euro-Arab dialogue, as well as the new tendency of the Nixon administration to explicitly make a continuing US military presence in Europe dependent on European compliance in the sphere of foreign policy demonstrated a determination to reconstitute the primacy of Atlantic cooperation, at the expense of EPC. Kissinger's demand that the Nine stay out of politics in the Middle East and his insistence on giving the US a say in their political consultations did not augur well for EPC's future.

The ever more dramatic oil (price) crisis and the rapidly advancing economic downturn in Europe posed a second external challenge that by 1974 definitely made it much more difficult for the Nine to speak with one voice in international politics. True, the oil crisis was a decisive factor for the Nine to embrace the concept of a Euro-Arab dialogue, which in 1974 became an important aspect of their collective Middle East policy and in that sense meant an advancement of EPC. Of more fundamental importance for EPC, however, was the recognition that the energy and economic challenges further increased the power gap between the Nine and the US, making most European governments dependent on Washington to deal with their mounting economic and monetary difficulties. The US continued to be unable to protect the Europeans from the energy threat in the same way as it protected them from a Soviet military attack. Yet, the US became indispensable for Europe to cope with the consequences of the crisis. This, in turn, rendered the Nine more vulnerable to American pressure and prone to meet Kissinger's demands. As the former US ambassador Robert Schaetzel, who accused the Nixon administration of dealing with Europe like a hostile state, aptly put it: 'Already staggering under the energy crisis, harried European leaders were unprepared to face as well an aggrieved America.'[196]

The profound economic crisis also affected the intra-European level. It deepened the EC crisis, which, in turn, also eroded the basis of EPC. As member states increasingly sought national or Atlantic rather than European solutions to their economic problems, EC solidarity collapsed. The indefinite postponement of the RDF project, the further weakening of the currency 'snake', and the inability to implement a comprehensive common energy policy were all manifestations of the breakdown of a joint Community spirit. This inevitably had negative repercussions on EPC too, as it weakened the sense of mutual trust that constituted an essential basis of a common foreign policy. For example, had Schmidt not been irritated by Pompidou's withdrawal from the 'snake' and the French policy of seeking bilateral oil deals, he might well have been less acrimonious towards Jobert at the energy conference, and less receptive to Kissinger's objective of isolating France. The economic crisis also became a severe handicap for EPC in that it widened the gap between the individual economies of the Nine. As much as the crisis weakened the Nine as a group in relation to the US, as much did it increase West Germany's relative power among the Nine. The Washington Energy Conference revealed how the growing economic supremacy of the FRG increasingly translated into political predominance in Europe, which negatively affected the balance of power between Bonn, Paris, and London. The prospect, or at least possibility, of a

German-dominated European foreign policy must have concerned the French as well as the British and presumably reduced their attraction to EPC to some extent. Was Pompidou's decision not to accept Bonn's financial support in order to keep France in the 'snake' not perhaps characteristic of a more general attitude of precaution to avoid excessive dependence on the FRG in order to escape West German political influence?

The EPC agreement to set up a Euro-Arab dialogue demonstrated that the Nine, despite their eroding economic basis and the shift of power among them, still possessed the political will to embark on common political enterprises when their interests converged. But, it seemed, the visions and ambitions that had marked their political cooperation in 1973 had receded into the background. Foreign policy coordination in March 1974 was one possible means for the European governments to deal with their overwhelming economic problems. However, there was some tangible disillusionment as to the objective of promoting EPC as a way of enhancing Europe's role in the world. This was all the more so since EPC appeared to have fostered transatlantic turmoil more than a European impact on world affairs. While the Middle East policy of the Nine so far had achieved little in terms of advancing peace in the region and securing Europe's oil supplies, it had definitely contributed to the worsening of European–American relations.

The constellation for effective political cooperation had also become less conducive because of changes at the individual level of decision-making in London, Bonn, and Paris. Heath was no longer able to maintain his policy of subordinating transatlantic relations to the unity of Europe and to prosperous Anglo-French relations in early 1974. The British economy had become so weak that he had little choice but to lean further towards the US. The rupture at the Washington Energy Conference marked a heavy defeat for his own foreign policy priorities, as well as for the pro-Community course steered by the FCO. As will be outlined in Chapter 7, Heath was no longer even in office by the time of the renewed transatlantic crisis in March 1974, which meant a serious loss for EPC. Meanwhile, Helmut Schmidt's position in West German politics gained further strength in the first three months of 1974. This had to do as much with the new predominance of economic and monetary issues in international politics as with the continuing weakness of Brandt. The chancellor's eroding authority over his government and his party was one of the reasons why his minister of finance in Washington had been able to take a more anti-French line that Brandt had wanted. At the same time, however, the chancellor also sought more backing from Washington himself in early 1974, as his *Ostpolitik* stagnated and required US help. Finally, in France, Jobert's role as a locomotive of European political unification had become severely compromised. His solitary, and hopeless, fight against Kissinger at the Washington Energy Conference mirrored the infeasibility of his aspiration to drag European unity forward against American misgivings. Without the moderating influence of Pompidou, Jobert went too far in risking a confrontation with the US for the sake of his conception of a *Europe européenne* – and ended up in isolation. What was more, his position as foreign minister of France was put in jeopardy by the fact that the French president was terminally ill. As it turned out, the second quarter of 1974 witnessed a change of guards in European politics, which had further negative consequences for the evolution of EPC. With new leaders in power in France, Britain, as well as West Germany, foreign policy priorities changed. This is what the final chapter is about.

Chapter 7
The transatlantic prerogative

In the history of European unification, the spring of 1974 marked an extraordinary period of crisis. EC institutions were paralysed by profound disagreements among member states on just about every important issue. Most national economies became ever harder hit by the rising inflation, and the oil crisis refused to go away. Foreign policy cooperation was in disarray, with American resistance unyielding. So deep were the divisions among the Nine that the eventuality of a break-up of the Community was no longer ruled out. To make matters worse, there was also an unusual degree of domestic political instability in Europe. Many governments possessed small parliamentary majorities only, or were even minority governments proper. Significant for the turbulences and profound changes that shook European politics at the time, all European leaders who had participated at the memorable Paris Summit of 1972 were out of office by June 1974.

Changes of leadership in London, Bonn, and Paris occurred in rapid succession. On 4 March 1974, after a surprise victory in the national elections, the Labour Party returned to power in Britain. Harold Wilson became prime minister again, with James Callaghan taking over as secretary of state in the FCO. On 16 May 1974, Helmut Schmidt replaced Brandt as chancellor of the FRG, with Hans-Dietrich Genscher succeeding Scheel as foreign minister. Finally, on 27 May 1974, Valéry Giscard d'Estaing moved into the Elysée Palace as the third president of the Fifth French Republic, appointing Jacques Chirac as Prime Minister and Jean Sauvagnargues, the former ambassador in Bonn, as new head of the Quai d'Orsay.

The context, extent, and significance of the political changes in the three countries varied. The Labour Party in Britain had received its mandate to govern on the basis of its electoral promise to deal more effectively with the huge economic problems at home. With the return of Wilson, a new government came into office eager to break with the Conservative era under Heath. In the FRG, there was much more continuity in terms of the domestic distribution of power. As Brandt resigned over a domestic scandal and Scheel was elected federal president on 15 May 1974, Schmidt was promoted as chancellor during an ongoing political term, without national elections. He took over the SPD/FDP coalition government without large modifications, with Genscher as new leader of the Liberals being his main coalition partner. The situation in France lay somewhere in the middle. Giscard symbolised a break with the past, as he did not belong to the Gaullist movement but came to power as leader of the small party of the Independent Republicans. Also, he was much younger than his two predecessors, being only 48 years old in 1974. Yet, Giscard's domestic power base was too weak to escape a continuing, strong Gaullist influence on French politics.

As this chapter will show, the changes of leadership in London, Paris, and Bonn contributed to the decline of EPC that occurred between March and June 1974, as it rendered the trilateral leadership in Europe a thing of the past. While Wilson, Giscard, and Schmidt all shared the recognition that Atlantic cooperation had to be reinforced in order to meet the global economic challenges, the British prime minister came to differ sharply with his two colleagues as to the desirability, objectives, and relevance of the European Community. Both the new Atlantic consensus and the rift over European unity impacted on EPC. On the one hand, it meant that the objective of Europe speaking with one voice in international diplomacy became subordinate to other goals, such as economic recovery and Western cohesion. On the other hand, the decline of trust and solidarity among the Community members made cooperation in EPC much more difficult, despite the fact that foreign policy cooperation constituted the one aspect of European unification that Britain remained interested in.

New governments, new priorities

On 1 April 1974, Callaghan in the Council of Ministers in Luxembourg outlined the policy of his Labour Party towards the EC. It was the first meeting with his new colleagues of the Nine. As it turned out, it became a watershed in the history of European unification, marking the beginning of Britain's policy of 'semi-detachment'[1] towards Europe. The speech revealed a stark difference with Labour's European policy of the late 1960s, when the first Wilson government had vehemently pressed to get into the Community. It was tough on Europe and arrogant towards Britain's partners, referring to the option of withdrawing from the EC as if Labour cared little about the consequences of such a move. The secretary of state opened his statement by underscoring that the Labour government opposed British membership of the Community 'on the terms negotiated'. The purpose of his speech was, consequently, to urge a renegotiation of these entry terms. Labour would negotiate in good faith, he assured, but if the results turned out unacceptable, the party would regard the treaty obligations as non-binding and consult the British people on 'the advisability of negotiating the withdrawal' of Britain from the EC. Callaghan added that there would be a consultative referendum on the new terms of entry in any case, and that Labour would advise its people pending the outcome of the renegotiations. It was another way of saying that if the Eight failed to comply with Labour's demands, Britain's withdrawal from the Community would likely ensue. Having outlined specific fields for renegotiation, Callaghan made it clear that Labour also rejected the project of EMU, which it considered 'dangerously overambitious'. Similarly, it opposed the notion of a European Union, on the grounds that it was both 'unrealistic' and 'not desired'. Concerning foreign policy, he expressed his concern about the degree of disagreement between the Nine and the US, implying that an effective Alliance was more important to Britain than the EC. Callaghan concluded that his government was ready to intensify EPC, but only if the Nine were able to agree beforehand on their 'broader aims'.[2]

The speech was a big blow to Europe, because of both its substance and its tone. Gone was the constructive and keenly pro-European approach of the Heath government. It was all the more troubling since the Community had already been in deep crisis. Callaghan's performance was also a slap in the face for the Brandt/Scheel government in West Germany, which had done much to help Britain get into the EC. Furthermore, it was a huge disappointment for the French, with Pompidou and Jobert having firmly based their European aspirations on the concept of a Franco-British axis of leadership in the Community. Yet, as the governments in the FRG and France changed too in the spring of 1974, Labour's attack on Europe was, first and foremost, a challenge for Schmidt and Giscard as the new leaders in Bonn and Paris.

The return of Wilson: Was de Gaulle right?

Rare are the examples of an incoming government executing such a stark change of course in foreign policy as in the case of Labour's return to power in 1974. Wilson's victory at the polls had come unexpectedly. When Heath had asked the Queen on 6 February 1974 to dissolve parliament in order to obtain a new public mandate in his struggle with the miners, most observers had assumed that the Conservative Party would win. Yet, the election ended with a hung parliament, and a slim majority for Labour.[3] As it turned out, Wilson's comeback as prime minister was to have a huge impact on Britain's outlook towards, and standing in, Europe. To be sure, the FCO, even under Heath, had begun in early 1974 to contemplate all sorts of options of how to best meet the new foreign policy prerogative of securing national economic survival and achieving economic growth. In a Planning Paper on the 'scope for change' of February 1974, scenarios including 'reducing European burdens' by obstructionist policies, withdrawal from the EC, or 'tilting the triangle towards America', that is, shifting emphasis from Europe's identity to closer Anglo-American relations, had all been assessed. However, the FCO top officials, who were on the whole strongly pro-European, had criticised this study, on the grounds that Britain's foreign policy needed some adjustment only, rather than change.[4] A look at the preparations by the European Unit in the Cabinet for a returning Heath government also indicates that Britain would have stressed continuity in its European policy in the case of a victory by the Conservative Party. It is true that the prepared policy drafts had pointed to the need for a more favourable arrangement for Britain's contribution to the EC budget as well. Yet, this specific concern had been placed in a wider British policy of finding ways of getting the Community back on the road as sketched by the Paris Summit, with a key objective being to re-establish confidence in the EMU project. Heath had even personally asked for sustained efforts by all departments to promote the case of Britain's membership in the Community, and to counter criticism as much as possible.[5]

Labour's approach to Europe was very different. In one of its first meetings, the new cabinet of Wilson agreed that 'the commitments of the Paris Summit to economic and monetary union and political union did not bind the present Government'.[6] There was no emotional attachment to the idea of Europe, nor did the new government in Whitehall seem to consider British interests adequately represented by EC membership. In fact, ever since Wilson had lost office in 1970, Labour had swung to a distinct Euro-sceptic course, both to placate the many anti-Europeans in its party and to accentuate its opposition policy. By dragging 'Europe' into domestic politics and fuelling anti-Community sentiments, Wilson had shattered the bipartisan support for Europe. Although analysts at the time were near-certain that Labour in 1972 would have accepted the same terms of entry as Heath had done, the party had launched a ferocious attack on the outcome of the entry negotiations and had begun to generally blame the EC for many of Britain's economic ills.[7]

Wilson's opportunism vis-à-vis Europe definitely paid off in that it helped him get back into power. Conversely, it was Heath's misfortune that the

Community had been struck by economic crisis just after Britain's accession. Moreover, there is no doubt that Heath had not done enough to convey to the British people an adequate picture of what the Community was about, how it worked, and the ways in which it affected everyday life in Britain. His hope, expressed in an interview in 1971, to be able to convince the 'housewife who is worried about food' and 'the trade unionist who may be worried about competition' of the benefits of membership on the ground of 'wider issues', such as peace, prosperity, and European defence, turned out to be one of the biggest misjudgements of his premiership.[8] If Heath had neglected the domestic angle to his Community policy, but had been fully engaged on the European level in carrying the project of unification forward, it was the other way round with Wilson in 1974. Compared to the first Wilson government between 1964 and 1970, there were far fewer pro-Europeans in the new cabinet, with the key positions being occupied by Euro-sceptics. Denis Healey, the new chancellor of the exchequer, had shifted dramatically from a position of benevolence to one of opposition towards Europe in the early 1970s.[9] As for Callaghan, he described himself as 'agnostic' about the Community, but he appeared to regard the EC much more as a necessary evil than an opportunity for Britain.[10]

Callaghan, in fact, became the key representative of the Wilson government to shape Britain's European policy. The new prime minister himself seemed to lack in 1974 the vigour and interest in foreign policy of his first period, leaving dealings with both Europe and the US largely to his secretary of state. Callaghan was one of those British politicians who had not only rejected British involvement in the European project in the early 1950s, but had also failed to warm to the idea of EC membership even once the country's economic decline and geopolitical marginalisation had begun to look inevitable. Having served as chancellor of the exchequer and home secretary in Wilson's first government, Callaghan became one of the foremost Labour campaigners against 'rushing into Europe'.[11] He claimed to have invented Labour's magic word 'renegotiation',[12] and, indeed, he had been one of the key figures to ensure Labour's opposition to the Conservative terms of entry to the EC.

Callaghan vividly displayed his critical attitude towards Europe and his confrontational trade union style in bilateral conversations with his Community partners. 'I am sick and tired of the word "European identity"', he told the West German government during his first visit abroad on 21 March 1974,[13] causing even greater anxiety in Bonn by signalling that he believed that the Community's role should be limited to a 'business arrangement'.[14] Callaghan was also very harsh with Ortoli during their first exchange of views, ridiculing the Community's inability to define any successful policies in the preceding months.[15] Unsurprisingly, Callaghan's negative beliefs about Europe made his working relationship with many of his officials in the FCO difficult. 'You care about Europe? I care about the Labour Party', he told one of the FCO officials responsible for Community policies in early March 1974. 'I want you to understand that all this European enthusiasm is not what we are in business for', he is reported to have instructed another diplomat. In his first talk with Brimelow, Callaghan expressed concern that his officials were 'zealots for integration' and much more European than himself, and he accordingly ordered that they should henceforth 'moderate their aims'.[16]

It is noteworthy that the one aspect about the Nine that came to interest Callaghan was EPC. Here too, his scepticism initially prevailed. Upon moving into the FCO, his first idea was to build up the OECD as a forum for political consultation, rather than EPC. He viewed the latter merely leading to friction with the US. In the weeks thereafter, he became more positive about EPC, presumably not only because his staff had warned him that opposition to political cooperation would have negative repercussions on the renegotiations, but also because he discovered the amenities of pragmatic cooperation outside the Brussels machinery. By the end of March 1974, Callaghan signalled his readiness to continue and intensify EPC, which, according to him, could even go on without the Community. By the summer of 1974, he went so far as to propose an EPC secretariat, located in Paris, if necessary.[17] Callaghan made his support for EPC contingent on two essential factors, however. First, EPC should remain an intergovernmental forum of non-binding consultation and should in no way represent a means of working towards political union. As eager as he was to take the dynamic elements and projects out of the economic Community, as determined was he to remove any evolutionary perspective from EPC. As he told Ortoli, EPC for him did not mean the convergence of positions, but the 'classification of what members had in common on any given issue and giving added impetus to those common elements'.[18] The goal should be to foster mutual understanding of national policies and, perhaps, achieve a certain degree of coordination, rather than work towards any common foreign policy. Second, and even more important, Callaghan was only willing to back EPC if the Nine took a different direction in their relations with the US. As long as EPC provoked dissatisfaction in Washington, it was of no interest to London.[19]

This last point typified the supreme importance Callaghan attached to reconstituting the special relationship with the US. Neither he nor Wilson left out any opportunity in talks with foreign leaders in the spring of 1974 to emphasise that the new Labour government would apply a broader outlook to foreign policy than Heath had and would pursue a distinctly Atlanticist approach. One of Callaghan's first acts in office was to assure Kissinger that close Anglo-American relations would become the cornerstone of British foreign policy again.[20] When the US secretary of state came to London at the end of March 1974, Wilson welcomed him by exclaiming that both he and Callaghan were 'Atlanticists'.[21] Upon Kissinger's complaints about how British foreign policy had evolved under Heath, the new British prime minister expressed some understanding for the Conservatives' reorientation towards France in order to get into the EC, but added that it had been excessive and was now a thing of the past. A few days later, on the occasion of Pompidou's funeral in Paris, he assured Nixon that Britain was back to a 'strong Atlantic tinge' in its approach to world affairs, recounting his answer to a journalist on whether he was a European or an Atlanticist: 'I said I was an Atlanticist, always have been, but more fundamentally I was a Seven Seas man because of my feelings about the Commonwealth.'[22]

In a seminal speech at the National Press Club in Washington on 21 May 1974, Callaghan argued that regional solutions no longer measured up to the vastness of the world's problems. Strongly arguing in favour of a transatlantic approach, he proposed that a policy of 'three C's' should be applied on all levels – political, economic, and defence: 'consult' as soon as a problem of common concern emerged; 'coordinate' to prepare a joint solution; and 'cooperate' in order to put forward this solution in other forums. Callaghan rejected the view that Europe should construct its own policies first before discussing them with the US. He did so not without mocking the French, who, he argued, 'still have to be convinced that this is where their best interests lie'.[23] So committed was Callaghan to winning US favour again that Wilson by the summer of 1974 expressed some concern that British foreign policy became too 'obsequious' and drew attention to the fact that 'HK is not God'.[24] Kissinger himself noted in his memoirs how Callaghan, being neither strategist nor geopolitician, had appeared to make it the basic line of his foreign policy to leave the broad design of strategy to the US and seek to bring in British preferences on a more tactical level only.[25]

Little wonder, then, that the US secretary of state was most pleased with the change of government in London in 1974 and later underlined how Callaghan had managed to gain his trust.[26] Conversely, the Brandt/Scheel government, as well as Pompidou and Jobert, were disturbed and disappointed with the reorientation of Britain's foreign policy. The West German leaders were not so much concerned about Labour's Atlantic prerogatives than its Euroscepticism. Brandt deplored that Britain had been schizophrenic about Europe ever since Churchill and in its attitudes and discussions appeared to have fallen back again to the beginnings of the 1950s. Internally, he called Wilson an opportunist and 'partially a madcap' (*partiell ein Spinner*), but regarded him at least as more European than Callaghan.[27] When the new British prime minister asked for West German support in Britain's quest for renegotiations in early April 1974, Brandt dryly answered that 'we can all survive, even if you decide to leave'.[28] He added that there would be no European concessions as long as London considered withdrawal from the EC an option. This view was shared by the Auswärtige Amt, where the objective of preserving the existence of the Community was judged to be more important than preventing Britain's exit from the EC. Scheel bemoaned that Callaghan seemed to have an 'inbred reservation against Europe' (*eine angeborene Reserve gegenüber Europa*).[29] There was much frustration and lamenting in his department about the conspicuous lack of any British vision concerning the unification of Europe.[30]

In France, Callaghan's speech in Luxembourg was initially overshadowed by Pompidou's death on 2 April 1974. Still, for the French government Labour's new foreign policy was highly unwelcome because of both the lack of European zeal and the re-established priority of Atlantic intimacy. The French had already been suspicious of Wilson's intentions in Europe in the late 1960s (see Chapter 1). They now had to realise that Heath's extraordinary enthusiasm for European unity had been an exception to what seemed to be a continuing British preference for Anglo-American cooperation. There was, thus, a widespread feeling in Paris that de Gaulle had been right after all in his warnings.[31] Labour's rejection of EMU and EU was particularly disturbing for the French government, since Pompidou had been a driving force behind both projects. It was also a blow to Jobert, who had reoriented French foreign policy towards building *l'Europe politique* together with Heath. Close Franco-British cooperation seemed all the less feasible now, given that French relations with the US were heavily strained. Pompidou's diplomatic adviser in the Elysée could, thus, only note that for France, a Europe without Heath was a Europe without hope.[32] Jobert firmly rejected the British case for renegotiations, arguing that it was impossible to overhaul Community arrangements every time a new government reassessed its interests. He insisted that it was not up to the Community to adapt itself to joining countries, but rather the other way round.[33] Yet, Jobert must have realised that his cause was lost and that France now was even more isolated than in early 1974. His sarcastic comment just after Labour's election victory that Kissinger, so eager to consult with the Nine, could act as a substitute for Britain at the European table until a new British delegation was formed also implied that French foreign policy had reached a dead end.[34]

There is no doubt that a triangle with Wilson, Pompidou, and Brandt would have had little potential to foster strong cooperation in either European or Atlantic relations. The new Labour government lacked the European commitment and ambitions of Pompidou/Jobert and Brandt/Scheel, who, in return, failed to share Wilson's and Callaghan's one-sided Atlantic zeal. Yet, as it turned out, it fell no longer to Pompidou and Brandt to find an answer to the British challenge.

Giscard d'Estaing and Schmidt: Britain marginalised in Europe

It was by coincidence that with Giscard and Schmidt, two close friends became the leaders of their respective countries at almost the same moment in history. Less surprising was that these two particular candidates were chosen as Pompidou's and Brandt's successors. With their economic and monetary competence, they were regarded as qualified to meet the most pressing challenges of the time. For Britain, the advent of Giscard and Schmidt as a new tandem of power in Europe was an inconvenient development, as it was to show in due time the limits of Labour's Community policy. For Atlantic cooperation, it was to be a positive impulse, with the new French president and the new chancellor both being anxious to repair and intensify relations with the US. For the EC, Franco-German leadership was to be a blessing, ensuring the preservation and ongoing functioning of the EC, despite the many crises and challenges it faced. As for EPC, the balance sheet was mixed.

The change of leadership in Bonn came out of the blue. According to Bahr's memoirs, Brandt was in the midst of planning a reshuffling of his government and a new policy statement calling for 'new élan for Europe' (*Neuer Schwung für Europa*), when he suddenly announced his resignation on 6 May 1974.[35] The chancellor took responsibility for a domestic scandal over his personal assistant, Günter Guillaume, who had been uncovered as an East German spy. Many observers considered the resignation unnecessary and an over-reaction, as the insufficient security checks of Guillaume were not Brandt's personal fault. Speculations about the background of the resignation are still rife to this day. Was Brandt just tired of the relentless accusations, even within his own party, of lacking leadership? Was he afraid of extra-marital affairs being disclosed by deeper investigations into the Guillaume case? Was he generally worn out and, being a *homo politicus*, lacking the interest or competence to deal with the economic problems of the time? Or did his own party, as Kissinger has suggested, even use the scandal as a pretext to remove him from office, as he had nothing left to say once *Ostpolitik* as his one major mission had been accomplished?[36] Whatever the answer, Schmidt was the obvious choice as new chancellor, not only because of his expertise in economic and security affairs, but also because of his dominant position within the SPD.

If Schmidt's election by his party and, on 16 May 1974, by the Bundestag was about the replacement of a leader, the change in France went deeper. The presidential elections following Pompidou's death were a struggle between candidates who represented very different policies and ideologies. After two rounds of elections on 19 May 1974, Giscard prevailed both against Jacques Chaban-Delmas, the Gaullist candidate, and against François Mitterand of the left-wing opposition.[37] His victory was widely perceived as a new start for France, implying a break with 16 years of Gaullist reign. It also terminated the power vacuum that had existed in France since early April. Although Jobert was acting as foreign minister until the end of May, he had been a lame duck during his last two months in office, lacking the authority of his deceased president.

Giscard and Schmidt had become friends during their days as ministers of finance. Frequent meetings and numerous phone calls, conducted in English, had led to a relationship of trust and understanding, or, as Schmidt described it after their first summit meeting, to 'first-class personal ties' (*erstklassiges persönliches Verständnis*).[38] Both new leaders were strong personalities. At least in the first few months in office, they also dominated the foreign policies of their respective governments. Genscher, as former minister of the interior, had moved to the Auswärtige Amt as a complete novice in international diplomacy. As Kissinger put it, his grasp of foreign policy in 1974 'could be charitably described as incomplete'.[39] Sauvagnargues in the Quai d'Orsay, by contrast, did not suffer from a lack of experience in foreign affairs. However, he continued to act more as an ambassador than a minister and appeared to be predominantly engaged in implementing Giscard's policies.[40]

In a very limited sense, Giscard and Schmidt agreed with Labour's criticism of the Community. They too had some doubts about the timeliness of the projects of EMU and EU. Their two major priorities lay in a return to the domestic stability of the European economies and the preservation of the EC as such. 'At a time of growing international problems, we shall concentrate realistically and soberly on essentials, on what needs to be done now, leaving other matters aside', Schmidt argued in his policy statement to the Bundestag on 17 May 1974.[41] It reflected his very realist and down-to-earth approach to politics, which contrasted him from more visionary and idealist colleagues, such as Brandt, Scheel, Heath, and Jobert. Schmidt criticised the fact that key European leaders in 1972/73 had not been up to their job as they had lacked economic competence.[42] At one stage, he also called the Paris Summit a 'disaster' (*verheerend*), as it had raised high expectations and formulated ambitious objectives, without taking the formidable economic obstacles sufficiently into account.[43] In an internal paper that he had produced for his party just weeks before becoming chancellor, Schmidt argued that the economic disparities and problems in Europe had simply become too big for any more courageous measures and leaps forward by the EC.[44] Although more ardently European than his West German counterpart, Giscard essentially agreed with this kind of analysis. As he had been more directly involved in working out the EMU project and had been a member of the government coining the term 'European Union', Giscard would have been subtler in his words. However, he too was well aware that this was not a time for visions but for sober crisis management.[45]

Yet, the big difference between Giscard and Schmidt, on the one hand, and the new Labour government, on the other, was that the former did not view the dynamic elements and perspectives of European unification as principally undesirable, but rather as temporarily unachievable. Giscard, identifying Monnet's thinking as one of his major sources of influence,[46] was more eager about a further deepening of the Community than Schmidt. However, they both agreed that the EC should be much more than a static scheme of economic cooperation, and both were strongly pro-European.[47] They accordingly had little sympathy for Labour's sabre-rattling about Europe, taking their distance from the Wilson government. Giscard considered the British prime minister opportunistic and untrustworthy. Schmidt too denounced Wilson's primary concern with party politics and called Heath's election defeat a calamity for Europe, his friendships with Callaghan and Healey notwithstanding.[48]

A major consequence of this was Britain's (self-)marginalisation in Europe. As soon as they were in office, Schmidt and Giscard re-forged a strong Franco-German axis of leadership in Europe.[49] They did this also in reaction to Labour's confrontational EC policy, with a view to protecting the Community and signalling that London could not shape it according to its own liking. As Schmidt once put it, he and Giscard 'played the Elysée card' to bring home to Wilson the dangers and negative effects of Labour's policy.[50] Britain should realise that it would become a 'third-class power' (*drittklassige Macht*) if it chose to withdraw.[51] The new leaders in Bonn and Paris, thus, remained cool about Britain's requests for renegotiation and largely ignored the pressure from Whitehall. By June 1974, London realised that the environment for renegotiations was far from promising. With France and the FRG giving overriding priority to their bilateral relations, each of the Nine being occupied with their own domestic problems, and the feeling of lacking European commitment by

Britain being ubiquitous, there was little prospect for the European partners to make major concessions.[52] Callaghan's follow-up speech to the Council of Ministers in Luxembourg on 4 June 1974, where he laid out specific British proposals of how to go about renegotiation, was already much more moderate in its tone, as well as in Labour's demands. A few weeks later, he came close to admitting the failure of his strategy, telling Sauvagnargues that he would personally regard it as a misfortune if Britain were to leave the Community and adding: 'The French might say that the British Government had set a trap for themselves and had fallen into it. Even if that were so, they had to get out of it.'[53] Callaghan went so far as to ask France for help, proposing to search for a convergent path that would enable France to maintain that the results did not amount to renegotiation, while Labour could still claim that its objectives had been met.

Giscard and Schmidt eventually did lend a hand to reaching such a deal. Offering some minor alterations to the original terms of entry, they allowed Wilson and Callaghan to recommend to the British electorate a positive vote in the referendum. Held on 5 June 1975, the referendum ended with 67 per cent votes in favour of staying in the Community.[54] If this in itself could be considered a success for Wilson, the whole renegotiation campaign had done great damage to Britain's standing in Europe. Not only had it failed to bring about significant improvements in Britain's conditions of membership, with the outcome having been described as 'linguistic blurring', 'cosmetic', or 'a bad joke'.[55] Worse, it had also led to a loss of influence of Britain in the Community, with the dominant Anglo–French–German triangle of the early 1970s being reduced to a Franco-German axis.

As for EPC, it lost its dominant position in the European conceptions of the FRG and, to a lesser extent, France. In 1973, European leaders, and especially the French, had put the development of EPC at the centre of their European policies, in part as a consequence of the economic stagnation of the Community. Their successors, however, refocused attention on economic crisis management in the EC, partly at the expense of EPC. This had to do with the fact that the economic crisis had become much more severe in 1974, requiring urgent action. But it also was a consequence of the predominantly economic view on international affairs by both Schmidt and Giscard. Moreover, with the new constellation of leaders in Europe, the psychology of cooperation among the big three powers became adversely affected in general. There were no more relations of trust between Wilson, Schmidt, and Giscard as had existed between Heath, Brandt, and Pompidou. With no more shared visions and ambitions for a strong Europe, EPC lost much of its dynamic.

Britain was interested in EPC to the extent that it served to increase its influence in the world. Yet, Wilson lacked Heath's zeal for promoting Europe as a cohesive actor in world politics.

What was more, at least two of the three foreign ministers in office were unfamiliar with the common conceptions and policies built up by their predecessors. Neither Callaghan nor Genscher had any idea of why and how the 'Year of Europe' had become a catalyst for the Nine to shape their own identity, nor were they aware of the specifics that had led the Nine to accentuate their position vis-à-vis the Arab–Israeli conflict. They were, thus, little involved emotionally in the details of the ongoing EPC projects. While this was no long-term handicap for the evolution of EPC, it was an important factor in the short term for how they approached the 'hot' issues of EPC and the American challenge in the first months of being in office. Of course, there were still the national bureaucracies, which guaranteed a degree of continuity in EPC. But, as will be shown below, the new ministers, and Callaghan above all, did have a personal impact on policies and left a strong mark on the course EPC took between April and June 1974.

Atlantic solutions to global problems: Towards the G7

Neither the new West German chancellor nor his French counterpart were 'Atlanticists' in the sense of Wilson and Callaghan. Yet, both of them were convinced of the need for close relations with the US. As former ministers of finance, they were well aware that Europe's economic recovery was impossible without cooperation with the world's biggest economy. Too interdependent were the industrial democracies already and too weakened were most economies in Europe for the Nine to go it alone.[56] Schmidt had already made it clear at the Washington Energy Conference that he regarded Atlantic cohesion as more important than the manifestation of any particular European identity (see Chapter 6). He had become Kissinger's main ally in Europe at that time, a role he would share with Callaghan once he was chancellor. As a former minister of defence and his party's foremost security expert, Schmidt was also devoted to the Alliance, being well aware of the supreme importance of the US to the security of West Germany.

In his policy statement to the Bundestag of 17 May 1974, Schmidt emphasised that the political unification of Europe should proceed 'in partnership' with the United States.[57] It was more than just a linguistic deviation from the previous position of the Nine in their negotiations with Washington on a European–American declaration. Against the background of the heated debates between the Nine and the US on the notion of 'partnership', it clearly signalled a break with the previous European policy of insisting on the political autonomy of the Nine, even at the expense of transatlantic unity. Significantly, Giscard too embraced the notion of 'partnership' between Europe and the US immediately after coming into office.[58] Although the new French president agreed that Kissinger paid lip service only to the project of European unification,[59] he generally appeared more relaxed about relations between the Nine and the US. Giscard was eager to restore Franco-American relations and to render the acerb controversies between Kissinger and Jobert a thing of the past.[60] His Atlantic policies, in fact, became the one realm of French foreign policy where a change of course became discernible after the death of Pompidou.[61] Yet, the degree of change should not be exaggerated. On the one hand, Franco-American relations had already improved between 1969 and 1973, with the sharp dispute between Paris and Washington in early 1974 being an exception, rather than the rule of the Pompidou presidency. On the other hand, Giscard's shaky domestic power base prevented him from moving towards a thorough rapprochement with the US, even if he had wanted to. Although organised Gaullism had partly disintegrated, Gaullist ideology was still a dominant feature of French politics. Furthermore, Giscard owed his victory to no little extent to the fact that Gaullist exponents, such as Chirac, had backed him. A strong, anti-American left was another obstacle to a sharp turn around in French policy towards the US.[62]

Still, Giscard's more positive attitude towards the US laid the basis for a marked improvement in relations between all major Atlantic powers. Allied cooperation became characterised by a constructive atmosphere again, rather than frequent European–American rows. Atlantic consultations became further institutionalised in the form of the Group of Seven (G7). At the root of these regular summits of the heads of the major industrial democracies stood the so-called 'Library Group' of the ministers of finance of West Germany, France, Britain, the US, and, occasionally, Japan. In the early 1970s, this group had held frequent, and often secret, meetings to discuss issues such as the monetary turbulences and the energy crisis, with Schmidt and Giscard as two of its protagonists. Once Schmidt had become chancellor, he lost little time in proposing that the Library Group should be reactivated.[63] Kissinger, for his part, in the autumn of 1974 summoned a conference of the five foreign and finance ministers in Washington to deal with the oil crisis again.[64] While this meeting caused unease among the European participants, who feared a confrontation with OPEC again, the idea of the 'Five' lingered on. By the end of the year, Giscard and Ford, who had assumed the US presidency after Nixon's resignation, agreed to set up an informal group of personal advisers to work out a common conception to deal with the economic challenges. In August 1975, Giscard suggested that the heads of state should pursue a similar dialogue among themselves. The first such summit of the G6 (including Italy) took place in November 1975 in Rambouillet, with Canada joining the process the year after.[65]

The impact of improved Atlantic relations on the significance and viability of EPC was ambiguous. On the one hand, the fact that the leaders in London, Bonn, Paris, and Washington all shared the perception that close transatlantic ties were essential and in their national interest removed a key source of tension from EPC. As will be shown below, the new European decision-makers, eager to re-establish harmonious relations between the Nine and the US, largely complied with Kissinger's requests about EPC. This, in turn, diminished American dissatisfaction with EPC. With US pressure and hostility gone, the Nine had more breathing space again. If events in early 1974 had made it clear that they would not be able to preserve their unity if faced with firm American opposition, the relaxation of tension in transatlantic relations under new European leaders implied improved conditions for effective European foreign policy cooperation.

On the other hand, meeting Kissinger's requests meant giving up important aspects of EPC as formed in the years before. The price for the new Atlantic prerogative was, thus, a decreased relevance of EPC. Whereas Heath, Brandt, and Pompidou had come to give priority to building Europe, the new leaders all believed that the pressing issues of the time required Atlantic solution. The G7 mirrored well this difference of perception. As Kissinger noted in his memoirs, this new grouping was a de facto political directorate of the great powers of the West.[66] As such, it was partly in competition with EPC, as well as with the Community (and, indeed, with the Alliance of Fifteen). Whereas Kissinger had in vain proposed such great power consultations in the context of the 'Year of Europe', the new leaders in London, Paris, and Bonn now readily embraced them.

No European identity vis-à-vis Washington

Having been a major driving force behind EPC's rapid development in 1973, the issue of European–American relations by March 1974 constituted its biggest source of strain. In the following, I will investigate into how the Nine, with new leaders in London, Paris, and Bonn, dealt with the American

challenge to EPC. The first issue to address is how they went about the problem of taking US views into account in EPC without compromising Europe's
autonomous decision-making. Subsequently, the outcome of the negotiations
on the 'Year of Europe' declarations will be examined. Finally, I will discuss the
reinforcement of NATO political consultations. As will be shown, while the
degree of influence of the new leaders on the European policy choices varied
in each of these cases, they all agreed to discontinue the project of formulating
a European policy vis-à-vis the US, and they generally subordinated the
objective of a European identity in world politics to smooth transatlantic
relations.

The Gymnich Agreement

In view of the harsh American reaction to the Euro-Arab dialogue in mid-
March 1974, the most urgent problem for the Nine to resolve was the issue of
consultation with the US. The challenge for the Nine to come up with a common solution was all the more complex since the new Labour government in
Britain defended a rather radical position on this. Callaghan received
Sonnenfeldt on 15 March 1974 in order to learn first hand about American
grievances. While his own officials defended EPC's procedures to work out
common policies, Callaghan explicitly sided with the American point of view.
Arguing that any contest with the US would be 'between a flyweight and a
heavyweight in the person of Dr Kissinger', he proposed that the Nine and the
US should henceforth sit at the same table for consultation.[67] A few days later,
the new British secretary of state informed Scheel that Britain would no longer
accept secret EPC consultations without informing the US and would always
first consult bilaterally with Washington before taking a stand among the Nine.
When Scheel protested that the US wanted to become the tenth member of
Europe, Callaghan insisted that Britain would change its policy and reserved
the right to talk to the Americans at any time about any matter. The new British
credo was, as Callaghan told Kissinger, that the Eight should not tell London
anything they did not want the US to know.[68]

   This was not how EPC had worked before. Scheel continued to argue that
an American seat at each European table was as unrealistic as a European representative permanently consulting in the White House.[69] Yet, the West
Germans were well aware that something had to be done to placate Kissinger.
The sharp US criticism of Europe had provoked a huge domestic affair, with
the opposition parties accusing Brandt and Scheel of having alienated both
Washington and Paris. There were, thus, fears in the Auswärtige Amt that

without a solution on consultation, EPC could be abolished entirely.[70] Accordingly, the FRG, as acting presidency of EPC, made great efforts in March and April 1974 to find a compromise solution between meeting American and British requirements, and preserving EPC's autonomy and viability. To this end, Bonn devised a formula according to which the Nine would still consult via the presidency, but would no longer do so after EPC ministerial decisions only. Rather, consultations with the US should take place once the Nine had reached tentative agreement on any given policy on the level of the Political Committee. This, so the reasoning of the FRG went, would allow Washington to outline its views prior to the deliberations by the foreign ministers while avoiding both excessive American influence in EPC and a return to bilateral consultations with Washington.[71] Yet, when the West Germans aired their idea to their European colleagues, they encountered criticism from both France and Britain.

On the level of the Political Committee, it was mainly the French who raised objections. Lamenting that such a procedure would equate EPC with NATO and mean the end of Europe's autonomy and raison d'être, they warned that France would lose all interest in EPC under such circumstances. This led to, as the FCO put it, a 'battle royal'[72] between the French and some of their colleagues, who insisted that some concession had to be made towards the US.[73] When Scheel floated the same West German suggestion during the EPC ministerial meeting in Luxembourg on 1 April 1974, it was Callaghan who was the most outspoken. Having outlined the British request for renegotiations just hours earlier in the Council of Ministers, Callaghan in his first appearance in EPC took particular exception to Scheel's explanation that the presidency would consult with the US only if all Nine agreed on such a move. Callaghan underlined that Britain would no longer allow any other government to exert a veto over its consultations with Washington. He also expressed disapproval of the language the Nine used with regard to the US, claiming that it resembled that of adversaries rather than partners, and he generally showed himself so Atlanticist that the Irish foreign minister had to remind him that he was in a European forum, rather than NATO. Scheel deplored Callaghan's emphasis on bilateralism as much as Kissinger's pressure for permanent consultations with EPC, pointing out that both trends made it much more difficult for the Nine to speak with one voice. Jobert, however, rejected the formula too and indicated that he would much rather block a European solution now than risk a long-term dilution of European unity. Surprisingly, however, Jobert added that the Nine should return to bilateral consultations with the US and work out no formula at all.[74] What appeared like a French move towards the British point of view was, in fact, motivated by rather different reasoning. Faced with a choice between abandoning EPC altogether and making concessions on consultation, Jobert and Pompidou had come to consider the latter option the lesser evil. Yet, rather than concede any institutional link between the Nine and the US, they preferred to drop the notion of a common European position vis-à-vis the US entirely. With Callaghan around, it was unlikely that any European policy would emerge that would be remotely of interest to France anyway. From a French perspective it was better to go one step back with EPC than move in the wrong direction.[75]

This was not how Scheel and other European partners saw it, however. The Belgians, in particular, indefatigably urged their colleagues to agree on a common formula, which they considered vital to ensuring EPC's survival. Debates went on into the early hours and continued on 2 April 1974, without producing any consensus. Worse still for EPC, the lack of agreement also had negative repercussions on the Euro-Arab dialogue. Although Callaghan indicated during the meeting Labour's general consent to the dialogue, he made his approval of launching it contingent on a solution to the consultation issue. The meeting ended, therefore, in complete deadlock, with EPC's future being less certain than ever before.[76]

Already in early March 1974, Scheel had come up with the idea of an informal meeting of the nine foreign ministers for a weekend at Gymnich, a castle near Bonn. Presumably taking inspiration from Pompidou's earlier proposal for foreign policy summits in closed circles, the idea in Bonn had been to organise a fireside chat between ministers only, the objective being to discuss EPC's future and restore relations of trust. As the situation had further deteriorated since the official West German invitation in mid-March 1974, the Gymnich meeting of 20/21 April 1974 seemed timely indeed.[77] During the days before the gathering, the Political Committee again tried to hammer out a compromise formula on how to consult with the US. During these deliberations, it became increasingly evident that no agreement on general principles could be established. Instead, the idea of working out an informal gentlemen's agreement, rather than an official written formula, was gaining ground.[78]

It was this approach that prevailed at the Gymnich meeting. The foreign ministers agreed to have a pragmatic procedure, deciding on consultations with any third party on a case-by-case basis and by consensus, with the presidency being in charge of subsequently executing the mandate.[79] It was a compromise solution, taking into account some concerns of each party involved. The British and the French could both be pleased with the informal and case-by-case solution, the former because it did not explicitly rule out bilateral consultations and the latter because it did not amount to an institutionalised link between the Nine and the US. The West Germans, in contrast, could point to the role attributed to the presidency in conducting the consultations, which they considered important in preserving the vitality of EPC. To the dismay of the British especially, Bonn, nevertheless, insisted on transforming the agreement into a written form after the Gymnich meeting. The West German government did so both because it needed some formula to show to the Bundestag and because it wanted to make sure that all governments involved interpreted the agreement along the same lines.[80] It took another month of negotiations before the Nine eventually agreed that Genscher, as EPC's new acting president, would distribute to his colleagues during the next EPC ministerial meeting a non-paper with an agreed formula on consultations, which he would read out but which was not to become an official EPC text.[81]

Thus, on 10 June 1974, the Gymnich Agreement in its written form was finally taken note of by the nine foreign ministers. It read as follows:

> Concerning the question of consultations of the Nine with allied or friendly states by means of the presidency, ministers have agreed to proceed in a pragmatic and case-by-case fashion. Where one of the partners raises the question of informing or consulting an allied or friendly state, the Nine will discuss the matter and will, after consensus has been reached, request the Presidency to proceed accordingly.[82]

As previously agreed among the Nine, Genscher on the occasion also drew the attention of his colleagues to an EPC document approved on 12 April 1972, according to which third parties could only be informed about EPC consultations and documents through the presidency and on the basis of consensus. This too became part of the Gymnich Agreement.[83]

What was the significance of the Gymnich formula for EPC? Any answer must take into account two rather different aspects, namely the abstract, conceptual dimension of the formula, and the question of its implementation in practice. To start with the former, a positive reading could point to the fact that the Nine had reached agreement on how to resolve EPC's most pressing challenge. By finding a way of organising consultations with the US that was acceptable to all Nine, as well as to Washington (see below), the Community members liberated EPC from its major source of tension and secured its continuing existence. Yet, they did so at a considerable price. By implication, the formula meant that failure of the Nine to reach consensus on consulting with the US on any particular issue would result in the removal of this issue from the EPC agenda. Jobert had been fully aware of this when he had warned his colleagues that EPC would lack any substance within one year with such a formula.[84] Scheel too had realised only too well the consequences of the formula.[85] If the Auswärtige Amt still had pushed its quasi-notification, it was because the FRG considered it inevitable to pay this price for the sake of both Atlantic unity and EPC's preservation. Seen in this light, the Gymnich Agreement could hardly conceal the subordination of European interests to US leadership. Given that the question of consultation would come up mainly in instances where the US potentially disagreed with European views, and given the likelihood that at least one EC member in such cases would insist on US involvement in the decision shaping, it was likely that the Nine would be able to pursue common polices in issues only on which they by and large agreed with Washington anyway. But, as the French in particular argued, what then was the point of a distinct European foreign policy?[86]

On the other hand, it is important to note that on the practical level of policy-making, the Gymnich Agreement came to play a very limited role only, as it was simply ignored by some governments. No matter how much the agreement of 10 June 1974 stressed the importance of the presidency, Callaghan, in particular, continued to interpret 'Gymnich' as 'full bilateral consultation all the time'.[87] This was also because Kissinger, although he had accepted the formula as a 'big step forward', came to show little interest in consulting with the Nine and was, above all, eager to pursue close bilateral consultations with London and Bonn.[88] If he initially showed some reservation about the 'case-by-case' procedure, he made no more fuss about it, and he too came to define the formula as meaning a blank check for bilateral consultations with each of the Nine.[89] Indeed, there was little reason for Kissinger to remain concerned. The Labour government provided him with comprehensive and permanent information about EPC and took US views into account in EPC to an extent that made an institutional link between the Nine and Washington less necessary. Anglo-American cooperation became so close that *The Economist* noted at the end of June 1974 that Peter Ramsbotham, the British Ambassador to Washington, was 'keeping himself in Kissinger's good books by cheerfully informing him of every confidential detail of political discussions among the Nine'. Even though Ramsbotham was distressed about this accusation, he could only defend himself by arguing that all his contacts with the US government had been 'on the understanding that the Americans would keep to themselves what we were telling them'.[90]

Another reason why Kissinger could be more relaxed was precisely because the Gymnich accord implied reduced political ambitions of the Nine, or, as Kissinger saw it, a reduced likelihood that European political unity would be organised against the US.[91] The US secretary of state could note that the new French government professed no intention of resuming further attempts to formulate a common European position vis-à-vis Washington. Sauvagnargues, indeed, made it clear that he supported full bilateralism between each European government and the US again. In contrast to Jobert, who had given up forming a European identity with respect to the US on the assumption that it was impossible to do so, Sauvagnargues seems to have considered such an undertaking also less desirable, calling the whole issue of consultation simply an artificial problem.[92] According to Kissinger's memoirs, there was even an agreement between the US and France on this: Washington would continue to deal bilaterally with the national governments in Europe, with Paris ceasing its efforts to enable the Nine to speak with one voice to the US; in return, France could continue to pursue European integration, with Kissinger refraining from placing any more obstacles in the way of the French.[93] Officials in the Auswärtige Amt were distraught that the US administration seemed to know everything about EPC even before the FRG, as presidency, had a chance to inform it. They criticised the British, in particular, for their excessive use of bilateral channels. Yet, there was little they could do, the less so since Genscher and Schmidt, in contrast to Scheel and Brandt, appeared to take no exception at how other governments buried the notion of a common European performance vis-à-vis the US.[94]

The Gymnich Agreement, although it did not bring about the kind of institutional link between the Nine and the US that Kissinger had wanted, was a reflection of the shift from the European dreams of 1973 to the Atlantic prerogatives and necessities of 1974. It stood for changes in EPC that were very much in accordance with American requests. It symbolised a recognition that pursuing common European policies which the US considered detrimental to its own interests was unfeasible and undesirable. Furthermore, it marked an end to Europe's ambition of acting as an entity vis-à-vis Washington and signified a return to bilateral relations between European governments and the US. While the formula had been mainly conceptualised by the FRG, its practical meaning became strongly influenced by Callaghan. The fact that even Jobert and Scheel had been involved in the Gymnich compromise mirrored the inevitability of a reduced standing of EPC, with the combination of US pressure and a British reorientation towards the special relationship proving too much to keep up the high ambitions of 1973. The impact of Giscard and Schmidt in this particular case was, thus, limited, relating mainly to backing or tolerating the Labour-inspired return to government-to-government consultations. The same assessment does not hold true in the case of the 'Year of Europe', where Giscard and Schmidt explicitly broke with the policy of their predecessors in order to restore Atlantic unity.

The Ottawa Declaration of NATO: The 'Year of Europe' at a close

There is no better mirror for the rise and decline of EPC in 1973 and 1974 than the course of the 'Year of Europe'. Being at first a catalyst for arousing Europe's political ambitions, the outcome of Kissinger's initiative in 1974 symbolised the failure of the Nine to put their objective of becoming a recognised, unitary actor in world politics into effect. Above all, it demonstrated the impossibility of pursuing a common European policy vis-à-vis the US. Rather than ending with two documents on the Alliance and on European–American relations, the 'Year of Europe' came to a close with an Atlantic declaration only, approved by the foreign ministers during a NATO ministerial meeting in Ottawa on 19 June 1974. This so-called 'Ottawa Declaration' was signed at summit level when Nixon stopped off in Brussels on his way to Moscow on 26 June 1974. Although the substance of the declaration fell well short of what Kissinger had originally asked for, it marked a victory for his Atlantic conception over the European political aspirations as entertained by Heath, Jobert, and Scheel/Brandt. The importance of allied cooperation in matters of defence, foreign policy, and economics was reaffirmed, while the draft on European–American relations was shelved for good.

Analytically, the evolution of the negotiations on the 'Year of Europe' in 1974 can be divided into four different phases. The weeks prior to the Washington Energy Conference were marked by continuing, if limited, American interest in bringing both declarations to an end. This period also witnessed a collective effort by the Nine to overhaul their draft on relations with Washington, in compliance with Kissinger's request of mid-December 1973 (see Chapter 5). The second phase, from 13 February 1974 to the positive European verdict on the Euro-Arab dialogue of 4 March 1974, was characterised by the Franco-American polarisation over Europe's future, as described in Chapter 6. Paris now lost a great deal of interest in the exercise of working out declarations, while the US remained ready to sign two declarations, but was no longer willing to attribute France any prominent role in this. In phase three, spanning from early March to late May 1974, Kissinger, as a sign of dissatisfaction with EPC, interrupted the process of negotiations and together with Callaghan embarked on a secret manoeuvre to kill the European–American declaration and push through a single Atlantic declaration of the Alliance. While Jobert and Scheel/Brandt tried to prevent such a move, Giscard and Schmidt subsequently acquiesced to it. Phase four of June 1974 was accordingly marked by a new transatlantic consensus on the primacy of reconstituting allied relations and subordinating any European quest for an autonomous foreign policy. The fact that the final negotiations in NATO on the new British–American draft were brought to a successful end reflected some degree of Franco-American reconciliation. At the same time, intra-European controversies on the declaration ended with a victory for Callaghan, who stubbornly refused any reference to European political unity in the text.

Already in January 1974, Kissinger was well aware that the 'Year of Europe' would no longer result in a document of historic significance. As he told the West German ambassador to Washington, the Europeans had begun to emphasise their own identity at the wrong moment in time, which is why historians later would argue that the decision-makers in 1973/74 had failed to live up to the real challenges of the time.[95] To Douglas-Home, Kissinger even confessed that he would not mind getting rid of the documents entirely, as they served little purpose. At the same time, he had to admit that there was no feasible way of doing so.[96] Watergate certainly made it very difficult for Kissinger to sink a major US foreign policy project entirely, since this would have further weakened Nixon domestically. The US secretary of state, therefore, was willing to continue the negotiations on the Atlantic as well as the European–American declaration. He indicated that Nixon might come to Europe in the context of NATO's twenty-fifth anniversary in April 1974 and could sign both documents on that occasion.[97]

During this phase, Kissinger even made another attempt to shape the remainder of the 'Year of Europe' by secret Franco-American cooperation. During his stay in Paris on 19/20 December 1973, he assured Pompidou and Jobert that the bilateral tensions of the autumn of 1973 had been caused by a philosophical misunderstanding. Whereas it was true that the US bureaucracy fostered hegemonic aspirations, Kissinger said, the Nixon administration was still in favour of a strong and independent Europe led by France. All it asked for was to build up a relationship to the emerging identity of the Nine. Pompidou reacted rather grumpily to these US efforts to get bilateral cooperation started again. Jobert, however, was more receptive. Although he sarcastically pointed out that the US demand to redo and shorten the European–American draft was a good device to divide the Nine again, he complied with Kissinger's request that the French should take the lead in working out a new draft, at least to the extent that he promised the US secretary of state a letter on how to go about it.[98]

Kissinger erroneously claimed in his memoirs that Jobert had never lived up to this promise. The fact is that the French foreign minister sent a letter on 8 January 1974, but indicated his preference of modifying the draft on European–American relations in EPC rather than through confidential Franco-American exchanges.[99] France, accordingly, in the Political Committee tabled a revised draft for discussion with its European partners. With Britain and Italy coming up with new drafts too, the FRG presidency eventually produced an amalgamated version of all papers.[100] A new joint European draft was ready by 8 February 1974, with a last paragraph on energy being scheduled to be added after the Washington Energy Conference. The political part of this draft was heavily based on the French proposal, while the economic sections closely followed the British draft.[101]

Rather than being a complete overhaul, the new European draft was a watered-down version of the original text. It was considerably shorter, warmer, and more forthcoming vis-à-vis the US. In the preamble, the Nine and the US were no longer explicitly contrasted by 'on the one hand' and 'on the other hand'. Instead, there was now simply a vertical spacing:

The European Community and its Member States,
The United States of America

Also, much more emphasis was put on highlighting the close links between Europe and the US. In the first paragraph it was stated that as the Nine had decided to define their relations with the rest of the world, they considered it 'natural to do so first with the United States'. The Nine also underscored that they were ready to work in harmony and in 'a spirit of creativity' with Washington and that they would undertake to 'intensify the existing cooperation and consultation by using to the full all the means which are at their disposal'. Having said that, the European draft continued to be primarily about winning US recognition of the Nine as a new factor in global diplomacy and of the EU as being beneficial to the West. The text still failed to take important US amendments into account. There was, largely because at French insistence, still no reference to 'partnership'. Nor did the revised draft signal any European readiness to set up new machinery of consultation between EPC and the US.

The situation was similar in the case of the Atlantic declaration. As in the autumn of 1973 (see Chapter 5), the French, as the original sponsors of the draft, continued to show willingness to modify their text in NATO. Two new French drafts of 14 December 1973 and 15 January 1974 contained minor concessions, in accordance with American requirements.[102] Yet, a small number of key points remained heavily disputed. Most importantly, the French refused to take into account US misgivings about a passage that drew attention to the increasingly specific character of the defence of Europe. They were supported in doing so by the FRG, which considered this statement to be the heart of the entire draft.[103] The price of such continuing differences was that progress in the negotiations slowed down. In consequence, a small drafting group comprising the NATO permanent representatives of the US, France, and Belgium was set up in the hope of finding compromise solutions. Yet, after the Washington Energy Conference, negotiations in NATO became ever more difficult, with the gap of expectations between the US and France widening. Even a joint trip by Rumsfeld and de Rose to the Tassili rock paintings in the Sahara failed to resolve the differences over the Atlantic declaration. Instead, the text was now replete with square brackets, which reflected the growing polarisation between Paris and Washington.[104]

With regard to the European–American declaration, France now lost much interest in it. As the European split in Washington had demonstrated the impossibility of building a European identity *à la française*, the working out of a declaration between the Nine and the US became a purely academic exercise from a French point of view. In the EPC ministerial meeting on 4 March 1974, Jobert still accepted that the Nine propose to the US a new round of negotiations between the Political Committee and the American representatives. However, he rejected Scheel's idea that the Nine should officially invite Nixon to sign the declaration with them.[105] Since there was little in the European draft that could have induced Nixon himself to propose signing it, this made it difficult to see how the European–American declaration would ever come about. As for Kissinger, he was still ready to sign both declarations at the end of February 1974. Yet, he now discarded his earlier idea of signing the Atlantic declaration in Paris to make it easier for Pompidou to participate. Instead, he proposed to celebrate NATO's anniversary in London, with the declaration on relations between the Nine and the US to be signed in Brussels.[106]

All this changed again after 4 March 1974. As shown in Chapter 6, the Nixon administration put the entire 'Year of Europe' exercise on ice in protest against what it regarded as insufficient consultations on the Euro-Arab dialogue. Not only did Kissinger stall the two processes of negotiations. More symbolically even, he also ruled out a visit to Europe by Nixon in April, which implied that any NATO celebrations had to be postponed too. As for the question of how to proceed, Kissinger listed three options in mid-March 1974. One possibility was to drop both declarations. This, argued the US secretary of state, would have to be done implicitly and step-by-step. A second option was to complete both declarations. In this case, the European draft would have to be redone, as it was still unbalanced and comprised nothing for the US. The Atlantic draft, in Kissinger's view, was more advanced, but it would require further French concessions in key parts. Finally, Kissinger also raised the idea of dropping the European draft only. Under this scenario, he said, the provisions on consultation between the Nine and the US would have to be transferred into the NATO document. Kissinger emphasised that he had not made his mind up as to which option to embrace and was eager to hear other opinions.[107]

The French were now decidedly fed up with the 'psychodrama' about the declarations.[108] Similarly to the discussions about the Gymnich formula on European–American consultation, the Quai d'Orsay now strongly argued in favour of giving up the EPC project of defining relations vis-à-vis the US entirely. EPC, so the French argued, should be reduced to dealing with the CSCE and the Euro-Arab dialogue. In consequence, the Atlantic declaration should be dropped too, as French support for it had been closely tied to the US acknowledging Europe's distinct identity by means of a parallel declaration between the Community members and Washington. The reasoning in Bonn was different, and the FRG remained strongly supportive of completing both texts. Dropping the Atlantic declaration from a West German perspective could have imponderable consequences with regard to US policy towards Europe and might even accelerate a withdrawal of American troops from Europe. Dropping the European declaration, on the other hand, implied a return to bilateral relations between the West European governments and Washington, which would both diminish the relevance of EPC and heighten the risk of a superpower condominium.[109] As for the British, they professed to come up with a compromise solution. Callaghan made the case for putting both declarations on hold temporarily while beefing up a NATO communiqué to dignify NATO's twenty-fifth anniversary at the upcoming ministerial meeting in Ottawa.[110] It was more or less along these British lines that the foreign ministers at their informal EPC meeting at Gymnich on 20/21 April 1974 decided to proceed. As far as the Nine were concerned, work on both declarations should continue. A majority of the EPC members were still eager for the US to acknowledge the political dimension of European unification, with the Italians going even so far as to make an explicit link between the two declarations. But there was also agreement at Gymnich that the Ottawa communiqué could be given extra substance if the US pressed for it, or that it could perhaps even take the form of a declaration to mark the occasion.[111]

Immediately after the Gymnich meeting, Callaghan wrote to Kissinger that the Nine had reacted favourably to the 'Ottawa declaration idea'. Interestingly, he misreported that there had been a tacit understanding that the European declaration was 'moribund'. The British secretary of state ended his letter with another noteworthy comment, cautioning his American counterpart that the other Europeans 'do not know that we already have had talks' on what to do with the 'Year of Europe'.[112] In fact, Britain and the US had secretly consulted on how to proceed ever since Kissinger had raised his three options, and they had bilaterally decided to drown the European–American declaration long before Callaghan outlined at Gymnich his alleged interim solution of giving priority to a NATO communiqué. It was a manoeuvre instigated by Kissinger, but readily embraced by Callaghan, who became his key man beguiling the other Europeans into bringing the 'Year of Europe' to an end in accordance with US preferences.

On 18 March 1974, Kissinger revealed to the British that he was thinking of proceeding with the NATO declaration alone and expanding the existing draft to take into account relations between the Nine and the US. Five days later, his aides confidentially handed an according US draft to Ramsbotham, not without hinting that Washington would not care too much this time if France refused to go along.[113] The US paper left little doubt that Kissinger wanted to go back to square one in the 'Year of Europe', coming out with a substantive Atlantic declaration that stressed the globalisation of issues and reaffirmed American leadership in the West. What was outstanding about the draft was the extraordinary emphasis it attached to consultations between the Nine and Washington. The conclusion the draft drew from the emerging European identity was 'the need to add fresh dimensions' to allied cooperation and consultation. The draft suggested that the Community members and the US should pursue 'closest consultations on the widest possible range of policies in all spheres'. The goal should be 'to harmonize policies to the greatest possible extent', to which end a 'broad new policy of cooperation' was proposed. In particular, this meant that the Nine and the US should 'establish new multilateral and bilateral channels as may be necessary to ensure that there is the fullest and frankest consultation before final decisions are taken on all political, security and economic issues affecting their common interests'.[114]

When Kissinger personally told Callaghan about his idea on 28 March 1974, he explained that he had decided against dropping both declarations so as not to display to the Soviet Union the image of a weakened West.[115] Two weeks later, he admitted that his decision also had to do with France: 'The more I think about a situation where we may not have any declarations at the end of this process, the more I come to the conclusion that this would be handing the French an undeserved victory.'[116] Kissinger indicated that Callaghan could also produce his own Atlantic draft, which they could then discuss bilaterally. He added that Nixon could sign a declaration in Europe in June, during a stop-over on his way to Brezhnev.

The US secretary of state's preferred interlocutor of the Nine in the 'Year of Europe' was now clearly Callaghan, rather than Jobert. He was, of course, preaching to the converted in London. On 29 March 1974, Callaghan gave orders to his officials to go along with Kissinger's plan, his goal being to 'put NATO on the map with Western public opinion again'.[117] Callaghan asked for a new British draft to be put together, mainly to get rid of the references to European political union that still figured in the US draft.[118] Unsurprisingly, his active support for Kissinger's manoeuvre brought him into confrontation with his own department. Those responsible in the FCO for the 'Year of Europe' had serious reservations about working towards a declaration in Ottawa, rather than a beefed up ministerial communiqué as Britain had communicated to its partners. They were against removing references to the EU, not only because of their own positive attitude towards the idea, but also because even Kissinger had accepted the notion of the political unification of the Nine in his draft. They were also against the single declaration approach, as this implied a failure of EPC and was certain to arouse fierce protest by the EC partners.[119]

But Callaghan had his way. By 19 April 1974, a new British draft was ready, in part worked out by the secretary of state himself. It was less radical than the US draft in the sense that it was still, to some extent, based on the French draft. While it did take US requirements into account, it introduced them in alleviated form, so as to present them as less openly anti-French than Kissinger had done. In contrast to the US draft, however, it barely treated the Nine as a unit any longer, referring merely to the contributions made by the 'United States and other individual members of the Alliance to the preservation of international security and world peace'.[120] Kissinger was not entirely happy with the British draft. The US continued to press for a much more forthcoming paragraph on consultation, and it was unwilling to acknowledge any specific character of the allied defence of Western Europe. Also, Washington wanted Britain to table its draft in NATO without advance warning, which London declined. Yet, such Anglo-American differences remained limited to the tactical level, with broad consensus existing on the strategic goal of jointly getting the allies to accept the single declaration approach.[121]

On 15 May 1974, Britain finally tabled its draft in NATO, with official discussions starting nine days later.[122] The draft was announced as emanating from the direct responsibility of Callaghan, who professed to have had 'some general exchanges' with the US about it. Rumsfeld strongly supported the British text in NATO, while circulating specific amendments that mainly referred to the issue of consultation.[123] Britain's European partners, however, received the draft with much reserve. The representatives of the FRG and Belgium immediately reminded the British of the decision the Nine had taken at Gymnich. Emotions soon ran high, with no serious work being possible on the draft.[124] In the EPC Political Committee, Britain encountered strong criticism on two particular points. First, Davignon and other political directors accused the Labour government of having deliberately misled its European partners in order to kill the declaration between the Nine and the US. Second, the FRG, France, Italy, and Belgium all vehemently protested against the exclusion of the concept of European Union from the text. Failure to include such a reference, these officials argued, would hand a victory to Kissinger by helping him in his objective of preventing the unity of Europe. The West German political director even insisted that his government would sign no Atlantic declaration without a reference to the EU. The deplorable FCO official tried to counter-attack that the negotiations on a European–American draft had only brought dissension in transatlantic relations. Yet, he received some support from the Dutch and the Danish only.[125] After this acrimonious discussion, the FCO had grave concerns that the British manoeuvre might not only fail to produce an agreed declaration in time for the Ottawa meeting, but could also have negative repercussions on the climate of renegotiations. Such gloom seemed all the more justified since there were signs that officials in the Auswärtige Amt tried to both redirect negotiations in NATO to the previous French draft and resuscitate work on the European–American draft.[126]

Then came Giscard and Schmidt. In contrast to their predecessors, they accepted the single declaration approach and were disposed to follow Callaghan and Kissinger in giving up the attempt to specifically define relations between the Nine and the US. One of Giscard's first acts in office was to let it be known that Paris was prepared to work towards getting a declaration ready for Ottawa.[127] In Bonn, officials in the Auswärtige Amt continued to be rueful about Callaghan's manoeuvre, but they received little support from the new leaders, as Schmidt and Genscher were mainly interested in resolving the European–American controversy.[128] Thus, the field was cleared to focus attention on the specifics of how to redefine Atlantic relations in a unitary text. Work in NATO began in earnest at the end of May 1974, with three weeks of intensive consultations leading to the Ottawa Declaration of mid-June.[129]

The two major remaining points of contention were the reference to the EU and the provisions concerning allied consultation. The former was an exclusively intra-European controversy, while the latter was above all a Franco-American dispute. Callaghan was vehemently against any mention of the notion of European political union in the declaration. So hostile was he towards the whole concept that he would rather have withdrawn the British draft from NATO than have made any substantive concessions. As he told his FCO officials, he could not recommend to the Labour Cabinet to subscribe 'to the kind of phrase that crept in late one afternoon when M. Pompidou was grappling with an idea'. Heath, according to Callaghan, had been 'foolish enough to be beguiled down this road'. He insisted that '[i]f "Union" is symbolic to them – it is equally symbolic to me'.[130]

In order to prevent a complete breakdown of the negotiations, Callaghan came up with what he called a 'compromise' solution. He was ready to accept a paragraph that read as follows:

> It is also recognised that growing unity among those member states of the EC which are also members of the Atlantic Alliance should, in due course, have a beneficial effect on their contribution to the Alliance.[131]

This proposition still met with opposition from Britain's European partners, however. The Belgians called it unacceptable, as it fundamentally contradicted the decisions of Paris and Copenhagen. The West Germans continued to question the whole declaration if there was no reference to the notion of *l'Europe politique*.[132] In his first EPC ministerial meeting on 10 June 1974, Genscher as acting president urged Callaghan to acknowledge the EU as an overriding objective of the Nine and accept at least a reference to 'European unification' in the declaration. Yet, it was to no avail, as the British secretary of state declined to accept any 'magic words' about Europe. Callaghan's partners, therefore, had little choice but to accept the meagre expression of 'growing unity', with the Political Committee being mandated to liven up the wording of the respective paragraph as much as possible.[133]

The issue of consultation remained disputed too. As will be outlined below, the range of topics for consultation and the geographic area to cover were significant questions in the Alliance at the time that went beyond the discussions on the 'Year of Europe' declaration. With respect to the specific negotiations prior to Ottawa, the controversy boiled down to three different versions of one key sentence. Since Kissinger insisted upon a wide range of issues for allied consultation, the US proposal was as follows:

> They undertake to keep each other fully informed and to strengthen the practice of frank and timely consultations on matters relating to their common interests, using all appropriate means, and bearing in mind that these interests can be affected by events in other areas of the world.

The French, by contrast, were not willing to accept anything beyond 'matters relating to the interests of the Alliance', with a compromise proposal of 'matters relating to their common interests as members of the Alliance' being rejected by both Paris and Washington.[134]

It was not before the actual Ottawa meeting that agreement could be established on the consultation issue. Sauvagnargues, to the surprise of his fellow ministers, criticised his own officials' text during the meeting. Calling the controversy over allied consultation 'the most pointless quarrel in the world',[135] the new French foreign minister was obviously eager to now put an end to it. With Franco-American differences settled amicably, the Ottawa gathering became the kind of successful meeting aspired to by Callaghan, Kissinger, Giscard, and Schmidt. The approval of the Ottawa Declaration by the foreign ministers on 19 June 1974 was broadcasted by TV, demonstrating to the public the re-established Atlantic consensus on the need for allied cooperation.[136]

NATO received an even bigger boost when the heads of government of the Fifteen gathered in Brussels on 26 June 1974 to celebrate its anniversary and officially sign the declaration.[137] Kissinger's plan that Nixon should have a stop-over in Europe on his way to a superpower summit in Moscow, which had already been revealed to the British in March 1974, was conveyed to the other allies at very short notice only.[138] Although the thought of meeting the American lame-duck president did not arouse enthusiasm among European leaders, most of them came to comply with the US proposal. With the heads of Canada and Iceland being absent due to national elections, it was only Giscard who, for domestic reasons, deliberately declined to go to the NATO summit in Brussels, sending Chirac instead. Yet, whereas Pompidou would have refused to go as a matter of principle, Giscard at least came up with the pretext of being visited by the Shah of Iran.[139]

With the Ottawa Declaration signed, the 'Year of Europe' had finally come to an end. As Flora Lewis reported for the *New York Times* from Brussels, there was 'no sense of solemn achievement or historic advance, just a sense of relief that the stormy quarrels that had undermined the alliance seemed to have calmed if not actually resolved'.[140] Kissinger was well aware that the resulting declaration lacked the kind of substance he had originally envisaged. Yet, given the emancipatory intentions of the Nine inadvertently instigated by the US in 1973, he was content that the prerogative of allied cooperation had at last been reaffirmed. As he recalled in his memoirs, although his initiative had 'failed in its objective of giving a new moral and psychological impetus to Atlantic relations, concluding the exercise in a cooperative manner at least removed the element of discord and served as an augury of a new era'.[141] Jobert was naturally less kind about the Ottawa Declaration, calling it the 'remaining frazzle of an overambitious plan' (*un lambeau d'un plan trop ambitieux*).[142] Although the declaration still contained passages echoing his original draft of October 1973, his successor had approved modifications that he would never have tolerated, the less so without a complementary European–American draft.

What was the significance of the Ottawa Declaration? Three different functions come to mind. First, it symbolised a rededication of the allies to the North Atlantic Treaty of 1949, confirming their commitment to the indivisibility of their common defence. Against the background of East–West détente and the ubiquitous domestic pressure for troop reductions, this was by no means self-evident. The declaration, in fact, contained important pledges and concessions by both the Europeans and the US for the sake of effective Atlantic defence. The Europeans acknowledged that American nuclear forces and the presence of US troops in Europe 'remained indispensable' for their own security. By this formula, they recognised their structural dependence on the US more explicitly than in the original French draft. The Europeans also undertook to make the necessary contributions to maintain the common defence at a level capable of credible deterrence, and they approved the principle of burden-sharing. These clauses, inspired by the French draft, were vague and, to some extent, sounded hollow, as several allies were in the process of cutting their defence expenditures. Nevertheless, they were important, as they increased the normative barriers to unilateral moves of reducing the defence effort.[143]

The US, in turn, acknowledged that the Europeans provided three-quarters of the conventional strength of the Alliance in Europe, and it recognised for the first time that French and British nuclear forces were capable of playing a deterrent role of their own and contributed to the overall deterrence of the Alliance. Washington also accepted an implicit interpretation of the superpower agreement on the prevention of nuclear war of June 1973, with the declaration reaffirming the freedom of the Alliance to use all forces at its disposal in the event of an attack. Most importantly, the Nixon administration stated its resolve to maintain forces in Europe at the level required to sustain the credibility of allied deterrence. Given Congressional pressure to cut troop levels in Europe, as well as Nixon's earlier threats to withdraw troops as a sign of dissatisfaction with EPC, this reassurance was particularly important for the Europeans.

A second function of the declaration was to both confirm and specify the substance of the Harmel Report of 1967. The Ottawa Declaration did confirm that the Alliance had two complementary tasks of deterring a military aggression and promoting détente in East–West relations. However, it went further

than the Harmel Report in that it declared security as a precondition for a
policy of détente. So far, the relationship between defence and détente in
NATO had been undefined, which had allowed each ally to emphasise either
notion, depending on domestic needs. Now, however, the declaration rendered détente a function of defence, to the extent that it argued that the pursuit
of détente was made possible by the security provided by the North Atlantic
Treaty only. This qualification of détente was all the more remarkable since the
Labour government, together with the Dutch and the Scandinavians, had tried
hard to insert a reference into the text according to which détente and defence
were equal tasks of the Alliance.[144]

Finally, and most importantly for this study, the Ottawa Declaration
also signified the failure of the policy of the Nine to use the 'Year of Europe'
as an opportunity to advance and demonstrate their political unity and
foreign policy aspirations. It would have been impossible to guess from the
timid reference to the Nine as an entity that most of the negotiations in the
course of the 'Year of Europe' had been about Europe's ambition to play a
bigger role within the West. The relevant passage in the declaration now read
as follows:

> It is also recognised that the further progress towards unity, which the member
> states of the European Community are determined to make, should in due
> course have a beneficial effect on the contribution to the common defence of
> the Alliance of those of them who belong to it. Moreover, the contributions
> made by members of the Alliance to the preservation of international security
> and world peace are recognised to be of great importance.

This was hardly a demonstration of European self-confidence. On the contrary, a comparison of this passage with the references, contained in leaked earlier drafts, to the political unity of the Nine and the benefits of the EU for allied
security revealed to anyone interested the near-complete removal of the notion
of a collective European identity from the declaration.

Even more symbolic for the failure of the collective EPC policy in the 'Year
of Europe' was the fact that the declaration on relations between the Nine and
the US never saw the light of day. A further consequence of this was that the
efforts by the Nine to define their collective relations with Japan and Canada
and sign respective declarations with Tokyo and Ottawa were also stalled in the
spring of 1974.[145] The one leftover of the EPC members' strategy in the 'Year
of Europe' was the Declaration on European Identity of December 1973. Yet,
this declaration was a purely European document and was never acknowledged by the US. Moreover, it seemed so out of touch with reality just months

after its publication that it soon became a largely forgotten piece of paper even among the Europeans.

If the Ottawa Declaration signified the decline of EPC in 1974, it would be too much to say that it removed all sources of strain from the Alliance. Indeed, the declaration could only insufficiently obscure the fact that beneath the reaffirmation of the general principle of collective defence, fundamental differences remained among the Western governments. These differences related mainly to the adequate level of defence spending in a time of détente and the question of whether the nuclear parity between the superpowers made Europe particularly vulnerable within the Alliance and rendered the nature of its defence distinct. Moreover, the paragraph on consultation was extensive but vague enough to conceal the divergent expectations that lay behind it. Owing to the Franco-American last-minute agreement, the declaration now defined the range of topics for consultation by the compromise formula of 'matters relating to their common interests as members of the Alliance' – a clause both Paris and Washington could interpret according to their linking.

Still, for all these weaknesses, the Ottawa Declaration did stand for a restored consensus among the major powers about the indispensability and, indeed, desirability of Atlantic cooperation. It was no longer, as Jobert had originally intended, a means to the larger objective of obtaining American recognition of the legitimacy of a distinct European foreign policy. Rather, it was an important statement in its own right, reflecting the regeneration of NATO as much as the collapse of the high-flying European dreams of 1973.

EPC weakened, NATO reinvigorated

The Ottawa Declaration was not an isolated expression of reaffirmed allied solidarity. Rather, it emerged in the wider context of a general reinvigoration of the Alliance. Discussions on how to strengthen NATO had been going on since mid-December 1973, when Kissinger had suggested that the political directors of the foreign ministries should be regularly involved in the political consultations of the NATO Council in permanent session (see Chapter 5). Kissinger's initiative did not really materialise in the way he would have wanted, for lack of European interest. Still, NATO political consultations received a remarkable boost in the spring of 1974, with procedures being improved and governments demonstrating more political will to consult meaningfully with their allies. NATO's regeneration did not necessarily have to be at the expense of EPC's viability and relevance. Yet, the strengthening of the Alliance did contrast with EPC's decline. Moreover, there were issues, such as crisis management, where the Nine abandoned their efforts deliberately so as not to duplicate those of NATO. These developments too reflected a primacy of effective allied cooperation over progress in forging a distinct European foreign policy.

In early February 1974, Rumsfeld in a letter to NATO Secretary-General Luns outlined in more detail what Kissinger had in mind with his idea of 'reinforced' NATO meetings. These specifications revealed that the US was thinking of a very ambitious design. Rather than just having an informal lunch between the NATO permanent representatives and the 15 political directors, as the Belgians had proposed, Washington made the case for joint working sessions in the context of regular Council meetings. Furthermore, Rumsfeld came up with a comprehensive agenda for the first such gathering, suggesting the issues of East–West relations in general, the CSCE and MBFR, the 'Year of Europe', the Mediterranean and the Middle East, as well as the Soviet presence in the Indian Ocean. Washington obviously was out to expand consultations both institutionally and in terms of the subjects covered.[146]

The Europeans were lukewarm at best about the American idea. Some, such as the Belgians, feared that the new kind of 'reinforced' meetings would negatively affect the effectiveness of regular NATO consultations. Others, such as the West Germans, added that the political directors were overloaded with work already. The British, for their part, saw little merit in fostering political consultations in NATO and were eager to treat the whole US proposal as a 'public relations exercise' only.[147] The FCO argued that while Alliance consultations were important on security and defence, the Fifteen could not expect to share a community of interest on other issues. While there was Alliance machinery for tackling other topics, the benefits had always been minimal. In the biannual meetings of regional working groups, national experts were comparing notes and producing a report. Yet, according to the FCO, it was neither feasible nor desirable for the allies to consult with one another on these matters, in the sense of asking for other views and taking them into account in the formation of national policy. This was the less so since the Americans themselves had 'never shown any disposition to consult substantively on broader aspects of their foreign policy'.[148]

Whereas most Europeans were still willing to have a first 'reinforced' meeting to further discuss the matter, the French were utterly hostile to the whole American idea. To Paris, Kissinger's initiative smelled of a plot to institutionalise relations between the Nine and the US through the back door, by creating an Atlantic counterweight to the Political Committee of EPC. Paris consequently launched a French counter initiative, proposing to restrict NATO consultations to security and defence, and limiting them to issues directly related to the Alliance area only. As the West Germans noted, the Quai d'Orsay was obviously out to turn NATO's clock back to 1949.[149] It was Davignon who formulated a compromise proposal to allow all Europeans to participate at a first 'reinforced' meeting, making three key points: first, the meetings should not take place periodically, but when deemed necessary only; second, it was up to the capitals whom to send there, political directors being only one of several options; and, third, the meetings should be issue-specific, rather than covering a broad range of topics. The British added to this their recommendation that there should be no talk of 'political directors' in NATO, as the use of such Euro jargon nourished suspicions about US motives along French lines.[150]

When the first 'reinforced' meeting on 14 March 1974 did take place, all delegations, with the exception of France, were represented by senior officials from capitals. Luns enthusiastically placed the gathering in a tradition dating back to a NATO report of 1956 on the improvement of political consultations.[151] Yet, the fact was that the character of the meeting had become such that it looked hardly innovative any longer in terms of allied consultations. The US not only accepted to drop the term 'political directors', but also agreed to limit the topics to the sphere of competence of the Alliance and to deal with one issue at the time. Most importantly, Kissinger agreed not to institutionalise such gatherings, but convene them on an ad hoc basis, by which he de facto embraced the established practice.[152]

Despite this failure of Kissinger's initiative, the allies did take measures to strengthen the Alliance in the spring of 1974. As shown above, it proved impossible to expand the scope of consultation explicitly and unambiguously in a document such as the Ottawa Declaration. Still, there were developments that clearly brought about a revitalisation of the Alliance. The procedure for NATO ministerial meetings was modified so as to make consultations more substantive. The Danish idea of December 1973 of copying the EPC approach and replacing the sterile global ministerial speeches with issue-by-issue discussions (see Chapter 5) was adopted by the Alliance and applied for the first time in Ottawa. The next NATO ministerial meeting, held in December 1974, was again based on the procedure of free discussions in closed circles, which, indeed, became the norm of Alliance consultations at the level of foreign ministers.[153]

A second discernible improvement was a shared political will by allied governments to informally expand the range of subjects for consultation by paying more attention to economic issues. In the Ottawa Declaration, the reference to the interdependence between security and economics remained much below what Kissinger had initially advocated in the 'Year of Europe'. The allies merely expressed their wish to 'ensure that their essential security relationship is supported by harmonious political and economic relations' and vowed to 'work to remove sources of conflict between their economic policies and to encourage economic cooperation with one another'. Yet, when Nixon proposed at the Brussels summit to multilaterally consult in NATO on economic issues, Schmidt enthusiastically agreed. Arguing that the Alliance was not so much threatened by armies as by economic problems, the West German chancellor made the case for rendering economic cooperation an essential pillar of NATO.[154] In marked contrast to 1973, when the Europeans had rejected treating security and economics as interlinked issues, there was no objection to the idea this time. Indeed, one of the major subjects at the NATO ministerial meeting in December 1974 was the repercussions of the economic and energy crisis on the common defence of the Alliance.[155] The subsequent establishment of the G7 by the major allied powers might have reflected recognition that NATO was not after all suited to dealing with economic questions in any depth. Still, the fact that economic issues moved onto the agenda of allied consultations was remarkable. It mirrored a changing international environment, as much as new policy preferences of national leaders.

Finally, it is worth noting the Kissinger himself appears to have rediscovered the merit of substantive multilateral cooperation and significantly improved the US habit of consultation in NATO. At the Ottawa meeting, he took great pains to assure his audience that Washington intended to meticulously fulfil its commitment to comprehensive and early consultation. As if to demonstrate how serious he was, Kissinger extensively briefed NATO on 4 July 1974 on Nixon's talks with Brezhnev in Moscow.[156] If his reorientation towards allied consultations might have had many different reasons, the gradual collapse of superpower détente is likely to have been crucial. Kissinger's unilateralist policy in the Middle East had seriously strained relations with Moscow. Furthermore, US domestic forces were increasingly undermining his course of détente. Congress not only drained SALT of much of its substance, but also made an American–Soviet trade agreement on the basis of most-favoured nation status contingent upon modified Soviet practices with regard to Jewish emigration. There was also the ever-growing conventional armament of the Soviet Union, which added to the fact that the US was gradually shifting its priority in 1974 from fostering a rapprochement with Moscow to consolidating its position of leadership in the West again.[157]

Apart from the deliberate measures by allied governments to regenerate the Alliance, it was the regime changes in Portugal and Greece in the spring and summer of 1974 that gave NATO much of its new dynamism. On 25 April 1974, Portugal's authoritarian government was overthrown in the so-called 'carnation revolution', with a series of new left-wing governments embarking on a course of democratisation and decolonisation. Together with the Greek transition from military rule to a civilian government, this allowed NATO to present itself more credibly as a community of values than in the years before. Indicative of the new allied vigour in this respect were the strong references to democracy and human rights in the Ottawa Declaration.[158]

While all these events were not specifically EPC-related, they did signify a shift of attention from EPC to the reinvigorated Alliance. Whereas governments were at loggerheads with each other about the future course of Europe, all were in agreement about the need to build up Atlantic ties. Characteristic for this shift was the fate of the EPC project of establishing European crisis management capabilities, as proposed by Pompidou in October 1973 and embraced by the Copenhagen summit. While the Political Committee did come up with a first report on the issue in March 1974, any follow-up work simply petered out. Some ministers, such as Scheel and van Elslande, called for the matter to be studied further, and for more substantial suggestions than ambassadorial meetings to enable consultation in the capital of the presidency in times of crisis. These voices pressed for crisis prevision and monitoring facilities as well as a clear concept for EPC crisis management. Yet, there was no longer any consensus by the Nine on the desirability of such an EPC tool, with some members, such as the Dutch, arguing that consultations should be focused on NATO in times of crisis. Moreover, since Luns too came to complain that the European project would duplicate and negatively affect NATO's crisis management system that was set up in the autumn of 1968, the whole idea was eventually adjourned.[159] Clearly, it was not the time to develop anything in EPC that might weaken the Alliance or renew upheaval in transatlantic relations. Little wonder, then, that Kissinger exulted in his memoirs that mid-1974 'ushered in one of the best periods of Atlantic cooperation in decades'.[160]

The collapse of other European policies and visions

The complete European retreat from defining a common identity vis-à-vis the US was the most symbolic, as well as the most substantive, expression of EPC's decline in the spring of 1974. Yet, there were other negative developments going on too, which together cemented the impression of a profound crisis in European foreign policy-making. With regard to the Middle East, the Nine came to accept a division of labour with the US, with Kissinger being in charge of peacemaking in the Arab–Israeli conflict and the Europeans limiting their engagement to the economic sphere. Talks on European defence collapsed too, as attention shifted from the Community to the Eurogroup and the Alliance again. Unsurprisingly, work on the European Union failed to get anywhere either. Both the growing structural divergences of the national economies and the Labour government's unwillingness to accept a dynamic concept of integration made any consensus on how to proceed look unattainable.

Exit from peacemaking in the Middle East

It would be excessive to claim that the Europeans had ever played an important role in the process of peacemaking in the Arab–Israeli conflict in 1973/74. The Nine had neither been able to assure a seat at the table in the multilateral peace conference in Geneva, nor had they been in a position to exert influence on Kissinger's unilateral shuttle diplomacy. Their declaration of 6 November 1973 had been a remarkable achievement in its own right, signalling rapid progress in European political unity. However, in terms of resolving the decade-old conflict between Israel and its Arab neighbours, such a declaratory policy alone could as yet do little to defuse tension and bring the conflicting parties closer together. Still, the early 1970s had witnessed a gradually growing political will, or perceived necessity, among the EPC members to define a common position and get involved in any emerging peace process. Much of this changed in the spring of 1974, however. The Nine now agreed to refrain as an entity from getting involved in Middle East politics and to concentrate their efforts on economically stabilising the region. They declined to further refine their collective attitude about the specifics of a peace agreement, and they embarked on their dialogue with the Arab League on the double premise that neither the Arab–Israeli conflict nor oil would figure on the agenda. What Jobert initially had conceded as a short-term measure to get the Euro-Arab dialogue started at all, became a basic European principle for its general conduct: the dialogue was to remain a technical affair that might have political implications, but shunned the most pressing issues of the time.

There were several reasons for Europe's withdrawal from attempting to shape Middle East politics. Clearly the most important one was American pressure. A second factor was the insufficient benefit the Nine had been able to draw from their engagement in Middle East diplomacy. To the consternation of the Europeans, OAPEC lifted its oil embargo against the US on 17 March 1974, but continued its discrimination of the Netherlands and Denmark, with the former receiving no supplies at all and the latter still failing to qualify as 'friendly'.[161] A French demarche in Arab capitals at the end of March 1974, designed to express European indignation about such treatment, did not achieve any tangible result, with OAPEC terminating its discriminating measures as late as July 1974.[162] The fact that Kissinger's confrontational policy paid off earlier than EPC's constructive approach towards the Arabs was a heavy defeat for the Nine.

Bonn's wavering position between Israel and the Arabs continued to be another problem for any sustainable European position in the Arab–Israeli conflict. Faced with unrelenting pressure for support from both sides, the West Germans changed their course between a pro-Arab and pro-Israeli stance so frequently in early 1974 that any cohesive EPC policy appeared unfeasible. When two Arab oil ministers of Algeria and Saudi Arabia urged Brandt and Scheel in mid-January 1974 to be more explicit about the precise extent of Israeli withdrawal from the occupied territories, the West German leaders at first declined to unilaterally interpret the EPC Declaration on the Middle East. Yet, when the Italians gave way to OAPEC pressure a few days later and issued a public pro-Arab statement, Bonn fell too, with Scheel specifying the FRG position in a confidential letter to the two oil ministers. Bonn, Scheel argued, generally supported the concept of peaceful border changes by mutual agreement. Yet, should such an agreement in the case of the Arab–Israeli conflict not be possible, any peace settlement should 'provide for the complete termination of the occupation of foreign territory and hence the total withdrawal of foreign troops'. Scheel added that West Germany also supported an 'equitable solution for the Palestinians'.[163] These were unambiguous formulations, which earned Bonn the status of a 'friendly' country in the OAPEC classification.[164] The FRG won further sympathies among Arab leaders when Brandt during a trip through the Middle East shortly before his resignation repeatedly argued in favour of a political Euro-Arab dialogue including a ministerial conference, which in his eyes should deal with issues such as the Arab–Israeli conflict and the interrelatedness of European and Mediterranean security.[165] But then again, the West Germans also came up with very pro-Israeli acts of policy. When Scheel's letter was published by the Arab press at the end of March 1974 and aroused a storm of protest in Israel, the West Germans did everything to diminish the relevance of their policy specification and declared that they were on the side of Israel.[166] The Auswärtige Amt was also adamantly opposed to any political substance in the Europe–Arab dialogue. Bonn's behaviour was extremely confusing and ruled out any credible political role by the FRG in the Arab–Israeli conflict, which by extension complicated any effective EPC course too.

Finally, Europe's exit from peacemaking in the Middle East also had to do with the changes of leadership in Britain and the FRG. During his first conversation with Kissinger on 28 March 1974, Wilson pointed out that he 'fundamentally differed' with Heath on the Middle East and that his Labour government would no longer be 'looking for a contrived European position' in relation to either the Arab–Israeli conflict or energy.[167] During NATO's Ottawa meeting, Callaghan explicitly embraced Kissinger's idea that the US should deal with the politics of bringing peace to the Middle East, while the Nine were to concentrate on economic relations with the region.[168] Quite generally, Labour's traditional pro-Israeli stance made it difficult to see how the new British government's position in the Arab–Israeli conflict could be reconciled with previous EPC policy. As for the FRG, Schmidt had already argued at the Washington Energy Conference that the Nine lacked the means to play any meaningful political role in the Middle East (see Chapter 6). There is no evidence that he changed his position in the months after becoming chancellor.

A consequence of Europe's retreat from politics in the Middle East was that a dialogue between the Nine and Israel, despite first tentative steps, never really took off. As indicated in Chapter 5, Tel Aviv had, in reaction to the European Declaration on the Middle East, reversed its policy from vehemently denying the legitimacy of a European involvement to proposing to the Nine a bilateral dialogue on the Arab–Israeli conflict. On 28 January 1974, the government in Tel Aviv officially answered the enquiry made by the Nine in mid-December 1973 as to Israel's views on Europe's role in the Middle East. Foreign Minister Eban now talked of past 'misunderstandings' and assured the Nine that Israel had 'taken with satisfaction notice of the desire and readiness of the governments of the community to assist in promoting peace in the Middle East and to contribute to its maintenance and furtherance'.[169] Nevertheless, although some confidential contacts between the Nine and Israel did take place in the spring of 1974,[170] by May it was clear that no formal dialogue would be established. This was partly because for all their warmer words, the Israeli remained hostile to any European political involvement in the peace process, proposing a European engagement in the economic and social sphere only. But it was also because of the decision by the Nine to keep their hands off the issues of peace and oil in the Middle East.[171]

The one major feature of EPC's Middle East policy that remained on the agenda was the economically oriented Euro-Arab dialogue. Yet even here, the Nine soon ran into difficulties. The start of the dialogue already became significantly delayed as a result of internal European differences on consultations with Washington. Although the FRG presidency in May 1974 had informal contacts with the Arab League on how to go about the dialogue, Europe's first official move could only take place once the Nine on 10 June 1974 approved the Gymnich Agreement.[172] One day later, Kissinger signalled that he would no longer oppose the dialogue and the ministerial conference, but he warned Genscher that the EPC plan was a good example of 'European masochism'.[173]

He did have a point. For more than a year, the Euro-Arab dialogue remained stuck in its preparatory phase, with procedural and substantive disagreements prevailing among the Nine as much as among the Arabs and between the two groupings. Within EPC, France continued to press for some political issues to be tackled in the dialogue, a proposition categorically rejected by most of its partners.[174] As for the Arab League, it had great difficulty in establishing consensus on any possible subject of the dialogue, being an even more heterogeneous entity than the Nine. The one issue all Arabs agreed upon was that the Palestine Liberation Organization (PLO) under Yasser Arafat should take part in the dialogue – which was anathema to most Europeans, however, as this by implication would have rendered the forum highly political. It was this question of PLO representation that proved most difficult to resolve, with the actual Euro-Arab dialogue only being launched in the second half of 1975.[175]

As it turned out, the Euro-Arab dialogue became more notable for the effects it had on the Nine than for any significant impact that the Europeans achieved with it in the Middle East. It represented the first interregional dialogue that the Europeans set up, thus standing at the beginning of what became a very prominent feature of the Community's external relations and foreign policy efforts. Moreover, the Euro-Arab dialogue brought about a further rapprochement between the Davignon mechanism and the Brussels machinery, since the Nine required a coordinating group to supervise the European side of the scheme that reported to both EPC and COREPER.[176] Yet, with regard to Europe's presence in the Middle East, the dialogue failed to deliver noteworthy results. Its limited effectiveness and its purely economic dimension reflected the Nine's continuing incapability, as well as their deflated ambition, to play any significant role in either the Arab–Israeli conflict or the region at large.

The mirage of European defence

The bilateral talks between Paris, Bonn, and London on a European defence identity to complement EPC collapsed too in the spring of 1974. Pompidou during his last months in office already began to disassociate himself from European defence cooperation again, and the notion became ever less realistic with the new leaders, as disagreements about the role and relevance of European unity widened. With Wilson turning to the US and Giscard remaining trapped in French Gaullist tradition, it became clear that the dream of a Community defence dimension, as harboured by Heath, Scheel, and Jobert, remained unrealisable.

Following Scheel's talks with Jobert in November 1973 (see Chapter 5), the Auswärtige Amt strenuously studied in early 1974 the possibilities of building up Europe's defence identity.[177] Yet, already the first Franco-German consultations about European defence at the level of officials in mid-January 1974 led to a degree of consternation in Bonn, as the differences between the respective ideas as laid out by the two sides were considerable.

The West Germans argued that the EU should have a defence component which in the long run should include nuclear weapons too. As for the short run, they made the case for constructing the emerging European defence cooperation in parallel to the integrated defence of the Fourteen in NATO. Keeping up allied integration, so the West Germans claimed, was essential to tie the US to Europe and preserve the German–American link that was vital to maximising Western deterrence. Concerning procurement cooperation, Bonn preferred the Eurogroup, but was ready to contemplate the benefits of the WEU. Scheel's officials showed themselves concerned, however, about the consequences of alienating the flank countries with a WEU solution. They also pointed out that there would be international protests if the discriminations of West Germany in the WEU were abolished. With respect to the Nine, Bonn suggested that defence cooperation should begin by consulting on security issues and by pre-discussing Alliance matters, such as MBFR and the role of tactical nuclear weapons, before taking a stand in NATO.

The response by the French was far from encouraging. They agreed that no European defence would ever be credible without a nuclear component. Yet, they envisaged an integration of European troops without the US. Washington, they argued, should remain the main ally of Europe, but US troops could not be linked to the Europeans on the same level of integration. Regarding procurement, France would only cooperate in WEU, and it considered relations with the flank countries less important than a cohesive nucleus of European defence. For the same reason, defence consultations according to the French should initially take place in the WEU too, as both neutral Ireland and Denmark had no interest in Community defence and were, therefore, bound to block progress among the Nine.[178]

Interestingly, despite this somehow disappointing start, Jobert proposed to Scheel regular meetings between the planning groups of the two foreign ministries to discuss the sensitive issues more freely. The secret Franco-British defence talks between planners that had begun in the summer of 1973 were, thus, complemented by respective Franco-German consultations. Yet, these exchanges brought about as little progress as the parallel debates in the WEU on a potential reactivation of the organisation.[179] This was because, as the British were the first to realise, for all the ambitions and zeal of Jobert, the French foreign minister lacked the necessary domestic support for his ideas. He was unable to escape the Gaullist ideology that still prevailed in France, which made it impossible for him to accept the kind of compromise solutions on defence that would have been necessary to bring the other Europeans on board.[180]

In early February 1974, Pompidou, in fact, decided to return to an orthodox Gaullist defence policy himself. In a confidential memorandum to Prime Minister Messmer and Defence Minister Galley, the French president instructed them to concentrate all defence efforts on the national deterrent again. Regarded by French researchers as his strategic 'testament', the memorandum revealed a very pessimistic assessment of the international environment. Pompidou argued that as each problem tended to be tackled by a tête-à-tête between the superpowers, the humiliations and dangers for Europe were evident. The energy and monetary crises contributed to a climate of permanent disquiet. In the majority of hypothetical crises, France would intervene in the framework of the Alliance, but it needed its freedom of manoeuvre. This was all the more so since the FRG, haunted by fear of nuclear war on its soil, continued to oscillate between an unconditional attachment to American protection and the temptations of neutralism. Nuclear cooperation with Great Britain was out of the question for the foreseeable future, since London would remain dependent on the US, Europe would gain insufficient protection, Bonn would be humiliated, and Moscow enraged. The only solution left, Pompidou concluded, was national dissuasion, which is why he ordered priority to be given to further building up both the French strategic nuclear force and tactical nuclear weapons.[181] Also indicative of France's retreat from the notion of defence cooperation, Pompidou left it to his successor to formally approve a revision of the 'Lemnitzer–Ailleret' agreement of 1967 on French participation in NATO operations in the case of Soviet attack. As much as Pompidou's willingness in the early 1970s to expand the agreement to include the whole first French army had mirrored attempts at improving Franco-American relations, his reluctance to codify it now reflected French isolation among the allies. The new 'Valentin–Ferber' agreement between the commanders of the first French army and NATO Central Europe was only signed on 3 July 1974, in the context of a general improvement of relations between Paris and Washington.[182]

Already reluctant about European defence in 1973, Pompidou obviously came to conclude in early 1974 that the time was not ripe to approach the issue further. With the Community paralysed and EPC in crisis, he considered it unrealistic and undesirable to expand European cooperation from the economic-political sphere to defence. As Pompidou told Brezhnev during his last visit abroad in mid-March 1974, he would continue to try to foster common European positions in the Middle East and elsewhere, but France would go its own way in matters of defence. Jobert too indicated in March that France would drop the issue for a while, while Scheel was forced to acknowledge that the FRG could not possibly go along with any French call for European defence as long as this meant the de facto end of NATO.[183]

With Wilson's return to office in Britain, the prospect of defence cooperation among the Nine diminished still further. His public rejection of any nuclear cooperation with France did not do much damage, as the idea had died down anyway after Heath and Jobert had left the scene.[184] Yet, when Callaghan made a formal representation to the French ambassador to London in June 1974 about France's nuclear tests, Paris was shocked and suspended all Franco-British politico-military talks.[185] As the close relations between Heath and Pompidou were a thing of the past, the idea of common defence became rather improbable. This was all the more so since the incompatible attitudes towards the Community between Wilson, on the one hand, and Giscard and Schmidt, on the other, left little room for any consensus on European defence. Indicative of this development, Callaghan also terminated cooperation among the Eight within the framework of the Alliance. As the West Germans came to complain, Britain's renewed courting of a special relationship with the US in NATO led to the disintegration of the fragile European identity that had been emerging within the Alliance since 1973.[186]

It is true that with Schmidt, a new champion of European defence entered the stage of European policy-making in 1974. As former minister of defence, Schmidt appeared to be much more interested in coordinating European defence policies than promoting EPC. In the autumn of 1974, for instance, he was in favour of applying the EPC model of consultation to the nine defence ministries, so as to bring about a gradual harmonisation of views. Yet, nothing ever resulted from such ideas and concepts, not least because Schmidt did not succeed in carrying Giscard along. As Brandt's successor recalled in his memoirs, he did have many intensive discussions on defence with his French counterpart, without interpreters and without any records being taken. However, these talks did not lead far. In part, this had to do with the fact that Giscard was less competent in defence matters than the West German chancellor. Yet, it was first and foremost the result of strong domestic Gaullist forces preventing the French president from substantially deviating from his predecessors' course.[187]

The one manifestation left of the Nine's brief flirtation with cooperation in the realm of security and defence was EPC consultations on MBFR. Launched in 1973 (see Chapter 5), these consultations actually became more intensive in the first half of 1974. This was because the Soviet Union now was displaying much more interest in reducing European forces than American troops at the MBFR negotiations in Vienna, which caused increased worries among the Nine that Moscow was out to make any later defence unification of Europe impossible. Those seven EC members participating at the talks in Vienna, therefore, jointly worked out specific guidelines for MBFR in EPC, referred to as the 'European reservation'. According to these guidelines, MBFR should not include provisions which could permit others to interfere in the development of the Community. Moreover, the Europeans would not accept national ceilings on their forces, as this would prevent them from replacing any withdrawing US troops. Significantly, however, these MBFR consultations took place in the ad hoc group set up in 1973 to analyse the Soviet–American agreement on the prevention of nuclear war.[188] There was still no official EPC working group dealing with issues of security and defence, which is another indication that the whole notion of European defence in the early 1970s remained a mirage. True, there was still cooperation in the Eurogroup. Yet, this forum was linked to the Alliance, rather than European unification, and, accordingly, had little to do with European defence proper. Moreover, as even the West German Defence Minister Leber, one of its more ardent proponents, had to concede in mid-1974, the Eurogroup might have been better than any 'French speculative idea' on Community defence, but other than splendid declarations and a proliferation of working parties, it had not accomplished much either.[189]

The EU shelved

It seems appropriate to end this overview of EPC's crisis in the spring of 1974 with a look at the debates of the Nine on European Union. Although the two projects of forging a European foreign policy and establishing a European Union had been separated at the Paris Summit in 1972 (see Chapter 2), EPC's rise in 1973 had had much to do with the political will manifest in the decision to advance the political unification of Europe and set up an EU by 1980. Work on defining the EU began in early 1974, but it did not get very far. Even with the old guard of European leaders, there were differences as to the preferred model of unification. With Labour coming to power in Britain, the whole enterprise became thoroughly hopeless, as the controversy shifted from what kind of union to build to whether any kind of union was desirable at all. Although the topic of European Union after mid-1974 formally remained on the Community agenda, the project became de facto shelved, to be reactivated in the mid-1980s only.

As acting presidency of the Nine, the FRG in early 1974 was very active in getting substantive discussions on the EU started. At the Copenhagen Summit, the Nine had decided to accelerate their respective work, which is why Bonn now suggested that an initial report should be worked out for discussion at the next summit, envisaged for May or June 1974.[190] On 4 February 1974, the EC Council of Ministers adopted the FRG proposal of tasking COREPER with the job, to be supported by an ad hoc group of senior government representatives, who would do the actual report. Debates in these two bodies started at the end of February and early March 1974, based on a West German paper which raised questions and laid out ideas concerning the issues and structure of a European Union.[191] Although the original Paris Summit mandate had made no explicit reference to EPC being involved in the process of defining the EU, the nine foreign ministers accepted on 4 March 1974 a proposition by Scheel that the Davignon machinery should produce a report on the matter too.[192]

From the beginning, the discussions on the EU proved to be difficult and unproductive, however. The Community already was in deep crisis in early 1974, with the EMU project stuck, RDF postponed, and the hopes for a common energy policy undone by the Washington Energy Conference. It was, thus, an unfortunate moment for attempting to outline a joint concept for a visionary venture such as the EU. What was more, national expectations about the shape and meaning of EU continued to be diverse. The French advocated a model along the lines of Fouchet. They supported a political confederation of states based on regular summitry and a weak European Parliament. The existing EC would be left intact, but would be embedded into, or complemented by, a bigger Community of an intergovernmental kind, which would comprise all those issues not covered by the Treaty of Rome. EC and EPC should be kept separate, and EMU was to evolve in a way that did not require a major shift of sovereignty to any new Community institutions.[193] The British under Heath, for their part, believed that the character of the EU would be largely determined by how EMU developed. They expected a considerable degree of central machinery to develop in support of economic and monetary matters by 1980, though they did not want a full federation. From their perspective, the EU should also include areas such as law, education, employment, migration, foreign policy, and defence, with decision-making on major questions remaining unanimous. EPC should, thus, be closely linked to or united with the EC. London hoped that the Community by 1980 would take common decisions on all key issues of foreign policy concerning Western Europe. By then, the Nine should have defined their foreign policy towards most important third countries, with diplomacy in these cases being conducted on a joint basis. There should also be machinery for defence coordination. In the longer term, the common foreign policy would be answerable to the European Parliament, and there would be a European Ministry of Foreign Affairs in Brussels.[194]

As for the West Germans, Brandt delineated the EU as a kind of federation with confederal components. There would be several communities in the main areas, such as economics, foreign policy, and defence, with other issues being covered on the national level. Regular summits could constitute the nucleus of a European executive, which in time would be answerable to the European Parliament.[195] In his last months in office, Brandt continued to recommend a functional approach so as to avoid theological disputes about any detailed blueprints. Yet, even his rather cautious design was too ambitious for others, such as the Danish and the Irish, who had joined the EC for economic reasons and remained reticent about any distinct political dimension to European unification.[196]

As work on the EU report failed to make progress on the level of officials, the issue of European Union became the major item on the agenda of the unofficial EPC ministerial meeting at Gymnich on 20/21 April 1974. Yet here too, the foreign ministers could only note their differences. Moro and van der Stoel argued in favour of a federation, Scheel proposed the FRG's mixed model of Bund and Länder, while Jobert insisted that any new French government would want a confederal scheme. The one thing almost all ministers present agreed upon was that the basic objective of establishing the EU was right. As Thorn put it, there was consensus about the label on the bottle, but the challenge was to define its contents. Or, in the words of Jobert, the Europeans had agreed on a skeleton, but were as yet divided on how to clothe it.

The one minister to take exception to such an interpretation was Callaghan, who suggested dropping the idea of EU entirely. As he entered the debate, the problem became no longer one of achieving consensus on any adequate conception for the European Union, but rather on the principle of political union at large. Callaghan argued that the notion of union aroused 'mixed feelings' in

Britain, as the act of union with Ireland had been unsuccessful and the union with Scotland signified a degree of harmonisation – in the sense of common citizenship, loyalty to a common crown, and a common currency – which the British people would not want for Europe. He tried to persuade his colleagues that it was good enough for national decision-makers to meet regularly and have exchanges, such as at Gymnich, without constructing an entity such as the EU.[197] A few weeks later, Wilson too indicated that he was opposed to European Union, suggesting to Thorn that the term should be abandoned and be replaced by 'some long German word like Gemütlichkeit'.[198]

Eventually, Wilson and Callaghan did come round to accepting that the EU as an objective would be maintained. They had to realise that abolishing the project of EU entirely would cause huge domestic troubles for some governments such as the West Germans. More importantly, speaking out openly against the idea was bound to negatively affect Britain's chances of winning economic concessions in the renegotiations. Unsurprisingly, however, with Labour at the European table, work on the EU report became even more tedious than before. In fact, the only result that COREPER and the ad hoc group in Brussels managed to achieve by June 1974 was a nine-page document filled with questions about the EU.[199] All these questions stood for differences concerning the structure and purpose of a European Union. As for EPC, it failed to produce any report at all, being preoccupied with its own crisis.[200] Conversely, the expectations by the Commission and the European Parliament, formulated in two reports later in the year, were so out of touch with reality that the West Germans were probably relieved never to have convened their summit, which would only have exposed to the public the total variance of European views.[201]

By the summer of 1974, the plan of the Community members to set up an EU by 1980 was effectively dead. Sauvagnargues, as new acting president of the Nine, proposed in the second half of 1974 to no longer talk about the EU. Rather, he argued, the Europeans in 1980 should simply fix on paper the progress in unification they had made until then and sell this as the European Union.[202] As this pragmatic approach was rejected by several governments, the Nine finally tasked Belgian Prime Minister Leo Tindemans to produce a report on the meaning of the EU, based on the reports already available and the individual views held by the national governments. It was an impossible mission, serving little other purpose than camouflaging that the project of working out the details of the European Union by mid-1974 had failed. As Christopher Hill and Karen Smith observed, the 'Tindemans Report' of 1975, while noteworthy for its emphasis on a common foreign policy, 'caught the downslope, not the crest, of the wave of enthusiasm which had characterized the EC in the early 1970s' and, accordingly, caused some embarrassment among the European leaders.[203]

Although the ideal of European Union survived in many capitals, building the EU was no longer an operational project after mid-1974, with the time-frame of 1980 being dropped from all subsequent statements on the issue. The one major lesson that the FRG presidency learnt from the work on EU in the first half of 1974 was that any European Union realistically could only ever be built as a roof construction, with the two pillars of EC and EPC being linked, but remaining separate.[204] Seen from this perspective, the debates in early 1974 already pointed to the negotiations on the EU that were taken up more than a decade later. With regard to the state of Europe and the decline of EPC in 1974, however, they above all reflected the impossibility of preserving and putting into effect the high-flying hopes and ambitions of a *Europe politique* that had characterised EPC in the extraordinary year of 1973.

No end to EPC: The European Sisyphus labours on

Many factors accounted for the decline of EPC between March/April and June 1974. Indeed, conditions for effective European foreign policy-making during this period worsened further on all levels. With regard to the extra-European level of the international environment, American resistance to collective European diplomacy in the way it had developed in 1973 could only be overcome by re-establishing the Atlantic prerogative. Strengthening NATO and setting up the G7 was also deemed essential in response to the needs deriving from the changing international system. With superpower détente being on the wane, and the global economic and energy crisis deepening, the Europeans in 1974 became more dependent on the US again for their security and prosperity. This, in turn, negatively affected the possibility of defining a distinct European foreign policy. At the same time, the return to a more antagonistic American–Soviet bilateralism also put an end to European fears of a superpower condominium and made American leadership in the West more reliable again, which removed a negative incentive for the Nine to unite politically.

With respect to the intra-European level, factors such as the quasi-paralysis of the EC and the widening divergences between the national economies of the Nine continued to exert a highly negative impact on EPC. A key new element here was the profound change in Britain's European policy, with Britain in March 1974 switching to a Eurosceptic position that rendered it the kind of 'awkward partner' it was to remain for many years.[205] Britain's new maverick policy towards the EC gave additional cause for the Nine to shift their attention from advancing and deepening the Community to preventing its dissolution and a re-nationalisation of European policies. With the EC existentially threatened and any Community spirit gone, a basic foundation for effective cooperation in the realm of foreign policy was now conspicuously lacking.

Finally, there was the individual level of decision-makers. With the coming to power of new leaders in Britain, France, and the FRG, trilateral leadership in Europe ceased to function. Although Wilson/Callaghan, Giscard, and Schmidt were by no means against EPC, the sum of their individual beliefs and policy preferences was not conducive to advancing political cooperation by the Nine to the same extent as had been the case with their predecessors. On the one hand, these new leaders were determined to restore the primacy of close Atlantic cooperation over any European enterprise to shape a common foreign policy. They were convinced that the pressing challenges of the time required global, rather than European, solutions and that the Nine in such a situation should no longer quarrel with Washington about the lofty goal of a European identity. Lacking their predecessors' emotional affinity to EPC, they were largely ready to meet American requirements regarding EPC and accepted its subordination to Atlantic exigencies.

On the other hand, the polarisation between Wilson/Callaghan and Schmidt and Giscard with regard to the relevance and purpose of European unification had negative implications for EPC too. Callaghan's ruthless demands for renegotiation and his denial of any dynamic perspective for the political unification of the Nine mirrored a new incongruity of role conceptions among key European leaders that caused the previous spirit of common vision and ambition to disappear. As Labour questioned the European enterprise at large, the psychology of cooperation among the Nine deteriorated, with the bonds of trust that had marked the trilateral relations between Heath, Pompidou/Jobert, and Brandt/Scheel vanishing. There is no doubt that EPC in view of the ever-growing external challenges would have fallen into a crisis in 1974 anyway. Yet it seems equally clear that Europe's foreign policy aspirations would not have lost so much dynamic if it had not been for the leadership changes in London, Paris, and Bonn.

EPC's crisis in 1974 obviously did not mean that European foreign policy cooperation would have come to an end. For one thing, as outlined in Chapter 3, the policy field of the CSCE remained largely unaffected by the transatlantic turmoil and intra-European differences in 1974. The CSCE continued to be EPC's showpiece after mid-1974, with the cohesion of the Nine remaining strong and their joint policies achieving impact and being internationally acknowledged. Moreover, the issues covered by EPC multiplied in the follow-ing years. By the end of the decade, EPC dealt with such diverse topics as the crises in Cyprus and Iran, the processes of democratisation in Southern Europe, conflicts in Africa, and the relations between Europe and Latin America.[206] This proliferation of issues and working groups in EPC stood in some contrast to the development of the EC, which, despite specific areas of progress, became characterised by a long period of stagnation and 'eurosclero-sis'. Furthermore, there was some institutional progress in EPC after mid-1974 too. The Gymnich-type weekends of informal consultations became a tradi-tion, taking place biannually in splendid castles and chateaus of the respective presidency. The frequency of ministerial meetings, thereby, rose from four to six gatherings per year. Also, the idea of regular European summits became adopted by the Nine at the Paris Summit of December 1974. The heads of state and government and their foreign ministers were subsequently to meet three times a year as the 'European Council', dealing with both Community matters and EPC, according to the respective procedures.[207] EPC and the EC were also brought closer together by a growing presence of Commission representatives in EPC consultations, as well as by the fact that there was no more French resistance to EPC meetings taking place at the same location as EC Councils.[208] Finally, although less tangible, EPC also made progress in the sense of contin-uing socialisation among the foreign ministries, with a degree of 'we-feeling' existing at least on the level of national bureaucracies.[209]

However, all this progress remained very limited and must be put into per-spective. Compared to the early 1970s, EPC after mid-1974 developed only slowly, consultations being marked by quantitative expansion, rather than qualitative improvement. There was no more substantive breakthrough for the remainder of the decade, with the next notable declaration being issued in 1980 only. This 'Venice Declaration' on the Middle East of June 1980 is sometimes referred to as the Europeans' one major policy achievement during the Cold War, outside the bounds of the CSCE. Such a perception is all the more signif-icant since the substance of the declaration did not go significantly beyond the declaration of 1973, except for recognising the Palestinian right to self-deter-mination and proposing to associate the PLO with the peace negotiations.[210] Even in the CSCE process, the role of the Nine became less prominent after 1975. This was because the US under President Jimmy Carter was eager to play a much more prominent role itself. Moreover, Washington adopted a course of propagandistically blemishing the Soviet human rights record, which was incompatible with the more subtle policy of the Europeans. Another problem facing the Nine was Moscow's diminished interest in getting anything out of the ongoing CSCE process, which reduced the leverage of the Europeans in obtaining further Soviet concessions.[211] As for the institutional development of EPC, it is worth noting that both the Gymnich meetings and the institutionalised summitry had already been shaped and anticipated by the old guard of leaders. Seen in this light, EPC institutionally stagnated in the late 1970s. This also finds reflection in the fact that a third report on EPC occurred as late as 1981 and then contained modest improvements only, such as the 'troika' of the past, present, and upcoming presidencies and a flimsy procedure for crisis management.[212]

Yes, EPC after mid-1974 evolved further. But it lacked the kind of dynamic that had become characteristic of its development in the early 1970s. To be sure, there were renewed efforts to make progress, and it would be unfair to conclude that Europe's interest in formulating a distinct foreign policy had ceased in 1974. To take up Stanley Hoffmann's metaphor again, the European Sisyphus, after his first fiasco in 1974, was bound to try to move the stone of cooperation up the slope time and again. Yet, the fact is that EPC after 1974 was no longer perceived as a vehicle with which to rapidly forge a European identity and establish the Nine as a cohesive actor in world politics. There was a routine of consultation, which was valuable in itself. However, there was no longer the same kind of joint ambition and shared optimism about the possibilities of European foreign policy-making that had once existed. The extraordinary constellation of factors that had enabled the noteworthy rise of political cooperation in 1973 was no longer there.

Conclusion

In retrospect, the effective performance of the Europeans in speaking with one voice in the early 1970s looks almost like an episode. It was the exception to the rule of division and lack of success that has marked European Political Cooperation through much of its history. EPC became remembered as an 'alibi for inaction, a means of deflecting external pressure, and a cover for shifts in national policy',[1] rather than as a tool for advancing European interests in the world. Although it had a remarkable start, it failed to substantiate many of its policy achievements over the long run. By mid-1974, the initial dynamism in European foreign policy cooperation was largely gone, and it was clear that no European identity was likely to emerge anytime soon. Indeed, no European foreign policy ever took shape during the remainder of the Cold War, which is why the promising beginnings of EPC became a largely forgotten affair.

Even though the rise of Europe as a collective actor in world politics was a limited experience, it was a noteworthy phenomenon. The substance of EPC policies and ambitions in the early 1970s was truly stunning. This study has offered a detailed examination of this extraordinary period in European foreign policy-making. It has done so with a view to both fostering understanding of the *special* conditions that enabled the dynamic start of EPC, and learning about the *general* conditions for an effective European foreign policy. Having applied a chronological and analytical framework, it has identified various factors affecting the psychology of cooperation between the Six and later Nine over the course of time. In these concluding remarks, a concise interpretation of the evolution of EPC between 1969 and 1974 will be offered. Based on these findings, there will be some final reflections on those key factors that have strongly influenced the potentiality of European foreign policy cooperation throughout its history – and that are still with us today.

One of the major findings of this study is that the positive performance of the Europeans in the early 1970s was only possible because of a favourable constellation of factors on all levels of European foreign policy-making. While the emergence and initial consolidation of EPC between 1969 and 1972 was primarily the result of developments on the individual and intra-European levels, its rise in 1973 was triggered by extra-European challenges that provided additional reasons and opportunities to act. Conversely, the psychology of cooperation deteriorated sharply in 1974 because of negative developments on the extra-European, intra-European, and individual levels, which accounted for EPC's rather abrupt decline into crisis.

The launch and establishment of EPC was enabled by two major developments: a shift in the intra-European balance of power, and the coming into office of a new generation of leaders. Mounting concerns about the FRG's growing economic might and its impending *Ostpolitik* led France to seek a rapprochement with Britain, with a view to counterbalancing and controlling West German power. If the Franco-British controversy over London's accession to the EC had prevented the emergence of any European foreign policy cooperation during the 1960s and had thrown the Community into deep crisis, this 'British question' became resolved once the recurring 'German question' compelled Paris to change the status quo in Europe. However, the old generation of leaders proved unable to find a viable solution to the changing distribution of power within Europe. In early 1969, de Gaulle sought to realign his country with Britain outside of the existing European institutions, proposing a new structure for political cooperation among the European great powers that was unacceptable to both London and the Five. Wilson and Stewart, for their part, misread the signs of movement in Paris. Their aggressive anti-French policy of hammering their way into the EC, reflected in the 'Soames Affair' and their attempt to build up political consultations with the Five in the WEU, rendered any genuine Anglo-French rapprochement impossible even after de Gaulle left office.

It was only with the advent to power of new governments in Paris, London, and Bonn that the European deadlock could be overcome. Pompidou's approach of solving the 'British question' within the existing EC framework paved the way for the comprehensive *relance européenne* at the Hague Summit in December 1969, with the Six defining an ambitious programme of widening and deepening the Community. The change of leadership in the FRG, though comparatively less significant, was still important for the success of this summit, as Brandt's European priorities and role conceptions were more compatible with Pompidou's ideas than those of Kiesinger. The departing chancellor had been sceptical about Britain's intentions in Europe and had one-sidedly emphasised the need for a political unification of Europe, which collided with Pompidou's caution in this regard. By contrast, Brandt's balanced and more realistic policy of accepting the French prerogative of consolidating the CAP, working towards EMU, launching enlargement negotiations, and making a modest start at political cooperation paved the ground for the Franco-German compromise solution that stood at the heart of the breakthrough in The Hague.

However, none of the subsequent dynamics in Europe would have been possible if it had not been for the coming into power of Heath in Britain. As long as Wilson stayed in office, Europe was still on shaky ground. By keeping the EC application on the table after de Gaulle's veto in 1967, the Labour government had no doubt contributed to France's eventual acceptance of enlargement. Yet, the price of its unnecessarily obstructionist policies was felt in the continuous strains in Anglo-French relations. Pompidou regarded British membership in the EC merely as the lesser of two evils, which is why the accession talks made little progress initially. Similarly, the discussions by the Six on the Davignon Report in 1970 were conducted in a climate of continuing distrust, as France feared new manoeuvres by Britain and did not expect anything substantial to emerge from the political consultations of an enlarged Europe that included London anyway. By contrast, Heath's enthusiasm for Europe, his unsentimentality about the Anglo-American special relationship, and his conspicuously pro-French policies by mid-1971 allowed for a genuine Anglo-French rapprochement, convincing Pompidou of the large political potential that a widened Europe could have if the member states joined forces. Heath deserves credit for forging a new Anglo-French axis of trust in Europe, a rarity in Euroepan post-war history that provided the basis for the trilateral Anglo–French–German leadership that came to mark the 'New Europe' in the early 1970s. With Brandt and Scheel being more interested and active in *Westpolitik* than many had anticipated, a political constellation was gradually forming in Europe where the three big powers shared an ambition to establish Europe as a powerful actor in world politics that would be able to speak with one voice.

It was this Anglo–French–German triangle that provided the essential foundation upon which EPC could flourish. Of course, extra-European developments also played a part in enabling the Europeans to move to the realm of foreign policy and asserting their own views in international diplomacy. The prospect of nuclear parity between East and West implied a growing relevance of economic power and allowed for a multipolarisation of the international order and the emergence of new regional units. Furthermore, superpower détente reduced European fears of the Soviet Union and at the same time increased concerns about the credibility of the American security guarantee, which again induced the Europeans to forge their own political identity. However, these processes had started well before the early 1970s. Moreover, the Europeans had recognised both the need for and specific opportunities for political cooperation throughout the 1950s and 1960s, without ever being able to make their respective negotiations succeed. The creation of EPC in 1970 was, accordingly, not the result of any sudden European urge to respond collectively to the challenges and possibilities of the international environment. Rather, it was the French decision to let Britain into Europe that unblocked the process of European unification, with the subsequent dramatic amelioration of Anglo-French relations standing at the beginning of effective European foreign policy cooperation.

One important factor for EPC's successful consolidation in 1971/72 was the lesson, learnt from previous failures: that political cooperation could only come about when based on a modest, pragmatic mechanism of consultation, rather than any grand design. The Davignon Report signified a shift from the futile 'theological' debates on the desirable to the art of the possible. The separation of EPC from the EC and its intergovernmental character meant that it was essentially a question of the political will of the member states whether anything substantial would come out of Europe's political consultations. In this regard, the balance sheet was as yet mixed on the eve of enlargement, but the glass was clearly already half full at this stage. On the one hand, basic normative issues concerning the 'New Europe' remained contested in 1971/72. The controversial discussions on relations between the Nine and the US and on European defence reflected an ongoing disagreement on Europe's role and purpose in the world. Similarly, the lack of agreement on the location of a political secretariat mirrored wider differences as to Europe's conceptual end state. On the other hand, the operational start of EPC was already remarkably effective. On the sensitive issue of the Arab–Israeli conflict, a considerable amount of common ground was already achieved, even though there were diverging opinions as to what to do with any joint European position. Moreover, preparations for the CSCE became an unqualified success, with the Europeans by 1972 taking the lead from NATO in preparing the Western position for this pan-European conference and developing a common policy on both tactics and substance. Although EPC's potential on the eve of enlargement was as yet undecided, the decision of the nine leaders at their first summit in Paris in October 1972 to establish a European Union reflected a degree of optimism and ambition that boded well for the future of European foreign policy cooperation.

EPC's noteworthy rise in 1973 was again spurred by several factors. Trilateral leadership became reinforced by further changes on the individual level of European foreign policy-making. In France, Jobert as the new French foreign minister was much more eager to build *l'Europe politique* than Schumann had been, and his old friendship with Heath further strengthened Franco-British relations. Debré's departure from government was equally important, symbolising another French move away from orthodox Gaullism. Also helpful was the stronger position of Scheel, an EPC-zealot, within the West German cabinet, as well as the fact that the Brandt government was ever more eager to demonstrate its loyalty to the West and to advance European unity following its *Ostpolitik*. A second factor was the historic success of EC enlargement on 1 January 1973, which provided an extra boost to the political self-confidence and will of the Europeans. Becoming an economic giant increased both the need and the opportunity for Europe to define a common foreign policy. Given that even the technical and economic decisions of the enlarged Community were bound to have significant political implications, a common political framework was ever more urgent.

Third, the fact that 1973 was a peak year in détente fostered the readiness of the Europeans to promote their political unity as well. Between 1969 and 1972, the rise of détente had already had a positive impact on the *economic* unification of Europe, with EC enlargement and EMU having been conceived, inter alia, as means of tying the FRG to the West. If *Ostpolitik* had been an inhibiting factor for effective political cooperation in 1971/72, with Pompidou being sceptical about West Germany's whole-hearted commitment to a European political identity, this changed in 1973. Although some concerns about Germany's future lingered on, they now contributed to the *political* unification of Europe too, not least because EMU was in crisis. While London and Paris pushed for *l'Europe politique* to engage the West Germans, Bonn was eager to support this development in order to dispel all doubts about its commitment to the West. With respect to superpower détente, worries that Washington might compromise European interests for the sake of stable superpower relations came to a head in 1973, particularly in the context of the American–Soviet Agreement on the Prevention of Nuclear War. This agreement had a strong effect especially on France, which saw a superpower condominium emerging that threatened its own special status within the West and its role as a permanent member of the UN Security Council, as well as Europe's autonomy. Together with the Watergate scandal and the growing domestic isolationism in the US that resulted from the Vietnam War, the climax of superpower détente in 1973 reduced the reliability of US leadership in the West to an extent that added considerably to the Nine's determination to advance their own political unity.

Yet, the accelerated evolution of EPC in 1973 was triggered mainly by three specific external challenges that provided concrete opportunities and requirements for the Europeans to articulate their common interests, get involved in various diplomatic processes, and strengthen their capacities to act jointly. The first such challenge was the CSCE. This multilateral European variant of détente implied a role for the Nine, not least because the Soviet Union was believed to be intent on subordinating the Community to a new pan-European security framework. However, in contrast to all other manifestations of détente, the CSCE also provided a chance for the EPC countries to collectively get involved in shaping East–West relations. It was an opportunity for the Nine to engage the Soviet Union in a dialogue about the parameters of European security, to present to the East their own model of multilateral cooperation based on shared values and equal participation, and to attempt to bring the two parts of Europe closer together.

While there were various reasons why the Nine became an actor group in their own right within the Western delegations at the CSCE, differences with the US concerning Western objectives and the potential of the conference were particularly important. To the Nixon administration, détente was about managing superpower relations and the geopolitical status quo, which is why the US was primarily concerned about hard-power issues and little interested in a multilateral dialogue on a multitude of largely non-military topics. The Nine, by contrast, pursued a dynamic notion of détente. Being eager to render the security of individuals a legitimate concern of inter-state relations, they sought to reconceptualise security in Europe by adding concepts such as human rights and freer movement of people and ideas, that is, concepts that were not part of the US idea of détente.

Because it constituted EPC's first major test, the Europeans were determined to make the CSCE a success for their foreign policy cooperation. Already during the Multilateral Preparatory Talks in Helsinki in the first half of 1973, they surprised the other delegates by their joint approach. Their cohesive and effective performance enabled them to shape the agenda and structure of the CSCE largely according to their own preferences, and to become the collective actor with the single biggest impact on the conference negotiations in Geneva. Such features as a high intensity of consultation and a division of labour during the conference reflected an extraordinary community of interests in jointly facing the Soviet Union. The recognition that the Nine could collectively make an impact and defend their own interests provided a tremendous boost to EPC from the very beginning of the CSCE, demonstrating both the feasibility and the benefits of working together in international diplomacy.

It was against the background of such increasing political self-confidence that the Nine in the course of 1973 also transformed Kissinger's 'Year of Europe' initiative, the second external challenge, into a catalyst for European political unity. The US call to redefine NATO and expand Atlantic political and economic cooperation was probably not designed as a specific attack against EPC, which Washington could not have been too familiar with by the time of Kissinger's speech. Yet, the American proposal to adapt NATO to the requirements of the changing international system, which can be seen as a follow-up to the Harmel exercise in 1966/67, was bound to create friction with the Europeans. Just when the EC countries were finally moving towards forging their own political identity, the US was eager to strengthen NATO as a platform for Western political consultation and orchestration. Although the US might well have intended to assure the Europeans of continuing American leadership in times of superpower bilateralism, the Nine overwhelmingly perceived the Kissinger initiative as a provocation. The 'Year of Europe' came across as a US attempt to bring the European approach to détente into line with US policies, to wrest economic concessions from the Nine in return for American military protection, and generally to subordinate any autonomous role of the enlarged Community to the principles of transatlantic cohesion and US predominance.

Yet, the initiative also implied opportunities. Several EPC members, and Britain and the FRG in particular, were eager to use the occasion to demonstrate to the US the reality of a unifying Europe. If France was initially sceptical about the feasibility of a collective EPC response, it gradually came round to the idea too, not least because of British assurances that the Nine would give priority to stressing their own interests before meeting American requirements. By the summer of 1973, the Nine had embarked on the great adventure of defining their collective relations with the US. Their decision to speak with one voice to Washington was also prompted by their shared anger at the working methods of Kissinger, who chose to discuss his initiative in bilateral great power consultations rather than with the Nine as a unit, and who swore Paris, London, and Bonn each to a degree of secrecy that resulted in great confusion and irritation among the Europeans as to the state of the deliberations.

Interpreting the state of transatlantic affairs in a less negative light than Kissinger, and being keen on preserving their own room of manoeuvre, the Nine had little desire to intensify Atlantic cooperation, which is why they refused to go along with Kissinger's call for a new Atlantic Charter. If they accepted the idea of working on a transatlantic declaration to confirm the relevance of the Alliance, they came up with their own draft for a second declaration on European–American relations. This European draft, which was presented to Kissinger at the end of September 1973, constituted a milestone in the development of EPC. It introduced the revolutionary aspect of the 'Year of Europe' by asking the US to recognise the Nine as a new factor in international politics and an equal partner within the West. Kissinger's acceptance of the idea of such a parallel declaration came about in a trade-off with France, which simultaneously tabled a substantial draft on a NATO declaration. It meant that the Nine in the autumn of 1973 began to negotiate with the Nixon administration on a new European–American bilateralism, which was all the more remarkable since the issue of European relations with the US had always proven highly divisive in post-war European history.

As for the third external challenge prompting the rise of EPC in 1973, the October War and the oil crisis differed from the CSCE and the 'Year of Europe' in that these Middle East-related issues one-sidedly brought pressure to bear upon the Nine. European action was urgently required since the Arab–Israeli military confrontation and the oil crisis, linked by the Arab 'oil weapon', brought home to the Nine that their security and European détente were becoming ever more dependent on stability in the Middle East. American–Soviet rivalry in the region had the potential to trigger a global confrontation, all talk of superpower détente notwithstanding. Moreover, as energy moved to the top of the security agenda and introduced a new North–South dimension to the international system, the Europeans painfully came to feel the consequences of the fact that they were as dependent on Arab oil for their economic security as they were dependent on the US for their military security.

A major reason why the Europeans decided to become actively involved in Middle East politics was their realisation that Washington was incapable of protecting their specific interests. The US was much less dependent on energy imports than the Nine, and it had no power to secure Arab oil supplies to Europe. European and American threat perceptions also diverged strongly with regard to the Arab–Israeli conflict. Kissinger treated the October War much more as a Cold War confrontation than a local conflict with indigenous causes, and he was preoccupied with getting the Soviets out of the region. Moreover, the Nine disagreed with his unilateralist post-war diplomacy and his step-by-step approach, advocating a leading role for the UN in the peace process and a comprehensive solution to the conflict instead.

Europe's concrete response to the Middle East challenge was twofold. On the one hand, the Nine issued a declaration on the Middle East in which they not only offered their assistance in the peace process, but also came up with their own position regarding key aspects of the Arab–Israeli conflict, pointing in particular to the need for Israel to end its territorial occupation. On the other hand, the Nine also embraced the idea of a scheme of comprehensive cooperation with the Arab countries. As they remained excluded from the peace process, they developed a long-term approach to increase the interdependence between Europe and the Arab world, so as to enhance their own security. The objective of the Euro-Arab dialogue was not only to contribute to the stabilisation of the Middle East, but also to raise the Arab stakes in sound European economies in order to reduce the incentives for the oil producers to use the 'oil weapon' against Europe again.

As an indirect consequence of the October War and the oil crisis, the Nine increased their general efforts to improve Europe's ability to assert itself in international politics. In response to a French initiative on EPC summitry, the nine leaders for the first time discussed issues of European foreign policy cooperation at their Copenhagen meeting in December 1973. In view of the tense international situation, the Copenhagen summit did not allow for the planned strategic discussions on EPC's future, as the Nine had to deal with pressing EPC and EC matters of the day. Still, the principle of involving the European leaders in political cooperation marked an important strengthening of EPC, which was officially endorsed when the Nine institutionalised European summit meetings one year later. It is also noteworthy that discussions between Britain, the FRG, and France on European defence cooperation gained much momentum during the last three months of 1973. Jobert repeatedly urged his partners to do something about Europe's lack of military power. The principal issue was no longer the desirability of a European defence entity, but whether to initiate cooperation within the WEU, the Eurogroup, or among the Nine. This in itself was a major development, and there were certainly grounds in Paris, London, and Bonn for hoping that the Europeans would be able to agree on a common forum in 1974 and translate their discussions into practical progress.

The symbolic peak of EPC's rise in 1973 was the Declaration on European Identity, issued by the Nine in mid-December 1973. Originating in the context of the European deliberations on the 'Year of Europe', the process of working out this document took on a life of its own in the second half of 1973. It was heavily influenced by both the external challenges that beset the Nine and their policy successes regarding the CSCE, European–American relations, and the Middle East crisis. While the paper lacked a strategic focus and sketched the relations of the Nine with other individual powers or regions in vague terms only, it was notable for its expression of Europe's determination to act as a distinct entity and increasingly speak with one voice in international politics. By identifying the common ideational foundations of the European nation states and developing a conceptual framework for a European foreign policy, it not only marked an early attempt at defining a joint perception of the world (pointing to the European Security Strategy in this respect), but also reflected a degree of ambition and optimism concerning EPC that was never matched again during the remainder of the Cold War.

Remarkable though EPC's progress may have been in 1973, it is equally striking how many of its achievements were undone again in 1974. The favourable constellation of factors that enabled EPC's rise in the early 1970s turned out to be a temporary phenomenon only, and within a few months, EPC fell into a deep crisis. Of the many manifestations of EPC's decline, the European decision to terminate efforts at defining a common identity vis-à-vis the US was the most glaring one. The issue of transforming transatlantic relations into a new European–American bilateralism completely disappeared from the European agenda in the spring of 1974. The fact that the 'Year of Europe' ended with a single Atlantic declaration and the reinvigoration of NATO consultations spoke volumes in this respect. The Gymnich Agreement of the Nine was revealing too: its substance reflected the impossibility of conducting European policies against American interests, and the fact that several EPC members chose to simply ignore it meant that speaking with one voice to Washington was definitely out of the question. Also conspicuous was the European retreat from attempts to shape the political developments in the Middle East. The Nine de facto gave up their attempt at getting involved in resolving the Arab–Israeli conflict, and they put on hold their consultations on further refining their substantive position regarding the peace process. Instead, they subsequently focused their attention on the economic stabilisation of the Arab world, which is why they excluded the Arab–Israeli conflict and the oil crisis from the Euro-Arab dialogue – much to the dismay of the Arab participants. Finally, in a move that was highly symbolic of their reduced political ambitions, the Europeans stalled their talks on European defence in 1974, and they mandated a single sage, Leo Tindemans, to find consensus where they collectively had failed, that is, in defining the concept of and path towards the European Union.

The CSCE was the only field of cooperation that remained unaffected by the crisis in 1974. In fact, EPC's effective performance at the CSCE not only endured through the early 1970s, but became Europe's biggest foreign policy success during the Cold War. This raises the twin question of why EPC lapsed into crisis in 1974 and what was different about the CSCE that allowed the Nine to preserve their cohesion and continue their successful cooperation in this particular case. In a nutshell, the answer proposed in this book is that conditions for speaking with one voice deteriorated comprehensively at all levels of European foreign policy-making, but that this had little bearing on the CSCE because of a series of peculiarities of this multilateral long-term conference that rendered it a rather uncommon kind of policy challenge.

On the extra-European level, the situation in 1974 worsened in two major respects for EPC. First, there was now strong US resistance to an autonomous European role in foreign policy, which had a very negative impact on the psychology of European cooperation. Between 1969 and 1972, Washington had not been especially concerned with the political unification of Europe, being preoccupied with its own policies towards the Soviet Union, China, and Vietnam. Although there had been transatlantic frictions, the major points of contention had related more to economic and monetary issues than to Europe's foreign policy aspirations. This had changed in 1973, when the Europeans had demonstrated that their collective weight could make a difference in international diplomacy. While European dissatisfaction with US policies had played an important role in the rise of EPC, it is equally true that Kissinger's frustration with EPC now became a major handicap for Europe to forge a common political identity. In the initial phase of the 'Year of Europe', Kissinger had still professed at least a measure of benevolence towards EPC by accepting negotiations on a redefinition of European–American relations. His attitude had become more hostile, however, once the Middle East crisis and Europe's policy of engagement with the Arab oil-producers revealed that diplomatic action by the Nine could negatively affect vital US interests and put Europe in a competitive position with Washington.

Accordingly, by 1974 the 'Year of Europe' had turned into a European–American battle over how to reorganise the West. With his new proposals for strengthening Atlantic unity, Kissinger was obviously intent on dividing the Nine and restoring US leadership. The Washington Energy Conference was not only about managing the oil crisis, but also, and first and foremost, a US-inspired test of Atlantic solidarity. Confronting the Nine with the choice of tackling the most pressing challenge of the time on their own or in an Atlantic framework, Kissinger managed to make the European front crumble for a first time, employing both carrots and sticks. When the Nine decided weeks later, nevertheless, to launch the Euro-Arab dialogue, the US reacted strongly and even came to question EPC in principle. By March 1974, Kissinger and Nixon demanded a US say in the decision-making process of EPC, and made the case for a division of labour in the Middle East, with Washington being in charge of the peace process and the Nine focusing on economic matters. By linking continuing US military protection of Europe with European compliance in foreign policy affairs, they greatly raised the stakes in the European–American confrontation over the role of the Nine in the world, which contributed significantly to the fragmentation of Europe. Relations between Washington and Paris, in particular, deteriorated sharply. Kissinger no longer regarded France as his preferred partner, but saw it as his main problem in Europe, and he now blamed Pompidou and Jobert for just about every aspect of EPC he took exception to.

It is interesting that in their own analyses of what went wrong with EPC in 1974, the key protagonists of this study all pointed to the overwhelming importance of the 'Kissinger factor'. In his memoirs, Jobert regarded Kissinger's contempt for coordinated European policies and his insistence on great power bilateral consultations as a major reason for the inability of the Nine to assert their own identity. Brandt accused Kissinger in retrospect of treating the Europeans as mere pawns in the great chess game of the superpowers and playing Paris, London, and Bonn off against each other by pursuing diplomatic methods of times long gone. Heath, too, blamed Kissinger for approaching Europe as if it was still marked by the balance-of-power system of the nineteenth century and argued that the US secretary of state tended to suffer from schizophrenia, denouncing Europe for not being able to act collectively, but also complaining when the Europeans eventually gave it a try.[2] Kissinger's seminal role in truncating EPC in 1974 seemed the more ironic to these European leaders since he himself, prior to his political career, had actually foreseen the troublesome independence of Europe, had accused the US of being paternalistic towards its European allies, and had called for 'wisdom and delicacy in handling the transition from tutelage to equality' in transatlantic relations. In his reappraisal of the Atlantic Alliance in 1966, Kissinger had written:

> In short, a united Europe is likely to insist on a specifically European view of world affairs – which is another way of saying that it will challenge American hegemony in Atlantic policy. This may well be a price worth paying for European unity; but American policy has suffered from an unwillingness to recognize that there is a price to be paid [...]. Some autonomy in political decisions for Europe is psychologically important for the cohesion of the Alliance. Though this proposition will be granted by most American policymakers in the abstract, they tend to resist independence when it takes the form of challenging our judgments.[3]

Having read these lines in the context of Kissinger's attacks on EPC, the FCO could only observe that '[p]ain, whatever the dentist would like us to believe, does not become easier to bear merely because it has been predicted', and that wisdom is difficult 'even when the philosophers become princes'.[4] In his own memoirs, Kissinger called accusations that he did not really favour European political unity 'breathtakingly cynical' and 'demagogic'.[5] Yet, as this study has shown, he did play an important role in the decline of EPC in 1974.

The CSCE remained unaffected by US dissatisfaction with EPC because Washington's interest in this East-West process was limited. Although Kissinger was repeatedly frustrated with the slow European negotiating tactics and occasionally disagreed with the substance of European policies, he always kept his pressure moderate in this case and never combined it with threats. He did not believe in the feasibility of inducing reform and a degree of liberalisation in the Communist East, but he let the Nine have their way and accepted a European lead in intra-Western policy coordination in the CSCE. NATO–EPC relations were thus largely non-competitive in this case, which gave the Europeans the necessary leeway to shape and implement their own policy.

The second extra-European development negatively affecting EPC concerned a two-fold change in the international system. On the one hand, superpower détente was on the wane, which also limited the scope for autonomous European action. There was a growing European dependence on US protection again, while Washington for its part was keen on re-establishing Western unity under American leadership. This meant bringing Europe in line with US policies in the Middle East and putting an end to general ideas of European political emancipation. By contrast, in the case of the CSCE, this change meant that Kissinger more actively supported European positions, as he no longer feared negative repercussions on US–Soviet relations.

On the other hand, new security challenges that the Europeans were only partly able to cope with came to dominate the international agenda. The years 1973–75 witnessed a remarkable redefinition and broadening of the notion of security, in two quite different ways. The CSCE came up with an additional normative dimension of security that referred to human rights and the security of individuals. Its approach of cooperative security based on multilateral dialogue and the joint working out of principles was very much in line with Europe's own conception of security and was indeed heavily influenced by the Nine. But there was also a new economic dimension to security coming to the foreground, with energy emerging as a key security issue for industrial democracies. This development had a much more negative impact on Europe, which became badly hit by economic crisis, marked by recession, structural unemployment, and a capital drain to oil-producing countries. Rather than strengthening the Community, the economisation of international politics in 1974 actually weakened it. The era of instability and crisis that began to emerge in 1974 increased the power gap not only between Europe and the US (whose economy became less affected and which – after years of weakness – managed to re-establish its economic and monetary leadership), but also among EC member states, nurturing fragmentation in Europe.

If Europe only proved itself able to perform effectively in the realm of normative security, but failed when it came to energy security or more traditional challenges of power politics, such as in the Middle East, this was also due to intra-European developments. Europe's power base was not sufficient to sustain an effective foreign policy. This was at least in part the result of the failure of the Nine to develop a coherent vision of a united Europe and to agree on its conceptual end state and ultimate purpose. The separation of EPC and the EC, and the inconclusive debates on European defence, had been of little significance as long as the external challenges consisted in producing declarations and defining principles, as was the case in the CSCE and during the first phase of the 'Year of Europe'. But the missing link between EPC and the EC's economic instruments and the lack of European hard power became severe handicaps when the nature of the challenges changed, with the oil crisis affecting core material interests and being felt in the everyday lives of European citizens. These handicaps made it impossible for the Nine to influence events in a confrontational environment outside of Europe and to shape the policy preferences of actors with whom they were not in an ongoing dialogue.

While the Nine had established themselves as a respected actor group at the CSCE, they conspicuously failed to do so in the case of the Middle East. Concerning the Arab–Israeli conflict, neither Israel nor the US was ready to accept a European role in the search for peace. As regards the oil crisis, the Arabs refused to treat the Nine as a unit, while the US had little difficulty in compelling most Europeans to participate in its confrontational approach towards OPEC. Policy declarations and expressions of European identity proved largely irrelevant in the Middle East as long as the Europeans were perceived as being unable to change the status quo in the region. Furthermore, negative repercussions now also resulted from the lack of European agreement on a central EPC organ. Without a secretariat and an international bureaucracy, it proved very difficult to forge common positions under conditions of crisis and time pressure. One reason why the CSCE became a success for the Nine was that its conference diplomacy provided them with a permanent structure for consultation, an advantage badly missed in the other fields of EPC.

Several other intra-European factors contributed to the decline of EPC in 1974. The inability of EC member states to agree on a common energy policy and some form of 'oil solidarity', caused by the varying treatment by the Arab oil-producers, diverging energy needs, and different policy priorities, had a very negative impact on European cooperation in general. Furthermore, differences within the Community as to the implementation of the ambitious Paris Summit programme added to the economic weakening of Europe and the return of distrust among the Nine. These differences were partly due to the fact that the treasuries of Britain and the FRG pursued a less pro-European course than their respective foreign ministries, which contributed to the collapse of the EMU project and made consensus on projects such the Regional Development Fund impossible. The élan of the *relance européenne* of the early 1970s was, thus, gradually petering out in 1974, with the Community plunging into a crisis that was as severe as Europe's deadlock in the late 1960s. Moreover, national idiosyncrasies played a role too, albeit a more limited one. Events in 1974 had made it clear that for all its growing power, the FRG remained an extremely vulnerable element in any European foreign policy, be it because of its dependence on the US or because of its Nazi past and its special relations with Israel. In addition, France under Pompidou had failed to ever resolve its basic dilemma of how to build a strong and cohesive Europe without diminishing its national room of manoeuvre, while the Dutch and the Danish had never really warmed to the idea of a European foreign policy and probably were not unhappy about EPC's new modesty.

Finally, changes at the level of individual decision-makers also contributed to the decline of EPC in 1974. There is no doubt that EPC would have fallen into some sort of crisis anyway, given the transatlantic row over Europe's foreign policy, the profound EC crisis, and the weak power base of the Nine. Also, Jobert during his last months in office clearly went too far with his emphasis on building a *Europe européenne*, and it is significant that even Heath as his closest ally had to side with the Americans at the Washington Energy Conference. Yet, the changes of leaders in Britain, the FRG, and France further weakened EPC, in two different ways. On the one hand, Wilson/Callaghan, Schmidt, and Giscard all emphasised a transatlantic prerogative and supported Kissinger's case for great power consultations to meet the challenges of the time, which to some extent came at the expense of EPC. On the other hand, they sharply differed in their role conceptions of Europe, which meant that the trilateral leadership that had provided the essential basis for Europe's rapid development in the early 1970s became a thing of the past. The Labour government pursued a much less constructive European policy than Heath had, demanding that the British terms of entry be renegotiated, and advocating a static conception of Europe without EMU and the EU. Although Wilson and Callaghan were more interested in EPC than in the EC, Labour's policy of semi-detachment vis-à-vis the Community nurtured a general climate of distrust in Europe, resulting in Britain's self-marginalisation among the Nine and the return to bilateral Franco-German leadership in Europe. Again, the effects of such leadership changes were felt much less strongly in the CSCE than elsewhere. This was because the CSCE had become a bottom-up driven, bureaucratic project, largely run by an anonymous group of middle-rank diplomats and national experts. This provided for a continuity of political will and policy preferences unmatched in any other field of cooperation in EPC, where new governments and leaders all too often meant new policy priorities.

An overall assessment of EPC's rise and decline between 1969 and 1974 points to two general conclusions. First, European foreign policy cooperation is an extremely fragile endeavour under any circumstances. This study has revealed both the broad variety of factors that can influence the psychology of cooperation and the extraordinary constellation of factors that is needed for the Europeans to be able to speak with one voice. While the conditions for effective joint foreign policy-making were gradually improving during the early 1970s and eventually made possible EPC's *annus mirabilis* in 1973, the first six months of 1974 painfully demonstrated how easily cohesion and trust among the Europeans could be swept away again.

Second, even though the broad variety of relevant factors renders any stringent theorising of multilateral political cooperation near-impossible, the results of this study suggest three key factors that had a large share in shaping the course of EPC during the period under investigation and appear to be of general importance for the viability and effectiveness of any European foreign policy. These factors concern the American role in, and attitude towards, Europe's joint diplomacy, the issue of political will and perceived common purpose at the level of member states and specific national decision-makers, and the means Europe has at its disposal to engage in international politics. It is noteworthy that the debates on all these issues still continue today, albeit partly in modified form.

The transatlantic angle to European foreign policy-making has been a major challenge ever since the launch of EPC. During the Cold War, uncertainties about the US security guarantee and dissatisfaction with US policies repeatedly prompted the Europeans to try to assert their own interests. After the events of 1973/74, Europe's Venice Declaration on the Middle East in the early 1980s was another case in point. Yet, Europe's military dependence on the US meant that it was almost impossible to pursue a common foreign policy without US goodwill, and once Washington had realised during the 'Year of Europe' that a united Europe risked creating a split in the West, its enthusiasm for a European foreign policy cooled off decidedly. In the changed environment of the twenty-first century, the US, although it continues to alternate between treating the Europeans as a unit and dealing with them bilaterally, has less direct lever-age on influencing Europe's policy. Still, US policies and the issue of European–American relations continue to be highly divisive among the Europeans, making the common European determination of 1973 to speak with one voice to Washington look like a curious moment in the history of transatlantic relations. The basic dilemma that has haunted Europe for decades is unlikely to go away anytime soon: a European foreign policy only makes lim-ited sense if it predominantly does the same things as the US, but it all too often leads to intra-European and transatlantic friction if it tries to be distinct from the US.

As for the political will of actors, it has proven to be a very volatile factor over the past decades. This study has underlined the great impact that individ-ual decision-makers can exert on the formation of national preferences in the realm of foreign policy and the feasibility of multilateral political cooperation. While there has been a process of socialisation at the bureaucratic level between the national foreign ministries over the years, the same 'coordination reflex' and sense of 'we-feeling' has proven more difficult to establish among the elected policy-makers. With governments coming and going, the constella-tions for European cooperation vary constantly, and the convergence of national role conceptions and interests has become more difficult with every round of European enlargement.

Although the willingness to 'think European', to search for common ground, and to act jointly is a formidable requirement for all EU member states, it has turned out to be a particular challenge in the case of Britain. Events in 1974 made clear that the excitement in the early 1970s about Britain's role in Europe being eventually clarified had been premature. While France had given up its policy of opposing British accession that had perturbed European inte-gration during the 1960s, Britain revived the 'British question' itself after 1974 with its wavering commitment to Europe, thus returning to the discussions of the 1950s. As important as Heath's European zeal was for the advancement of the Community, his administration turned out to be the great exception in British post-war history. Subsequent Conservative governments joined

Labour in taking up a rather sceptical stance towards Europe, which was famously reflected in Prime Minister Margaret Thatcher demanding Britain's money back at the European summit in 1984. With its public remaining largely Euro-sceptic today, Britain's relationship with the EU is bound to remain ambivalent. While this does not rule out occasional tri- or multilateral leadership in Europe, it is detrimental to a strong and sustainable European presence in world affairs.

Whereas the problems of political disunity and external disturbances are bound to be recurring phenomena that will not go away, there has been clear progress with regard to the third key factor, that is, the instruments and power bases that Europe can use to back its policies. Given that this intra-European factor constitutes the one element that the Europeans can actually influence collectively, recent developments in this field provide ground for some optimism about the EU's foreign policy aspirations. First of all, although Europe's attempt at speaking with one voice is still largely based on intergovernmental cooperation, today these efforts are backed by numerous organs in Brussels and a centralised bureaucracy. The considerable degree of institutionalisation of the Common Foreign and Security Policy (CFSP) and the European Security and Defence Policy (ESDP) contrasts notably to the case of EPC, which had no secretariat before 1986 and was run almost exclusively by the rotating presidency. Second, the gap between the Economic Community and Europe's foreign-policy element has significantly narrowed in recent years. Undeniably, problems of coherence between the three pillars of the EU remain, and the CFSP has not been able yet to take full advantage of Europe's economic instruments and power to further its objectives. Still, barriers are no longer as doctrinaire as they used to be, and the EU's predominant success in stabilising Europe and its neighbourhood since the end of the East–West divide is a prime example of a foreign policy achievement by a combination of structural approaches of enlargement and association and more traditional diplomacy.

Finally, it is particularly noteworthy that the EU today is also in the process of building up its military capabilities. As this study has shown, Europe in the 1970s developed into a rather peculiar 'civil power' by necessity and not by deliberate choice. Europe was, of course, particularly suited and eager to make itself felt in the world and to shape the preferences of other states by its moral and economic force. However, countries such as France, Britain, and even the FRG were well aware that defending European interests in an environment marked by power politics required complementary hard power too. If it was no coincidence that the issue of a European defence identity returned to the

European agenda with the launch of EPC, the failure of the respective deliberations resulted in Europe's one-sided emphasis on 'soft power' during the Cold War. It was the consequence not only of an insufficient French departure from the Gaullist paradigm of national defence but also, and above all, of the impossibility of resolving the basic European dilemma of how to build up military capabilities without diminishing the US commitment to the defence of Europe.

Although many came to regard Europe's 'soft power' as its special strength, the one-sided nature of this power in fact constituted a major handicap. This is why the building up of ESDP is of seminal importance for the viability of Europe's foreign policy. Since the launch of EPC, Europe has made much progress in complementing its competence in normative security with instruments to cover other aspects of the ever-broader spectrum of security challenges. It has long demonstrated that it has adapted well to the economic requirements of security that came to the forefront with the oil crisis in 1973/74 – despite the fact that it is still struggling to formulate a cohesive common energy policy. Also, it has set up a series of institutions and developed expertise to deal with the civilian challenges of conflict resolution. As the EU now has begun to build up its own hard-power capacities, it is further improving its ability to respond to the complex contemporary challenges with a uniquely broad range of tools. Yet, the key question is whether Europe will prove willing to use its new military power when circumstances require it to do so. Only then can we rightfully talk of a European strategic culture. And only then will the EU have the potential to establish itself as a credible and effective actor in international politics. The jury is still out.

Notes

Introduction

1. François Duchêne, 'The European Community and the Uncertainties of Interdependence', in Kohnstamm and Hager (1973), 1–21.
2. Hoffmann (1995) and (2000).
3. Norway was a candidate country too, but failed to join the EC following a negative referendum in 1972.
4. Morgan (1973).
5. According to Moravcsik's theory of Liberal Intergovernmentalism (1993 and 1998), the process of preference formation in the economic realm is dominated by bargaining among interest groups. Far fewer such groups are mobilised in the case of foreign policy cooperation, where gains and losses for societal groups are usually lower and generally less calculable.
6. Loth and Osterhammel (2000); Conze, Lappenküper, and Müller (2004); Westad (2000).
7. Wendt (1999).
8. Elman and Elman (2001).
9. Mayer (2004).
10. Hill (2002).
11. Vertzberger (1990); Jervis (1976); Little and Smith (1988); Holsti (1962); James F. Voss and Ellen Dorsey, 'Perception and International Relations: An Overview', in Singer and Hudson (1992), 3–30.
12. Walker (1987); DiMaggio (1997).
13. Allison and Zelikow (1999); Hart, Stern, and Sundelius (1997).
14. Milner (1992); Jervis (1999); Keohane (1984); Haftendorn and Keck (1997); Risse-Kappen (1995); Adler and Barnett (1998).
15. Particularly worth mentioning are three volumes edited by a transnational study group on EPC: Allen, Rummel, and Wessels (1982); Hill (1983); Allen and Pijpers (1984). See also Regelsberger (1992); Regelsberger, de Schoutheete de Tervarent, and Wessels (1997); Mayer (2001); Schwarz (2004).
16. De Schoutheete (1986); Ifestos (1987); Nuttall (1992).
17. Knipping and Schönwald (2004); Ludlow (2007); van der Harst (2007).

18. Bitsch (2001); Gerbet (1999); Knipping and Schönwald (2004); Brunn (2002).

19. Berstein and Rioux (2000). See also Association Georges Pompidou (2001).

20. Association Georges Pompidou (1995); Elisabeth du Réau, 'Georges Pompidou, l'élargissement et le renforcement de la Communauté', in du Réau and Frank (2002), 55–75; Soutou (1996), (2000), and (2004); Soutou, 'Präsident Georges Pompidou und die Ostpolitik', in Niedhart, Junker, and Richter (1997), 171–9; Pierre Mélandri, 'La France et l'alliance atlantique sous Georges Pompidou et Valéry Giscard d'Estaing', in Vaïsse, Mélandri, and Bozo (1999), 519–58; Bussière (2003).

21. Roussel (1994); Weed (1981) and (1988).

22. Möller and Vaïsse (2005); Andreas Wilkens, 'Willy Brandt et la place de l'Allemagne en Europe', in Catala (2002), 261–74; Wilkens (1999b); Claudia Hiepel, 'Willy Brandt, Georges Pompidou und Europa: Das deutsch–französische Tandem in den Jahren 1969–1974'; and Hubert Zimmermann, 'Der unschlüssige Hegemon: Deutschland und die Anfänge der europäischen Währungsintegration', both in Knipping and Schönwald (2004), 28–46 and 203–16. On *Ostpolitik*, see the important research project 'Détente and Ostpolitik' by Gottfried Niedhart and Oliver Bange: (www.ostpolitik.net).

23. Merseburger (2002).

24. Werner Link, 'Aussen- und Deutschlandpolitik in der Ära Brandt 1969–1974', in Bracher, Jäger, and Link (1986), 163–282; Baring (1982); Müller-Roschach (1980).

25. Daddow (2003); Pine (2007); Anne Deighton, 'The Second British Application for Membership of the EEC', in Loth (2001), 391–405.

26. A notable exception is N. Piers Ludlow, 'Constancy and Flirtation: Germany, Britain, and the EEC, 1956–1972', in Noakes, Wende, and Wright (2002), 95–112.

27. Ball and Seldon (1996); Young (1998); Lord (1993).

28. Campbell (1993).

29. Höhn (1978). Höhn was not allowed to reveal the identity of his sources – which limits the value of his book.

30. Götz von Groll, 'The Nine at the Conference on Security and Cooperation in Europe', in Allen, Rummel, and Wessels (1982), 60–8; Crispin Tickell, 'The Enlarged Community and the European Security Conference', in John (1975), 115–24; Schwerin (1975).

31. Dosenrode and Stubkjær (2002); Kaiser and Steinbach (1981).

32. Lieber (1976); Krämer (1974).

33. For an early historical account, see Pierre Mélandri, 'Une relation très spéciale: la France, les Etats-Unis et l'Année de l'Europe, 1973–1974', in *Association Georges Pompidou* (1995), 89–131. See also various contributions in Schultz, Schwartz, and Schäfer (forthcoming).

34. For a recent study, see Hanhimäki (2004).

35. Schaetzel (1975); Kaiser (1973); Hanrieder (1973).
36. Wilfried Loth, 'European Political Co-operation and European security in the policies of Willy Brandt and Georges Pompidou', and Helen Parr, 'Anglo-French nuclear collaboration and Britain's policy towards Europe, 1970-1973', both in van der Harst (2007), 21–34 and 35–60. See also Smart (1971); Cromwell (1992), Chs 2–6; Aybet (2001), Ch. 4; Ifestos (1988).
37. Important memoirs include Brandt (1978); Jobert (1974) and (1976); Kissinger (1999), (2000a), and (2000b).
38. See the bibliography for the list of interviews.

Part I: Towards a European Foreign Policy, 1969–72

1. On the operative phase of *Ostpolitk*, see note 22 in the introduction. See also Haftendorn (2001), Ch. 5; Link, 'Aussen- und Deutschlandpolitik in der Ära Brandt', in Bracher, Jäger, and Link (1986), 178–241; Bahr (1996), Chs 6f.
2. Garthoff (1994), Chs 1–12; Vojtech Mastny, 'Superpower Détente: US–Soviet Relations, 1969–1972', in Geyer and Schaefer (2004), 19–25.

1 New leaders and the relaunch of Europe

1. 'Communiqué of the Conference of the Heads of State and Government of the Member States of the European Community (The Hague Summit Declaration), The Hague, 2 December 1969', *European Foreign Policy: Key Documents*, 72–4.
2. Ibid., 72.
3. Greenwood (1996); Ralph Dietl, 'Kontinuität und Wandel – Zur Geschichte der europäischen Zusammenarbeit auf dem Gebiet der Sicherheits- und Verteidigungspolitik 1948–2003', in Meier-Walser (2004), 19–86, at 27–36.
4. Kim (2000). The EDC treaty and the draft on Political Community are reproduced in *European Foreign Policy: Key Documents*, 16–39. The Political Community foresaw an executive council, a council of ministers, and a two-chambered parliament, as well as a mechanism for the permanent coordination of foreign policy.
5. Cabalo (1999); Dietl (2002).
6. The Treaty of Rome of 25 March 1957 is reproduced in *European Foreign Policy: Key Documents*, 42–6.
7. Kramer (2003), 222–33.
8. Georges-Henri Soutou, 'Le Général de Gaulle et le Plan Fouchet d'union politique européenne: un projet stratégique', in Deighton and Milward (1999), 55–71. The Fouchet drafts are reproduced in *European Foreign Policy: Key Documents*, 47–62.
9. Krüger (2003).

10. Hoffmann (1995), 84; Vaïsse (1998).

11. Giauque (2002); Ralph Dietl, "Sole Master of the Western Nuclear Strength'? The United States, Western Europe and the Elusiveness of a European Defence Identity, 1959–64', in Loth (2004), 132–72.

12. Ludlow (1997); Bange (2000); Milward (2002). During the Fouchet negotiations, West German Chancellor Konrad Adenauer accepted de Gaulle's Europe à Six. Mayer (1996).

13. Note FCO (Research Department), 'European Political Cooperation: French Policies and Attitudes 1949–70', January 1970, FCO 30/565.

14. Bozo (2001).

15. Maurice Vaïsse, 'La politique européenne de la France en 1965: pourquoi 'la chaise vide'?', in Loth (2001), 193–214.

16. In 1967, the executives of the EEC, the European Coal and Steel Community, and the European Atomic Energy Community were fused. Technically, the abbreviation 'EC' stood for the 'European Communities' (plural).

17. Albonetti (1972). On the Harmel Report, see Wenger (2004).

18. Ideas to revive the Fouchet talks in 1964 came to nothing. See Carine Germond, 'Les projets d'Union politique de l'année 1964', in Loth (2001), 109–30.

19. See also Ludlow (2006).

20. As Secretary of State Michael Stewart warned Wilson, if Britain did not take its chance now, 'the Community may then resume its development, under French leadership today, under German leadership tomorrow'. Stewart (from New York) to Wilson, 13 November 1968, FCO 30/533 [telegram numbers are only listed when several telegrams with the same date are in the file].

21. Haftendorn (2001), Chs 3 and 6.

22. Young (1998), 203.

23. Taschler (2001), 352 and 388f.

24. For Soames' report, see the attachment to note FCO (John Robinson, head EID), 'General de Gaulle's proposal to Mr. Soames', 17 February 1969, FCO 30/414; note Elysée to Maurice Couve de Murville, French prime minister, 'Entretien du Président de la République avec l'Ambassadeur de Grande-Bretagne le Mardi 4 Février 1969', 7 February 1969, Archives d'histoire contemporaine, Maurice Couve de Murville papers 9.

25. UK embassy Paris (Soames) to FCO, 5 February 1969, no. 125, FCO 30/414.

26. Daddow (2003).

27. Note FCO (Hugh Morgan, head WED, to Viscount Hood, Deputy Under-Secretary of State, WED), 'General de Gaulle's Proposals on Europe', 7 February 1969, FCO 30/416.

28. Note PMO (Arthur Michael Palliser, Private Secretary to the Prime Minister) to FCO (Donald Maitland, Private Secretary to the Secretary of State), 12 September 1968, FCO 30/411.

29. Note FCO (Hood), 'Europe', 3 October 1968, FCO 30/533.

30. Stewart to Wilson (in Bonn), 11 February 1969, FCO 30/414.

31. Record of conversation between Kiesinger and Wilson in Bonn on 12 February 1969, CAB 164/407; note FCO (Robinson to Patrick Hancock, Deputy Under-secretary of State, and Greenhill), 'Should we leak the full de Gaulle proposal?', 21 February 1969, FCO 30/415.

32. Dismayed at how London had deliberately provoked 'ultra-strained relations' by 'bashing' the French, Soames in several letters listed numerous examples of how Stewart and the British media had distorted the contents of the proposals. UK embassy Paris (Soames) to FCO, 24 February 1969, no. 199, FCO 30/415; to Stewart, 25 February 1969, no. 205, FCO 30/416; to Wilson, 11 March 1969, FCO 30/418.

33. Political consultations at WEU had taken place even before 1963, but on a pragmatic and sporadic basis. See note MAE, 'Les consultations politiques au sein de l'U.E.O.', 18 February 1969, ADMAE Gén. 2025.

34. For the respective plans of the FRG and Belgium, see note AA (Frank to Brandt), 4 September 1968, PA B1/325; and Dujardin (2004), 469–512.

35. Letter FCO (Robinson) to UK embassy Brussels, 25 October 1968, FCO 30/533; Stewart to UK embassy Bonn (Roger Jackling), 16 January 1969, FCO 30/536.

36. Stewart (from Luxembourg) to FCO, 7 February 1969, no. 41–3, FCO 30/537. Britain also agreed with Italy and the Benelux countries on compulsory advance consultations on a range of issues to be determined, while the FRG stuck to the idea of voluntary consultations.

37. Note FCO (Hood to WOD), 'W.E.U.', 17 February 1969, FCO 41/505.

38. Record of conversation between Debré and Stewart in Washington on 11 April 1969, ADMAE EM 37.

39. Ibid.

40. N. Piers Ludlow, 'A Short-Term Defeat: The Community Institutions and the Second British Application to Join the EEC', in Daddow (2003), 135–50.

41. Pine (2004), 76. See also Pine (2007).

42. Record of conversation between Wilson and Brandt in Bonn on 13 February 1969, CAB 164/407; AAPD 1969, no. 94.

43. AAPD 1969, no. 99.

44. Even a personal letter from Wilson to Kiesinger (21 February 1969, PA B21/666), requesting that the FRG 'take account of the new and developing role we see for Western European Union', could not persuade the chancellor to leave France behind and go along with Britain. AAPD 1969, no. 70.

45. The final declaration was much less substantial than the FCO had wished and contrasted with a far-reaching Anglo-Italian declaration of April 1969. Note AA (Georg Duckwitz, state secretary) to BKA (Karl Carstens), 5 February 1969, PA B150/146; FRG embassy London (Herbert Blankenhorn) to AA, 29 April 1969, PA B130/266.

46. Note AA (IA1), 'Weiteres deutsches Vorgehen', 3 March 1969, PA B21/666.

47. Letter Stewart to French embassy Paris (Soames), 20 March 1969, FCO 30/418.

48. 'Poher Stresses Role in Alliance', *New York Times*, 28 May 1969.

49. On the French elections of 1969, see Berstein and Rioux (2000), 4–15.

50. Stewart (1980), 227.

51. Stewart (from The Hague) to FCO, 6 June 1969, FCO 41/501; Schmidt to Brandt, 'Betr.: Meine Gespräche in London vom 19.–21.5.1969', 27 May 1969, WBA, Bundesaussenminister 9; note FCO to UK embassy The Hague, undated, with Stewart's instructions for Soames' conversation with Schumann prior to the summit, FCO 30/271.

52. In an interview with the author, Sir Michael Palliser added that Pompidou's reservations about Wilson were also due to the disregard with which the British prime minister had treated him when Pompidou served as premier during de Gaulle's presidency. According to Sir Michael, if Wilson had won the elections in 1970, he would probably not have managed to convince Pompidou to accept Britain as a member of the EC.

53. Note FCO (Hancock), 'Some Political Aspects of our European Policy', 2 April 1969, FCO 30/397.

54. Record of conversation between Pompidou and Soames in Paris on 10 October 1969, AN 5AG2 1014.

55. Brandt's proposal during the WEU ministerial meeting of 5 June 1969, AAPD 1969, no. 194, note 2.

56. Berstein and Rioux (2000), 11.

57. Alain de Boissieu, 'La politique militaire', in Messmer (1990), 208–21; Marie-Pierre Rey, 'Georges Pompidou, l'Union soviétique et l'Europe', in Association Georges Pompidou (1995), 140–70.

58. Roussel (1994). The term was coined by Alain Peyrefitte, a close associate of de Gaulle. On Pompidou's background and political career prior to his presidency, see ibid., 23–280.

59. Maurice Schumann, 'La politique étrangère', in Messmer (1990), 267–82; Soutou (2000), 114.

60. Maurice Vaïsse, 'Changement et continuité dans la politique européenne de la France', in Association Georges Pompidou (1995), 29–43.

61. Soames' portrait of Schumann in a letter to Stewart, 21 January 1970, FCO 73/52; Debré (1996), 48; Chaban-Delmas' self-characterisation in his conversation with Luns on 17 July 1969, ADMAE EM 37; Roussel (1994), 163 and 196.

62. Pompidou's hand-written annotation on a record of conversation between Schumann and Luns in Paris on 8 July 1969, AN 5AG2 1049.

63. Testimony of Peyrefitte in Association Georges Pompidou (1995), 254.

64. Translated from Kiesinger's welcome address to Pompidou at their summit on 8 September 1969. *Europäische Politische Einigung*, vol. II, 70. On Kiesinger and the 'British question', see note FRG embassy Paris (von Braun), 'Vorbesprechungen

im BKA', 11 March 1969, PA SvB 138; 'Kiesinger: Die Sicherheit Westeuropas planen', *Die Welt*, 25 August 1969. On Kiesinger, Brandt, and Europe, see Türk (2006).

65. One of Kiesinger's most insistent argumentations in favour of the political unification of Europe took place during his summit with Pompidou in Bonn on 8 and 9 September 1969, AAPD 1969, nos. 279 and 282.

66. On the West German election campaign, see two analyses by French embassy Bonn (François Seydoux de Clausonne) to MAE, 25 and 27 August 1969, ADMAE RFA 1554.

67. AAPD 1973, no. 198.

68. 'Das Wünschenswerte darf uns nicht daran hindern, das Mögliche zu tun.' Speech by Brandt in Bad Godesberg, 'Europas Weg in die siebziger Jahre', 21 July 1969, AdsD SPD PV-Neuer Bestand, Abteilung Internationale Beziehungen 2776.

69. Hiepel (2003), 66.

70. Important factors included a principled rejection of the Small Europe à Six, and the desire to make the EC more democratic and legitimate. Interview with Hans Apel (INT639). In the AA, frequently mentioned reasons for expanding the EC included the desire to strengthen Europe vis-à-vis the superpowers, balancing French leadership, expanding markets for German exports, and gaining influence on British policies. Notes AA (IA2), 'Politische und wirtschaftspolitische Aspekte der Erweiterungsfrage', 31 July 1969, PA B20/1595; (IA, Berndt von Staden), 'Interministerielle Arbeitsgruppe 'Europ. Gemeinschaften/Grossbrit.", 15 September 1969, PA B20/1432.

71. See Brandt's 'Regierungserklärung vor dem Bundestag' of 28 October 1969, reproduced in *Bundeskanzler Brandt*, vol. I, 13–30.

72. Brandt (1978), 296.

73. AAPD 1969, no. 353.

74. AAPD 1969, no. 221; record of conversation between Pompidou and Carlo Schmid, FRG coordinator for the Elysée Treaty, in Paris on 7 November 1969, AN 5AG2 1010. Pompidou argued during the latter conversation: 'Le désir profond du Gouvernement allemand, c'est que la possibilité soit donnée d'ouvrir des négociations avec la Grande-Bretagne. Je dis tout de suite que nous n'y ferons pas obstacle. Après avoir obtenu ce que nous souhaitons, nous ne créerons pas de nouvelles difficultés. Vous pouvez le dire au Chancelier: nous serons ouverts, coopératifs, mais nous voulons l'achèvement du Marché Commun et le règlement financier.' Schmid replied: 'Le Chancelier le sait et est d'accord.'

75. Note AA (von Staden), 20 November 1969, PA B20/1439.

76. For the three meetings on 15 September, 17 October, and 10 November 1969, see EUROGERMA to AA, 15 September 1969, PA B21/736; note AA (Frank), 20 October 1969, PA B130/2667; AAPD 1969, no. 356.

77. See the French *Conseil restreint* of 18 November 1969, AN 5AG2 1042.

78. Brandt's opening speech is reproduced in *Bundeskanzler Brandt*, vol. I, 63–9; 'Statement by Georges Pompidou (The Hague, 1 December 1969)', *Bulletin of the European Communities* no. 2 (February 1970): 33–5; 'The Proposals by France', *The Times*, 3 December 1969. For comprehensive records of the summit deliberations, see note AA (IA2), 5 January 1970, PA B20/1441; ADMAE Gén. 2724.

79. Brandt (1978), 321.

80. Letter Don Cook, *Los Angeles Times*, to Con O'Neill, 3 December 1969, on Luns' summit report; UK embassy Luxembourg (Dugald Malcolm) to FCO, 10 December 1969, on Thorn's summit report, both in FCO 30/273.

81. Note FCO (John Waterfield, head WOD, to David Bendall, Assistant Under-Secretary of State), 'France and Western European Union', 13 October 1969, FCO 41/509.

82. Notes FCO (Waterfield to Maitland), 'Western European Ministerial Meeting', 5 June 1969, FCO 41/501; AA (IA1), 'WEU; politische Zusammenarbeit', 20 June 1969, PA B1/327; FCO (Waterfield to Bendall), 'France and Western European Union', 13 October 1969, FCO 41/509.

83. Draft note MAE (Occ.), 25 September 1969, ADMAE Gén. 2025; note FCO (Waterfield to Bendall), 'Harmel's proposals for French re-entry to WEU', 17 September 1969, FCO 41/477; Dujardin (2004), 522–30. See also Pompidou's hand-written annotation of 19 September 1969: 'Je ne suis pas d'accord sur l'UEO. Je n'accepte rien. On nous a agressé, on doit se retirer.' AN 5AG2 1049.

84. Record of conversation between Brandt and Schumann in Bonn on 8 September 1969, PA B20/1437.

85. Pompidou made his proposal during a press conference on 10 July 1969. *Europäische Politische Einigung*, vol. II, 62.

86. Record of a meeting of the French *Conseil restreint* concerning the summit at The Hague on 18 November 1969, AN 5AG2 1042.

87. French embassy Bonn (Seydoux) to MAE, 4 June 1969, on Kiesinger's concept of Europe as presented during his election campaign, ADMAE RFA 1554; AAPD 1969, no. 267. For Brandt, see note 67 in this chapter.

88. EUROGERMA to AA, 15 September 1969, PA B21/736.

89. Notes AA (Frank to Brandt), 4 September 1969, PA B1/325; AA (Frank), 11 November 1969, PA B21/719.

90. Note AA (IA1), 'Stand der politischen Zusammenarbeit in Europa', 6 October 1969, PA B21/667.

91. West German draft communiqué of 20 November 1969, PA B20/1439. Early drafts had contained proposals for the foreign ministers of the candidate states to join the Six in their study after a certain time. Shortly before the summit, such a clause had been relegated to a secondary option that Brandt intended to table only if the conference went really well. Note AA (Frank to Brandt), 'Sitzung Bundeskabinett', 5 September 1969, PA B20/1438.

92. See note 77 in this chapter.

93. Note Elysée (Jean-Bernard Raimond, counsellor of the President, to Pompidou), 6 January 1970, AN 5AG2 1035.

94. The issue was also discussed among the foreign ministers, but there is no indication that the Six sought a summit agreement on substantive or procedural questions concerning EPC. UK embassy Brussels (James Marjoribanks) to FCO, 4 December 1969, on the impressions by the FRG representative at the EC in Brussels, Hans-Georg Sachs, FCO 30/273; interviews with Egon Bahr and Etienne Davignon.

95. Record of conversation between Con O'Neill and Günther Harkort, State Secretary AA, in Bonn on 14 November 1969, FCO 30/437. For Britain's efforts to mobilise the Five against a definitive financial agreement of CAP, see Dujardin (2004), 543. For Wilson's lack of support for the CAP, see Milward (2003).

96. Note FCO (O'Neill to Bendall), 4 December 1969, FCO 41/484.

97. Stewart to UKDEL NATO, 'Political Consultation between the Six', 14 August 1969, FCO 41/508.

98. Note FCO (O'Neill to Thomas Brimelow, Deputy Under-Secretary of State), 'France and WEU', 21 October 1969, FCO 41/509: 'After all that has been said it would be, and would be seen to be, a reverse for Her Majesty's Government, and for the Secretary of State personally, if the Six were now to embark on political consultations from which we were excluded.'

99. Wilkens (1999b), 93.

100. 'Text of reply from Chancellor of the Duchy of Lancaster, Mr. George Thomson, to paper communicated to him by Monsieur Harmel on 12 March', 19 March 1970, ADMAE Gén. 2723.

101. Circular MAE (Hervé Alphand, Secretary-General MAE), 20 April 1970, ADMAE Gén. 2025.

102. Note MAE (Occ.), 6 February 1970, ADMAE Gén. 2723.

103. As Soames put it, Britain had 'every right to be in on the act and the more we can get involved, the more we shall be able to help the economic negotiations along'. Letter to FCO (Thomson), 'European Political Unification', 13 May 1970, FCO 30/566.

104. FRG embassy Paris (Sigismund von Braun) to AA, 20 April 1970, on a conversation with Schumann, PA B130/2667; note MAE (Occ. to Jacques de Beaumarchais, political director), 27 March 1970, ADMAE Gén. 2723.

105. Record of conversation between Schumann and Thomson in Paris on 17 April 1970, CAB 164/467.

106. Record of conversation between Wilson and Frank in London on 3 December 1969, FCO 30/273.

107. Stewart to UK embassy Bonn, 15 April 1970, FCO 30/565; AA (IA1) to FRG embassy London, 15 April 1970, PA B21/748; FRG embassy London (Karl-Günther von Hase) to AA, 16 April 1970, on a conversation with Con O'Neill, PA B130/2667.

108. Letter UK embassy Paris (Soames) to FCO (Thomson), 'European Political Unification', 13 May 1970, FCO 30/566.

109. Note FCO (Waterfield), 'WEU and European political unification', undated, FCO 30/566.

110. See Schumann's statement at a meeting of EC foreign ministers in Brussels (Val Duchesse), 6 March 1970, according to the Belgian record of conversation of 12 March 1970, PA B21/748; record of conversation between Pompidou and Heath (as opposition leader) in Paris on 5 May 1970, AN 5AG2 1014.

111. Note FCO (Martin Morland, EID, to Norman Statham and Adams), 'Political Unification and WEU', 18 May 1970, FCO 30/567. Similarly, Con O'Neill argued that 'there was now no question of the Six wishing to [...] operate an agreement on political union without full British participation'. Record of a 'Meeting of Heads of Mission from certain European Posts 9/10 March, 1970', 10 March 1970, FCO 73/53.

112. Note FCO (Bendall to Con O'Neill), 2 January 1970, FCO 41/712. According to the French archives, the British also proposed to transfer the WEU to Brussels for interim consultations before working out a definite Community mechanism after enlargement. Overview of incoming telegrams by Elysée of 9 January 1970, and Pompidou's respective annotation: 'à exclure.' AN 5AG2 1049.

113. Note AA (IA1), 8 June 1970, on the WEU ministerial meeting of 5 June 1970, PA B21/740.

114. Focke possessed neither the conceptual brilliance of Bahr nor the personal closeness to Brandt that would have been required to achieve a significant impact on West German policies. In an interview (INT643), she pointed out that it had been a spontaneous idea of Brandt and Horst Ehmke, the new head of the chancellery, to create this post in the chancellery for representational purposes.

115. Baring (1982), 269–71 and 351.

116. Brandt also encountered criticism from Ralf Dahrendorf and Focke, the two parliamentary state secretaries, who argued that the conceptual basis of his foreign policy was too narrowly focused on Bahr's planning papers and on *Deutschlandpolitik*. Notes AA (Dahrendorf) to BKA (Bahr), 16 February 1970, AdsD EB 247/2; and BKA (Focke to Brandt), 10 March 1970, AdsD KF 191.

117. Bahr (1996), Chs 4–7.

118. On Bahr's thinking concerning a European security system, see AAPD 1969, no. 111. On his views about political unification, see his memoires (1996), 174–84.

119. Brandt according to Katharina Focke, 'Erinnerungen an Jean Monnet', in Wilkens (1999a), 23–30, 25 (*ein preussischer Patriot*); and Harpprecht (2000), 236 (*für Europa farbenblind*) and 323 (*er weiss nicht wo Frankreich liegt*).

120. French embassy Bonn (Seydoux) to MAE, 15 January 1970, on a conversation with von Staden, ADMAE Gén. 2723.

121. Note FCO, 3 March 1970, on Brandt's comments at the Foreign Press Association in London, FCO 30/564. Significantly, the FRG now argued that it

had been mistaken to speak of 'political unification' at The Hague and that it pre-ferred to think and talk of 'political cooperation.' Letter UK embassy Bonn (Robin O'Neill) to FCO (Robinson), 'European Political Cooperation', 8 April 1970, on a conversation with Horst Holthoff (AA), FCO 30/565.

122. Record of conversation between Pompidou/Schumann and Moro in Paris on 20 May 1970, ADMAE EM 42.

123. Georges-Henri Soutou, 'L'attitude de Georges Pompidou face à l'Allemagne', in Association Georges Pompidou (1995), 267–313.

124. Pompidou's annotation on a note MAE of 1 June 1970, AN 5AG2 1035.

125. Note MAE (Jean de Lipkowski, minister of state), 6 January 1970, on a conversa-tion with Pompidou, AN 5AG2 1035. Accordingly, Pompidou turned down a secret proposal by Harmel, who was deeply worried about *Ostpolitik*, that France should take an initiative on a European political and defence community. Letter Harmel to Schumann, 23 September 1970, ADMAE Gén. 2723.

126. Note AA (IA1), 'Gesprächsvorschlag zu TO 'EPZ und gesamteuropäische Kooperation'', 30 December 1970, PA B130/2667.

127. The Belgian presidency presented a questionnaire on 4 March 1970 that was meant to structure the discussions of the Six. However, by raising all the touchy points concerning the institutions and substance of European unification, this paper threatened to block work before it could really start. On 25 February 1970, the Italian delegation even put forward a three-stage plan for a federal European Political Organisation that was sure to raise the same unfruitful debates that had dominated the 1950s and 1960s. ADMAE Gén. 2723.

128. Notes BKA (Carl Sanne to Focke), 'Besorgnisse westlicher Verbündeter über einen möglichen Kurswechsel in unserer Europapolitik', 24 March 1970, BA B136/6417; AA (Niels Hansen, head IA1, to Scheel), 'Deutsche Ostpolitik und europäische politische Integration', 3 September 1970, PA B21/740.

129. Note AA (IA1), 6 January 1970, PA B21/740.

130. Note AA (Frank to Scheel), 6 February 1970, PA B1/327.

131. Notes AA (Frank), 9 March 1970, PA B21/748; BKA (Per Fischer to Focke), 13 March 1970, BA B136/6417.

132. Meetings took place on 14 April, 11 May, and 22 June 1970. Note AA (IA1), 16 April 1970, PA B21/748; circular MAE (Claude Arnaud, Chargé des Affaires d'Europe), 14 May 1970; and note MAE (Occ.), 23 June 1970, both in ADMAE Gén. 2723.

133. This was to occur during an intensive two-day ministerial meeting in Viterbo (close to Rome) at the end of May, and immediately before the report was provi-sionally approved in Bonn on 20 July 1970. AAPD 1970, nos. 243 and 326.

134. The Davignon Report of 27 October 1970 is reproduced in *European Foreign Policy*, 75–80.

135. For the French paper 'Avant-projet de schéma de coopération politique', see ADMAE Gén. 2723.

136. Preparatory note AA (IA1 to Scheel), 30 June 1970, for a meeting with Schumann, PA B21/740; note AA (IA1), 'Erörterung des Berichtsentwurfs', 15 July 1970, PA B21/749.

137. Interview with Etienne Davignon.

138. Note FCO to PMO, 'Political Unification – The Davignon Report', 10 November 1970, FCO 30/569.

139. Note AA (IA1), 'EPZ: Stellungnahmen der 4 Beitrittskandidaten', 30 September 1970, BA B136/6418.

140. Ifestos (1987), 142.

141. William Wallace and David Allen, 'Political Cooperation: Procedures as Substitute for Policy', in Wallace, Wallace, and Webb (1977), 227–47, 231; Hanns Jürgen Küsters, 'Die Entstehung und Entwicklung der Europäischen Politischen Zusammenarbeit aus deutscher Perspektive', in Knipping and Schönwald (2004), 131–49, 140.

142. Reinhardt Rummel and Wolfgang Wessels, 'Federal Republic of Germany: new responsibilities, old restraints', in Hill (1983), 40–50.

143. AAPD 1970, no. 571; notes AA (Dirk Oncken, head of planning unit), 'Verbesserung und Ausbau der europäischen Zusammenarbeit', 17 July 1970, PA B20/1968.

144. See Pompidou's annotations to two notes by de Beaumarchais of 15 December 1970 (*Tout cela n'a pas de sens*), and 29 January 1971 (*bouillie pour les chats*), both in AN 5AG2 1035.

145. French embassy Bonn (Commines) to Paris, 19 August 1970, on a conversation with Fischer (BKA), ADMAE RFA 1554.

146. 'Der Staatsbesuch Königin Elisabeths in Paris', *Neue Zürcher Zeitung*, 18 May 1972: 'Pompidou bemüht sich, einen Schlussstrich unter die Zeit des gegenseitigen Misstrauens zu ziehen. Die neue Aera, die jetzt mit der Erweiterung der Europäischen Gemeinschaften angebrochen sei, müsse auf die Basis eines gegenseitigen Vertrauens gestellt werden.'

147. Campbell (1993), xv.

148. Young (1998), 220.

149. Kissinger (2000a), 937.

150. Heath (1998), 472.

151. Heath saw in the decline of British power and in the attitude of the previous Conservative government towards Vietnam two main reasons for London's diminishing stance in Washington. See his remarks in 'President Nixon's Visit', undated, PREM 15/714.

152. FCO paper 'Future Relations with the US', sent to PMO on 5 November 1971, PREM 15/712; note FCO (John Graham, Private Secretary to Douglas-Home, to Greenhill), 'Relations with the U.S.', 9 September 1971, FCO 73/148.

153. Kissinger (2000a), 965.

154. Heath (1998), Chs 4–13.

155. Ibid., 25, 69, 83f.

156. Ibid., 84f.

157. Heath (1970), 73; (1969); (1976).

158. Young (1998), 198.

159. The FCO Planning Staff report 'What sort of Western Europe do we want?', undated [summer 1970], FCO 30/568, depicted the goal of a comprehensive community that by 1980–85 would comprise both a common foreign policy and defence cooperation, including the coordination of military policy, the harmonisation of tactical doctrine, a European Staff College, a European Defence Centre, European Defence Policy Staff, a European Advanced Weapon Agency, and a European Logistics Agency, as well as common procurement programmes. Britain's interests were elaborated in: Working Group on Europe, 'European Political Unification: Note by the Foreign and Commonwealth Office', 26 October 1971, FCO 30/842. The FCO also produced six detailed policy papers on the Community's external relations with different regions of the world. See FCO 49/385–91 and 49/456–61.

160. Two notoriously anti-French (but pro-European) top officials in the FCO in the late 1960s were Robinson and Hancock. In December 1970, Heath ordered a planning paper of December 1970 making the case for a genuine Anglo-French rapprochement to 'be seen, absorbed and acted on by all Whitehall.' Note Douglas-Home to Anthony Barber, Chancellor of the Exchequer, 'Anglo–French Relations', 19 December 1970, PREM 15/1560.

161. Campbell (1993), 296f; Thorpe (1997), 404.

162. The summit idea was first voiced in February 1971. For the preparations, see 'Compte rendu d'un entretien ayant pour but de préparer la visite de M. Heath à Paris', 15 May 1971, AN 5AG2 1014. The two foreign ministries were largely circumvented, Schumann being informed as late as 7 May 1971 of the upcoming summit. Jobert (1974), 190.

163. *Britain's Entry into the European Community: Report on the Negotiations of 1970–1972*, 40.

164. Ibid., 326.

165. Ibid., 355. On the negotiations, see Kitzinger (1973), Chs 3–5.

166. For the records of conversation, see AN 5AG2 1014.

167. Soames' despatch of 9 June 1971, reproduced in *Britain's Entry into the European Community: Report on the Negotiations of 1970–1972*, 402–8, at 407.

168. Note Elysée (Jean-René Bernard, counsellor of the President, to Pompidou), 25 August 1970, AN 5AG2 1035.

169. For the list, dated 24 May 1971, see 'Meetings between the President of the French Republic and the Prime Minister of the United Kingdom held at the Palais de l'Elysée, Paris, on Thursday 20 and Friday 21 May 1971', PREM 15/372.

170. English translation taken from Heath (1998), 372. For the original, see 'Déclaration à l'occasion de la visite de M. Edward Heath à Paris', 21 May 1971, in *Georges Pompidou*, vol. II, 126.

171. Donald Maitland, '1975–1979', in Menon (2004), 11–3, at 11.

172. FRG embassy Paris (Hans Ruete) to AA, 12 November 1971, PA B20/1822; 'Der Staatsbesuch Königin Elisabeths in Paris', *Neue Zürcher Zeitung*, 18 May 1972.

173. Testimony of Michael Palliser in Association Georges Pompidou (1995), 259.

174. Letter Pompidou to Brandt, 26 May 1971, WBA BK 51.

175. Note MAE, 'Comité d'animation de la coopération Franco-britannique', 27 April 1972, AN 5AG2 1014.

176. AAPD 1971, no. 218.

177. Heath (1998), 434 (caption). For the 'Great Debate', see ibid., 380.

178. Uwe Kitzinger, 'Entry and Referendum Revisited', in Broad and Preston (2001), 79–94, at 82.

179. Britain first participated in EPC at the meeting of the Political Committee on 15 February 1972; Ireland, Denmark, and Norway joined on 11 April 1972. Norway dropped out again in September 1972.

180. AAPD 1971, no. 228.

181. 'Entretien radiotélévisé avec M. Ferniot (O.R.T.F.)', 24 June 1971, in *Georges Pompidou*, vol. II, 126–9; Roussel (1994), 448.

182. Gérard Bossuat, 'Le président Georges Pompidou et les tentatives d'Union économique et monétaire', in Association Georges Pompidou (1995), 405–47, 419–21; Wilkens, 'Une tentative prématurée? L'Allemagne, la France et les balbutiements de l'Europe monétaire (1969–1974)', in du Réau and Frank (2002), 77–103; Müller-Roschach (1980), 245–8.

183. 'Allocution prononcée à l'occasion du déjeuner offert en l'honneur de S.E.M. Gaston Eyskens, Premier ministre de Belgique', 2 June 1972, *Georges Pompidou*, vol. II, 97 (*la coopération politique, grande espérance de l'Europe, mais encore petite flamme vacillante qu'on ne peut entretenir et faire grandir qu'au prix de beaucoup de patience, de prudence et d'obstination*).

184. Knipping and Schönwald (2004).

2 Political cooperation: Operative beginnings

1. AAPD 1970, no. 499.

2. 'Aufzeichnung über das Aussenministertreffen der Gemeinschaftsländer vom 19.11.1970 in München über politische Zusammenarbeit gemäss Ziffer 15 des Haager Kommuniqués', undated, PA B150/217.

3. 'Politische Zusammenarbeit gemäss Ziffer 15 Haager Kommuniqué: Meinungsaustausch zu Zehnt am 2.12.70 in Brüssel', undated, PA B150/219.

4. Tickell, 'The Enlarged Community and the European Security Conference', in John (1975), 115–24, 118.

5. Loth (1998), Chs 1–5; *Sicherheitskonferenz in Europa*; Maresca (1985), 5.

6. Memorandum of the conference of Warsaw Pact foreign ministers in Budapest on 21/22 June 1970, reproduced in *Sicherheitskonferenz in Europa*, 520–2.

7. According to Thomas (2001), 43f., the formula 'freer movement of people, ideas, and information' had already been proposed in the autumn of 1969 as a substantive issue for the CSCE by a Belgian delegation at a meeting of the Inter-Parliamentary Union. Other evidence found by the same author suggests that the formula originated in the US Information Agency, with a view to preventing the conference altogether by tabling an issue that Moscow would refuse to discuss.

8. Kenneth Dyson, 'The Conference on Security and Cooperation in Europe: Europe before and after the Helsinki Final Act', in Dyson (1986), 83–112, here 86–93; Altmeppen (1972).

9. 'North Atlantic Council Ministerial Communiqué of 10 December 1971, Brussels' (www.nato.int/docu/).

10. 'North Atlantic Council Ministerial Communiqué of 27 May 1970, Rome' (www.nato.int/docu/).

11. AAPD 1970, no. 291.

12. AAPD 1969, no. 301. On the MBFR priority, see AAPD 1971, no. 311; Bluth (2000), 223.

13. Becker (1992), 135.

14. Note AA (IIA3 to Scheel), 'Europäische Sicherheitskonferenz', 3 April 1970, PA B150/200; Schlotter (1999), 65.

15. For the 'Leitlinien', see AAPD 1972, no. 138. For the comprehensive FRG dossier of 25 April 1972, see AdsD KF 192.

16. DBPO III/I, no. 50.

17. DBPO III/II, no. 3; brief FCO, 'European Security: meeting with Mr. Hillenbrand on 19 November', 19 November 1970, FCO 41/746; DBPO III/II, no. 1.

18. AAPD 1971, no. 120.

19. DBPO III/II, no. 1, note 7.

20. Heath (1998), 475.

21. Note AA (IIA3), 5 November 1970, BA B136/6419.

22. Rey (1991).

23. France sought to underline its privileged relations with the East by issuing bilateral declarations with the Soviets (*Sicherheitskonferenz in Europa*, 246f.) and the Poles ('Déclaration Franco-Polonaise sur l'amitié et la coopération' of 6 October 1972 (www.doc.diplomatie.fr)), identifying possible principles of relations between states and 'contacts among people' as a CSCE goal.

24. In his conversation with Heath at Chequers on 19 March 1972, Pompidou spoke of a 'pénétration pacifique des idées' and the French hope to be able to 'diffuser le virus de la liberté.' AN 5AG2 1014. He also argued that as long as the Eastern Europeans sat at a common conference table with the West, the Soviets would be

more reluctant than in 1968 to apply military means against them. Record of conversation with Rogers in Paris on 8 December 1969, ADMAE EM 40.

25. DBPO III/II, no. 8; note MAE (Ori.), 'Conférence sur la Sécurité et la Coopération en Europe', 27 September 1971, ADMAE Gén. 2922.

26. Circular AA (Walter Gehlhoff, IA1), 11 November 1970, PA B130/2667. For the Belgian view of the CSCE, see Dujardin (2004), 659–82.

27. FRG embassy Paris (von Braun), 2 January 1973, on a conversation with Schumann, PA SvB 172.

28. Note AA (IIA3), 29 October 1970, PA B130/2667; note AA (Klaus Simon, IA, to von Staden), 5 March 1971, PA B21/735; Höhn (1978), 139.

29. Philip Williams, 'Britain, Détente and the Conference on Security and Cooperation in Europe', in Dyson (1986), 221–36, 225.

30. See the annex to DBPO III/I, no. 89.

31. 'La Conférence sur la Sécurité et la Coopération en Europe dans l'optique de la négociation', NATO report C-M(71)69(Révisé), 29 November 1971, ADMAE Gén. 2922.

32. Note AA (IIA3), 'Stand der KSE-Diskussion in NATO, Politischer Konsultationen der 'Sechs' und Bonner Vierergruppe', 17 September 1971, PA B150/238; AAPD 1972, nos. 133 and 399; DBPO III/II, no. 1.

33. DBPO III/II, no. 12; Hanhimäki (2003).

34. Note Elysée (Raimond to Pompidou), 7 December 1971, on a conversation between Kissinger and de Beaumarchais, AN 5AG2 1022; Frank (1981), 287.

35. Maresca (1985), 64.

36. AAPD 1972, no. 379, note 3.

37. Maresca (1985), 89; Michael Clarke, 'Britain and European Political Cooperation in the CSCE', in Dyson (1986), 237–53, 242.

38. Vojtech Mastny, 'Superpower Détente: US–Soviet Relations, 1969–1972', in Geyer and Schaefer (2004), 19–25; Kissinger (2000b), Ch. 7; Maresca (1985), 11 and 34.

39. NATOGERMA (Franz Krapf) to AA, 26 November 1971, PA B150/243; note MAE (CSCE), 16 November 1972, ADMAE Gén. 3791; Stewart (1980), 228.

40. AAPD 1970, no. 586.

41. AAPD 1973, no. 404.

42. The first mission listed in the draft on European political community of 1953 was 'to contribute towards the protection of human rights and fundamental freedoms' in member states. The third aim of the political union according to the first Fouchet Plan was 'to contribute in member states to the defence of human rights, fundamental freedoms and democracy'. The Davignon Report of 1970 maintained that a 'united Europe must be founded upon the common heritage of respect for the liberty and the rights of men, and must assemble democratic states having freely elected parliaments'. Further, in the Declaration on European Identity of 1973, the Nine identified human rights, together with representative

democracy, the rule of law, and social justice, as key principles of their common identity. See *European Foreign Policy: Key Documents*, 33, 48, 76, 93.

43. Coufoudakis (1977).

44. One conclusion of the consultations by the Six was EPC's special suitability to deal with the freer movement issue. Note AA (IIA3, Götz von Groll, to von Staden), 'KSE: 2. Bericht des politischen Komitees an die Minister', 5 November 1971, BA B136/6419. See also Thomas (2001), 28 and 51.

45. See the 'CSCE Dossier on Freer Movement of People' of the NATO secretariat, 30 March 1972, ADMAE Gén. 2923. Interview with John Maresca.

46. DBPO III/II, no. 15, note 10.

47. Note FCO (Rodric Braithwaite, head EID external, to Crispin Tickell, head WOD), 'EEC Political Consultations: Sub-Committee on the European Security Conference (CSCE)', 1 March 1972, FCO 41/1052.

48. Note AA (von Staden), 'Zusammenfassendes Protokoll der Ressortbesprechung vom 25.8.1971 im AA', 26 August 1971, BA B136/6419.

49. On the FRG proposal to take up this issue in EPC because of ongoing controversies in NATO, see note AA (IIA3 to Jürgen Diesel, IIA), 18 January 1972, BA B136/6419.

50. Höhn (1978), 182.

51. 'Allocution prononcée au dîner offert à Versailles en l'honneur de M. L.I. Brejnev, Secrétaire Général du comité central du parti communiste de l'Union Soviétique', 25 October 1971, in *Georges Pompidou*, vol. II, 182; note AA (von Groll), 'KSE; hier: Multiple bilaterale Gespräche', 13 September 1971, PA B150/237; Becker (1992), 145.

52. The FRG chancellery insisted that a conference on security could not leave out the problem of the high troop levels in Central Europe. The French argued that political détente should precede military détente, as troop reductions would only tackle the symptoms of East–West tension. They refused to talk about MBFR in any framework and consequently rejected any link between the two negotiations. A middle path was taken by Britain, which seemed indifferent as to the link between the negotiations, but supported a symbolic reduction of stationary troops to help Nixon mitigate domestic calls for unilateral withdrawals by placing them in a multilateral framework. Müller (1988); note MAE (Pactes) to Debré, 26 June 1972, AN 5AG2 117; DBPO III/III, no. 2.

53. Note MAE (Ori.) 'Thèmes d'études sur la Conférence de sécurité européenne en vue de la coopération politique à Six', 27 January 1971, ADMAE Gén. 2921; note AA (IIA3), 'Europäische Politische Einigung und KSE: Sachstand, französische, belgische und deutsche Haltung', 3 February 1971, BA B136/6419.

54. Circular AA (von Staden), 10 March 1971, BA B136/6419; 'Compte rendu de la réunion du groupe d'étude consacré à la C.S.C.E. (5–6 avril 1971)', undated, ADMAE Gén. 2921. The topics were: 'L'attitude de l'U.R.S.S. et de ses alliés d'un part, des pays neutres ou non alignés d'autre part, à l'égard de la C.E.E.' (FRG);

'les initiatives intéressant la C.E.E., que ces pays sont susceptibles de prendre lors d'une C.S.C.E.' (Italy); 'les initiatives que pourraient prendre, lors d'une C.S.C.E., les Etats membres de la C.E.E. ou d'autres pays occidentaux' (Belgium); 'les questions touchant la préparation, la dur et les suites d'une C.S.C.E.' (France); 'le rôle que pourrait jouer la Commission économique des Nations-Unies pour l'Europe en liaison avec une C.S.C.E.' (Netherlands).

55. 'Rapport du Comité Politique consacré à la Conférence sur la Sécurité et la Coopération en Europe', approved by the Six on 14 May 1971, ADMAE Gén. 2921.

56. Circular AA (von Groll), 21 October 1971, PA B150/240; note MAE (Ori.), 'Rapport du Comité politique sur la C.S.C.E.', 30 October 1971, ADMAE Gén. 2922.

57. Note FCO (Braithwaite to Brimelow), 'EEC Political Consultation: European Security Conference', 10 February 1972, FCO 41/1052.

58. 'Note de la Présidence: Coopération politique – sous-comité sur la C.S.C.E.: Rapport oral du Président au Comité politique des 18 et 19 mai 1972', (CSCE(72)30 P), 18 May 1972, with two documents on 'Questions de procédure lors de la phase de préparation multilatérale et à la conférence: règles sur les commissions' (CSCE(72)8); and 'Suite de la C.S.C.E.' (CSCE(72)14), ADMAE Gén. 2923. For a list of all documents produced by the 'sous-comité' in the first half of 1972, see FCO 30/1253.

59. Circular MAE (Alphand), 30 September 1972, ADMAE Gén. 2924; Höhn (1978), 196.

60. 'Activités récentes du sous-Comité sur la C.S.C.E.', 12 September 1972, ADMAE Gén. 2924; Douglas-Home to UKDEL NATO, 9 October 1972; and 'CSCE (72) 48 UK 2nd Revise [sic], 'Conference on Security and Co-operation in Europe (CSCE): the Work of the Sub-Committee and of the North Atlantic Alliance', 16 October 1972, both in FCO 41/1054. For the French draft mandates, see FCO 30/1253.

61. The reports CP(72)54 (recommendations of the ad hoc group), and CP(72)57 (recommendations of the 'sous-comité') were approved by the Political Committee on 7 November 1972, and the foreign ministers resolved the remaining disagreements during their fifth EPC meeting on 20 November 1972. For the final version of the report of the ad hoc group, RM (72) 8, 23 November 1972, see FCO 30/1254. The final report of the 'sous-comité' could not be found in the archives. For a description, see Brief FCO, 'Meeting of the Foreign Ministers of the Nine 20/21 November in The Hague, Agenda Item 1: Conference on Security and Co-operation in Europe', undated, FCO 41/1055.

62. UK embassy Bonn (Reginald Alfred Hibbert) to Charles D. Wiggin, Assistant Under-Secretary of State, 'German Attitude to the Proposed Conference on Security and Cooperation in Europe', 5 April 1972, FCO 41/1070.

63. UK embassy Luxembourg (James N. Allan) to FCO, 29 February 1972, FCO 41/1052.

64. UKDEL NATO (Edward Peck) to FCO, 17 November 1972, FCO 41/1055.

65. REPAN-Bruxelles (François de Rose) to MAE, 17 November 1972, ADMAE Gén. 2925.

66. Circular AA (Gerhard Dohms, Informationsreferat Ausland), 23 November 1972, BA B136/6417.

67. See the report CSCE 72(57), as well as a French working document, 'Question de procedure concernant le deroulement de la conférence sur la sécurité et la coopération en Europe', distributed on 21 October 1971 in NATO, ADMAE Gén. 2922.

68. Interviews by the author with Jacques Andréani and Luigi Vittorio Ferraris. For the US model, see the US paper 'Procedures' of 6 April 1971, as enclosed in a note of Lawrence S. Eagleburger, US Mission to NATO, to Hans Jörg Kastl, NATO Assistant Secretary General and head of Division of Political Affairs, and the commentary by de Rose, 7 April 1971, ADMAE Gén. 2921. The FRG and Italy had initially supported the US concept, but had come to embrace a unitary MPT along the French concept, as outlined in the paper 'Préparation de la Conférence sur la Sécurité et la Coopération en Europe', 30 December 1971, ADMAE Gén. 2921.

69. This idea again first appeared in French documents. See note MAE (Ori.), 'C.S.C.E.: Eléments pour la définition d'une position française lors de sa préparation multilatérale', 12 January 1972, ADMAE Gén. 2923.

70. Record of the Franco-German meeting of political directors on 9 October 1972, 25 October 1972, ADMAE Gén. 2924.

71. Circular MAE (François Puaux, Political Director), 21 November 1972, ADMAE Gén. 2925.

72. Note FCO (Tickell to Brimelow), 'Political Directors, Luxembourg, 18/19 May', 17 May 1972, FCO 41/1052.

73. 'Conversations multilatérales préparatoires sur le volet culturel et humain de la C.S.C.E.' (Sous-Comité sur la CSCE, Délégation française, CSCE [72]F) of 23 October 1972, FCO 28/1682. For the US position, see their paper on the 'Freer Movement of People, Ideas and Information', presented to NATO on 8 April 1971, and enclosed in a note of Eagleburger to Kastl on the same day, ADMAE Gén. 2921.

74. 'Développement des contacts entre les hommes, accroissement des échanges culturels et en matière d'enseignement et élargissement de la diffusion de l'information.' Consensus on a non-provocative approach had only been achieved after much haggling with the Dutch and the Italians. Note MAE (CSCE), 9 November 1972, ADMAE Gén. 3791.

75. Note AA (von Staden to Scheel), 'Allianz- und europapolitische Ausführungen Schumanns am 7.12.1972 im NATO-Ministerrat', 12 December 1972, PA B24/667.

76. DBPO III/II, no. 6.

77. REPAN-Bruxelles (de Rose) to MAE, 29 April 1971, on US concerns; and to MAE, 27 May 1971, on Turkish criticism, both in ADMAE Gén. 2921; FRG embassy London (von Hase) to AA, 6 April 1972, on complaints by NATO Secretary-General Luns in London concerning EPC faits accomplis, BA B136/6419; DBPO III/II, no. 15; UKDEL NATO (Peck) to FCO, 17 November 1972, FCO 41/1055.

78. Provisional rules for EPC–NATO relations, worked out by the end of 1972, foresaw that the NATO secretary-general and the permanent representatives of the non-EC countries would be informed on a case-by-case basis by the permanent representative of the EPC presidency. There was a special agreement on providing information to Turkey. See 'Information de la Turquie', 26 May and 20 November 1972, ADMAE Gén. 3786.

79. AAPD 1972, no. 378.

80. Douglas-Home to UKDEL NATO, 16 November 1972, FCO 41/1055; note FCO (Michael D. Butler, head EID, to Tickell), 'CSCE Discussions in Davignon', 8 November 1972, FCO 41/1055; note French embassy The Hague (Senard) to MAE, 17 November 1972, ADMAE Gén. 2925.

81. The following is based on Kissinger (2000a), Ch. 10, and (2000b), Ch. 6; Bickerton and Klausner (2005), Chs 1–6.

82. For Resolution 242, see (www.un.org/Docs/sc/unsc_resolutions.html).

83. Kissinger (2000a), 1278.

84. Ibid., 107, 352–4; Jobert (1974), 259.

85. Kissinger (2000a), 375, 558f., 1280.

86. Dosenrode and Stubkjær (2002), 35–51.

87. Note MAE (*Ori.*), 27 November 1970, ADMAE RFA 1634.

88. Notes Elysée (Georges Gaucher, councellor, to Pompidou), 'Problèmes d'actualité au Moyen-Orient', 26 June 1969; MAE (de Lipkowski to Schumann), 'Notre politique au Moyen-Orient', 27 April 1970, both in AN 5AG2 1034. On de Gaulle's proposal to set up Four-Power talks, see the record of his conversation with Nixon on 28 February 1969, AN 582AP 33.

89. Brosio (1974), 116.

90. See Pompidou's annotation to a note by Raimond of 18 December 1970 on Four-Power talks, AN 5AG2 1034.

91. Note MAE (Occ.), 25 September 1970, ADMAE Gén. 2723.

92. Note French embassy Cairo to MAE, 'D'une initiative française possible dans la question palestinienne', 10 July 1970, AN 5AG2 1034; record of conversation between Schumann and Soames in Paris on 7 September 1970, ADMAE EM 44.

93. Record of the 'Anglo–French Talks on the Middle East, London 10 February 1972', FCO 30/1256.

94. Vaïsse (1998), 615–40.

95. Berstein and Rioux (2000), 23. Schumann, 'La politique étrangère', in Messmer

(1990), 267–82, claims that he lost the election in 1973 because of this decision by Pompidou, which he had opposed.

96. Note Elysée (Raimond to Pompidou), 'Etude du projet français d'un réglement du conflit israélo–arabe', 16 September 1969, AN 5AG2 1034.

97. AAPD 1970, no. 566; note AA (IB4, Helmut Redies), 15 February 1971 [erroneously dated 1970], PA B21/753.

98. Records of Franco-German meetings of the political directors in Paris, 7 January and 3 October 1969, PA B21/674 and B20/1437.

99. AAPD 1972, no. 128.

100. Friedemann Büttner and Peter Hünseler, 'Die politischen Beziehungen zwischen der Bundesrepublik Deutschland und den arabischen Staaten', in Kaiser and Steinbach (1981), 11–152, 112–28.

101. Record of a Franco-German meeting of the political directors in Paris on 3 October 1969, PA B20/1437.

102. Neustadt (1983), 63.

103. Note FCO (Philip Adams, Arabian Department, to EID), 24 November 1970, FCO 17/1168.

104. Geoffrey Edwards, 'Britain', in Allen and Pijpers (1984), 47–59.

105. Douglas-Home to UK embassy Brussels, 26 November 1970, FCO 17/1168.

106. Note CO, 'President Nixon's Visit', 30 September 1970, PREM 15/714.

107. Note FCO (Greenhill to Douglas-Home), 'Summary of Current Problems in H.M.G's Foreign Policy', June 1970, PREM 15/64. Greenhill further pointed out the 'conflict between the need to protect our material interests […] and the pressure of public and Parliamentary opinion in favour of Israel'.

108. Note FCO (Adams to Brimelow), 'Middle East: European Political Consultation', 17 December 1970, FCO 17/1168. The Harrogate speech is reproduced in Douglas-Home (1976), 296–301.

109. Record of conversation between Schumann and Soames in Paris on 1 December 1970, ADMAE GB, 269.

110. Circular MAE (Alphand), 5 May 1971, AN 5AG2 1035.

111. Note AA (Redies to Frank), 10 December 1970, PA B130/2667.

112. AAPD 1971, no. 143. Other important points concerned the notion of demilitarised zones and buffer areas with UN observers and peacekeepers; a system of international guarantees for the peace agreement; the administrative internationalisation of Jerusalem (a problem not touched on in Resolution 242); and the freedom of choice of refugees to return to Palestine or receive compensation.

113. Note Elysée (Raimond to Pompidou), 12 May 1971, AN 5AG2 1035; AAPD 1971, no. 174.

114. See the record of the ministerial meeting, ADMAE EM 48 and PA B150/229.

115. Note MAE (Occ.), 9 June 1971, AN 5AG2 1011.

116. Note AA (von Staden to IB4), 21 December 1970, on a conversation with the

Israeli ambassador to Bonn, Eliashiv Ben-Horin, PA B130/2667; AAPD 1971, nos. 43 and 153.

117. For the letter, dated 7 May 1971, see PA B150/229.

118. Italy declared the contents of the report non-binding, with Moro suggesting in a letter to Schumann that political cooperation should be reduced again to a simple exchange of views. Note AA (IA1), 'Vorschau PK am Rande Lissaboner NATO-Konferenz 4.6.71', 1 June 1971, PA B21/744. On Belgium, see AAPD 1971, no. 238.

119. Record of conversation between Scheel and Schumann in Bonn on 5 July 1971, ADMAE EM 49.

120. Frank (1981), 253–5.

121. AAPD 1971, no. 237; note AA (von Staden), 'Gespräch des Herrn Bundesministers mit Ministerpräsident Frau Meir am 8.7.1971', 13 July 1971, PA B150/233.

122. 'Gespräche des Herrn Bundesministers mit Aussenminister Abba Eban am 7. und 8. Juli', 12 July 1971, PA B150/233. After Scheel's visit, the puzzled West German ambassador to Tel Aviv, Jesco von Puttkamer, sent a list with some of Scheel's key comments in Israel to Bonn and enquired about the official West German policy, only to be told that these were complex and difficult matters. See von Puttkamer to AA (von Staden), 28 July 1971, and the latter's reply, 5 August 1971, PA B150/234.

123. AAPD 1971, no. 241, note 2.

124. Schumann to Pompidou, 12 July 1971, AN 5AG2 1035; Frank to FRG embassy Paris (Ruete), 13 July 1971, PA B150/233; note AA (von Staden to Scheel), 'EG-Nahost-Konsultationen; hier: Wunsch der französischen Regierung nach Veröffentlichung des gemeinsamen Berichts der Politischen Direktoren über die Lage im Nahen Osten', 19 July 1971, PA B150/233.

125. 'Wortlaut des 'Nahost-Papiers' der sechs EWG-Mitgliedstaaten', *Die Welt*, reproduced in Neustadt (1983), 536f.

126. Letter Scheel to Mohammed Abdel Khalek al-Hassouna, General Secretary of the Arab League, 23 August 1971, PA 150/236. On the resumption of diplomatic relations with individual Arab countries, see AAPD 1973, no. 184, note 8.

127. Note Elysée (Raimond to Pompidou), 4 November 1971, AN 5AG2 1009.

128. Circular MAE (Alphand), 14 April 1972, ADMAE Gén. 3795. For the papers 'Garanties de l'accord de paix' and 'Engagements de paix', as well as the West German *Aide Mémoire* of 29 March 1972, see FCO 30/2511.

129. Record of 'Anglo–French Talks on the Middle East, London 10 February 1972', FCO 30/1256.

130. Douglas-Home to UK embassy The Hague, 31 July 1972, FCO 30/1256; FRG embassy Cairo to AA, 31 August 1972, PA B21/753.

131. 'Kampf ums Mittelmeer', *Die Zeit*, 20 October 1972; Udo Steinbach, 'Die

europäische Gemeinschaft und die arabischen Staaten', in Kaiser and Steinbach (1981), 185–204, 185f.

132. Note Elysée (Raimond to Pompidou), 'Note pour Monsieur le Président de la République', 19 September 1972, AN 5AG2 1025. On Schumann's soundings with the Egyptians, see his telegram 493/505 to French embassy Cairo, 28 July 1972, AN 5AG2 1034, as well as the document collection in AN 5AG2 1025.

133. The incident also marked the beginning of European cooperation in internal security and judicial affairs. See note FCO, 'Meeting of the Political Directors of the Ten: The Hague 21 September: Terrorism – Counter Measures', 21 September 1972, FCO 30/1257.

134. AAPD 1972, no. 318.

135. AAPD 1972, no. 352; Ilan Greilsammer and Joseph Weiler, 'European Political Cooperation and the Palestinian-Israeli conflict', in Allen and Pijpers (1984), 121–60, 134.

136. See the document collection in AN 5AG2 1035.

137. Circular MAE (Puaux), 23 November 1972, ADMAE Gén. 3791.

138. FRG representation at UN New York (Gehlhoff) to AA, 8 December 1972, PA B21/753.

139. On Pompidou's summit initiative, see his communiqué and press conference of 18 August and 23 September 1971, both reproduced at (www.ena.lu) (Centre Virtuel de la Connaissance sur l'Europe, European Navigator). On the chronology of initiatives calling for another summit, see note AA (IA1), 'Vorgeschichte und Vorstellungen der Regierungen sowie der Kommission', 29 October 1971, PA B21/745. The final agenda comprised EMU, EC external relations and world responsibilities, institutional strengthening, and political progress. Record of the EC foreign ministers' meeting on 28 February 1972 by the Luxembourg presidency, 10 March 1972, PA B20/1970.

140. There were three ministerial preparatory meetings on external relations (20 March 1972), EMU (24 April 1972), and institutions and political progress (26 May 1972). For the respective records, see PREM 15/890f. Subsequently, an ad hoc group was in charge of preparing the summit, which resulted in a common report: 'Preparation of the Conference of Heads of State or of Government: Report by the Ministers of Foreign Affairs, final version', 12 October 1972, PREM 15/894, ADMAE Gén. 3787, PA B21/745.

141. PMO (Robert Armstrong, principal private secretary) to Heath (in Munich), 5 September 1972, PREM 15/893; letter Pompidou to Brandt, 15 September 1972, WBA BK 51

142. Brandt (1978), 360.

143. For the French and British records of the summit, see AN 5AG2 257 and PREM 15/895.

144. For the communiqué, see *Bulletin of the European Communities* no. 10 (1972): 14–26.

145. For national verdicts on the summit, see AAPD 1972, no. 344; Brandt (1978), 358f.; circular MAE (Alphand), 24 October 1972, and note MAE (Occ.), 30 October 1972, both in ADMAE Gén. 3787; FRG embassy London (von Hase) to AA, 23 October 1972, on British press reactions, PA B20/1974.

146. Jean-René Bernard, 'Pragmatisme et ambition dans l'action européenne du président Pompidou', in Association Georges Pompidou (1995), 45–54, 49. Some 40 per cent of the French abstained from voting. Of those participating, 11 per cent cast an empty vote and 60 per cent voted 'yes'.

147. On Britain and the RDF, see note CO (Deputy Cabinet Secretary John Hunt) to PMO (Armstrong), 'European Summit Meeting', 10 May 1972, PREM 15/890.

148. For Pompidou's initiative, see *Europäische Politische Einigung*, vol. II, 150–2; record of the Conseil restreint of 9 December 1970, and Bernard's brief to Pompidou, 7 December 1970, both in AN 5AG2 1043.

149. AAPD 1972, no. 148.

150. Note AA (IA4), 1 September 1972, on a conversation between Scheel and Italian Foreign Minister Giuseppe Medici in Munich on 30 August 1972, PA B21/750.

151. AAPD 1972, no. 109; note AA (von Staden to Frank), 'Künftige Bezeichnung des westeuropäischen Zusammenschlusses', 27 January 1972, PA B21/743.

152. Letter Pompidou to Brandt, 16 October 1972, with French draft communiqué, WBA BK 51; Jobert (1976), 164.

153. For the FRG memorandum of 25 November 1971, see PA B20/1892.

154. Note MAE (Occ.), 'Réflexions sur le Secrétariat de la Coopération Politique', 6 March 1972, ADMAE Gén. 3786; record of conversation between Pompidou and Barzel in Paris on 22 March 1972, AN 5AG2 1011.

155. For the debate, see note 149 in this chapter.

156. Debré argued in a note to Pompidou (15 May 1972, AN 5AG2 89) that a secretariat in Brussels would be the 'amputation of France'.

157. DELFRA Bruxelles (Etienne Georges Burin des Roziers) to MAE, 30 March 1972, with Pompidou's annotations, AN 5AG2 1035; AAPD 1972, no. 196. Already during the secret preparations for the Anglo-French summit in spring 1971, the French delegation had suggested that the British should propose a political secretariat to be seated in Paris. 'Preparatory Discussions about the Meeting between the Prime Minister and the French President in Paris on 20 and 21 May 1971', 15 May 1971, PREM 15/372.

158. Note AA (IA1), 10 May 1972, PA B21/742.

159. Note AA (von Staden to Scheel), 12 June 1972, PA B21/745; minutes of a Cabinet meeting, 'Preparations for the European Summit', 24 May 1972, CAB 130/586; AAPD 1972, no. 196.

160. AAPD 1972, no. 150.

161. Letter Brandt to Heath, 7 July 1972, on talks with Pompidou, WBA BK 52.

162. AAPD, no. 240; note Schumann to Pompidou, 23 August 1972, AN 5AG2 1011; 'Record of a Telephone Conversation Between the Prime Minister and Herr

Brandt at 6.00 PM on Wednesday, 23 August, 1972', PREM 15/893; record of conversation between Heath and Schumann at Chequers on 24 August 1972, PREM 15/893; note Schumann to Pompidou, 24 August 1972, AN 5AG2 1014.

163. Note AA (IA1), 9 September 1972, PA B21/750; note Elysée (Bernard and Raimond to Pompidou), 'Note pour Monsieur le Président de la République', 2 October 1972, AN 86AJ 142.

164. UK embassy Paris (Soames) to FCO, 'Some Thoughts on the Paris Conference – 19–20 October', 27 October 1972, FCO 30/1262.

165. Brandt discussed the issue with many of his Western interlocutors between 1970 and 1972.

166. Brandt (1978), 404. The chancellery favoured a much more ambitious design for an EC–US dialogue than the Auswärtige Amt. Note BKA (II/1 and IV/1) to AA (IA1), 'Ausgestaltung eines Dialogs EG–USA', 21 September 1972, and reactions of IA1 and von Staden of 28 and 29 September 1972, all in PA B21/747.

167. Record of conversation between Pompidou and Nixon on the Azores on 13 December 1971, AN 5AG2 102; note AA (IA1) to BKA (Fischer), 'Bleiben wir mit den Füssen auf der Erde', 9 February 1972, BA B136/6422.

168. Note BKA (Fischer) to AA (Büro Staatssekretäre), 16 October 1972, with UK document 'US/EEC Institutional Link', PA B20/1973.

169. Brandt (1978), 52.

170. Duchêne (1972), 191.

171. 'Draft Brief for a meeting with Dr Kissinger', 16 April 1971, CAB 130/493. See also 'European Defence Cooperation: Paper by the Foreign and Commonwealth Office for Discussion with the Prime Minister and Defence Secretary', 2 November 1970, FCO 41/759.

172. 'Defence and Overseas Policy Committee DOP(71): 26th Meeting', 15 December 1971, CAB 148/115.

173. 'European Defence Co-Operation: Report by the Chairman of the Official Working Party', 2 March 1971; and 'European Defence Co-Operation: Report to Ministers by the Chairman of the Official Working Party', 13 September 1971, both in CAB 130/517; 'Report by the Joint Study Group on European Defence Cooperation', October 1971, CAB 148/117; 'GEN 29(72) 3: Cabinet: Interdepartmental Study on European Defence Co-Operation: Report to Ministers', 4 August 1972, FCO 41/1080.

174. Minutes of a Cabinet meeting with Heath, Douglas-Home, and Carrington on 'Anglo–French Defence Collaboration', 18 November 1970, CAB 130/490; minutes of the meetings of the Working Party in Cabinet Office on 24 November 1970, 6 January, and 5 February 1971, as well as two interim reports, undated and 10 February 1972, all in CAB 130/493. The MOD was generally more sceptical about nuclear cooperation than Heath and the FCO.

175. Heath (1970), 73 and 4; Campbell (1993), 341.

176. Minutes of a Cabinet meeting with Heath, Douglas-Home, and Carrington on Anglo-French Defence Collaboration, 5 March 1971, CAB 130/506; 'Summary of a Discussion Held at the Residence of Sir E Peck, at Hoeilaart on the Evening of 23 February 1972', FCO 41/1078.

177. Record of conversation between Brandt and Pompidou in Bonn on 5 July 1971, AN 5AG2 1011; AAPD 1971, no. 429.

178. UK embassy Bonn (Robin O'Neill) to FCO (Braithwaite), 'European Defence Cooperation', 16 February 1972, on a conversation with Franz Pfeffer, head of AA NATO department (IA7), FCO 41/1078.

179. Notes AA (Wolfgang Behrends, IIA7), 'Europäische politische Zusammenarbeit gem. Ziffer 15 des Haager Kommuniqué; hier: Vorbereitung der ersten Konsultationen der Aussenminister', 22 October 1970, PA B150/215; (IA7 to Simon), 'Europäische Zusammenarbeit im Verteidigungsbereich', 9 July 1971, PA B150/233; AAPD 1971, no. 451.

180. FRG embassy London (von Hase) to AA, 17 July 1970, on talks between Scheel and Douglas-Home, PA B150/207; note Barzel, 'Zur Verteidigung Westeuropas', 25 May 1972, ACDP 08–010–143/2; AAPD 1971, no. 121.

181. Record of conversation between Carrington and Schmidt in Brussels on 12 November 1971, FCO 41/893; Schmidt to Brandt, 12 July 1972, HSA 10624; Smart (1971), 44.

182. Two notes Debré to Pompidou, 'Note à l'attention du président de la République' and 'Relations Franco-britannique dans le domaine militaire', 11 February 1972, AN 5AG2 1014; record of conversation between Carrington and Debré on 20 November 1970, PREM 15/299; note Admiral Hill-Norton, UK Chief of Defence Staff, 'Conversation with M. Debré', 12 December 1972, 14 December 1972, PREM 15/1357.

183. Pierre Mélandri, 'La France et l'alliance atlantique sous Georges Pompidou et Valéry Giscard d'Estaing', in Vaïsse, Mélandri, and Bozo (1999), 519–58, 531.

184. Record of conversation between Pompidou and Soames in Paris on 20 November 1970, AN 5AG2 1014, and UK embassy Paris (Soames) to FCO on the same day, PREM 15/1560.

185. When Pompidou came into office, only an air-delivered system using Mirages was operational, with the land-based component and a first submarine boat being about to be introduced. 'Brief for the Prime Minister', including annex MOD: 'The scope of possible co-operation between British and French strategic nuclear forces', 10 March 1972, CAB 130/49; note MOD to PMO (Bridges), with MO 18/5 annex 'Anglo/French Nuclear Collaboration', 21 November 1972, PREM 15/1357.

186. See the 'top secret' part of the record of the second conversation between Heath and Pompidou at Chequers on 19 March 1972, PREM 15/904, and the 'partie confidentielle' in the French record, AN 5AG2 1014.

187. Soames to Carrington, 18 July 1972, with a note on talks between the UK defence attaché and the French Sous Chef, Plans, Etats-Major des Armées, Général Saint-Cricq, in Paris, PREM 15/1357.

188. Heath (1998), 4; note CO (Cabinet Secretary Burke Trend) to Heath, 'Anglo–French Nuclear Co-operation', 28 January 1972, on talks between Nixon and Heath on Bermuda in December 1971, PREM 15/787.

189. Minutes of the 14th and 15th meeting of the Working Party in Cabinet Office, 24 August and 25 August 1971, CAB 130/493; note CO (Trend) to Heath, 'Discussions with Dr. Kissinger at Washington', 31 July 1972, PREM 15/1362.

190. Note Elysée (Raimond to Pompidou), 28 June 1971, AN 5AG2 1050; record of conversation between Pompidou and Kissinger in Paris on 15 September 1972, AN 5AG2 1022; Debré (1994), 107f.

191. UK embassy Paris (Christopher Ewart-Biggs) to FCO (Clive Martin Rose, Assistant Under-Secretary), 'Franco/American Defence Discussions', 19 April 1972, PREM 15/787.

192. Memorandum MOD, 'Strategic Nuclear Options', 2 November 1972; and note CO, 'Extract from Note of a Meeting of Ministers 14.11.72', 15 November 1972, both in PREM 15/1359.

193. Note CO (Trend) to Heath, 'European Defence and British Defence Policy', 10 November 1972; and 'Defence Policy: Note of a Meeting of Ministers held at 10 Downing Street on Wednesday 14 November at 10.30 am', both in PREM 15/789.

194. Presse- und Informationsamt der Bundesregierung/Ostinformationen, 'EWG-Militarismus', 3 March 1972, translating a feature by Radio Moscow, BA B136/6422.

195. Note MAE (Jean Jurgensen, Directeur-adjoint des Affaires politiques) to Debré, 15 October 1970, ADMAE RFA 1457; note PMO (Bridges to Heath), 'Politico Military Talks with France', 11 February 1972, PREM 15/903.

196. 'Report by the Joint Study Group on European Defence Cooperation', October 1971, Annex 13, 'The Eurogroup', CAB 148/117; note Debré to Pompidou, 22 June 1971, AN 5AG2 1009; Cromwell (1992), Ch. 3; Kissinger (2000a), 401f.

197. Nuttall (1992), 318, has made the interesting point that this had to do with the foreign ministries' loss of influence in formulating national EC policies.

198. A system of classification that was analogous to the one applied in NATO was introduced in EPC. 'Caractère confidentiel des travaux: Nomenclature et classification des documents', adopted by EPC foreign ministers on 5 November 1971, ADMAE Gén. 3786.

199. William Wallace and David Allen, 'Political Cooperation: Procedures as Substitute for Policy', in Wallace, Wallace, and Webb (1977), 227–47, 238.

200. See note 164 in this chapter.

Part II: External Challenges

1. Dettke (1976), 91; Morgan (1973), 1.
2. 'Regierungserklärung vor dem Deutschen Bundestag am 18. Januar 1973', *Bundeskanzler Brandt*, vol. II, 519–37.
3. Merseburger (2002), 667; Brandt (1994), 305–10.
4. Debré (1994), 146.
5. On these meetings, see Weed (1981), annex II.
6. Heath (1998), 365.
7. Letter Focke to Brandt, 9 April 1973, HSA 9121.
8. Weed (1981), 235.

3 Facing the Soviet Union

1. Renk (1996), 54.
2. Uwe Nerlich, 'Der Wandel des 'europäischen Systems' und die Idee einer gesamt-europäischen Konferenz', in Volle and Wagner (1976), 23–32.
3. Kissinger (2000b), 114.
4. For the text of the agreement, see (www.state.gov/t/ac/trt/5186.htm).
5. Kissinger (2000b), 274–86.
6. Notes CO (Trend) to Heath, 'Discussions with Dr. Kissinger at Washington', 31 July 1972; and 'Anglo–American nuclear relations', 11 August 1972, PREM 15/1362; note CO (Trend) to Heath, 'Personal Record of a Discussion in the British Embassy, Washington DC, on 19th April, 1973', 24 April 1973, PREM 15/1359.
7. Both learnt about the Soviet request in September 1972 and, subsequently, received occasional updates on the negotiations. See Brandt (1978), 416; back-channel notes Kissinger to Bahr, 15 May and 15 June 1973, AdsD EB 439; French embassy Washington (Kosciusko-Morizet) to MAE, 3 May 1973, AN 5AG2 1021.
8. Czempiel (1973), 781–90, 786. For French and West German analyses of the agreement, see French embassy Washington (Kosciusko-Morizet) to Jobert, 4 May 1973; and notes Elysée (Raimond to Pompidou), 10 and 18 May 1973, AN 5AG2 1021; AAPD 1973, no. 204.
9. Letter Leber to Brandt, 25 July 1973, AdsD EB 332; record of a meeting of the 'Deutsch–französische Studiengruppe' in Paris on 21 September 1973, 24 September 1973, PA B150/289; record of conversation between Pompidou and Kissinger in Paris on 18 May 1973, AN 5AG2 1022; letters Nixon to Pompidou, 20 and 24 June 1973, AN 5AG2 1021.
10. Record of conversation between Jobert and Brezhnev in Oreanda on 27 July 1973, AN 5AG2 1019; Jobert (1974), 232; Soutou (2004), 99.

11. Record of conversation between Pompidou and Brezhnev in Paris on 26 June 1973, AN 5AG2 1019.

12. Jobert (1974), 246f: 'résolution à ne jamais consentir l'abandon de soi-même aux fausses sécurités [...]. La sécurité se mérite, on ne la gagne pas à la tombola.'

13. DBPO III/III, no. 10.

14. AAPD 1973, no. 207; note MAE (Pactes), 7 May 1973, ADMAE RFA 3019.

15. AAPD 1973, no. 397.

16. AAPD 1972, no. 189.

17. On the intra-FRG debate, see AAPD 1973, nos. 10, 81, 95, 144, 160, 171, and 273.

18. Note Elysée (Raimond to Pompidou), 8 November 1973, AN 5AG2 1015.

19. DBPO III/III, no. 2.

20. DBPO III/III, no. 9.

21. MAE (Pactes), 'Note de Synthèse', 1 June 1973, ADMAE RFA 3005.

22. Record of fourth conversation between Pompidou and Brezhnev in Paris on 29 October 1971, AN 5AG2 1018.

23. AAPD 1971, no. 401.

24. French embassy Bonn (Sauvagnargues) to MAE, 20 September 1973, on a conversation with Bahr, ADMAE RFA 2997; letter Leber to Brandt, 20 February 1973, on a conversation between Luns and Bahr in Brussels, WBA BK 12. Bahr in a letter to Brandt (15 April 1973, AdsD EB 439) argued that a modest result of MBFR would be a reduction of 60 per cent in 10 years.

25. Note Elysée (Raimond to Pompidou), 23 November 1973, AN 5AG2 1012.

26. Note MAE (Cent.), 1 June 1973, on Brezhnev's visit to Bonn, ADMAE RFA 3005, Jobert (1976), 141. For a contemporary attack on Bahr in 1973, see Hahn (1973).

27. Note FCO (Cynlais James, head WED, to Wiggin and Brimelow), 'Ostpolitik and Westpolitik', 2 July 1973, FCO 33/2160.

28. Already in February 1971, Heath expressed his concern in Parliament that 'one of the more exposed members of the Alliance lapse into neutrality'. FRG embassy London (von Hase) to AA, 1 March 1971, PA B31/371. Another British analysis of the FRG's foreign policy concluded that '[t]he continued division of Germany, despite its potential for friction, is the one fact of international life in which every nation in Europe except the two Germanies can happily acquiesce, reluctant as we or others may be to say so publicly'. Note FCO to PMO (Peter Moon, Private Secretary), 'Herr Brandt's Foreign Policies', 25 November 1971, PREM 15/1575.

29. London limited its reaction to watching developments carefully and paying particular attention to the actions of Bahr. See the despatch of UK embassy Bonn (Nicholas Henderson), 5 October 1973, with a 21-page portray of Bahr, FCO 33/2161. Conversely, Pompidou during a Franco-German summit on 21 June 1973 put the issue on the table: 'Comment voyez-vous, à la lumière de ce qui se

passe, l'avenir de l'Allemagne?', he asked Brandt, not without adding that this was the most fundamental question for France and that his country would not want either an armed or a neutralised Germany between the two blocs. Brandt in his reply assured Pompidou of the FRG's commitment to Western Europe even in case of seductions by the Soviet Union. AN 5AG2 106.

30. Record of first conversation between Pompidou and Heath in Paris on 21 May 1973, 'Partie de l'entretien très secrète', AN 5AG2 1015. In a conversation on 15 October 1973 with Helmut Kohl, the new opposition leader in the FRG, Pompidou indicated that he did not fear so much a top-down decision of the FRG government to move East than a bottom-up 'espèce de flambée' and 'poussée profonde' (AN 5AG2 1012).

31. Record of second conversation between Heath and Pompidou at Chequers on 16 November 1973, AN 5AG2 1015.

32. AAPD 1971, no. 408; UK embassy Bonn (Henderson), 'Mr Brezhnev's Visit to Bonn', 18 June 1973, on Frank's fears regarding uncontrollable dynamics of *Ostpolitik*, and on a new West German urge to accelerate European unification, FCO 33/2160.

33. See, for example, von Staden, 'Fortschritte im politischen Bereich', 16 April 1972, PA B21/750.

34. On Coudenhove's activities and arguments concerning the CSCE and European unification, see his numerous letters to Brandt, BA B136/6409. See also his letter to Pompidou of 4 June 1971, AN 5AG2 1050.

35. Record of a meeting of the 'Staatssekretärausschuss für Europafragen', 20 April 1972, PA B20/1978.

36. Pompidou's argument as recorded in the circular AA (Dohms), 24 January 1973, on the Franco-German summit of 22/23 January 1973, PA B1/499.

37. Thomas (2001), Chs 5–7.

38. DBPO III/II, no. 37; Renk (1996), 53.

39. AAPD 1972, no. 406.

40. FRG delegation MPT, report no. 125, 6 April 1973, PA ZA 100002.

41. For the 'Final Recommendations of the Helsinki Consultations', subsequently referred to as 'Blue Book', see (www.osce.org/documents).

42. Ibid.

43. AAPD 1973, no. 221.

44. Interview with John Maresca.

45. DBPO III/II, no. 94.

46. DBPO III/II, no. 81.

47. Höhn (1978), 251; interview with Helmut Liedermann.

48. Maresca (1985), 138.

49. For the 'Helsinki Final Act', subsequently referred to as 'Final Act', see (www.osce.org/documents).

50. Maresca (1985), 18–21.

51. Hanspeter Neuhold, 'Die neutralen Staaten Europas und die Konferenz über Sicherheit und Zusammenarbeit in Europa', in Volle and Wagner (1976), 55–61; Renk (1996), 127–35; interview with Helmut Liedermann.

52. Record of conversation between Scheel and Schumann in Paris on 22 January 1973, ADMAE Gén. 3784; AAPD 1973, no. 138.

53. DBPO III/II, no. 37. For a West German verdict of the MPT, see FRG delegation MPT, report no. 212, 8 June 1973, PA ZA 100002.

54. Circular MAE (Alphand), 7 December 1972, ADMAE Gén. 2925; record of 'Sitzung der IMAG/KSZE am 9. Januar 1973 im Auswärtigen Amt', 17 January 1973, PA B150/272.

55. Belgium presented the proposals for the agenda and for the economic realm, Italy for the security realm (principles and CBMs), and Denmark for the human realm, that is, the later basket III. While Britain initially wanted one member to present the whole package and France made the case for tabling the proposals only for one realm at the time, it was finally agreed to come up with three separate, but simultaneous presentations. Notes MAE (CSCE), 'Activités récentes du sous-comité sur la CSCE', 9 January 1973, ADMAE RFA 3019; and 12 January 1973, ADMAE Gén. 3795.

56. AAPD 1973, no. 42.

57. FRG delegation MPT, report no. 32, 14 December 1972, PA ZA 100001.

58. Brief FCO 'European Political Cooperation: Ministerial Meeting 16 March 1973, Agenda Item 3: CSCE', 16 March 1973, FCO 41/1295.

59. DBPO III/II, no. 26; FRG delegation MPT, report no. 62, 26 February 1973, PA ZA 100001.

60. Note AA (Diesel to Frank), 'Sitzung des Unterausschusses KSZE der PZ in Brüssel am 3.3.1973', 7 March 1973, PA ZA 100020; Renk (1996), 61.

61. AAPD 1973, no. 32; Renk (1996), 80.

62. AAPD 1973, nos. 28 and 101; Douglas-Home to UK embassy Brussels, 5 March 1973, FCO 41/1295.

63. Interview with Helmut Liedermann.

64. Blue Book. On this principle, see Thomas (2001), 61; Maresca (1985), 154.

65. FRG delegation MPT, report no. 128, 6 April 1973, PA ZA 100002.

66. Maresca (1985), 156.

67. Thomas (2001), 60; Renk (1996), 124.

68. Renk (1996), 140.

69. Blue Book; FRG delegation MPT, report no. 104, 29 March 1973, PA ZA 100002.

70. AAPD 1973, no. 25; 'Rapport du Président du Comité Politique aux Ministres', RM(73)3P. (définitif), 12 March 1973, ADMAE Gén. 2926.

71. FRG delegation MPT, report no. 127, 6 April 1973, PA ZA 100002; DBPO III/II, no. 37.

72. Blue Book.

73. Ibid.

74. For an overview of the final months of negotiation, see DBPO III/II, xxx–xxxiii.

75. AAPD 1973, no. 418.

76. REPAN-Bruxelles, 'Projet révisé de Déclaration sur les Principes Gouvernant les Relations entre les Etats Participant à la C.S.C.E. (2. révision)', 6 September 1973, PA B150/288; Höhn (1978), 259–62.

77. DBPO III/II, xxiv.

78. Maresca (1985), 113–6. The FRG, in view of strong domestic pressure, initially tried to put the clause back into the inviolability principle, but found limited enthusiasm among the Nine to reopen this debate. Some of the Nine would have been content to replace the clause to other principles, such as 'non-use of force' or 'territorial integrity', but loyally supported Bonn's preference in the end. Note AA (von Groll), 'KSZE-Abstimmung der 'Neun'; hier: Sitzung des Souscomité CSCE am 17.12.1974', 18 December 1974, PA ZA 100020.

79. Note AA (von Groll to 500), 'Revidierter französischer Prinzipienkatalog', 10 September 1973, PA B150/288; Höhn (1978), 303.

80. Renk (1996), 87; Thomas (2001), 71.

81. Final Act.

82. Andréani (2005).

83. Gerhard Henze, 'Freizügigkeit und verbesserte Informationsmöglichkeit als Ziele der KSZE', in Volle and Wagner (1976), 77–86.

84. DBPO III/II, nos. 57 and 68.

85. Maresca (1985), 52.

86. DBPO III/II, no. 42.

87. DBPO III/II, no. 94.

88. DBPO III/II, no. 57; Maresca (1985), 95–8; Thomas (2001), 74.

89. DBPO III/II, nos. 63 and 94.

90. Maresca (1985), 147–9.

91. Interview with Helmut Liedermann.

92. Renk (1996), 115.

93. AAPD 1973, no. 418; DBPO III/II, no. 55; Höhn (1978), 277–9.

94. AAPD 1973, no. 347; 'The Position of the Nine at the CSCE', RM(74) 7P, 10 June 1974, FCO 30/2486.

95. Höhn (1978), 270f.

96. Renk (1996), 109–14; Maresca (1985), 169–73. Major controversies about CBM concerned the area to be covered in Europe and in the Soviet East, the number of days of advance notice, and the notification threshold.

97. AAPD 1973, no. 347. The idea of labelling this single volume the 'Final Act' was put forward by the British in a paper for discussion by the Nine in October 1973. FRG delegation CSCE, report no. 67, 15 October 1973, PA ZA 100003.

98. 'Draft Final Act', CSCE (74) 62 P rev., 13 February 1974; and note AA (Otto von Stempel, FRG delegation CSCE) to NATOGERMA, 13 February 1974, PA ZA 100020.

99. DBPO III/II, no. 63; note AA (von Groll), 'Konferenz über Sicherheit und Zusammenarbeit in Europa (KSZE): Sachstand', 2 April 1974, PA B1/553; 'The Position of the Nine at the CSCE', RM(74) 7P, 10 June 1974, FCO 30/2486.

100. Renk (1996), 154–8

101. Maresca (1985), 159.

102. For an assessment of the Final Act, see Schwarz (1977), Ch. 2.

103. See, for instance, AAPD 1974, no. 326; Maresca (1985), 44f.

104. Substantive disagreement occurred, for example, in early 1974, when the Nine were attempting to develop a more constructive and specific position in the field of CBM. FRG delegation CSCE, report nos. 235, 258, and 259, 31 January and 13 February 1974, PA ZA 100005.

105. Callaghan (from the Ottawa NATO ministerial meeting) to FCO, 19 June 1974, no. 426, FCO 41/1418.

106. DBPO III/II, no. 25, note 6.

107. Ibid.

108. AAPD 1973, no. 214.

109. Record of conversation between Brimelow and Kissinger at the British embassy, Washington, on 5 March 1973, FCO 73/135.

110. Ibid.

111. FRG embassy Washington (von Staden) to AA, 17 May 1973, PA B150/280.

112. AAPD 1974, nos. 197 and 199; DBPO III/II, nos. 92 and 94.

113. Brief FCO (no. 6), 'Visit of Dr Kissinger on 8 July: CSCE', undated [1974], PREM 16/290; Callaghan to UK embassy Paris, 12 July 1974, FCO 30/2486; Thomas (2001), 79.

114. Via back channel in early 1973, Kissinger contacted Bahr and proposed to accept Brezhnev's secret proposal of settling the outcome of the MPT among the great powers. However, as Bahr had to inform Kissinger, it turned out to be impossible to informally steer a multilateral framework like the Nine with the same secretive back-channel methods that had proven so effective in the case of the four-power negotiations over Berlin. AdsD EB 439.

115. Record of conversation between Heath and Brandt at Chequers on 6 October 1973, PREM 15/1564; Van Well (1973), 586.

116. Note Elysée (Raimond to Pompidou), 10 January 1973, AN 5AG2 100: 'Tout se passe comme si les Américaines avaient maintenant d'autres priorités (du type réduction des forces, SALT, coopération américano–soviétique) et comme s'ils laissaient, dans le cadre de la Conférence sur la Sécurité européenne, aux Européens le rôle de l'infanterie.'

117. FCO steering brief, 'Prime Minister's Visit to Brussels: 25/26 June', undated [1974], PREM 16/11; AAPD 1974, nos. 7 and 90.

118. AAPD 1974, nos. 198 and 360; Maresca (1985), 46.

119. UK delegation MPT (Elliott) to FCO, 18 December 1972, FCO 41/1295.

120. Note AA (Diesel to Frank), 27 February 1973, PA B150/274: 'De facto sind die Neun in der Lage, die NATO-Haltung vorzuprogrammieren.' See also DBPO III/II, no. 94; interview with Barthold C. Witte.

121. According to Höhn (1978), 246, NATO delegations met about once a week in the embassy of the acting presidency of the Fifteen. These meetings had been inspired by the EPC model, but changed on a monthly rather than semi-annual basis. On differences of NATO and EPC consultations, see also Pijpers (1984).

122. Record of 'Sitzung der IMAG/KSZE am 22. Februar 1973 im Auswärtigen Amt', 9 March 1973, PA B150/275.

123. DBPO III/II, no. 36.

124. During the MPT, the EPC presidency was in charge of informing the US. Other couples were France and Portugal, Britain and Canada, Italy and Turkey, the FRG and Greece, and Denmark with Norway and Iceland. Conversely, the Dutch were in charge of informing Ireland about NATO decisions. FRG delegation MPT, report no. 77, 15 March 1973, PA ZA 100001. During the Geneva negotiations, the EPC presidency often informed the Fifteen collectively on behalf of the Nine. AAPD 1974, no. 161.

125. Concerning the neutrals, the couples were the FRG and Austria, Italy and Switzerland, and Denmark with Sweden and Finland. Renk (1996), 186.

126. Höhn (1978), 346.

127. Interview with Helmut Liedermann.

128. UK embassy Brussels (John Beith) to FCO, 5 January 1973, FCO 41/1295; note MAE (CSCE), 12 January 1973, ADMAE Gén. 3795.

129. Record of 'Sitzung der IMAG/KSZE am 9. Januar 1973 im Auswärtigen Amt', 17 January 1973, PA B150/272.

130. Interview with Barthold C. Witte.

131. For example, in the second semester of 1973, more than 50 national papers or EPC reports were discussed in the sous-comité. For the list, see FCO 30/2482.

132. DBPO III/II, no. 37; Becker (1992), 220.

133. DBPO III/II, no. 51; von Groll, 'The Nine at the Conference on Security and Cooperation in Europe', in Allen, Rummel, and Wessels (1982), 60–8, 64.

134. DBPO III/II, no. 57.

135. DBPO III/II, nos. 73 and 94.

136. Note FCO (Wiggin to Brimelow), 'Impressions of 'Davignon Committee' Meeting in Brussels on 25 April', 26 April 1973, FCO 41/1296.

137. French delegation MPT (Gérard André) to MAE, 21 December 1972, no. 1034-1028, ADMAE Gén. 2925; interview with Barthold C. Witte.

138. 'C.S.C.E. – Organisation du travail de la prochaine session', 16 February 1973, enclosed to NATOGERMA (von Groll/Krapf) to AA, 19 February 1972, PA B150/274; 'Les suites de la CSCE (Rapport du Comité Politique)', CSCE RM(74)2 CP, 6 February 1974, FCO 30/2482.

139. 'Rapport oral du président du Comité Politique à la Réunion des Ministres du 16 mars 1973', and 'Rapport oral du Président du Comité Politique à la Réunion des Ministres du 16 mars 1973: C.S.C.E. – Problèmes économiques', RM(73)5P, 16 March 1973, ADMAE Gén. 2926; 'Rapport du Sous-Comité CSCE sur 'Les problèmes à résoudre'', CP (74)21 P, 18 April 1974, FCO 30/2486; 'The Position of the Nine at the CSCE', RM(74) 7P, 10 June 1974, FCO 30/2486; 'Rapport du Président du Sous-Comité C.S.C.E. au Comité Politique', C.S.C.E. (74) 140 P Rév. 1, 10 July 1974, FCO 30/2486; 'Rapport du Comité Politique à la Réunion Ministérielle', RM(74) 8 CP., 10 September 1974, FCO 30/2480.

140. 'Objectifs et Stratégie des Neuf à la CSCE: Rapport au Comité Politique', RM(73)20CP, 13 November 1973, ADMAE Gén. 2926. For assessments, see AAPD 1973, no. 377; DBPO III/II, no. 53.

141. DBPO III/II, no. 44. By 1974, the Nine came to support the idea of a declaration on security in the Mediterranean in the Final Act. 'Projet: Déclaration de la CSCE sur les Rapports de l'Europe avec la Région Méditerranéenne', CSCE (74)70 I rev. 4, 19 March 1974, FCO 30/2486.

142. AAPD 1973, no. 62; note MAE (Direction des Affaires Politiques) to Pompidou, 14 November 1973, AN 5AG2 92; brief FCO for EPC ministerial meeting in Brussels, 'Agenda Item 3: CSCE', 4 March 1974, FCO 30/2466.

143. FRG delegation CSCE, report no. 196, 3 December 1973, PA ZA 100004.

144. According to Höhn (1978), 220, an early compromise package comprised French acceptance of CBM in return for the FRG supporting the largely state-centred French approach towards cultural cooperation.

145. Becker (1992), 221.

146. FRG delegation MPT, report no. 125, 6 April 1973, PA ZA 100002.

147. Denmark at times linked up with the Nordic countries, Italy with the Mediterranean group, and the Dutch with the NNA delegations. Pijpers (1984), 141.

148. Record of 'Sitzung der IMAG/KSZE am 9. Januar 1973 im Auswärtigen Amt', 17 January 1973, PA B150/272.

149. For two French assessments of the role of the FRG at CSCE, see note MAE (Direction des Affaires Politiques) to Pompidou, 14 November 1973; and note MAE (Occ.) to Pompidou, 19 November 1973, AN 5AG2 92.

150. Note AA (Diesel to Frank), 'Stichworte für das Gespräch mit dem Herrn Bundeskanzler über KSZE am 8.3.73', 7 March 1973, PA B150/275; AAPD 1974, no. 90.

151. Note MAE (CSCE), 'Préliminaires C.S.C.E.: Rapport du président du Comité Politique aux Ministres', ADMAE Gén. 3792; Douglas-Home to UK embassy Brussels, 5 March 1973, FCO 41/1295; circular AA (Otto von der Gablentz, 200), 9 July 1973, PA B150/284.

152. DBPO III/II, no. 20.

153. Douglas-Home to UK embassy Brussels, 14 April 1973; and FCO 'Briefing for the Political Directors' Meeting on 25 April', 25 April 1973, FCO 41/1296.

154. For instance, in reaction to a Soviet campaign against dissidents in 1973/74, the Dutch tabled a paper on the free accessibility of works of art and literature, the purpose of which was clearly to provoke Moscow. This did not go down well with partners such as France and the FRG. FRG delegation CSCE, reports nos. 40 and 58, 5 and 11 October 1973, PA ZA 100003.

155. DBPO III/II, no. 63.

156. FRG delegation CSCE, report no. 387, 9 April 1974, PA ZA 100006.

157. DBPO III/II, appendix II. The description referred to the conference proceedings in basket III specifically.

158. AAPD 1973, no. 42; DBPO III/II, no. 46.

159. DBPO III/II, no. 31. Italics original.

160. DBPO III/II, no. 37. For a characterisation of the positions of individual EPC members at the CSCE, see also note Elysée (Raimond to Pompidou), 10 December 1973, AN 5AG2 1036.

161. Pijpers (1984), 139.

162. Record of 'Sitzung der IMAG/KSZE am 9. Januar 1973 im Auswärtigen Amt', 17 January 1973, PA B150/272; DBPO III/II, no. 39; Höhn (1978), 248–87.

163. See, for example, the 'Rapport du Comité Politique à la Réunion Ministérielle', RM(74) 8 CP., 10 September 1974, FCO 30/2480, urging *de patience et de fermeté*.

164. DBPO III/II, no. 75, on the Nine's discouragement but 'disposition to see things through'.

165. Record of conversation between Pompidou and Brezhnev in the Soviet Union on 11 January 1973, 'Deuxième Partie de la réunion plénière', AN 5AG2 1019; AAPD 1973, no. 31.

166. AAPD 1973, nos. 145, 146, and 148; record of conversation between Jobert and Brezhnev in Oreanda on 27 July 1973, AN 5AG2 1019.

167. AAPD 1974, nos. 37, 45, and 80; note AA (von Groll), 'Konferenz über Sicherheit und Zusammenarbeit in Europa (KSZE): Sachstand', 2 April 1974, PA B1/553; record of conversation between Jobert and Gromyko in Paris on 16 February 1974, in possession of author, courtesy of Mary Weed. After Anglo-Soviet relations had improved in 1973, the UK too was an addressee of the Soviet campaign. DBPO III/II, nos. 62 and 71.

168. AAPD 1973, no. 351; AAPD 1974, no. 14.

169. FRG delegation MPT, report no. 167, 12 May 1973, PA ZA 100002.

170. DBPO III/II, no. 94.

171. Letter Kissinger to Genscher, 2 September 1974, HSA 6579; AAPD 1974, no. 262.

172. Tickell, 'The Enlarged Community and the European Security Conference', in John (1975), 115–24, 115; interview with Philippe de Schoutheete de Tervarent.

173. Thomas (2001), 43; DBPO III/II, nos. 58 and 60.

174. Interview with Etienne Davignon.

175. Maresca (1985), 158.

176. Kissinger (1999), 642.

177. Rüdiger Lentz, 'Die Entwicklung der deutschen Position zur KSZE – multilaterale Problemstellung und innerorganisatorische Innovation', in Haftendorn *et al.* (1978), 151–65, 163.

178. Note MAE (CSCE), 'Réunion ministérielle des Neuf du 20 Novembre: C.S.C.E.', 16 November 1973, ADMAE Gén. 3792; 'Rapport du Comité Politique à la Réunion Ministérielle', RM(74) 8 CP., 10 September 1974, with an attached: 'Projet de directives à l'intention des délégations à la C.S.C.E.', FCO 30/2480.

179. AAPD 1974, no. 171, note 13.

180. Interviews with Barthold C. Witte, Jacques Andréani, and Luigi Vittorio Ferraris.

181. Note AA (von Staden to von Groll), 'Zusammenfassendes Protokoll der Ressortbesprechung vom 25.8.1971 im AA', 26 August 1971, BA B136/6419; record of 'Anglo/German Planning Talks', 13 April 1973, 16 April 1973, FCO 49/488.

182. DBPO III/II, no. 50.

183. Draft note FCO, 'CSCE Preparations Within the Community Framework', undated [Nov 1972], FCO 28/1687.

184. Note AA, 'Kurzbericht über Sitzung der Europa-Beauftragten', 27 April 1973, PA B20/1979.

185. Douglas-Home to UK embassy Brussels, 26 June 1973, FCO 41/1297.

186. *Conference on Security and Cooperation in Europe: Stage I – Helsinki: Verbatim Records, July 3–7, 1973*, 24.

187. Höhn (1978), 245.

188. FRG delegation CSCE, report no. 38, 5 October 1973, PA ZA 100003.

189. AAPD 1973, no. 319.

190. Final Act.

191. FRG delegation CSCE (von Groll) to AA, 17 April 1974, PA ZA 100020.

192. Ferraris (1979), 373–83.

193. Interview with Philippe de Schoutheete de Tervarent.

194. Höhn (1978), 345.

195. AAPD 1974, nos. 37 (note 5) and 64.

196. 'Statement by the European Council on the Conference for Security and Cooperation in Europe, Brussels, 17 July 1975', *European Foreign Policy: Key Documents*, 257.

197. DBPO III/II, no. 37.

198. DBPO III/II, no. 29; record of conversation between Pompidou and Brandt in Paris on 21 June 1973, AN 5AG2 106.

199. Scheel (1973), 436.

200. Record of conversation between Scheel and Jobert in Bonn on 12 June 1973, AN 5AG2 106: '[…] le meilleure exemple pour montrer la réalité des progrès de

l'Europe.' Jobert added that the Nine 'ont montré la meilleure disponabilité et la meilleure entente.'

201. Brief FCO, 'European Political Cooperation: Ministerial Meeting 16 March 1973, Agenda Item 3: CSCE', 16 March 1973, FCO 41/1295; DBPO III/II, no. 21, note 3.

4 Facing the US

1. The speech is reproduced in Mally (1974), 29–37. The following quotes are taken from there.
2. Ibid.
3. Kissinger (2000b), 193.
4. Kaiser (1973). For a survey of European and US grievances, see note AA (204), 'Zusammenstellung der wichtigsten, die europäisch–amerikanischen Beziehungen belastenden Konfliktthemen', 27 March 1973, PA B21/747.
5. 'Fourth Annual Report to the Congress on United States Foreign Policy', 3 May 1973, *Public Papers of the Presidents of the United States: Richard Nixon – 1973*, 348–518, 404f.
6. Ibid., 416.
7. FRG embassy Washington (Hans Heinrich Noebel) to AA, 'Europäische–amerikanische Konferenz in Amsterdam', 2 April 1973, BA B136/6425.
8. French embassy London (Philippe Cuvillier) to MAE, 25 April 1973, ADMAE Etats-Unis 1137; note FCO, 'Extract from a Speech made by the Foreign and Commonwealth Secretary at Dunblane on 27th April 1973', PREM 15/1541.
9. Kissinger (2000b), 154.
10. Record of conversation between Jobert and Kissinger in Paris on 17 May 1973, National Archives at College Park, MD, Nixon Presidential Materials Staff, HAK Office Files, French Memcons 1973, Box 56; Jobert (1976), 288; note PMO (Armstrong) to FCO (Antony Acland, principal private secretary to the secretary of state), 19 June 1973, PREM 15/1542; letter Brandt to Nixon, 4 August 1973, AdsD EB 332.
11. Kissinger (2000b), 149 and 153.
12. Testimony of Kosciusko-Morizet in Association Georges Pompidou (1995), 209f.
13. AAPD 1972, no. 357, note 10.
14. AAPD 1973, no. 52; records of conversation of Peterson with Debré in Paris on 18 February 1973, and with Douglas-Home and Carrington on 22 and 23 February 1973, AN 5AG2 117, and FCO 30/1745.
15. AAPD 1973, no. 64.
16. Kissinger (2000b), 143; Record of conversation between Brimelow and Kissinger at the British embassy, Washington, on 5 March 1973, FCO 73/135.

17. Note CO, 'Record of a Meeting in the British Embassy, Washington, on Thursday 19 April 1973', undated, FCO 82/311; note CO (Trend) to Heath, with a first draft on 'The Next Ten Years in East–West and Trans–Atlantic Relations: Assumptions and Questions', 16 March 1973, PREM 15/1540; note PMO (Hunt to Heath), 'East/West Relations in the Next Decade', 5 April 1973, PREM 15/1541.

18. Notes CO (Trend), 'Personal Record of a Discussion in the British Embassy, Washington DC, on 19th April, 1973', undated; and 'Discussion with Dr. Kissinger', 24 April 1973, PREM 15/1359.

19. Kissinger (2000b), 129f. Kissinger might have read too much into it when Pompidou after the meeting in an interview with the *New York Times* ('Pompidou favors U.S.–Europe Talks', 14 December 1972) indicated his support of transatlantic consultations 'at the highest level' to clarify European–US relations and think about 'common political objectives' before starting to quarrel about money and commerce. Internally, Pompidou claimed that his arguments had been overstated, and that he would continue to support bilateral summits only. See Pompidou's annotation to French embassy Bonn (Sauvagnargues) to MAE, 16 January 1973, AN 5AG2 1036.

20. Note French embassy Washington (Kosciusko-Morizet), 'Déjeuner en tête à tête avec M. Kissinger', 16 March 1973, AN, Kosciusko-Morizet Papers (582AP) 37; Kissinger (2000b), 149.

21. Notes Kissinger to Bahr, and Bahr to Kissinger, 12 and 15 March 1973, AdsD EB 439; Harpprecht (2000), 63.

22. Letters Kissinger to Bahr, 9 April 1973, and Bahr to Brandt, 15 April 1973, AdsD EB 439; Kissinger (2000b), 147f. On Bahr's meeting with Kissinger on 5 January 1973, see his note to Brandt of 10 January 1973, AdsD EB 436, where he reported that no agreement had been found on how to redefine European–US relations.

23. Note FCO (Acland) to PMO (Thomas Bridges, private secretary), 10 January 1973, PREM 15/1540; circular AA (Gisbert Poensgen, IIIE), 17 January 1973, PA B1/503; note MAE (Gén.), 18 January 1973, ADMAE Etats-Unis 1137; note Kissinger to Bahr, 18 January 1973, AdsD EB 439.

24. UK embassy Brussels (Beith) to FCO, 16 March 1973, FCO 30/1731; 'Note personnelle du Président du Comité Politique', CP(73)30 P, 17 April 1973, FCO 30/1732.

25. Note FCO, 'Extract from a Speech made by the Foreign and Commonwealth Secretary at Dunblane on 27th April 1973', 27 April 1973, PREM 15/1541.

26. AAPD 1973, no. 115.

27. Kissinger (2000b), 154.

28. Note FCO (Butler to Cable), 12 September 1973, FCO 30/1740.

29. Record of first conversation between Pompidou and Heath in Paris on 21 May 1973, AN 5AG2 1015.

30. Ibid.; Brandt's interview in *Der Spiegel* of 27 September 1971, *Bundeskanzler Brandt*, vol. II, 39–46.

31. Stanley Hoffmann, 'Toward a Common European Foreign Policy?', in Hanrieder (1973), 79–105, 91; Schaetzel (1973), 74.

32. AAPD 1971, no. 426; note Bahr to Kissinger, 17 January 1973, AdsD EB 439; AA draft statement, 'Premières observations sur le discours prononcé le 23 avril 1973 par le Dr. Kissinger', 3 May 1973, PA B21/747.

33. Kissinger's press statement of 12 May 1973, reproduced in *Europa-Archiv* 28, no. 19 (1973), D531–34.

34. *Public Papers of the Presidents of the United States: Richard Nixon – 1973*, 326f.

35. Kissinger (2000b), 101 and 153.

36. UK embassy Washington (Cromer) to FCO, 23 April 1973, PREM 15/1541; AAPD 1973, no. 118; Brandt (1978), 371.

37. Note CO (Trend) to Heath, 'Discussion with Dr. Kissinger', 24 April 1973, PREM 15/1359; Kissinger (2000b), 126.

38. Record of conversation between Pompidou and Heath in Paris on 21 May 1973, PREM 15/1541.

39. AAPD 1973, no. 118; UK embassy Bonn (Brian Crowe) to FCO, 'Reactions to Dr Kissinger's Speech', FCO 82/283; Harpprecht (2000), 101; letter Wehner to Brandt, 27 April 1973, WBA BK 21.

40. WB (1978), 370.

41. French embassy Bonn (Sauvagnargues) to MAE, 27 April 1973, ADMAE Gén. 3795; AAPD 1973, no. 182.

42. Harpprecht (2000), 98 and 117; Brandt (1978), 413; Kissinger (2000b), 157.

43. Brandt (1978), 413; AAPD 1973, no. 124.

44. 'Joint Statement Following Discussions With Chancellor Brandt of the Federal Republic of Germany', 2 May 1973, in *Public Papers of the Presidents of the United States: Richard Nixon – 1973*, 343–5.

45. Letter Scheel to Renaat van Elslande, Belgian foreign minister since January 1973, 10 May 1973, PA B21/747; AAPD 1973, no. 139; Kissinger (2000b), 155–9.

46. Note Kissinger to Bahr, 14 May 1973, AdsD EB 439.

47. Draft letters Brandt to Pompidou and Heath, 4 May 1973, WBA BK 51; Brandt (1978), 371; AAPD 1973, no. 145.

48. UK embassy Bonn (Henderson) to FCO, 17 May 1973, PREM 15/1541.

49. Letter PMO (Armstrong) to FCO (Acland), 12 December 1972, PREM 15/1540.

50. Letter UK embassy Washington (Cromer) to FCO (Greenhill), 'The US and Europe', 19 January 1973, PREM 15/1540.

51. Note CO (Trend) to Heath, 2 May 1973, PREM 15/1541; note MOD (Patrick D. Nairne) to CO (B. M. Norbury, private secretary), 'Talks with Dr. Kissinger: NATO Defence Policy', 9 May 1973, FCO 41/1192.

52. Heath (1998), 493.

53. Heath's comments, as recorded in note POM (Armstrong) to FCO (Acland), 19 June 1973, PREM 15/1542.

54. Note PMO (Armstrong to Heath), 29 June 1973, PREM 15/1542.

55. Note FCO (Hugh Overton, North America Department, to Wiggin), 'US Policy towards Europe', 9 May 1973, FCO 82/284.

56. Letter UK embassy Washington (Cromer) to FCO (Brimelow), 'Dr Kissinger's Speech on US/European Relations', 8 May 1973, FCO 82/283.

57. Note FCO (Tickell to Wiggin), 'Draft Declaration of Principles on US/European relations', 18 June 1973, FCO 41/1185; FCO (Greenhill) to UK embassy Washington (Cromer), 8 June 1973, FCO 82/284.

58. See Kissinger's account of the meeting to Jobert during their conversation in Paris on 17 May 1973, National Archives at College Park, MD, Nixon Presidential Materials Staff, HAK Office Files, French Memcons 1973, Box 56.

59. Record of conversation between Douglas-Home and Kissinger in London on 10 May 1973, FCO 82/307; Kissinger (2000b), 162f.

60. Note Elysée (Raimond to Pompidou), 3 May 1973, AN 5AG2 1021.

61. Note Elysée (Raimond to Pompidou), 4 July 1973, AN 5AG2 1023; two telegrams French embassy Washington (Kosciusko-Morizet) to MAE, 23 and 25 April 1973, ADMAE Etats-Unis 1137.

62. Jobert (1976), 308 and 306.

63. Circular MAE (de Courcel), 28 April 1973, ADMAE Etats-Unis 1137; note MAE, 'Note de synthèse', 18 May 1973, AN 5AG2 1023; Jobert (1976), 294.

64. Record of conversation between Pompidou and Heath in Paris on 21 May 1973, PREM 15/1541.

65. Note MAE, 'Note de synthèse', 18 May 1973, AN 5AG2 1023.

66. The phrase stems from Ewart-Biggs and is quoted in UK embassy Paris (Edward Tomkins) to FCO, 7 June 1973, PREM 15/1542.

67. Jobert's line of reasoning at the EPC ministerial meeting of 5 June 1973, as recorded by draft note AA (Hansen), 5 June 1973, PA B21/747.

68. Letter Pompidou to Brandt, 22 May 1973, AN 5AG2 1009.

69. See note 58 in this chapter.

70. Soutou (2000), 133.

71. Record of conversation between Pompidou and Kissinger in Paris on 18 May 1973, AN 5AG2 1022; Kissinger (2000b), 167.

72. Memorandum Kissinger to Jobert, 'Proposed Outcome of the Meeting Between Presidents Nixon and Pompidou in Iceland', 26 May 1973, AN 582AP 37.

73. Kissinger (2000b), 175; record of conversation between Trend and Kissinger at the British embassy in Washington on 4 June 1973, PREM 15/1542.

74. Records of the first two conversations between Pompidou and Nixon in Reykjavik on 31 May 1973, AN 5AG2 1023. See also Roussel (1994), 550–70; Jobert (1976), 293.

75. Record of the second conversation between Pompidou and Nixon in Reykjavik on 31 May 1973, AN 5AG2 1023.

76. UK embassy Paris (Tomkins) to FCO, 5 June 1973, PREM 15/1542; 'Europe: Hopes and Realities', *The International Herald Tribune*, 11 June 1973; Kissinger (2000b), 180.

77. REPAN-Bruxelles (de Rose) to MAE, 27 April 1973, ADMAE Etats-Unis 1137; UKDEL NATO (Peck) to FCO, 11 May 1973, FCO 30/1734.

78. Jobert famously argued: 'Nous avons une bonne alliance, gardons-la.' Note FCO (Tickell to Wiggin), 'Draft Declaration of Principles on US/European relations', 18 June 1973, FCO 41/1185.

79. Deputy Under-Secretary of State John O. Wright (from Brussels) to FCO, 25 May 1973, FCO 30/1734; note MAE, 25 April 1973, ADMAE Gén. 3795; circular MAE (de Courcel), 30 May 1973, ADMAE Etats-Unis 1137; Wright (from Brussels) to FCO, 26 May 1973, FCO 30/1734.

80. Circular FCO (Douglas-Home), 6 June 1973, no. 450, FCO 30/1736.

81. French embassy Rome (Charles Lucet) to MAE, 25 July 1973, on the Italians reporting from a meeting with Kissinger, ADMAE Etats-Unis 1137.

82. UK embassy Washington (Cromer) to FCO, 1 July 1973, on an unofficial meeting of Nixon and Kissinger with the NATO permanent representatives in San Clemente, FCO 41/1185.

83. Letter Kissinger to Jobert, undated [about 20 July 1973], AN 5AG2 1021.

84. Record of conversation between Trend and Kissinger at the British embassy in Washington on 4 June 1973, and letter UK embassy Washington (Cromer) to CO (Trend), 5 July 1973, PREM 15/1542; letter Nixon to Heath, 18 July 1973, PREM 15/1543.

85. Letter FCO (Greenhill) to UK embassy Washington (Cromer), 8 June 1973, FCO 82/284; AAPD 1973, no. 225.

86. Jobert (1974), 232; (1976), 289.

87. UK embassy Paris (Tomkins) to FCO, 7 June 1973, PREM 15/1542.

88. Note MAE, 'Entretiens de Reykjavik 31 mai – 1er juin 1973: Note de synthèse', 18 May 1973, ADMAE Gén. 3810.

89. Record of conversation between Jobert and Kissinger in Paris on 8 June 1973, AN 5AG2 1023; Kissinger (2000b), 181.

90. Record of conversation between Jobert and Nixon in San Clemente, 29 June 1973, AN 5AG2 1023; Jobert (1974), 242f.; Weed (1988), 110f. For the drafts of the NSC ('Joint Declaration of Principles', 16 pages) and the State Department ('Illustrative Declaration', 6 pages), see PREM 15/1542 and AdsD EB 332.

91. Note CO (Trend) to Heath, 'United States–European Relations', 19 June 1973, PREM 15/1542; notes FCO, 'Mr Wright's Talks with Monsieur Puaux', 20 June 1973, and (Butler to Brimelow), 'Meeting of Political Directors Helsinki 5/6 July: Europe/US Relations (Item 2)', 4 July 1973, FCO 30/1736. For the first series of British drafts, see note FCO, 'Problems of a Declaration of Principles and

Drafts', undated [June 1973], PREM 15/1541. See also Douglas-Home to Heath, 'US/European Relations', 19 July 1973, PREM 15/1543, with revised British drafts: 'Declaration of principles by members of the North Atlantic Alliance' (third draft); and 'Outline for a Declaration of Principles between the Community and the US' (third draft).

92. Note FCO (Private Secretary to Minister of State Marrack Goulding to Private Secretary), 'Anglo/French Relations', 8 May 1973, PREM 15/1560.

93. Jobert (1974), 245: 'combien les vues du Premier minister et sa volonté pouvaient faciliter la naissance d'une Europe et preserver son identité de la fatalité américaine'.

94. Note PMO (Armstrong), 'Note for the record', 3 July 1973, PREM 15/1542.

95. See the FCO study 'The Year of Europe: The Impact on Transatlantic and Anglo–American Relations – An Analytical Account – February–July 1973', 17 October 1973, PREM 15/2089.

96. Record of conversation between Scheel and Jobert in Bonn on 12 June 1973, AN 5AG2 106; AAPD 1973, no. 186; letter Brandt to Nixon, 6 July 1973, AdsD EB 332.

97. AAPD 1973, nos. 201 and 259.

98. AAPD 1973, no. 222; BKA (Abt. II) to Guillaume (in Norway) 18 July 1973, AdsD EB 322; Kissinger (2000b), 185–7. For the West German draft, dated 11 July 1973, see PA B150/284.

99. Record of conversation between Douglas-Home and Guido Brunner, head of AA Planungsstab, in London on 18 July 1973, FCO 30/1737.

100. Note FRG embassy Paris (von Braun), 'Gespräche des Bundesministers in Washington', 19 July 1973, PA SvB 172.

101. Note FCO (Butler to Cable) 12 September 1973, 12 September 1973, FCO 30/1740; Brandt (1994), 459.

102. Draft record of conversation between Douglas-Home and Scheel in Helsinki on 4 July 1973, FCO 30/1756.

103. Note PMO (Armstrong) to FCO (Wright), 26 July 1973; UK embassy Paris (Tomkins) to FCO, 31 July 1973, PREM 15/1543.

104. UK embassy Bonn (Henderson) to Douglas-Home (in Ottawa), 1 August 1973, PREM 15/1544.

105. AAPD 1973, no. 234. On the Italian consultations in Washington, see French embassy Rome (Lucet) to MAE, 11 July 1973, AN 5AG2 1035; and French embassy Washington (François de la Gorce) to MAE, 21 July 1973, ADMAE Etats-Unis 1137.

106. FCO speaking notes, 'President Nixon's message of July 26 to the Prime Minister', 27 July 1973, PREM 15/1543; note FCO, 'Calendar of Meetings and exchanges: Transatlantic relations: Britain and USA', undated [second half of 1973], with a list of Anglo-American meetings Britain was asked not to reveal to its partners, FCO 30/1738.

107. BKA (Wolf-Dietrich Schilling) to Guillaume (in Norway), 17 July 1973, on Brunner's talks in Paris and London, AdsD EB 332; AAPD 1973, no. 227.

108. Note FCO (Cable to Brimelow), 'Transatlantic relations: Declarations of Principles', 18 July 1973, FCO 30/1736; note FCO (Greenhill) to CO (Trend), 6 July 1973, with enclosed 'Analysis of American Draft Declarations on Transatlantic Relations', PREM 15/1542.

109. Letter Jobert to Kissinger, 14 July 1973, AN 582AP 38; note Elysée (Raimond to Pompidou), 4 July 1973, AN 5AG2 1023.

110. Record of conversation between Jobert and John Davies, chancellor of the Duchy of Lancaster, in Paris on 17 July 1973, FCO 30/2008.

111. 'EEC ministers go to two capitals in search of an identity', *The Times*, 24 July 1973. See also Schoutheete (1986), 28. Scheel had to talk a reluctant Douglas-Home into making the extra trip to Copenhagen for the sake of a unifying Europe. AAPD 1973, no. 218.

112. Circular MAE (de Courcel), 10 July 1973, no. 415, ADMAE Etats-Unis 1137; circular FCO (Douglas-Home), 14 July 1973, PREM 15/1543.

113. Circular MAE (de Courcel), 24 July 1973, no. 476, ADMAE Gén. 3810, quoting Jobert as demanding that Europe should 'affirmer son identité tous azimuts, à tous usages, et pour elle-même'.

114. Jobert quoted in AAPD 1973, no. 229.

115. Circulars FCO (Douglas-Home), 24 July 1973, nos. 1528–31, PREM 15/1543.

116. Jobert (1976), 314.

117. Letter Heath to Nixon, 25 July 1973, PREM 15/1543.

118. AAPD 1973, no. 232.

119. AAPD 1973, no. 230 (*hemmende Missverständnisse*).

120. Letter Nixon to Heath, 26 July 1973, PREM 15/1543.

121. Letter Nixon to Brandt, 30 July 1973, and letter BKA (Sanne) to AA (Frank), 9 August 1973, AdsD EB 332; UK embassy Bonn (Henderson) to UK embassies Paris and Ottawa, 9 August 1973, PREM 15/1544.

122. Letter Kissinger to Scheel, 20 July 1973, AdsD EB 332.

123. Letter Kissinger to Scheel, 27 July 1973, AdsD EB 332. For Scheel's renewed reply, see AAPD 1973, no. 240.

124. Kissinger (2000b), 701 and 191.

125. The following quotes are taken from the record of conversation between Trend and Kissinger in Washington on 30 July 1973, FCO 82/311.

126. Ibid. See also Kissinger (2000b), 191f.

127. Note FCO (Michael Alexander, assistant private secretary to the secretary of state, to James Cable, head of planning staff), 'US/Europe Relations', 29 August 1973, FCO 30/1739.

128. Draft note FCO, 'Information Communautaire: Conversation between Dr. Kissinger and Sir Burke Trend, Sir John Hunt and Sir Thomas Brimelow,

Washington, 30 July, 1973', 30 July 1973, PREM 15/1543; French embassy London (de Beaumarchais) to MAE, 7 August 1973, AN 5AG2 1021.

129. Letter Brandt to Nixon, 4 August 1973, AdsD EB 332 (*ein falsches Gefühl des Ausgeschlossenseins*).

130. Letter Heath to Nixon, undated [early August 1973], CAB 164/1235.

131. Letter Nixon to Brandt, 11 August 1973, AdsD EB 332.

132. Letters Heath to Pompidou and Brandt, 3 August 1973, PREM 15/1544.

133. AAPD 1973, no. 242; UK embassy Paris (Ewart-Biggs) to Heath (in Ottawa), 8 August 1973, with a translation of Pompidou's answer, PREM 15/1544; letter Heath to Brandt, 8 August 1973, PREM 15/1544.

134. UK embassy Bonn (Henderson) to FCO, 17 August 1973, no. 895, FCO 30/1739.

135. Letter UK embassy Washington (Richard A. Sykes) to FCO (Brimelow), 24 August 1973, quoting Brimelow's own assessment in a preceding letter, FCO 82/286.

136. Harpprecht (2000), 274, quoting Brandt.

137. UK embassy Bonn (Henderson) to FCO (Brimelow), 3 August 1973, on a conversation with Frank, PREM 15/1544.

138. Harpprecht (2000), 344.

139. Letters Heath to Pompidou and Brandt, 3 August 1973, PREM 15/1544.

140. UK embassy Bonn (Henderson) to UK embassy Ottawa, 3 August 1973, PREM 15/1544; letter UK embassy Washington (Sykes) to FCO (Brimelow), 22 August 1973, FCO 82/286.

141. Record of conversation between Jobert and Brimelow in Paris on 29 August 1973, ADMAE Gén. 3810.

142. UK embassy Bonn (Henderson) to FCO, 17 August 1973, no. 894, on talks between Brimelow and Frank, FCO 30/1739.

143. Letters Heath to Brandt, and Brandt to Heath, 3 and 7 August 1973, PREM 15/1544.

144. Record of conversation between Jobert and Brimelow in Paris on 29 August 1973, PREM 15/1546; AAPD 1973, no. 267.

145. For the West German draft Atlantic declaration, as completed after Scheel's trip to Washington, see 'Entwurf einer Atlantischen Erklärung', 19 July 1973, PA B150/285.

146. For Bonn's draft declaration between the Nine and the US, see 'Contribution allemande en vue de l'exécution du mandate donné au Comité Politique par les Ministres le 23 juillet à Copenhague', GC(73)39D, undated [August 1973], FCO 30/1740. See also AAPD 1973, no. 254.

147. Harpprecht (2000), 275.

148. Note AA (Hansen), 'US–Europa; hier vorbereitende Gespräche mit Frankreich', PA B21/747; AAPD 1973, no. 265.

149. Note MAE (Puaux to Jobert), 'Entretien avec M. Ewart-Biggs – Relations Europe – Etats-Unis', 9 August 1973, ADMAE Gén. 3810.

150. For the UK draft, see 'Outline for a Declaration of Principles between the Community and the United States', reproduced as document no. 10 in the internal FCO study 'The Year of Europe: The Impact on Transatlantic and Anglo-American Relations – An Analytical Account – February–July 1973', 17 October 1973, PREM 15/2089. For earlier draft versions, see PREM 15/1542f.

151. Note PMO (Heath), 'Record of a Meeting with the Prime Minister and M. Jobert, French Foreign Minister at Knoll Farm, Aldington, Ashford on Sunday 26 August 1973', 26 August 1973, PREM 15/1546; Jobert (1974), 252.

152. Note MAE (Puaux to Jobert), 'Europe – Etats-Unis', 20 August 1973, ADMAE Gén. 3810.

153. Memorandum Douglas-Home to Jobert, 'Message from the Secretary of State for Foreign and Commonwealth Affairs to the Minister for Foreign Affairs', 3 September 1973, ADMAE Gén. 3792.

154. Record of conversation between Jobert and Brimelow in Paris on 29 August 1973, PREM 15/1546.

155. UK embassy Bonn (Hibbert) to FCO, 'Western European Political Consultation and the relationship with the United States', 18 September 1973, FCO 30/1741.

156. Circular MAE (de Courcel), 31 August 1973, on Jobert's parallel talks with Brimelow and Frank, ADMAE Etats-Unis 1137; AAPD 1973, no. 267.

157. Note AA (200/411), 'Europa/US: Stand der Vorbereitungen für eine Begegnung der 9 mit Präsident Nixon', 7 September 1973, PA B21/747.

158. Note MAE (Puaux to Jobert), 6 September 1973, AN 86AJ 149.

159. The draft declaration of the Nine is reproduced in Mally (1974), 385–8. For the French version, see Le Monde, 27 September 1973.

160. Note MAE (Puaux to Jobert), 6 September 1973, AN 86AJ 149: 'Jamais, à ma connaissance, ne s'était manifesté spontanément un état d'esprit aussi authentiquement européen dans une affaire mettant en jeu au premier chef les Etats-Unis.'

161. Wright (from Brussels) to FCO, 5 September 1973, no. 320, FCO 30/1740.

162. UK embassy Bonn (Hibbert) to FCO, 'Western European Political Consultation and the relationship with the United States', 18 September 1973, quoting Wright, FCO 30/1741.

163. For the initial West German list of 'Gesprächsthemen', tabled in EPC on 21 August 1973, see PA B150/287. For the final list agreed by ministers, see circular MAE (Puaux), 12 September 1973, ADMAE Etats-Unis 1137. See also circular MAE (Puaux), 6 September 1973, ADMAE Gén. 3795.

164. The ministerial meeting had also been diplomatically prepared by trips of the Danish and Italian political directors, Trøls Oldenbourg (to London, Bonn, and Paris) and Roberto Ducci (to Paris, Bonn, and Brussels). AAPD 1973, no. 280.

165. Douglas-Home (from Copenhagen) to FCO, 11 September 1973, no. 339, FCO 30/1740.

166. 'Die Stimme der EG in der Welt', Neue Zürcher Zeitung, 13 September 1973.

167. 'Antwort über den Atlantik', *Frankfurter Allgemeine Zeitung*, 12 September 1973.

168. Scheel's address to the West German Bundestag on 13 September 1973, repro-duced in *Europa-Archiv* 28, no. 19 (1973): D534–9; 'Record of a Conversation with M. Ortoli at Chequers after Dinner at 9.30 pm on Wednesday 12 September 1973', 12 September 1973, PREM 15/1546.

169. Jobert (1976), 330.

170. Note AA (von der Gablentz), 'EPZ: Beziehungen Europa/USA – Sprechzettel vom 2.10.1973 für die Unterrichtung des Bundeskabinetts', PA B21/747.

171. For Brandt's speech during a 'Civic Luncheon' on 27 September 1973, see WBA Publikationen 523.

172. French embassy Washington (Kosciusko-Morizet) to MAE, 21 September 1973, ADMAE Etats-Unis 1137.

173. The draft was published in the *New York Times* on 24 September 1973.

174. Note MAE to Pompidou, 27 September 1973, AN 5AG2 1021; Kissinger (2000b), 703f. See also AAPD 1973, no. 296.

175. AAPD 1973, no. 298.

176. Kissinger quoted in AAPD 1973, no. 297, note 5.

177. Douglas-Home to UK embassy Washington (Cromer), 6 September 1973, no. 1815, FCO 30/1740; Brandt (1978), 416–9.

178. Record of conversation between Douglas-Home and Kissinger in the Waldorf Towers Hotel in New York on 24 September 1973, FCO 30/1743.

179. Kissinger (2000b), 705.

180. Record of conversation between Jobert and Kissinger in New York on 26 September 1973, National Archives at College Park, MD, Nixon Presidential Materials Staff, Country Files Europe, France vol. XI, Box 679.

181. Handwritten note de Rose (25 pages), 'Origine et mise au point du Papier Français de déclaration sur les relations Atlantiques', undated [after 24 September 1973], in possession of author, courtesy of Mary Weed.

182. Ibid.; Jobert (1976), 333; Weed (1988), 121.

183. For the French draft, see AN 5AG2 1021, FCO 41/1189. For assessments, see AAPD 1973, no. 315; Soutou (2000), 141.

184. Letter Kissinger to Jobert, 28 September 1973, AN 5AG2 1021.

185. Letter Jobert to Kissinger, 2 October 1973, AN 582AP 37; UKDEL NATO (Peck) to FCO, 10 October 1973, FCO 41/1189.

186. REPAN-Bruxelles (de Rose) to MAE, 3 October 1973, AN 582AP 37.

187. 'Netherlands Draft for an Atlantic Declaration of Principles (provisional transla-tion)', 25 June 1973, FCO 41/1185; NATO draft (PO/73/103), 11 July 1973, ADMAE Etats-Unis 1137; Turkish 'Draft Declaration on Atlantic Relations', circulated on 27 August 1973, FCO 41/1187; Canadian 'Draft declaration on transatlantic relations', 19 September 1973, PA B150/289; 'British Draft for a Declaration of Principles by Members of the North Atlantic Alliance', 8 August 1973, reproduced as document no. 9 in the internal FCO study 'The Year of

Europe: The Impact on Transatlantic and Anglo-American Relations – An Analytical Account – February–July 1973', 17 October 1973, PREM 15/2089. For the FRG draft, see AAPD 1973, no. 245.

188. Douglas-Home to UKDEL NATO, 24 August 1973, PREM 15/1546.

189. Von Staden (2005), 136.

190. Wright (from New York) to FCO, 29 September 1973, PREM 15/1546.

191. Kissinger (2000b), 189.

192. 'Record of a Conversation with M. Ortoli at Chequers after Dinner at 9.30 pm on Wednesday 12 September 1973', 12 September 1973, PREM 15/1546.

193. Letter UK embassy Washington (Cromer) to FCO (Brimelow), 'Transatlantic Relations', 2 October 1973, FCO 30/1741.

194. UK embassy Washington (Cromer) to FCO, 2 December 1973, no. 3752, FCO 82/289; 'Annual Message to the Congress: The Economic Report of the President', 1 February 1974, *Public Papers of the Presidents of the United States: Richard Nixon – 1974*, 104–10.

195. Political Director Günther van Well (from Paris) to AA, 1 October 1973, on his talks with Jobert and the situation of the Nine, PA B150/290.

196. Record of conversation between Heath and Brandt at Chequers on 6 October 1973, PA B150/290.

5 Into the Middle East

1. Weed (1988), 86.

2. See the introduction to the document collection *The October War and U.S. Policy*; See also Kissinger (2000b), 205f., 225, 450, and 461; Parker (2001). The following outline is heavily based on these accounts.

3. Quandt (2001), 136; Kissinger (2000b), 226 and 460.

4. Rabinovich (2004), 497f.; *Crisis: The Anatomy*, 145; Bickerton and Klausner (2005), 173f.; Parker (2001), 6.

5. Kissinger (2000b), 161, 192, 221, and 303.

6. Ibid., 542–56 and 1246f.

7. Ibid., 1247.

8. Ibid., 569–92 and 1247.

9. Ibid., 610–54 and 799–1111.

10. Ibid., 749–92; Bickerton and Klausner (2005), 176–98.

11. Venn (2002), 7 and 45f; Hohensee (1996).

12. Maull (1975), 1 and 6; Venn (2002), 18f.; Sus (1974).

13. Lieber (1976), 15–17; Venn (2002), 149–54 and 202; interview with Henry Kissinger.

14. Maull (1975), 6.

15. Circular AA (Dohms), 'Zu unserer Haltung im Nahostkonflikt', 19 October 1973, PA B1/576.

16. Hohensee (1996), 133–5; Thorpe (1997), 434; Morgan (1992), 426.

17. Lieber (1976), 13.

18. Maull (1975), 6.

19. Letter Assad to Heath, 8 October 1973, FCO 93/256; note AA (Redies to van Well), 'PK-Sitzung am 11./12. Oktober in Kopenhagen; hier: TOP Nahost', 11 October 1973, PA ZA 104978; UK embassy Bonn (Henderson) to FCO, 12 October 1973, no. 1086, FCO 93/259.

20. Record of conversation between Pompidou and Qadhafi in Paris on 24 November 1973, AN 5AG2 1026.

21. Record of conversation between Pompidou and Hafez Ismail, Sadat's security adviser, in Paris on 16 May 1973, AN 5AG2 1025. Several European statesmen blamed Kissinger personally for the outbreak of the October War. Interview with Henry Kissinger.

22. Draft brief FCO, 'European Political Co-operation: Ministerial Meeting 16 March 1973', FCO 93/196.

23. Note MAE (ANL), 3 August 1973, ADMAE RFA 3019.

24. Note FCO, 'Record of Anglo/German Talks on the Middle East Held at the Auswaertiges Amt on 18 May 1973', 18 May 1973, FCO 93/201.

25. Note MAE (Levant), 'Réunion des Experts du Proche-Orient', 14 March 1973, ADMAE Gén. 3792.

26. 'Situation au Moyen-Orient: Rapport du Président du Groupe Moyen-Orient', CP(73) 50 P, 22 May 1973, FCO 93/198.

27. Record of conversation between Douglas-Home and Kissinger in London on 10 May 1973, PREM 15/1984.

28. Note FCO (Anthony Parsons, NENAD) 'Western Interests in the Middle East over the Next Fifteen Years', 7 June 1973, FCO 93/250.

29. Ibid.

30. Record of third conversation between Pompidou and Nixon in Reykjavik on 1 June 1973, AN 5AG2 1023; AAPD 1973, no. 276.

31. Record of conversation between Heath, Brandt, and members of the West German Cabinet in the Federal Chancellor's House in Bonn-Venusberg on 29 May 1973, PREM 15/1577; record of the first conversation between Pompidou and Heath in Paris on 21 May 1973, AN 5AG2 1015.

32. Letter Heath to Nixon, 15 June 1973, PREM 15/1981.

33. AAPD 1973, no. 184.

34. 'Situation au Moyen-Orient: Rapport du Président de Groupe Moyen-Orient', CP(73) 19P, 13 March 1973, ADMAE Gén. 3804.

35. Brief FCO, 'European Political Co-operation: Political Directors Meeting 25 April: The Middle East', 25 April 1973, FCO 93/197; note FCO (David Gore-Booth to James Craig and Parsons, NENAD), 'The Italian Memorandum on the

Middle East', 15 May 1973, FCO 93/198; 'Situation au Moyen-Orient', RM(73) 9P, 30 May 1973, ADMAE Gén. 3804.

36. Note MAE, 'Réunion du groupe de travail Moyen-Orient: Note pour la direction des affaires politiques, sous-direction d'Europe occidentale', 3 September 1973, ADMAE Gén. 3804.

37. Letter FCO (Gore-Booth) to UK embassy Cairo (David Gladstone), 'Europe and the Middle East', 13 June 1973, FCO 93/198.

38. Note FCO, 'Record of Anglo/German Talks on the Middle East Held at the Auswaertiges Amt on 18 May 1973', 18 May 1973, FCO 93/201; record of MAE (Levant) on Franco-German talks on 9 August 1973, ADMAE RFA 2997.

39. AAPD 1973, no. 49; FRG embassy Cairo (Hans-Georg Steltzer) to AA (Frank), 18 June 1973, PA B150/283.

40. Note MAE (Pactes), 'Note de Synthèse', 1 June 1973, ADMAE RFA 3005.

41. AAPD 1973, no. 170; FRG embassy Tel Aviv (von Puttkamer) to AA, 8 June 1973, PA B150/282.

42. AAPD 1973, nos. 211 and 309; note Hans-Eberhard Dingels, SPD foreign policy expert, 'Der Nahost-Konflikt und seine Auswirkungen auf uns', 16 October 1973, WBA BK 28; note MAE (Levant), 30 May 1973, ADMAE RFA 3005.

43. Note MAE, 'Entretiens Franco-Britannique, Paris 21–22 Mai 1973: Note de Synthèse', 10 May 1973, ADMAE GB 3294; note FCO, 'Anglo/French Talks on the Middle East Held at the Quai d'Orsay on 12 January 1973', FCO 93/184; letter FCO (Gore-Booth) to UKMIS NY, Michael Weir), 'Anglo/French Talks on the Middle East', 23 November 1973, FCO 93/184.

44. Parson's comment to note FCO (Craig to Parsons and Wright), 'European Political Consultation: Meeting of Middle East Experts, Brussels, 12 March 1973', 12 March 1973, FCO 93/196.

45. Letter FCO (Gore-Booth) to UK embassy Cairo (Gladstone), 'Europe and the Middle East', 13 June 1973, FCO 93/198.

46. FCO Planning Paper, 'The External Relations of the European Community: Relations with the Middle East Oil Producers', 4 June 1973, FCO 49/461.

47. Note FCO (Parsons) 'Western Interests in the Middle East over the Next Fifteen Years', 7 June 1973, FCO 93/250; note Douglas-Home to Heath, 'Middle East', 7 June 1973, FCO 93/249; note Ministère des Armées (Délégation ministérielle pour l'armement), Fiche 356/DMA/DAI/33/SD, 'Vente du Crotale – Version Cobra – à la Libye', 19 September 1973, AN 582AP 38; Weed (1988), 301–3.

48. AAPD 1973, no. 156; note Premier Ministre to Pompidou, 6 December 1973, AN 5AG2 1036; Krämer (1974), 23–6; Lieber (1976), 5–7.

49. Fiona Venn, 'International Co-operation versus National Self-Interest: The United States and Europe during the 1973–1974 Oil Crisis', in Burk and Stokes (1999), 71–98, 77; Maull (1975), 9.

50. Weed (1988), 134.

51. UK embassy Paris (Tomkins) to FCO, 18 October 1973, no. 1388, on Jobert's speech in the National Assembly, FCO 93/265; Jobert (1974), 260.

52. Record of conversation between Douglas-Home and the Board of Deputies of British Jews in London on 15 October 1973, FCO 93/264; FRG embassy Cairo (Steltzer) to AA, 29 November 1973, PA ZA 104979; Sus (1974), 70f.

53. Note FCO (Parsons to Alexander), 'Our Objectives in the Present Middle East Crisis', 11 October 1973, PREM 15/1765; brief FCO, 'Cabinet 16 October 1973: The Middle East', 15 October 1973, FCO 93/263; circular MAE, 13 October 1973, AN 582AP 38.

54. Note Cabinet CM(73)48th, 'Conclusions of a Meeting of the Cabinet held at 10 Downing Street on Thursday 18 October 1973 at 11.00 am, Confidential Annex, Minute 2', CAB 128/53; Sus (1974), 70; Thorpe (1997), 433.

55. UK embassy Paris (Tomkins) to FCO, 10 October 1973, no. 1343, FCO 93/257; Jobert (1976), 336–8.

56. AAPD 1973, nos. 322, 335, and 337.

57. Note AA (Walter Jesser, Dg 31), 'Entwicklung des Verhältnisses zwischen der Bundesrepublik Deutschland und der arabischen Welt seit Ausbruch des Nahost-Kriegs am 6.10.1973', 23 October 1973, PA B1/576.

58. 'Der falsche Verdacht: Eine geheime Episode in der Geschichte deutsch–amerikanischer Beziehungen', *Die Zeit*, 27 April 2000.

59. Friedemann Büttner and Peter Hünseler, 'Die politischen Beziehungen zwischen der Bundesrepublik Deutschland und den arabischen Staaten', in Kaiser and Steinbach (1981), 11–152, 137, quoting and translating the Israeli paper Maariv: 'Einmal haben sie aus ideologischen Gründen gemordet, diesmal wegen Öl. Der Unterschied ist nicht gross.'

60. For an example, see UK embassy Tel Aviv (Sydney Giffard) to FCO, 8 October 1973, no. 432, FCO 93/255.

61. AAPD 1973, no. 329.

62. Note AA (Redies to Hansen), 'Sachstand I: Bisherige europäische Schritte in der Nahostkrise', 4 November 1973, PA B150/292; note MAE (Levant) to Pompidou, 'Le Proche-Orient et l'Europe', 3 December 1973, AN 86AJ 123.

63. For the text, see FCO 93/266.

64. UK embassy Copenhagen to FCO (for Parsons from Wright), 12 October 1973, nos. 392 and 397, FCO 93/259.

65. UK embassy Cairo (Adams) to FCO, 15 October 1973, no. 844, FCO 93/262; minute by Danish embassy in Bonn to AA (von der Gablentz), 16 October 1973, PA ZA 104978.

66. Circular MAE (Puaux), 15 October 1973, no. 598, ADMAE Gén. 3804.

67. Letter van Elslande to Douglas-Home, 16 October 1973, FCO 93/267.

68. FCO (Douglas-Home) to UK embassy Copenhagen, 22 October 1973, no. 275, FCO 93/268; UK embassy Paris (Tomkins) to FCO, 23 October 1973, no. 1406, FCO 93/270; circular MAE (Puaux), 17 October 1973, ADMAE

Gén. 3804; FCO record 'Meeting of Middle East Experts of the Nine at the Foreign and Commonwealth Office in London on 22 October 1973', 25 October 1973, FCO 30/1674.

69. Despatch UK embassy Washington (Cromer) to Douglas-Home, 'The Middle East and US/UK Relations', 9 January 1974, FCO 82/304.

70. Record of conversation between Douglas-Home and Kissinger at London Airport on 22 October 1973, PREM 15/1766.

71. Note FCO (Middle East Unit), 'European Political Cooperation: Political Committee Meeting on 5 November: The Middle East Crisis', 3 November 1973, FCO 30/1675.

72. FCO to UK embassy Paris (for Robin Renwick from Gore-Booth), 23 October 1973, no. 791, FCO 93/270; French embassy Brussels (Francis Huré) to MAE, 25 October 1973, no. 1163–68, ADMAE Gén. 3804; UKMIS NY (Maitland) to FCO, 29 October 1973, no. 1253, FCO 30/1675.

73. Frank (1981), 275; record of conversation between Heath and Rumour at Chequers on 8 December 1973, PREM 15/1768. In a letter to Nixon (31 October 1973, PREM 15/1981), Heath urged the US to take a different course of action, but to no avail.

74. Note FCO (Cable to Elliott), 'Anglo–French Planning Talks: 23 October 1973', 25 October 1973, PREM 15/1556.

75. Record of conversation between Heath and the Egyptian Foreign Minister Muhammad al-Zayyat in London on 7 November 1973, PREM 15/1767.

76. UK embassy Paris (Tomkins) to FCO, 26 October 1973, no. 1436, FCO 93/273; FRG embassy Brussels (Peter Limbourg) to AA, 30 October 1973, PA ZA 104978.

77. FCO (Douglas-Home) to UK embassy Washington, 2 November 1973, no. 2207, FCO 93/225.

78. 'Note de la Présidence', CPE/MUL 57, 31 October 1973; French embassy Copenhagen (Olivier Pelen) to MAE, 31 October 1973, no. 1009/15, ADMAE Gén. 3804.

79. FCO (Parson) to Wright (in Paris), 5 November 1973, PREM 15/1767.

80. AAPD 1973, no. 363.

81. *European Foreign Policy: Key Documents*, 300f.

82. 'Britain and a Middle East Settlement', enclosed to note FCO (Parsons to Private Secretary) 'Arab/Israel', 24 October 1973, FCO 93/274; note Elysée (Raimond to Pompidou), 'Positions soviétique et française sur le règlement du conflit israélo–arabe', 18 October 1973, AN 5AG2 1034.

83. UK embassy Tel Aviv (Bernard Ledwidge) to FCO, 11 November 1973, no. 595, with the text of Eban's statement of 9 November 1973, FCO 30/1675.

84. 'Erpressung und Appeasement', *Neue Zürcher Zeitung*, 11 November 1973; Sus (1974), 75.

85. Maull (1975), 8.

86. Venn (2002), 124.

87. FRG embassy Bonn (Sauvagnargues) to MAE, 7 November 1973, no. 5003/06, ADMAE Gén. 3804; brief FCO, 'Visit of Herr Walter Scheel, Minister for Foreign Affairs, FRG: 22–23 November', PREM 15/1571; Jobert (1976), 343.

88. UK embassy Bonn (Henderson) to FCO, 13 November 1973, FCO 93/226.

89. Note FCO (Gore-Booth to Craig), 'Meeting of Middle East Working Group in Copenhagen on 12 November', 11 November 1973, FCO 93/226.

90. FCO (Craig) to UK embassy Cairo (Richard Faber), 'European Political Cooperation and the Middle East', 29 November 1973, FCO 93/227.

91. UK embassy Paris (Tomkins) to FCO, 22 November 1973, FCO 93/226.

92. For the *Aide Mémoire*, see FCO 93/227.

93. Circular MAE (de Courcel), 21 November 1973, no. 714, ADMAE Gén. 3804.

94. For the text of the demarche, see FCO 30/1675.

95. Ilan Greilsammer and Joseph Weiler, 'European Political Cooperation and the Palestinian–Israeli conflict', in Allen and Pijpers (1984), 121–60, 136.

96. See note 90 in this chapter.

97. Krämer (1974), 51.

98. The resolutions were secret, but leaked to the Arab press on 4 December 1973. Hohensee (1996), 88.

99. 'Aux émissaires du pétrole: pourquoi punir les Neuf?' *Le Monde*, 28 November 1973.

100. Kissinger (2000b), 883.

101. Translated by the author from Jobert (1976), 344.

102. For Jobert's speech, see FCO 30/1763.

103. Jobert's idea was for Brandt to act as Community spokesman in 1974, Heath in 1975, and Pompidou in 1976. Note PMO (Armstrong), 'Note for the Record', undated [early September 1973], PREM 15/1507; Jobert (1974), 252f.

104. 'Déclaration à l'issue du Conseil des Ministres', 31 October 1973, in *Georges Pompidou*, vol. II, 267f.

105. Record of conversation between Heath and Pompidou at Chequers on 16 November 1973, AN 5AG2 1015; circular MAE (Jobert), 5 November 1973, AN 5AG2 1036; AAPD 1973, nos. 382 and 394.

106. 'Pompidou proposerait de doter l'Europe d'une sorte de 'conseil de sécurité'', *Le Monde*, 13 December 1973.

107. Kissinger (2000b), 719.

108. AAPD 1973, no. 365.

109. See the dossier 'Verstärkung der Westpolitik', in AdsD KF 194. While there was an extraordinary, all-day Cabinet session on European and security policy in November 1973, it produced little more than guidelines for upcoming EC negotiations. AAPD 1973, no. 361; note BKA (Strehlke and Fischer), 'Vermerk für die Kabinettssitzung am 15. November 1973: EG und EPZ', 9 November 1973, BA B136/6417.

110. Note BKA (Schilling to Fischer), 13 November 1973, BA B136/6417.

111. Record of conversation between Douglas-Home and Scheel in London on 23 November 1973, FCO 30/1758.

112. Note AA (200/411), 31 October 1973, PA B21/751; note AA (van Well), 'Gespräch zwischen dem Herrn Bundesminister und dem niederländischen Aussenminister', 19 November 1973, PA B150/293.

113. *European Foreign Policy: Key Documents*, 83–92. An annex 'relatif aux fonctionnements de la Coopération Politique' was kept confidential (AN 5AG2 1035). On the EPC negotiations that led to the report, see circulars MAE (Puaux), 19 January 1973, MAE (de Courcel), 22 February 1973, MAE (Puaux), 30 March 1973, and MAE (Puaux), 29 May 1973, all in ADMAE Gén. 3795.

114. 'Statement made by Sir Alec Douglas-Home at the Ministerial Meeting (Political European Co-operation) in Brussels on 16 March', FCO 30/1670.

115. Letter UKREP Brussels (Palliser) to FCO (Wright), 'A Community Foreign Policy', 14 March 1973, FCO 30/ 1654.

116. Note FCO (Butler to Wright), 'European Political Cooperation: Relationship between Political Cooperation and Institutions of the Community', 28 June 1973, FCO 30/1673.

117. Note CO (Nairne, now second permanent secretary) to PMO (Armstrong), 'Regular and more frequent summit meetings', 26 October 1973, PREM 15/1523; letter Heath to Pompidou, 5 November 1973, PREM 15/1523; letter Brandt to Pompidou, 7 November 1973, AN 5AG2 1009.

118. Letter Pompidou to Anker Jørgensen, prime minister of Denmark, 15 November 1973, ADMAE Gén. 3789.

119. Monnet (1988), Ch. 21. In London, Monnet suggested that additional frequent informal coordination meetings among the Big Three (through personal advisers of the leaders) would be necessary to give impetus to Europe. Note PMO (Armstrong), 'Note for the Record', 20 September 1973, PREM 15/1527.

120. Note Elysée (Raimond to Pompidou), 10 December 1973, AN 5AG2 1036.

121. Note FCO (Wright to Private Secretary), 15 November 1973, FCO 30/1637; Douglas-Home (from Copenhagen) to FCO, 20 November 1973, FCO 30/1638; circular MAE (Puaux), 22 November 1973, no. 722, ADMAE Gén. 3789.

122. Jobert (1974), 279.

123. Note FCO (Tickell), 'European Defence Co-operation', 23 May 1973, FCO 41/1158; AAPD 1973, no. 102.

124. Jobert (1974), 267; record of conversation between Carrington and Galley in London on 26 June 1973, AN 5AG2 1014.

125. Note FCO (Wiggin to Tickell), 'Anglo/French Defence Relations', 26 June 1973, FCO 41/1133; record of conversation between Galley and Carrington in Paris on 16 November 1973, FCO 41/1134.

126. Note MOD (K. T. Nash), 'France and the Western Alliance', 20 February 1973, FCO 41/1131; UK embassy Bonn (Hibbert) to FCO, 2 November 1973, FCO 41/1356; AAPD 1973, no. 275.

127. Note FCO (Tickell to Brimelow), 'European Defence Co-operation', 26 July 1973, FCO 41/1356.

128. AAPD 1973, no. 300; letter UK embassy Bonn (Hibbert) to FCO (Wiggin), 3 December 1973, with an enclosed paper of the Auswärtige Amt on European defence cooperation, FCO 41/1357.

129. Georges-Henri Soutou, 'L'attitude de Georges Pompidou face à l'Allemagne', in Association Georges Pompidou (1995), 267–313, 301.

130. AAPD 1973, no. 198 and 201. The French records (AN 5AG2 106 and 1012) differ in key passages and provide extra details.

131. Ibid.

132. Note FRG embassy Paris (von Braun), 'Gespräch mit Jobert', 20 September 1973, PA SvB 172.

133. Jobert (1974), 268f.

134. AAPD 1973, nos. 367 and 368. For the French record, see AN 5AG2 1012. On Scheel's view about a European nuclear force, see AAPD 1973, no. 274.

135. Weed (1988), 73–7; 'M. Jobert a crée au Quai d'Orsay un "centre d'analyse et de prévision"', *Le Monde*, 27 December 1973.

136. Note FCO (Cable to Elliott), 'Anglo–French Planning Talks', 17 September 1973, FCO 49/489; note FCO (Cable to Elliott), 'Anglo–French Planning Talks: 23 October 1973', 25 October 1973, PREM 15/1556. In London on 2 July 1973, Jobert had already suggested a European Defence Group and meetings of the General Staffs of the Nine. Note Bundesministerium für Verteidigung to BKA (Horst Grabert), 6 September 1973, AdsD EB 441.

137. Record of conversation between Pompidou and Heath in Paris on 21 May 1973 (top secret version), PREM 15/1357.

138. 'C'est pourquoi, si le gouvernement britannique le désire, je considère que la question est posée et qu'il faut s'y attaquer, contrairement à ce qui a souvent été l'attitude de la France.' Record of first conversation between Pompidou and Heath in Paris on 21 May 1973 (Partie de l'entretien très secrète), AN 5AG2 1015.

139. Letter Heath to Pompidou, 18 June 1973, and Pompidou's answer of 29 June 1973, PREM 15/1357.

140. Carrington to Heath, 'Improvement of the Strategic Nuclear Deterrent', 13 July 1973, PREM 15/1360; minutes of a Cabinet meeting of 30 October 1973 on 'Defence Expenditure', 1 November 1973, PREM 15/2038.

141. 'Britain should rely on Polaris fleet of four and not purchase the costly Poseidon, MPs advised', *The Times*, 23 August 1973.

142. Record of third conversation between Pompidou and Nixon in Reykjavik on 1 June 1973, AN 5AG2 1023.

143. Letter Galley to Jobert, 2 December 1973, in possession of author, courtesy of Mary Weed; MAE (Directeur du Cabinet) to French embassy Washington (Kosciusko-Morizet), 16 January 1975, AN 582AP 38; Soutou (2000), 137f.; Ullman (1989).

144. Assembly of Western European Union, Proceedings 19th Session, second part (November 1973), IV (Minutes), 124–34.

145. Note MAE (Pactes) to Pompidou, 11 November 1973, AN 5AG2 1054; record of second conversation between Heath and Pompidou at Chequers on 16 November 1973 (partie secrète), AN 5AG2 1015.

146. AAPD 1973, nos. 390 and 393.

147. AAPD 1973, no. 385; note FCO to UK embassy Bonn (Hibbert), 'German Views on European Defence Co-operation', 13 December 1973, FCO 41/1357.

148. Assembly of Western European Union, Proceedings 19th Session, second part (November 1973), IV (Minutes), 169–80.

149. 'Comment by the British Government Spokesman on M. Jobert's Speech at the WEU Assembly', 30 November 1973, ADMAE Gén. 2909; record of conversation between Heath and Edmond Leburton, prime minister of Belgium, in Brussels on 3 December 1973, FCO 41/1357; AAPD 1973, no. 403.

150. Brief MOD for summit, 7 December 1973, FCO 41/1357.

151. AAPD 1973, no. 367; note MAE (de Lipkowski to Jobert), 21 November 1973, AN 5AG2 1014.

152. Note FCO (Wright to Tickell), 'The Political Directors and MBFR', 22 February 1973, FCO 41/1214; note Elysée (Raimond to Pompidou), 10 December 1973, AN 5AG2 1036.

153. 'Rapport du président du groupe de travail ad hoc chargé d'analyser les aspects politiques de l'accord soviéto–américain sur la prévention de la guerre nucléaire', CP(73) 59 P, 29 August 1973, FCO 41/1174.

154. FCO record of 'Anglo/German Politico–Military Talks London 4 October 1973', FCO 41/1158.

155. Circular FCO (Douglas-Home), 31 August 1973, FCO 30/1750.

156. 'The Identity of the Nine vis à vis the United States', undated [August 1973], PREM 15/1544; note FCO (Butler to Cable), 'US/European relations', 27 July 1973, FCO 30/1738.

157. 'Rapport du président du Comité politique sur les délibérations du Comité concernant l'identité européenne', RM(73) 17 P, 7 September 1973, ADMAE Gén. 3792.

158. 'De l'identité européenne', CP (73)65 F, 4 September 1973, AN 5AG2 1035.

159. Circular FCO (Douglas-Home), 18 September 1973, FCO 30/1750.

160. UKMIS NY (Maitland) to FCO, 28 September 1973, FCO 30/1750.

161. Brief FCO, 'The European Identity Paper', 26 September 1973, FCO 30/1750; letter FCO (Elliott) to PMO (Bridges), 15 November 1973, FCO 30/1637. A revised French draft of late October 1973 (FCO 30/1750) did include an annex

with rules for European–US relations. See FCO (Butler) to UK embassy Paris (Ewart-Biggs), 'European Identity exercise', 29 November 1973, FCO 30/1751.

162. Circular FCO (Douglas-Home), 31 August 1973, FCO 30/1750.

163. Notes MAE (Occ. to Jobert), 9 November 1973, AN 5AG2 1035; 8 November 1973, ADMAE Gén. 3795.

164. Note FCO (Butler to Cable), 'European identity paper', 12 September 1973, FCO 30/1750; circular FCO (Douglas-Home), 7 November 1973, FCO 30/1750; note MAE, 'Fiche III: Identité Européenne', 7 December 1973, AN 86AJ 123.

165. 'Declaration on European Identity by the Nine Foreign Ministers, Copenhagen, 14 December 1973', *European Foreign Policy: Key Documents*, 93–7.

166. Werner Link, 'Aussen- und Deutschlandpolitik in der Ära Brandt 1969–1974', in Bracher, Jäger, and Link (1986), 163–282, 257: 'Ein imponierender Check, der auf die Zukunft ausgestellt und machtpolitisch nicht gedeckt war.'

167. Dettke (1976), 166; AAPD 1973, no. 341

168. French embassy Washington (Kosciusko-Morizet) to MAE, 31 October 1973, ADMAE Etats-Unis 1137; Kissinger (2000b), 884.

169. Despatch UK embassy Washington (Cromer) to Douglas-Home, 'The Middle East and US/UK Relations', 9 January 1974, FCO 82/304; Kissinger (2000b), 708.

170. UK embassy Washington (Cromer) to FCO (Douglas-Home), 13 October 1973, no. 3208, PREM 15/1765.

171. Record of telephone conversation between Cromer and Kissinger on 13 October 1973, in *Crisis: The Anatomy*, 239. Kissinger eventually had to admit that his information from Moscow had been wrong. UK embassy Washington (Cromer) to FCO (Douglas-Home), 13 October 1973, no. 3210, PREM 15/1765.

172. Heath (1998), 501; Kissinger (2000b), 709.

173. Kissinger (2000b), 714; note FCO (Tickell to Wiggin), 29 November 1973, PREM 15/1766.

174. Harpprecht (2000), 375; Frank (1981), 268–72.

175. UKDEL NATO (Peck) to FCO, 16 October 1973, FCO 41/1178.

176. Van Well (1976), 124.

177. Kissinger (2000b), 710.

178. UK embassy Washington (Cromer) to FCO (Douglas-Home), 'The US, Europe and the Middle East', 15 November 1973, FCO 30/1676.

179. *Crisis: The Anatomy*, 352; note FCO (Tickell to Wiggin), 'The Middle East and the Alliance', 30 October 1973, FCO 41/1180.

180. Brosio (1974), 116.

181. UK embassy Moscow (Killick) to FCO, 19 October 1973, on the assessment of EC ambassadors in Moscow, FCO 41/1178.

182. French embassy Washington (Kosciusko-Morizet) to MAE (Jobert), 3 November 1973, no. 7184–88, AN 582AP 37. Kissinger did not edit the conciliatory passage of Brezhnev's letter in his memoirs (2000b), 583.

183. Nixon (1990), 928–35.

184. *The October War and U.S. Policy*, no. 90; Kissinger (2000b), 713.

185. Note FCO (Tickell to Wiggin), 29 October 1973, PREM 15/1766.

186. Kissinger (2000b), 716.

187. *Crisis: The Anatomy*, 390.

188. French embassy Washington (Kosciusko-Morizet) to MAE (Jobert), 25 October 1973, no. 6865–70, AN 582AP 37 (*absence totale du sens des responsabilités*).

189. *The October War and U.S. Policy*, no. 75.

190. Ibid., no. 81.

191. AAPD 1973, no. 341.

192. Kissinger (2000b), 635, 711, and 718; interview with Henry Kissinger.

193. Record of conversation between Carrington and Schlesinger in The Hague on 7 November 1973, FCO 41/1154.

194. 'Note for the Record: Prime Minister's Dinner with American Correspondents on 28.11.73', 29 November 1973, FCO 82/308; Kissinger (2000b), 721.

195. Record of conversation between Douglas-Home and Jobert at Dorneywood on 17 November 1973, FCO 30/1638.

196. Note CO (Hunt) to PMO (Armstrong), with an enclosed paper of the Joint Intelligence Committee Assessments Staff, 'The Effects of the Middle East War', 12 November 1973, PREM 15/1768.

197. AAPD 1973, no. 323; circular MAE (Puaux), 15 October 1973, and French embassy Copenhagen (Pelen) to MAE, 18 October 1973, ADMAE Etats-Unis 1137.

198. 'European second draft for a declaration of principles between the United States of America and the European Community and its Member States (articles 1–16)', ADMAE Etats-Unis 1137.

199. Note MAE (Puaux), 'Consultation Franco-britannique: Europe/Etats-Unis', 8 October 1973, AN 582AP 43.

200. Circular MAE (Puaux), 20 October 1973, with the text of the EPC briefs, ADMAE Etats-Unis 1137.

201. Wright (from Copenhagen) to FCO, 19 October 1973, no. 418, FCO 30/1741; circular MAE (Puaux), 20 October 1973, ADMAE Etats-Unis 1137; AAPD 1973, no. 333.

202. Circular French embassy Copenhagen (Pelen), 19 October 1973, ADMAE Etats-Unis 1137.

203. French embassy Washington (Kosciusko-Morizet) to MAE (Jobert), 25 October 1973, no. 6865–70, AN 582AP 37.

204. AAPD 1973, nos. 341 and 356.

205. UK embassy Washington (Cromer) to FCO, 31 October 1973, nos. 3415f., PREM 15/1767.

206. Kissinger (2000b), 714.

207. MAE (de Courcel) to French embassy London, 8 November 1973, with a 'Projet révisé de déclaration à quinze sur les relations atlantiques' as well as a synopsis of the first French draft, US amendments, and French comments on these amendments, AN 86AJ 123.

208. 'Projet de Déclaration a Quinze sur les Relations Atlantiques (révisé)', AN 5AG2 92; note MAE (Pactes) to Pompidou, 15 November 1973, AN 5AG2 92.

209. 'Projet de déclaration à 15 sur les relations atlantiques, 3ème révision', 28 November 1973, FCO 41/1191; REPAN-Bruxelles (de Rose) to MAE, 3 December 1973, AN 5AG2 1021.

210. Letter Jobert to Kissinger, 2 November 1973, AN 582AP 37.

211. Circular MAE (Puaux), 15 November 1973, ADMAE Etats-Unis 1137. The meeting produced a joint 'Third draft for a declaration of principles between the United States of America and the European Community and its Member States', 15 November 1973, AN 86AJ 123.

212. Wright (from New York) to FCO, 26 September 1973, no. 972, FCO 82/287; note AA (Koenig to Armin Zimmermann), 'US–Europa–Japan: Einbeziehung Japans in Grundsatzerklärung EG–US', 29 November 1973, PA B21/751.

213. 'Text of the Modified Draft of a U.S.–Common Market Statement', *New York Times*, 9 November 1973; UKDEL NATO (Peck) to FCO, 16 November 1973, on the leakage of the first French draft in *Le Figaro*, FCO 41/1190; 'French draft for NATO Declaration of Purpose', *New York Times*, 19 November 1973.

214. UK embassy Washington (Cromer) to FCO, 30 November and 5 December 1973, FCO 30/1751.

215. UK embassy Washington (Cromer) to FCO, 24 November 1973, no. 3674, FCO 82/309.

216. Brief FCO (WOD) for Douglas-Home, 'Cabinet: NATO Ministerial Meeting', 12 December 1973, FCO 41/1143.

217. AAPD 1973, nos. 410 and 411; 'Dîner quadripartite du 9 Décembre 1973 à Bruxelles', AN 582AP 38.

218. Kissinger (2000b), 723f.

219. AAPD 1973, no. 413; Douglas-Home (from Brussels) to FCO, 10 December 1973, no. 590–97; and UKDEL NATO (Peck) to FCO, nos. 877 and 879, 11 December 1973, FCO 41/1143.

220. Kissinger (2000b), 724.

221. FCO (Douglas-Home) to UK embassies in EC capitals, 27 November 1973, no. 910, FCO 30/1742; note FCO (John E. Killick, deputy under-secretary of state, to Wright), 'Proposed Nine–US Meeting', 11 December 1973, FCO 30/1743;

circular MAE (de Courcel), 12 December 1973, ADMAE Gén. 3810; note Elysée (Raimond to Pompidou), 13 December 1973, AN 5AG2 1021.

222. Catlin (1974).

223. The address to The Pilgrims of Great Britain (Pilgrims Society) is reproduced in Mally (1974), 39–46.

224. Note FCO (Wright to Douglas-Home), 'Britain and the European Community – Retrospect: 1973', 21 December 1973, FCO 30/1651.

225. Note FCO, 'The Summit Programme and the negotiating possibilities', 6 July 1973, FCO 30/1639.

226. See note 224 in this chapter; note FCO (Patrick Grattan to Goulding), 'Internal Development of the Community', 23 July 1973, FCO 30/1650.

227. AAPD 1973, nos. 50, 69, and 70; Brandt (1978), 329f.

228. AAPD 1973, no. 75, note 9.

229. AAPD 1973, no. 80.

230. Record of second conversation between Pompidou and Heath in Paris on 21 May 1973, AN 5AG2 1015; note Elysée (Michel Freyche, counsellor of the president, to Pompidou), 10 December 1973, AN 5AG2 1036.

231. Note Elysée (Bernard to Pompidou), 'Note pour Monsieur le Président de la République', 16 January 1973, AN 86AJ 150; French embassy London to Pompidou, 4 May 1973, AN 5AG2 1015.

232. Note BKA (Koordinierungsgruppe Europa), 29 October 1973, BA B136/30659.

233. AAPD 1973, no. 345.

234. Note AA (Hans Lautenschlager to Scheel), 'Behandlung der Erdölkrise in der EG', PA B1/577.

235. Draft telegram FCO (Nicholas Fenn, Energy Department) to UK embassy The Hague, undated [November 1973], FCO 30/1675; note FCO 'Economic Strategic Committee: 11 December – Energy: Scope for Practical Cooperation in the EEC', 10 December 1973, FCO 30/1652.

236. AAPD 1973, no. 390.

237. Circular Douglas-Home (from Brussels), 5 November 1973, FCO 93/225.

238. EUROGERMA (Lebsanft) to AA, 6 November 1973, BA B136/6421.

239. Heath (1998), 502.

240. Lieber (1976), 14.

241. UKREP Brussels (Palliser) to FCO, 26 November 1973, FCO 30/1638.

242. Cabinet CP(73)139, 'Energy Situation: Public Expenditure Measures: Memorandum by the Chancellor of the Exchequer', 12 December 1973, CAB 129/173; Brunn (2002), 187.

243. Venn (2002), 121 and 158; Campbell (1993), 565.

244. Note PMO (Armstrong), 'Note for the Record', undated [early September 1973], PREM 15/1507; record of conversation between Heath and Brandt at Chequers on 6 October 1973, PREM 15/1564.

245. AAPD 1973, no. 399; letter Apel to Brandt, 6 December 1973, WBA BK 1.

246. Bahr's speech at the Centre d'Etudes de Politique Etrangère in Paris on 20 November 1973, 'Réflexions sur la politique étrangère de la République Fédérale d'Allemagne', AdsD EB 302; Harpprecht (2000), 427.

247. Circular FCO (Douglas-Home), 17 December 1973, FCO 30/1639.

248. Frank (1981), 365.

249. Jobert (1976), 354; Heath (1998), 393; Brandt (1978), 371.

250. FCO (Douglas-Home) to UK embassy Copenhagen, 12 December 1973, FCO 30/1652; Jobert (1974), 278.

251. Circular MAE (Puaux), 'Entretiens avec les Ministres Arabes', 18 December 1973, ADMAE Gén. 3789; Brandt (1978), 372.

252. For the final communiqué, see *Bulletin of the European Communities* no. 12 (1973): 9–12.

253. Note FCO, 'Discussion of the Middle East at the Copenhagen Summit', undated, FCO 30/1652; FCO (Douglas-Home) to UK embassy Amman, 17 December 1973, FCO 30/1639; note BKA (Fischer), 'Konferenz der Staats- und Regierungschefs der Neun in Kopenhagen am 14./15. Dezember 1973; hier: Äusserungen des Bundeskanzlers zum Nahost-Problem', 21 December 1973, PA ZA 104979. On British and French summit proposals concerning the Middle East, see note MAE, 14 December 1973, ADMAE Gén. 3789.

254. AAPD 1973, no. 382; Jobert (1976), 363.

255. Note MAE (Levant) to Pompidou, 'Le Proche-Orient et l'Europe', 3 December 1973, AN 86AJ 123.

256. 'Die europäische Identität in der Erdölkrise', *Neue Zürcher Zeitung*, 16 December 1973.

257. Record of conversation between Heath and Kissinger in London on 12 December 1973, FCO 41/1191.

258. Note PMO (Bridges) to FCO (Elliott), 'Message from the Prime Minister to President Nixon', FCO 30/1639; circular MAE (Puaux), 18 December 1973, ADMAE Gén. 3789.

259. For the respective summit proposals of individual delegations, see BA B102/201338.

260. Note BKA (Fischer), 'Treffen der Staats- und Regierungschefs der Neun in Kopenhagen am 14./15. Dezember 1973; hier: Debatte über Energiepolitik', 21 December 1973, BA B102/201338.

261. AAPD 1973, no. 422; note AA (Alois Jelonek, 412), 'Ergebnisse der EG-Gipfelkonferenz: hier: Energiepolitik/Innerer Ausbau', 19 December 1973, PA ZA 104979; Krämer (1974), 91.

262. FCO (Butler) to UK embassy Washington (Graham), 18 December 1973, FCO 30/1638.

263. Note AA (von der Gablentz), 'Sprechzettel für Kabinettssitzung', 18 December 1973, PA B21/751; 'Entretien radiotélévisée avec M. Cavada (O.R.T.F.)',

20 December 1973, in *Georges Pompidou*, vol. II, 269; circular FCO (Douglas-Home), 17 December 1973, FCO 30/1639.

264. Brandt (1978), 373.

265. Record of telephone conversation between Heath and Brandt on 16 December 1973, FCO 30/1758.

266. AAPD 1973, no. 425.

267. 'What went wrong in Bonn', *The Economist*, 22 December 1973.

268. Merseburger (2002), 657f.

269. Scheel (2004), 134–7.

Part III: US Discontent

1. The US journal *Foreign Affairs* in April 1974 grouped several articles on the energy crisis under the heading of 'The Year of Economics'.

2. 'Allocution prononcée à l'occasion de la présentation des vœux du corps diplomatique', 31 January 1974, *Georges Pompidou*, vol. II, 277: 'Nous sommes entrés dans l'ère des incertitudes.' On the economic crisis, see Grosser (1976); Venn (2002), 154–62.

3. Note FRG embassy Paris (von Braun), 'Flottierung des Franc', 11 February 1974, PA SvB 172; Müller-Roschach (1980), 335.

4. AAPD 1974, no. 19; note Elysée (Gabriel Robin, counsellor to the president, to Pompidou), 24 January 1974, AN 5AG2 1054; note CO (Nairne) to PMO (Bridges), 'Regional Development Fund: Where we are', 31 January 1974, PREM 15/2081.

5. Note AA (Jelonek), 'Europäische Energiepolitik', 27 February 1974, PA ZA 105693. For an overview of deals and negotiations by EC members, see note Apel to Helga Köhnen, SPD parliamentary party (Koordinierungsstelle Europapolitik), 6 March 1974, AdsD HJW 819.

6. Note FRG BMWi (Everling, head Abteilung E, to Minister Hans Friederichs), 'Lage der Europäischen Gemeinschaft', 22 May 1974, BA B102/185797.

7. See the analysis by Schmidt of 15 April 1974, AdsD KF 207, reproduced as 'Der Politiker als Ökonom' in *Helmut Schmidt: Kontinuität und Konzentration*, 128–44.

8. Note BKA (Manfred Lahnstein and Fischer to Brandt), 'Europäische Integration: Vorbereitung eines neuen Integrationsprogramms', 6 May 1974, BA B136/17654.

9. FCO draft paper 'Surviving the Seventies', 10 October 1974, FCO 49/522.

10. *Bulletin of the European Communities* no. 1 (January 1974): 5–8.

11. Schaetzel (1975), 140.

12. See the various studies by BKA (Lahnstein and Fischer) regarding 'Europäische Integration; hier: Erste Überlegungen für die Präsidentschaftskonferenz im Mai 1974', February and March 1974, BA B136/6417.

13. UK embassy Washington (Sykes) to FCO (Brimelow), 'Dr Kissinger's Visit to Europe', 25 January 1974, FCO 82/424.

14. Hanhimäki (2004), xvi and 330.

15. Note FCO (Butler to Wright and Private Secretary), 'Political Implications of Issues Likely to Arise at the Washington Meeting on Energy', undated [early February 1974], FCO 30/2494.

16. Note BKA (Thiele, IV/1), 'Europapolitische Bilanz', undated [February 1974], BA B136/6417; FCO Planning Paper, 'British Foreign Policy: The Scope for Change', 12 February 1974, FCO 30/2457.

6 The Washington Energy Conference

1. 'Un nouveau 'Discours de Harvard'', *Le Monde*, 14 December 1973; 'Alone or Together?' *New York Times*, 16 December 1973; Kissinger (2000b), 897.

2. US embassy London (Earl D. Sohm, chargé d'affaires) to Douglas-Home, 14 December 1973, PREM 15/2178.

3. Letter Kissinger to Scheel, 12 December 1973, HSA 8999.

4. Note BKA (AL IV to Brandt), 'Initiative des amerikanischen Präsidenten auf dem Energiegebiet', 10 January 1974, WBA BK 60; 'Special Message to the Congress on the Energy Crisis', 23 January 1974, *Public Papers of the Presidents of the United States: Richard Nixon – 1974*, 17–32.

5. Interview with Henry Kissinger.

6. Note Douglas-Home to Heath, 'Copenhagen Summit: Kissinger's Proposal on Energy', 13 December 1973, FCO 82/289.

7. Letter Heath to Nixon, 15 October 1973, PREM 15/1981.

8. Note FCO (Wright to Killick), 'An Assessment of Dr Kissinger's Visit', 7 January 1974 [erroneously dated 1973], FCO 30/2495.

9. Note FCO (Amery to Douglas-Home), 18 December 1973, FCO 73/152; letter Douglas-Home to Kissinger, 20 December 1973, FCO 82/325.

10. Note MAE (Occ.), 'Relations Europe/Etats-Unis: Discours de M. Kissinger (Londres, 12 décembre)', 18 December 1973, ADMAE Gén. 3810; note Elysée (Robin to Pompidou), 19 December 1973, AN 5AG2 1023.

11. FRG embassy Paris (Blomeyer-Bartenstein) to AA, 22 December 1973, PA ZA 104992.

12. Record of conversation between Jobert and Kissinger in Paris on 19 December 1973, National Archives at College Park, MD, Nixon Presidential Materials Staff, HAK Office Files, French Memcons 1973, Box 56; record of conversation between Pompidou and Kissinger in Paris on 20 December 1973, AN 5AG2 1023; Kissinger (2000b), 898.

13. Circular FCO (Douglas-Home), 13 December 1973, PREM 15/2178.

14. FCO (Douglas-Home) to UK embassy Washington, 20 December 1973, no. 2503; note Douglas-Home to Heath, 'Appointment of a United Kingdom Representative to the High Level Energy Action Group suggested by Dr. Kissinger', 28 December 1973, PREM 15/2178.

15. UKDEL OECD (Francis Gallagher) to FCO, 27 December 1973; and circular FCO (Douglas-Home), 31 December 1973, PREM 15/2178.

16. Note FCO (Wright to Killick), 'An Assessment of Dr Kissinger's Visit', 7 January 1974, FCO 30/2495.

17. AAPD 1974, no. 5, note 9.

18. Record of conversation between Heath and Schmidt in London on 29 January 1974, PREM 15/2178; letters Kissinger to Schmidt (via back channel Bahr–Kissinger), 27 November and 8 December 1973, AdsD EB 439; Schmidt (1987), 201f.

19. For Jobert's letter, see Kissinger (2000b), 899.

20. Hohensee (1996), 90f; Krämer (1974), 51f.

21. French embassy Bonn to AA (Poensgen), 20 December 1973, PA ZA 104992.

22. Kissinger (2000b), 885–93.

23. Letter Nixon to Heath, 6 January 1974, PREM 15/2178; AAPD 1974, no. 5.

24. For Nixon's letters to Brandt, Heath, and Pompidou of 9 January 1974, see WBA BK 60, PREM 15/2178, and AN 5AG2 1021.

25. Letter Nixon to Brandt, 9 January 1974, WBA BK 60.

26. 'Transcript of a Press Conference Discussion on the Energy Crisis and the Middle East, Held in Washington Yesterday (January 10th) by U.S. Secretary of State Henry Kissinger and Federal Energy Administrator William Simon', 11 January 1974, PREM 15/2178.

27. For the specific US proposals, submitted on 30 January 1974, see UK brief, 'Council of Ministers: 3/4 February, Item 1: Washington Energy Conference', undated, CAB 164/1255.

28. Note FCO (Nicholas Fenn, energy department, to John Taylor and Private Secretary), 'Nixon Proposal on Energy', 9 January 1974, PREM 15/2178.

29. Record of conversation between Hunt and Kissinger in Washington on 30 January 1974, CAB 164/1255.

30. AAPD 1974, no. 30, notes 3 and 4; 'Nixons Ölkonferenz', *Frankfurter Allgemeine Zeitung*, 17 January 1974.

31. Note Elysée (Robin to Pompidou), 10 January 1974, AN 5AG2 1021; note AA (Christel Steffler), 'Deutsch–französische Direktorenkonsultation am 24.1.1974 in Bonn; hier: Französische Haltung zur Energiekonferenz in Washington am 14.2.1974', 24 January 1974, PA B150/297; Debré (1996), 211.

32. AAPD 1974, no. 30 (*Gleichschaltung der europäischen und japanischen Haltung mit der amerikanischen*).

33. Record of conversation between Carrington and Simonet in London on 31 January 1974, CAB 164/1255.

34. See, for example, FRG embassy Washington (von Staden) to AA, 30 January 1974, PA B150/29; note FRG BMF (Georg-Dieter Gotschlich to Schmidt), 'Energiekonferenz in Washington', 29 January 1974, HSA 6005.

35. Kissinger (2000b), 901 and 906.

36. Record of conversation between Wilson and Nixon in Paris on 6 April 1974, PREM 16/95; Nixon (1990), 970–88.

37. Wright (from Bonn) to FCO, 10 January 1974; UKREP Brussels (Palliser) to FCO, 11 January 1974; UK embassy Paris (Tomkins) to FCO, 11 January 1974, PREM 15/2178; FRG embassy Paris (Blomeyer-Bartenstein) to AA, 11 January 1974, WBA BK 60.

38. Circular Douglas-Home, 17 January 1974, PREM 15/2178.

39. Note CO (Hunt) to PMO (Heath), 'Steering Brief for the Washington Energy Conference', 28 January 1974, PREM 15/2178; Douglas-Home to UK embassy Washington, 8 February 1974, no. 340, PREM 15/2179; note AA (412), 'Energiekonferenz in Washington; hier: Deutsche Haltung', 5 February 1974, PA ZA 105693.

40. Letter Heath to Nixon, 17 January 1974, PREM 15/2178; letter Brandt to Nixon, 18 January 1974, WBA BK 60.

41. UK brief, 'Council of Ministers: 3/4 February, Item 1: Washington Energy Conference', undated, CAB 164/1255.

42. Record of conversation between Douglas-Home and Kissinger at London Airport on 20 January 1974; Douglas-Home to UK embassy Washington, 3 February 1974; letter Heath to Nixon, 17 January 1974, PREM 15/2178; letter Douglas-Home to Kissinger, 9 February 1974, PREM 15/2179.

43. AAPD 1974, no. 33.

44. UK brief, 'Council of Ministers: 3/4 February, Item 1: Washington Energy Conference', undated, CAB 164/1255; note CO (Hunt) to PMO (Heath), 'Steering Brief for the Washington Energy Conference', 28 January 1974, PREM 15/2178.

45. Note FCO (Butler to Wright and Private Secretary), 'Political Implications of Issues Likely to Arise at the Washington Meeting on Energy', undated [early February 1974], FCO 30/2494.

46. Note FCO (Braithwaite to Butler), 'Europe, Energy and the Arabs', 16 January 1974, FCO 30/2344.

47. Letter Heath to Nixon, 25 January 1974, PREM 15/2178.

48. Letter Douglas-Home to Scheel, 9 February 1974, PREM 15/2179.

49. CO (Hunt) to UK embassy Washington (Sykes), 28 January 1974, PREM 15/2178.

50. Record of conversation between Hunt and Kissinger in Washington on 30 January 1974, CAB 164/1255; Hunt (from Washington) to FCO, 30 January 1974, nos. 367 and 368, PREM 15/2178.

51. AAPD 1974, no. 30.

52. Letter Brandt to Nixon, 28 January 1974, WBA BK 60.

53. Letter Brandt to Scheel, 8 February 1974, WBA BK 45.

54. Note Elysée (Robin to Pompidou), 10 January 1974, AN 5AG2 1021; note MAE (C.A.P. to Jobert), 21 January 1974, AN 5AG2 203.

55. Letter Jobert to Waldheim, 18 January 1974, FCO 30/2344.

56. For the French *Aide Mémoire*, see PA ZA 105693.

57. Weed (1981), 320–8 and 343; Jobert (1976), 367–73.

58. Debré (1996), 211; Jobert (1974), 285; Robin's retrospective note on Pompidou's foreign policy, undated [1974], AN 5AG2 1163.

59. 'Déclaration à l'issue du Conseil des Ministres', 6 February 1974, in *Georges Pompidou*, vol. II, 308f. See also letter Pompidou to Nixon, 7 February 1974, AN 5AG2 1021.

60. 'Mandat der Vertreter der Gemeinschaft für die Washingtoner Konferenz', undated, PA ZA 105693.

61. Jobert (1976), 376; AAPD 1974, no. 23.

62. 'Mandat des Représentants de la Communauté à la Conférence de Washington: Proposition française', undated, FCO 30/2345; note BMWi, 'Aufzeichnung zur Behandlung der Vorbereitung der Washingtoner Konferenz im EG-Rat am 5.2.1974', 4 February 1974, PA ZA 105693.

63. Note FCO (Fenn to Taylor), 'Washington Energy Conference: EEC Council of Ministers, Brussels, 5 February', 6 February 1974, FCO 30/2345.

64. EUROGERMA (Ulrich Lebsanft) to AA, 6 February 1974, PA ZA 105693; Lieber (1976), 21.

65. AAPD 1974, no. 42; Kissinger (2000b), 904.

66. Kissinger (2000b), 904f.; record of telephone conversation between Kissinger and Sonnenfeldt on 8 February 1974, as in 'Kissinger Telephone Transcripts (1973–1976)' (foia.state.gov).

67. Letters Nixon to Heath, 3 February 1974, and Heath to Nixon, 4 February 1974, PREM 15/2178; letters Nixon to Brandt, 4 February 1974, and Bahr to Kissinger (back channel), 4 February 1974, AdsD EB 439; note PMO (Bridges) to FCO (Alexander), 4 February 1974, CAB 164/1255.

68. Kissinger (2000b), 907f.; AAPD 1974, no. 42.

69. Record of conversation between Heath and Schmidt in London on 29 January 1974, PREM 15/2178.

70. Kissinger (2000b), 909.

71. Walton (1976), 188.

72. Jobert (1976), 378.

73. Von Staden (2005), 139.

74. Jobert (1976), 379; (1974), 287; Kissinger (2000b), 910f.

75. Kissinger's speech is reproduced in Mally (1974), 47–55.

76. Kissinger (2000b), 912.

77. Scheel's speech is reproduced at (www.ena.lu).

78. Schmidt's speech, as published on 12 February 1974 in 'BMF Finanznachrichten' (13/74), BA N1371 63.

79. Douglas-Home (from Washington) to FCO, 12 February 1974, no. 540, PREM 15/2179.

80. Jobert's speech is reproduced at (www.ena.lu).

81. FRG embassy Washington (Peter Hermes and von Staden), 'Energiekonferenz; hier: Delegationsbericht Nr. 1', 12 February 1974, BA N1371 63.

82. Jobert (1976, 380) quotes Schmidt as saying: 'S'il faut choisir entre l'Europe et l'Amérique, je choisis l'Amérique et je le dis bien haut!'

83. 'Remarks at a Working Dinner of the Washington Energy Conference', 11 February 1974, *Public Papers of the Presidents of the United States: Richard Nixon – 1974*, 150–6; Kissinger (2000b), 915f.

84. AAPD 1974, no. 49.

85. FRG embassy Washington (Brunner and von Staden), 'Energiekonferenz; hier: Delegationsbericht Nr. 2', 12 February 1974, BA N1371 63; Schmidt (1987), 202.

86. Harpprecht (2000), 488; AAPD 1974, no. 189.

87. Kissinger (2000b), 917–20.

88. 'Washington Energy Conference Final Communiqué', FCO 30/2345.

89. FRG embassy Washington (Hermes and von Staden), 'Energiekonferenz; hier: Delegationsbericht Nr. 3', 13 February 1974, BA N1371 63.

90. Note AA (Hans-Günter Sulimma, press division, to Scheel) '"Europäische" Pressekonferenz am Ende der Energiekonferenz von Washington vom 11./12. Februar 1974', 29 January 1974, PA B1/581; AAPD 1974, no. 49, note 10.

91. 'Press conference given in Washington by Mr Michel Jobert', 13 February 1974, reproduced at (www.ena.lu); Kissinger (2000b), 922; Jobert (1974), 289.

92. Kissinger (2000b), 922–4.

93. Schmidt (1990), 138 and 164.

94. Fiona Venn, 'International Co-operation versus National Self-Interest: The United States and Europe during the 1973–1974 Oil Crisis', in Burk and Stokes (1999), 71–98, 87.

95. AAPD 1974, nos. 68 and 203; record of telephone conversation between Kissinger and George P. Shultz, US secretary of the treasury, on 20 March 1974, as in 'Kissinger Telephone Transcripts (1973–1976)' (foia.state.gov).

96. Eric Varley, secretary of state for energy, to Wilson, 'Energy Co-ordinating Group', 26 April 1974, PREM 16/243.

97. Kissinger (1999), 680f.

98. AAPD 1974, no. 317, note 47; Kissinger (1999), 680–3.

99. Turner (1974).

100. FRG embassy Washington (Brunner and von Staden), 'Energiekonferenz; hier: Delegationsbericht Nr. 2', 12 February 1974, BA N1371 63.

101. Record of conversation between Wright, Fenn, Cuvillier and J. Fargue (the latter two: French embassy London) in London on 15 February 1974, FCO 73/151.

102. Note FCO (Braithwaite to Butler), 'Conversation with American Embassy', 20 February 1974, FCO 30/2345.

103. UK embassy France (Ewart-Biggs) to FCO, 'France, Europe and the Atlantic Relationship', 17 February 1974, PREM 15/2179; record of conversation between Pompidou and Brezhnev in the Soviet Union on 13 March 1974, AN 5AG2 1019.

104. Wright quoting Messmer, as in note 101 in this chapter; Weed (1981), 578.

105. Jobert (1976), 383.

106. AAPD 1974, no. 65; note Elysée (Robin to Pompidou), 20 February 1974, AN 5AG2 1035.

107. Wright's quote, as in note 101 in this chapter.

108. Note FCO (Braithwaite to Butler), 'Conversation with American Embassy', 20 February 1974, FCO 30/2345.

109. 'Festhalten Bonns am Kurs der Europäischen Union', *Neue Zürcher Zeitung*, 18 February 1974.

110. Note MAE (de Lipkowski to Jobert), 'Note pour le Ministre', 12 December 1973, AN 5AG2 1025.

111. For the French paper 'Coopération Europe – Pays Arabes', see BA B102/185797.

112. The three meetings took place on 18 and 25 January and 1 February 1974. See note MAE (Levant), 'Coopération européo–arabe (Groupe d'experts Proche-Orient)', 21 January 1974, ADMAE Gén. 3807; notes AA (Christoph Niemöller, Referat Naher Osten), 'Sitzung der Gruppe 'Naher Osten' am 25. Januar 1974', 25 January 1974; and 'Sitzung der Nahostgruppe am Freitag, dem 1. Februar 1974', 5 February 1974, PA B150/297 and B150/298.

113. 'Entretien avec les journalistes à l'Elysée', 3 January 1974, in *Georges Pompidou*, vol. II, 285; draft record of conversation between Douglas-Home and Kissinger in London on 12 December 1973, FCO 82/309; note AA (Niemöller), 'Sitzung der Nahostgruppe am Freitag, dem 1. Februar 1974', 5 February 1974, PA B150/298.

114. For example, see note BMWi (Everling), 'Europäisch–arabischer Dialog über eine künftige Kooperation', BA B102/185797.

115. Paper FCO, 'Euro/Arab Dialogue: Objectives', undated, FCO 30/2520.

116. FCO (Butler) to UK embassy Bonn, 7 February 1974, FCO 30/2494.

117. AAPD 1974, no. 41; MAE (Arnaud) to Jobert (in Baghdad), 7 February 1974, no. 516/22, ADMAE Gén. 3807.

118. AAPD 1974, no. 29.

119. Brief FCO, 'European Political Cooperation: Political Committee 6/7 February 1974, Agenda Item 2: Middle East', undated, FCO 30/2512; 'Proche-Orient: Rapport du Comité Politique aux Ministres des Affaires étrangères en vue de la réunion du 14 février 1974', RM (74) 1 CP, 7 February 1974, B150/298.

120. Note BMF (State Secretary Manfred Schüler) to Brandt, 11 February 1974, on a telephone call by Schmidt, WBA BK 60 (*ernsthafte Krise im Bündnis*); AAPD 1974, nos. 42 and 65.

121. Telegram Brandt to Scheel (in Washington), note BMF (Schüler) to Brandt, telegram Scheel (from Washington) to Brandt, all 11 February 1974, WBA BK 60.

122. Note MAE (Levant), 'Réunion des Ministres des Affaires Etrangères (Bruxelles – 4 mars) – Proche orient', 27 February 1974, ADMAE Gén. 3804.

123. 'Note: Conférence euro–arabe', 28 February 1974, PA ZA 104989.

124. FCO (Douglas-Home) to UK embassy Washington, 20 February 1974, FCO 82/440.

125. Note AA to Brandt, 15 February 1974, WBA BK 60.

126. FCO (Douglas-Home) to UK embassy Bonn, 19 February 1974, FCO 30/2512.

127. FCO (Douglas-Home) to UK embassy Washington, 20 February 1974, FCO 82/440; paper FCO, 'Euro/Arab Dialogue: Objectives', undated, FCO 30/2520; note FCO (Michael Weir, NENAD, to Alan Campbell, deputy under-secretary of state, and to Private Secretary), 'Europe/Arab Dialogue', 6 March 1974, FCO 30/2513; FCO (Douglas-Home) to UK embassy Bonn, 19 February 1974, FCO 30/2512.

128. Circular MAE (de Courcel), 5 March 1974, no. 161, ADMAE Gén. 3807.

129. Record of conversation between Douglas-Home and Kissinger in London on 26 February 1974, FCO 82/440.

130. Record of conversation between Scheel and Kissinger in Bonn on 3 March 1974, PA B150/300; AAPD 1974, no. 67.

131. 'Brandt und Kissinger betonen gute deutsch–amerikanische Beziehungen', *Süddeutsche Zeitung*, 5 March 1974; AAPD 1974, no. 68.

132. AAPD 1974, no. 77.

133. Note MAE, 'Compte rendu de la réunion ministérielle du 4 mars 1974 au titre de la coopération politique européenne à Bruxelles', ADMAE Gén. 3792.

134. Circular MAE (de Courcel), 5 March 1974, no. 161, ADMAE Gén. 3792; Jobert (1976), 384.

135. The earlier draft can be found in PA ZA 108877, the final version in FCO 30/2516.

136. Record AA of the 'Pressekonferenz des Bundesministers Scheel als Vorsitzender der EPZ-Ministerkonferenz am 4.3.1974 in Brüssel', PA ZA 104987.

137. Kissinger (2000b), 929.

138. AAPD 1974, no. 69.

139. Pierre Mélandri, 'Une relation très spéciale: la France, les Etats-Unis et l'Année de l'Europe, 1973–1974', in Association Georges Pompidou (1995), 89–131, 125.

140. Letter Nixon to Brandt, 6 March 1974, ADMAE Etats-Unis 1138.

141. AAPD 1974, no. 81.

142. Letter Jobert to Scheel, 21 March 1974, HSA 8999. See also note MAE (Occ.), 'L'information des Etats-Unis en matière de coopération euro–arabe', 30 March 1974, ADMAE Gén. 3807.

143. Letter Nixon to Brandt, 15 March 1974, AdsD EB 440.

144. 'Question-and-Answer Session at the Executives' Club of Chicago', 15 March 1974, *Public Papers of the Presidents of the United States: Richard Nixon – 1974*, 261–77, 276.

145. 'Question-and-Answer Session at the Annual Convention of the National Association of Broadcasters, Houston, Texas', 19 March 1974, *Public Papers of the Presidents of the United States: Richard Nixon – 1974*, 282–98, 294f.

146. Note FCO (Braithwaite to Butler), 'Transatlantic Relations: Consultation and the Arab Dialogue', 8 March 1974, FCO 30/2495.

147. Note MAE (Arnaud), 'Comité Politique des 18 et 19 avril', 18 April 1974, ADMAE Gén. 3811.

148. AAPD 1974, nos. 75, 76, and 96.

149. Record of telephone conversation between Kissinger and Sonnenfeldt on 5 March 1974, as in 'Kissinger Telephone Transcripts (1973–1976)' (foia.state.gov).

150. Note French embassy Paris (von Braun), 'Amerikanische Europa-Politik in französischer Sicht', 20 March 1974, PA SvB 172.

151. Note FCO (Acland) to PMO (Bridges), 'Relations with the United States', 25 March 1974, FCO 82/424.

152. Kissinger quoted in the *Daily Telegraph* of 8 March 1974, as in Allen (1977), 327.

153. French embassy Bonn (Sauvagnargues) to MAE, 25 March 1974, ADMAE Etas-Unis 1138; French embassy Washington (Kosciusko-Morizet) to MAE, 19 April 1974, no. 3273–82, ADMAE Gén. 3804; record of conversation between Douglas-Home and Kissinger in London on 26 February 1974, FCO 82/440.

154. AAPD 1974, no. 75.

155. Record of conversation between Scheel and Kissinger in Bonn on 3 March 1974, PA B150/300.

156. Record of conversation between Brandt and Nixon in Paris on 8 April 1974, AdsD EB 440.

157. UK embassy Washington (Ramsbotham) to FCO (Killick), 20 March 1974, with the record of his conversation with Kissinger on the same day ('Europe–US Cooperation'), FCO 82/424.

158. AAPD 1974, no. 97.

159. AAPD 1974, no. 104; note FRG embassy Paris (von Braun), 'Mitteilung Frl. Steffler über gestrige Unterrichtung Kissingers in Bonn', 25 March 1974, PA SvB 172; note AA (von der Gablentz), 'Beziehungen Europa/USA', 8 May 1974, PA ZA 108860.

160. Record of conversation between Ramsbotham and Kissinger in Washington on 6 March 1974, FCO 30/2496. See also Kissinger (2000b), 927–9.

161. AAPD 1974, no. 97.

162. Record of conversation between Scheel and Kissinger in Bonn on 3 March 1974, PA B150/300.

163. AAPD 1974, no. 75.

164. Record of conversation between Ramsbotham and Kissinger in Washington on 6 March 1974, FCO 30/2496.

165. French embassy Washington (Kosciusko-Morizet) to MAE, 14 March 1974, ADMAE Etats-Unis 1138; French embassy Bonn (Sauvagnargues) to MAE, 28 March 1974, no. 1376/82, ADMAE Gén. 3811.

166. AAPD 1974, no. 17.

167. Note FCO (Braithwaite to Butler), 'Transatlantic Relations: Consultation and the Arab Dialogue', 8 March 1974, FCO 30/2495.

168. UK embassy Paris (Tomkins) to FCO, 8 March 1974, FCO 30/2495.

169. Record of conversation between Ramsbotham and Kissinger in Washington on 6 March 1974, FCO 30/2496.

170. Note FCO (Wright to Killick), 'An Assessment of Dr Kissinger's Visit', 7 January 1974, FCO 30/2495.

171. Note FCO, 'Meeting Between Secretary of State and Mr Sonnenfeldt on Friday 15 March: Euro–Arab Dialogue', 14 March 1974, FCO 30/2514.

172. See note 157 in this chapter.

173. Letter UK embassy Paris (Ewart-Biggs) to FCO (Brimelow), 15 January 1974, FCO 30/2494.

174. Note FCO (James to Wiggin), 'France and the Atlantic Relationship', 14 February 1974, FCO 30/2494.

175. Note BKA (Thiele), 'Europapolitische Bilanz', undated [February 1974], BA B136/6417.

176. AAPD 1974, no. 97.

177. Note AA (von der Gablentz), 'Beziehungen Europa/USA', 8 May 1974, PA ZA 108860.

178. Kissinger proposed that the Four or Five (with Italy) should meet informally for a weekend every two months. AAPD 1974, nos. 65 and 104.

179. AAPD 1974, no. 115.

180. Record of telephone conversations between Kissinger and Scowcroft on 15 March 1974, between Kissinger and Graubard on 18 March 1974, between Kissinger and Haig on 20 March 1974, and between Kissinger and Bundy on 23 March 1974, as in 'Kissinger Telephone Transcripts (1973–1976)' (foia.state.gov).

181. AAPD 1974, no. 65.

182. Note FCO (Braithwaite to Butler), 'Political Co-operation and Consultation with the Americans', 14 March 1974, FCO 30/2496.

183. Kissinger (1999), 605.

184. Letter Fox to Jobert, 18 December 1973, in possession of author, courtesy of Mary Weed.

185. Weed (1988), 175.

186. Ibid.; Ambassade de France, Service de Presse et d'Information, 'Text of a letter addressed by H.E. Jacques Kosciusko-Morizet to the Washington Post March 24: Formal Protest by the French Ambassador: France has never advised Arab countries not to lift the oil embargo', in possession of author, courtesy of Mary Weed.

187. For an example, see Kissinger's assurances in his conversation with Scheel in Bonn on 24 March 1974, AAPD 1974, no. 104.

188. Weed (1988), 357f.

189. 'A Visit With Jobert', *New York Times*, 10 March 1974. See also French embassy Washington (Kosciusko-Morizet) to MAE, 10 March 1974, no. 1902, ADMAE Gén. 3811.

190. UK embassy Paris (Nicholas Spreckley) to FCO (MacInnes), 'M. Jobert's Interview with 'Le Monde'', 17 April 1974, FCO 41/1480.

191. French embassy Washington (Kosciusko-Morizet) to MAE, 22 March 1974, nos. 2479/87, 2488/500, and 2501/09, AN 5AG2 117.

192. UK embassy Paris (Tomkins) to FCO (Brimelow), 'Transatlantic Relations', 30 November 1973, FCO 82/289.

193. For example, see note AA (Redies to Scheel), 'US-Haltung zu dem in der EPZ erörterten Vorhaben einer europäisch–arabischen Kooperation', 15 February 1974, PA B150/298.

194. Note FCO (Wright to Killick), 'Kissinger and France', 26 April 1974, FCO 30/2498.

195. UK embassy Paris (Tomkins) to FCO, 8 March 1974, FCO 30/2495.

196. Schaetzel (1975), 79.

7 The transatlantic prerogative

1. George (1992).

2. 'Statement by James Callaghan (Luxembourg, 1 April 1974)', *Bulletin of the European Communities* no. 3 (1974): 14–19.

3. Heath (1998), 513–25.

4. FCO Planning Paper, 'British Foreign Policy: The Scope for Change', 12 February 1974, with the enclosed 'Minutes of the 53rd meeting of Planning Committee', FCO 30/2457.

5. Note CO (Nairne) to FCO (Wright), 'European Community: Future Policy', 25 February 1974, PREM 15/2076; note FCO (Norman Reddaway, Information Research Department, to Wright), 'Europe –Presentation', 18 December 1973, FCO 30/2456.

6. 'Cabinet Minutes of a meeting of the Ministerial Committee on European Community Strategy', 13 March 1974, FCO 30/2388.

7. Uwe Kitzinger, 'Entry and Referendum Revisited', in Broad and Preston (2001), 79–94, 85–7; Wolfram Kaiser, "What alternative is open to us?': Britain', in Kaiser and Elvert (2004), 9–30.

8. Heath (1998), 378.

9. Note BKA (Fischer), 2 December 1974, HSA 6642.

10. Record of conversation between Callaghan, Sonnenfeldt and Arthur A. Hartman, US assistant secretary for European affairs, in London on 15 March 1974, FCO 30/2497.

11. Morgan (1997), 394.

12. Record of telephone conversation between Brimelow and Wright on 5 March 1974, with Brimelow reporting on a conversation with Callaghan, FCO 30/2456.

13. AAPD 1974, no. 100.

14. Note CO (Nairne to Hunt), 25 March 1974, PREM 16/92.

15. Record of conversation between Callaghan and Ortoli in Luxembourg on 1 April 1974, FCO 30/2435.

16. Interview with Michael Butler (INT565); Young (1998), 279; record of telephone conversation between Brimelow and Wright on 5 March 1974, FCO 30/2456.

17. Notes FCO (Butler to Wright), 'European "Political Cooperation"', 13 March 1974, FCO 30/2496; 'Political Cooperation: The Need for a Single Spokesman', 22 March 1974, FCO 30/2457; record of conversation between Callaghan and Genscher at Dorneywood on 15 June 1974, FCO 30/2451; record of conversation between Wilson, Callaghan, Chirac, and Sauvagnargues at NATO headquarters in Brussels on 26 June 1974, PREM 16/11. On Paris being a possible location, see Tomkins' 'Record of Conversation during and after lunch given by President Giscard d'Estaing for the Prime Minister at the Elysée on Friday, 19 July', PREM 16/97.

18. Record of conversation between Callaghan and Ortoli in Luxembourg on 1 April 1974, FCO 30/2435.

19. Callaghan to Wilson, 26 March 1974, PREM 16/92.

20. Record of conversation between Ramsbotham and Kissinger in Washington on 6 March 1974, FCO 30/2496.

21. Record of conversation between Wilson and Kissinger in London on 28 March 1974, PREM 16/290.

22. Record of conversation between Wilson and Nixon in Paris on 6 April 1974, PREM 16/95.

23. 'Text of Secretary of State's Speech at National Press Club in Washington on Tuesday 21 May', 21 May 1974, FCO 30/2476.

24. Handwritten comments Wilson on brief FCO, 'Visit of US Secretary of State – 8 July 1974', PREM 16/290.

25. Kissinger (1999), 609.

26. Ibid.

27. Harpprecht (2000), 539; AAPD 1974, no. 110.

28. Record of conversation between Wilson and Brandt in Paris on 6 April 1974, PREM 16/95.

29. AAPD 1974, no. 109.

30. AAPD 1974, no. 133.

31. Robin's retrospective note on Pompidou's foreign policy, undated [1974], AN 5AG2 1163.

32. Ibid.

33. 'Interview de M. Jobert, lors de la réunion de concertation politique des ministres des Affaires étrangères européens, à Luxembourg (1er avril 1974)', reproduced at (www.ena.lu).

34. AAPD 1974, no. 65.

35. Bahr (1996), 457.

36. Merseburger (2002), 657–738; von Staden (2005), 87; Kissinger (2000b), 733.

37. Abadie and Corcelette (1997), 236.

38. AAPD 1974, no. 157. See also Giscard (1988), 124–8.

39. Kissinger (1999), 615. See also Hans-Dieter Lucas, 'Politik der kleinen Schritte – Genscher und die deutsche Europapolitik 1974–1983', in Lucas (2002), 85–113.

40. Callaghan (from Ottawa) to FCO, 19 June 1974, no. 432, FCO 41/1418; Samy Cohen, 'La politique extérieure de la France de 1974 à 1981: Un seul homme? Un homme seul?', in Cohen and Smouts (1985), 18–37.

41. 'Continuity and Concentration: Policy Statement Delivered to the Bundestag (May 17, 1974)', in *Helmut Schmidt: Perspectives on Politics*, 105–23, 105.

42. AAPD 1974, no. 162.

43. Ibid.

44. 'Der Politiker als Ökonom', in *Helmut Schmidt: Kontinuität und Konzentration*, 128–44.

45. Note FRG embassy Paris (von Braun), 31 May 1974, on a conversation between Schmidt and Giscard, PA SvB 172.

46. Giscard (1988), 117–24.

47. On Giscard and Europe, see Berstein and Sirinelli (2006). On Schmidt and Europe, see Werner Link, 'Aussen- und Deutschlandpolitik in der Ära Schmidt 1974–1982', in Jäger and Link (1987), 273–432.

48. Giscard (1988), 145; AAPD 1974, no. 247.

49. Young (2000), 120.

50. Ibid. See also Schmidt (1990), 94; Weinachter (2004).

51. AAPD 1974, no. 162.

52. Comment Wright, 30 May 1974, to note FCO (Tickell), 29 May 1974, FCO 82/425.

53. Record of conversation between Sauvagnargues and Callaghan in Paris on 19 July 1974, PREM 16/97; 'Speech by James Callaghan (Luxembourg, 4 June 1974)', *Bulletin of the European Communities* no. 6 (1974): 6–15.

54. Uwe Kitzinger, 'Entry and Referendum Revisited', in Broad and Preston (2001), 79–94, 89.

55. Young (1998), 281; interview with Crispin Tickell (INT577).

56. Miard-Delacroix (1993), 175.

57. 'Continuity and Concentration: Policy Statement Delivered to the Bundestag (May 17, 1974)', in *Helmut Schmidt: Perspectives on Politics*, 111.

58. Brief BKA (Fischer) for a meeting between Schmidt and Giscard, 30 May 1974, HSA 6638.

59. Note FCO (John Leahy to Braithwaite), 'European Political Consultation and the United States', 7 November 1974, FCO 82/426.

60. Kissinger (1999), 621; von Staden (2005), 140.

61. Marie-France Toinet, 'Valéry Giscard d'Estaing et les Etats-Unis', in Cohen and Smouts (1985), 45–62; Weed (1988), 194.

62. Note Richard Löwenthal, member of the SPD, 'Frankreich zwischen den Wahlgängen', 9 May 1974, WBA BK 12; Kissinger (1999), 623.

63. Letter BMF (Gotschlich to Schmidt), 3 December 1973, HSA 6005; record of conversation between Schmidt and Wilson in Bonn on 19 June 1974, HSA 6927; AAPD 1974, no. 249; Miard-Delacroix (1993), 175.

64. AAPD 1974, nos. 285, 289, and 292.

65. Kissinger (1999), 689–92.

66. Ibid., 696.

67. Record of conversation between Callaghan, Sonnenfeldt, and Hartman in London on 15 March 1974, FCO 30/2497.

68. AAPD 1974, no. 100; record of conversation between Callaghan and Kissinger in London on 28 March 1974, PREM 16/290.

69. See the record of the debate on Europe in the Bundestag on 28 March 1974, HSA 6067.

70. Note MAE (Puaux), 'Réunion des directeurs politiques français et allemand: Relations euro–américaine', 20 March 1974, ADMAE Etats-Unis 1138.

71. AAPD 1974, no. 89.

72. Note FCO (Wright to Braithwaite), 'Political Directors' Dinner: Bonn: 12 March', 13 March 1974, FCO 30/2496.

73. Note MAE (Puaux), 14 March 1974, AN 582AP 43; note AA (von der Gablentz), 'Deutsch–französische Direktorenkonsultation am 20. März 1974 in Paris; hier: EPZ; Grundsatzerklärung Europa/US', 21 March 1974, PA B150/301.

74. Note MAE, 'Réunion ministérielle de la coopération politique', 1 April 1974, ADMAE Gén. 3792; Callaghan to UK embassy Bonn, 3 April 1974, FCO 30/2498.

75. Note MAE (Puaux), 21 March 1974; and note Elysée (Robin to Pompidou), 28 March 1974, with annotations by Pompidou, both in AN 5AG2 1021.

76. AAPD 1974, no. 111.

77. Circular AA (von der Gablentz), 15 March 1974, PA B150/300.

78. Note AA (van Well to Scheel), 'Konsultationsfrage', 19 April 1974, PA ZA 108877; note MAE (Arnaud), 'Comité Politique des 18 et 19 avril', 18 April 1974, ADMAE Gén. 3811.

79. Note FCO, 'Gymnich: German Briefing Given to US Embassy (US Account)', undated, FCO 30/2463.

80. Note MAE (Puaux), 'Entretien des directeurs politiques français et allemande', 8 May 1974, ADMAE Gén. 3811.

81. AAPD 1974, no. 155; note MAE (Occ.), 'Entretiens entre le Président de la République et le Chancelier de la République Fédérale d'Allemagne: relations Europe-Etats Unis', 29 May 1974, ADMAE Gén. 3811.

82. For the original French text, see AAPD 1974, no. 168.

83. Circular MAE (Puaux), 11 June 1974, no. 402, ADMAE Etats-Unis 1138; note FCO, 'Extract from Bonn telegram No 733 of 12 June to FCO', undated, FCO 30/2459.

84. Note MAE, 'Réunion ministérielle de la coopération politique', 1 April 1974, ADMAE Gén. 3792.

85. AAPD 1974, no. 100; note AA (200), 'Beziehungen Europa/US; hier: Konsultationen', 5 April 1974, PA ZA 108860.

86. Note MAE (Puaux to Jobert), 14 March 1974, AN 582AP 43.

87. UK embassy Washington (Graham) to FCO (Butler), 'European Political Cooperation: Consultations with the United States', 18 June 1974, FCO 30/2501.

88. AAPD 1974, no. 104 (*ein grosser Schritt vorwärts*). See also Kissinger (2000b), 933; record of conversation between Callaghan and Kissinger in London on 28 March 1974, PREM 16/290.

89. UK embassy Washington (Ramsbotham) to FCO, 23 April 1974, no. 1417, FCO 30/2463; AAPD 1974, no. 149; FRG embassy Washington (von Staden) to AA, 22 May 1974, PA B150/305.

90. 'A stitch in time?', *The Economist*, 29 June 1974; letter UK embassy Washington (Ramsbotham) to FCO (Brimelow), 2 July 1974, FCO 30/2501.

91. AAPD 1974, no. 171.

92. Note MAE (Occ.), 'Entretien entre le Ministre et l'Ambassadeur des Etats-Unis', 7 June 1974, AN 582AP 43.

93. Kissinger (1999), 626.

94. Note FCO (Braithwaite to Wright), 'Political Cooperation: The Role of the Presidency in Washington', 28 May 1974, FCO 82/425; letter UK embassy Washington (Ramsbotham) to FCO (Wright), 'US/European Consultation', 23 May 1974, FCO 82/425.

95. AAPD 1974, nos. 3 and 4.

96. Record of conversation between Douglas-Home and Kissinger at London Airport on 20 January 1974, PREM 15/2153.

97. Note MAE (Puaux to Jobert), 4 January 1974, AN 5AG2 1021.

98. Record of conversation between Pompidou and Kissinger in Paris on 20 December 1974, AN 5AG2 1023; record of conversation between Jobert and Kissinger in Paris on 19 December 1973, National Archives at College Park, MD, Nixon Presidential Materials Staff, HAK Office Files, French Memcons 1973, Box 56.

99. Kissinger (2000b), 728; letter Jobert to Kissinger, 8 January 1974, in possession of author, courtesy of Mary Weed.

100. For the drafts by France, Italy, and the UK, see FCO 30/2504. See also the 'Declaration of Principles: Synopsis of French, Italian and British Drafts', 17 January 1974, PA B150/297.

101. 'Declaration of Principles', 8 February 1974, PA B150/298, ADMAE Etats-Unis 1138. See also the FCO brief for Ramsbotham, 'US/Nine Declaration', 30 January 1974, FCO 30/2504; AAPD 1974, no. 41.

102. Despatch UKDEL NATO (Peck), 'Atlantic Relations', 11 July 1974, FCO 82/426.

103. AA (van Well) to NATOGERMA, 14 January 1974, PA B150/296.

104. Despatch UKDEL NATO (Peck), 'Atlantic Relations', 11 July 1974, FCO 82/426; NATOGERMA (Walter Boss) to AA, 19 February 1974, PA B150/299.

105. Circulars MAE (de Courcel), 5 March 1974, no. 161; and 6 March 1974, no. 106, ADMAE Gén. 3792; French embassy Bonn (Sauvagnargues) to MAE, 14 February 1974, no. 643/47, ADMAE Gén. 3811.

106. FRG embassy Washington (von Staden) to AA, 28 February 1974, PA B150/299; record of conversation between Douglas-Home and Kissinger in London on 26 February 1974, FCO 82/440.

107. AAPD 1974, no. 97; note FCO (Mark Elliott, private secretary to permanent under-secretary, to Wright), 18 March 1974, FCO 30/2496.

108. Note AA (von der Gablentz), 'Deutsch–französische Direktorenkonsultation am 20. März 1974 in Paris; hier: EPZ; Grundsatzerklärung Europa/US', 21 March 1974, PA B150/301.

109. Ibid.

110. Note MAE (Arnaud), 'Comité Politique des 18 et 19 avril', 18 April 1974, ADMAE Gén. 3811.

111. AAPD 1974, no. 128; note FCO, 'Gymnich: German Briefing Given to US Embassy (US Account)', undated, FCO 30/2463.

112. Letter Callaghan to Kissinger, 24 April 1974, FCO 82/471.

113. UK embassy Washington (Ramsbotham) to FCO, 23 March 1974, FCO 41/1469.

114. For the American draft declaration of 23 March 1974, see FCO 82/441; note FCO (John Kerr to Robin McLaren, both WOD), 'Revised US Version of the Alliance Declaration', 26 March 1974, FCO 30/2497.

115. Record of conversation between Callaghan and Kissinger in London on 28 March 1974, PREM 16/290.

116. Letter Kissinger to Callaghan, 13 April 1974, FCO 82/471.

117. Callaghan to UK embassy Washington, 19 April 1974, no. 875, FCO 41/1470; note FCO (Acland to Tickell), 'Nato 25th Anniversary', 29 March 1974, FCO 30/2498.

118. Note FCO (Acland to Tickell), 'Nato 25th Anniversary', 29 March 1974, FCO 30/2498.

119. Notes FCO (Acland to Wiggin), 'Declarations', 8 April 1974; and (McLaren to Wiggin), 'Declarations', 11 April 1974, FCO 30/2498.

120. 'Draft Declaration', 19 April 1974, FCO 41/1470.

121. Note FCO (Tickell to Wiggin), 'Alliance Declaration', 30 April 1974; Callaghan to UK embassy Washington, 2 May 1974, no. 978; UK embassy Washington (Ramsbotham) to FCO, 3 May 1974, no. 1589, FCO 41/1470.

122. 'British draft for an Alliance declaration as at 3 May 1974', FCO 30/2499.

123. Letter Callaghan to Scheel, 13 May 1974, FCO 30/2499; NATOGERMA (Krapf) to AA, 24 May 1974, with enclosed 'United States suggested revisions to United Kingdom draft NATO declaration', PA B150/305.

124. Despatch UKDEL NATO (Peck), 'Atlantic Relations', 11 July 1974, FCO 82/426.

125. Wright (from Bonn) to FCO, 28 May 1974, no. 657, FCO 41/1471; brief FCO, 'European Political Cooperation: Ministerial Meeting Bonn 10/11 June, Agenda Item 3: Europe/US Relations', undated, FCO 30/2500.

126. Note FCO (Braithwaite to Wright), 'US/European Relations', 15 May 1974, FCO 30/2499; note FCO (Tickell to Wiggin and Private Secretary), 'Alliance Declaration', 29 May 1974, FCO 30/2500.

127. Despatch UKDEL NATO (Peck), 'Atlantic Relations', 11 July 1974, FCO 82/426.

128. UK embassy Bonn (Crowe) to FCO (Braithwaite), 'European Political Cooperation', 5 July 1974, FCO 82/425; Werner Link, 'Aussen- und Deutschlandpolitik in der Ära Schmidt 1974–1982', in Jäger and Link (1987), 273–432, 275.

129. Despatch UKDEL NATO (Peck), 'Atlantic Relations', 11 July 1974, FCO 82/426.

130. Note FCO (Alexander to Tickell), 'Alliance Declaration', 6 June 1974, FCO 30/2500.

131. Note FCO (Acland) to PMO (Bridges), 'Atlantic Declaration', 6 June 1974, FCO 41/1472.

132. NATOGERMA (Boss) to AA, 6 June 1974, PA B150/306; note AA (van Well to Genscher), 'Atlantische Erklärung; hier: Europa-Passage', 7 June 1974, PA B150/306.

133. Callaghan to UKDEL NATO, 11 June 1974, no. 135, FCO 41/1472; AAPD 1974, no. 164, note 7.

134. NATOGERMA (Krapf) to AA, 13 June 1974, no. 875, PA B150/306.

135. Sauvagnargues quoted in the French press, according to UK embassy Paris (Tomkins) to FCO, 20 June 1974, FCO 41/1418.

136. For the 'Declaration on Atlantic Relations issued by the North Atlantic Council ('The Ottawa Declaration')', 19 June 1974, see (www.nato.int/docu/). See also Callaghan (from Ottawa) to FCO, 19 June 1974, no. 432, FCO 41/1418; AAPD 1974, no. 183.

137. Despatch UKDEL NATO (Peck), 'Atlantic Relations', 11 July 1974, FCO 82/426.

138. Steering brief FCO for 'Prime Minister's Visit to Brussels: 25/26 June', undated, PREM 16/11.

139. 'Ce qui reste de la 'nouvelle charte'', *Le Monde*, 27 June 1974.

140. 'New Sense of Alliance', *New York Times*, 28 June 1974.

141. Kissinger (1999), 624.

142. Jobert (1976), 298.

143. Cogan (1994), 167.

144. NATOGERMA (Krapf) to AA, 13 June 1974, no. 864, PA B150/306.

145. French draft declaration 'Avant-Projet d'une Déclaration de Principes Europe–Canada', tabled in EPC on 4 March 1974, ADMAE Gén. 3792; 'Aide Mémoire of Canada', 22 April 1974, FCO 2476; AAPD 1974, no. 129.

146. Douglas-Home to UK embassy Washington, 11 February 1974, FCO 41/1413; note Elysée (Robin to Pompidou), 11 February 1974, AN 5AG2 1021.

147. PA B150/296; AA (van Well) to NATOGERMA, 2 January 1974, PA B150/296; brief FCO, 'Reinforced meeting of the North Atlantic Council 13 March 1974', undated, FCO 41/1413.

148. Note FCO (Tickell to Wiggin, Killick, Goulding), 'Consultation in NATO', 13 May 1974, FCO30/2491.

149. Note AA (van Well), 'Gemeinsame Treffen der NATO-Botschafter und der Politischen Direktoren der Fünfzehn', 11 January 1974, PA B150/296; note FCO, 'Background Note on Reinforced Meetings of the North Atlantic Council', undated [early March 74], FCO 30/2491; AAPD 1974, no. 60.

150. Note Elysée (Robin to Pompidou), 11 February 1974, AN 5AG2 1021; Douglas-Home to UK embassy Washington, 11 February 1974, FCO 41/1413.

151. UKDEL NATO (Peck) to FCO, 14 March 1974, FCO 41/1413.

152. Brief FCO, 'Reinforced meeting of the North Atlantic Council 13 March 1974', undated, FCO 41/1413.

153. AAPD 1974, nos. 183 and 372.

154. AAPD 1974, no. 191.

155. AAPD 1974, no. 376.

156. Callaghan (from Ottawa) to FCO, 19 June 1974, no. 421, FCO 41/1418.

157. Hanhimäki (2004), xix and 328; Kissinger (1999), 243, 251, and 305.

158. Kissinger (1999), 631.

159. Note MAE, 'Compte rendu de la réunion ministérielle du 4 mars 1974 au titre de la coopération politique européenne à Bruxelles', ADMAE Gén. 3792; AAPD 1974, no. 93.

160. Kissinger (2000b), 934.

161. Letter Jobert to Scheel, 20 March 1974, PA ZA 104981.

162. Circulars MAE (de Courcel), 22 March 1974, no. 217; and 10 April 1974, no. 264, ADMAE Gén. 3804; Hohensee (1996), 94.

163. AAPD 1974, nos. 10 and 13; French embassy Bonn (Sauvagnargues) to MAE, 30 March 1974, no. 1422/25, ADMAE Gén. 3804; letter Scheel to Ahmed Yamani, oil minister of Saudi Arabia, 30 January 1974, PA ZA 104663.

164. Hohensee (1996), appendix, no. 19.

165. AAPD 1974, nos. 123 and 125.

166. FRG embassy Tel Aviv (Helmut Rückriegel) to AA, 26 March 1974, PA B150/301; record of conversation between Frank and Ben-Horin in Bonn on 28 March 1974, PA B1/576; 'CDU/CSU-Fraktion des Deutschen Bundestages: Presserefeerat: Carstens in Europa-Debatte heute', 28 March 1974, ACDP 08–010–143/2.

167. Record of conversation between Wilson and Kissinger in London on 28 March 1974, PREM 16/290.

168. Callaghan (from Ottawa) to FCO, 19 June 1974, no. 425, FCO 41/1418.

169. FRG embassy Tel Aviv (von Puttkamer) to AA, 28 January 1974, PA B1/576.

170. Circular AA (von der Gablentz), 14 March 1974, PA B150/300.

171. 'Proche-Orient: Rapport du Comité Politique aux Ministres des affaires étrangères en vue de la réunion du 14 février 1974', RM (74) 1 CP, 7 February 1974, FCO 30/2474; note AA (Redies to van Well), 'Nahostexpertensitzung am 10. Mai 1974', 13 May 1974, PA ZA 104981.

172. Note MAE (Levant), 'Dialogue euro–arabe', 29 May 1974, ADMAE Gén. 3807; EPC 'Rapport relatif à la marche à suivre des neuf à l'avenir en ce qui concerne le dialogue euro–arabe et les contacts avec Israël', undated, ADMAE Gén. 3807.

173. AAPD 1974, no. 171.

174. Circular MAE (Puaux), 12 June 1974, no. 413, ADMAE Gén. 3807; note FCO (Gore-Booth to Caroline Sinclair and Giles FitzHerbert), 'Euro–Arab Dialogue', 6 August 1974, FCO 82/426.

175. Jacobs (2003), Ch. 5.3; van Well (1976), 127; Jawad (1992).

176. Memorandum FCO, 'Euro/Arab Dialogue: Procedural Questions', 23 May 1974, ADMAE Gén. 3796; Allen (1977), 331.

177. Note AA (van Well to Frank) 'Möglichkeiten einer stärkeren europäischen Zusammenarbeit auf dem Gebiet der Verteidigung', 28 December 1973, PA B150/295; AA (van Well) to London, NATOGERMA, and Paris, 18 January 1974; FRG embassy London (von Hase) to AA, 24 January 1974; note AA (Pfeffer and Claus Vollers, 201, to Frank), 'Stärkere Zusammenarbeit der europäischen Staaten auf dem Gebiet der Verteidigung', 25 January 1974; note

AA (Dedo von Schenck, head Rechtsabteilung, to Frank), 'Stärkere Zusammenarbeit der europäischen Staaten auf dem Gebiet der Verteidigung', 29 January 1974, all in PA B150/297.

178. Note AA (van Well), 'Deutsch–französische Studiengruppe; hier: Protokoll der Sitzung vom 15.1.1974 in Bonn', 17 January 1974, PA B150/297.

179. AAPD 1974, no. 65; note AA (Brunner to Scheel), 'Deutsch–französische Planungsstabsgespräche in Paris am 5. März 1974; hier: Sicherheitsfragen', 7 March 1974, PA B150/300; note AA (Brunner to Scheel), 'Gespräch mit dem Planungsstab des französischen Aussenministeriums in Bonn am 24. April 1974; hier: Verteidigungsfragen', 26 April 1974, PA B150/303; AAPD 1974, no. 253.

180. FCO (Wiggin) to MOD (Arthur Hockaday), 'Defence and France: Talks with M Jobert's Planners', 3 January 1974, PREM 15/2040; UK embassy Paris (Spreckley) to FCO (Planning staff), 'Contacts with French Planning Staff', 8 April 1974, FCO 49/522.

181. Soutou (2004), 105–7.

182. Soutou (1996), 325; AAPD 1970, no. 291; record of conversation between Nixon and Pompidou in the US on 24 February 1970, AN 5AG2 1022.

183. Record of conversation between Pompidou and Brezhnev in the Soviet Union on 13 March 1974, AN 5AG2 1019; UK embassy Paris (Spreckley) to FCO (Tickell), 'French Defence Policy', 13 March 1974, FCO 41/1408; AAPD 1974, no. 104.

184. Note FCO (Tickell to Wiggin), 'Anglo/French Joint Nuclear Force: Parliamentary Question by Mr Frank Allaun MP', undated, FCO 41/1480.

185. UK embassy Paris (Ewart-Biggs) to FCO (Tickell), 'Politico–Military Talks', 21 June 1974, FCO 41/1406.

186. NATOGERMA (Krapf) to AA, 13 June 1974, no. 864, PA B150/306.

187. AAPD 1974, no. 253; Schmidt (1990), 272; Weinachter (2004), Ch. 3.

188. Note AA (Friedrich Ruth to van Well), 'Erörterung der Auswirkungen von MBFR-Ergebnissen auf Europa im Kreise der Neun', 17 January 1974, PA B150/297; circular MAE (Puaux), 15 March 1974, ADMAE Etats-Unis 1138; note FCO (Tickell to Wiggin and Private Secretary), 'MBFR: The European reservation', 21 June 1974, FCO 41/1495.

189. Record of conversation between Leber and Roy Mason, British secretary of state for defense, in Bonn on 21 May 1974, FCO 41/1478.

190. Note BKA (Koordinierungsgruppe Europa), 22 January 1974, BA B136/30659.

191. Note MAE (Occ.), 27 February 1974, ADMAE Gén. 3789; note MAE (Occ.), 28 February 1974, ADMAE Gén. 3789; EUROGERMA (Lebsanft) to AA (Hans M. Ruyter, 410), 'Europäische Union; hier: 1. Sitzung der ad hoc-Gruppe', 11 March 1974, BA B136/6428.

192. Circular MAE (de Courcel), 6 March 1974, ADMAE Gén. 3771.

193. Note MAE (Occ.), 22 November 1973, AN 5AG2 1012; note MAE (Occ.), 'De l'Union Européenne', 27 February 1974, ADMAE Gén. 3771; note AA

(Christian Feit, 202), 'Französische Vorstellungen zur Europäischen Union', 26 March 1974, PA ZA 108860.

194. Note FCO, 'European Union: Summary of Foreign & Commonwealth Office Thinking', 30 October 1973, FCO 30/1607; note FCO, 'Foreign Policy as an Element in European Union', undated [January 1974], FCO 30/2472.

195. Note MAE (Occ.), 'Rencontre Franco-allemande du 4 avril: Union européenne', 20 March 1974, ADMAE Gén. 3771; record of conversation between Brandt and Nixon in Paris on 8 April 1974, AdsD EB 440.

196. Note FCO, 'Attitude of EEC Member States Towards European Union', undated [end of 1973], FCO 30/1608.

197. AAPD 1974, no. 128; note FCO (Wright), 'Meeting of the Foreign Ministers of the Member States of the European Community at Schloss Gymnich – 20/21 April 1974', 24 April 1974, FCO 30/2463.

198. Record of conversation between Wilson and Thorn in Brussels on 25 June 1974, PREM 16/11.

199. Europäische Gemeinschaften: Der Rat, 'Europäische Union', R/1620/74 (AG 116), 21 June 1974, BA B136/6428.

200. Note MAE (Occ.), 'Union Européenne', 25 July 1974, ADMAE Gén. 3771.

201. Political Commission of the European Parliament, 'Projet de Rapport intérimaire sur l'Union européenne, rapporteur Alfred Bertrand', PE 37.998, 9 September 1974; and Commission des Communautés européennes, 'Rapport du groupe ad hoc sur l'Union européenne', SEC(74) 5206, 19 December 1974, both in ADMAE Gén. 3771.

202. Brief BKA, 'Treffen der Regierungschefs der Europäischen Gemeinschaft 9. und 10. Dezember 1974 Paris', undated, HSA 6645.

203. 'Report on European Union, by Leo Tindemans (The Tindemans Report), 29 December 1975', *European Foreign Policy: Key Documents*, 100–11. The quote is taken from the introductory comment, 99f.

204. Note AA (Ruyter), 'Ausarbeitung des Berichts zur Europäischen Union', 1 March 1974, BA B136/6428.

205. George (1994).

206. William Wallace, 'Introduction: cooperation and convergence in European foreign policy', in Hill (1983), 1–16, 2. See also my 'Speaking with one voice? The evolution of a European foreign policy', in Deighton and Bossuat (2007), 132–51.

207. AAPD 1974, no. 369.

208. AAPD 1974, no. 222. Giscard even wanted to transfer EPC into the Council of Ministers. AAPD 1974, no. 250.

209. Interview with Philippe de Schoutheete de Tervarent.

210. 'Declaration by the European Council on the Situation in the Middle East (Venice Declaration), Venice, 12–13 June 1980', *European Foreign Policy: Key Documents,* 302–4.

211. Kenneth Dyson, 'The Conference on Security and Cooperation in Europe: Europe before and after the Helsinki Final Act', in Dyson (1986), 83–112, 100f.

212. 'Report Issued by the Foreign Ministers of the Ten on European Political Co-operation (The London Report), London, 13 October 1981', *European Foreign Policy: Key Documents*, 114–9.

Conclusion

1. William Wallace, 'Introduction: cooperation and convergence in European foreign policy', in Hill (1983), 1–16, 10.

2. Jobert (1976), 290; Brandt (1994), 190–2; record of conversation between Heath and Rumor at Chequers on 8 December 1973, PREM 15/2076.

3. Kissinger (1966), 232 and 40.

4. Note FCO (Planning Staff), 'Too True to be Good, or Dr Kissinger Then and Now', 31 October 1973, PREM 15/1546.

5. Kissinger (2000b), 926.

Bibliography

Archival sources

Britain

The National Archives

Records of the Prime Minister's Office (PREM)
PREM 13: Correspondence and Papers, 1964–70
PREM 15: Correspondence and Papers, 1970–74
PREM 16: Correspondence and Papers, 1974–78
Cabinet Office Records (CAB)
CAB 129: Memoranda
CAB 130: Miscellaneous Committees: Minutes and Papers
CAB 148: Defence and Oversea Policy Committees and Sub-committees: Minutes and
    Papers
CAB 164: Subject (Theme Series) Files
Records of the Foreign and Commonwealth Office (FCO)
FCO 17: Foreign Office, Eastern Department and successors
FCO 26: Information, News and Guidance Department
FCO 28: Northern Department and East European and Soviet Department
FCO 30: European Economic Organisations Department and successors
FCO 33: Western European Department
FCO 41: Western Organisations Department
FCO 49: Planning Staff and Commonwealth Policy and Planning Department
FCO 73: Private Offices: Michael Stewart, Dennis Greenhill, Alec Douglas-Home
FCO 82: North America Department
FCO 93: Near East and North Africa Department

France

Archives Nationales (AN)

*Archives de la présidence de la République: La Ve République: Georges Pompidou 1969–1974
    (5AG2)*

Fonds
Jacques Kosciusko-Morizet (582AP)
Jean-René Bernard (86AJ)
Michel Jobert (89AJ)

Archives Diplomatiques du Ministère des Affaires Etrangères (ADMAE)

Direction d'Amérique
Etats-Unis 1971–75 (inventaire provisoire)
Direction Europe
Généralités 1966–70; 1971–76 (inventaire provisoire)
République fédérale d'Allemagne 1944–70; 1971–76 (inventaire provisoire)
Grande Bretagne 1944–70; 1971–76 (inventaire provisoire)
Secrétariat Général
Entretiens et messages

Archives d'histoire contemporaine (Centre d'histoire de l'Europe du vingtième siècle)

Maurice Couve de Murville

West Germany

Politisches Archiv des Auswärtigen Amts (PA)

Akten des Neuen Amts
Ministerbüro (B1)
Büro Staatssekretäre (B2)
NATO, WEU, Verteidigung (B14)
Europäische Politische Integration (B20–200)
Europäische Politische Integration (B21)
Frankreich, Benelux (B24)
KSZE (B28)
Grossbritannien, USA (B31)
Nahost (B36)
Offengelegte Verschlusssachenregistraturen (B130)
B150
Europäische Wirtschaftliche Integration (B200)
Zwischenlager
Nachlässe
Freiherr Sigismund von Braun (SvB)

Bundesarchiv Koblenz (BA)

Bundesministerium für Wirtschaft (B102)
Bundeskanzleramt (B136)

Nachlässe und Deposita
Rainer Barzel (N1371)
Herbert Blankenhorn (N351)
Karl Carstens (N1337)

Archiv der sozialen Demokratie (AdsD)

Willy Brandt Archiv (WBA)
Bundesaussenminister 1966–69
Bundeskanzler und Bundesregierung 1969–74 (BK)
Publikationen
Helmut Schmidt Archiv (HSA)
Depositum Egon Bahr (EB)
Depositum Katharina Focke (KF)
Depositum Hans-Jürgen Wischnewski (HJW)
SPD PV-Neuer Bestand, Abteilung Internationale Beziehungen

Archiv des Liberalismus (AdL)

Bundesparteitag (A1)
Walter Scheel (A35)

Archiv für Christlich–Demokratische Politik (ACDP)

CDU/CSU-Fraktion des Deutschen Bundestages: Europabüro (08–010)
Kurt Birrenbach (I–433)
Gerhard Schröder (I–483)

United States

National Archives

Nixon Presidential Materials Staff
Country Files Europe, France vol. XI
HAK Office Files: French Memcons 1973

Published sources

Document editions

Akten zur Auswärtigen Politik der Bundesrepublik Deutschland. 16 vols 1969–74. Munich: Oldenbourg.
Britain's Entry into the European Community: Report on the Negotiations of 1970–1972. By

Con O'Neill. Edited and with a Foreword by David Hannay. London: Whitehall History Publishing in association with Frank Cass, 2000.

Bundeskanzler Brandt: Reden und Interviews. 2 vols. Edited by Presse- und Informationsamt der Bundesregierung, 1971 and 1973.

Conference on Security and Cooperation in Europe: Stage I – Helsinki: Verbatim Records, July 3–7, 1973. Helsinki, 1973.

Crisis: The Anatomy of Two Major Foreign Policy Crises. By Henry Kissinger. New York: Simon & Schuster, 2003.

Documents on British Policy Overseas, Series III.

Vol. I: *Britain and the Soviet Union, 1968–72.* London: Frank Cass, 2001.

Vol. II: *The Conference on Security and Cooperation in Europe, 1972–75.* London: Frank Cass, 1997.

Vol. III: *Détente in Europe, 1972–76.* London: The Stationary Office, 1997.

Vol. IV on 'The Year of Europe: America, Europe and the Energy Crisis, 1972–1974' (Routledge 2006) was published after the completion of the draft manuscript.

Europäische Politische Einigung: Dokumentation von Vorschlägen und Stellungnahmen. Vols II (1968–73) and III (1973–76). Edited by Heinrich Siegler. Bonn: Siegler, 1973 and 1977.

European Foreign Policy: Key Documents. Edited by Christopher Hill and Karen E. Smith. London: Routledge, 2000.

Georges Pompidou: Entretiens et Discours 1968–1974. 2 vols. Paris: Plon, 1975.

Helmut Schmidt: Kontinuität und Konzentration. Bonn: Neue Gesellschaft, 1975.

Helmut Schmidt: Perspectives on Politics. Edited by Wolfram F. Hanrieder. Boulder: Westview Press, 1982.

Public Papers of the Presidents of the United States: Richard Nixon. 5 vols 1970–74. Washington: United States Government Printing Office.

Sicherheitskonferenz in Europa: Dokumentation 1954–1972. Edited by Friedrich-Karl Schramm, Wolfram-Georg Riggert, and Alois Friedel. Frankfurt: Alfred Metzner, 1972.

The October War and U.S. Policy, documents edited and commented by William Burr, National Security Archive, 7 October 2003 (www.gwu.edu/~nsarchiv – accessed on 1 April 2007).

Documents on the world wide web

All web pages were accessed on 1 April 2007.
- Déclarations françaises de politique étrangère (www.doc.diplomatie.fr)
- European Navigator (www.ena.lu)
- NATO Summits and Ministerial Meetings (www.nato.int/docu/)
- OSCE documents (www.osce.org/documents)
- UN Security Council Resolutions (www.un.org/Docs/sc/unsc_resolutions.html)

- US Department of State, Kissinger Telephone Transcripts (1973–1976) (foia.state.gov)
- US Department of State, Treaties and Agreements (www.state.gov/t/ac/trt/)

Memoires and other writings by policy-makers

Andréani, Jacques (2005). *Le Piège: Helsinki et la chute du communism.* Paris: Odile Jacob.

Bahr, Egon (1996). *Zu meiner Zeit.* Munich: Karl Blessing Verlag.

Brandt, Willy (1978). *Begegnungen und Einsichten: Die Jahre 1960–1975.* Paperback edition. Munich: Droemer Knaur [Hamburg: Hoffmann und Campe, 1976].

—— (1994). *Erinnerungen: mit den 'Notizen zum Fall G'.* Expanded edition. Berlin: Ullstein.

Brosio, Manlio (1974). 'Consultation and the Atlantic Alliance'. *Survival* 16, no. 3: 115–21.

Debré, Michel (1994). *Trois Républiques pour une France: Mémoires V – Combattre Toujours, 1969–1993.* Paris: Albin Michel.

—— (1996). *Entretiens avec Georges Pompidou 1971–1974.* Paris: Albin Michel.

Douglas-Home, Alec (1976). *The Way the Wind Blows: An Autobiography.* New York: Quadrangle/The New York Times Book.

Ferraris, Luigi Vittorio, ed. (1979). *Report on a Negotiation: Helsinki – Geneva – Helsinki 1972–1975.* Translated from the Italian by Marie-Claire Barber. Alphen aan den Rijn: Sijthoff & Noordhoff International Publishers BV.

Frank, Paul (1981). *Entschlüsselte Botschaft: Ein Diplomat macht Inventur.* Stuttgart: Deutsche Verlags-Anstalt.

Giscard d'Estaing, Valéry (1988). *Le pouvoir et la vie.* Paris: Compagnie 12.

Harpprecht, Klaus (2000). *Im Kanzleramt: Tagebuch der Jahre mit Willy Brandt.* Reinbek: Rowohlt.

Heath, Edward (1969). 'Realism in British Foreign Policy'. *Foreign Affairs* 48, no. 1: 39–50.

—— (1970). *Old World, New Horizons: Britain, the Common Market and the Atlantic Alliance.* London: Oxford University Press.

—— (1976). *A British Approach to European Foreign Policy.* Cambridge: Leeds University Press.

—— (1998). *The Course of My Life: My Autobiography.* London: Hodder & Stoughton.

Jobert, Michel (1974). *Mémoires d'avenir.* Paris: Grasset.

—— (1976). *L'autre regard.* Paris: Grasset.

Kissinger, Henry A. (1966). *The Troubled Partnership: A Re-appraisal of the Atlantic Alliance.* New York: Anchor Books [Mc Graw-Hill, 1965].

—— (1999). *Years of Renewal.* New York: Simon & Schuster.

—— (2000a). *White House Years.* London: Phoenix Press [Weidenfeld & Nicolson, 1979].

—— (2000b). *Years of Upheaval*. London: Phoenix Press [Weidenfeld & Nicolson, 1982].

Maresca, John J. (1985). *To Helsinki: The Conference on Security and Cooperation in Europe 1973–1975*. Durham: Duke University Press.

Monnet, Jean (1988). *Erinnerungen eines Europäers*. Baden-Baden: Nomos.

Nixon, Richard (1990). *The Memoirs of Richard Nixon*. New York: Touchstone.

Renk, Hans-Jörg (1996). *Der Weg der Schweiz nach Helsinki: Der Beitrag der schweizerischen Diplomatie zum Zustandekommen der Konferenz über Sicherheit und Zusammenarbeit in Europa (KSZE), 1972–1975*. Berne: Paul Haupt.

Scheel, Walter (1973). 'Aktuelle Probleme der Aussenpolitik der Bundesrepublik Deutschland'. *Europa–Archiv* 28, no. 13: 433–38.

—— (2004). *Erinnerungen und Einsichten: Walter Scheel im Gespräch mit Jürgen Engert*. Stuttgart: Hohenheim.

Schmidt, Helmut (1987). *Menschen und Mächte*. Berlin: Siedler.

—— (1990). *Die Deutschen und ihre Nachbarn*. Berlin: Siedler.

Staden, Berndt von (2005). *Zwischen Eiszeit und Tauwetter: Diplomatie in einer Epoche des Umbruchs – Erinnerungen*. Berlin: wjs Verlag.

Stewart, Michael (1980). *Life and Labour: An Autobiography*. London: Sidgwick & Jackson.

Van Well, Günther (1973). 'Die Europäische Politische Zusammenarbeit in der aussenpolitischen Sicht der Bundesrepublik Deutschland'. *Europa–Archiv* 28, no. 17: 581–90.

—— (1976). 'Die Entwicklung einer gemeinsamen Nahost-Politik der Neun'. *Europa–Archiv* 31, no. 4: 119–28.

Interviews

Interviews conducted by the author

Jacques Andréani (French delegation CSCE), 9 September 2005; Egon Bahr, 15 March 2004; Etienne Davignon, 3 March 2006; Luigi Vittorio Ferraris (Italian delegation CSCE), 9 September 2005; Henry Kissinger, 20 September 2005; Helmut Liedermann (Austrian delegation CSCE), 2 November 2004; John Maresca (US delegation CSCE), 6 October 2004; Michael Palliser (FCO), 7 September 2007; Philippe de Schoutheete de Tervarent (Belgian diplomat), 21 January 2005; Crispin Tickell (FCO), 9 September 2005; Barthold C. Witte (FRG delegation CSCE), 6 December 2004.

Oral history project: 'Voices on Europe'

European University Institute, Florence (www.arc.iue.it/oh/OralHistory.html – accessed on 1 April 2007), interview nos. 565, 577, 598, 614, 639, 642, 643, 650, 652.

Scholarly books and articles

Abadie, Frédéric and Jean-Pierre Corcelette (1997). *Valéry Giscard d'Estaing*. Paris: Balland.

Adler, Emanuel and Michael Barnett, eds (1998). *Security Communities*. Cambridge: Cambridge University Press.

Albonetti, Achille (1972). *Hegemonie oder Partnerschaft in der europäischen Aussenpolitik*. Nomos: Baden-Baden.

Allen, David (1977). 'The Euro–Arab Dialogue'. *Journal of Common Market Studies* 16, no. 1: 323–42.

—— and Alfred Pijpers, eds (1984). *European Foreign Policy-Making and the Arab–Israeli Conflict*. The Hague: Martinus Nijhoff Publishers.

—— Reinhardt Rummel, and Wolfgang Wessels, eds (1982). *European Political Cooperation: Towards a Foreign Policy for Western Europe*. London: Butterworth Scientific.

Allison, Graham and Philip Zelikow (1999). *Essence of Decision: The Cuban Missile Crisis*. 2nd edn. New York: Longman.

Altmeppen, Hans (1972). 'Entspannungsinitiativen von NATO und Warschauer Pakt seit 1966: Eine synchronoptische Darstellung'. *Beiträge zur Konfliktforschung* 3: 65–96.

Association Georges Pompidou, ed. (1995). *Georges Pompidou et l'Europe*. Paris: Editions Complexe.

—— ed. (2001). *Un politique: Georges Pompidou*. Paris: Presses Universitaires de France.

Aybet, Gülnur (2001). *The Dynamics of European Security Cooperation, 1945–91*. London: Palgrave.

Ball, Stuart and Anthony Seldon, eds (1996). *The Heath Government 1970–1974: A Reappraisal*. London: Longman.

Bange, Oliver (2000). *The EEC Crisis of 1963: Kennedy, Macmillan, de Gaulle and Adenauer in Conflict*. Basingstoke: Macmillan.

Baring, Arnulf, in cooperation with Manfred Görtemaker (1982). *Machtwechsel: Die Ära Brandt–Scheel*. Stuttgart: Deutsche Verlags-Anstalt.

Becker, Peter (1992). *Die frühe KSZE-Politik der Bundesrepublik Deutschland: Der aussenpolitische Entscheidungsprozess bis zur Unterzeichnung der Schlussakte von Helsinki*. Münster: Lit.

Berstein, Serge and Jean-Pierre Rioux (2000). *The Pompidou Years, 1969–1974*. Paris: Cambridge University Press.

Berstein, Serge and Jean-François Sirinelli, eds (2006). *Les années Giscard: Valéry Giscard d'Estaing et l'Europe, 1974–1981*. Paris: Armand Colin.

Bickerton, Ian J. and Carla L. Klausner (2005). *A Concise History of the Arab–Israeli Conflict*. Updated 4th edn. Upper Saddle River, NJ: Prentice Hall.

Bitsch, Marie-Thérèse (2001). *Histoire de la construction européenne de 1945 à nos jours*. Paris: Editions Complexe.

Bluth, Christoph (2000). 'The Origins of MBFR: West German Policy Priorities and Conventional Arms Control'. *War in History* 7, no. 2: 199–224.

Bozo, Frédéric (2001). *Two Strategies for Europe: De Gaulle, the United States, and the Atlantic Alliance*. Lanham: Rowman and Littlefield.

Bracher, Karl Dietrich, Wolfgang Jäger, and Werner Link (1986). *Republik im Wandel, 1969–1974: Die Ära Brandt*. Stuttgart: Deutsche Verlags-Anstalt.

Broad, Roger and Virginia Preston, eds (2001). *Moored to the Continent? Britain and European Integration*. London: University of London.

Brunn, Gerhard (2002). *Die Europäische Einigung von 1945 bis heute*. Stuttgart: Reclam.

Burk, Kathleen and Melvyn Stokes, eds (1999). *The United States and the European Alliance Since 1945*. Oxford: Berg.

Bussière, Eric, ed. (2003). *Georges Pompidou face à la mutation économique de l'Occident, 1969–1974*. Paris: Presses universitaires de France.

Cabalo, Thorsten (1999). *Politische Union Europas 1956–1963*. Cologne: PapyRossa.

Campbell, John (1993). *Edward Heath: A Biography*. London: Jonathan Cape.

Catala, Michel, ed. (2002). *Histoire de la construction européenne: cinquante ans après la déclaration Schuman*. Nantes: Quest Editions.

Catlin, George (1974). *Kissinger's Atlantic Charter*. Gerrards Cross: Colin Smythe.

Cogan, Charles G. (1994). *Oldest Allies, Guarded Friends: The United States and France Since 1940*. Westport: Praeger.

Cohen, Samy and Marie-Claude Smouts, eds (1985). *La politique extérieure de Valéry Giscard d'Estaing*. Paris: Presses de la Fondation nationale des sciences politiques.

Conze, Eckart, Ulrich Lappenküper, and Guido Müller, eds (2004). *Geschichte der internationalen Beziehungen: Erneuerung und Erweiterung einer historischen Disziplin*. Cologne: Böhlau.

Coufoudakis, Van (1977). 'The European Economic Community and the 'Freezing' of the Greek Association, 1967–1974'. *Journal of Common Market Studies* 16, no. 1: 114–31.

Cromwell, William C. (1992). *The United States and the European Pillar: The Strained Alliance*. New York: St. Martin's Press.

Czempiel, Ernst-Otto (1973). 'Entwicklungslinien der amerikanisch–europäischen Beziehungen'. *Europa–Archiv* 28, no. 22: 781–90.

Daddow, Oliver J., ed. (2003). *Harold Wilson and European Integration: Britain's Second Application to Join the EEC*. London: Frank Cass.

Deighton, Anne and Gérard Bossuat, eds (2007). *The EC/EU: A World Security Actor?* Paris: Soleb.

Deighton, Anne and Alan S. Milward, eds (1999). *Widening, Deepening and Acceleration: The European Economic Community 1957–1963*. Baden-Baden: Nomos.

Dettke, Dieter (1976). *Allianz im Wandel: Amerikanisch–europäische Sicherheitsbeziehungen im Zeichen des Bilateralismus der Supermächte*. Frankfurt am Main: Alfred Metzner Verlag.

Dietl, Ralph (2002). '"Une Déception Amoureuse"? Great Britain, the Continent and European Nuclear Cooperation, 1953–57'. *Cold War History* 3, no. 1: 29–66.

DiMaggio, Paul (1997). 'Culture and Cognition'. *Annual Review of Sociology* 23: 263–87.

Dosenrode, Søren and Anders Stubkjær (2002). *The European Union and the Middle East.* New York: Sheffield Academic Press.

Du Réau, Elisabeth and Robert Frank, eds (2002). *Dynamiques européennes: Nouvel espace, nouveaux acteurs, 1969–1981.* Paris: Publications de la Sorbonne.

Duchêne, François (1972). 'A New European Defense Community'. *Revue militaire générale* 2: 183–99.

Dujardin, Vincent (2004). *Pierre Harmel: biographie.* Brussels: Le Cri.

Dyson, Kenneth, ed. (1986). *European Détente: Case Studies of the Politics of East–West Relations.* New York: St. Martin's Press.

Elman, Colin and Miriam Fendius Elman, eds (2001). *Bridges and Boundaries: Historians, Political Scientists, and the Study of International Relations.* Cambridge, Mass.: MIT Press.

Garthoff, Raymond L. (1994). *Détente and Confrontation: American–Soviet Relations from Nixon to Reagan.* Rev. edn. Washington, DC: The Brookings Institution.

George, Stephen, ed. (1992). *Britain and the European Community: The Politics of Semi-Detachment.* Oxford: Clarendon Press.

—— (1994). *An Awkward Partner: Britain in the European Community.* 2nd edn. Oxford: Oxford University Press.

Gerbet, Pierre (1999). *La construction de l'Europe.* Paris: Imprimerie Nationale.

Geyer, David C. and Bernd Schaefer, eds (2004). *American Détente and German Ostpolitik, 1969–1972.* Washington, DC: Supplement no. 1 to the Bulletin of the German Historical Institute.

Giauque, Jeffrey Glen (2002). *Grand Designs and Visions of Unity: The Atlantic Powers and the Reorganization of Western Europe, 1955–1963.* Chapel Hill: The University of North Carolina Press.

Greenwood, Sean (1996). *The Alternative Alliance: Anglo–French Relations before the Coming of NATO, 1944–48.* Montreux: Minerva Press.

Grosser, Alfred (1976). *Les politiques extérieures européennes dans la crise.* Paris: Presses de la Fondation Nationale des Sciences Politiques.

Haftendorn, Helga (2001). *Deutsche Aussenpolitik zwischen Selbstbeschränkung und Selbstbehauptung, 1945–2000.* Stuttgart: Deutsche Verlags-Anstalt.

—— and Otto Keck, eds (1997). *Kooperation jenseits von Hegemonie und Bedrohung: Sicherheitsinstitutionen in den internationalen Beziehungen.* Baden-Baden: Nomos.

—— et al., eds (1978). *Verwaltete Aussenpolitik: Sicherheits- und entspannungspolitische Entscheidungsprozesse in Bonn.* Cologne: Verlag Wissenschaft und Politik.

Hahn, Walter F. (1973). 'West Germany's Ostpolitik: The Grand Design of Egon Bahr'. *Orbis* 16: 859–80.

Hanhimäki, Jussi M. (2003). '"They Can Write it in Swahili": Kissinger, the Soviets, and the Helsinki Accords, 1973–75'. *Journal of Transatlantic Studies* 1, no. 1: 37–58.

—— (2004). *The Flawed Architect: Henry Kissinger and American Foreign Policy.* New York: Oxford University Press.

Hanrieder, Wolfram F., ed. (1973). *The United States and Western Europe: Political, Economic and Strategic Perspectives.* Cambridge, Mass.: Winthrop.

Hart, Paul, Eric K. Stern, and Bengt Sundelius, eds (1997). *Beyond Groupthink: Political Group Dynamics and Foreign Policy-Making.* Ann Arbor: University of Michigan Press.

Hiepel, Claudia (2003). 'In Search of the Greatest Common Denominator: Germany and the Hague Summit Conference 1969'. *Journal of European Integration History* 9, no. 2: 63–81.

Hill, Christopher, ed. (1983). *National Foreign Policies and European Political Cooperation.* London: Allen & Unwin.

—— (2002). *The Changing Politics of Foreign Policy.* Basingstoke: Palgrave.

Hobsbawm, Eric (2003). *The Age of Extremes: The Short Twentieth Century, 1914–1991.* London: Abacus [1994].

Hoffmann, Stanley (1995). *The European Sisyphus: Essays on Europe, 1964–1994.* Boulder: Westview Press.

—— (2000). 'Towards a Common European Foreign and Security Policy?' *Journal of Common Market Studies* 38, no. 2: 189–98.

Hohensee, Jens (1996). *Der erste Ölpreisschock 1973/74: Die politischen und gesellschaftlichen Auswirkungen der arabischen Erdölpolitik auf die Bundesrepublik Deutschland und Westeuropa.* Stuttgart: Franz Steiner.

Höhn, Jan (1978). *Aussenpolitik der EG-Staaten: Im Fall der KSZE – Geschichte – Struktur – Entscheidungsprozess – Aktion – Möglichkeiten und Grenzen.* Munich: tuduv.

Holsti, Ole R. (1962). 'The Belief System and National Images: A Case Study'. *Journal of Conflict Resolution* 6: 244–52.

Ifestos, Panayiotis (1987). *European Political Cooperation: Towards a Framework of Supranational Diplomacy?* Aldershot: Avebury.

—— (1988). *Nuclear Strategy and European Security Dilemmas: Towards an Autonomous European Defence System?* Aldershot: Avebury.

Jacobs, Andreas (2003). *Problematische Partner: Europäisch–arabische Zusammenarbeit 1970–1998.* Cologne: SH-Verlag.

Jäger, Wolfgang and Werner Link (1987). *Republik im Wandel, 1974-1982: Die Ära Schmidt.* Stuttgart: Deutsche Verlags-Anstalt.

Jawad, Haifaa A. (1992). *Euro–Arab Relations: A Study in Collective Diplomacy.* Reading: Ithaca Press.

Jervis, Robert (1976). *Perception and Misperception in International Politics.* Princeton: Princeton University Press.

—— (1999). 'Realism, Neoliberalism, and Cooperation: Understanding the Debate'. *International Security* 24, no. 1: 42–63.

John, Ieuan G., ed. (1975). *EEC Policy Towards Eastern Europe.* Westmead: Saxon House.

Kaiser, Karl (1973). *Europe and the United States: The Future of the Relationship.* Washington, DC: Columbia Books.

—— and Udo Steinbach, eds (1981). *Deutsch–arabische Beziehungen: Bestimmungsfaktoren und Probleme einer Neuorientierung.* Munich: Oldenbourg.

Kaiser, Wolfram and Jürgen Elvert, eds (2004). *European Union Enlargement: A Comparative History*. London: Routledge.

Keohane, Robert O. (1984). *After Hegemony: Cooperation and Discord in the World Political Economy*. Princeton: Princeton University Press.

Kim, Seung-Ryeol (2000). *Der Fehlschlag des ersten Versuchs zu einer politischen Integration Westeuropas von 1951 bis 1954*. Frankfurt am Main: Peter Lang.

Kitzinger, Uwe (1973). *Diplomacy and Persuasion: How Britain Joined the Common Market*. London: Thames and Hudson.

Knipping, Franz and Matthias Schönwald, eds (2004). *Aufbruch zum Europa der zweiten Generation: Die europäische Einigung 1969–1984*. Trier: Wissenschaftlicher Verlag Trier.

Kohnstamm, Max and Wolfgang Hager, eds (1973). *A Nation Writ Large? Foreign-Policy Problems before the European Community*. London: Macmillan.

Kramer, Esther (2003). *Europäisches oder atlantisches Europa? Kontinuität und Wandel in den Verhandlungen über eine politische Union 1958–1970*. Baden-Baden: Nomos.

Krämer, Hans R. (1974). *Die Europäische Gemeinschaft und die Ölkrise*. Baden-Baden: Nomos.

Krüger, Dieter (2003). *Sicherheit durch Integration? Die wirtschaftliche und politische Zuammenarbeit Westeuropas 1947 bis 1957/58*. Munich: Oldenbourg.

Lieber, Robert J. (1976). *Oil and the Middle East War: Europe in the Energy Crisis*. Harvard Studies in International Affairs 35. Cambridge, Mass.: Harvard University Center for International Affairs.

Little, Richard and Steve Smith, eds (1988). *Belief Systems and International Relations*. Oxford: Basil Blackwell.

Lord, Christopher (1993). *British Entry to the European Community under the Heath Government of 1970–74*. Aldershot: Dartmouth Publishing Company.

Loth, Wilfried (1998). *Helsinki, 1. August 1975: Entspannung und Abrüstung*. Munich: DTV.

—— ed. (2001). *Crises and Compromises: The European Project 1963–1969*. Baden-Baden: Nomos.

—— ed. (2004). *Europe, Cold War and Co-existence, 1953–1965*. London: Frank Cass.

—— and Jürgen Osterhammel, eds (2000). *Internationale Geschichte: Themen – Ergebnisse – Aussichten*. Munich: Oldenbourg.

Ludlow, N. Piers (1997). *Dealing with Britain: The Six and the First UK Application to the EEC*. Cambridge: Cambridge University Press.

—— (2006). *The European Community and the Crises of the 1960s: Negotiating the Gaullist Challenge*. London: Routledge.

—— ed. (2007). *European Integration and the Cold War: Ostpolitik-Westpolitik, 1965-1973*. London: Routledge.

Lucas, Hans-Dieter, ed. (2002). *Genscher, Deutschland und Europa*. Baden-Baden: Nomos.

Mally, Gerhard, ed. (1974). *The New Europe and the United States: Partners or Rivals*. Lexington, Mass.: Lexington Books.

Maull, Hanns (1975). *Oil and Influence: The Oil Weapon Examined*. Adelphi Paper no. 117. London: The Institute for Strategic Studies.

Mayer, Hartmut (1996). 'Germany's Role in the Fouchet Negotiations'. *Journal of European Integration History* 2, no. 2: 39–59.

—— (2001). 'National Foreign Policy Through Multilateral Means: The Federal Republic of Germany and European Political Cooperation 1969–1986'. Unpublished Ph.D. thesis, University of Oxford.

Mayer, Sebastian (2004). 'Die EU als weltpolitischer Akteur: Anmerkungen zum Forschungsstand'. *WeltTrends* 12, no. 42: 65–77.

Meier-Walser, Reinhard C., ed. (2004). *Gemeinsam sicher? Vision und Realität europäischer Sicherheitspolitik*. Neuried: Ars una.

Menon, Anand, ed. (2004). *Britain and European Integration: Views from Within*. Oxford: Blackwell.

Merseburger, Peter (2002). *Willy Brandt, 1913–1992: Visionär und Realist*. Stuttgart: Deutsche Verlags-Anstalt.

Messmer, Pierre, ed. (1990). *Georges Pompidou hier et aujourd'hui: Témoignages*. Paris: Editions Breet.

Miard-Delacroix, Hélène (1993). *Partenaires de choix? Le chancelier Helmut Schmidt et la France (1974–1982)*. Berne: Peter Lang.

Milner, Helen (1992). 'International Theories of Cooperation Among Nations: Strengths and Weaknesses'. *World Politics* 44: 466–96.

Milward, Alan S. (2002). *The UK and The European Community, Vol. 1: The Rise and Fall of a National Strategy, 1945–1963*. London: Whitehall History Publishing, in association with Frank Cass.

—— (2003) 'The Hague Conference of 1969 and the United Kingdom's Accession to the European Economic Community'. *Journal of European Integration History* 9, no. 2: 117–26.

Möller, Horst and Maurice Vaïsse, eds (2005). *Willy Brandt und Frankreich*. Munich: Oldenbourg.

Moravcsik, Andrew (1993). 'Preferences and Power in the European Community: A Liberal Intergovernmentalist Approach'. *Journal of Common Market Studies* 31, no. 4: 473–524.

—— (1998). *The Choice for Europe: Social Purpose and State Power from Messina to Maastricht*. Ithaca: Cornell University Press.

Morgan, Austen (1992). *Harold Wilson*. London: Pluto Press.

Morgan, Kenneth O. (1997). *Callaghan: A Life*. Oxford: Oxford University Press.

Morgan, Roger P. (1973). *High Politics, Low Politics: Toward a Foreign Policy for Western Europe*. Beverly Hills: Sage.

Müller, Martin (1988). *Politik und Bürokratie: Die MBFR-Politik der Bundesrepublik Deutschland zwischen 1967 und 1973*. Baden-Baden: Nomos.

Müller-Roschach, Herbert (1980). *Die deutsche Europapolitik 1949–1977: Eine politische Chronik*. Bonn: Europa Union Verlag.

Neustadt, Amnon (1983). *Die deutsch–israelischen Beziehungen im Schatten der EG-Nahostpolitik*. Frankfurt: Haag+Herchen.

Niedhart, Gottfried, Detlef Junker, and Michael W. Richter, eds (1997). *Deutschland in Europa: Nationale Interessen und internationale Ordnung im 20. Jahrhundert*. Mannheim: Palatium.

Noakes, Jeremy, Peter Wende, and Jonathan Wright, eds (2002). *Britain and Germany in Europe, 1949–1990*. Oxford: Oxford University Press.

Nuttall, Simon J. (1992). *European Political Co-operation*. Oxford: Clarendon Press.

Parker, Richard B. (2001). *The October War: A Retrospective*. Gainesville: University Press of Florida.

Pijpers, Alfred (1984). 'European Political Co-operation and the CSCE Process'. *Legal Issues of European Integration* 10, no. 1: 135–48.

Pine, Melissa (2004). 'British Personal Diplomacy and Public Policy: The Soames Affair'. *Journal of European Integration History* 10, no. 2: 59–76.

—— (2007). *Harold Wilson and Europe: Pursuing Britain's Membership of the European Community*. London: I.B.Tauris.

Quandt, William B. (2001). *Peace Process: American Diplomacy and the Arab–Israeli Conflict since 1967*. Washington, DC: Brookings Institution Press.

Rabinovich, Abraham (2004). *The Yom Kippur War: The Epic Encounter that Transformed the Middle East*. New York: Schocken.

Regelsberger, Elfriede (1992). 'Westeuropa als Internationaler Akteur: Die Aussenbeziehungen der Europäischen Politischen Zusammenarbeit (EPZ)'. Unpublished Ph.D. thesis, Universität Tübingen.

—— Philippe de Schoutheete de Tervarent, and Wolfgang Wessels, eds (1997). *Foreign Policy of the European Union: From EPC to CFSP and Beyond*. Boulder: Lynne Rienner.

Rey, Marie-Pierre (1991). *La tentation du rapprochement: France et URSS à l'heure de la détente (1964–1974)*. Paris: Sorbonne.

Risse-Kappen, Thomas (1995). *Cooperation among Democracies: The European Influence on U.S. Foreign Policy*. Princeton: Princeton University Press.

Roussel, Eric (1994). *Georges Pompidou, 1911–1974*. Paris: Editions Jean-Claude Lattès.

Schaetzel, Robert J. (1973). 'Some European Questions for Dr. Kissinger'. *Foreign Policy* 12: 66–74.

—— (1975). *The Unhinged Alliance: America and the European Community*. New York: Harper & Row.

Schlotter, Peter (1999). *Die KSZE im Ost–West–Konflikt: Wirkung einer internationalen Institution*. Frankfurt: Campus.

Schoutheete, Philippe de (1986). *La coopération politique européenne*. 2nd edn. Paris: Fernand Nathan.

Schultz, Matthias, Thomas A. Schwartz, and Bernd Schäfer, eds (forthcoming). *The Strained Alliance: Conflicts and Cooperation in Transatlantic Relations from Nixon to Carter*. Cambridge: Cambridge University Press.

Schwarz, Hans-Peter (1977). *Zwischenbilanz der KSZE*. Stuttgart: Seewald.

Schwarz, Siegfried (2004). 'Zur Geschichte einer gemeinsamen europäischen Aussenpolitik'. *WeltTrends* 12, no. 42: 51–63.

Schwerin, Otto Graf (1975). 'Die Solidarität der EG-Staaten in der KSZE'. *Europa Archiv* 30, no. 15: 483–92.

Singer, Eric and Valerie Hudson, eds (1992). *Political Psychology and Foreign Policy*. Boulder: Westview Press.

Smart, Ian (1971). *Future Conditional: The Prospect for Anglo–French Nuclear Co-operation*. Adelphi Paper 78. London: The Institute for Strategic Studies.

Soutou, Georges-Henri (1996). *L'Alliance Incertaine: Les Rapports politico–stratégiques Franco-allemands, 1954–1996*. Paris: Fayard.

—— (2000). 'Le Président Pompidou et les relations entre les Etats-Unis et l'Europe'. *Journal of European Integration History* 6, no. 2: 111–46.

—— (2004). 'La problématique de la détente et le testament stratégique de Georges Pompidou'. *Cahiers du Centre d'Etudes d'Historie de la Défense* no. 22: 79–107.

Sus, Ibrahim (1974). 'Western Europe and the October War'. *Journal of Palestine Studies* 3, no. 2: 65–83.

Taschler, Daniela (2001). *Vor neuen Herausforderungen: Die aussen- und deutschlandpolitische Debatte in der CDU/CSU-Bundestagsfraktion während der Grossen Koalition (1966–1969)*. Düsseldorf: Droste.

Thomas, Daniel C. (2001). *The Helsinki Effect: International Norms, Human Rights, and the Demise of Communism*. Princeton: Princeton University Press.

Thorpe, D. R. (1997). *Alec Douglas-Home*. London: Sinclair-Stevenson.

Türk, Henning (2006). *Die Europapolitik der Grossen Koalition 1966-1969*. Schriftenreihe der Vierteljahrshefte für Zeitgeschichte, vol. 93. Munich: Oldenbourg Wissenschaftsverlag.

Turner, Louis (1974). 'The European Community: Factors of Disintegration – Politics of the Energy Crisis'. *International Affairs* 50, no. 3: 404–15.

Ullman, Richard H. (1989). 'The Covert French Connection'. *Foreign Policy* 75: 3–33.

Vaïsse, Maurice (1998). *La grandeur: Politique étrangère du général de Gaulle 1958–1969*. Paris: Fayard.

—— Pierre Mélandri, and Frédéric Bozo, eds (1999). *La France et l'OTAN 1949–1996*. Paris: Editions Complexe.

Van der Harst, Jan, ed. (2007). *Beyond the Customs Union: The European Community's Quest for Deepening, Widening and Completion*. Brussels: Bruylant.

Venn, Fiona (2002). *The Oil Crisis*. London: Longman.

Vertzberger, Yaacov Y. I. (1990). *The World in Their Minds: Information Processes, Cognition, and Perception in Foreign Policy Decisionmaking*. Stanford: Stanford University Press.

Volle, Hermann and Wolfgang Wagner, eds (1976). *Konferenz über Sicherheit und Zusammenarbeit in Europa: Beiträge und Dokumente aus dem Europa-Archiv*. Bonn: Verlag für Internationale Politik.

Walker, Stephen G., ed. (1987). *Role Theory and Foreign Policy Analysis*. Durham: Duke University Press.

Wallace, Helen, William Wallace, and Carole Webb, eds (1977). *Policy-Making in the European Communities*. London: John Wiley & Sons.

Walton, Ann-Margaret (1976). 'Atlantic Relations: Policy Co-ordination and Conflict – Atlantic Bargaining over Energy'. *International Affairs* 52, no. 2: 180–96.

Weed, Mary Kathleen (1981). 'Michel Jobert et la Diplomatie Française de 1973 à 1974'. Unpublished Ph.D. thesis, Institut d'Etudes Politiques de Paris.

—— (1988). *L'image publique d'un homme secret: Michel Jobert et la Diplomatie Française*. Paris: Fernand Lanore.

Weinachter, Michèle (2004). *Valéry Giscard d'Estaing et l'Allemagne: Le double rêve inachevé*. Paris: L'Harmattan.

Wendt, Alexander (1999). *Social Theory of International Politics*. Cambridge: Cambridge University Press.

Wenger, Andreas (2004). 'Crisis and Opportunity: NATO and the Multilateralization of Détente, 1966–1968'. *Journal of Cold War Studies* 6, no. 1: 22–74.

Westad, Odd Arne, ed. (2000). *Reviewing the Cold War: Approaches, Interpretations, Theory*. London: Frank Cass.

Wilkens, Andreas, ed. (1999a). *Interessen verbinden: Jean Monnet und die europäische Integration der Bundesrepublik Deutschland*. Bonn: Bouvier.

—— (1999b). 'Westpolitik, Ostpolitik and the Project of the Economic and Monetary Union: Germany's European Policy in the Brandt Era (1969–1974)'. *Journal of European Integration History* 5, no. 1: 73–102.

Young, Hugo (1998). *This Blessed Plot: Britain and Europe from Churchill to Blair*. Basingstoke: Macmillan.

Young, John W. (2000). *Britain and European Unity, 1945–1999*. 2nd edn. New York: St. Martin's Press.

Index